T0155847

Communications in Computer and Information Science 2067

Rationale

The CCIS series is devoted to the publication of proceedings of computer science conferences. Its aim is to efficiently disseminate original research results in informatics in printed and electronic form. While the focus is on publication of peer-reviewed full papers presenting mature work, inclusion of reviewed short papers reporting on work in progress is welcome, too. Besides globally relevant meetings with internationally representative program committees guaranteeing a strict peer-reviewing and paper selection process, conferences run by societies or of high regional or national relevance are also considered for publication.

Topics

The topical scope of CCIS spans the entire spectrum of informatics ranging from foundational topics in the theory of computing to information and communications science and technology and a broad variety of interdisciplinary application fields.

Information for Volume Editors and Authors

Publication in CCIS is free of charge. No royalties are paid, however, we offer registered conference participants temporary free access to the online version of the conference proceedings on SpringerLink (http://link.springer.com) by means of an http referrer from the conference website and/or a number of complimentary printed copies, as specified in the official acceptance email of the event.

CCIS proceedings can be published in time for distribution at conferences or as post-proceedings, and delivered in the form of printed books and/or electronically as USBs and/or e-content licenses for accessing proceedings at SpringerLink. Furthermore, CCIS proceedings are included in the CCIS electronic book series hosted in the SpringerLink digital library at http://link.springer.com/bookseries/7899. Conferences publishing in CCIS are allowed to use Online Conference Service (OCS) for managing the whole proceedings lifecycle (from submission and reviewing to preparing for publication) free of charge.

Publication process

The language of publication is exclusively English. Authors publishing in CCIS have to sign the Springer CCIS copyright transfer form, however, they are free to use their material published in CCIS for substantially changed, more elaborate subsequent publications elsewhere. For the preparation of the camera-ready papers/files, authors have to strictly adhere to the Springer CCIS Authors' Instructions and are strongly encouraged to use the CCIS LaTeX style files or templates.

Abstracting/Indexing

CCIS is abstracted/indexed in DBLP, Google Scholar, EI-Compendex, Mathematical Reviews, SCImago, Scopus. CCIS volumes are also submitted for the inclusion in ISI Proceedings.

How to start

To start the evaluation of your proposal for inclusion in the CCIS series, please send an e-mail to ccis@springer.com.

Guangtao Zhai · Jun Zhou · Long Ye · Hua Yang ·
Ping An · Xiaokang Yang

Editors

Digital Multimedia Communications

20th International Forum on Digital TV and
Wireless Multimedia Communications, IFTC 2023
Beijing, China, December 21–22, 2023
Revised Selected Papers, Part II

Springer

Editors
Guangtao Zhai 🔟
SEIEE Building 5-411
Shanghai Jiao Tong University
Shanghai, China

Long Ye
Communication University of China
Beijing, China

Ping An
Shanghai University
Shanghai, China

Jun Zhou 🔟
Shanghai Jiao Tong University
Shanghai, China

Hua Yang 🔟
Shanghai Jiao Tong University
Shanghai, China

Xiaokang Yang
Shanghai Jiao Tong University
Shanghai, China

ISSN 1865-0929   ISSN 1865-0937 (electronic)
Communications in Computer and Information Science
ISBN 978-981-97-3625-6   ISBN 978-981-97-3626-3 (eBook)
https://doi.org/10.1007/978-981-97-3626-3

This Springer imprint is published by the registered company Springer Nature Singapore Pte Ltd.
The registered company address is: 152 Beach Road, #21-01/04 Gateway East, Singapore 189721, Singapore

If disposing of this product, please recycle the paper.

Preface

This volume contains the selected papers presented at IFTC 2023: 20th International Forum of Digital Multimedia Communication, held in Beijing, China, on December 21–22, 2023.

IFTC is a summit forum in the field of digital media communication. The 20th IFTC served as an international bridge for extensively exchanging the latest research advances in digital media communication around the world. The forum also aimed to promote technology, equipment, and applications in the field of digital media by comparing the characteristics, frameworks, and significant techniques and their maturity, analyzing the performance of various applications in terms of scalability, manageability, and portability, and discussing the interfaces among varieties of networks and platforms.

The conference program included invited talks focusing on Artificial Intelligence for Multimedia Communication by four distinguished speakers from University of Rochester (USA), Communication University of China (China), Tsinghua University (China), and Baidu (China), as well as an oral session of eleven papers, and a poster session of forty-six papers. The topics of these papers ranged from audio/image/video processing to artification intelligence as well as multimedia communication. This book contains the 57 papers selected for IFTC 2023.

The proceeding editors wish to thank the authors for contributing their novel ideas and visions that are recorded in this book, and all reviewers for their contributions. We also thank Springer for their trust and for publishing the proceedings of IFTC 2023.

IFTC 2023 was hosted by the Shanghai Image and Graphics Association (SIGA). It was organized by the State Key Laboratory of Media Convergence and Communication, the School of Data Science and Media Intelligence of Communication University of China, and was co-organized by Key Laboratory of Media Audio & Video of Ministry of Education (Communication University of China), and Guangdong South New Media Inc.. The Forum was co-sponsored by Shanghai Jiao Tong University (SJTU), the Shanghai Institute for Advanced Communication and Data Science, Shanghai Telecom Company, Shanghai Key Laboratory of Digital Media Processing and Communication, and Shanghai Qing Assistant Technology Company Ltd.

January 2024

Guangtao Zhai
Jun Zhou
Long Ye
Hua Yang
Ping An
Xiaokang Yang

Organization

General Chairs

Xiaokang Yang   Shanghai Jiao Tong University, China
Ping An   Shanghai University, China
Long Ye   Communication University of China, China
Guangtao Zhai   Shanghai Jiao Tong University, China

Program Chairs

Yue Lu   East China Normal University, China
Jun Zhou   Shanghai Jiao Tong University, China
Yuan Zhang   Communication University of China, China
Haonan Cheng   Communication University of China, China
Hua Yang   Shanghai Jiao Tong University, China

Tutorial Chairs

Xiangyang Xue   Fudan University, China
Yuming Fang   Jiangxi University of Finance and Economics,
            China
Jiantao Zhou   University of Macau, China

International Liaisons

Weisi Lin   Nanyang Technological University, Singapore
Patrick Le Callet   Nantes Université, France
Lu Zhang   INSA Rennes, France

Finance Chairs

Yi Xu   Shanghai Jiao Tong University, China
Hao Liu   Donghua University, China

| Beibei Li | Shanghai Polytechnic University, China |
| Xuefei Song | Shanghai Ninth People's Hospital, China |

Publications Chairs

Hong Lu	Fudan University, China
Feiniu Yuan	Shanghai Normal University, China
Menghan Hu	East China Normal University, China
Liquan Shen	Shanghai University, China

Award Chairs

Zhijun Fang	Donghua University, China
George Wang	Guangdong South New Media Inc., China
Xiaolin Huang	Shanghai Jiao Tong University, China
Hanli Wang	Tongji University, China
Yu Zhu	East China University of Science and Technology, China

Publicity Chairs

Bo Yan	Fudan University, China
Wei Zhong	Communication University of China, China
Juanjuan Cai	Communication University of China, China
Gang Hou	Central Research Institute of INESA, China

Industrial Program Chairs

Yiyi Lu	China Telecom Shanghai Company, China
Zhiye Chen	Guangdong South New Media Inc., China
Guozhong Wang	Shanghai University of Engineering Science, China
Chen Yao	Third Research Institute of the Ministry of Public Security, China
Yan Zhou	Renji Hospital, China

Arrangements Chairs

Cheng Zhi   Shanghai Image and Graphics Association, China
Jia Wang   Shanghai Jiao Tong University, China

Program Committee

Xiaokang Yang   Shanghai Jiao Tong University, China
Ping An   Shanghai University, China
Guangtao Zhai   Shanghai Jiao Tong University, China
Jun Zhou   Shanghai Jiao Tong University, China
Long Ye   Communication University of China, China
Haonan Cheng   Communication University of China, China
Wei Zhong   Communication University of China, China
Cong Bai   Zhejiang University of Technology, China
Juanjuan Cai   Communication University of China, China
Patrick Le Callet   Nantes University, France
Xun Cao   Nanjing University, China
Zhenzhong Chen   Huazhong University of Science and Technology,
                                    China
Zhiye Chen   Guangdong South New Media, China
Chenwei Deng   Beijing Institute of Technology, China
Lianghui Ding   Shanghai Jiao Tong University, China
Weisheng Dong   Xidian University, China
Xiaopeng Fan   Harbin Institute of Technology, China
Xin Fan   Dalian University of Technology, China
Li Fang   Communication University of China, China
Lu Fang   University of Science and Technology of China,
                                    China
Zhijun Fang   Donghua University, China
Yuming Fang   Jiangxi University of Finance and Economy,
                                    China
Hanlong Guo   China Telecom Shanghai Company, China
Junwei Han   Northwestern Polytechnical University, China
Menghan Hu   East China Normal University, China
Fei Hu   Communication University of China, China
Ruimin Hu   Wuhan University, China
Xiaolin Huang   Shanghai Jiao Tong University, China
Yongmin Huang   Southeast University, China
Huiyu Duan   Shanghai Jiao Tong University, China
Rongrong Ji   Xiamen University, China

Xiangyang Ji	Tsinghua University, China
Tingting Jiang	Peking University, China
Ke Gu	Beijing University of Technology, China
Jianhuang Lai	Sun Yat-sen University, China
Beibei Li	Shanghai Polytechnic University, China
Dapeng Li	Nanjing University of Posts and Telecommunications, China
Fanchang Li	Soochow University, China
Hongliang Li	University of Electronic Science and Technology, China
Dingxiang Lin	Shanghai Oriental Pearl (Group) Co. Ltd., China
Weisi Lin	Nanyang Technological University, Singapore
Dong Liu	University of Science and Technology of China, China
Hao Liu	Donghua University, China
Jing Liu	Tianjin University, China
Jiaying Liu	Peking University, China
Ju Liu	Shan Dong University, China
Tangyou Liu	Donghua University, China
Xianming Liu	Harbin Institute of Technology, China
Yebin Liu	Tsinghua University, China
Yingying Liu	Yinrui Information Technology Co. Ltd., China
Yue Liu	Beijing Institute of Technology, China
Zhi Liu	Shandong University, China
Fuxiang Lu	Lanzhou University, China
Guo Lu	Shanghai Jiao Tong University, China
Hong Lu	Fudan University, China
Ke Lu	University of Chinese Academy of Sciences, China
Yiyi Lu	China Telecom Shanghai Company, China
Yue Lu	East China Normal University, China
Lizhuang Ma	Shanghai Jiao Tong University, China
Siwei Ma	Peking University, China
Lin Mei	Third Institute of The Ministry of Public Security, China
Xiongkuo Min	Shanghai Jiao Tong University, China
Bingbing Ni	Shanghai Jiao Tong University, China
Yi Niu	Xidian University, China
Feng Shao	Ningbo University, China
Liquan Shen	Shanghai University, China
Xiaofeng Shen	East China Normal University, China
Zhenwei Shi	Beihang University, China

Li Song	Shanghai Jiao Tong University, China
Xuefei Song	Shanghai Ninth People's Hospital, China
Qiudong Sun	Shanghai Polytechnic University, China
Shiliang Sun	East China Normal University, China
Wei Sun	Shanghai Jiao Tong University, China
Xinmei Tian	University of Science and Technology of China, China
Yonghong Tian	Peking University, China
Hanli Wang	Tongji University, China
Jicheng Wang	Tongji University, China
Meng Wang	Hefei University of Technology, China
Pei Wang	Shanghai Normal University, China
Shigang Wang	Jilin University, China
George Wang	Guangdong South New Media, China
Guozhong Wang	Shanghai University of Engineering Science, China
Zhou Wang	Waterloo University, Canada
Fei Wu	Zhejiang University, China
Jinjian Wu	Xidian University, China
Shiming Xiang	Institute of Automation of Chinese Academy of Sciences, China
Jian Xiong	Shanghai Jiao Tong University, China
Ruiqin Xiong	Peking University, China
Xiangmin Xu	South China University of Technology, China
Yi Xu	Shanghai Jiao Tong University, China
Xiangyang Xue	Fudan University, China
Junchi Yan	Shanghai Jiao Tong University, China
Jie Yang	Shanghai Jiao Tong University, China
Chao Yang	Shanghai University, China
Hua Yang	Shanghai Jiao Tong University, China
Jingyu Yang	Tianjing University, China
Xinyan Yang	Communication University of China, China
You Yang	Huazhong University of Science and Technology, China
Haibing Yin	Hangzhou Dianzi University, China
Li Yu	Huazhong University of Science and Technology, China
Jun Yu	Hangzhou Dianzi University, China
Bin Zeng	University of Electronic Science and Technology, China
Chongyang Zhang	Shanghai Jiao Tong University, China
Lu Zhang	INSA de Rennes, France

Wenjun Zhang	Shanghai Jiao Tong University, China
Wenqian Zhang	Shanghai Maritime University, China
Ya Zhang	Shanghai University, China
Yuan Zhang	Communication University of China, China
Zhao Zhang	Zhejiang Normal University, China
Cheng Zhi	Shanghai Image and Graphic Association, China
Yao Zhao	Beijing Jiaotong University, China
Chengxu Zhou	Beijing University of Technology, China
Jiantao Zhou	University of Macau, China
Yuchen Zhu	Shanghai Jiao Tong University, China
Yu Zhu	East China University of Science and Technology, China
Li Zhuo	Beijing University of Technology, China

Contents – Part II

Application of AI

Contents – Part I

Image Processing

Media Computing

Metaverse and Virtual Reality

Multimedia Communication

Quality Assessment

AUIQE: Attention-Based Underwater Image Quality Evaluator

Baochao Zhang[1], Chenghao Zhou[2], Runze Hu[3], Jingchao Cao[1], and Yutao Liu[1]([✉])

[1] School of Computer Science and Technology, Ocean University of China, Qingdao, China
zhangbaochao@stu.ouc.edu.cn, {caojingchao,liuyutao}@ouc.edu.cn
[2] School of Management Engineering, Qingdao University of Technology, Qingdao, China
[3] School of Information and Electronics, Beijing Institute of Technology, Beijing, China

Abstract. Underwater image quality assessment (UIQA) is critical to many underwater application scenarios, including marine biology research, marine resource development, underwater exploration, and more. Due to the different attenuation rates of light at different wavelengths and the effects of the absorption and scattering of light by suspended particles in the water, there are many types of distortion in the acquired underwater images. Most underwater images often show color casts, reduced contrast, low brightness, blurred object edges, local texture distortion, etc. degradation phenomena compared to natural images. This renders many of the image quality assessment (IQA) methods designed for natural images inapplicable to underwater images. Currently, there is a lack of UIQA methods that are accurate and efficient. In this paper, we proposed an Attention-Based Underwater Image Quality Evaluator (AUIQE), a novel end-to-end IQA approach suitable for UIQA tasks. Specifically, we introduced channel and spatial dual attention mechanisms on the basis of the distortion characteristics of underwater images to make the network focus on some channels and spatial regions that are relevant to image quality. A large number of experiments were designed and carried out on an underwater image quality assessment dataset, and the experimental results indicate that the prediction performance of AUIQE outperforms some of the latest IQA and UIQA methods. The code of AUIQE will be available at https://github.com/ibaochao/AUIQE.

Keywords: Image quality assessment (IQA) · Underwater image · Channel attention · Spatial attention

G. Zhai et al. (Eds.): IFTC 2023, CCIS 2067, pp. 3–15, 2024.
https://doi.org/10.1007/978-981-97-3626-3_1

1   Introduction

Different from natural images taken in the air, underwater images are susceptible to factors such as the complex underwater environment and the attenuation characteristics of the light itself, often showing color casts, reduced contrast, low brightness, blurred object edges, local texture distortion, etc. degradation phenomenon. The quality of underwater images crucially influences underwater tasks, including marine biology study, marine resource development, and underwater exploration. Therefore, for a variety of underwater tasks, accurate and efficient assessment of underwater image quality is a vital aid. Subjective quality assessment may not meet standards of timeliness and requires significant time, personnel, and resources. Research on objective IQA methods is the current mainstream direction of IQA development. Due to the huge difference between underwater images and natural images, most IQA methods designed for natural images often have low prediction performance when applied to underwater IQA tasks. Current UIQA approaches are limited, mainly relying on manual feature design to ascertain several image attributes for quality evaluation. The cultivation of objective and specialized UIQA methods is therefore urgently needed.

For one thing, affected by the attenuation of light underwater, underwater images commonly manifest significant color casts, such as a greenish or bluish tint. For another, affected by factors such as suspended impurities in underwater shooting environments such as different regions and depths, underwater images are prone to exhibiting regions of local overexposure or underexposure in their spatial distribution. Inspired by CBAM [18] and LANet [6], we proposed AUIQE, a novel UIQA method by combining the distortion characteristics of underwater images. Our AUIQE method can obtain powerful feature representations related to underwater image quality by integrating channel and spatial dual attention mechanisms. Numerous experiments have confirmed the effectiveness of AUIQE. The main contributions of this paper are as follows:

- We proposed AUIQE, a novel end-to-end approach suitable for UIQA tasks. AUIQE incorporates both channel and spatial dual attention mechanisms. These mechanisms are utilized to emphasize the channels and spatial regions of the image that are pertinent to underwater image quality.
- We designed and carried out a large number of experiments on an underwater image quality assessment dataset, and the experimental results indicate that the prediction performance of AUIQE outperforms some of the latest IQA and UIQA methods.

2   Related Work

In this section we introduce some IQA methods for natural images and UIQA methods for underwater images.

2.1 Image Quality Assessment Methods

In recent years, many IQA methods for evaluating natural images have emerged. In [12], based on the principle of sparse representation and free energy, Liu et al. proposed a reduced-reference (RR) IQA method. A number of statistically based no-reference (NR) blind IQA methods [8,9,11] continue to appear. The advancement of IQA field has been significantly driven by the development of these methods. Quality evaluation methods designed specifically for high-definition (HD) videos [13] and blurred images [10] have also come to light. In recent times, with the rapid advancement of deep learning technology, there has been a proliferation of IQA methods based on convolutional neural networks (CNN) and vision transformer (ViT) [2], such as CNN-IQA [4], WaDIQaM-NR [1], DBCNN [22], HyperIQA [16], TReS [3], TRIQ [21], and others. The CNN-based HyperIQA method uses a content understanding hyper network to analyze the extracted semantic features of images for quality assessment. Both ViT-based TReS and TRIQ methods utilize the encoder from ViT for quality assessment. Due to the very large differences between underwater and natural images, the IQA method mentioned above is not applicable to UIQA task.

2.2 Underwater Image Quality Assessment Methods

Most existing UIQA methods usually evaluate image quality by manually designing several features such as contrast, brightness, color, etc. that are related to image quality and then weighting them to linearly combine them. In [17], Wang et al. evaluated image quality by analyzing properties such as fog density, colorfulness, and contrast in the images. A comprehensive metric for quality assessment of underwater images has been developed, called UCIQE [19]. Objective evaluation is ensured by considering image saturation, chromaticity, and contrast. Li et al. [5] devised a UIQA metric named URQ by evaluating the degree of colour deviation and visibility degradation in images. In [20], Yang et al. proposed a UIQA measurement method that incorporates image sharpness cues, contrast and colourfulness. The widely-used UIQA metric UIQM characterizes the image colorfulness, sharpness and contrast for quality evaluation [14]. The UIQI method [7] designed by Liu et al. integrates characterizes such as color shift, contrast, and noise, etc. The above UIQA methods still have moderate performance and slower prediction speeds. Therefore, there is an urgent need to research UIQA methods that deliver both superior predictive performance and faster predicting speed.

3 The Proposed Method

3.1 Overall Architecture

The architecture of AUIQE is shown in Fig. 1. As depicted in Fig. 1(a), the network of AUIQE consists of 3 main parts from left to right: a multi-scale feature extraction module, 6 channel and spatial attention modules, and a multilayer

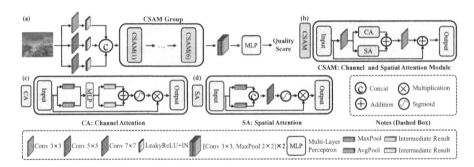

Fig. 1. The architecture of AUIQE.

perceptron (MLP) module. The multi-scale feature extraction module is responsible for extracting multi-scale features of the input image using convolution of different sizes. The 6 channel and spatial attention modules are responsible for focusing on feature information relevant to image quality in the channel and spatial dimensions. The MLP module generates the final quality score of the input image by analyzing feature vectors that incorporate information related to image quality.

Specifically, given an underwater image $I \in \mathbb{R}^{H \times W \times 3}$, notations H and W denote the height and width of the input image, while 3 represents the number of channels. The following process is carried out to obtain precise information on the features that are relevant to its quality. To start with, the image is subjected to convolution at three different scales to extract various features across multiple scales. Furthermore, the gathered feature information at multiple scales is combined in the channel dimension and then processed by consecutive CSAM in order to enhance the image quality feature information for both spatial and channel dimensions. Finally, the MLP module analyzes the feature information acquired and produces the quality score of the input image.

3.2 Multi-scale Feature Extraction Module

The diverse sizes of convolutional kernels correspond to distinct receptive field sizes. Our goal is to acquire a comprehensive feature representation of the input underwater image from multiple scales. Three parallel convolutional layers with varying kernel sizes were employed to produce characteristic maps of the input image at different scales. The sizes of the three convolution kernels are set as 3×3, 5×5, 7×7, respectively.

The feature maps acquired following convolution are combined in the channel dimension to produce a multi-scale feature representation $\boldsymbol{F}_0$, which can be formulated as:

$$
\begin{aligned}
\boldsymbol{S}_i &= \text{IN}(\text{LeakyReLU}(\text{Conv}_i(I))), \text{ for } i = 1 \sim 3, \\
\boldsymbol{F}_0 &= \text{Concat}_c(\boldsymbol{S}_1, \boldsymbol{S}_2, \boldsymbol{S}_3),
\end{aligned}
\tag{1}
$$

where instance normalization (IN) is used for normalization and LeakyReLU serves as the activation function. Conv_i ($i \in 1 \sim 3$) is the i-th convolutional layer.

3.3   Channel and Spatial Attention Module

We designed the channel and spatial attention Module (CSAM) based on the CBAM [18] and LANet [6]. $\boldsymbol{F}_0$ will be sent to the CSAM Group for further processing of the channel and spatial information of the feature map. As depicted in Fig. 1(b), before conducting channel and spatial attention operations, the information contained within the feature maps is initially blended along the channel dimension using a 3×3 convolutional layer. Subsequently, the feature maps will undergo separate processing in Channel Attention (CA) and Spatial Attention (SA), with the resultant outputs being combined. Afterward, a 3×3 convolutions within the feature maps blend information along the channel dimension. Ultimately, the processed feature map integrates with the feature map upon input to the CSAM. This process can be formulated as:

$$\hat{\boldsymbol{F}}_i = \text{Conv}_{3\times3}(\boldsymbol{F}_{i-1}), \text{ for } i = 1 \sim 6,$$
$$\boldsymbol{F}_i = \boldsymbol{F}_{i-1} + \text{Conv}_{3\times3}(\text{CA}(\hat{\boldsymbol{F}}_i) + \text{SA}(\hat{\boldsymbol{F}}_i)), \text{ for } i = 1 \sim 6,$$

(2)

where $\boldsymbol{F}_i$ ($i \in 1 \sim 6$) represents the output feature map of the i-th CSAM. The feature map outputted by the last CSAM is denoted as $\boldsymbol{F}_6$.

Channel Attention. On the one hand, because of different colors of light have different wavelengths, their attenuation coefficients under water are also different, with red light exhibiting the highest attenuation coefficient in particular, underwater images usually display considerable colour shifts that deviate from the natural images taken in the air. On the other hand, light transmission through water is influenced by a number of environmental factors, namely the water medium and suspended particles, which can cause light to become absorbed and scattered. These factors have the potential to cause problems in underwater images, such as colour distortion, low contrast, and loss of texture. As a result, underwater images are usually characterized by a predominance of green or blue in the colour cast. To address this effect, the Channel Attention (CA) mechanism has been introduced, which prioritises the quality-informative channels while suppressing the impact of less relevant or noisy channels when characterizing image quality.

As shown in Fig. 1(c), given the feature map $\hat{\boldsymbol{F}}_i \in \mathbb{R}^{C \times H \times W}$ ($i \in 1 \sim 6$), notation C represents the number of channels, we compress the spatial information by using average-polling and max-pooling. As a result, we can obtain two spatial context descriptors as in $\hat{\boldsymbol{F}}_{\text{CA-avg}(i)} \in \mathbb{R}^{C \times 1 \times 1}$ and $\hat{\boldsymbol{F}}_{\text{CA-max}(i)} \in \mathbb{R}^{C \times 1 \times 1}$. Both the average-pooling and the max-pooling can offer advantages for the calculation of the CA. The average-pooling acts as the global context descriptor for each channel, whereas the max-pooling describes the channel-wised essential information. Therefore, they are complementary, which enables the network to produce a more comprehensive CA map. They are then passed through an MLP block consisting of 1×1 convolutional layer, ReLU activation function, and 1×1 convolutional layer to establish the CA map, written by:

$$\mathcal{W}_{\text{CA}_i} = \sigma \left(\text{MLP}(\text{AvgPool}(\hat{\mathbf{F}}_i)) + \text{MLP}(\text{MaxPool}(\hat{\mathbf{F}}_i)) \right), \text{ for } i = 1 \sim 6, \quad (3)$$

where σ is the sigmoid activation function. We can acquire the feature map enhanced by CA as:

$$\hat{\mathbf{F}}_{\text{CA}_i} = \hat{\mathbf{F}}_i \odot_c \mathcal{W}_{\text{CA}_i}, \text{ for } i = 1 \sim 6, \quad (4)$$

where $\odot_c$ is the channel-wise multiplication.

Spatial Attention. Underwater images are susceptible to local quality degradation, such as an excess of brightness due to the introduction of an artificial light source during underwater shooting. Local distortions inevitably affect the quality of underwater images and therefore require greater consideration when assessing their overall quality. To overcome this problem, the Spatial Attention (SA) mechanism is used to highlight the regions that significantly affect image quality.

As shown in Fig. 1(d), the SA map is computed by studying the spatial relationship between the features. The feature map $\hat{\mathbf{F}}_i$ undergoes average-pooling and max-pooling operations in their respective channel dimensions, resulting in two descriptors, as in $\hat{\mathbf{F}}_{\text{SA-avg}(i)} \in \mathbb{R}^{1 \times H \times W}$ and $\hat{\mathbf{F}}_{\text{SA-max}(i)} \in \mathbb{R}^{1 \times H \times W}$. They are concatenated in channel dimension and sent to a 7×7 convolutional layer to produce the final SA map, formulated as:

$$\mathcal{W}_{\text{SA}_i} = \sigma \left(\text{Conv}_{7\times7}(\text{Concat}_c(\text{AvgPool}(\hat{\mathbf{F}}_i), \text{MaxPool}(\hat{\mathbf{F}}_i))) \right), \text{ for } i = 1 \sim 6, \quad (5)$$

The spatially-refined feature map can be obtained through the spatial-wised multiplication, written by:

$$\hat{\mathbf{F}}_{\text{SA}_i} = \hat{\mathbf{F}}_i \odot_s \mathcal{W}_{\text{SA}_i}, \text{ for } i = 1 \sim 6, \quad (6)$$

where $\odot_s$ denotes the spatial-wise multiplication. The order of CA and SA are applicable in either a parallel or sequential paradigm. We have chosen the parallel architecture in our ablation study. The feature map generated by the CSAM can also be described by the following formula:

$$\mathbf{F}_i = \mathbf{F}_{i-1} + \text{Conv}_{3\times3}(\hat{\mathbf{F}}_{\text{CA}_i} + \hat{\mathbf{F}}_{\text{SA}_i}), \text{ for } i = 1 \sim 6, \quad (7)$$

3.4   Underwater Image Quality Prediction

Given the relatively high number of parameters in the feature map $\mathbf{F}_6$ produced by the last CSAM, we contemplate utilizing convolutional and pooling operations to reduce dimensionality and decrease resolution of $\mathbf{F}_6$. The obtained feature map is defined as $\boldsymbol{F}_{fin}$. We adopt an MLP module with 2 hidden layers to generate the final prediction quality score by analyzing the feature information obtained in the previous step. The quality score of an underwater image is calculated as:

$$\begin{aligned} \boldsymbol{F}_{fin} &= \text{Pool}_{2\times2}(\text{Conv}_{3\times3}(\text{Pool}_{2\times2}(\text{Conv}_{3\times3}(\boldsymbol{F}_6)))), \\ \text{score} &= \text{MLP}(\boldsymbol{F}_{fin}), \end{aligned} \tag{8}$$

where score refers to the predicted quality score. We minimize the mean squared error (MSE) loss to train the entire network, which is defined as:

$$\mathcal{L}_{MSE} = \frac{1}{N}\sum_{i=1}^{N}(\text{score}_i - \text{mos}_i)^2, \tag{9}$$

where N refers to the total number of training images, score_i and mos_i are the predicted quality score and ground-truth MOS value of the i-th training image.

4 Experiments

4.1 Experimental Protocol

We measure the predictive performance of each of the IQA methods using four widely used evaluation metrics. We use Spearman rank order correlation coefficient (SRCC) and Kendalls rank order correlation coefficient (KRCC) to measure the predictive monotonicity of objective methods, Pearsons linear correlation coefficient (PLCC) to measure their predictive consistency, and root mean square error (RMSE) to measure their predictive accuracy [15]. The values of the first three of these metrics are in the range $[-1, 1]$. The closer the absolute value of the first three metrics is to 1 and the closer the value of the last metric is to 0, the higher the predictive performance of the objective assessment method.

The objective prediction scores need to be mapped to the subjective MOS values by a non-linear fitting function before calculating the values of the latter two metrics. The function as follows:

$$f(p) = \lambda_1\left(\frac{1}{2} - \frac{1}{1 + \exp(\lambda2 \cdot (p - \lambda3))}\right) + \lambda4 \cdot p + \lambda5, \tag{10}$$

with p stands for the predicted score of the objective methods, and $f(p)$ represents the mapped score. $\lambda_j(j \in 1 \sim 5)$ are the 5 free parameters automatically determined during the nonlinear fitting process.

4.2 Implementation Details

In our AUIQE, the quantity of output channels of each parallel branch in the multi-scale feature extraction module is set to 8. The quantity of CSAM is set to 6 to strike a balance between prediction accuracy and model parameters. The quantity of input and output nodes of the MLP is 3136 and 1, respectively.

We constructed an underwater image quality evaluation dataset. The dataset comprises a total of 5369 authentic underwater images, encompassing a diverse range of underwater scenes and typical distortions such as color cast and low contrast. We invited multiple observers to rate the quality of each image individually based on their subjective perceptions. The MOS value of each image is obtained by averaging. This dataset will be publicly available at https://github.com/ibaochao/UIQD. We performed 10 iterations of 10-fold cross-validation on the dataset, where the training dataset and testing dataset were split into 8:2 ratio. We utilized data augmentation procedures such as random horizontal flipping and cropping to the input images. The images were resized to meet the model's input size requirement of 224×224. Experimental results are the average of ten experiments.

We use PyTorch (1.13.0) as the deep learning framework. The deep learning-based models are trained for 10 epochs on 2 NVIDIA RTX 3090 GPUs. We optimize models by minimizing the $\mathcal{L}_{MSE}$ through Adam optimizer. We initially set the learning rate as 1×10^{-4} and the bath size as 32. The classic underwater IQA methods are tested on a CPU of 12th Gen Intel(R) Core(TM) i5-12400.

4.3 Experimental Results

To investigate the prediction performance of AUIQE, we provide overall prediction performance comparison with representative methods on the dataset. These methods include both IQA and underwater IQA methods. The IQA methods include CNN-IQA [4], WaDIQaM-NR [1], DBCNN [22], HyperIQA [16], TReS [3] and TRIQ [21], while the underwater IQA methods comprise CCF [17], UCIQE [19], URQ [5], FDUM [20] and UIQM [14].

Table 1. Comparison of prediction performance of AUIQE and other methods on the dataset. The best result is highlighted in bold.

Method	Type	SRCC($\uparrow$)	KRCC($\uparrow$)	PLCC($\uparrow$)	RMSE($\downarrow$)
CNN-IQA [4]	IQA	0.7961	0.6024	0.7769	0.6118
WaDIQaM-NR [1]	IQA	0.8959	0.7200	0.9003	0.4227
DBCNN [22]	IQA	0.9023	0.7319	0.9004	0.4463
HyperIQA [16]	IQA	0.9004	0.7303	0.8960	0.4313
TReS [3]	IQA	0.8648	0.6824	0.8618	0.4935
TRIQ [21]	IQA	0.9070	0.7400	0.9064	0.4393
CCF [17]	UIQA	0.7800	0.5889	0.7894	0.5965
UCIQE [19]	UIQA	0.7640	0.5708	0.7811	0.6063
URQ [5]	UIQA	0.6537	0.4864	0.6364	0.7497
FDUM [20]	UIQA	0.8547	0.6671	0.8109	0.5649
UIQM [14]	UIQA	0.6325	0.4592	0.6038	0.7715
AUIQE (Ours)	UIQA	**0.9125**	**0.7462**	**0.9109**	**0.4175**

Overall Prediction Performance Comparison. Our proposed AUIQE, like most deep learning-based IQA methods, requires pre-training a model before performing image quality prediction on it. Both our proposed approach and some other IQA methods based on deep learning were subjected to repeated experiments (10 times) on ten different training and testing datasets for training and testing purposes, as partitioned from the dataset of underwater image quality. The experimental results were averaged. It should be noted that IQA methods do not use their pre-trained weights. Traditional UIQA methods underwent a comparable process, conducting experiments on ten distinct testing datasets, and averaging the results. We show the prediction performance results of AUIQE and some other IQA and UIQA methods in Table 1. The symbol "($\uparrow$)" behind SRCC, KRCC and PLCC represents that a larger value signifies better performance for this method. In contrast, the symbol "$\downarrow$" behind RMSE indicates a smaller value is preferable.

In Table 1, we can see that the quality assessment methods designed for natural images can also be applied to underwater images. However, it is evident that the performance of most such models in UIQA is not as strong as it is for natural images. Observations show that the distortion characteristics of underwater images are far more complex than those of natural images. Traditional UIQA methods mostly rely on predicting image quality by assigning weights to various features extracted from the image, such as CCF [17]. Their predictive ability is inadequate. In contrast, we designed our method specifically for the distortion characteristics of underwater images, incorporating both channel and spatial dual attention mechanisms that utilize to emphasize the channels and spatial regions of the image that are pertinent to underwater image quality. Obviously, AUIQE outperforms the other methods presented in Table 1.

For visualization and ease of understanding, we plot scatterplots of subjective and objective scores for each method in Table 1 on the testing dataset. Each plus sign in Fig. 2 represents an image, and the curve in the middle is derived by nonlinear fitting. It can be observed that most of the images in the scatter plots of WaDIQaM-NR, TReS, TRIQ and AUIQE are located near the fitted curve, which suggests that there is a very high degree of agreement between the predicted results of these methods and the results of the subjective human assessments. This illustrates the superior prediction performance of AUIQE.

4.4   Ablation Study

In order to carry out a more in-depth analysis of the proposed model architecture, we did some ablation studies about the order of CA and SA and the number of CSAM, and the results are shown in Table 2 and Fig. 3.

The Order of CA and SA. CA emphasizes the channels related to image quality, while SA focuses on spatial positions related to quality. To investigate the optimal order of CA and SA within the CSAM, we conducted three experiments: first, CA before SA, second, SA before CA, and third, CA and SA in parallel. The experimental results are presented in Table 2.

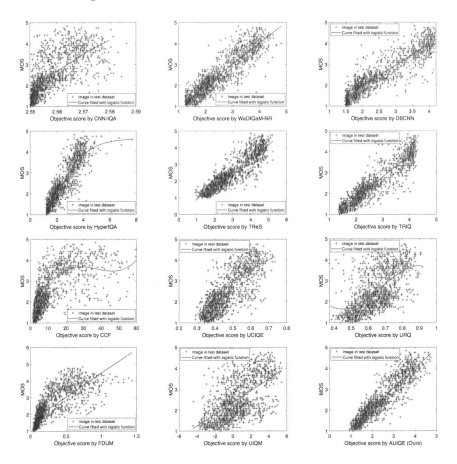

Fig. 2. Scatterplots of subjective and objective scores on the testing dataset.

Table 2. Comparison of prediction performance of the different module combination forms on the dataset. The optimal results are highlighted in bold.

The order of CA and SA	SRCC(↑)	KRCC(↑)	PLCC(↑)	RMSE(↓)
First CA, then SA	0.9124	0.7459	0.9104	**0.4172**
First SA, then CA	0.9109	0.7435	0.9085	0.4215
CA and SA in parallel (Ours)	**0.9125**	**0.7462**	**0.9109**	0.4175

In Table 2, it is evident that the combination of CA and SA in parallel form yields the best performance for the model, slightly outperforming the sequential combination of CA and SA. When CA and SA are combined sequentially, the order of CA before SA performs better than the order of SA before CA. Therefore, we decided to adopt the combination structure of CA and SA in parallel.

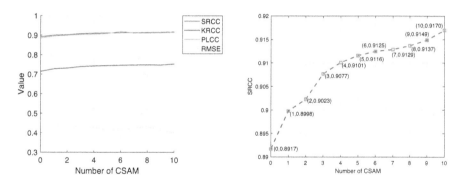

Fig. 3. Left: SRCC, KRCC, PLCC and RMSE curves graph. Right: SRCC curve graph.

The Number of CSAM. To strike a balance between efficiency and performance, we conducted experiments to test the better number of CSAM in AUIQE. We varied the number of CSAM from 0 to 10 as a variable and observed the model's performance across this range. The experiments were carried out once on each of the 10 different training and testing datasets mentioned earlier, and the results were averaged over ten runs, as depicted in Fig. 3.

From the left-hand side of Fig. 3, we observe that as the number of CSAM increases, there is a favorable trend in SRCC, KRCC, PLCC, and RMSE. The right-hand side of Fig. 3 provides an expanded view of SRCC from the left-hand side graph. Taking into consideration the increasing computational complexity with the growing number of CSAM, we ultimately decided to set the number of CSAM to 6.

4.5   Computational Time Evaluation

For assessing the efficiency of AUIQE, we carried out comparative experiments on the computation time required for predicting a single image. We tested the computation time for each IQA method when processing a single image, which, to a certain extent, reflect the efficiency and practicality of the IQA algorithms. Specifically, we selected a representative image from the testing dataset with resolution of 1920 × 1080. We executed all the objective IQA methods mentioned above on this single image in a CPU and recorded their respective computation time, measured in seconds. These results are shown in the Table 3. Obviously, AUIQE exhibits relatively fast prediction speed.

Table 3. Time cost of AUIQE and other methods. The top three results are emphatically highlighted in bold.

Method	CNN-IQA [4]	WaDIQaM-NR [1]	DBCNN [22]	HyperIQA [16]
Time cost(s↓)	**0.0011**	0.0165	**0.0064**	0.0210
Method	TReS [3]	TRIQ [21]	CCF [17]	UCIQE [19]
Time cost(s↓)	0.0393	0.0185	2.1718	0.3437
Method	URQ [5]	FDUM [20]	UIQM [14]	AUIQE (Ours)
Time cost(s↓)	0.1504	6.0321	0.7422	**0.0115**

5   Conclusion

In this paper, we proposed the Attention-Based Underwater Image Quality Evaluator (AUIQE), a novel method for UIQA task. Our AUIQE aggregates channel and spatial features via the channel and spatial attention dual mechanisms, for powerful representation competence. Addressing the unique characteristics of underwater images, we designed the channel and spatial attention module (CSAM) that enable the model to focus on channels and spatial regions relevant to image quality. Specifically, the Channel Attention (CA) mechanism prioritises the quality-informative channels while suppressing the impact of less relevant or noisy channels when characterizing image quality. Meanwhile, the Spatial Attention (SA) mechanism is used to highlight the regions that significantly affect image quality. Extensive experiments indicate that the prediction performance of AUIQE outperforms some of the latest IQA and UIQA methods.

Acknowledgements. This work was supported by the National Science Foundation of China under grants 62201538 and 62301041, and the Natural Science Foundation of Shandong Province under grant ZR2022QF006.

References

1. Bosse, S., Maniry, D., Müller, K.R., Wiegand, T., Samek, W.: Deep neural networks for no-reference and full-reference image quality assessment. IEEE Trans. Image Process. **27**(1), 206–219 (2017)
2. Dosovitskiy, A., et al.: An image is worth 16x16 words: Transformers for image recognition at scale. arXiv preprint arXiv:2010.11929 (2020)
3. Golestaneh, S.A., Dadsetan, S., Kitani, K.M.: No-reference image quality assessment via transformers, relative ranking, and self-consistency. In: Proceedings of the IEEE/CVF Winter Conference on Applications of Computer Vision, pp. 1220–1230 (2022)
4. Kang, L., Ye, P., Li, Y., Doermann, D.: Convolutional neural networks for no-reference image quality assessment. In: Proceedings of the IEEE Conference on Computer Vision and Pattern Recognition, pp. 1733–1740 (2014)
5. Li, L.: Underwater color image quality assessment. https://github.com/LangtaoLi/Underwater-color-image-quality-assessment

6. Liu, S., Fan, H., Lin, S., Wang, Q., Ding, N., Tang, Y.: Adaptive learning attention network for underwater image enhancement. IEEE Robot. Autom. Lett. **7**(2), 5326–5333 (2022)
7. Liu, Y., et al.: Uiqi: a comprehensive quality evaluation index for underwater images. IEEE Trans. Multimed. (2023)
8. Liu, Y., Gu, K., Li, X., Zhang, Y.: Blind image quality assessment by natural scene statistics and perceptual characteristics. ACM Trans. Multimed. Comput. Commun. Appl. (TOMM) **16**(3), 1–91 (2020)
9. Liu, Y., Gu, K., Wang, S., Zhao, D., Gao, W.: Blind quality assessment of camera images based on low-level and high-level statistical features. IEEE Trans. Multimedia **21**(1), 135–146 (2018)
10. Liu, Y., Gu, K., Zhai, G., Liu, X., Zhao, D., Gao, W.: Quality assessment for real out-of-focus blurred images. J. Vis. Commun. Image Represent. **46**, 70–80 (2017)
11. Liu, Y., et al.: Unsupervised blind image quality evaluation via statistical measurements of structure, naturalness, and perception. IEEE Trans. Circuits Syst. Video Technol. **30**(4), 929–943 (2019)
12. Liu, Y., Zhai, G., Gu, K., Liu, X., Zhao, D., Gao, W.: Reduced-reference image quality assessment in free-energy principle and sparse representation. IEEE Trans. Multimedia **20**(2), 379–391 (2017)
13. Liu, Y., Zhai, G., Zhao, D., Liu, X.: Frame rate and perceptual quality for hd video. In: Advances in Multimedia Information Processing–PCM 2015: 16th Pacific-Rim Conference on Multimedia, Gwangju, South Korea, September 16-18, 2015, Proceedings, Part II 16, pp. 497–505. Springer (2015)
14. Panetta, K., Gao, C., Agaian, S.: Human-visual-system-inspired underwater image quality measures. IEEE J. Oceanic Eng. **41**(3), 541–551 (2015)
15. Rohaly, A.M., Libert, J., Corriveau, P., Webster, A., et al.: Final report from the video quality experts group on the validation of objective models of video quality assessment. ITU-T Standards Contribution COM, pp. 9–80 (2000)
16. Su, S., et al.: Blindly assess image quality in the wild guided by a self-adaptive hyper network. In: Proceedings of the IEEE/CVF Conference on Computer Vision and Pattern Recognition, pp. 3667–3676 (2020)
17. Wang, Y., et al.: An imaging-inspired no-reference underwater color image quality assessment metric. Comput. Electr. Eng. **70**, 904–913 (2018)
18. Woo, S., Park, J., Lee, J.Y., Kweon, I.S.: Cbam: convolutional block attention module. In: Proceedings of the European Conference on Computer Vision (ECCV), pp. 3–19 (2018)
19. Yang, M., Sowmya, A.: An underwater color image quality evaluation metric. IEEE Trans. Image Process. **24**(12), 6062–6071 (2015)
20. Yang, N., Zhong, Q., Li, K., Cong, R., Zhao, Y., Kwong, S.: A reference-free underwater image quality assessment metric in frequency domain. Sig. Process. Image Commun. **94**, 116218 (2021)
21. You, J., Korhonen, J.: Transformer for image quality assessment. In: 2021 IEEE International Conference on Image Processing (ICIP), pp. 1389–1393. IEEE (2021)
22. Zhang, W., Ma, K., Yan, J., Deng, D., Wang, Z.: Blind image quality assessment using a deep bilinear convolutional neural network. IEEE Trans. Circuits Syst. Video Technol. **30**(1), 36–47 (2018)

I2QED: A Benchmark Database for Infrared Imaging Quality Evaluation

Chengxun Zhou[1,2,3,4,5,6](✉), Xiaojie Fan[5], Guangcheng Wang[7],
Yanlin Jiang[1,2,3,4], Yuchen Liu[1,2,3,4], Hongyan Liu[1,2,3,4], and Ke Gu[1,2,3,4]

[1] Faculty of Information Technology, Beijing University of Technology, Beijing, China
zhouchengxu@lnut.edu.cn

[2] Engineering Research Center of Intelligent Perception and Autonomous Control of Ministry of Education, Beijing, China

[3] Beijing Laboratory of Smart Environmental Protection, Beijing, China

[4] Beijing Artificial Intelligence Institute, Beijing, China

[5] School of Electronic and Information Engineering, Liaoning University of Technology, Liaoning, China

[6] Key Laboratory of Intelligent Control and Optimization for Industrial Equipment of Ministry of Education, Dalian University of Technology, Dalian, China

[7] School of Transportation and Civil Engineering, Nantong University, Nantong, China

Abstract. The infrared images have wider practical value in industry, medicine and military. They capture the long wave at the infrared camera, which will cause unique distortions differently to natural images. The current research of image quality assessment (IQA) for infrared images has been largely overlooked so far. To fill this void, we describe a novel benchmark infrared imaging quality evaluation database, dubbed I2QED. The database includes 50 reference (original) images from other available infrared image datasets. The pristine images are distorted by introducing white noise, blur, non-uniformity and compression for the acquisition and transmission of the long wave signals. The 5000 distorted images with various human visual perception quality are obtained by five different levels of degradation for each type. The 5050 images including reference and distorted images are evaluated by 30 inexperienced observers to obtain mean opinion scores (MOS). We analyze the I2QED database using 13 traditional and advanced objective quality evaluation measures. Experimental results confirm the effectiveness and versatility of the proposed database, and weaknesses of existing algorithms.

Keywords: Image quality assessment · infrared image quality database · subjective and objective evaluation

This work was supported in part by the National Science Foundation of China under Grant 62322302, Grant 62273011, Grant 62076013, Grant 62021003; in part by the Beijing Natural Science Foundation under Grant JQ21014; in part by the Key Laboratory of Intelligent Control and Optimization for Industrial Equipment of Ministry of Education, Dalian University of Technology under Grant LICO2022TB03.

G. Zhai et al. (Eds.): IFTC 2023, CCIS 2067, pp. 16–27, 2024.
https://doi.org/10.1007/978-981-97-3626-3_2

1 Introduction

The infrared images have been significant in many applications and areas such as industry [1], medicine [2], firefighting [3], science [4], military and security surveillance [5,6]. The infrared images are generated by non-illumination based imagers, which can capture images in cases of low light or even complete darkness scenes [3]. We focus on infrared image analysis since they have been a significant field of research in humans' life. We store and transmit the infrared images by different types media channels. There are various signal distortions on the transmission channels. The infrared camera itself or scene condition may cause artifacts. The compression and non uniformity noise often affect the infrared image quality. The image quality assessment (IQA) can be used to guide the construction and adjustment of image acquisition equipment and processing system, as well as optimize image processing algorithms and parameter setting. Therefore, evaluating image quality becomes an important step for both applicational development and scientific research for image signal analysis and processing system. Commonly, IQA includes two types, subjective evaluation and objective evaluation. The subjective assessment achieves mean opinion score (MOS) by time-consuming and expensive human tests. Though it is known as the best performance IQA standard, this can not satisfy the requirements of real-time. Over the last decades, the objective IQA approaches including full-reference (FR), reduced-reference (RR) [7] and no reference (NR) [8,10] have attracted lots of researchers' attention at home and abroad. Recently, many scholars have devoted to explore the novelty of RR and NR IQA [11–13] due to a lack of the original image. However, the RR and NR IQA techniques have good performance for specific types of distortion, such as noise, blur, contrast change and compression, and they are not effective for other conditions.

Extensive FR IQA work has been conducted on research of evaluating image quality. The most well-known FR IQA models are perhaps structural similarity index (SSIM) and peak signal-to-noise ratio (PSNR) [14] assuming we know the reference image. Then many advanced SSIM-type of FR IQA models have been proposed to have good performance [15,16]. Other different types FR IQA metrics are also devised. It is developed from the perspective of information measure called visual information fidelity (VIF) [17]. The plan based on detection and appearance is utilized by the most apparent distortion (MAD) [18]. Afterwards, gradient similarity index (GSIM) [19], feature similarity index (FSIM) [20], VS-based index (VSI) [21], internal generative mechanism (IGM) [22] and spectral residual (SR) SR-SSIM [23] have been presented owing to explore the IQA method for extracting low-level features including phase and gradient. The measures above are based on limited hand-crafted features of images. However, it is difficult to keep consistent with human visual system which is a complicated process. In contrast, FR-IQA metrics based on deep learning networks have grown in popularity over the past 10 years [26–28], because they extract features without prior knowledge. Gao et al. [24] firstly proposed the deep learning-based IQA model by computing the local features similarities from VGGNet [25] between pristine and distorted images.

Nonetheless, the infrared image quality assessment (IIQA) work has been little done. Only some statistics of infrared images have been studied. [29] developed the Natural Scene Statistics (NSS) model of long wave infrared (LWIR) images, and the statistical regularities of LWIR images are similar to visible light images. The NSS model of LWIR images can present global and local distortion evaluations, and predict human subjective quality assessment performance. [30] studied the NSS model of images fused with LWIR images and visible light images. The fused images processed by divisively normalized and band-pass filtered have statistical regularities, and we can use them to build IIQA models to obtain the fused image quality scores. [31] analyzed the NSS model of fused images affected by different kinds of distortions, studied the subjective IQA model of original and distorted fused images was studies, and proposed an opinion-aware fused image IQA algorithm which correlate better with human perceptual evaluations compared with other methods.

The IQA of visible light images containing noise, compression distorted, and commonly encountered blur has been studied in depth in previous years, the IQA for infrared images has been mostly overlooked in the papers. Therefore, we focus on exploring the IIQA in this paper. In this research, due to lack of the infrared image database, we create a novel database for assessing infrared imaging quality evaluation algorithms, dubbed I2QED, before analyzing the subjective and objective quality of infrared images. The database consists of 5000 distorted infrared images obtained from 50 original ones in the three infrared datasets including CVC-09 [32], CVC-14 [33] and IR Data. The pristine images are distorted by introducing white noise, blurring, non-uniformity and compression for the acquisition and transmission of the long wave signals. The 5000 distorted images with various human visual perception quality are obtained by five different levels of degradation for each type. In terms of the standard ITU-R BT.500-13 [34], we invited 30 inexperienced observers to evaluate the 5050 images including reference and distorted images in the suitable illuminance and distance setting. In the subjective experiment, we recorded the mean opinion scores (MOSs) coming form these viewers. In the objective experiment, we used 13 existing IQA measures including traditional methods (e.g., SSIM [29], VIF [17], MAD [17], GSIM [19], FSIM [20], Gradient Magnitude Similarity Deviation (GMSD) [41], and local-tuned-global (LTG) VIF [42]).

The rest of this article is structured as follows. Section 2 describes the database construction by a description of the original datasets, and introduces the degradations for various types of distortion created the proposed database. Section 3 provides an analysis of the new database by the subjective experiment and objective experiment. In Sect. 3, we obtain initial subjective evaluation results and use the traditional perceptual metrics to describe the image objective quality and analyze the results. Section 4 gives a general conclusion.

2   Construction of I2QED

In this section, both sources and distortion of infrared images are introduced.

Fig. 1. Display of 9 representative original infrared images of the I2QED database from three public datasets. Those in the blue box are from CVC-09 [32], those in the red box are from CVC-15 [33], and those in the green box are from METU Multi-Modal Stereo Datasets [34,35]. (Color figure online)

2.1 Sources of Infrared Images

The I2QED database consists of 50 source infrared images which were collected from three public databases namely CVC-09 [32], CVC-14 [33] and METU Multi-Modal Stereo Datasets [34,35]. CVC-09 is FIR Sequence Pedestrian Dataset. Two sets of sequences, named as the night and day sets, which represent the moment of the day and night they were acquired. Two sets of images include 5990 frames and 5081 frames respectively for training and testing of each sequence. CVC-15 [33] include 100 pairs of visible and LWIR images. In order to find all the images in horizontal lines, they were aligned and rectified. There are outdoor images containing different city scenarios. The METU Multi-Modal Stereo Datasets consists of two sets which are the synthetically altered stereo images and visible-infrared images using a Kinect device. Figure 1 shows 9 representative original infrared images of the I2QED database from three public datasets.

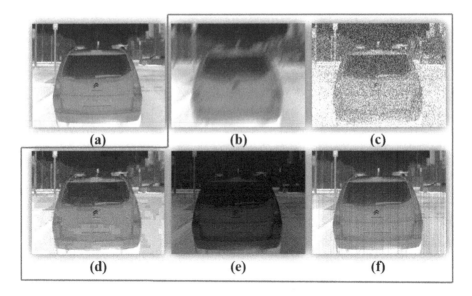

Fig. 2. Examples of distorted infrared images after some distortions as follows: (a) original image, (b) Blur, (c) AWGN, (d) JPEG compression, (e) Brightness, (f) Non-Uniformity.

2.2 Distortion of Infrared Images

It is known to all that IIQA is a meaningful and significant topic in scientific development and applicational research due to distortions in the LWIE spectrum. These applications include distortion recognition in some given infrared images, improving infrared image quality by avoiding distortion, and making better performance and more accurate thermal imagers. We introduce the I2QED dataset to simulate the process of distorted image generation.

Several distorted infrared image research have been conducted to characterize and model distortions in signal transmission process. Non-uniformity (NU) fixed pattern noise [37] can be seen in infrared images obtained from focal plane arrays, resulting in a grid like pattern. We use the spectral additive model of NU fixed pattern noise reported in [29,38] in this work.

We used some frequent types of distortions that can affect infrared images, such as additive white gaussian noise (AWGN), blur, JPEG compression, and NU noise. The standard deviation parameter NU, which adjusts the dynamic range of the NU noise, is used to manage the distortion level. Throughout the study, three distortion levels were utilized for each distortion type, which were applied to the infrared images of 50 source infrared images from three public databases. The standard deviation for AWGN and NU was modified as AWGN = 0.001, 0.005, 0.01, 0.005, 0.1, NU = 0.001, 0.005, 0.01, 0.05, 0.1, 0.5; for blur, a Gaussian blur kernel of size 384 * 288 pixels was used with blur = 0, 5, 10, 15,

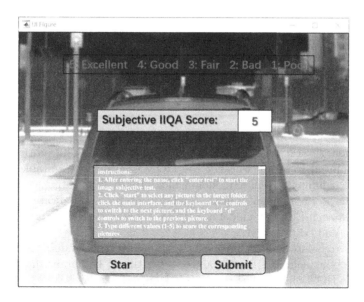

Fig. 3. Graphical user interface utilized to rate image quality

20, 25; and for JPEG compression, the quality was set to 80, 60, 40, 20, 10, 5. Figure 2 shows various examples of distorted infrared images.

3   Analysis of I2QED

In this section, we will analyze the subjective experiment and the performance of traditional objective IQA methods to assess the perceptual quality of the infrared images in the I2QED database.

3.1   Subjective Experiment

This section aims to collect the subjective quality scores of the infrared images in our database. Since obtaining an image with no distortion is difficult, we use the single stimulus method recommended by the ITU. Our subjective assessment experiment involves 30 college students whose ages in range from 18 to 22. All of them have either corrected or normal vision. We ensure all students know the aim and the testing processing of the subjective experiment, before the formal personal experiment begins. Our subjective evaluation include two steps. In the first step, we teach all the students how to evaluate the quality of various infrared images by a brief train. The train can assist participants in becoming acquainted with the scoring techniques and criteria in order to increase their accuracy. In the second step, the users use GUI to score the 5050 infrared images, which is a formal test. Each student rest every few minutes to avoid unnecessary mistakes because of visual fatigue. The GUI allows viewers to switch between and score the infrared images in our dataset, which can become more efficient for the subjective experiment since there are 5050 infrared images. The quality scores of images can then be saved as a form by clicking on the "Submit" button. For the subjective experiment, we set the following image quality ratings: 1: poor, 2: bad, 3: fair, 4: good, and 5: excellent, as shown in Fig. 3.

3.2   Objective Experiment

In this section, several existing IQA models including existing traditional methods are employed to study whether the I2QED database is suitable to IIQA. We have 13 common FR IQA models which are good performance for visible images. Then, some frequently used standards are used to indicate the correlation between each FR IQA model and MOS. Finally, we elaborate the analysis by the table and scatter figure.

In order to remove the nonlinearity of the correlation values, a monotonic logistic function including five parameters is utilized to obtain the prediction scores of the IIQA metric. The monotonic logistic function is set as following:

$$W(x) = \beta_1(0.5 - \frac{1}{1 + e^{\beta_2(x - \beta_3)}}) + \beta_4 x + \beta_5 \qquad (1)$$

We draw on four statistical standards in [31] to measure the correlation between objective IQA models predicted value and subjective scores. These performance results can show various information and represent the predictive power of the IQA methods by different ways. We analyze the I2QED dataset by comparing 13 traditional and advanced objective quality evaluation measures methods for infrared images in Figs. 4, 5, 6 and 7. We sum up four conclusions:

(1) The first index is the Pearson linear correlation coefficient (PLCC) which is used to evaluate accuracy by computing the correlation between subjective

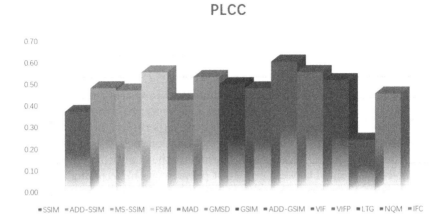

Fig. 4. PLCC performance comparison of existing FR IQA metrics on the I2QED.

SROCC

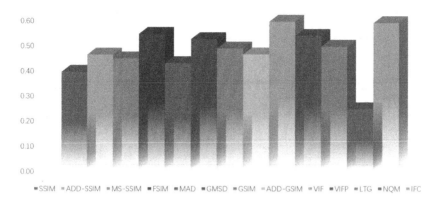

Fig. 5. SROCC performance comparison of existing FR IQA metrics on the I2QED.

KROCC

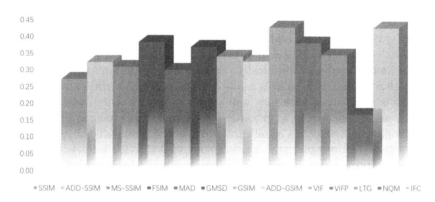

Fig. 6. KROCC performance comparison of existing FR IQA metrics on the I2QED.

and objective values as shown in Fig. 4. It is evident that all the existing objective IQA methods for nature scene images not have good performance. The FR IQA methods such as VIP and FSIM [20] do not achieve values of 0.7 for PLCC. The nature scene image evaluation algorithms are not good at assessing infrared images quality due to their unique characteristics. It is necessary to develop high-performance objective IQA modes specifically tailored for infrared images.

(2) The second index is the Spearman rank-order correlation coefficient (SROCC). It reflects the monotonicity, and it is known that it is not influenced by monotonic nonlinear as shown in Fig. 5. The performance of FR IQA metrics such as IFC and GSIM are found to be high when applied to visible images due to the significance of image gradients in these images. On

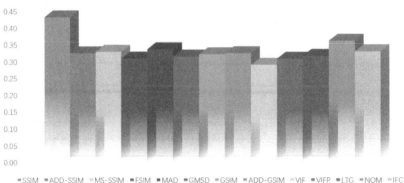

Fig. 7. RMSE performance comparison of existing FR IQA metrics on the I2QED.

the other hand, VIF and VIFP [44] metrics outperform most other FR IQAs by being less affected by motion blur. It shows that the visual saliency features extracted by VIF, and VIFP models are valuable for evaluating image quality for infrared images. It is notable that the saliency models used in these models were not specifically designed for infrared images.

(3) The third index is Kendall's rank-order correlation coefficient (KROCC) which is used to measure how well subjective scores match with objective scores as shown in Fig. 6. It can be seen that some hand-craft FR IQA methods do not exhibit a significantly high correlation with subjective quality scores. For instance, the performance of NQM for infrared images is unsatisfactory. This advises that the commonly-used assessment evaluation methods for infrared images may not be suitable. The limited presence of distortions such as NU noise, JPEG artifacts and brightness change in infrared images makes the NQM model less effective compared to state-of-the-art methods used for natural images.

(4) The last two indices are root mean-squared error (RMSE) and mean absolute error (MAE) as shown in Fig. 7. We inspected the performance of SSIM [14] and SSIM-based FR IQA metrics on infrared images. All SSIM-based IQA models show an improvement over SSIM, which indicates their ability to analyze some distortion of infrared images. Both ADD-SSIM [39] and MS-SSIM [40] specifically are good at analyzing the impact of distortion on image structure. Among these SSIM-based IQA methods, ADD-SSIM performs better. On the other hand, SSIM exhibits inferior performance.

For these four statistical standards, the values of PLCC, SROCC, and KROCC close to 1 representing the better performance of IQA metrics, while the values of RMSE and MAE close to 0. The scatter plots serve as a frequently-used visualization tool in IQA studies to provide direct comparisons among different metrics. We depict the versus results obtained from testing some traditional objective FR IQA methods on our proposed the I2QED database. The algorithms research include NQM, FSIM, GMSD, LTG, VIFP, and VIF. It can be seen that all the methods exhibit bad convergence and linearity which implies that these models not yield more consistent results between objective ratings and subjective scores. Particularly, the NQM for infrared images is worst performance showing sample points are situated further away from 1.

4 Conclusion

In this study, we conducted a comprehensive investigation into the issue of assessing the quality of infrared images. To facilitate research on evaluating the quality of these images, we created a meticulously designed the I2QED database. This database consists of 5050 distorted images with varying levels of AWGN, motion blur, JPEG compression, and specific NU noise. We also collected MOS values from both experienced and inexperienced individuals to associate with each infrared image including reference and distorted images. Furthermore, we compared and analyzed 13 FR IQA models that contained some traditional IQA methods. Experimental results prove that the existing nature scene image evaluation algorithms are not good at assessing infrared images quality due to their unique characteristics. Moving forward, our involve expanding the size of the database by including more lossless images and developing high-performance objective IQA models specifically tailored for infrared images.

References

1. Usamentiaga, R., Venegas, P., Guerediaga, J., Vega, L., Molleda, J., Bulnes, F.G.: Infrared thermography for temperature measurement and non-destructive testing. Sensors **14**(7), 12305–12348 (2014)
2. Diakides, M., Bronzino, J.D., Peterson, D.R.: Medical infrared imaging: principles and practices. CRC Press (2012)
3. Gade, R., Moeslund, T.B.: Thermal cameras and applications: a survey, machine vision and applications. Mach. Vis. Appl. **25**(1), 245–262 (2014)
4. Zelmati, O., Bondžulić, B., Pavlović, B., et al.: Study of subjective and objective quality assessment of infrared compressed images. J. Electr. Eng. **73**(2), 73–87 (2022)
5. Haque, M.J., Muntjir, M.: Night vision technology: an overview. Int. J. Comput. Appl. **167**(13), 37–42 (2017)
6. Chen, G., Wang, W.: Target recognition in infrared circumferential scanning system via deep convolutional neural networks. Sensors **20**(7), 1–18 (2020)
7. Gu, K., Zhai, G., Yang, X., Zhang, W.: A new reduced-reference image quality assessment using structural degradation model. In: IEEE International Symposium on Circuits and Systems, pp. 1095–1098 (2013)
8. Gu, K., Lin, W., Zhai, G., et al.: No-reference quality metric of contrast-distorted images based on information maximization. IEEE Trans. Cybern. **47**(12), 4559–4565 (2017)

9. Gu, K., Tao, D., Qiao, J., et al.: Learning a no-reference quality assessment model of enhanced images with big data. IEEE Trans. Neural Networks Learn. Syst. **29**(4), 1301–1313 (2017)

10. Gu, K., Zhai, G., Lin, W., Yang, X., Zhang, W.: No-reference image sharpness assessment in autoregressive parameter space. IEEE Trans. Image Process. **24**(10), 3218–3231 (2015)

11. Liu, D., Xu, Y., Quan, Y., Yu, Z., Le Callet, P.: Directional regularity for visual quality estimation. Signal Process. **110**, 211–221 (2015)

12. Gu, K., Zhai, G., Yang, X., Zhang, W.: Hybrid no-reference quality metric for singly and multiply distorted images. IEEE Trans. Broadcast. **60**(3), 555–567 (2014)

13. Gu, K., Zhai, G., Yang, X., Zhang, W.: Using free energy principle for blind image quality assessment. IEEE Trans. Multimedia **17**(1), 50–63 (2015)

14. Wang, Z., Bovik, A.C., Sheikh, H.R., Simoncelli, E.P.: Image quality assessment: from error visibility to structural similarity. IEEE Trans. Image Process. **13**(4), 600–612 (2004)

15. Wang, Z., Simoncelli, E.P., Bovik, A.C.: Multi-scale structural similarity for image quality assessment. In: Proc. Conf. Record 37th Asilomar Conf. Signals Syst. Comput., pp. 1398–1402 (2003)

16. Wang, Z., Li, Q.: Information content weighting for perceptual image quality assessment. IEEE Trans. Image Process. **20**(5), 1185–1198 (2011)

17. Sheikh, H.R., Bovik, A.C.: Image information and visual quality. IEEE Trans. Image Process. **15**(2), 430–444 (2006)

18. Larson, E.C., Chandler, D.M.: Most apparent distortion: fullreference image quality assessment and the role of strategy. J. Electron. Imaging **19**(1), 011006-011006-21 (2010)

19. Liu, A., Lin, W., Narwaria, M.: Image quality assessment based on gradient similarity. IEEE Trans. Image Process. **21**(4), 1500–1512 (2012)

20. Zhang, L., Zhang, L., Mou, X., Zhang, D.: FSIM: a feature similarity index for image quality assessment. IEEE Trans. Image Process. **20**(8), 2378–2386 (2011)

21. Zhang, L., Shen, Y., Li, H.: VSI: a visual saliency induced index for perceptual image quality assessment. IEEE Trans. Image Process. **23**(10), 4270–4281 (2014)

22. Wu, J., Lin, W., Shi, G., Liu, A.: Perceptual quality metric with internal generative mechanism. IEEE Trans. Image Process. **22**(1), 43–54 (2013)

23. Zhang, L., Li, H.: SR-SIM: a fast and high performance IQA index based on spectral residual. In: 2012 19th IEEE International Conference on Image Processing, pp. 1473–1476 (2012)

24. Gao, F., Wang, Y., Li, P., et al.: Deepsim: deep similarity for image quality assessment. Neurocomputing **257**, 104–114 (2017)

25. Shi, S., Bai, Q., Cao, M., et al.: Region-adaptive deformable network for image quality assessment. In: In IEEE Conference on Computer Vision and Pattern Recognition Workshops, pp. 324–333 (2021)

26. Zhang, R., Isola, P., Efros, A.A., et al.: The unreasonable effectiveness of deep features as a perceptual metric. In: Proceedings of the IEEE Conference on Computer Vision and Pattern Recognition, pp. 586–595 (2018)

27. Krizhevsky, A., Sutskever, I., Hinton, G.E.: Imagenet classification with deep convolutional neural networks. Advances in neural information processing systems, pp. 25 (2012)

28. Ding, K., Ma, K., Wang, S., et al.: Image quality assessment: unifying structure and texture similarity. IEEE Trans. Pattern Anal. Mach. Intell. **44**(5), 2567–2581 (2020)

29. Goodall, T., Bovik, A.C., Paulter, N.G.: Tasking on natural statistics of infrared images. IEEE Trans. Image Process. **25**(1), 65–79 (2016)

30. Moreno-Villamarin, D.E., Benitez-Restrepo, H.D., Bovik, A.C.: Statistics of natural fused image distortions. In:2017 IEEE International Conference on Acoustics, Speech and Signal Processing (ICASSP), pp. 1243–1247 (2017)

31. Moreno-Villamarin, D.E., Benitez-Restrepo, H.D., Bovik, A.C.: Predicting the quality of fused long wave infrared and visible light images. IEEE Trans. Image Process. **26**(7), 3479–3491 (2017)

32. Socarrs, Y., Ramos, S., Vzquez, D., L®pez, A.M., Gevers, T.: Adapting pedestrian detection from synthetic to far infrared images. In: Proceedings of ICCV Workshops Vis. Domain Adaptation Dataset Bias, pp. 1–3 (2013)

33. CVC, Cvc-15: Multimodal stereo dataset2 (2016). http://adas.cvc.uab.es/elektra/enigma-portfolio/cvc-15-multimodal-stereo-dataset-2/

34. Yaman, M., Kalkan, S.: An iterative adaptive multi-modal stereo-vision method using mutual information. J. Vis. Commun. Image Represent. **26**, 115–131 (2015)

35. Yaman, M., Kalkan, S.: Multimodal stereo vision using mutual information with adaptive windowing. In: 13th IAPR Conference on Machine Vision and Applications, Kyoto, Japan (2013)

36. Yang, H., Wu, S., Deng, C., Lin, W.: Scale and orientation invariant text segmentation for born-digital compound images. IEEE Trans. Cybern. **45**(3), 533–547 (2015)

37. Rajic, N.: Nondestructive Testing Handbook: Infrared and Thermal Testing. American Society for Nondestructive Testing (2001)

38. Pezoa, J.E., Medina, O.J.: Spectral model for fixed-pattern-noise in infrared focal-plane arrays. In: Progress in Pattern Recognition, Image Analysis, Computer Vision, and Applications: 16th Iberoamerican Congress, pp. 55–63 (2011)

39. Gu, K., Wang, S., Zhai, G., Lin, W., Yang, X., Zhang, W.: Analysis of distortion distribution for pooling in image quality prediction. IEEE Trans. Broadcast. **62**(2), 446–456 (2016)

40. Wang, Z., Simoncelli, E.P., Bovik, A.C.: Multiscale structural similarity for image quality assessment. In: Proceeding 37th Asilomar Conference on Signals, 2, pp. 1398–1402 (2003)

41. Xue, W., Zhang, L., Mou, X., Bovik, A.C.: Gradient magnitude similarity deviation: a highly efficient perceptual image quality index. IEEE Trans. Image Process. **23**(2), 684–695 (2013)

42. Gu, K., Zhai, G., Yang, X., et al.: An efficient color image quality metric with local-tuned-global model. In: IEEE International Conference on Image Processing (ICIP), pp. 506–510 (2014)

43. Damera-Venkata, N., Kite, T.D., Geisler, W.S., et al.: Image quality assessment based on a degradation model. IEEE Trans. Image Process. **9**(4), 636–650 (2000)

44. Sheikh, H.R., Bovik, A.C., De Veciana, G.: An information fidelity criterion for image quality assessment using natural scene statistics. IEEE Trans. Image Process. **14**(12), 2117–2128 (2005)

45. Cheon, M., Yoon, S.J., Kang, B., et al.: Perceptual image quality assessment with transformers. In: Proceedings of the IEEE/CVF Conference on Computer Vision and Pattern Recognition, pp. 433–442 (2021)

46. Lao, S., Gong, Y., Shi, S., et al.: Attentions help cnns see better: attention-based hybrid image quality assessment network. In: Proceedings of the IEEE/CVF Conference on Computer Vision and Pattern Recognition, pp. 1140–1149 (2022)

Perceptual Blind Panoramic Image Quality Assessment Based on Super-Pixel

Shuyu Xiao[1], Yongfang Wang[1], Yinhan Wang[1(✉)], and Zhijun Fang[2]

[1] School of Communication and Information Engineering, Shanghai University,
Shanghai 200444, China
yfw@shu.edu.cn
[2] School of Computer Science and Technology, Donghua University, Shanghai 201620, China

Abstract. Blind objective quality assessment of panoramic images (PIQA) is a great challenge to perform highly consistent with human perception without the original panoramic images. In this paper, we propose a perceptual blind PIQA method based super-pixel, which exploits the equirectangular projection (ERP) and human perception characteristics for panoramic image to boost up the quality assessment performance. In particular, in order to make use of the local features of panoramic image, panoramic weights based on super-pixel is designed by combining ERP format and human perception. In addition, we propose panoramic-weighted structural features to predict the visual quality of panoramic images, which can reflect spherical quality accurately. Finally, we fuse and map extracted features into quality scores by applying support vector regression (SVR). The experiments demonstrate the effectiveness and superiority of our proposed metric compared with state-of-the-art PIQA methods on the public panoramic image datasets.

Keywords: Blind image quality assessment · super-pixel · panoramic weight

1 Introduction

Virtual reality has been developed rapidly in recent years. Users can acquire immersive experience when viewing panoramic images or videos through the head mounted displays (HMDs). This interactive experience forms the basis of virtual reality. Different from ordinary images and videos, panoramic images and videos require a larger field of view and higher resolution, which are important to immersive perception. However, due to the limitations of image capture and display devices and high-resolution compression processing, Quality of Experience will be affected severely by this distortion [1]. Therefore, it is of great significance to propose a new panoramic image quality assessment method (PIQA) for future virtual reality applications.

The traditional image is displayed on a flat screen, so the traditional image quality assessment (IQA) is also the evaluation of the image quality on the flat. While the observation space of panoramic images and videos is spherical and processing of evaluation is on the projected plane. As shown in Fig. 1, there is different distortion between

© The Author(s), under exclusive license to Springer Nature Singapore Pte Ltd. 2024
G. Zhai et al. (Eds.): IFTC 2023, CCIS 2067, pp. 28–38, 2024.
https://doi.org/10.1007/978-981-97-3626-3_3

Fig. 1. Distortion in ERP panoramic image and viewport image.

panoramic image from HDMs and its projected equirectangular projection (ERP) format image. At the same time, Fig. 1 shows that the nonlinear mapping from the spherical 3-D observation space to 2-D plane cannot reflect the aberration of the observation space [2].

Based on the nonlinear mapping between spherical panoramic image and its planar projection, researchers have proposed a variety of PIQA indicators. Craster parabolic projection peak signal noise ratio (CPP-PSNR) algorithm converts reference images and test images based on the Craster Parabolic projection, which can calculate the PSNR between panoramic sequences with different projection formats [3]. Spherical-PSNR (S-PSNR) evaluates quality of panoramic images based on the mean square error (MSE) and structural similarity (SSIM), which are calculated based on a set of sampling points uniformly distributed on the spherical surface [4]. Weighted spherical-PSNR (WS-PSNR) directly calculates the distortion of each pixel in the current projection format by weighting to avoid the error caused by interpolation [5]. Weighted to spherical uniform structure similarity (WS-SSIM) weights the structural similarity on the sphere based on nonlinear mapping relationships to more accurately evaluate the quality of spherical images [6]. In [7], a full reference PIQA method considering multi-level quality factors of region of interest (ROI) map is proposed.

Although the aforementioned PIQA indicators have good performance, they are all full-reference methods and have the limitation of requiring reference images. In addition, they are derived from traditional IQA indicators such as PSNR and lack the ability to match human eye perception [8, 9].

Recently, there have been some attempts to address the above limitations. Ding et al. propose a PIQA method without any reference utilizing the statistical characteristics of adjacent pixels correlation (APC) [10]. Multi-projection Fusion Attention Network (MFAN) which extracts features from projection images generated from multiple projection methods is proposed to improve the efficiency of features in PIQA [11]. Liu et al. propose simple linear iterative clustering (SLGC) by considering the hierarchical perception features of the human vision system, which includes specific information, local saliency information, global information, and color information [12].

At the same time, some researchers are trying to use mature deep learning frameworks to handle PIQA tasks. Sendjasni et al. use CNN to perform multiple regression on the quality score distribution of blocks to predict panoramic image quality scores [13]. Liu et al. propose the method of masked knowledge distillation to screen out effective information that characterizes the quality of panoramic images and then the student network extracts more comprehensive features from panoramic images for quality prediction [14].

Besides, researches on the characteristics of panoramic images show two findings. Firstly, the distortion measurement on the projection plane cannot linearly reflect the distortion on the spherical surface [15]. Secondly, according to the subjective experiment [16], when the human observes the panoramic image, the vicinity of the equator on the spherical surface will attract more attention. Inspired by the above two findings, we propose a perceptual blind PIQA algorithm based on super-pixel (SP-PIQA), which exploits the projection and human perception characteristics for panoramic image to boost up the assessment performance. The key idea is to formulate panoramic weighted structural features based on projection format and human perception, which can accurately reflect panoramic image distortions between observation space and projected plane. Meanwhile, in order to make use of the local features of panoramic image, the panoramic weight is calculated based on super-pixel segmentation. Experimental results show that the proposed SP-PIQA method can realize superior performance.

2 Proposed Method

In this paper, we propose a blind PIQA method to predict the visual quality of panoramic images. Figure 2 shows the framework of proposed model. Firstly, the local binary pattern (LBP) on the gradient map (GM) (GLBP) is used to represent the structural features of the ERP format, which is effective to capture the information degradation of image [17]. Secondly, considering that the spherical visual distortion cannot be reflected linearly by the features extracted from ERP format and the equator on the spherical surface will attract more attention, the fusion panoramic weight combining projection weight with perception weight is calculated based on super-pixel. Then we accumulate the panoramic weights of super-pixels with same GLBP pattern to generate the panoramic features, which ensure the structural feature extracted from ERP format can reflect spherical quality accurately. Finally, a quality predictor based on support vector regression (SVR) is adopted to predict scores of panoramic images.

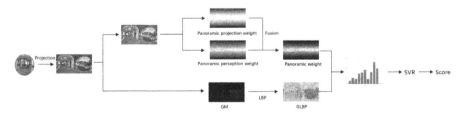

Fig. 2. The framework of proposed model.

Edge is an important feature of image. The second-order derivative can effectively capture the peak value of image edge, which plays an important role in image feature extraction [18]. In order to predict the visual quality of panoramic images, we first use Prewitt operator to extract the first-order derivative of ERP format panoramic images. Prewitt operator is used for image edge detection as a differential operator [19]. Its principle is to realize edge detection by using the difference generated by the gray value of pixels in a specific region. Then, the second-order derivative is extracted by encoding each pixel with rotation invariant uniform GLBP. Through computing gray-level differences, the LBP operator indicates the relationship between the center pixel and its surrounding neighbors [17]. We apply the LBP operator on the first-order derivative map, and the rotation invariant uniform GLBP is defined as:

$$GLBP_{P,R} = \begin{cases} \sum_{i=0}^{P-1} \theta(g_i - g_c), & u(GLBP_{P,R}) \leq 2 \\ p + 1, & others \end{cases} \tag{1}$$

$$\theta(g_i - g_c) = \begin{cases} 1, & g_i - g_c \geq 0 \\ 0, & g_i - g_c < 0 \end{cases} \tag{2}$$

$$u(GLBP_{P,R}) = \|\theta(g_{P-1} - g_c) - \theta(g_0 - g_c)\|$$
$$+ \sum_{i=0}^{P-1} \|\theta(g_i - g_c) - \theta(g_{i-1} - g_c)\| \tag{3}$$

where P is the number of neighbor pixel and R means the radius of neighborhood. g_c and g_i represent the gradient magnitudes of the center pixel and its neighbors, respectively. And u is a uniform index which is used to calculate the number of bitwise transitions. The types of the GLBP patterns are reduces to $P+2$ due to the limitation of u, as experiments in [17] show that rotation invariant uniform patterns are sufficient to represent the most edge of images. However, the GLBP on ERP format cannot linearly reflect the distortion in spherical observation surface. Therefore, we modify it by combining projection weight and perception weight based on panoramic characteristics.

Furthermore, super-pixel segmentation is used to segment images as a preprocessing step in visual detection models by some researchers [20, 21]. Compared with pixel-level methods, super-pixel method greatly reduces the complexity of subsequent image processing tasks [20]. Besides, the human eyes pay more attention to the region of an object (super-pixel) instead of pixel [21]. Therefore, we use super-pixel method to make use of the local features of panoramic image.

2.1 Panoramic Projection Weight Based on Super-Pixel

As the example shown in Fig. 3, the degree of pixel stretching is directly proportional to its longitude in the correspondence between ERP projection images and spherical images.

Based on the above observation, the stretched ratio (SR) from the ERP projection plane to the sphere is defined as the projection weight which ensures that the extracted features are more consistent with the perception of the human eyes. According to [5], SR is derived as:

$$SR(i, j) = cos \frac{(j + 0.5 - N/2)\pi}{N} \tag{4}$$

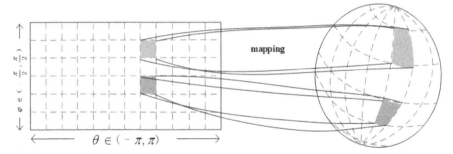

Fig. 3. The mapping from ERP to spherical space.

where M is the height of ERP panoramic image and N is the width of ERP panoramic image. (i, j) represents pixel coordinates, and $\{(i, j)|0 < i \leq M, 0 < j \leq N\}$. SR of other projection formats can also be obtained by the same method [5], and the SR is related to the projection format only.

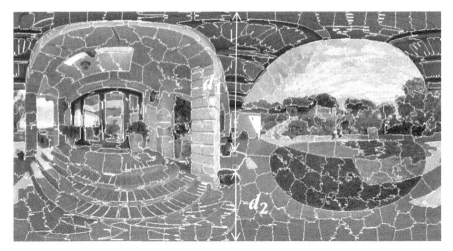

Fig. 4. Illustration of the calculation of distance.

In order to make use of the local features of panoramic image, we segment panoramic images into super-pixel using the simple linear iterative clustering (SLIC) algorithm [22]. We take the maximum pixel SR among the super-pixel as the SR of that super-pixel. Thus, panoramic projection weight of each super-pixel is defined as:

$$\omega_{1m} = SR(i, d_{min}) \tag{5}$$

$$d_{min} = min\{d_1^1, d_2^1, \cdots d_1^n, d_2^n\} \tag{6}$$

where m is the number of super-pixels in each panoramic image, n represents the number of pixels in each super-pixel. As shown in Fig. 4, d_1^n is the distance between pixel and the upper edge of image, and d_2^n is the distance between pixel and the lower edge of image. They can be calculated according to Eq. 7.

$$\begin{cases} d_1^n = y_n \\ d_2^n = N - y_n \end{cases} \tag{7}$$

where y_n is the ordinate of the nth pixel in the super-pixel, and N represent the height of the panoramic image.

2.2 Panoramic Perception Weight Based on Super-Pixel

When watching panoramic image, observers pay much more attention to the equatorial region of the sphere than other regions according to the subjective experiment in [15]. In order to make the predicted quality score more consistent with human perception, we propose panoramic perception weight based on super-pixel.

Firstly, we use SLIC method to segment the panoramic image into several super-pixels which have different possibility of attracting human attention. Then, we propose the perception weight ω_{2m} to describe the probability that each super-pixel attracts human attention. It is determined by the minimum distance between the pixels in super-pixel and the upper and lower edges of the panoramic image. The farther away from the upper and lower boundaries of the panoramic image, the closer the super-pixel is to the equator, and we give it a higher weight. Therefore, panoramic perception weight is able to calculate as Eq. 8.

$$\omega_{2m} = d_{min} \tag{8}$$

where the calculation of d_{min} is the same as Eq. 6.

Fig. 5. Fusion panoramic weight map.

Finally, we fuse the panoramic projection weight and panoramic perceptual weight into fusion panoramic weight. The fusion panoramic weight is defined in Eq. 9. And Fig. 5 shows the fusion weight map.

$$\omega = \omega_{1m} \times \omega_{2m} \tag{9}$$

2.3 Panoramic-Weighted Structural Feature

We use the panoramic weights ω to weight the GLBP coding of ERP panoramic images, and then accumulate based on super-pixels, which reflects the visual perception of the sphere observed by the human eye more accurately. The panoramic weighted GLBP histogram is defined as:

$$PW(k) = \sum\nolimits_{i=1}^{N} \omega \cdot \varphi(GLBP_{P,R}(i), k) \tag{10}$$

where N is the number of super-pixels, $N = 400$ works best in experiments. ω is the fusion panoramic weight. We set $P = 8$ and $R = 1$ according to [23], thus there are 10 bins for each $PW(k)$. GLBP value is k, and function $\varphi(\cdot)$ is calculated as:

$$\varphi(x, y) = \begin{cases} 1, x = y \\ 0, otherwise \end{cases} \tag{11}$$

In addition, combined with the multi-scale perception characteristics of human visual system (HVS), the proposed method combines the features of original image scale and five images scales.

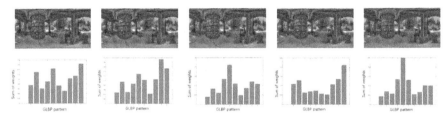

Fig. 6. Panoramic-weighted structural feature of different distortion type. The first row is original image, JPEG, JPEG2000, Gaussian noise, Gaussian blur. The second row is corresponding histogram of first row.

Figure 6 shows the features map obtained from images of different distortions. The result demonstrates that histogram distributions are affected by the kinds of distortion.

3 Experiment

3.1 Databases and Evaluation Methodology

The comparison experiments were conducted on the public panoramic image database [24]. There are 16 pristine reference images and 320 distorted images in this PIQA dataset. The distorted images are generated by introducing JPEG compression, JPEG2000 compression, Gaussian blur (GB) and Gaussian white noise (GN) to the pristine images.

We use Spearman rank-order correlation coefficient (SRCC), Kendall rank-over correlation coefficient (KRCC), Pearson linear correlation coefficient (PLCC) and root mean square error (RMSE) to measure the performance of PIQA indicators. Among them, the higher the values of SRCC, KRCC and PLCC, the closer the predicted score is to the subjective mean opinion scores (MOS). And RMSE shows the deviation between the predicted score and MOS. Smaller RMSE means smaller deviation.

3.2 Performance Comparison and Evaluation

In this section, we conduct comparative experiments between the proposed SP-PIQA and with several state-of-the-art PIQA methods, including S-PSNR, CPP-PSNR, WS-PSNR, WS-SSIM and traditional IQA metrics PSNR and SSIM. Among them, CPP-PSNR, WS-PSNR, and S-PSNR evaluate the quality only by Y component.

In the proposed model, the LIBSVM package [25] is employed to fuse the extracted features into quality scores. In detail, ε-SVR based on a radial basis function (RBF) kernel is utilized. We choose the parameters of SVR by optimizing function of parameter search [25]. In this experiment, we randomly selected 80% of the distorted images for training and the remaining 20% for testing. We repeated the above operation 1000 times and recorded the median as the final predicted score, because that the times of random splits decrease, the median results fluctuate very much. When times of the random training-testing split is1000, the median result is relatively stable.

Table 1. Performance Comparison with other metrics

Metrics	SRCC	KRCC	PLCC	RMSE
PSNR	0.4979	0.3382	0.5080	1.8211
SSIM	0.3483	0.2492	0.4373	1.9014
CPP-PSNR [3]	0.5182	0.3502	0.5186	1.8078
WS-PSNR [5]	0.5032	0.3414	0.5044	1.8256
S-PSNR [4]	0.5303	0.3588	0.5319	1.7904
WS-SSIM [6]	0.4311	0.2955	0.4591	1.8783
PW	0.7781	0.5792	0.7974	1.2843
HW	0.7908	0.5929	0.8131	1.2410
SP-PIQA	**0.8067**	**0.6072**	**0.8296**	**1.1898**

The predictive performance is listed in Table 1, the model with best performance highlighted in bold. In addition, to verify the effectiveness of the fusion strategy of weight map, the performance of projection weight (PW) and perception weight (HW) only is also listed.

From Table 1, we can draw a conclusion that the prediction results of panoramic quality by SP-PIQA model are more consistent to the subjective MOS. Compared with PSNR and SSIM, the proposed SP-PIQA makes significant improvements in SRCC, KRCC and PLCC. Specifically, SP-PIQA achieves 62.02% and 131.61% improvement on SRCC, respectively. Other methods [3–6] consider the panoramic features of the image, and perform better than PSNR and SSIM. However, SP-PIQA is still outstanding. The performance of SP-PIQA on SRCC, KRCC and PLCC improves 63.81%, 81.49% and 65.28% in average. In addition, the proposed method also achieved excellent performance in RMSE index, with an average reduction of 35%.

In particular, better performance is achieved with only projection weighted features or perception weighted features as well. Besides, owing to using the fusion weight map, the proposed SP-PIQA achieves better performance than PW by 4.83% and HW by 3.41% in KRCC.

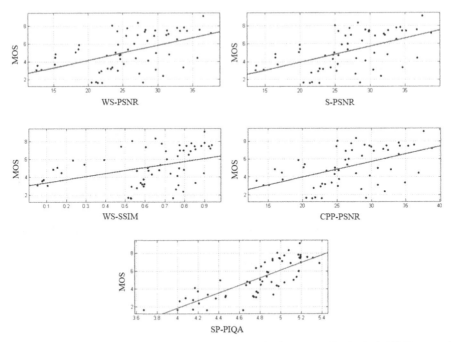

Fig. 7. Scatter plots of predicted quality scores and MOS. First row: WS-PSNR, S-PSNR; second row: WS-SSIM and CPP-PSNR; third row: SP-PIQA.

Figure 7 shows the comparisons of the scatter points of the predicted scores of the testing set versus mean opinion score (MOS). Based on the results in Fig. 7, it is concluded that the scatter points between SP-PIQA and MOS are concentrated near the fitting line, which is closer to the proportional relationship. Therefore, we deduce that proposed SP-PIQA model achieves best performance.

Table 2. PLCC of four types of different distortion

Metrics	JPEG	JPEG2000	GN	GB
CPP-PSNR [3]	0.5683	0.7039	0.9530	0.4979
WS-PSNR [5]	0.7368	0.7176	0.9483	0.4961
S-PSNR [4]	0.7526	0.7264	0.9540	0.5212
WS-SSIM [6]	0.7903	0.7401	0.9383	0.4232
SP-PIQA	**0.9006**	**0.9010**	**0.9678**	**0.9470**

In the second experiment, we compared the performance of SP-PIQA on different distortions with four methods [3–6]. The evaluation index PLCC results of the experiment is listed in Table 2.

From Table 2, it can be concluded that SP-PIQA exhibits high performance under different types of distortions. Meanwhile, the variance of SP-PIQA in four types of distortion PLCC is 8.55×10^{-4}, which is two orders of magnitude lower than other algorithms [3–6]. Therefore, SP-PIQA is more robust to different distortion types, which indicates that the feature extraction module of SP-PIQA can capture the changes caused by compression and other distortions.

4   Conclusion

In this paper, we introduce a perceptual blind PIQA method based on super-pixel by considering ERP format and the human perception. Panoramic structural features based on fusion weight which combines projection and perception are extracted to predict the quality scores of panoramic images. Comparative experiments on the public database show that SP-PIQA is superior to the existing PIQA methods.

Furthermore, since panoramic videos are usually filmed in a gentle way and do not have too much scene switching to avoid bringing uncomfortable feelings to viewers, the average quality of each frame can be regarded as the quality of the whole video. Therefore, our SP-PIQA model can be extended to panoramic video quality assessment conveniently.

Acknowledgments. This work was supported by National Natural Science Foundation of China under Grant No. 61671283, U2033218.

References

1. Battisti, F., Carli, M., Le Callet, P., et al.: Toward the assessment of quality of experience for asymmetric encoding in immersive media. IEEE Trans. Broadcast. **64**, 392–406 (2018)
2. Chen, S., Zhang, Y., Li, Y., et al.: Spherical structural similarity index for objective omnidirectional video quality assessment. In: 2018 IEEE International Conference on Multimedia and Expo (ICME), pp. 1–6 (2018)
3. Zakharchenko, V., Choi, K.P., Alshina, E., et al.: Omnidirectional video quality metrics and evaluation process. In: 2017 Data Compression Conference (DCC), pp. 472–472 (2017)
4. Yu, M., Lakshman, H., Girod, B.: A framework to evaluate omnidirectional video coding schemes. In: 2015 IEEE International Symposium on Mixed and Augmented Reality, pp. 31–36 (2015)
5. Sun, Y., Lu, A., Yu, L.: Weighted-to-spherically-uniform quality evaluation for omnidirectional video. IEEE Sign. Process. Lett. **24**, 1408–1412 (2017)
6. Zhou, Y., Yu, M., Ma, H., et al.: Weighted-to-spherically-uniform SSIM objective quality evaluation for panoramic video. In: 2018 14th IEEE International Conference on Signal Processing (ICSP), pp. 54–57 (2018)
7. Yang, S., Zhao, J., Jiang, T., et al.: An objective assessment method based on multi-level factors for panoramic videos. In: 2017 IEEE Visual Communications and Image Processing (VCIP), pp. 1–4 (2017)

8. Sun. W., Gu, K., Ma, S., et al.: A large-scale compressed 360-degree spherical image database: from subjective quality evaluation to objective model comparison. In: 2018 IEEE 20th International Workshop on Multimedia Signal Processing (MMSP), pp. 1–6 (2018)

9. Sun, W., Gu, K., Zhai, G., et al.: CVIQD: subjective quality evaluation of compressed virtual reality images. In: 2017 IEEE International Conference on Image Processing (ICIP), pp. 3450–3454 (2017)

10. Ding, W., An, P., Liu, X., et al.: No-reference panoramic image quality assessment based on adjacent pixels correlation. In: 2021 IEEE International Symposium on Broadband Multimedia Systems and Broadcasting (BMSB), pp. 1–5 (2021)

11. Li, H., Zhang, X.: MFAN: A multi-projection fusion attention network for no-reference and full-reference panoramic image quality assessment. IEEE Sig. Process. Lett. **30**, 1207–1211 (2023)

12. Liu, Y., Yin, X., Tang, C., et al.: A no-reference panoramic image quality assessment with hierarchical perception and color features. J. Vis. Commun. Image Represent. **95**, 103885 (2023)

13. Sendjasni, A., Larabi, M.C.: Self patch labeling using quality distribution estimation for CNN-based 360-IQA training. In: 2023 IEEE International Conference on Image Processing (ICIP), pp. 2640–2644 (2023)

14. Liu, L., Ma, P., Wang, C., et al.: Omnidirectional image quality assessment with knowledge distillation. IEEE Sig. Process. Lett. **30**, 1562–1566 (2023)

15. Xu, M., Li, C., Liu, Y., et al.: A subjective visual quality assessment method of panoramic videos. In: 2017 IEEE International Conference on Multimedia and Expo (ICME), pp. 517–522 (2017)

16. Zhu, Y., Zhai, G., Min, X.: The prediction of head and eye movement for 360 degree images. Sig. Process. Image Commun. **69**, 15–25 (2018)

17. Li, Q., Lin, W., Fang, Y.: No-reference quality assessment for multiply-distorted images in gradient domain. IEEE Sig. Process. Lett. **23**(4), 541–545 (2016)

18. Fang, Y., Yan, J., Li, L., et al.: No reference quality assessment for screen content images with both local and global feature representation. IEEE Trans. Image Process. **27**(4), 1600–1610 (2018)

19. Balochian, S., Baloochian, H.: Edge detection on noisy images using Prewitt operator and fractional order differentiation. Multimed. Tools Appl. **81**(7), 9759–9770 (2022)

20. Lei, J., Wang, B., Fang, Y., et al.: A universal framework for salient object detection. IEEE Trans. Multimedia **18**(9), 1783–1795 (2016)

21. Li, J., Liu, Z., Zhang, X., et al.: Spatiotemporal saliency detection based on superpixel-level trajectory. Sig. Process. Image Commun. **38**, 100–114 (2015)

22. Achanta, R., Shaji, A., Smith, K., et al.: SLIC superpixels compared to state-of-the-art superpixel methods. IEEE Trans. Pattern Anal. Mach. Intell. **34**(11), 2274–2282 (2012)

23. Ojala, T., Pietikainen, M., Maenpaa, T.: Multiresolution gray-scale and rotation invariant texture classification with local binary patterns. IEEE Trans. Pattern Anal. Mach. Intell. **24**(7), 971–987 (2002)

24. Duan, H., Zhai, G., Min, X., et al.: Perceptual quality assessment of omnidirectional images. In: 2018 IEEE International Symposium on Circuits and Systems (ISCAS), pp. 1–5 (2018)

25. Chang, C.C., Lin, C.J.: LIBSVM: a library for support vector machines. ACM Trans. Intell. Syst. Technol. (TIST) **2**(3), 1–27 (2011)

Image Aesthetics Assessment Based on Visual Perception and Textual Semantic Understanding

Yun Liu[1], Zhipeng Wen[1(✉)], Sifan Li[1(✉)], Daoxin Fan[1(✉)], and Guangtao Zhai[2]

[1] Faculty of Information, Liaoning University, Shenyang, Liaoning, China
`zhipengwen2023@163.com`, `sfl_lnu@163.com`, `fdx_0729@163.com`
[2] Institute of Image Communication and Network Engineering, Shanghai Jiao Tong University, Shanghai, China

Abstract. Our goal is to promote an effective image aesthetics assessment (IAA) model. In the current Internet era, it has become easier to obtain the text description of an image. With the dual-modal support of image and text, the image aesthetics assessment model will further reflect its superiority. To this end, we design a multimodal feature-driven guided image aesthetics assessment model (MFD). Firstly, multi-modal features are extracted through the feature extraction sub-network, including image-driven aesthetic features and content features, as well as text-driven semantic features. Each feature captures the implicit characteristics of different levels of human brain object analysis. Secondly, these multi-modal features are combined to form multi-modal combination features that contain multiple characteristics. Finally, the obtained multi-modal are combined for aesthetic assessment prediction. Experimental results on public image aesthetics assessment databases demonstrate the superiority of our model.

Keywords: Image Aesthetics Assessment · Multimodal Features · Feature Extraction Sub-network

1 Introduction

With the widespread use of social media and e-commerce platforms, image aesthetic prediction has become crucial for image retrieval systems [1], recommendation systems, and product marketing to enhance user experience and improve product sales [2]. With the development of machine learning technology [3, 4], image aesthetic analysis has attracted increasing attention. Aesthetic perception is a relatively subjective concept, and different individuals vary in different preferences for the same image, making it challenging to establish an objective evaluation standard [5].

The focus of image aesthetic prediction research is to build a model to automatically predict the aesthetic quality of images. The task involves analyzing various visual features such as composition, color, content, and texture in images [6]. By extracting relevant features from images and leveraging machine learning techniques [7, 8], researchers aim to build accurate models for predicting aesthetic quality. Traditional approaches for image aesthetic prediction typically rely on hand-crafted features [9]. These methods often fail to capture complex visual patterns and aesthetic concepts effectively. By using deep learning techniques [10, 11], researchers have gradually replaced hand-crafted features with learned features, leading to more accurate predictions [12, 13]. Convolutional neural networks (CNNs) in capturing hierarchical visual patterns in images present great promise [14, 15]. AlexNet and regression loss are used in some architecture to predict a moderate pattern of mean scores for images [16]. Moreover, Visual Geometry Group Networks (VGGNets) are also fine-tuned to apply to comprehend how humans rate an image in aesthetic ways [17]. Recently, for the use of processing multiple scales of images, adaptive spatial pooling has been applied [18], which shows us how a multi-net of pre-trained VGGs extracts features at multiple scales. As the research in the area deepens, ResNet CNNs are applied in the process of predicting the quality of photos [19]. Additionally, attention mechanisms [20] and reinforcement learning [21] have been employed to conduct image aesthetic prediction tasks. In summary, it can be observed that a series of applicable methods and tools have been used in the aesthetic prediction of images, which makes an unprecedented leap in the area to the hand-crafted era [22].

Despite considerable progress made in image aesthetic prediction tasks, there are still several challenges. One of the fundamental challenges is the subjectivity associated with aesthetics [23]. Aesthetic preferences vary across individuals, cultures, and preferences, making it difficult to develop a universally applicable evaluation metric [24]. Furthermore, there is a need for more modality content that provides sufficient information for image aesthetic prediction models [25]. Most of the above works are built based on a single modal content, which can provide a limited performance improvement [26]. Multimodality contents like text, video, and audio can play important roles in downstream tasks [27]. Some recent research works have proven that multimodal-based models yield better performance than single-modal-based methods [28, 29].

Motivated by the above works, we build an image aesthetics assessment method driven by multi-modal feature perceptions in the human brain, in which a specific feature extraction sub-network is designed to extract different categories of features from different modal content. Specifically, we design an Aesthetic Feature Extraction Sub-network (AFES) and a Content Feature Extraction Sub-network (CFES) to extract aesthetic features and content features of images respectively, which can well explain low-level visual perception. For high-level semantic understanding, we design a Semantic Feature Extraction Sub-network (SFES) to extract semantic features from text content. To fuse multiple types of features, a feature conversion (FV) module is built to change the dimensions and sizes of different features. Then the potential correlations of different categories of features are mined through Multi-Layer Perceptron (MLP), and finally, the aesthetic assessment prediction distribution that correlates multiple types of features is obtained.

Our contributions mainly include the following aspects:

1) Based on human aesthetic perception characteristics, we design a multi-modal feature extraction sub-network based on the image-driven aesthetic features and content features, and text-driven high-level semantic features to complement the above visual features, which can boost the overall performance.

2) Considering the mutual influences between visual features and textual words, our model can effectively capture the relationship between different modes and retain the characteristics of each mode by designing a feature conversion (FV) module, which can achieve accurate prediction.

3) The superior performance of our model is demonstrated through experimental results on a public image aesthetics assessment database, which can prove the rationality of the fusion of visual features from images and textual words.

2   Related Works

Image aesthetic quality evaluation models can be categorized into two types: subjective evaluation and objective evaluation models. Subjective evaluation relies on human opinions to rate, which is costly and time-consuming. Objective evaluation models attempt to propose a model to simulate human perception to automatically assess the aesthetic quality of an image, which is of low cost and fast and arouses more attention [30]. In early research, objective evaluation is proposed based on hand-crafted features to conduct image aesthetic quality classification. For example, Datta et al. [31] trained the SVM classifier based on some low-level features to classify the aesthetic quality, which is extracted according to photography rules. Wong et al. [32], based on the relationship between subject and background, and global features, built an aesthetic quality classification model. These features were extracted by detecting salient areas of the image. Overall, handcrafted features have clear physical meaning, and they tend to focus on specific physical features and struggle to fully capture the vital information of image aesthetics, which limits its development.

With the rapid development of deep learning, the models based on CNN are increasingly built-in image processing and have reliable results in predicting the quality of images. Compared with traditional handcrafted feature-based methods, these works have better performance in image perception assessment due to their ability to perform pixel-level quality assessment. The impressive results achieved by CNN provide us with a new way to evaluate the aesthetic quality assessment of images. By using patches randomly cropped from the original image, Lu et al. [33] proposed an architecture to categorize image aesthetic quality. Kao et al. [34] built a three-independent convolutional neural network model to extract objects, scenes, and textures for aesthetic learning. Mai et al. [35] proposed a model that did not require any image transformation, whose method is to use adaptive spatial convolution layers to train the model. To evaluate the photos' quality, Zeng et al. [36] present a method to retrain AlexNet and ResNet CNNs. To learn the ranking correlation between two input images, Kong et al. [37] proposed an aesthetics ranking network based on Alex Net. By using the saliency characteristics of images, Ma et al. [38] proposed a layout-aware framework to predict aesthetic scores. Considering the usefulness of multi-task learning, Li et al. [39] proposed a multi-task learning framework to predict the aesthetic evaluation. By using a universal aesthetic knowledge base, Li et al. [40] propose a new Knowledge Embedding model for image aesthetics assessment. She et al. [41] uses a novel graph convolution method to extract important image features to evaluate image aesthetics, which has improved the accuracy. Hosu et al. [42] and He et al. [43] simultaneously considered multi-level aesthetic features from a single modality and obtained good results. Li et al. [44] fully considered the image's visual attributes and proposed a TAVAR model, which yielded a high classification accuracy.

Although the above valuable studies have been previously conducted, image aesthetics assessment is an extraordinarily complex task. It is hard to continue to improve the overall performance by relying only on a single modality. Some recent research works have been built based on multimodal contents, which prove that multimodal-based methods can boost the result than single-modal-based models [28] [29]. For example, Zhang et al. [45] proposed an image retrieval model based on visual features and text features. Taking audio modality into consideration, Wu et al. [46] combined audio and visual features and proposed an action recognition method. To improve the classification results of images, He et al. [47] built a model that combines visual content and text information, which proves the nationality of visual and textual combination. Zhang et al. [48] encoded multimodal feature interactions by using the MFB pooling method. To conduct a multi-dimensional aesthetic analysis, Miao et al. [49] propose a stacked multimodal co-transformer module. Later, Zhu et al. [50] proposed a new image-text interaction network (ITIN) for multimodal sentiment analysis. Motivated by the above works, Li et al. [51] proposed a multimodal Network that extracts more discriminative aesthetic representations by utilizing visual and text contents. The above works provide us with a new way to conduct the image aesthetics assessment by utilizing multi-modal features.

3   Methodology

In this section, we introduce our proposed Multimodal Feature-Driven (MFD) image aesthetics assessment method. The specific structure of our model is present in Fig. 1. Firstly, the two different modal information, image, and text, are preprocessed separately. Resize the image to $224 \times 224 \times 3$ and normalize it using ImageNet's mean and standard deviation [16] to obtain a tensor. The text uses the pre-trained tokenizer [52] to convert the text into the corresponding token. Then, corresponding feature extraction sub-networks are designed for the preprocessed tensors and tokens to extract features of different modal information. Specifically, the Aesthetic Feature Extraction Sub-network (AFES) is designed for image information to extract aesthetic features and the Content Feature Extraction Sub-network (CFES) is designed to extract content features, and the Semantic Feature Extraction Sub-network (SFES) is designed for textual information to extract high-level semantic features. The feature conversion (FV) module within the feature extraction sub-network converts each extracted multi-modal feature into the same dimension. Finally, we splice three different types of features and use the Multi-Layer Perceptron (MLP) for aesthetic distribution prediction. Based on the aesthetic distribution prediction, the final aesthetic score $\widehat{Y}$ can be calculated.

3.1   Feature Extraction Sub-network

Aesthetic Feature Extraction Sub-network (AFES). The basic expression of the aesthetic characteristics of images is obscure, and mining the potential connections of aesthetics in images is a necessary step in the image aesthetics assessment method.

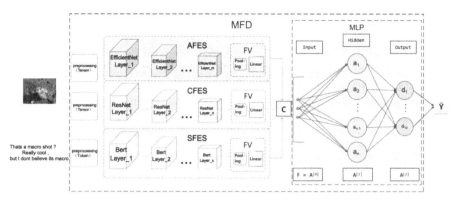

Fig. 1. Overall framework diagram of the proposed MFD

Therefore, aesthetic features, as the main features for judging the aesthetic quality of images, are also the core of the entire network. We design and use the efficient Efficient-Net_v2_s [53] as the backbone of the network to mine the implicit expressions of image aesthetic features. Specifically, the fully connected layer classifier of the last layer of EfficientNet_v2_s is removed to establish an aesthetic feature extraction sub-network and initialize it using parameters pre-trained on ImageNet. For the input image, the aesthetic feature extraction sub-network performs coding to extract a set of aesthetic feature tensors $AF^c_{b \times w \times h}$. The aesthetic feature tensors can be defined as follows:

$$AF^c_{b \times w \times h} = concat\{af^1_{b \times w \times h}, af^2_{b \times w \times h}, \cdots af^c_{b \times w \times h}\} \tag{1}$$

where, $af^i_{b \times w \times h} \in R^{b \times w \times h}$ represents an aesthetic feature tensor in the group of aesthetic feature tensors, and stores the data in the form of a three-dimensional matrix; $w \times h$ represents the width and height of the tensor, with a value of 7×7; b represents the number of images processed simultaneously; c belongs to the number of channels, with a value of 1280; $AF^c_{b \times w \times h} \in R^{b \times c \times w \times h}$ represents the tensor of the group Store data in the form of a four-dimensional matrix.

To better combine with other features, we change the size and dimension of $CF^c_{b \times w \times h}$ through a feature conversion (FV) module. The process is defined as follows:

$$AF^c_{b \times 1 \times 1} = meanpool(AF^c_{b \times w \times h}) \tag{2}$$

$$AF^c_b = squeeze(AF^c_{b \times 1 \times 1}) \tag{3}$$

$$AF^s = linear(AF^c_b, \theta) \tag{4}$$

where, $AF^s \in R^{b \times s}$ indicates that the tensor stores data; s is set to 256 in this article.

Content Feature Extraction Sub-network (CFES). The content presented by the image has a strong correlation with image aesthetics and can further complement the above aesthetic features. Therefore, we designed to use the classic network ResNet-50 [54] as the content feature extraction sub-network. Since unsupervised learning can have a better perception of image content than supervised learning, some works have chosen to use ResNet-50 as the backbone to perform unsupervised learning of image classification tasks on large public data sets [55]. We regard it as an upstream task, learning the content features of image modality information, and then remove the last fully connected layer classifier of ResNet-50 to establish a content feature extraction sub-network, and initialize it using the parameters pre-trained by the upstream task. For the input image, the content feature extraction sub-network performs coding and extraction to obtain a set of content feature tensors $CF^c_{b \times w \times h}$. The content feature tensors can be defined as follows:

$$CF^c_{b \times w \times h} = concat\{cf^1_{b \times w \times h}, cf^2_{b \times w \times h}, \cdots cf^c_{b \times w \times h}\} \tag{5}$$

where, $y^i_{w \times h} \in R^{w \times h}$ represents a certain content feature tensor in the group of content feature tensors, and stores the data in the form of a three-dimensional matrix; b represents batch size; $w \times h$ represents the width and height of the feature tensor, the value is 7×7; c belongs to the channel number, the value is 512; $CF^c_{b \times w \times h} \in R^{b \times c \times w \times h}$ represents that the group of tensors stores data in the form of a four-dimensional matrix.

Similarly, we also change the size and dimension of $CF^c_{b \times w \times h}$ through a feature conversion (FV) module. Specifically, we first mean-pool it to a smaller size and then compress it to a lower dimension, and then adjust the number of channels through a linear layer. The process is defined as follows:

$$CF^c_{b \times 1 \times 1} = meanpool\left(CF^c_{b \times w \times h}\right). \tag{6}$$

$$CF^c_b = squeeze(CF^c_{1 \times 1}) \tag{7}$$

$$CF^s = linear(CF^c_b, \theta) \tag{8}$$

where $CF^s \in R^{b \times s}$ represents that the tensor stores data in the form of a two-dimensional matrix; θ represents the parameters in the linear layer; s represents the vector length, which is set to 256 in this paper.

Semantic Feature Extraction Sub-network (SFES). Semantic analysis is an advanced way for humans to perceive things. At this level, the human brain further integrates middle-level visual information and associates it with semantic knowledge and context. Perception at this level is related to semantic analysis and conceptual cognition. Specifically, we build a semantic feature extraction sub-network through the pre-trained contextual language reasoning model Bert [52] to extract human high-level perception features, which can well complement the above visual features. For the corresponding comment text of the image, the semantic feature extraction sub-network infers the upper-level semantics with the help of comment context information and provides feedback with a set of one-dimensional semantic feature tensors SF^c_{length}. The semantic feature tensor can be defined as follows:

$$SF^c_{length} = concat\{sf^1_{length}, sf^2_{length}, \cdots sf^c_{length}\} \tag{9}$$

where, $sf^i_{length} \in R^{b \times length}$ represents a certain semantic feature tensor in the group of semantic feature tensors, and stores data with a two-dimensional matrix; $length$ represents the length of the embedding vector, which is fixed to 768; c belongs to the number of channels, with a value of 128; $SF^c_{length} \in R^{b \times c \times length}$ represents the group of tensors. Quantities store data in the form of three-dimensional matrices.

A feature conversion (FV) module is then applied to change the size and dimension of $CF^c_{b \times w \times h}$. The process is defined as follows:

$$SF^c_{b \times 64} = meanpool(SF^c_{b \times length}) \tag{10}$$

$$SF^d_b = squeeze(SF^c_{b \times 64}) \tag{11}$$

$$SF^s = linear(SF^d_b, \theta) \tag{12}$$

where, $SF^d_b \in R^{b \times d}$ indicates that the tensor stores data in a two-dimensional matrix, d and s both indicate the vector length, and the sizes are set to 128×64 and 256 respectively.

3.2 Model Training and Prediction Representation

The above three features, CF^s, AF^s and SF^s, extracted by the feature extraction subnetwork are spliced and combined to form a multi-modal feature group, denoted as F, which can be defined as follows:

$$F = concat\{CF^s, AF^s, SF^s\} \tag{13}$$

The extracted multi-modal feature group F is then sent to Multi-Layer Perceptron (MLP) for further prediction and output aesthetic distribution d. The process can be described as follows:

$$d = MLP(F, \theta) \tag{14}$$

where θ represents the trainable parameter in MLP. We set up two hidden layers, with the number of neurons being 256 and 128, respectively. The PRelu activation function is used between the hidden layers. Since the number of neurons is relatively small, we do not use Dropout.

The predicted image aesthetic score is obtained based on the aesthetic distribution $\hat{Y}$. The calculation method is as follows:

$$\hat{Y} = \sum_{i=1}^{10} d_i p_i \tag{15}$$

where d_i represents the i-th discrete point in aesthetic distribution d, and p_i represents the probability value of this discrete point.

Following the previous works [30, 41], we use the EMD loss function $L_{EMD}(d, \hat{d})$ to assist in optimizing our model, which is defined as follows:

$$L_{EMD}(d, \hat{d}) = (\frac{1}{N} \sum_{k=1}^{N} |CDF_d(k) - CDF_{\hat{d}}(k)|^r)^{1/r} \tag{16}$$

where $CDF_d(k)$ represents the probability value of a certain point in the predicted aesthetic distribution. $CDF_{\hat{d}}(k)$ represents the probability value label value of a certain point in the aesthetic distribution. N represents the number of aesthetic score values in the aesthetic distribution, and here it is set to 10, that is 1–10 points. r takes a value of 2 to speed up gradient convergence.

4 Experimental Results

We first introduce our experimental setup to demonstrate the performance of our model in this section. The superiority of our model is proved by extensive experiments on public image aesthetics assessment databases with some image aesthetics assessment models, and finally, some ablation experiments are conducted to demonstrate the effectiveness of each sub-network.

4.1 Experimental Setups

Implementation Details. For all input images I, we resize them to $224 \times 224 \times 3$, and for each review text, we convert it into a token through a pre-trained tokenizer as the input of the BERT model [52]. The Adam optimizer with an initial learning rate of 3×10^{-5}, and a decay rate of 0.5 times the original value after every 5 epochs. The batch size is set to 40. All experiments were implemented under the PyTorch framework and accelerated training was performed on a computer with a single NVIDIA GeForce RTX 3090 24G GPU.

Evaluation Criteria. We use several commonly used evaluation metrics to evaluate the prediction accuracy of the model: accuracy (ACC), Spearman's rank correlation coefficient (SRCC) [30], and Pearson's linear correlation coefficient (PLCC) [30]. Earth Mover Distance (EMD) was utilized to evaluate the performance of aesthetic distribution predictions. SRCC is calculated as follows:

$$SRCC = 1 - \frac{6\sum_{i=1}^{N}(d_i)^2}{N(N^2-1)} \tag{17}$$

where d_i represents the difference between the real score and the predicted score; N represents the number of images.

PLCC is calculated as follows:

$$PLCC = \frac{\sum_{i=1}^{N}(y_i - \bar{y})(\hat{y}_i - \bar{y})}{\sqrt{\sum_{i=1}^{N}(y_i - \bar{y})^2}\sqrt{\sum_{i=1}^{N}(\hat{y}_i - \bar{y})^2}} \tag{18}$$

where N is the number of images; y_i and $\hat{y}_i$ represent the real aesthetic value and predicted aesthetic score of the i-th image respectively; $\bar{y}$ and $\hat{y}$ represents the real aesthetic average and predicted average value respectively.

ACC is calculated as follows:

$$Acc = \frac{TP + TN}{TP + FN + FP + TN} \tag{19}$$

where *TP* represents the positive prediction, and the actual value is positive; *FP* means the positive prediction and the actual value is negative; *TN* means the negative prediction and the actual value is positive; *FN* means the negative prediction and the actual value is negative.

4.2 Databases

AVA Database [56]. All images in this database are collected from the DPChallenge website. The total number of images has exceeded 250,000. The database covers various common types of images. Following previous research [43], the images included a training set with 229,951 images, a validation set with 12,775 images, and a test set with 12,776 images.

AVA-Comments Database [57]. The AVA-Comments database crawls the user comments corresponding to all images in the AVA database on the DPChallenge website and obtains more than 1.5 million user comments. It removes all quotation marks and additional HTML tags in the crawled data and converts the data into the valid comments of each image into a single text file as the text modal data of the corresponding image.

4.3 Comparison with Advanced Methods

We applied 6 IAA models to conduct the fair comparison on the AVA database, and the experimental results are summarized in Table 1. Since some models are released without source code or related data in the paper, these results are marked with "-". The best performance for each metric is marked in bold. Overall, our model achieves superior performance. Specifically, NIMA [30] was a classic model for early image aesthetics assessment with a simple structure and didn't yield a good result. HLA-GCN [41] used a novel graph convolution method to extract image features, which has improved the accuracy compared to work [30]. MLSP [42], TANet [43], and TAVAR [44] all considered multi-level features of the image, so these models achieved further improvement on SRCC and PLCC indicators. It needs to be mentioned that the above works are all built based on a single modality. Multimodal co-TRM [49] took into account the aesthetic features and text features of multimodal information and has the best classification accuracy among all the models, which also proves reasonable for image and text feature fusion. Our MFD model not only considers multi-modal information, but also adds additional content features at the visual level as a supplement, which yields the best SRCC and PLCC indicators, and the model's classification accuracy also achieves competitive results.

4.4 Ablation Studies

To verify the effectiveness of each sub-network of the proposed model, in this section, we deeply explore the impact of each sub-network of the model on the overall performance of the model. All ablation studies are implemented based on the AVA database [56] and the AVA-Comments database [57]. We divide the model as a whole into Aesthetic Feature Extraction Sub-network (AFES), Content Feature Extraction Sub-network

Table 1. Comparison of SRCC, PLCC, and ACC between the proposed model and other image aesthetics assessment models.

Method	Backbone	SRCC	PLCC	ACC	EMD
NIMA [30]	Inception-v2	0.612	0.636	81.51	0.050
HLA-GCN [41]	ResNet-50	0.665	0.687	84.60	0.043
MLSP [42]	InceptionResNet	0.756	0.757	81.72	-
TANet [43]	MobileNet-v2	0.753	0.762	80.01	0.049
TAVAR [44]	ResNet-50	0.725	0.736	85.10	-
Multimodal co-TRM [49]	FCN	0.784	-	**85.63**	-
MFD(Ours)	Efficientnet_v2_s	**0.800**	**0.812**	82.49	**0.038**

(CFES), and Semantic Feature Extraction Sub-network (SFES). Table 2 shows the evaluation indicators under different sub-network combinations. The best performance for each metric is marked in bold. Experimental results show that when each sub-network is executed individually, the integrity of the model is low, and the performance of AFES is better than that of other sub-networks, which further illustrates that aesthetic features play an important role in image aesthetics assessment. When AFES and SFES are combined with CFES and SFES, the overall performance is good, while with only AFES and CFES, the model performance is average. This shows that different modal information can provide the model with richer feature representations, thereby improving the overall performance of the model. Compared with the combination of AFES, CFES, and SFES, the overall performance of the combination of AFES and SFES is relatively close. Our subjective analysis is due to the lack of expression ability of the content features extracted by CFES. Limited to upstream tasks, we are temporarily unable to explore CFES of other backbones, and we will further conduct related work in the future. Finally, it can be obtained that the combination of three sub-networks achieves the best model performance and prediction accuracy, which also proves the effectiveness of our proposed MFD method.

4.5   Performance of Different Backbones

Considering that different backbones have different feature representation capabilities, and the aesthetic features play a vital role in image aesthetics assessment, in this part, we explore the specific impact of different backbones in AFES on the model. The specific performance of each model can be seen in Table 3. The best performance for each metric is marked in bold.

It can be seen that when AFES uses Efficientnet_v2_s as the backbone, the model evaluation index is greatly improved compared to other backbones, with a maximum improvement of 0.034 for SRCC, a maximum improvement of 0.027 for PLCC, and a maximum improvement of ACC of 1.41%. The performance of the model is relatively good when using Densenet121 [59], but it is still slightly lower than Efficientnet_v2_s

Table 2. Comparison of SRCC, PLCC, and ACC of the proposed model for ablation studies of different feature extraction sub-networks.

Method	Backbone	SRCC	PLCC	ACC	EMD
AFES	Efficientnet_v2_s	0.704	0.716	80.60	0.045
CFES	ResNet-50	0.643	0.655	78.46	0.052
SFES	Bert	0.642	0.664	75.71	0.052
AFES + CFES	Efficientnet_v2_s+ ResNet-50	0.708	0.719	80.42	0.045
AFES + SFES	Efficientnet_v2_s+ Bert	0.795	0.808	82.45	0.038
CFES + SFES	ResNet-50 + Bert	0.770	0.785	81.54	0.040
AFES + CFES + SFES	Efficientnet_v2_s+ ResNet-50 + Bert	**0.800**	**0.812**	**82.49**	**0.038**

Table 3. Comparison of SRCC, PLCC, and ACC of the proposed model using different backbones on AFES.

Method	Backbone (AFES)	SRCC	PLCC	ACC	EMD
AFES + CFES (ResNet-50) + SFES (Bert)	AlexNet [16]	0.766	0.785	81.08	0.040
	VGG16 [17]	0.773	0.790	81.47	0.039
	ResNet-18 [54]	0.770	0.787	81.47	0.039
	ResNet-50 [54]	0.774	0.789	81.89	0.039
	Googlenet [58]	0.773	0.790	81.32	0.039
	Densenet121 [59]	0.780	0.796	82.04	0.038
	Efficientnet_v2_s [53]	**0.800**	**0.812**	**82.49**	**0.038**

in various evaluation indicators. In general, the backbones can slightly affect the overall performance, and the specific task can choose a suitable model for the task.

5 Conclusion

In this paper, we propose an image aesthetics assessment method (MFD) driven by multi-modal features from the perspective of different levels of object analysis by the human brain. For different modal information, a specific method of feature extraction sub-network is designed to extract dissimilar categories of features corresponding to the modal content. Specifically, for image content, the visual perception of the human eye dominates, so we design the Aesthetic Feature Extraction Sub-network (AFES) and Content Feature Extraction Sub-network (CFES) to extract image aesthetic features and image content features, respectively. For text content, high-level semantic understanding is the main analysis method of the human brain, and a Semantic Feature Extraction Subnetwork (SFES) is designed to extract text semantic features. To fuse multiple types of features, we designed a feature conversion (FV) module to change the dimensions and sizes of different features. The obtained three types of features are then used to predict the aesthetic score distribution.

Through experiments on a public image aesthetics assessment database, the effectiveness and superiority of our proposed model are proved compared with mainstream image aesthetics assessment methods.

Acknowledgments. This work is supported by Liaoning Province Natural Science Foundation under Grant 2023-MS-139, Shenyang science and technology plan project under Grant 23-407-3-32 and National Natural Science Foundation of China under Grant 61901205.

References

1. Ji, Z., Chen, K., He, Y., et al.: Heterogeneous memory enhanced graph reasoning network for cross-modal retrieval. Sci. China Inf. Sci. **65**(7), 172104 (2022)
2. Wang, L., Wang, X., Yamasaki, T.: Image aesthetics prediction using multiple patches preserving the original aspect ratio of contents. Multimed. Tools Appl. **82**, 2783–2804 (2023)
3. Mei, S., Geng, Y., Hou, J., et al.: Learning hyperspectral images from RGB images via a coarse-to-fine CNN. Sci. China Inf. Sci. **65**, 1–14 (2022)
4. Cheng, G., Lai, P., Gao, D., et al.: Class attention network for image recognition. Sci. China Inf. Sci. **66**(3), 132105 (2023)
5. Pandit, A., Animesh, Gautam, B.K., Agarwal, R.: Image aesthetic score prediction using image captioning. In: Kumar, A., Mozar, S., Haase, J. (eds.) Advances in Cognitive Science and Communications, ICCCE 2023. Cognitive Science and Technology. Springer, Singapore (2023)
6. Ke, J., et al.: VILA: learning image aesthetics from user comments with vision-language pretraining. In: Proceedings of the IEEE Computer Society Conference on Computer Vision and Pattern Recognition, 2023-June, pp. 10041–10051 (2023)
7. Wang, J., Li, Y., Pan, Y., et al.: Contextual and selective attention networks for image captioning. Sci. China Inf. Sci. **65**(12), 222103 (2022)
8. Yue, Y., Zou, Q., Yu, H., et al.: An end-to-end network for co-saliency detection in one single image. Sci. China Inf. Sci. **66**(11), 1–18 (2023)
9. Zhang, X., Gao, X., He, L., Lu, W.: MSCAN: multimodal self-and-collaborative attention Network for image aesthetic prediction tasks. Neurocomputing **430**, 14–23 (2021)
10. Yu, H., Wu, J.: A unified pruning framework for vision transformers. Sci. China Inf. Sci. **66**(7), 1–2 (2023)
11. Yan, P., Liu, X., Zhang, P., et al.: Learning convolutional multi-level transformers for image-based person re-identification. Visual Intell. **1**(1), 24 (2023)
12. Cui, Y., Jiang, G., Yu, M., et al.: Stitched wide field of view light field image quality assessment: benchmark database and objective metric. IEEE Trans. Multimed. Early Access (2023). https://doi.org/10.1109/TMM.2023.3330096
13. Chen, B., Fu, H., Chen, X., et al.: NeuralReshaper: single-image human-body retouching with deep neural networks. arXiv preprint arXiv:2203.10496 (2022)
14. Du, B., Du, C., Yu, L.: MEGF-Net: multi-exposure generation and fusion network for vehicle detection under dim light conditions. Vis. Intell. **1**(1), 1–13 (2023)

15. Guo, G., Han, L., Wang, L., et al.: Semantic-aware knowledge distillation with parameter-free feature uniformization. Vis. Intell. **1**(1), 6 (2023)
16. Krizhevsky, A., Sutskever, I., Hinton, G.E.: ImageNet classification with deep convolutional neural networks. Commun. ACM **60**(6), 84–90 (2017)
17. Simonyan, K., Zisserman, A.: Very deep convolutional networks for large-scale image recognition (2014). arXiv preprint arXiv:1409.1556
18. Mai, L., Jin, H., Liu, F.: Composition-preserving deep photo aesthetics assessment. In: Proceedings of the IEEE Computer Society Conference on Computer Vision and Pattern Recognition, pp. 497–506, December 2016
19. Zeng, H., Zhang, L., Bovik, A.C.: A probabilistic quality representation approach to deep blind image quality prediction. In: arXiv (2017)
20. Liu, L., Guo, X., Bai, R., Li, W.: Image aesthetic assessment based on attention mechanisms and holistic nested edge detection. In: Proceedings - 2022 Asia Conference on Advanced Robotics, Automation, and Control Engineering, ARACE 2022, pp. 70–75 (2022)
21. Black, K., Janner, M., Du, Y., Kostrikov, I., Levine, S.: Training Diffusion Models with Reinforcement Learning. In: arXiv (2023)
22. Valenzise, G., Kang, C., Dufaux, F.: Advances and challenges in computational image aesthetics. In: Ionescu, B., Bainbridge, W.A., Murray, N. (eds) Human Perception of Visual Information. Springer, Cham (2022)
23. Biswas, K., Shivakumara, P., Pal, U., et al.: Classification of aesthetic natural scene images using statistical and semantic features. Multimed. Tools Appl. **82**, 13507–13532 (2023)
24. Jang, H., Lee, Y., Lee, J.-S.: Modeling, Quantifying, and Predicting Subjectivity of Image Aesthetics. In: arXiv (2022)
25. Zhu, T., Li, L., Chen, P., Wu, J., Yang, Y., Li, Y., Guo, Y.: Attribute-assisted multimodal network for image aesthetics assessment. In: Proceedings of IEEE International Conference on Multimedia and Expo, 2023-July, pp. 2477–2482 (2023)
26. Withöft, A., Abdenebaoui, L., Boll, S.: ILMICA - interactive learning model of image collage assessment: a transfer learning approach for aesthetic principles. In: Þór Jónsson, B., et al. MultiMedia Modeling. MMM 2022. Lecture Notes in Computer Science, vol. 13142. Springer, Cham (2022)
27. Li, K., Guo, D., Wang, M.: ViGT: proposal-free video grounding with a learnable token in the transformer. Sci. China Inf. Sci. **66**(10), 202102 (2023)
28. Ramachandram, D., Taylor, G.W.: Deep multimodal learning: A survey on recent advances and trends. IEEE Signal Process. Mag. **34**(6), 96–108 (2017)
29. Zhu, W., Wang, X., Li, H.: Multi-modal deep analysis for multimedia. IEEE Trans. Circuits Syst. Video Technol. **30**(10), 3740–3764 (2019)
30. Talebi, H., Milanfar, P.: Nima: neural image assessment. IEEE Trans. Image Process. **27**(8), 3998–4011 (2018)
31. Datta, R., Joshi, D., Li, J., Wang, J. Z.: Studying aesthetics in photographic images using a computational approach. In: Proceedings of the European Conference on Computer Vision, pp. 288–301. Springer (2006)
32. Wong, L.-K., Low, K.-L.: Saliency-enhanced image aesthetics class prediction. In: Proceedings of the IEEE International Conference on Image Processing, pp. 997–1000 (2009)
33. Lu, X., Lin, Z., Shen, X., Mech, R., Wang, J.Z.: Deep multi-patch aggregation network for image style, aesthetics, and quality estimation. In: Proceedings of the IEEE International Conference on Computer Vision, pp. 990–998. 1 (2015)
34. Kao, Y., Huang, K., Maybank, S.: Hierarchical aesthetic quality assessment using deep convolutional neural networks. In: Signal Processing: Image Communication, vol. 47, pp. 500–510 (2016)

35. Mai, L., Jin, H., Liu, F.: Composition-preserving deep photo aesthetics assessment. In: Proceedings of the IEEE Conference on Computer Vision and Pattern Recognition, pp. 497–506 (2016)
36. Zeng, H., Zhang, L., Bovik, A.C.: A probabilistic quality representation approach to deep blind image quality prediction. In: arXiv preprint arXiv:1708.08190, 2017. 1 (2017)
37. Kong, S., Shen, X., Lin, Z., Mech, R., Fowlkes, C.: Photo aesthetics ranking network with attributes and content adaptation. In: European Conference on Computer Vision, pp. 662–679. Springer (2016), 1, 6, 7
38. Ma, S., Liu, J., Chen, C. W.: A-lamp: Adaptive layout-aware multipatch deep convolutional neural network for photo aesthetic assessment. In: 2017 IEEE Conference on Computer Vision and Pattern Recognition (CVPR). IEEE (2017). 1, 6, 7
39. Li, L., Zhu, H., Zhao, S., Ding, G., Lin, W.: Personality-assisted multitask learning for generic and personalized image aesthetics assessment. In: Proceedings of IEEE Transactions on Image Processing, vol. 29, pp. 3898–3910 (2020)
40. Li, L., Zhi, T., Shi, G., Yang, Y., Xu, L., Li, Y., Guo, Y.: Anchor-based knowledge embedding for image aesthetics assessment. In: Proceedings of Neurocomputing (2023)
41. She, D., Lai, Y. K., Yi, G., et al.: Hierarchical layout-aware graph convolutional network for unified aesthetics assessment. In: Proceedings of the IEEE/CVF Conference on Computer Vision and Pattern Recognition, pp. 8475–8484 (2021)
42. Hosu, V., Goldlucke, B., Saupe, D.: Effective aesthetics prediction with multi-level spatially pooled features. In: Proceedings of the IEEE/CVF Conference on Computer Vision and Pattern Recognition, pp. 9375–9383 (2019)
43. He, S., Zhang, Y., Xie, R., et al.: Rethinking image aesthetics assessment: Models, datasets, and benchmarks. In: Proceedings of the Thirty-First International Joint Conference on Artificial Intelligence, IJCAI-22. 2022, pp. 942–948 (2022)
44. Li, L., Huang, Y., Wu, J., et al.: Theme-aware visual attribute reasoning for image aesthetics assessment. IEEE Trans. Circuits Syst. Video Technol. (2023)
45. Zhang, R., Zhang, Z., Li, M., Ma, W.-Y., Zhang, H.-J.: A probabilistic semantic model for image annotation and multimodal image retrieval. In: Proceedings of the IEEE International Conference on Computer Vision, vol. 1, pp. 846–851. IEEE (2005)
46. Wu, Q., Wang, Z., Deng, F., Chi, Z., Feng, D.D.: Realistic human action recognition with multimodal feature selection and fusion. IEEE Trans. Syst. Man Cybern. Syst. 43(4), 875–885 (2013)
47. He, X., Peng, Y.: Fine-grained image classification via combining vision and language. In: Proceedings of the IEEE Conference on Computer Vision and Pattern Recognition, 2017, pp. 5994–6002 (2017)
48. Zhang, X., Gao, X., Lu, W., He, L., Li, J.: Beyond vision: a multimodal recurrent attention convolutional neural network for unified image aesthetic prediction tasks. IEEE Trans. Multimed. 23, 611–623 (2021)
49. Miao, H., Zhang, Y., Wang, D., Feng, S.: Multimodal aesthetic analysis assisted by styles through a multimodal co-transformer model. In: Proceedings of the IEEE 24th International Conference on Computational Science and Engineering (CSE), 2021 (2021)
50. Zhu, T., Li, L., Yang, J., Zhao, S., Liu, H., Qian, J.: Multimodal sentiment analysis with image-text interaction network. IEEE Trans. Multimed., 1–12 (2022)
51. Li, L., Zhu, T., Chen, P., Yang, Y., Li, Y., Lin, W.: Image aesthetics assessment with attribute-assisted multimodal memory network. IEEE Trans. Circuits Syst. Video Technol., 1 (2023)
52. Devlin, J., Chang, M.-W., Lee, K., Toutanova, K.: BERT: pre-training of deep bidirectional transformers for language understanding. In: NAACL HLT 2019 - 2019 Conference of the North American Chapter of the Association for Computational Linguistics: Human Language Technologies - Proceedings of the Conference, vol. 1, pp. 4171–4186 (2019)

53. Tan, M., Le, Q.: Efficientnetv2: smaller models and faster training. In: International Conference on Machine Learning. PMLR, 2021, pp. 10096–10106 (2021)
54. He, K., Zhang, X., Ren, S., et al.: Deep residual learning for image recognition. In: Proceedings of the IEEE Conference on Computer Vision and Pattern Recognition, pp. 770–778 (2016)
55. He, K., Fan, H., Wu, Y., et al.: Momentum contrast for unsupervised visual representation learning. In: Proceedings of the IEEE/CVF Conference on Computer Vision and Pattern Recognition, pp. 9729–9738 (2020)
56. Murray, N., Marchesotti, L., Perronnin, F.: AVA: a large-scale database for aesthetic visual analysis. In: 2012 IEEE Conference on Computer Vision and Pattern Recognition, pp. 2408–2415. IEEE (2012)
57. Zhou, Y., Lu, X., Zhang, J., et al.: Joint image and text representation for aesthetics analysis. In: Proceedings of the 24th ACM International Conference on Multimedia, pp. 262–266 (2016)
58. Szegedy, C., Liu, W., Jia, Y., et al.: Going deeper with convolutions. In: Proceedings of the IEEE Conference on Computer Vision and Pattern Recognition, pp. 1–9 (2015)
59. Huang, G., Liu, Z., Van Der Maaten, L., et al.: Densely connected convolutional networks. In: Proceedings of the IEEE Conference on Computer Vision and Pattern Recognition, pp. 4700–4708 (2017)

An Omnidirectional Videos Quality Assessment Method Using Salient Object Information

Kai Jia[1], Zelu Qi[2], Yunchao Xie[3], Da Pan[2], Shuqi Wang[2], Xin Xiong[2], Fei Zhao[2], Yichun Zhang[3(✉)], and Tianyu Liang[3]

[1] China Electronics Standardization Institute, Beijing, China
`jiakai@cesi.cn`
[2] School of Infomation and Communication Engineering, Communication University of China, Beijing, China
`theoneqi2001@cuc.edu.cn`
[3] China Institute of Arts Science and Technology, Beijing, China
`zhangyichun@vip.sina.com`

Abstract. Omnidirectional videos(ODVs) aim to provide an immersive viewing experience but are susceptible to various distortions during processing, leading to quality degradation. Accurately predicting their quality is crucial for ensuring a satisfying users' Quality of Experience (QoE). While watching ODVs, users' visible areas are confined to specific portions, referred to as viewports. The choice of a viewport extraction method significantly influences evaluation results, yet existing methods often underutilize advanced semantic information, such as salient objects in videos. In response to this limitation, this study introduces a two-stage model comprising a viewport extraction stage and a quality assessment stage. During the viewport extracion stage, we first employ a viewport extraction network to generate multiple candidate viewports. Subsequently, we introduces an innovative non-maximum suppression algorithm based on salient objects (SO-NMS) to filter the recommended viewports. In the quality assessment stage, we utilizes a dense network to predict the quality scores of each viewport and then integrates these scores to obtain the video quality score. Experimental results demonstrate that the proposed model exhibits exceptional performance, surpassing the majority of existing omnidirectional videos objective quality assessment models.

Keywords: Omnidirectional Video · Objective Quality Assessment · Viewport

1 Introduction

With the rapid growth of Internet and communication technology, Virtual Reality (VR) has found widespread applications in various fields such as cultural tourism, medical care, and game production. Omnidirectional videos, also known

G. Zhai et al. (Eds.): IFTC 2023, CCIS 2067, pp. 54–67, 2024.
https://doi.org/10.1007/978-981-97-3626-3_5

as 360° or panoramic videos, serve as crucial carriers of visual information for VR content [1]. They offer users a 360° immersive viewing environment, garnering significant attention in academia and industry. To ensure a high QoE for users, ODVs often require ultra-high resolutions like 8K, 16K, or higher. However, this poses challenges for current transmission and storage technologies, resulting in quality degradation and impacting the user's QoE [2]. Hence, there is a pressing need to explore methods for evaluating the quality of omnidirectional videos accurately to enhance the visual perception quality of ODVs and improve the overall QoE of VR systems.

In recent years, researchers have introduced various objective Omnidirectional Video Quality Assessment methods [3–12]. For example, Yu et al. proposed to calculate the PSNR based on a spherical uniform sampling point set, and derived two variants of S-PSNR-NN and S-PSNR-I based on different neighborhood sample prediction algorithms. Zakharchenkoa et al. proposed CPP-PSNR, which converts both the reference image and the output image into Craster parabolic projection(CPP) format, and calculates PSNR based on the resampling points obtained by interpolation in the CPP domain. However, these methods will bring high computational complexity and cause excessive consumption of computing resources. In fact, for ODVs, more than 30% of the content is not viewed by the audience [10], so the salient areas of ODVs contribute more to the video quality score.

For omnidirectional videos, visual saliency is primarily reflected in two aspects: Eye Movement (EM) and Head Movement (HM). HM determines the viewport that user sees, while EM determines the gaze point location within that viewport. Currently, many endeavors have integrated the visual attention mechanism into the objective quality assessment of panoramic videos. The aim is to guide quality evaluation models to prioritize human areas of interest, achieving higher performance with minimal computational resource consumption. However, in most quality assessment models based on visual saliency, the focus is limited to pixel-level semantic information such as optical flow, texture, and color. Higher-level semantic information, like salient objects, is overlooked. In fact, when humans watch videos, particularly immersive ones, their attention is more likely to be captivated by salient objects within the video. For example, people will pay more attention to the singer at a concert. Relevant psychological experiments have also proven that users' arousal (intensity of emotion) levels in immersive environments are more closely related to high-level saliency (such as faces, salient objects, etc.) [13], but there is currently little work that considers this influence.

In view of this, we proposes an objective omnidirectional video quality assessment model that integrates salient object information. The main work contents are as follows:

1. We adopts a two-stage model, including the viewport extraction stage and the viewport quality assessment stage.
2. The viewport extraction stage comprehensively uses motion information (optical flow, etc.), spatial information (texture, chroma, structure, etc.) and

salient object information to obtain a set of recommended viewport center point coordinates, and obtains 2D viewports through a viewport alignment module.

3. The quality evaluation stage takes the 2D viewport image as input, predicts the EM distribution within viewport and evaluates the viewport quality score, and finally weights the panoramic video quality score.

2   Related Work

Currently, research on objective OVQA is still in its early stages. This section will provide a retrospective overview of the development and evolution of objective OVQA. According to the development history of omnidirectional video quality assessment methods, they can be divided into two categories: sampling-based methods and perception-based methods.

2.1   Sampling-Based OVQA Methods

Objective quality assessment for 2D videos is well-established, and the idea of applying these methods directly to ODVs seems intuitive, since ODVs are essentially projected onto a 2D surface for encoding and transmission. However, existing projection methods introduce uneven sampling densities, making direct application of 2D-VQA methods problematic [3].

To tackle the above problem, one solution is to reproject ODVs into another domain with uniform sampling density, referred to as re-projection approaches. Yu et al. [3] proposed Spherical PSNR based on a uniformly sampled spherical point set and derived two variants, S-PSNR-NN and S-PSNR-I. Zakharchenkoa et al. [4] introduced CPP-PSNR, transforming both reference and output images to CPP format and calculating PSNR based on resampled points obtained through interpolation in the CPP domain. While re-projection approaches effectively address non-uniform sampling issues, secondary projections introduce high computational complexity, leading to excessive resource consumption [14]. Therefore, researchers further proposed weight allocation approaches, combining weight allocation in the calculation of quality scores to balance contributions from different pixel positions. Sun et al. [5] first proposed Weighted Spherical PSNR (WS-PSNR), generating weight maps for different projections based on the stretch ratio in continuous spatial domain, balancing non-uniform sampling density. Xiu et al. [6] based weight map generation on the area covered by each pixel on the spherical surface, further introducing Area-Weighted Spherical PSNR (AW-SPSNR). Additionally, Lopes [7], Zhou [8], and others computed structural assessment metrics using a similar approach, introducing Weighted SSIM (W-SSIM), Weighted Multi-Scale SSIM (WMS-SSIM), and Weighted Spherical Uniform SSIM (WS-SSIM), respectively. However, the aforementioned methods do not take into account human visual perception characteristics.

2.2   Perception-Based OVQA Methods

Traditional perception-based methods such as NCP-PSNR [9], CP-PSNR [9], SAL-PSNR [11] are still improvements upon basic models like PSNR and SSIM. These methods initially generate EM/HM weight maps for the entire video frame, utilizing this map for quality weight allocation. This process, requiring a single calculation, is referred to as frame-based. With the rapid development of deep learning theory and applications, patch-based methods have emerged. Li et al. [10] proposed a Convolutional Neural Network (CNN) model for OVQA, embedding predicted HM and EM information into the CNN structure. The ODV is then cropped into multiple patches, and quality scores for each patch are predicted after sampling using HM weights. Finally, quality scores are weighted based on corresponding EM data. Li et al. [12] introduced V-CNN, consisting of Viewport Proposal Network (VP-Net) and Viewport Quality Network (VQ-Net). VP-Net utilizes the spatiotemporal information of ODVs to generate multiple potential viewports for each frame. These viewport images are then fed into VQ-Net, which predicts EM distribution within the viewport and assigns a quality score. The above-mentioned methods have demonstrated excellent performance across multiple databases. However, when describing visual saliency, these models exclusively depend on low-level semantic information such as optical flow, structure, color, and brightness. They neglect the perceptual characteristics of the human visual system, which is more attuned to high-level semantic information such as scene types and salient objects in videos.

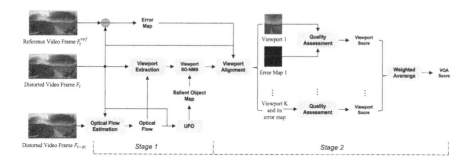

Fig. 1. Framework of our proposed approach

3   Method

Given that the quality of ODV hinges entirely on the viewports observed by the user, prioritizing the quality of these viewports becomes crucial when evaluating the overall video quality. As a result, the accuracy of viewport selection emerges as a pivotal factor in assessing OVQA performance, especially considering its intricate connection to visual attention. Based on this foundation, this paper introduces an objective OVQA model that integrates salient object information. The following sections delineate the comprehensive architecture of the model and offer detailed insights into the structure and functionality of each module.

3.1 Framework

The method framework proposed in this article is shown in Fig. 1, it comprises two stages: viewport extraction and quality assessment, utilized for extracting potential viewports and assessing the quality score of the distorted video frame F_t, respectively. As shown in Fig. 1, the model's inputs consist of three components: the tth distorted video frame F_t, the t reference video frame F_t^{ref}, and the $(t - \Delta t)$ distorted video frame $F_{(t-\Delta t)}$. In the first stage, we first extract a set of candidate viewports and their corresponding saliency weights via a viewport extraction network from [12]. Subsequently, a salient object based NMS algorithm is introduced, which coherently filters the recommended viewport set based on viewport weights and the predicted salient object map. In the quality assessment stage, we first obtains flat viewports through viewport alignment, followed by using a quality evaluation network to assess the quality scores of each viewport. In this paper, we directly employs DenseNet [15] to predict the saliency map representing the EM distribution within the viewport, and utilizes the error map and predicted saliency map to score the quality of each viewport.

The above describes the overall architecture and algorithmic workflow of the proposed model in this paper. Subsequent sections will focus on detailing the specific structure and functionality of the network models employed in each stage.

3.2 Viewport Extraction Stage

Candidate Viewport Extraction. The core task of this module is to extract the candidate viewports for each frame. We first employing an optical flow estimation model to generate the optical flow map F_t^{flow} for frame t. The optical flow map effectively represents the motion intensity and direction of each pixel in the frame, providing an intuitive reflection of regions with high motion intensity, which are more prone to distortion (such as motion blur). In this work, the RAFT-Net [16] model is utilized for optical flow estimation. RAFT-Net utilizes a pyramid structure to construct multi-scale image similarity features, enabling robust capture of abrupt motion and achieving more accurate optical flow outputs at motion boundaries.

Subsequently, as mentioned earlier, when ODVs are projected onto a plane, geometric distortions are introduced that are absent in the original video. Utilizing traditional convolutional methods may lead to reduced accuracy in feature extraction, affecting the algorithm's performance. Therefore, this paper initially employs Spherical Grid [17] to resample F_t^{flow} and F_t to the spherical domain. A 10-layer Spherical CNN (S-CNN) [18] is used to extract spherical features, connecting some shallow and deep layers to achieve fusion of low-level and deep features. After the final convolutional layer, the output is projected onto the unit

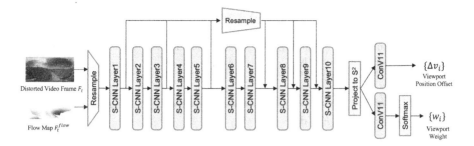

Fig. 2. Viewport extraction network structure

sphere S^2, denoted as T. T is then processed through two additional convolutional layers to obtain the set of viewport position offset $\{\Delta v_i = (\Delta\phi_i, \Delta\theta_i)\}_{i=1}^{N}$ and their corresponding saliency weights $\{w_i\}_{i=1}^{N}$, where N represents the number of viewports extracted from per-frame (Fig. 2).

SO-NMS. Considering the substantial number of viewports extracted within each video frame by the preceding module, which could impose a significant computational burden on the model, we introduce SO-NMS to further refine the set of candidate omnidirectional viewports. Specifically, SO-NMS filters the candidate viewport set using salient object information to obtain the proposal omnidirectional viewports. To achieve this, the first step is to detect salient objects in the video frames. The UFO model [19] is employed in this paper to obtain the salient object map F_t^{SOD} for each frame of the panoramic video. The salient object map is then resampled to the spherical domain using the same spherical grid, ensuring a consistent spatial coordinate domain for both the candidate omnidirectional viewports and the salient object map.

To guide the selection of viewports using salient objects, the salient object map F_t^{SOD} is weight-fused with viewport weights. This process assigns higher weight values to omnidirectional viewports in the salient object region. Subsequently, we define a Great-circle distance threshold d_{th} [20] and search for the omnidirectional viewport v_l with the maximum weight in the set V, located in the salient object region. Finally, it aggregates all candidate omnidirectional viewports within the d_{th} range and removes these viewports from the set V. This process is repeated to obtain the refined set of recommended omnidirectional viewports. These viewports incorporate both low-level semantic cues (structure, texture, color, optical flow) and high-level semantic cues (salient objects) from ODVs, offering a more nuanced representation of the perceptual characteristics of the human visual system in immersive environments. The selected viewports will be further evaluated in the next stage for quality assessment. The pseudocode for the SO-NMS algorithm is presented below.

Algorithm 1. Salient Object based Viewport NMS

Require: Candidate viewport set $V = \{v_1, v_2, \ldots, v_N\}$, viewport weight $W = \{w_1, w_2, \ldots, w_N\}$, salient map F^{sod}, Great-circle distance threshold d_{th}, Number of recommended viewports K_{th}.

$k \leftarrow 1, V^p \leftarrow \emptyset, W^p \leftarrow \emptyset$

$F_{sph}^{sod} \leftarrow Grid(F^{sod})$

$W_{sod} \leftarrow weight(F_{sph}^{sod}, W)$

while $V \neq \emptyset$ **and** $k \leq K_{th}$ **do**

    $l \leftarrow argmax_{\{l | w_l \in W_{sod}\}} w_l$

    $I' \leftarrow \{l' | d(v_{l'}, v_l) < d_{th}, v_{l'} \in V\}$

    $w_k^p \leftarrow \sum_{l' \in I'} w_{l'}$

    $v_k^p \leftarrow (\sum_{l' \in I'} w_{l'} \cdot v_{l'}) / w_k^p$

    $V^p \leftarrow V^p \cup \{v_k^p\}, W^p \leftarrow W^p \cup \{w_k^p\}$

    $V \leftarrow V \setminus \{v_{l'} | l' \in I'\}, W_{sod} \leftarrow W_{sod} \setminus \{w_{l'} | l' \in I'\}$

    $k \leftarrow k + 1$

end while

return V^p, W^p

3.3 Quality Assessment Stage

In this stage, the recommended omnidirectional viewports are first projected onto a 2D plane using the viewport alignment module. The aligned viewports are then fed into the quality assessment network for quality scoring.

Viewport Alignment. Assuming the recommended viewport set is $\{v_k = (\phi_k, \theta_k)\}_{k=1}^K$, where K is the total number of recommended viewports. We project both the recommended viewports and their corresponding error maps onto a 2D plane, denoted as C_k and C_k^{err}, respectively. For each pixel value in C_k and C_k^{err}, we apply bilinear interpolation at the corresponding pixel position in the distorted video frame F_t and the error map F_t^{err}. Specifically, this paper defines the size of the 2D plane viewports as $W \times H$. For any given pixel position (x, y) on C_k, where $x \in [1, W]$ and $y \in [1, H]$, we need to find the corresponding spherical position $(\phi_{x,y}, \theta_{x,y})$ through geometric projection inversion [21]. First, the pixel coordinates (x, y) are transformed into (f_x, f_y):

$$f_x = \frac{2x - 1 - W}{W} \times \tan\frac{a_W}{2},$$
$$f_y = -\frac{2y - 1 - H}{H} \times \tan\frac{a_H}{2} \tag{1}$$

where a_W and a_H describe the angular range of the viewport. The corresponding spherical coordinates $(\phi_{x,y}, \theta_{x,y})$ can be obtained from the following equations:

$$\phi_{x,y} = \phi_k + \arctan\left(\frac{f_x \sin c}{\rho \cos\theta_k \cos c - f_y \sin\theta_k \sin c}\right) \tag{2}$$

$$\theta_{x,y} = \arcsin\left(\cos c \sin\theta_k + \frac{f_y \sin c \cos\theta_k}{\rho}\right) \tag{3}$$

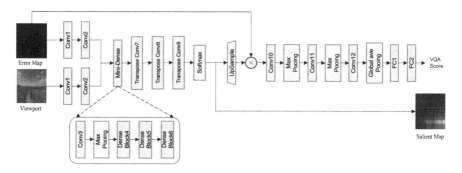

Fig. 3. Quality assessment network structure

In addition, where $\rho = \sqrt{f_x^2 + f_y^2}$ and $c = \arctan(\rho)$.

The resulting spherical coordinates $(\phi_{x,y}, \theta_{x,y})$ corresponding to the pixel positions on F_t and F_t^{err} depend on the projection type of the omnidirectional video. Taking the ERP format as an example, the corresponding pixel positions $(p_{x,y}, q_{x,y})$ for $(\phi_{x,y}, \theta_{x,y})$ are given by:

$$
\begin{aligned}
p_{x,y} &= \left(\frac{\phi_{x,y}}{360°} + \frac{1}{2} \right) W_{\mathbf{F}} + \frac{1}{2}, \\
q_{x,y} &= \left(\frac{1}{2} - \frac{\theta_{x,y}}{180°} \right) H_{\mathbf{F}} + \frac{1}{2}
\end{aligned}
\tag{4}
$$

where W_F and H_F are the width and height of the ODV frame in the ERP format. Finally, the pixel value at (x, y) in C_k and C_k^{err} can be obtained by bilinear interpolation on F_t and F_t^{err} at $(p_{x,y}, q_{x,y})$.

Quality Assessment Module. The network structure is shown in Fig. 3. Each recommended viewport C_k and its corresponding error map C_k^{err} are fed into the network, and after passing through 2 convolutional layers, they are concatenated. Subsequently, a Mini-DenseNet with 3 DenseBlock layers, 3 transposed convolutional layers, and a Softmax activation function is employed to predict the saliency map M_k within each viewport. The predicted results can simulate the distribution of EM under stable fixation. Then, the Hadamard product is applied to the weighted sum of M_k and C_k^{err}. Finally, the obtained weighted error map is input into a CNN structure with 3 convolutional layers, 2 max-pooling layers, 1 global average pooling layer, and 2 fully connected layers, yielding the quality score s_k for each recommended viewport. The quality score for each frame can be obtained using the following formula:

$$
s_f = \frac{\sum_{k=1}^{K} s_k}{K}
\tag{5}
$$

4   Experimental Results and Analysis

4.1   Experimental Setup

Database. This paper adopts the VQA-ODV dataset [10] as the benchmark which consists of 60 reference videos and their corresponding 540 distorted videos. The projection formats include ERP, RCMP, and TSP, covering resolutions from 4K (3840×1920) to 8K (7680×3840). Three types of distorted videos are obtained by compressing them with H.265 encoding under the conditions of QP = 27, 37, and 42.

Implementation Details. In this paper, the weight parameters of the viewport recommendation network are initialized using the pre-training data provided by Li et al. [12], and the UFO model parameters are based on pre-training results on the YouTubeVOS database [22], we only need to train the quality evaluation network. Specifically, we freeze the gradients of the network before the softmax activation layer in the quality assessment network and only update the parameters of the subsequent network. This paper employs the AdamW optimizer with a learning rate of 1e−5, decay weight of 0.05, and selects the L1 loss as the loss function.

$$\mathcal{L} = \frac{1}{T} \sum_{t=1}^{T} (q'_t - q_t) \tag{6}$$

where q'_t denotes the subjective score of t-th ODV, q_t denotes the corresponding prediction score, and T denotes the batch size. The number of epochs is set to 100, and the batch size is set to 8. The dataset is divided into a training set and a test set in a 4:1 ratio, and other hyperparameters are specified in Table 1. The experiments were conducted on an Intel Xeon (R) CPU E5-2630, with an Nvidia V100 32G GPU, running Linux Ubuntu 18.04. The programming language used is Python, and the deep learning framework is PyTorch.

Table 1. Hyperparameter settings

Hyperparameter	Value
Great-circle Distance d_{th}	$13.75°$
Number of proposal viewports K_{th}	20
Viewport size W,H	$W = 540, H = 600$
Angular Range α_w, α_H	$\alpha_w = 71°, \alpha_H = 74°$

4.2   Performance Comparison

This paper employs four performance metrics, including Pearson Linear Correlation Coefficient (PLCC), Spearman Rank Correlation Coefficient (SROCC), Kendall Rank Correlation Coefficient (KRCC), and Root Mean Square Error (RMSE). We compare the performance of our model with other classical models, including S-PSNR [3], WS-PSNR [5], CPP-PSNR [4], VR-IQA-NET [23], Li et al. [10], Jiang et al. [24], Meng et al. [25] and V-CNN [12]. Among them, S-PSNR, WS-PSNR, and CPP-PSNR are VR video quality assessment methods recognized in the Moving Picture Experts Group (MPEG) standard [26]. VR-IQA-NET, Li et al., Jiang et al., Meng et al. and V-CNN are deep learning-based omnidirectional video quality assessment methods. Table 2 presents the results of PLCC, SROCC, KROCC, and RMSE for the 9 models participating in the performance comparison on the dataset used. The results in red and bold indicate the optimal performance.

Table 2. Performance comparison experimental results

Approaches	Attributes		Evaluation			
	Deep Learning	Full Reference	PLCC	SROCC	KROCC	RMSE
S-PSNR	✗	✓	0.6929	0.6976	0.4981	8.5407
WS-PSNR	✗	✓	0.6721	0.6839	0.4860	8.7707
CPP-PSNR	✗	✓	0.6812	0.6896	0.4912	8.6718
Li et al	✓	✓	0.7821	0.7953	0.5902	7.3817
VR-IQA-NET	✓	✗	0.3713	0.3379	0.2260	10.9984
V-CNN	✓	✓	0.9122	0.9079	0.7492	6.3209
Jiang et al.	✓	✗	0.8863	0.8721	0.6957	5.3469
Meng et al.	✗	✗	0.8600	0.9100	✗	6.320
Ours	✓	✓	0.9004	0.9065	0.7301	6.4964

4.3   Ablation Analysis

As previously discussed, the precision and appropriateness of viewport extraction play a pivotal role in determining the quality assessment outcomes. Consequently, we first conducts ablation experiments on the viewport extraction strategy to validate the effectiveness of the proposed SO-NMS algorithm. Recognizing that the number of recommended viewports can also impact VQA performance, striking a balance is crucial-too few recommended viewports may lead to incomplete coverage of the user's actual viewing content, while an excess may introduce unnecessary interference. Therefore, following the ablation of the viewport extraction strategy, we delves into the further exploration of the key hyperparameter, the recommended number of viewports K_{th}, within the SO-NMS framework.

Ablation of the Viewport Extraction Strategy. While maintaining a consistent number of recommended viewports, the viewport extraction strategy determines whether the extracted viewports effectively reflect the audience's actual viewing behavior. The experiment considers three viewport extraction strategies: SO-NMS, NMS used in [12], and randomly selected viewports. These strategies are tested and their performances are compared on the VQA-ODV dataset. The experimental results are illustrated in Fig. 4.

The results unequivocally highlight the superior performance of the model when adopting the SO-NMS strategy in contrast to the random selection approach, showcasing its impressive competitiveness. SO-NMS meticulously accounts for perceptual intricacies, particularly viewers' inclination towards higher-level semantic cues such as salient objects in immersive environments. The extracted set of recommended viewports effectively spans the content observed by users, yielding quality scores that closely align with users' subjective perceptual assessments.

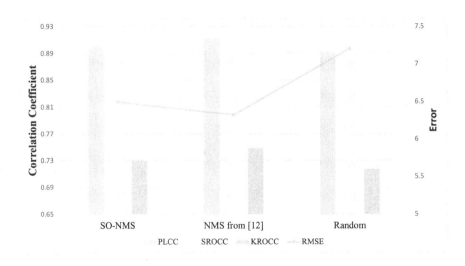

Fig. 4. Results of viewport extraction strategy ablation

Ablation of Recommended Viewport Quantity. The number of extracted viewports plays a crucial role in determining the effectiveness and comprehensiveness of capturing the video content observed by users. Moreover, the viewport quantity significantly impacts the computational time of the model. Therefore, we conducted experiments with four recommended viewport quantities ($K_{th} = 15, 20, 25, 50$) to assess their corresponding performance metrics and computation times. The experimental results are presented in Table 3, with the optimal results highlighted in red-bolded font.

It is evident that when the number of recommended viewports is relatively low (e.g., $K_{th} = 15$), the model exhibits the minimum computational time (about 191.1637 s). However, the performance declines compared to $K_{th} = 20$ due to inadequate coverage of the observed video content. Conversely, with a higher number of recommended viewports (e.g., $K_{th} = 25, 50$), there is an increase in computational time (210.0509 s and 241.4257 s, respectively), along with the introduction of disruptive noise in the recommended viewports, leading to a noticeable decrease in model performance compared to $K_{th} = 20$. This underscores that the chosen number of recommended viewports, $K_{th} = 20$, strikes a favorable balance between computational efficiency and superior performance.

Table 3. Results of ablation experiment on recommended viewport quantity

Value of K_{th}	Time cost	Evaluation			
		PLCC	SROCC	KROCC	RMSE
15	191.1637 s	0.8852	0.9052	0.7016	6.8587
20	201.7381 s	0.9004	0.9065	0.7301	6.4964
25	210.0509 s	0.8981	0.9005	0.7238	6.6321
50	241.4257	0.8854	0.8849	0.7143	7.0338

5   Conclusion

Omnidirectional videos, emerging as a novel multimedia format, are garnering extensive attention from both the academic and industrial sectors. Accurate and effective algorithms for OVQA plays a pivotal role in high-quality image coding, optimizing presentation parameters, and elevating the overall visual experience for users. It is noteworthy that many perception-based quality assessment models primarily focus on pixel-level semantic details like optical flow, texture, and color during saliency detection, often overlooking advanced semantic cues such as salient objects.

In response to this challenge, we introduces the SO-NMS algorithm. This method amalgamates multi-level saliency information to extract recommended omnidirectional viewports, paving the way for subsequent quality assessments solely on these identified viewports. The experimental results underscore the highly competitive performance of the model proposed in this study on the test dataset, surpassing the majority of objective OVQA methods.

References

1. Xu, M., Li, C., Zhang, S., Le Callet, P.: State-of-the-art in 360 video/image processing: perception, assessment and compression. IEEE J. Sel. Top. Signal Process. **14**(1), 5–26 (2020)
2. Yang, L., Xu, M., Liu, T., Huo, L., Gao, X.: Tvformer: trajectory-guided visual quality assessment on 360° images with transformers. In: Proceedings of the 30th ACM International Conference on Multimedia, pp. 799–808 (2022)
3. Yu, M., Lakshman, H., Girod, B.: A framework to evaluate omnidirectional video coding schemes. In: 2015 IEEE International Symposium on Mixed and Augmented Reality, pp. 31–36. IEEE (2015)
4. Zakharchenko, V., Choi, K.P., Park, J.H.: Quality metric for spherical panoramic video. In: Optics and Photonics for Information Processing X, vol. 9970, pp. 57–65. SPIE (2016)
5. Sun, Y., Lu, A., Yu, L.: Weighted-to-spherically-uniform quality evaluation for omnidirectional video. IEEE Signal Process. Lett. **24**(9), 1408–1412 (2017)
6. Xiu, X., He, Y., Ye, Y., Vishwanath, B.: An evaluation framework for 360-degree video compression. In: 2017 IEEE Visual Communications and Image Processing (VCIP), pp. 1–4. IEEE (2017)
7. Wang, Z., Simoncelli, E.P., Bovik, A.C.: Multiscale structural similarity for image quality assessment. In: The Thrity-Seventh Asilomar Conference on Signals, Systems & Computers, 2003, vol. 2, pp. 1398–1402. IEEE (2003)
8. Zhou, Y., Yu, M., Ma, H., Shao, H., Jiang, G.: Weighted-to-spherically-uniform ssim objective quality evaluation for panoramic video. In: 2018 14th IEEE International Conference on Signal Processing (ICSP), pp. 54–57. IEEE (2018)
9. Luz, G., Ascenso, J., Brites, C., Pereira, F.: Saliency-driven omnidirectional imaging adaptive coding: modeling and assessment. In: 2017 IEEE 19th International Workshop on Multimedia Signal Processing (MMSP), pp. 1–6. IEEE (2017)
10. Li, C., Xu, M., Du, X., Wang, Z.: Bridge the gap between vqa and human behavior on omnidirectional video: a large-scale dataset and a deep learning model. In: Proceedings of the 26th ACM International Conference on Multimedia, pp. 932–940 (2018)
11. Xu, M., Li, C., Chen, Z., Wang, Z., Guan, Z.: Assessing visual quality of omnidirectional videos. IEEE Trans. Circuits Syst. Video Technol. **29**(12), 3516–3530 (2018)
12. Xu, M., Jiang, L., Li, C., Wang, Z., Tao, X.: Viewport-based CNN: a multi-task approach for assessing 360° video quality. IEEE Trans. Pattern Anal. Mach. Intell. **44**(4), 2198–2215 (2020)
13. Guimard, Q., et al.: On the link between emotion, attention and content in virtual immersive environments. In: 2022 IEEE International Conference on Image Processing (ICIP), pp. 2521–2525. IEEE (2022)
14. Tran, H.T., Pham, C.T., Ngoc, N.P., Pham, A.T., Thang, T.C.: A study on quality metrics for 360 video communications. IEICE Trans. Inf. Syst. **101**(1), 28–36 (2018)
15. Huang, G., Liu, Z., Van Der Maaten, L., Weinberger, K.Q.: Densely connected convolutional networks. In: Proceedings of the IEEE Conference on Computer Vision and Pattern Recognition, pp. 4700–4708 (2017)
16. Teed, Z., Deng, J.: Raft: Recurrent all-pairs field transforms for optical flow. In: Computer Vision–ECCV 2020: 16th European Conference, pp. 402–419. Springer (2020)

17. Healy, D.M., Rockmore, D.N., Kostelec, P.J., Moore, S.: FFTs for the 2-sphere-improvements and variations. J. Fourier Anal. Appl. **9**, 341–385 (2003)
18. Cohen, T.S., Geiger, M., Köhler, J., Welling, M.: Spherical cnns. arXiv preprint arXiv:1801.10130 (2018)
19. Su, Y., Deng, J., Sun, R., Lin, G., Su, H., Wu, Q.: A unified transformer framework for group-based segmentation: Co-segmentation, co-saliency detection and video salient object detection. IEEE Transactions on Multimedia (2023)
20. Kells, L.M.: Plane and Spherical Trigonometry With Tables by Lyman M. Willis F. Kern, James R. Bland. US Armed Forces Institute, Kells (1940)
21. Snyder, J.P.: Map projections–A working manual, vol. 1395. US Government Printing Office (1987)
22. Xu, N., et al.: A large-scale video object segmentation benchmark. arXiv preprint (2018)
23. Kim, H.G., Lim, H.T., Ro, Y.M.: Deep virtual reality image quality assessment with human perception guider for omnidirectional image. IEEE Trans. Circuits Syst. Video Technol. **30**(4), 917–928 (2019)
24. Jiang, Z., Xu, Y., Sun, J., Hwang, J.N., Zhang, Y., Appleby, S.C.: Tile-based panoramic video quality assessment. IEEE Trans. Broadcast. **68**(2), 530–544 (2021)
25. Meng, Y., Ma, Z.: Viewport-based omnidirectional video quality assessment: Database, modeling and inference. IEEE Trans. Circuits Syst. Video Technol. **32**(1), 120–134 (2021)
26. Ye, Y., Alshina, E., Boyce, J.: Joint video exploration team (jvet) of itu-t sg 16 wp 3 and iso/iec jtc 1/sc 29/wg 11

A No-Reference Stereoscopic Image Quality Assessment Based on Cartoon Texture Decomposition and Human Visual System

Yun Liu[1], Yan Bai[1], Yaohui Wang[1(✉)], Minzhu Jin[1(✉)], and Bo Liu[2(✉)]

[1] College of Information, School of Cyber Science and Engineering, Liaoning University, Shenyang, Liaoning, China
{cangsheng.why,mmmzzz0826}@foxmail.com
[2] Lianyungang Aids to Navigation Department of Donghai Navigation Safety Administration, Lianyungang, Jiangsu, China
531837035@qq.com

Abstract. It has become important to develop an objective stereoscopic image quality assessment (SIQA) method that aligns with human visual system characteristics. To enable an accurate and efficient assessment of stereoscopic image quality, this study introduces a no-reference stereoscopic image quality assessment model, aiming to address the limitations of existing assessment methods. Considering that natural images typically contain information like textures and contours, we decompose stereoscopic views into cartoon and texture images to effectively extract monocular perception features. We also take binocular difference information to explain binocular perception features. Subsequently, a CNN multi-branch architecture is employed to feed images into the network for extracting relevant feature mappings. Finally, all sub-networks are used for quality scoring predictions, resulting in the final perceptual quality score. Experiments conducted on the LIVE dataset have demonstrated the superiority of this approach.

Keywords: Stereoscopic Image Quality · Cartoon Texture Decomposition · Human Visual System · Binocular Vision

1 Introduction

With the rapid development of modern digital technology and computer vision field, Image Quality Assessment (IQA) [1] has become an important research topic. In various applications, such as image compression, enhancement, restoration, transmission, etc., the quality of images needs to be accurately assessed to achieve better results and user experience. In recent years, due to the rapid development of three-dimensional imaging technology, more and more stereoscopic (3D) images emerge in people's daily life, and 3D movies and videos

G. Zhai et al. (Eds.): IFTC 2023, CCIS 2067, pp. 68–81, 2024.
https://doi.org/10.1007/978-981-97-3626-3_6

bring people an immersive viewing experience. However, 3D images in the compression, transmission and display process will introduce a variety of noise, such as JPEG (JPEG) [2] compression distortion, JPEG2000 (JP2K) [3] compression distortion, additive white noise (WN) [4] distortion, fast decay (FF) [5] distortion, Gaussian fuzzy (Blur) [6] distortion, and so on, which inevitably caused quality degradation. As image receivers, image quality degradation will seriously affect the visual experience of the viewers, which may cause dizziness, eye pain, and perceptual discomfort, etc. Therefore, how to establish an effectiveSIQA [7] method has become an important research topic and research direction in image quality assessment.

Although there are many objective assessment metrics that have been widely used, such as PSNR [8], SSIM [9] and VIF [10] etc., they still have some limitations, especially in complex and diverse real-world 3D scenes. In recent years, deep learning method has made remarkable progress in the field of computer vision. These methods have the ability to capture more complex and abstract image features and structures by learning from a large amount of data, thus providing a new way for image quality assessment. Convolutional Neural Networks (CNNs) [11–14] have shown great potential in image quality assessment tasks due to their powerful feature extraction capabilities. Like traditional SIQA [7] methods, monocular and binocular quality features are both utilized to map the quality scores in the CNN-based models.

Recent works [15–17] have presented that cartoon texture decomposition can provide rich visual information. They indicated that cartoon images tend to emphasize low-frequency information [18], such as overall structure and shape, and can learn the basic shapes and structures, aiding in global understanding and conceptual abstraction. Texture images, on the other hand, are typical representatives of high-frequency information [19], which can provide rich details, such as the texture of object surfaces and subtle changes in light and shade. Texture images enable the model to learn about local details and texture information, which is crucial for understanding surface properties of objects and for tasks requiring fine classification. Motivated by the above works, we assumption that cartoon texture decomposition can help to learn rich monocular information. Therefore, in this paper, we first perform cartoon texture decomposition on left view, dividing it into cartoon images and texture images. We also introduced the right view image to compensate the above left view information and learn more monocular features, especially asymmetric information, to represent binocular rivalry information. Then, we calculate the disparity map by subtracting the left and right view images to extract the binocular features related to depth information. Subsequently, we utilize powerful deep learning networks to extract features to regress the final quality score. The newly designed SIQA model has strong portability and low computational requirements, which has great potential for development and broad application prospects.

This paper is structured as follows: Sect. 2 outlines relevant literature and previous research in the field. Section 3 introduces our novel Non-Reference Image Quality Assessment (NR-IQA) metric. Section 4 details the experiments conducted and analyzes the results, demonstrating that our proposed algorithm performs on par with leading non-reference algorithms in the industry. Finally, Sect. 5 summarizes our findings and conclusions

2 Related Works

Image quality assessment methods can be broadly categorized into two main types: subjective and objective assessment methods [20–22]. Subjective assessment relies on human observers to perceive and rate the quality of an image, while objective assessment attempts to simulate the human visual system [23] to automatically assess the quality of an image. The former method relies on human rating opinions to determine quality, which is costly and time consuming, while the latter method relies on machine algorithmic scoring, which is low cost and fast, and has more potential in practical applications. Based on the availability of reference images, objective SIQA algorithms consist of three main types: full-reference stereoscopic image quality assessment (FR-SIQA) [24], reduced-reference stereoscopic image quality assessment (RR-SIQA) [25] and no-reference stereoscopic image quality assessment (NR-SIQA) [26]. Compared to FR-SIQA and RR-SIQA approaches, NR-SIQA techniques have the unique ability to evaluate the visual quality of images without needing any reference data. As a result, NR-SIQA methods are increasingly becoming the primary focus of research in this field.

Nowadays, in the field of non-referenced image quality assessment (NR IQA), convolutional neural networks (CNNs) [27,28] have made great success in computer vision tasks due to their powerful ability to automatically extract features. As a result, a large number of CNN-based SIQA methods have been proposed. For instance, Feng et al. [29] developed a two-channel CNN [30,31] to extract monocular features and then concatenated as a binocular feature for quality score prediction. Similarly, Li et al. [32] employed a sparse CNN for SIQA by simply fusing left and right view features in alignment with human brain's stereoscopic image processing. Additionally, Fang et al. [33] Devised an innovative method for no-reference quality assessment of stereoscopic images using a deep learning-based approach. It leverages a Siamese Network to extract essential semantic features from both views, effectively reducing data redundancy. Shi et al. [34] Presented a unique three-column, multi-mask CNN framework, which separately analyzes the left and right views, along with the aligned distortion representation, for simultaneous prediction of image quality and identification of distortion types. Ding et al. [35] Introduced a SIQA method employing a compact two-column dense CNN, using cyclopean views and disparity images from distorted stereo pairs as inputs. Yan et al. [36] designed a DNN by considering feature fusion in various cortical areas of the human visual system (HVS). Si et al. [37] introduced StereoIF-Net with a Binocular Interaction Module (BIM) and a Binocular Fusion Module (BFM) to model binocular interaction in the HVS.

Most existing no-reference SIQA methods are ignored deeply dig rich monocular features, such as the properties of texture and cartoon information, even in traditional 2D IQA methods. To fill this gap, researchers have begun to develop 2D IQA methods by taking into account the unique characteristics of these image information [38,39] based on cartoon texture decomposition, which provide us a new way to learn monocular features.

3   Proposed Model

In this paper, we introduce a new no-reference method to evaluate image quality. Figure 1 outlines the framework of our model. This model integrates four sub-networks to collaboratively process stereoscopic imaging inputs, enabling the capture and analysis of image information from each independent perspective. These sub-networks are tasked with processing the left cartoon image, left texture image, disparity map, and right image from a pair of stereoscopic images. This multi-channel processing strategy allows the model to independently assess the quality of each view while maintaining sensitivity to the binocular information inherent in stereoscopic images. Subsequently, we fuse and concatenate the information from all views into a single vector to extract deeper visual features. Then, we perform regression on all the obtained features to predict the quality score. Overall, our model's design reflects a comprehensive and hierarchical approach to processing.

3.1   Cartoon Texture Decomposition

In this paper, we adopt a cartoon-texture decomposition method based on total variation (LTV) structure for image decomposition into cartoon images and texture images [40]. For any given pixel, designated as "x", within an image, its LTV

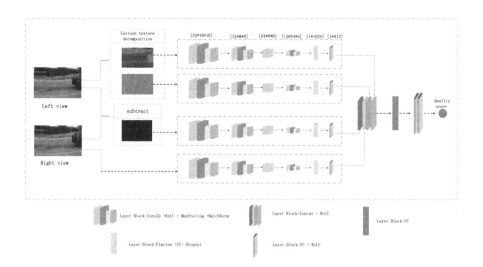

Fig. 1. The Framework of Our Model

is characterized as follows:

$$LTV_\sigma(x)(I) = G_\sigma * |\nabla I|(x) \tag{1}$$

where G_σ is a Gaussian kernel characterized by a standard deviation sigma, where * symbolizes the convolution process. We define $x \to \lambda_{\sigma(x)}$, The measure of how the Local Tonal Value (LTV) varies at a specific point x within the image is defined as:

$$\lambda_\sigma(x) = \frac{LTV_\sigma(x)(I) - LTV_\sigma(x)(L_\sigma * I)}{LTV_\sigma(x)(I)} \tag{2}$$

where L_σ represents a low-pass filter, and the scale parameter L for decomposition is determined by this kernel function. When LTV decays quickly under low-pass filtering conditions, $\lambda_{\sigma(x)}$ can reveal its local oscillation conditions. Evidently, the equation can also be equivalently expressed as:

$$LTV_\sigma(x)(L_\sigma * I) = (1 - \lambda_\sigma(x)) LTV_\sigma(x)(I) \tag{3}$$

Equation indicates that when λ_σ approaching 0, there's a minimal decrease in LTV following lowpass filtering, indicating a negligible effect of the low-pass filter on the LTV at that location. This implies that such points are part of the cartoon component U; In contrast, as λ_σ approaching 1, we observe a significant relative change rate, marked by a rapid decrease, identifying these points as part of the texture component V. Therefore, by evaluating the relative rate of change of LTV in the image, we can derive a pair of efficient nonlinear high-pass and low-pass filters. These are obtained from the weighted mean of $L_\sigma * I*I$ and I, and are represented as follows:

$$U(x) = \left(1 - w\big(\lambda_\sigma(x)\big)\right)I(x) + w(\lambda_\sigma(x))(L_\sigma(x))(L_\sigma * I)(x) \tag{4}$$

$$V(x) = I(x) - U(x) \tag{5}$$

where $w(x)$ has a range of [0,1], and represents a segmented, progressively non-diminishing, soft threshold function. It takes a constant value of 0 near 0, and a constant value of 1 near 1. In the experiment, this paper sets the soft threshold function as:

$$w(x) \begin{cases} 0, & x \leq a_1 \\ (x - a_1)/(x - a_2), & a_1 < x \leq a_2 \\ 1, & x > a_2 \end{cases} \tag{6}$$

where the values assigned to the parameters a_1 and a_2 are 0.25 and 0.5 respectively. When $\lambda_\sigma \to 0$ is small, the function I(x) oscillates less near x, so it is correct that it is a cartoon at x with U(x) = I(x); on the contrary, when $\lambda_{\sigma(x)}$ is large, the function I(x) shows local oscillation around x, and U(x) is locally replaced by $(L_\sigma * I)(x)$. The texture component V takes the difference between the cartoon component and the original image I. Cartoon texture images are shown in Figs. 2.

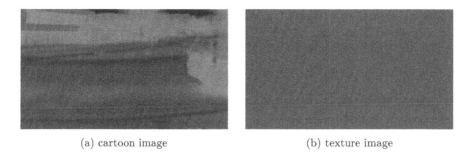

(a) cartoon image   (b) texture image

Fig. 2. Cartoon Texture Decomposition Image

3.2 Binocular Difference Information

The difference information in stereoscopic images is a key factor distinguishing them from 2D images. Binocular differences [41], This phenomenon, manifesting as the eyes focus on a singular object, is characterized by the disparity in the projection points from dual perspectives. Binocular difference is an important attribute of stereoscopic vision, helping the brain extract depth information from stereoscopic images. Considering the significant influence of binocular vision on human perception in actual visual experiences, our approach incorporates a binocular difference information to effectively replicate the visual traits of the HVS [42], as follows:

$$\Delta I = I_{left} - I_{right} \tag{7}$$

where ΔI represents the binocular difference image calculated from the left view I_{left} and the right view I_{right}, which reveals the depth information and potential visual distortions in the 3D image.

3.3 Network Architecture of IQA

In our deep learning methodology for image quality assessment, we integrate the characteristics of the HVS with the mechanism of binocular rivalry. The HVS is a sophisticated processing mechanism highly sensitive to visual elements such as brightness, contrast, color, and spatial frequency. Notably, the HVS exhibits varying sensitivities to different spatial frequencies, implying that human perception varies across different levels of image detail. To simulate this complex process, we designed a deep learning model that assesses image quality by emulating how the HVS processes visual information. The model incorporates a series of convolutional layers to mimic the retina's initial response to image details, followed by deeper network structures that simulate how the brain cortex synthesizes this information to make a comprehensive judgment of image quality.

Motivated by the above analysis, we propose a multi-score architecture comprising four sub-CNN structures, shown in Fig. 1. Each sub-network utilizes five groups of convolutional layers (Convs) and three groups of max-pooling layers for feature extraction. And each convolutional layer is activated by a 3×3 Conv with a rectified linear unit (ReLU) [43], and followed by a max-pooling layer. Finally, a $[1 \times 1]$ fully connected (FC) layer is required to generate the quality score.

3.4   Loss Function

In our stereoscopic image quality assessment model, the quality prediction phase employs a dual loss function strategy to mimic the human visual system's perception of visual fidelity in an image, as follows:

$$LOSS = (\lambda * loss_G) + (\theta * loss_D) \tag{8}$$

where $loss_G$ is designed to capture the overall visual quality by aggregating the outputs of the left cartoon image, left texture image, disparity map, and right image sub-networks. This function ensures comprehensive assessment of global features. $loss_D$ focuses on stereoscopic vision and depth perception, assessing the loss from the disparity map. This approach is essential for understanding and evaluating the subtle differences in stereoscopic images, a dimension often overlooked in traditional quality assessments. λ and θ are parameters to adjust their contributions in the total loss. Based on the human visual system's sensitivity to overall visual quality, λ is set higher than θ ($\lambda=2$, $\theta=1$). This weighting reflects the importance of global quality while incorporating disparity impacts, providing a comprehensive image quality assessment method.

4   Experimental Results and Analysis

4.1   Experimental Data Set

To test the performance of the algorithm in this paper, two stereoscopic image quality evaluation databases: LIVE 3D IQA Database Phase I (Live-I) [44], LIVE 3D IQA Database Phase II [45], are used to evaluate the proposed algorithm.

LIVE 3D Phase I [44] (LIVE-I)contains 20 original reference stereoscopic image pairs and 365 symmetric distortion stereoscopic image pairs, including five types, as shown below :JPEG compression [2], JP2K compression [3], additive white noise (WN) [4], Gaussian Blur (Blur) [6], and fast fading (FF) [5].

LIVE 3D Phase-II [45] (LIVE-II)contains 8 pairs of original stereoscopic images and 360 pairs of distorted stereoscopic images (including symmetric and asymmetric distortion). It has the same distortion type as LIVE-I with one distortion type per 72 pairs.

4.2   Experimental Setting

The training set consists of 80% randomly selected distorted stereoscopic images, and the remaining 20% is used to evaluate the performance of the algorithm as a test set. The experiment was carried out 1000 times, and the average value was taken as the final experimental result. The experimental environment of this paper is: Xeon(R) Platinum 8358P CPU; NVIDIA GeForce RTX 3090 GPU; 80 GB RAM; Python 3.8.

4.3   Experimental Result

Overall Performance Analysis. Three commonly used evaluation indexes are used to evaluate the performance of objective image quality evaluation algorithm in the experiments: Pearson linear correlation coefficient (PLCC), Spearman rank coefficient (SROCC) and root mean square error (RMSE) [46]. Where PLCC represents the correlation between the predicted value of the algorithm and the subjective value of human eyes. The closer the absolute value of PLCC is to 1, the better the performance of the algorithm.SROCC measures the monotonicity of the algorithm prediction. The closer the absolute value is to 1, the better the monotonicity of the subjective evaluation of human eyes and the predicted value of the algorithm. RMSE measures the accuracy of an algorithm's predictions. The closer the value is to 0, the higher the accuracy of the algorithm's prediction value and human eyes' subjective evaluation value.

In order to verify the effectiveness of the objective evaluation model proposed in this paper for the prediction of single distortion stereoscopic image quality, one RR-SIQA models Wan2020 [9] is selected and eight NR-SIQA models were selected as follows: Hu2022 [47], Messai2021 [48], Si2021 [49], Sun2020 [2], Messai2020 [50], Liu2020 [51], Wang2020 [11] and Jiang2020 [52] are used as comparison algorithms. For each performance metric , the best results are shown in bold.

Table 1. Overall performance comparison of several methods in the LIVE database

Type	LIVE 3D Phase I			LIVE 3D Phase II		
	PLCC	SROCC	RMSE	PLCC	SROCC	RMSE
Hu2022	0.945	0.948	NA	0.928	0.919	NA
Messai2021	0.956	0.911	5.905	0.948	0.932	4.629
Si2021	0.944	0.943	5.313	0.927	0.924	6.194
Sun2020	0.951	0.959	4.573	0.938	0.918	3.809
Messai2020	0.939	0.930	5.605	0.922	0.913	4.352
Liu2020	**0.960**	0.952	4.905	**0.958**	0.956	3.508
Wang2020	0.938	0.868	NA	0.851	0.831	3.508
Jiang2020	**0.960**	0.953	NA	0.932	0.927	NA
Wan2020	0.944	0.928	NA	0.945	0.932	NA
Ours	0.959	**0.967**	**4.105**	**0.958**	**0.968**	**3.132**

As can be seen from Table 1, the overall performance index of the proposed algorithm on the LIVE 3D phaseI and LIVE 3D phaseII databases is better than other algorithms, with PLCC and SROCC values of more than 0.95 and small RMSE values. The PLCC index of Liu2020 [51] algorithm and Jiang2020 [52] on LIVE-I is slightly better than that of the proposed algorithm, while the PLCC value of Liu2020 [51] algorithm on LIVE-II is the same as that of this paper.

However, the Liu2020 [51] algorithm network separation extracts the left and right view features, which does not reflect the binocular interaction. Wang2020 [11] extracts image features through dictionary learning, which does not perform as well as deep learning to extract features, so it does not get good results on SROCC and RMSE.In terms of overall performance, the proposed algorithm is superior to the two algorithms. Compared with other deep learning feature extraction algorithms, Hu2022 [47] and Messai2021 [48] both obtain local features based on image blocks, ignoring the integrity of the global information of the image, limiting their performance. At the same time, the deep learning algorithm is used to comprehensively consider the global information of the image, binocular fusion features and monocular cartoon texture features, and better prediction results are obtained, which verifies the rationality of the algorithm.

Result Analysis of Different Distortion Types. In order to more accurately evaluate the performance of the model, we listed the SROCC and PLCC of 5 different types of distorted images in the LIVE 3D Phase II database, and the two optimal results for each distorted image were highlighted in bold, as shown in Table 2. The performance of our algorithm is outstanding in JPEG,WN and FF distortion types. The PLCC values in Blur and SROCC values in JP2K slightly worse than the top two values. In general, our method is generally superior to the other methods with four times good performance in the PLCC index and four times good performance in the SROCC index. The above analysis shows that our model is consistent with human subjective perception and can simulate human visual system to evaluate symmetric and asymmetric stereoscopic images.

Table 2. Values for different distortion types in LIVE 3D Phase II

Type	PLCC					SROCC				
	JP2K	JPEG	WN	Blur	FF	JP2K	JPEK	WN	Blur	FF
Hu2022	0.877	0.837	0.928	0.959	0.946	0.860	0.841	0.911	0.943	0.946
Messai2021	0.835	0.859	0.953	0.978	0.925	0.842	0.837	0.943	0.913	0.925
Sun2021	0.900	0.823	0.956	**0.996**	0.901	0.897	0.579	0.933	**0.964**	0.918
Si2021	0.910	0.901	0.899	0.961	0.940	0.872	0.882	0.876	0.945	**0.951**
Messai2020	0.835	0.859	0.953	0.978	0.925	0.842	0.837	0.943	0.913	0.925
Liu2020	**0.920**	0.875	**0.969**	**0.984**	**0.954**	**0.917**	0.858	**0.944**	0.915	0.932
Wang2020	NA	NA	NA	NA	NA	0.850	0.847	0.942	0.914	0.903
Jiang2020	0.942	**0.924**	0.917	0.920	0.919	**0.909**	**0.889**	0.873	0.865	0.887
Ours	**0.950**	**0.975**	**0.959**	0.976	**0.977**	0.907	**0.956**	**0.966**	**0.951**	**0.965**

4.4   Ablation Experiment

In order to understand the impact of different image feature on the prediction results of image quality in detail, four different experimental schemes are designed and the performance of four algorithms on the LIVE 3D Phase II database are compared. The prediction results of the algorithm are shown in Table 3. In the M1 scheme, we keep other experimental conditions unchanged and remove the left-view cartoon image subnetwork in the model. In the M2 scheme, the subnetwork of the texture image in the left view is removed by keeping other experimental conditions unchanged. In M3 scheme, other experimental conditions remain unchanged and the subnet of the right view is removed. In M4, keep other experimental conditions unchanged and remove the left and right view parallax information subnet.The experiment sets are the same as the above experiments.

Table 3. Performance comparison of this paper's algorithms using different characteristics on LIVE II

Type	LIVE 3D Phase II		
	SROCC	PLCC	RMSE
M1	0.951	0.958	4.201
M2	0.947	0.952	4.225
M3	0.945	0.946	4.421
M4	0.949	0.951	4.356
Ours	**0.958**	**0.968**	**3.132**

As can be seen from Table 3, the values of SROCC and PLCC are all above 0.945, and the value of RMSE is below 4.4, and there is little difference in the evaluation of M2, M3 and M4 in the LIVE 3D PhaseII database, while M1 present a slight high improvement. The probable reason is that the left view cartoon features contain part of the overall features of the left view, and the image feature information contained in the M1 scheme is relatively comprehensive. Due to the absence of features of the right view, M3 only contains one-eyed monocular features in its prediction, and cannot accurately predict stereoscopic images. Therefore, the M3 scheme has a low value, which indicating that the features of the right view have a greater influence in our algorithm, and also proves the necessary of combination of right monocular information. As LIVE-II database contains asymmetric distorted stereoscopic images, the left and right views differ greatly, so M4 scheme without left and right parallax feature cannot further improve the accuracy of evaluation results. Overall, our model can achieve good overall performance, which proves the reasonable of our model.

5   Conclusion

In this paper, we proposed a NR-SIQA model based on comprehensive monocular information learning with right view and cartoon texture decomposition of left view, and disparity information learning. The texture information allows the model to learn more about local details and texture information, and cartoon images can learn the basic shapes and structures, aiding in global understanding and conceptual abstraction. Utilizing four CNN subnetwork architectures, the model can extract rich monocular and binocular features for quality score prediction. Experimental results on the widely-used LIVE database indicate that the proposed method has achieved competitive performance with common NR IQA models.

Acknowledgments. This work is supported by Shenyang science and technology plan project under Grant 23-407-3-32, Liaoning Province Natural Science Foundation under Grant 2023-MS-139 and National Natural Science Foundation of China under Grant 61901205.

References

1. Rajagopal, H., et al.: A no-reference image quality assessment metric for wood images. J. Rob. Network. Artif. Life **8**(2), 127–133 (2021)
2. Das, T.K.: Anti-forensics of JPEG compression detection schemes using approximation of DCT coefficients. Multimedia Tools Appl. **77**(24), 31835–31854 (2018). https://doi.org/10.1007/s11042-018-6170-7
3. Voo, K.H.B., Bong, D.B.L.: Quality assessment for stereoscopic images with JPEG compression errors. In: IEEE International Conference Consumer Electronics, pp. 220–221 (2015)
4. Ibrar-ul Haque, M., Qadri, M.T., Siddiqui, N., Altaf, T.: Combined blockiness, blurriness and white noise distortion meter. Wirel. Pers. Commun. **103**(3), 1927–1939 (2018)
5. Ahmed, I.T., Der, C.S., Hammad, B.T.: Impact of contrast-distorted image on curvelet coefficients. In: 2018 1st Annual International Conference on Information and Sciences (AiCIS), Fallujah, Iraq, pp. 28–32 (2018)
6. Amor, M.B., Kammoun, F., Masmoudi, N.: A quality evaluation model for calculating block and blur effects generated by H.264 and MPEG2 codecs. Comput. Stan. Interfaces **61**, 36–44 (2019)
7. Li, S., Wang, M.: No-reference stereoscopic image quality assessment based on convolutional neural network with a long-term feature fusion. In: 2020 IEEE International Conference on Visual Communication and Image Processing (VCIP), pp. 318–321 (2020)
8. Keles, O., Yilmaz, M.A., Tekalp, A.M., Korkmaz, C., Dogan, Z.: On the computation of PSNR for a set of images or video. In: Image Coding Workshop 2021 (PCS), pp. 286–290 (2021)
9. Sasaki, T., Fukushima, N., Maeda, Y., Sugimoto, K., Kamata, S.I.: Constant-time gaussian filtering for acceleration of structure similarity. In: Sudantha, B. (Ed.), 2020 International Conference on Image Processing and Robotics (ICIPROB) (2020)
10. Sheikh, H.R., Sabir, M.F., Bovik, A.C.: A statistical evaluation of recent full reference image quality assessment algorithms. IEEE Trans. Image Process. **15**(11), 3440–3451 (2006)
11. Zhao, J., Mao, X., Chen, L.: Learning deep features to recognise speech emotion using merged deep CNN. IET Signal Proc. **12**(6), 713–721 (2018)

12. Yue, G., et al.: Dual-constraint coarse-to-fine network for camouflaged object detection. IEEE Trans. Circuits Syst. Video Technol. **34**, 3286–3298 (2023)

13. Yue, G., Gao, J., Cong, R., Zhou, T., Li, L., Wang, T.: Deep pyramid network for low-light endoscopic image enhancement. IEEE Trans. Circuits Syst. Video Technol. **34**, 3834–3845 (2023)

14. Yue, G.: Specificity-aware federated learning with dynamic feature fusion network for imbalanced medical image classification. IEEE J. Biomed. Health Inform. **99**, 1–11 (2023)

15. Yin, W., Goldfarb, D., Osher, S.: Image cartoon-texture decomposition and feature selection using the total variation regularized L^1 functional. In: Paragios, N., Faugeras, O., Chan, T., Schnörr, C. (eds.) VLSM 2005. LNCS, vol. 3752, pp. 73–84. Springer, Heidelberg (2005). https://doi.org/10.1007/11567646_7

16. Ono, S., Miyata, T., Yamada, I.: Cartoon-texture image decomposition using blockwise low-rank texture characterization. IEEE Trans. Image Process. **23**(3), 1128–1142 (2014)

17. Yin, W., Goldfarb, D., Osher, S.: Total variation based image cartoon-texture decomposition. Columbia Univ. CORC Rep. TR-2005-01, UCLA CAM Rep. 05–27 (2005)

18. Shi, B., Zhu, C., Li, L., Huang, H.: Cartoon-texture guided network for low-light image enhancement. Digit. Signal Process. **144**, 104271 (2024)

19. Oechsle, M., Mescheder, L., Niemeyer, M., Strauss, T., Geiger, A.: Texture Fields: learning texture representations in function space. In: Proceedings of the IEEE/CVF International Conference on Computer Vision, pp. 4531–4540 (2019)

20. Gu, K., Zhai, G., Lin, W., Liu, M.: The analysis of image contrast: from quality assessment to automatic enhancement. IEEE Trans. Cybern. **46**(1), 284–297 (2016). https://doi.org/10.1109/TCYB.2015.2401732

21. Gu, K., et al.: Saliency-guided quality assessment of screen content images. IEEE Trans. Multimedia **18**(6), 1098–1110 (2016)

22. Cui, Y., Jiang, G., Yu, M., Chen, Y., Ho, Y.S.: Stitched wide field of view light field image quality assessment: benchmark database and objective metric. IEEE Trans. Multimedia (2023)

23. Tong, F., Meng, M., Blake, R.: Neural bases of binocular rivalry. Trends Cogn. Sci. **10**(11), 502–511 (2006)

24. Li, L., Li, Y., Wu, J., Ma, L., Fang, Y.: Quality evaluation for image retargeting with instance semantics. IEEE Trans. Multimedia **23**, 2757–2769 (2020)

25. Ma, L., Wang, X., Liu, Q., Ngan, K.N.: Reorganized DCT-based image representation for reduced reference stereoscopic image quality assessment. Neurocomputing **215**, 21–31 (2016)

26. Chen, Y., Zhu, K., Huanlin, L.: Blind stereo image quality assessment based on binocular visual characteristics and depth perception. IEEE Access **8**, 85760–85771 (2020)

27. Cheng, G., Lai, P., Gao, D., Han, J.: Class attention network for image recognition. Sci. China Inform. Sci. **66**(3), 132105 (2023). https://doi.org/10.1007/s11432-021-3493-7

28. Tang, J., Wang, J., Hu, J.F.: Predicting human poses via recurrent attention network. Vis. Intel. **1**(1), 18 (2023). https://doi.org/10.1007/s44267-023-00020-z

29. Jinhui, F., Li, S., Chang, Y.: No-reference stereoscopic image quality assessment considering binocular disparity and fusion compensation. In: 2021 International Conference on Visual Communications and Image Processing (VCIP), pp. 1–5. IEEE (2021)

30. Zhang, D.: Onfocus detection: identifying individual-camera eye contact from unconstrained images. Sci. China Inform. Sci. **65**(6), 160101 (2022). https://doi.org/10.1007/s11432-020-3181-9

31. Wu, T., Duan, F., Chang, L., Lu, K.: Human-object interaction detection via interactive visual-semantic graph learning. Sci. China Inform. Sci. **65**(6), 160108 (2022). https://doi.org/10.1007/s11432-021-3427-2

32. Li, S., Han, X., Zubair, M., Ma, S.: Stereo image quality assessment based on sparse binocular fusion convolution neural network. In: IEEE Visual Communications and Image Processing (VCIP), pp. 1–4. IEEE (2019)

33. Fang, Y., Yan, J., Liu, X., Wang, J.: Stereoscopic image quality assessment by deep convolutional neural network. J. Vis. Commun. Image Represent. **58**, 400–406 (2019)

34. Shi, Y., Guo, W., Niu, Y., Zhan, J.: No-reference stereoscopic image quality assessment using a multi-task CNN and registered distortion representation. Pattern Recogn. **100**, 107168 (2020)

35. Ding, Y., Li, S., Chang, Y.: Stereoscopic image quality assessment weighted guidance by disparity map using convolutional neural network. In: IEEE Visual Communications and Image Processing (VCIP), pp. 1–4. IEEE (2019)

36. Yan, J., Fang, Y., Huang, L., Min, X., Yao, Y., Zhai, G.: Blind stereoscopic image quality assessment by deep neural network of multi-level feature fusion. In: 2020 IEEE International Conference on Multimedia and Expo (ICME), pp. 1–6. IEEE (2020)

37. Si, J., Huang, B., Yang, H., Lin, W., Pan, Z.: A no-reference stereoscopic image quality assessment network based on binocular interaction and fusion mechanisms. IEEE Trans. Image Process. **31**, 3066–3080 (2022)

38. Chen, Y., Zhao, Y., Li, S., Zuo, W., Jia, W., Liu, X.: Blind quality assessment for cartoon images. IEEE Trans. Circuits Syst. Video Technol. **30**(9), 3282–3288 (2020). https://doi.org/10.1109/TCSVT.2019.2931589

39. Chen, H., et al.: Perceptual quality assessment of cartoon images. IEEE Trans. Multimedia **25** 140–153 (2023). https://doi.org/10.1109/TMM.2021.3121875

40. Zhang, F., Roysam, B.: Blind quality metric for multidistortion images based on cartoon and texture decomposition. IEEE Signal Process. Lett. **23**(9), 1265–1269 (2016)

41. Servos, P., Goodale, M.A., Jakobson, L.S.: The role of binocular vision in prehension: a kinematic analysis. Vis. Res. **32**(8), 1513–1521 (1992)

42. Thorpe, S., Fize, D., Marlot, C.: Speed of processing in the human visual system. Nature **381**(6582), 520–522 (1996)

43. Du, B., Du, C., Yu, L.: MEGF-Net: multi-exposure generation and fusion network for vehicle detection under dim light conditions. Vis. Intel. **1**(1), 28 (2023). https://doi.org/10.1007/s44267-023-00030-x

44. Moorthy, A.K., Su, C.-C., Mittal, A., Bovik, A.C.: Subjective evaluation of stereoscopic image quality. Signal Process. Image Commun. **28**(8), 870–883 (2013)

45. Chen, M.-J., Cormack, L.K., Bovik, A.C.: No-reference quality assessment of natural stereopairs. IEEE Trans. Image Process. **22**(9), 3379–3391 (2013)

46. Mei, S., Geng, Y., Hou, J., Du, Q.: Learning hyperspectral images from RGB images via a coarse-to-fine CNN. Sci. China Inform. Sci. **65**(5), 1–14 (2021). https://doi.org/10.1007/s11432-020-3102-9

47. Hu, J., Wang, X., Chai, X., Shao, F., Jiang, Q.: Deep network based stereoscopic image quality assessment via binocular summing and differencing. J. Vis. Commun. Image Representation **82**, 103420 (2022). https://doi.org/10.1016/j.jvcir.2021.103420

48. Messai, O., Chetouani, A., Hachouf, F., Seghir, Z.A.: No-reference stereoscopic image quality predictor using deep features from cyclopean image. Electron. Imaging **33**(9), 297-1–297-9 (2021).https://doi.org/10.2352/issn.2470-1173.2021.9.iqsp-297

49. Si, J., Yang, H., Huang, B., Pan, Z., Su, H.: A full-reference stereoscopic image quality assessment index based on stable aggregation of monocular and binocular visual features. IET Image Process. **15**(8), 1629–1643 (2021). https://doi.org/10.1049/ipr2.12132

50. Messai, O., Hachouf, F., Seghir, Z.A.: Adaboost neural network and cyclopean view for no-reference stereoscopic image quality assessment. Signal Process. Image Commun. **82**, 115772 (2020). https://doi.org/10.1016/j.image.2019.115772

51. Liu, L., Zhang, J., Saad, M.A., Huang, H., Bovik, A.C.: Blind S3D image quality prediction using classical and non-classical receptive field models. Signal Process. Image Commun. **87**, 115915 (2020)

52. Jiang, Q., Zhou, W., Chai, X., Yue, G., Shao, F., Chen, Z.: A full-reference stereoscopic image quality measurement via hierarchical deep feature degradation fusion. IEEE Trans. Instrum. Meas. **69**(12), 9784–9796 (2020). https://doi.org/10.1109/TIM.2020.3005111

Decoding the Flow Experience in Video Games: An Analysis of Physiological and Performance Metrics

Di Zhang[1], Qi Wu[1], Xinhui Huang[1], and Boning Zhang[2(✉)]

[1] School of Data Science and Intelligent Media, Communication University of China, Ministry of Education, Beijing 100024, China
dizhang@cuc.edu.cn
[2] Beijing Geospatial Smart Technology Co., Ltd., Beijing 100024, China
zhangboning@geospatialsmart.com

Abstract. We explore the application of psychophysiological measures to gain real-time and objective insights into the flow experience of gamers, aiming to overcome the limitations of traditional self-report surveys, which can be intrusive and lack real-time capabilities. In this study, a self-developed game platform is employed to capture users' real-time performance data and physiological responses. The recorded data includes in-game process logs, eye movement patterns, and galvanic skin response (GSR). To objectively quantify gaming performance, a novel method employing a gradient boosting model is introduced, offering a comprehensive understanding of the gaming experience. The experimental results indicate that gaming performance tends to improve during flow states compared to non-flow states. Flow states are characterized by specific physiological markers, including saccade number in the area of interest (AOI), average peak velocity of saccades, pupil diameter, blink rate, and fixation number. Additionally, GSR signals exhibit significant differences between flow and non-flow states, with an increased peak frequency during the flow state. The integration of real-time multi-modal measurements offers a novel approach to investigating the flow experience in games, providing valuable insights for future research in immersive game design and user experience evaluation.

Keywords: Flow · Performance Measures · Physiological Indicator · Game User Experience

1 Introduction

Flow is a phenomenon that describes a holistic sensation experienced by individuals who are fully engaged in an activity. This concept has attracted considerable attention in various fields, leading to numerous studies aimed at understanding its nature and psychological correlates [1]. While self-report scales have been the primary method of measuring flow, they are typically administered post-task [2], and may not provide a complete picture of the phenomenon. Real-time measurements of flow are crucial for

G. Zhai et al. (Eds.): IFTC 2023, CCIS 2067, pp. 82–95, 2024.
https://doi.org/10.1007/978-981-97-3626-3_7

gaining insights into the dynamics of the flow state [3]. However, obtaining such measures can be challenging, as it requires researchers to collect feedback from participants without disrupting their engagement in the activity [4]. Therefore, exploring alternative, less obtrusive methods of measuring flow in real-time is essential to further our understanding of this important psychological construct.

Research on game user experience (GUX) has garnered significant attention as a representative paradigm of human-computer interaction (HCI) due to the elicitation of rich and varied experiences that games provide, making them an excellent test-bed for investigating flow [5]. However, accurately capturing flow during gameplay poses challenges. Post-hoc questionnaires have limitations in providing dynamic insights. Flow states manifest through diverse objective indicators including physiological responses and gameplay performance metrics. Gameplay metrics reflect behavioral engagement, while physiology offers biological correlates. Fusing these multimodal objective markers of users' states could enable more accurate real-time detection of flow. Gameplay performance metrics also often emphasize singular dimensions like scores or progression, rather than a comprehensive assessment. Notably, prior work on quantifying gameplay performance has focused on isolated metrics like completion times, points accrued, or player rank [6, 7]. Composite formulas integrating multiple performance facets are less common. Recently, researchers have begun exploring the correlation between nervous system features and flow [8]. Physiological responses, such as EEG, heart rate variability, and galvanic skin response (GSR), have been proven to be effective indicators of flow state detection [9–11]. However, the signal acquisition for these studies relied on professional physiological instruments, making preparation work complicated, and wearing the equipment (such as a large number of electrode patches) uncomfortable for participants, potentially affecting their game experience and introducing noise into physiological data [12–14]. Consequently, some researchers have tried to use cheaper and commercially available wearable devices, such as blood oxygen meters and physiological signal sensors, to collect users' physiological signals and study the role of various physiological signals in detecting the user's experience status in games [15, 16]. These works lay the foundation for analyzing game user experience based on wearable devices, improving the practical science of relevant research to some extent. However, there are still very few relevant studies, and experiments carried out with wearable devices may disturb the user's performance [17].

The objective of this paper is to investigate the flow experience by using a self-developed game, which allows the recording of game logs simultaneously with physiological responses. The performance score is extracted from the game log by utilizing a performance calculation formula [6], while the physiological responses are measured by an eye tracker and a galvanic skin response device. This approach contributes to the understanding of physiological flow by identifying the performance measurement and correlation of physiological signals. Therefore, the research question formulated is: "What are the real-time flow state features from the perspective of performance and physiological responses?" To address this question, a lab experiment was conducted with 42 participants, and statistical analysis was carried out to evaluate the significant parameters of the flow experience.

2 Experimental Setup

Current psychophysiological research posits that physiological responses serve as the underpinnings of psychological activities. This implies that a range of human emotional states and cognitive processes can be effectively characterized or quantified through corresponding physiological metrics. In alignment with this perspective, our study aims to assess flow experiences during gameplay by meticulously analyzing physiological data, encompassing GSR and eye movement metrics, alongside user performance data. These quantitative analyses are further augmented by integrating subjective responses obtained from a flow questionnaire. Our experiments delve into the intricate relationship between flow states and physiological indicators, as well as the influence of these flow states on user performance, thereby providing a comprehensive understanding of the interplay between physiological responses, psychological states, and gaming performance.

2.1 Experimental Equipment and Participant

The present study utilized a Tobii Glasses 3 eye tracker and a custom-built electrodermal activity measurement device to record participants' physiological data, along with real-time gameplay metrics including death count, difficulty level, and scores. The sample consisted of 42 teachers and students aged 18 to 35 years from the Communication University of China. Participants were deliberately sampled to ensure baseline homogeneity in daily gaming habits, with mean daily playtime not exceeding 2 h. Stringent inclusion criteria minimized variability in gaming fluency and understanding of research participation, better isolating interindividual differences in experiential flow states. Before data collection, detailed experimental information was relayed, and written informed consent was obtained from all participants by institutional ethical regulations. This cross-section represented an appropriately uniform baseline in terms of gaming literacy, allowing investigation into the variability of user flow absorption. The integrative setup enabled synchronized capture of organic gameplay patterns, gaze behavior, and electrodermal activity within a naturalistic paradigm.

2.2 Flow Experience Assessment Scale (FEAS)

Self-reported flow experiences were evaluated using a customized 12-item Flow Experience Assessment Scale (FEAS) questionnaire rated on a 5-point Likert scale. The initial 3 questions elicited overall impressions of game difficulty, enjoyability, and global flow. These were designed to limit respondent fatigue which could confound experiential self-reports. The subsequent 9-item module simplified the validated 36-item Flow State Scale (FSS) [18], Refining the core elements while steering clear of potential negative emotional states that could be triggered by prolonged assessments. As hypothesized by Csikszentmihalyi [19], flow encompasses perceived challenge-skill balance, attentional focus, sense of control, and intrinsic reward. The abridged scale isolated indicators spanning these major dimensions, as confirmed by prior psychometric evaluations [20, 21]. Using established questionnaires while mitigating boredom and frustration enabled clean self-quantification of flow absorption. The 5-point scale captured nuanced oscillations across various facets during the game. Overall, the FEAS consolidated validated items to efficiently survey multifaceted flow episodes.

2.3 Test Games

Achieving flow requires balancing perceived challenges and skills. Excess difficulty induces anxiety; insufficient challenge brings boredom. This study aimed to elicit varied experiential states by manipulating game difficulty to align with skill levels. A customized instrument was thus developed per the following criteria:

(1) Familiar, simple gameplay mitigates cognitive load.
(2) Adjustable difficulty accommodates players across competencies.
(3) Configurable duration prevents fatigue.

The implemented game improved the classic "Snake" format using Java programming. Participants controlled a perpetually moving snake to eat randomly spawned apples using the arrow keys. Each apple eaten increased snake length while adding to the score. Colliding with walls or itself reset the score and increased the death tally. To sustain engagement, a special coin appeared when the snake length reached multiples of 4. Consuming this coin conferred 10 s of "invincibility" immunity against collisions. The coin disappeared after 10 s. Background music, sound effects, and graphical snippets responded to events like eating, dying, and invincibility. Speed determined difficulty across 8 levels of 300 s each. "Game Over" displayed upon session completion (Fig. 1).

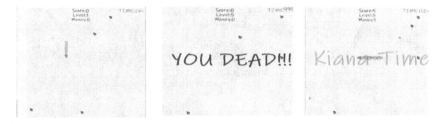

Fig. 1. The screenshots of the test game

Game logs auto-recorded metrics including participant name, scores, coins acquired, deaths, and difficulty level in real-time. Timestamps of apple/coin consumptions enabled distinguishing flow/non-flow periods based on performance. This instrumentation enabled fine-grained analysis between experiences and behaviors.

2.4 Experimental Procedure

The experiment encompassed preparation and data collection phases (Fig. 2). Preparatory activities encompassed briefing participants on protocols, surveying gaming literacy, and determining skill-matched difficulty settings per participant to elicit varied psychological states. Specifically, a 3–5 min test play session combined with self-appraised competency identified easy, normal, and hard difficulty conditions by incrementally adjusting the game challenge. Participants were then outfitted with biosensing devices.

A resting baseline recording of physiological signals preceded the gaming session. Participants subsequently played 5 min of randomly assigned difficulty levels to minimize order effects. Snake's simple, repetitive nature conferred consistent theming. Postgame self-reports via a customized Flow Experience Assessment Scale questionnaire

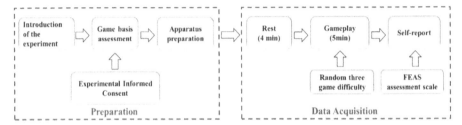

Fig. 2. Experiment process including preparation and data acquisition

surveyed absorption. Experiments occurred in a controlled, minimized-distraction environment mitigating confounds (Fig. 3). Proctors provided necessary guidance while limiting interference.

Fig. 3. The experimental environment

3   Result and Analysis

3.1   Flow Mode Verification

Post-game questionnaires surveyed flow state occurrence. The easy, medium, and difficult game conditions aimed to elicit boredom, flow, and anxiety respectively based on the challenge-skill dynamic [22]. We analyzed mean flow scores across difficulty levels using ANOVA.

Figure 4 illustrates significantly higher boredom in easy mode ($F = 80$, $p < 0.001$); stronger flow in medium difficulty ($F = 17$, $p < 0.001$); and greater anxiety from hard conditions ($F = 78$, $p < 0.001$). Though the difficult mode had a lower flow than the balanced medium setting, scores exceeded the easy mode, indicating greater focus and engagement despite excessive challenge. Nonetheless, participants reported degrees of flow across all settings, aligned with subtle gameplay variations within static difficulty parameters [19].

Additionally, we investigated links between gaming habit and flow proneness via a gameplay literacy survey, categorizing participants as non-gamers, occasional players, and habitual gamers. ANOVA found no significant group differences in flow scores ($p > 0.05$), indicating pre-existing gaming fluency did not impact state induction success.

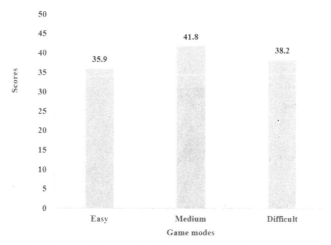

Fig. 4. Subjects' flow experience evaluation scores across three modes (Total score: 50)

3.2 Performance Assessment

Flow state, as articulated by Chen [7], is inherently a subjective aspect of the user's experience and cannot be sufficiently captured through simplistic metrics such as aggregate scores or kill counts. This subjectivity is further compounded by individual gaming preferences. For example, some players, like one who indulges in executing suicidal stunts in GTA, exhibit behaviors that lead to atypical statistical outcomes, such as a sharp increase in death count. Recognizing these nuances, we have developed an integrated performance evaluation method. This method combines elements of game design with a holistic analysis of all user performance data, moving beyond reductive, single-metric assessments. This comprehensive approach allows for a deeper investigation into the relationship between the flow state and user performance in gaming, acknowledging the multifaceted nature of player interaction and experience.

To quantify participants' gameplay achievement, we constructed a machine learning-based performance assessment model. Specifically, we extracted multiple variables impacting scores including death tallies, coin acquisitions, and finish times from the gameplay logs of 42 participants. We implemented a random forest regression with optimized hyperparameters like maximum tree depth and minimum leaf samples obtained via grid search. The tuned random forest model achieved: an R^2 Score: 0.664, MSE: 2002.911. Though improved from baseline, accuracy could be further enhanced. Hence, we adopted a gradient-boosting decision tree approach, which significantly improved performance: R^2 Score: 0.984, MSE: 95.67. The strong correlation between predicted and actual values demonstrated effective gameplay performance quantification. We will leverage these gradient-boosting-derived achievement scores along with psychophysiological markers like electrodermal activity and gaze metrics to examine variations across the flow and non-flow states. This will shed light on the heterogeneous characteristics of absorption from a multidimensional perspective.

We adopted a gradient-boosting-based model to predict gameplay achievement from multivariate logs. To further evaluate effectiveness and diagnose relationships, we generated a correlation heatmap between predictive variables and performance forecasts (Fig. 5).

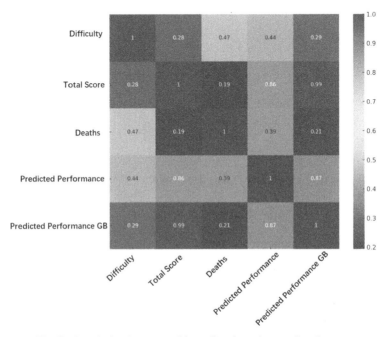

Fig. 5. Correlation heatmap with gradient boosting predicted scores

The heatmap distinctly illustrates the varying degrees of significance among features, as determined by their correlations with the modeled scores. 'Predicted Performance' represents the projections derived from the baseline random forest regressor, whereas 'Predicted Performance GB' refers to the outcomes forecasted by the gradient-boosted decision trees. Notably, the gradient boosting methodology demonstrates a more pronounced correlation with the aggregate total points compared to its random forest counterpart, thereby affirming a heightened level of realism in its predictions. Meanwhile, factors like game duration and difficulty level appear to have a more marginal connection. Additionally, a scatter diagram (Fig. 6) provides a direct juxtaposition of the actual scores against those predicted by the models. The close clustering of data points near the line of equality in this diagram is indicative of the robustness and precision inherent in the gradient boosting-based analysis, underscoring its efficacy in quantifying gaming performance.

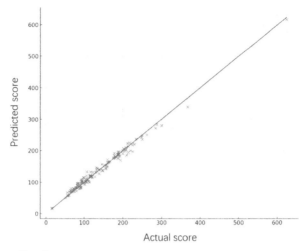

Fig. 6. Actual and predicted scores with gradient boosting

By leveraging our comprehensive gameplay performance model, we executed an ANOVA to examine the variations in quantified achievement across different levels of game difficulty. The analysis yielded an F-statistic of 3.286 ($p = 0.041$), indicating statistically significant differences in scores among the varying difficulty settings. Further exploration through Honest Significant Difference (HSD) tests highlighted a distinct performance edge in the medium difficulty over the easy mode. Although less pronounced, performance in the medium difficulty also tended to surpass that in the hard setting. This trend is visually corroborated by the box plots, suggesting that gameplay performance can serve as a sensitive indicator of flow states, in line with prior research [23, 24].

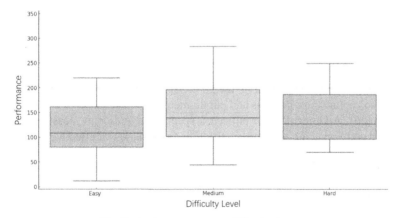

Fig. 7. Performance across difficulty levels

Moreover, our analysis revealed subtle yet significant influences of gaming habits on performance scores. In scenarios featuring simpler gameplay, both casual and habitual gamers exhibited superior performance on average, outshining non-gamers. This performance disparity became more pronounced at medium and hard difficulty levels, where frequent players consistently achieved the highest scores. Occasional gamers followed closely, maintaining a competitive edge, while non-gamers recorded considerably lower average scores, as depicted in Figs. 7 and 8. These findings highlight the intricate relationship between gaming frequency and player proficiency, particularly evident in more challenging gaming environments.

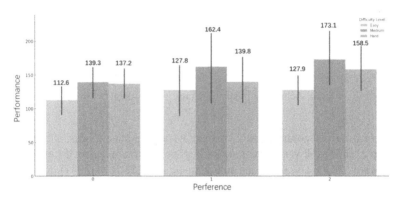

Fig. 8. Performance by preference across difficulty levels

3.3 Physiological Indicator Extraction

Recognizing that self-reported flow is susceptible to participant biases [25], we turned to physiological signals for more objective assessments. In our study, we simultaneously monitored various aspects of the participants' peripheral nervous system activity during gameplay, ensuring minimal interference with task engagement. This approach facilitated the direct quantification of natural and transient physiological responses to the dynamic challenges presented by the game. Specifically, eye-tracking glasses were employed to capture gaze patterns and pupillometry data, indicative of cognitive focus and effort [26]. Additionally, we utilized a specialized sensor to measure skin conductance, thereby gauging electrodermal activity as a marker of affective arousal [27]. The collected multivariate physiological data underwent a rigorous preprocessing routine, which involved noise filtering, outlier management, and addressing missing values. This comprehensive preprocessing culminated in the production of clean, well-labeled datasets, primed for subsequent comparative analyses.

As illustrated in Fig. 9 through representative electrodermal traces, periods of flow were characterized by an increased frequency of skin conductance peaks, in contrast to the states of boredom or anxiety. Furthermore, both the amplitude and the frequency of the skin conductance peaks exhibited a notable enhancement during flow periods, underscoring a distinct physiological response pattern. The mean galvanic amplitude showed an upward trend as well, resonating with the intense engagement typically associated with flow states [5]. Notably, the onset of gameplay triggered rapid Skin Conductance Response (SCR) spikes across participants, marking a transition from resting states to active, effortful concentration.

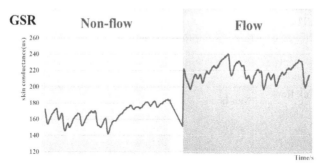

Fig. 9. Changes in skin conductance levels

In our analysis of eye movements, we focused on distinguishing flow from non-flow states, concentrating on three key aspects: pupillometry, blink dynamics, and visual fixation patterns. Utilizing a random forest-based feature selection on extensive multivariate gaze data, we methodically ranked variables by importance. This led to identifying crucial metrics: Number of Saccades in the Area of Interest (AOI) Rectangle, Average Peak Velocity of Saccades, Pupil Diameter, Blink Rate, and Number of Whole Fixations.

Our findings, illustrated in Figs. 10, 11, 12 and 13, reveal that flow states are characterized by reduced blink frequency, significantly enlarged pupil size, and a higher number and velocity of saccades, suggesting enhanced cognitive engagement and visual searching activities. Specifically, Figs. 10 and 11 display line graphs detailing changes in blink rate and pupil diameter, respectively, highlighting these marked differences between flow and non-flow states. Furthermore, Figs. 12 and 13, presenting cumulative saccade velocity and fixation point data in stacked area charts, indicate that both the intensity and the quantity of eye movements are considerably higher in flow states. These observations underscore a more dynamic and intense visual processing and information gathering during flow, as evidenced by the higher cumulative velocity and increased fixation points.

This pattern indicates a heightened frequency of ocular movements, reflecting an intensified cognitive engagement and a dynamic visual exploration process, characteristic of the flow state. Such findings underscore the nuanced interplay between various oculometric parameters and the psychological state of the user, offering valuable insights into the cognitive and perceptual aspects of the gaming experience. By distilling key eye movement signatures of absorption, we can efficiently identify flow states without complex analytics. The practical viability of these lean eye-tracking feature sets suggests appreciable utility as experience sampling biosensors.

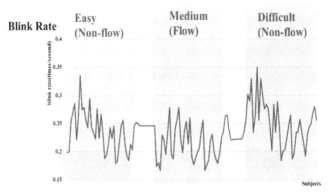

Fig. 10. Blink rate in different states

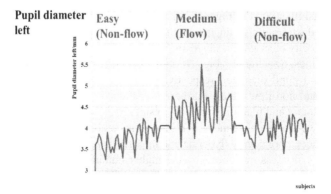

Fig. 11. Pupil diameter left in different states

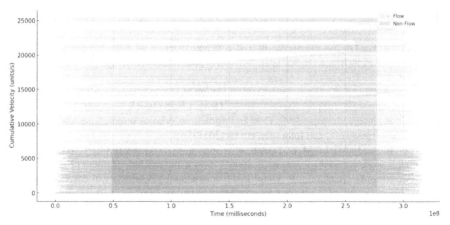

Fig. 12. Comparison of time-based cumulative eye movement velocity in flow and non-flow states. The y axis represents the cumulative eye movement velocity over time, calculated by aggregating the velocity at each time point. The x axis denotes time in milliseconds. Each point on the graph signifies the cumulative velocity at that specific time point.

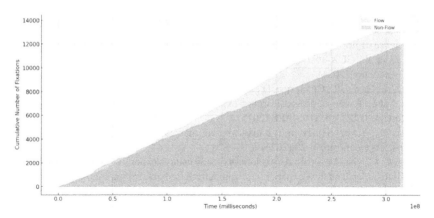

Fig. 13. Cumulative number of fixations over time: flow and non-flow state comparison

4 Conclusion

Aiming to explore the real-time flow state features from the perspective of performance and physiological responses, this paper investigated users' flow experiences during gameplay by analyzing their physiological responses and performance data. Based on the flow model of Csikszentmihalyi, an experiment was designed to acquire the user's GSR, eye movement signals, and game performance in different game experience states. Our findings may serve as the foundation for future game design aiming to build physio-adaptive systems that can improve user experience. For instance, these systems could modify game strategy regarding the user's flow state by analyzing the user's psychological and physiological reaction in the entire interactive game-play process.

References

1. Moneta, G.B.: On the measurement and conceptualization of flow. In: Engeser, S. (ed.) Advances in Flow Research. Springer, New York (2012). https://doi.org/10.1007/978-1-4614-2359-1_2
2. Jackson, S., Marsh, H.: Development and validation of a scale to measure optimal experience: the flow state scale. J. Sport Exerc. Psychol. **18**(1), 17–35 (1996)
3. Rissler, R., Nadj, M., Adam, M.: Flow in information systems research: review, integrative theoretical framework, and future directions (2017)
4. Rissler, R., Nadj, M., Li, M.X., Loewe, N., Knierim, M.T., Maedche, A.: To be or not to be in flow at work: physiological classification of flow using machine learning (2020)
5. Ye, X., Ning, H., Backlund, P., Ding, J.: Flow experience detection and analysis for game users by wearable-devices-based physiological responses capture. IEEE Internet Things J. **8**(3), 1373–1387 (2020)
6. Sapienza, A., Zeng, Y., Bessi, A., Lerman, K., Ferrara, E.: Individual performance in team-based online games. R. Soc. Open Sci. **5**(6), 180329 (2018)
7. Chen, J.: Flow in games (and everything else). Commun. ACM **50**(4), 31–34 (2007)
8. Knierim, M.T., Rissler, R., Dorner, V., Maedche, A., Weinhardt, C.: The psychophysiology of flow: a systematic review of peripheral nervous system features. In: Davis, F., Riedl, R., vom Brocke, J., Léger, PM., Randolph, A. (eds.) Information Systems and Neuroscience. LNISO, vol. 25, pp. 109–120. Springer, Cham (2018). https://doi.org/10.1007/978-3-319-67431-5_13
9. Khoshnoud, S., Alvarez Igarzábal, F., Wittmann, M.: Brain–heart interaction and the experience of flow while playing a video game. Front. Hum. Neurosci. **16**, 819834 (2022)
10. Liu, Z., et al.: GUX-analyzer: a deep multi-modal analyzer via motivational flow for game user experience (2021)
11. Sinha, A., Gavas, R., Chatterjee, D., Das, R., Sinharay, A.: Dynamic assessment of learners' mental state for an improved learning experience. In: 2015 IEEE Frontiers in Education Conference (FIE), pp. 1–9. IEEE (2015)
12. Cakar, S., Yavuz, F.: Hybrid statistical and machine learning modeling of cognitive neuroscience data, pp. 1–22 (2023)
13. Wang, C.-C., Hsu, M., et al.: An exploratory study using inexpensive electroencephalography (EEG) to understand flow experience in computer-based instruction. Inf. Manag. **51**(7), 912–923 (2014)
14. Wang, Y., Han, B., Li, M., Li, J., Li, R.: An efficiently working brain characterizes higher mental flow that elicits pleasure in Chinese calligraphic handwriting. Cereb. Cortex **33**(12), 7395–7408 (2023)
15. Di Lascio, E., Gashi, S., Debus, M.E., Santini, S.: Automatic recognition of flow during work activities using context and physiological signals. In: 2021 9th International Conference on Affective Computing and Intelligent Interaction (ACII), pp. 1–8. IEEE (2021)
16. Michailidis, L.: Exploiting physiological changes during the flow experience for assessing virtual-reality game design. Bournemouth University (2021)
17. Hafiz, P., Bardram, J.E.: Design and formative evaluation of cognitive assessment apps for wearable technologies. In: Adjunct Proceedings of the 2019 ACM International Joint Conference on Pervasive and Ubiquitous Computing and Proceedings of the 2019 ACM International Symposium on Wearable Computers, pp. 1162–1165 (2019)
18. Tenenbaum, G., Fogarty, G.J., Jackson, S.: The flow experience: a Rasch analysis of Jackson's flow state scale. J. Outcome Meas. **3**(3), 278–294 (1999)
19. Csikszentmihalyi, M.: The flow experience and its significance for human psychology, vol. 2, pp. 15–35 (1988)

20. Riva, E.F., et al.: Measuring dispositional flow: validity and reliability of the dispositional flow state scale 2, Italian version. PLoS ONE **12**(9), e0182201 (2017)
21. Kalcev, G., et al.: Development and validation of the questionnaire for adaptive hyperactivity and goal achievement (AHGA). Clin. Pract. Epidemiol. Mental Health **19**(1), e174501792303281 (2023)
22. Mirvis, P.H.: Flow: the psychology of optimal experience. JSTOR **16**, 636 (1991)
23. Perttula, A., Kiili, K., Lindstedt, A., Tuomi, P.: Flow experience in game based learning–a systematic literature review. Int. J. Ser. Games **4**(1), 57 (2017)
24. Admiraal, W., Huizenga, J., Akkerman, S., Dam, G.T.: The concept of flow in collaborative game-based learning. Comput. Hum. Behav. **27**(3), 1185–1194 (2011)
25. Kreitchmann, R.S., Abad, F.J., Ponsoda, V., Nieto, M.D., Morillo, D.: Controlling for response biases in self-report scales: forced-choice vs. psychometric modeling of Likert items. Front. Psychol. **10**, 2309 (2019)
26. Mahanama, B., et al.: Eye movement and pupil measures: a review. Front. Comput. Sci. **3**, 733531 (2022)
27. Sanchez-Comas, A., Synnes, K., Molina-Estren, D., Troncoso-Palacio, A., Comas-González, Z.J.S.: Correlation analysis of different measurement places of galvanic skin response in test groups facing pleasant and unpleasant stimuli. Sensors (Basel) **21**(12), 4210 (2021)

Source Coding

ULIC: Ultra Lightweight Image Coder on Wearable Devices

Muchen Dong, Hongwei Sha, Ming Lu$^{(\boxtimes)}$, and Zhan Ma

School of Electronic Science and Engineering, Nanjing University, Nanjing, China
{dmc,hongweisha}@smail.nju.edu.cn, {minglu,mazhan}@nju.edu.cn

Abstract. Visual display-equipped wearable devices desire efficient-yet-fast image compression methods for pervasive visual computing. However, block-based JPEG is still computationally-expensive and power-exhaustive, which is hardly affordable by most low-power and general-purpose Micro Controller Units (MCUs). This paper thus proposes the ULIC - a pixel-based, ultra-lightweight lossy image coder to fulfill the purpose. The proposed ULIC is extended substantially from the lossless QOI (Quite OK Image Format) by applying a distortion-allowable copy of pixels or blocks. Through extensive evaluations on a low-power chip, ULIC outperforms well-optimized JPEG coders with about 6%–22% compression efficiency gains, 10× - 30× faster decoding, and 17% less power consumption, making it practically attractive in applications.

Keywords: Image coder · lossy compression · wearable devices

1 Introduction

Since the invention of digital displays like LCD, LED, OLED, etc., they have been equipped with excessive devices, from wall-size TV screens to SmartPhone touch displays, for visual content rendering, processing, and consumption. Recent years have also witnessed the fast growth of wearable devices with sizeable screens (e.g., smart watches, glasses), making pervasive visual computing tractable [10,11].

1.1 Motivation

In practice, an excessive number of digitalized images are utilized on these wearable devices, including visual icons used in applications' graphical user interfaces, photo images for social sharing, etc. However, on-device computing and storage are highly constrained concerning wearable devices' form factor, battery capacity, and thermal control. This urges the development of image compression to save storage and reduce data I/O when fetching images from external memory to

Ming Lu is also with Interdisciplinary Research Center for Future Intelligent Chips (Chip-X), Nanjing University, Suzhou, China.

© The Author(s), under exclusive license to Springer Nature Singapore Pte Ltd. 2024
G. Zhai et al. (Eds.): IFTC 2023, CCIS 2067, pp. 99–113, 2024.
https://doi.org/10.1007/978-981-97-3626-3_8

on-chip buffers for processing. Apparently, such an image compression method must be *ultra-lightweight* to avoid intensive computing and exhaustive power consumption and *platform agnostic* to support all kinds of embedded MCUs (e.g., ARM) in a software-defined manner without requiring any dedicated hardware support.

Image compression generally has lossless and lossy coding modes. This work focuses on lossy image compression as the lossy mode can trade unperceivable pixel loss for a much higher compression gain. For the past decades, famous lossy image compression standards, including JPEG [6], WebP [7], and BPG [1], have been widely adopted in applications for their outstanding compression performance. Unfortunately, these methods are still computing- and power-intensive, owing to serial computations involved in block-based transform coding, e.g., prediction/transform, quantization, and entropy coding. This makes them hardly affordable on most wearable devices with only general-purpose MCUs. For instance, even for the transform module alone, it requires a sequence of operations (ops) like multiplication, addition, etc.

1.2 Approach

Recently, a very competitive, pixel-based lossless image compression method – QOI (The Quite OK Image Format) was developed [8]. It offers similar lossless coding performance to the PNG (Portable Network Graphics[1]) with 20× - 50× faster encoding and 3× - 4× faster decoding, showing the potential to be used on highly resource-constrained wearable devices. However, such a lossless QOI only offers a mild compression ratio, which cannot effectively reduce the data I/O and storage space yet.

As a result, this work attempts to extend the lossless QOI to support lossy compression, termed ULIC, for which we basically allow the introduction of unperceivable distortion for much better compression performance. To this end, we introduce a distortion-allowable copy that can be applied on both block and pixel levels. Such a distortion allowance copy is controlled by an intensity threshold between pixels that can be either a fixed value (determined by extensive simulations) or a user-defined input. If the difference between pixels or blocks (of pixels) is lower than such a distortion threshold, they are treated the same, then compressed using the run-length codes in the encoder, and directly copied for reconstruction in the decoder. Apparently, adapting the threshold can make the trade-off between compression efficiency and reconstruction distortion.

The proposed ULIC successfully runs on an ultra-low-power embedded system (see Sect. 4.1) widely deployed in wearable devices (e.g., wristbands, watches, etc.). Upon a collection of typical testing images (e.g., 331 samples), ULIC outperforms well-optimized JPEG coders, e.g., libjpeg [5], and turbo-jpeg [9], with 6% - 22% compression efficiency improvement measured by BD-rate (Bjøntegaard Delta Rate) [2]. Compared to the TjpgDec [4], the only JPEG

---

[1] https://en.wikipedia.org/wiki/PNG.

decoder successfully running on the same MCU, ULIC offers 10× - 30× faster decoding and about 17% power consumption reduction.

2 Background

2.1 System Architecture

Figure 1 illustrates the system architecture of a wearable device that implements our algorithms. Image codecs are stored in (on-chip) FLASH memory and loaded into the fastest Static Random-access Memory (SRAM) for computing using the Micro Controller Unit (MCU). Both uncompressed and compressed images are cached in the external memory, e.g., Secure Digital (SD) card. They are transferred to Pseudostatic RAM (PSRAM) for subsequent processing. For example, the MCU fetches compressed images into PSRAM and decodes them for display on an LCD screen, while the MCU can also encode the raw images and send them back to the SD card. In practice, a lightweight file system, dubbed FatFs [3], is widely deployed on wearable devices, and the Direct Memory Access (DMA) unit is also supported to transfer data between off-chip and on-chip storage.

Although some high-end wearable devices may use better hardware units for improved computing capacity, this work enforces strict assumptions with limited resources to exemplify the image coding on a low-end system detailed in Sect. 4.1. In this way, our solution can generally apply to almost all wearable devices.

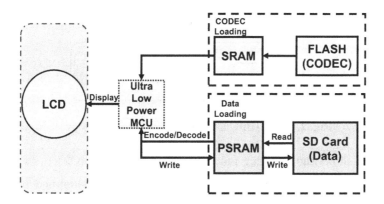

Fig. 1. System architecture used in typical wearable device

2.2 Lossless Image Coding Using QOI

Recently, the QOI [8] is emerged as a simple-yet-efficient lossless image compression approach. Its lossless compression performance rivals that of PNG, while its encoding and decoding speeds surpass PNG's significantly. Lossless QOI avoids expensive block-based transform, quantization, and entropy coding used in popular image codecs by adopting the pixel-wise processing pipeline. Specifically,

QOI recurrently compares the current pixel with its preceding neighbor for compression: if the current pixel equals a neighbor (e.g., one from the dictionary or the nearest one), it is signaled using INDEX or RUN mode; if the RGB[2] or color difference is less than pre-defined thresholds, the current pixel is encoded using DIFF or LUMA mode to signal the difference, respectively; otherwise, the RGB value of the current pixel is explicitly signaled using fixed-length codes and cached in a local pixel dictionary. Such a local pixel dictionary can be used to represent repeated-color pixels with shorter-length color indices. As long as more than two successive pixels share the same color, RUN mode is triggered. In summary, QOI uses five modes, e.g., RGB/RGBA, DIFF, LUMA, INDEX, and RUN, to compactly signal an input image. More details of the QOI can be found at [8].

3   Method

3.1   From Lossless QOI to Lossy ULIC

Yet, lossless QOI still faces data storage and I/O bottleneck because of its mild compression performance. We thus introduce Distortion-allowable Copy into the QOI to greatly improve compression efficiency through the reconstruction distortion tradeoff. Such a copy mechanism can be applied on both block and pixel levels, assuming the difference of blocks (of pixels) or pixels lower than a pre-defined threshold are the same.

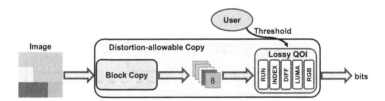

Fig. 2. Lossy ULIC using distortion-allowable copy

Figure 2 shows the encoding process of the proposed ULIC.

- A given input image is first sliced into multiple non-overlapped blocks for compression. In default, the block size is set at 64×64.
- For each block, we first examine whether it can be directly copied from a pre-defined block dictionary (see Sect. 3.2); otherwise, we need to encode it later.
- We then apply the similar pixel-wise processing as the default QOI, in which we additionally introduce a user-defined threshold. In the encoder, we use RUN mode to signal pixels that present a difference to the neighbor less than the threshold. In the decoder, we can directly perform pixel copy for reconstruction. (see Sect. 3.3).

---

[2] We primarily use RGB format in discussions. Images with RGBA format can be easily extended.

Compared with the lossless QOI, a novel block copy mode, i.e., BCOPY, is defined, with which an additional block dictionary is maintained for compression; And, the pixel copy mode is merged with RUN mode in default QOI while keeping other modes without change. With such a hybrid block/pixel copy mechanism, ULIC still appreciates the ultra-lightweight nature of QOI.

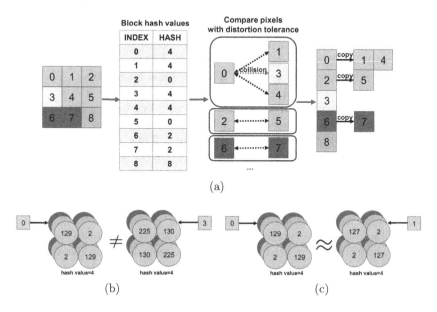

Fig. 3. Block copy mode: squares are pixel blocks, and circles are pixels with RGB values. Same-color blocks are signaled using BCOPY mode.

3.2   Block Copy

The Block Copy mode BCOPY is to directly reuse similar image blocks in the past. Figure 3(a) shows its processing pipeline.

First, we initialize a block dictionary to store each block's index and corresponding hash value. The dictionary's size depends on the number of blocks defined for each image. Assuming that the input image size is $H \times W$, we divide it into blocks at a size of $H_B \times W_B$, having the size of the block dictionary

$$N = \lceil \frac{H}{H_B} \rceil \times \lceil \frac{W}{W_B} \rceil, \tag{1}$$

where $\lceil \cdot \rceil$ represents rounding up. As a toy example shown in Fig. 3(a), $H = W = 6$, and $H_B = W_B = 2$, there are nine 2×2 blocks in total, and $N = 9$.

Concerning the limited computational resources of low-power wearable devices, a very simple hash function is proposed below to derive the hash value of each block, e.g.,

$$HASH(B) = \sum_{i=1}^{H \times W} ((R_i \wedge 2) \oplus (G_i \wedge 2) \oplus (B_i \wedge 2)), \qquad (2)$$

where R_i is the red channel intensity of i-th pixel, G_i and B_i correspond to the intensities of respective green and blue channels. $\oplus$ is the bitwise XOR and $\wedge$ is for bitwise AND. Specifically, we perform a bitwise AND ($\wedge$) operation between each channel value of a pixel and 00000010, and then the bitwise XOR operation to derive the hash value for that pixel. The hash value of each pixel within the block is summed to obtain the block's hash value. Here, we introduce the bitwise AND ($\wedge$) with 00000010 to neglect the value of the last bit. This intentionally allows blocks with small differences to have the same hash value.

From the hash table in Fig. 3(a), we can see that blocks #0, #1, and #3 have the same hash value of 4. Figure 3(b) and 3(c) further detail pixels in blocks #0, #1 and #3. We see that blocks #0 and #1 have the same hash value and their pixel differences are all less than 2. Thus, they might be treated the same block. On the other hand, even though blocks #0 and #3 present the same hash value, their pixels are very different, for which directly copying blocks with the same hash value will lead to large distortions. This is termed the hash collision. To solve it, a pixel-by-pixel comparison for blocks with the same hash value is critical and necessary. In this work, if each channel of a pixel at the corresponding position of two blocks is less than a pre-defined threshold, e.g., 2 used in this work after extensive simulations, we consider them the same.

In this toy example, we use a 2×2 block for explanation. As a result, there are only five hash values in total. Hash collisions are more likely to happen then. In the ULIC using 64×64 block, there are 4097 different hash values. The probability of hash collision is quite low.

Apparently, if the hash value of the current block is not the same as anyone in the block dictionary, we code it using Lossy QOI detailed next.

3.3 Lossy QOI

We use the modes pre-defined in QOI [8] to encode each pixel of a given block. The main change is introducing a user-defined threshold T to obtain different compression qualities. Specifically, given the image block B_i, we first initialize a 64-pixel color table. Such a table is dynamically updated during the encoding and decoding process. Then, pixels within a block are read sequentially for encoding. When the difference of the successive pixels (per channel) is less than T, the RUN mode, as in default QOI, is triggered until a different pixel is encountered, i.e., the difference of the successive pixels (any channel) is larger than T. We will signal the RUN and reset the counter. We turn to the color table to see if there is a similar pixel that presents the difference to the current one less than T. If so, we compress it using the INDEX mode with the color table. In case there is no similar pixel in the color table, we use the DIFF mode and LUMA mode to predict the value of the current pixel based on the previous pixel, denoted as p_{DIFF} and p_{LUMA}, respectively, for which we calculate whether the current pixel is similar to these two predicted values. If so, we use DIFF or LUMA mode to encode it. Otherwise, we store its pixel value directly. Algorithm 1 illustrates the details of the encoding process of our Lossy QOI.

Algorithm 1: Encoding process for each block

1. **Input:** B_i
2. **Output:** b
3. **Initialization:** $run = 0$, $ColorTable = Null$, $p_{pre} = \{0,0,0\}$, $\Delta_{res} = \{0,0,0\}$
4. **for each** p_{cur} **in** B_i
5.   **if** $compare(p_{cur}, p_{pre}) < T$
6. $run++$
7.   **continue**
8.   **else**
9.   **if** $run > 0$
10. $b.append(run)$
11. $run = 0$
12.   **for** idx **in** $len(ColorTable)$
13.   **if** $compare(p_{cur}, ColorTable[idx]) < T$
14. $b.append(idx)$
15.   **continue**
16.   **end for**
17. $\Delta_{res}.R = p_{cur}.R - p_{pre}.R$
18. $\Delta_{res}.G = p_{cur}.G - p_{pre}.G$
19. $\Delta_{res}.B = p_{cur}.B - p_{pre}.B$
20. $p_{DIFF}.R = p_{pre}.R + clamp(\Delta_{res}.R, -2, 1)$
21. $p_{DIFF}.G = p_{pre}.G + clamp(\Delta_{res}.G, -2, 1)$
22. $p_{DIFF}.B = p_{pre}.B + clamp(\Delta_{res}.B, -2, 1)$
23. $p_{LUMA}.G = p_{pre}.G + clamp(\Delta_{res}.G, -32, 31)$
24. $p_{LUMA}.R = p_{pre}.R + clamp(\Delta_{res}.R - \Delta_{res}.G, -8, 7)$
25. $p_{LUMA}.B = p_{pre}.B + clamp(\Delta_{res}.B - \Delta_{res}.G, -8, 7)$
26.   **if** $compare(p_{cur}, p_{DIFF}) < T$
27. $b.append(\Delta_{res}.R, \Delta_{res}.G, \Delta_{res}.B)$
28.   **continue**
29.   **else if** $compare(p_{cur}, p_{LUMA}) < T$
30. $b.append(\Delta_{res}.G, \Delta_{res}.R - \Delta_{res}.G, \Delta_{res}.B - \Delta_{res}.G)$
31.   **continue**
32.   **else**
33. $b.append(p_{cur})$
34. $Update\ p_{cur}\ to\ the\ ColorTable$
35. $p_{pre} = p_{cur}$
36. **end for**

Fig. 4. Testing samples including natural & screen content.

4   Experiments

4.1   Experimental Settings

An embedded system using an ultra-low power MCU with a maximum frequency of 120MHz, 2MB FLASH, 640KB SRAM, and 2MB PSRAM is chosen to represent a typical wearable device upon which we perform image compression studies. As mentioned, a more recent device with better hardware capacity can run our algorithm with better performance.

We then collect 331 images to form a testing dataset. The generation of such a dataset fully considers the characteristics of images used on various wearable devices, such as low spatial resolution (up to 466×466), diverse content (including GUI icons, screens, and natural images), and different bit-depths (e.g., 16-bit and 24-bit). Several testing images are visualized in Fig. 4 for illustration.

4.2   Comparative Studies

Compression Efficiency. We first evaluate the efficiency of ULIC through comparisons with prevalent JPEG coders. We choose two famous implementations, e.g., libjpeg [5] and turbojpeg [9], for their leading performance as reported. However, both libjpeg and turbojpeg cannot be run on the embedded system easily. We run them on a PC and collect the data for analysis.

Figure 5(a) and 5(b) plot averaged Rate-Distortion (R-D) curves of turbojpeg, libjpeg, and our ULIC. Our method performs better than libjpeg and

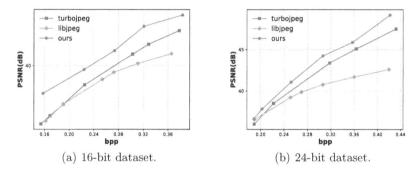

(a) 16-bit dataset.   (b) 24-bit dataset.

Fig. 5. The performance of ULIC and JPEG coders for 16-bit dataset and 24-bit dataset, respectively.

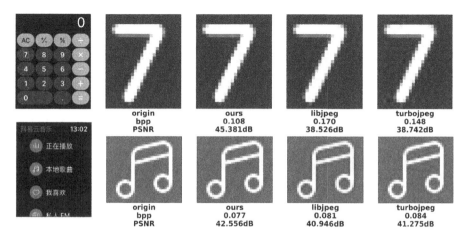

Fig. 6. Visual reconstructions of images encoded by libjpeg, turbojpeg and ours.

turbojpeg on 16-bit and 24-bit image samples consistently. For 16-bit images, ULIC provides about 22.26% and 15.51% BD-rate reductions [2] to that of libjpeg and turbojpeg, respectively. As for the 24-bit dataset, the BD-rate gains are 15.50% and 6.91%. Besides, Fig. 6 visualizes compressed reconstructions of different algorithms. Our algorithm presents the best visual quality, while the other two methods show clear blurring and blocky artifacts.

Decoding Time. In this experiment, we evaluate the decoding complexity of the ULIC. We use TjpgDec [4], a lightweight JPEG decoder that can be successfully run on the same testing systems, for comparison. Since TjpgDec [4] only provides a decoder, we utilize turbojpeg to encode all the images for decoding. For a fair comparison, we try our best to ensure the same compression ratios between ULIC and turbojpeg. The resulting compressed files will then be stored on the SD card and decoded using the low-power MCU on the embedded system

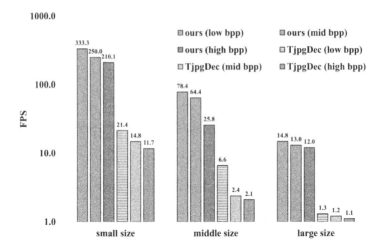

Fig. 7. Decoding speed comparison between TjpgDec and ours (ULIC) at various compression ratios

shown in Fig. 1. We measure the decoding time to assess the performance of the different methods.

We compress images with three bitrate settings: large, small, and medium, to experiment with different application scenarios. As depicted in Fig. 7, the experimental results present the Frames Per Second (FPS) for corresponding decoders, where higher values indicate faster decoding. The results demonstrate that our algorithm outperforms TjpgDec with much lower decoding complexity at all compression bitrates. Specifically, our algorithm shows approximately 10 to 30 times faster than TjpgDec.

Power Consumption. We further measure the power consumption when running the proposed ULIC and TjpgDec. To fulfill this purpose, we consider the following scenarios: standby mode without any running application and image decoding mode with ULIC or TjpgDec running. Similarly, we ensure the files are (almost) the same size in decoding for a fair study. Testing results are shown in Table 1, which includes the power consumption of both algorithms for decoding compressed 24-bit samples. As a result, the proposed ULIC presents a 16.56% decrease in total power consumption compared to TjpgDec, e.g., from 0.4627w to 0.3861w. When we only count the MCU power, the reduction is about 37% from 0.1980w used by TjpgDec to 0.1254w consumed by ULIC.

Table 1. Power Consumption

Method	Total	Standby	Running	
			MCU	LCD
TjpgDec	0.4627W	0.1485W	+0.1980W	+0.1162W
Ours	0.3861W	0.1485W	+0.1254W	+0.1122W

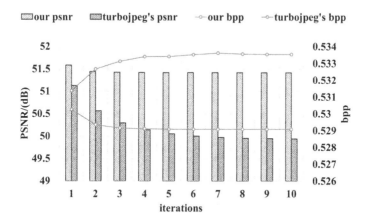

Fig. 8. Recompression stability

4.3 Ablation Studies

Recompression. Images on wearable devices may have to be compressed and decompressed several times, raising the stability issue. To tackle it, we propose to measure the compression rate and PSNR (Peak signal-to-noise ratio) for each iteration. Note that the PSNR is evaluated against the uncompressed image accordingly. We iteratively compressed the same image ten times using the proposed ULIC and turbojpeg. The experiment is performed using widely-used 24-bit images from our dataset.

The results are presented in Fig. 8. Our algorithm's compression rate (e.g., bpp) and PSNR gradually decrease and converge to 0.529 bpp and 51.42 dB. In contrast, the turbojpeg compression rate increases and then converge to 0.534 bpp, while the PSNR gradually decreases and converges to 49.93 dB. These results reveal that our algorithm is less affected by the distortion or noise caused by successive compression, promising a much more stable image compression solution when compared with the well-known turbojpeg.

Block Size. In default, we use 64×64 blocks for block copy in ULIC. Here, we further investigate the performance when we adapt the block sizes to 16 × 16 and 32 × 32. We do not allow for a block size larger than 64×64 because the maximal size of images used on wearable devices for testing is less than 466×466, and a noticeable percentage of testing images are with the size less than 128×128.

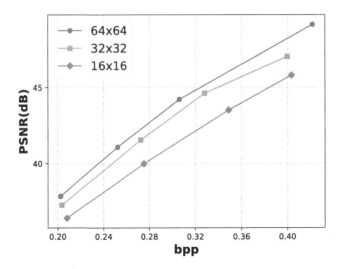

Fig. 9. Impact of different block sizes on compression performance

Figure 9 shows that optimal efficiency is obtained when setting block size at 64×64. We then analyze the mode distribution with different block sizes for further understanding. As in Table 2, when adapting the block size of 64×64 to that of 16×16, more blocks are compressed using BCOPY mode. Since we independently process each block, the percentage of other modes except RUN also increases. However, the compression efficiency degrades as the block size reduces. As seen, using smaller block sizes incurs more distortions (e.g., lower PNSR) and a slight increase in bit rate consumption (e.g., points in rate-distortion curves right-shifted slightly). This suggests that even if we allow a small pixel difference threshold, e.g., 2, in block copy mode, it may bring noticeable block-level distortions when aggregating all pixel errors (e.g., 256 pixels for 16×16 block).

Table 2. Compression mode distribution at various block sizes ($T = 3.0$). Other settings of T share similar behaviors.

Block Size	RUN	INDEX	LUMA	DIFF	RGB/RGBA	BCOPY
64	**86.7%**	12.0%	0.6%	0.2%	0.5%	17.42%
32	82.7%	14.7%	1.2%	0.4%	1.0%	33.21%
16	77.0%	**17.4%**	**2.7%**	**0.8%**	**2.1%**	**47.78%**

User-Defined Threshold. In Sect. 4.2, we can balance the compression trade-off by adjusting the threshold T. The larger T, the smaller the compressed image, and vice versa.

As in Fig. 10, we statistically show the distribution of different modes for compressed images with natural or screen content. We observe that the percent-

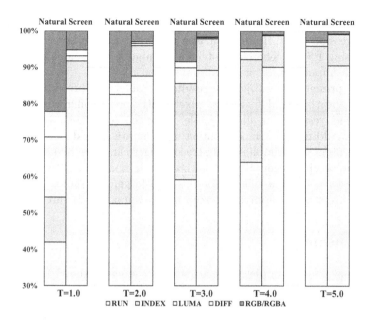

Fig. 10. Effect of threshold on the distribution of lossy QOI modes

ages of the RUN mode and INDEX mode increase as the threshold enlarges, while the percentages of other modes decrease correspondingly. This coincides

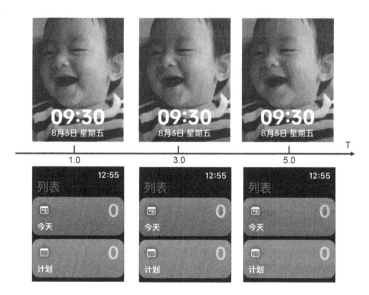

Fig. 11. Visual reconstructions of compressed natural and screen images at different thresholds T

with the fact that larger thresholds consider more pixels the same, leading to lower compression rates. However, it also results in a decrease in image quality measured using PSNR. Therefore, striking a balance between compression rate and PSNR is important for practical applications.

We also present the subjective results for different thresholds, as Fig. 11 depicts. As the threshold increases, pixels with larger differences are considered the same, resulting in more visible distortion (e.g., color banding in the baby's face). Additionally, screen content can tolerate more distortion compared to natural content. This implies that screen images can allow higher compression while still preserving acceptable visual quality. In contrast, natural images are easier to perceive visual artifacts when using a larger threshold. An interesting topic for future study is applying perceptual-driven adaptive thresholding.

5   Conclusion

This work develops a simple and efficient lossy image coder, ULIC, for ultra-low-power wearable devices. The proposed ULIC is extended from the lossless QOI by purposely introducing a distortion-allowable copy mechanism. Note that the proposed distortion-allowable copy can be executed at either block or pixel level. Such a distortion allowance is motivated by the fact that a small pixel difference cannot be perceived visually. We can also pre-define a pixel difference threshold to balance the compression ratio and distortion manually. The proposed ULIC outperforms the famous JPEG coders regarding compression efficiency and exhibits much faster decoding and less power consumption than a JPEG decoder specifically optimized for an embedded system. As for future exploration, we plan to extend the ULIC to support motion images.

References

1. Bellard, F.: BPG image format (2014). https://bellard.org/bpg/
2. Bjontegaard, G.: Calculation of average PSNR differences between RD-curves. ITU SG16 Doc. VCEG-M33 (2001)
3. ChaN: FatFs - generic FAT filesystem module (2006). http://elm-chan.org/fsw/ff/00index_e.html. Accessed 06 Nov 2022
4. ChaN: TJpgDec - tiny JPEG decompressor (2011). http://elm-chan.org/fsw/tjpgd/00index.html. Accessed 01 Jul 2021
5. Group, I.J.: JPEG software (1991). http://www.ijg.org/. Accessed 16 Jan 2022
6. Marcellin, M.W., Bilgin, A., Gormish, M.J., Boliek, M.P.: An overview of JPEG-2000. In: Proceedings of the Conference on Data Compression, p. 523. DCC '00, IEEE Computer Society, USA (2000)
7. Si, Z., Shen, K.: Research on the WebP image format. In: Ouyang, Y., Xu, M., Yang, L., Ouyang, Y. (eds.) Advanced Graphic Communications, Packaging Technology and Materials. LNEE, vol. 369, pp. 271–277. Springer, Singapore (2016). https://doi.org/10.1007/978-981-10-0072-0_35
8. Szablewski, D.: The quite ok image format for fast, lossless compression (2022). https://qoiformat.org/

9. libjpeg turbo: SIMD-accelerated libjpeg-compatible JPEG codec library (2010). https://libjpeg-turbo.org/. Accessed 31 Jan 2023
10. Wang, H., Zhang, X., Chen, H., Xu, Y., Ma, Z.: Inferring end-to-end latency in live videos. IEEE Trans. Broadcast. **68**(2), 517–529 (2021)
11. Zhang, X., Min, G., Li, T., Ma, Z., Cao, X., Wang, S.: AI and blockchain empowered metaverse for web 3.0: vision, architecture, and future directions. IEEE Commun. Mag. (2023)

Temporal Dependency-Oriented Deep In-Loop Filter for VVC

Ziyi Zhuang, Li Li, and Dong Liu$^{(\boxtimes)}$ ⓘ

University of Science and Technology of China, Hefei 230027, China
`zeay@mail.ustc.edu.cn`, {`lil1,dongeliu`}`@ustc.edu.cn`

Abstract. Video coding schemes exploit the temporal correlation between the video frames for high coding efficiency. Thus, the coding efficiency of one frame is dependent on the quality of its reference frames. Such temporal dependency is seldom considered in the existing in-loop filters, since they optimize the current frame reconstruction quality but ignore its effect on the subsequent frames. We address this limitation and propose a temporal dependency-oriented deep in-loop filter, namely TDOF. First, we design a deep network that uses several kinds of guiding information to help the network distinguish different regions of different temporal dependency importance. Second, we train the network using the combination of two losses to optimize not only the current frame reconstruction quality but also the next frame prediction quality. We implement the TDOF with a simple network structure for the Versatile Video Coding (VVC) standard. Our method achieves on average 1.77% BD-rate reduction compared to VTM-10.0 under the Low-delay P configuration. Ablation studies demonstrate the effectiveness of the proposed method.

Keywords: Deep network · In-loop filter · Temporal dependency · Versatile Video Coding (VVC)

1 Introduction

Video coding schemes are almost always lossy, incurring distortion and visible artifacts, especially at low bit rates. To alleviate the distortion and artifacts, a lot of studies have focused on in-loop filters, where the filters are applied to the reconstructed frames, and "in-loop" stands for the filtered frames being used as reference frames. In-loop filters may improve the reconstruction quality and thus achieve compression efficiency gain. Meanwhile, in-loop filters may improve the visual quality of the reconstructed frames as well. In the widely adopted video coding standard, H.265 also known as High Efficiency Video Coding (HEVC) [22], there are two in-loop filters, i.e. deblocking filter (DBF) [18] and sample adaptive offset (SAO) [6]. In the state-of-the-art standard, H.266 also known as Versatile Video Coding (VVC) [3], three in-loop filters have been adopted, i.e. DBF, SAO, and adaptive loop filter (ALF) [12].

© The Author(s), under exclusive license to Springer Nature Singapore Pte Ltd. 2024
G. Zhai et al. (Eds.): IFTC 2023, CCIS 2067, pp. 114–125, 2024.
https://doi.org/10.1007/978-981-97-3626-3_9

Beyond the existing standards, new in-loop filtering technologies remain a research focus in the video coding community. Recently, inspired by the success of deep learning, deep network-based in-loop filters have been intensively studied, for example in [4,5,10,11,13,14,16,19,23]. While earlier work performed single-frame filtering using a trained convolutional neural network (CNN), later work has explored multi-frame filtering by utilizing the spatial information and temporal correlation simultaneously, e.g. [14]. Another trend of deep in-loop filters is to use additional information for the filtering. For example, Lin *et al.* [16] proposed to use the block partition information to assist the CNN for filtering. Jia *et al.* [11] proposed a residual-reconstruction-based CNN, where the residual is fed into the CNN as a supplementary input. Chen *et al.* [4] proposed to use the quality map as an additional input to the CNN-based in-loop filter. Kathariya *et al.* [13] proposed a CNN-based in-loop filter that utilized discrete cosine transform (DCT) coefficients in addition to pixel values, to exploit the long-range correlated spectral features in the DCT domain.

By definition, in-loop filtered frames shall be used inside the video coding loop. That is to say, the filtered frames shall be used as reference frames for the subsequent frame coding. Video coding schemes naturally exploit the correlation between different frames using motion estimation and motion-compensated prediction. Thus, the coding efficiency of one frame is highly dependent on the quality of its reference frames. In other words, in-loop filters improve the reconstruction quality of the current frame and indirectly improve the coding efficiency of the subsequent frames. Unfortunately, such an indirect effect is seldom explicitly addressed in the existing in-loop filters, no matter whether deep or non-deep. The existing in-loop filters usually optimize the current frame reconstruction quality but do not explicitly consider its benefit for the subsequent frame coding.

Indeed, the temporal dependency—the coding efficiency of one frame is dependent on the quality of its reference frames—has been well known in the video coding literature, especially in the studies of frame bit allocation [7]. It has been observed that the temporal dependency is quite complex and varies significantly in natural videos. Moreover, the temporal dependency reflects the temporal correlation, so multi-frame filters have addressed the temporal dependency in an implicit fashion [14]. However, if we restrict ourselves to practical low-delay coding scenarios, where we do not know the subsequent frames during the current frame coding, the temporal dependency remains unexplored to our knowledge.

In this paper, we make the first attempt to address the temporal dependency explicitly in deep in-loop filters for video coding. As usual, we assume the subsequent frames are not available when applying the trained in-loop filter. However, when *training* the filter, we can easily build a multi-frame example, on which we apply the filter and evaluate not only the current frame reconstruction quality but also the next frame prediction quality. This idea is illustrated in Fig. 1, where we use the combination of two losses to optimize the two kinds of quality respectively. It is worth noting that the $Loss_2$ in Fig. 1 is not able to be

$$Loss = Loss_1 + \lambda Loss_2$$

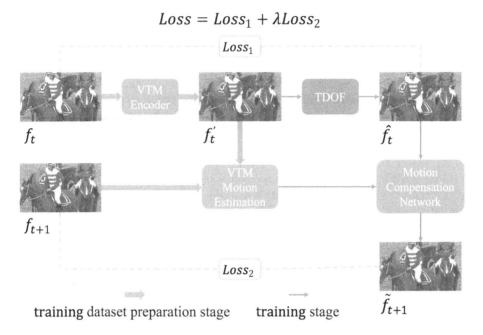

Fig. 1. Overview of the training process for our proposed TDOF. TDOF is optimized by minimizing the weighted sum of $Loss_1$ and $Loss_2$, which correspond to the current frame reconstruction quality and the next frame prediction quality, respectively. Note that the previous studies usually use only $Loss_1$.

evaluated in the inference stage, but we introduce the $Loss_2$ in the training stage and expect that the trained network may have learned a statistical rule about the temporal dependency from the training examples. Moreover, if we had used only the current frame as input to the network (without any hint of the temporal dependency), then it would be difficult for the network to learn the statistical rule. To ease the network learning, we design a network with several kinds of guiding information that we expect to be helpful, including residual information, mode information, position information, and quality information.

Based on the aforementioned ideas, we propose a CNN-based in-loop filter, namely Temporal Dependency-Oriented Filter (TDOF), for the VVC standard. We implement the TDOF with a simple network structure. We perform experiments on the VVC reference software, VTM version 10.0. The experimental results show that our TDOF achieves on average 1.77% BD-rate reduction under the Low-delay P (LDP) configuration. We also verify that the idea of using two losses and the idea of introducing multiple guiding information are both helpful.

2   Method

In this section, we present the proposed TDOF in detail. First, we introduce the temporal dependency-oriented loss function. Then, we introduce the guiding information as hints of the temporal dependency for TDOF. Finally, we elaborate on the network architecture of TDOF.

2.1 Temporal Dependency-Oriented Loss Function

As shown in Fig. 1, our proposed TDOF is trained by the following loss function:

$$Loss = Loss_1 + \lambda Loss_2, \tag{1}$$

where λ is a hyperparameter used to adjust the weight of $Loss_2$. Specifically, for one frame f_t, we use the VVC/VTM encoder to compress and obtain its reconstructed frame f'_t. Then, TDOF is applied onto f'_t to produce the filtered frame $\hat{f}_t$. $Loss_1$ measures the difference between the filtered frame $\hat{f}_t$ and its corresponding original frame f_t. By minimizing $Loss_1$, the difference/distortion is reduced and the frame reconstruction quality is improved. Moreover, the filtered frame $\hat{f}_t$ is warped towards the next timestamp $t + 1$ to provide the motion-compensated prediction $\tilde{f}_{t+1}$ for the next frame coding. $Loss_2$ measures the difference between the motion-compensated prediction $\tilde{f}_{t+1}$ and the next frame f_{t+1}. Less $Loss_2$ corresponds to a better prediction and leads to higher coding efficiency for the next frame.

It is worth noting that $\tilde{f}_{t+1}$ is obtained by warping the filtered frame $\hat{f}_t$ with the optical flow between f'_t and f_{t+1}. Here, the optical flow is obtained by using the motion estimation functionality of the VVC/VTM encoder *before* the training. The VTM motion estimation module produces block-level motion vectors (MVs). These MVs are spatially upsampled to pixel level and used as optical flow. The warping operation is differentiable [15] and depicted by the motion compensation "network" in Fig. 1. The motion compensation network remains constant during the training process. In summary, TDOF can be trained as a usual deep network once given f_t, f'_t, f_{t+1} and the optical flow.

For both $Loss_1$ and $Loss_2$ we use the mean-squared error (MSE) to calculate the difference. Before the training, we need to compress the frame f_t and compute the optical flow between f'_t and f_{t+1}, both accomplished by the VTM encoder.

2.2 Guiding Information

As mentioned before, if we had used only the current frame as input to the network (without any hint of the temporal dependency), the network may have difficulty learning how to address the temporal dependency. Inspired by the studies that provide additional information for the network [4,11,13,16], we design several kinds of guiding information to be input to the network. Here, the underlying idea is that such information may help the network identify which part shall be more important for the temporal dependency. Specifically, we try to use residual information, mode information, position information, and quality information to guide the network.

Residual Information. Residual is obtained by subtracting the motion-compensated prediction from the original signal. Since the motion estimation

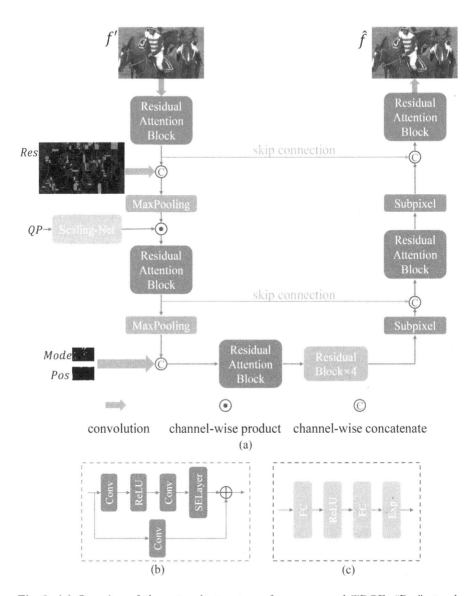

Fig. 2. (a) Overview of the network structure of our proposed TDOF. "Res" stands for the residual information. "Mode" stands for the mode information. "Pos" stands for the position information. "QP" stands for the quality information. (b) Structure of one residual attention block. (c) Structure of the Scaling-Net.

and motion compensation methods are imperfect, the prediction is usually not equal to the original signal, especially at the boundary of a moving object (where the motion is inaccurate or disocclusion happens). Thus, the pixel with a larger residual value is more likely to be on the boundary of a moving object and less likely to be referenced by the subsequent frames. The residual information is represented as a residual map recording per-pixel residual values. Since the original signal is not available when we apply the TDOF (at the decoder side), we use an approximate residual map by subtracting the motion-compensated prediction from the *reconstructed* frame.

Mode Information. There are many coding modes in VVC. One important mode decision is to choose intra-frame coding modes or inter-frame coding modes. Intra-frame coded content is more likely to be new appearing content and thus has a higher probability to be referenced by the subsequent frames. Thus, we use a binary map recording each block is either intra-frame coded or inter-frame coded. This binary map serves as the mode information.

Position Information. Due to motion, the content at frame borders may move out of the camera view in the next frame. Such "disappearing" content is less likely to be referenced by the subsequent frames. To find out such content, we use the position of each block as well as its MV (concerning the previous frame). If we assume the block has uniform linear motion, then its position in the next frame can be calculated. We then check whether the next-frame position is out or not. In this way, we have a binary map recording whether each block is "moving out" or not. This binary map serves as the position information.

Quality Information. VVC enables the use of different quality settings for different frames as well as the use of multiple reference frames for one frame to be coded. If multiple frames have similar content, then the frame with higher quality is more likely to be referenced. Thus, the frame with a higher quality is considered more likely to be referenced by the subsequent frames. Here, the quality can be indicated by the used quantization parameter (QP). In VVC, QP ranges from 0 to 51, the higher the QP, the lower quality [3]. Thus, we use the QP value as the quality information for each frame.

2.3   Network Architecture

Given the aforementioned guiding information, we designed a convolutional neural network (CNN) for TDOF. The network architecture is illustrated in Fig. 2. Here, the reconstructed frame and the filtered frame are denoted as f' and $\hat{f}$ respectively. To reduce the computational complexity, we adopt a structure similar to U-net [21], which consists of a contracting path and an expansive path. In the contracting path, there are two max-pooling layers to reduce the spatial resolution of the feature maps. In the corresponding expansive path, we use subpixel layers to restore the spatial resolution, where subpixel operation is computationally efficient. Considering the benefit of residual learning [8], we use multiple residual blocks in the network. In addition, we embed a squeeze-and-excitation (SE) layer into each of some residual blocks, which incorporates the attention mechanism [9]. Note that our designed guiding information can help learn the attention, so we did not use the complex multi-head self-attention in our network.

For the temporal dependency-oriented optimization, we integrate the guiding information into the network. For the residual information, the position information, and the mode information, we convert them into feature maps using convolutional layers respectively, and concatenate these feature maps into the contracting path. For the quality information, we convert the QP value into a vector using the Scaling-Net proposed in [15], and then scale the feature maps with the vector—one feature map with one component of the vector.

It is worth noting that the four kinds of guiding information are introduced at different locations of the U-net in Fig. 2. First, they have different spatial resolutions. The spatial resolution of the residual information is the same as that of the input frame; the spatial resolution of the mode information and that of the position information are both $1/4 \times 1/4$ of that of the input frame (since we use 4×4 blocks to record modes and MVs). Accordingly, the residual information is introduced after the first residual attention block (which does not change the spatial resolution); the mode information and position information are introduced after two pooling operations. Second, our empirical study implied that, in general, the guiding information shall be used in earlier modules of the network. Thus, all four kinds of guiding information are used in the contracting path of the U-net.

3   Experimental Results

In this section, we present extensive experimental results to verify the performance of our proposed TDOF. First, we describe the experimental settings. Then, both objective evaluations and subjective visualizations are provided.

3.1   Experimental Settings

We build a training dataset using BVI-DVC [17], which contains 800 sequences with diverse content. These sequences are all compressed by VTM-10.0 under the LDP configuration at four QPs: 22, 27, 32, and 37. For each QP we train an individual TDOF model. During the training, we consider the luma component but not the chroma components. We implement the model training with PyTorch [20].

We integrate the trained models into VTM-10.0 as an additional in-loop filter after ALF. We use LibTorch, the C++ interface provided by PyTorch, to integrate the trained models into VTM. We apply the filter on the luma component of all the P frames.

We use the common test sequences recommended by JVET [2] for performance evaluation, including Class A1 (3840×2160), Class A2 (3840×2160), Class B (1920×1080), Class C (832×480), Class D (416×240), and Class E (1280×720). BD-rate [1] is used to evaluate the compression efficiency.

Table 1. BD-rate results of the baseline (i.e. the U-net in Fig. 2 without the guiding information trained with $Loss_1$ only) and the proposed TDOF, using VTM as the anchor

Class	Sequence	Baseline			TDOF		
		Y	U	V	Y	U	V
Class A1	Tango2	−3.42%	0.02%	0.41%	−4.34%	0.15%	0.36%
	FoodMarket4	−2.47%	0.14%	0.30%	−3.06%	−0.04%	0.09%
	Campfire	−1.73%	−0.09%	0.60%	−2.09%	−0.07%	0.75%
Class A2	CatRobot	−2.07%	0.62%	0.62%	−2.54%	0.35%	0.53%
	DaylightRoad2	−3.01%	−0.17%	−0.23%	−3.52%	0.24%	−0.16%
	ParkRunning3	−1.47%	−0.13%	−0.09%	−1.86%	−0.14%	−0.03%
Class B	MarketPlace	−1.58%	−0.09%	0.24%	−1.86%	−0.12%	0.28%
	RitualDance	−2.17%	−0.07%	0.27%	−2.80%	0.01%	0.15%
	Cactus	−1.43%	−0.58%	−0.54%	−1.46%	−0.06%	−0.44%
	BasketballDrive	−1.75%	−0.11%	−0.01%	−2.14%	0.06%	−0.16%
	BQTerrace	−0.96%	0.55%	0.91%	−1.17%	−0.28%	−0.19%
Class C	BasketballDrill	−0.54%	0.61%	1.77%	−0.53%	0.30%	1.12%
	BQMall	−1.08%	0.06%	0.17%	−1.24%	0.37%	0.10%
	PartyScene	−0.79%	−0.15%	−0.15%	−0.82%	−0.18%	−0.14%
	RaceHorsesC	−1.11%	0.20%	0.26%	−1.39%	0.60%	0.66%
Class D	BasketballPass	−1.02%	0.21%	0.26%	−1.23%	0.31%	−0.11%
	BQSquare	−0.87%	0.40%	−0.08%	−0.97%	0.22%	1.27%
	BlowingBubbles	−0.82%	−0.25%	1.24%	−0.80%	0.20%	1.11%
	RaceHorses	−1.77%	−0.04%	−0.25%	−1.93%	0.20%	0.36%
Class E	FourPeople	−1.06%	−0.03%	0.74%	−1.13%	0.49%	0.79%
	Johnny	−0.56%	3.24%	0.31%	−0.82%	3.56%	0.63%
	KistenAndSara	−1.02%	−0.31%	0.71%	−1.14%	1.36%	−0.08%
Average		**−1.49%**	0.18%	0.34%	**−1.77%**	0.34%	0.31%
FLOPs per pixel		197.44k			203.35k		
Parameters		1,727,745			1,751,841		

3.2   Performance Analysis

Table 1 presents the BD-rate results of our proposed method. Compared with VTM-10.0, our proposed TDOF brings on average 1.77% BD-rate reductions for the luma component. To contrast, Table 1 presents the results of our baseline, which is the same network but without any guiding information and not using $Loss_2$ in Eq. (1) either. Compared to the baseline, our proposed temporal dependency-oriented in-loop filter achieves a better performance. For almost all the test sequences, our TDOF consistently outperforms the baseline. For the sequence Tango2, TDOF surpasses the baseline by 0.92% BD-rate

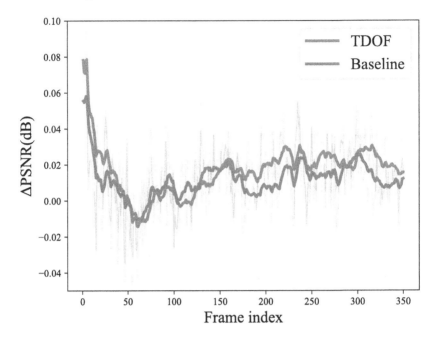

Fig. 3. Comparison of the PSNR gain of the baseline (i.e. the U-net in Fig. 2 without the guiding information trained with $Loss_1$ only) and TDOF. The gain is compared to the VTM-10.0 anchor on the sequence `BQTerrace` when QP is 32. Thin curves indicate per-frame gain and thick curves are sliding-window smoothed.

reduction, which is quite significant. In addition, Table 1 presents the computational complexity of TDOF and the baseline, including the number of floating-point operations (FLOPs) per pixel and the number of parameters. Compared to the baseline, TDOF has slightly increased FLOPs and parameters, but the increase is small.

Figure 3 shows the comparison of the PSNR gain for each P frame of the sequence `BQTerrace` when QP is 32. It can be observed that our proposed TDOF may not perform as well as the baseline on the frames closer to the I frame, but for the frames farther away from the I frame, TDOF outperforms the baseline. This is expected because TDOF is oriented to the temporal dependency and tries to improve the subsequent frame coding efficiency. Overall, TDOF has a better performance.

We also compare the reconstructed frames of our proposed TDOF and the baseline. Figure 4 illustrates some regions as examples. These results are obtained when QP is 37. In the sequence `RitualDance`, it can be observed that the wooden balls appear clearer when filtered by our TDOF. For the sequence `BasketballDrive`, the wrinkles on the short pants are better reconstructed by our method. These examples demonstrate that our method has improved the subjective quality of the filtered videos.

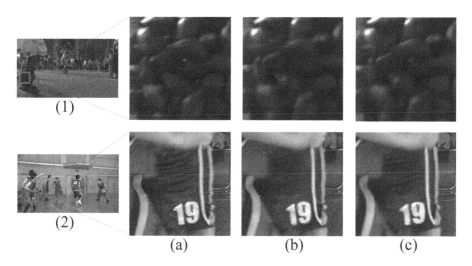

Fig. 4. Visual quality comparison. (1) One frame of the sequence `RitualDance`. (2) One frame of the sequence `BasketballDrive`. (a) Original frame. (b) Filtered frame of the baseline. (c) Filtered frame of TDOF.

Table 2. BD-rate results of ablation study, using VTM as the anchor

	Y	U	V
TDOF	−1.77%	0.34%	0.31%
w/o $Loss_2$	−1.68%	0.29%	0.37%
w/o Residual	−1.52%	0.19%	0.24%
w/o Mode	−1.27%	0.17%	0.40%
w/o Position	−1.64%	0.41%	0.30%
w/o Quality	−1.66%	0.25%	0.34%

3.3 Ablation Study

We conduct a series of ablation experiments to investigate the effectiveness of our proposed combined loss function and the different kinds of guiding information. Here, we summarize the average BD-rate results on all the test sequences in Table 2. It can be observed that the performance always drops, either without using $Loss_2$ in Eq. (1) or without any kind of guiding information. The performance drop due to not using $Loss_2$ is minor, which indicates that $Loss_2$ has difficulty providing significantly better guidance for network training. This may be attributed to the inaccuracy of the motion estimation and motion compensation, which incurs errors in $Loss_2$. Among the several kinds of guiding information, it appears that the mode information (intra-frame or inter-frame) is the most important one. This is interesting because previous studies usually believed the quality information is the most important [4]. Here, our results seem to confirm that the mode information is quite important for considering the temporal dependency, which is quite interpretable. In summary, these ablation experiments have verified that the proposed loss function and four kinds of guiding information help improve the performance of our TDOF.

4   Conclusion

We have proposed a temporal dependency-oriented deep in-loop filter, namely TDOF, for VVC. TDOF is designed to not only improve the quality of the current reconstructed frame but also make the filtered frame a better reference for the subsequent frame coding. For our purpose, we have proposed a temporal dependency-oriented loss function, and we have introduced the residual, mode, position, and quality information as guiding information for the network. Experimental results demonstrate that our proposed TDOF achieves an average 1.77% BD-rate reduction under the LDP configuration than the VTM anchor, and outperforms the baseline that ignores the temporal dependency.

Acknowledgement. This work is supported by the Fundamental Research Funds for the Central Universities under Grant WK3490000006.

References

1. Bjontegaard, G.: Calculation of average PSNR differences between RD-curves. Tech. Rep. VCEG-M33, ITU-T VCEG (2001). https://www.itu.int/wftp3/av-arch/video-site/0104_Aus/
2. Boyce, J., Suehring, K., Li, X., Seregin, V.: JVET common test conditions and software reference configurations. Tech. Rep. JVET-J1010, JVET (ISO/IEC MPEG and ITU-T VCEG) (2018). https://jvet-experts.org/
3. Bross, B., et al.: Overview of the Versatile Video Coding (VVC) standard and its applications. IEEE Trans. Circuits Syst. Video Technol. **31**(10), 3736–3764 (2021)
4. Chen, W., Xiu, X., Wang, X., Chen, Y.W., Jhu, H.J., Kuo, C.W.: Quality-aware CNN-based in-loop filter for video coding. In: Proceedings of SPIE (Applications of Digital Image Processing XLIV), vol. 11842. SPIE (2021)
5. Ding, D., Kong, L., Chen, G., Liu, Z., Fang, Y.: A switchable deep learning approach for in-loop filtering in video coding. IEEE Trans. Circuits Syst. Video Technol. **30**(7), 1871–1887 (2019)
6. Fu, C.M., et al.: Sample adaptive offset in the HEVC standard. IEEE Trans. Circuits Syst. Video Technol. **22**(12), 1755–1764 (2012)
7. Guo, H., Zhu, C., Li, S., Gao, Y.: Optimal bit allocation at frame level for rate control in HEVC. IEEE Trans. Broadcast. **65**(2), 270–281 (2019)
8. He, K., Zhang, X., Ren, S., Sun, J.: Deep residual learning for image recognition. In: Proceedings of the IEEE Conference on Computer Vision and Pattern Recognition, pp. 770–778 (2016)
9. Hu, J., Shen, L., Sun, G.: Squeeze-and-excitation networks. In: Proceedings of the IEEE Conference on Computer Vision and Pattern Recognition, pp. 7132–7141 (2018)
10. Huang, Z., Sun, J., Guo, X., Shang, M.: Adaptive deep reinforcement learning-based in-loop filter for VVC. IEEE Trans. Image Process. **30**, 5439–5451 (2021)

11. Jia, W., Li, L., Li, Z., Zhang, X., Liu, S.: Residual guided deblocking with deep learning. In: 2020 IEEE International Conference on Image Processing, pp. 3109–3113. IEEE (2020)
12. Karczewicz, M., et al.: VVC in-loop filters. IEEE Trans. Circuits Syst. Video Technol. **31**(10), 3907–3925 (2021)
13. Kathariya, B., Li, Z., Wang, H., Van Der Auwera, G.: Multi-stage locally and long-range correlated feature fusion for learned in-loop filter in VVC. In: 2022 IEEE International Conference on Visual Communications and Image Processing, pp. 1–5. IEEE (2022)
14. Li, T., Xu, M., Zhu, C., Yang, R., Wang, Z., Guan, Z.: A deep learning approach for multi-frame in-loop filter of HEVC. IEEE Trans. Image Process. **28**(11), 5663–5678 (2019)
15. Lin, J., Liu, D., Liang, J., Li, H., Wu, F.: A deeply modulated scheme for variable-rate video compression. In: 2021 IEEE International Conference on Image Processing, pp. 3722–3726. IEEE (2021)
16. Lin, W., et al.: Partition-aware adaptive switching neural networks for post-processing in HEVC. IEEE Trans. Multim. **22**(11), 2749–2763 (2019)
17. Ma, D., Zhang, F., Bull, D.R.: BVI-DVC: a training database for deep video compression. IEEE Trans. Multimedia **24**, 3847–3858 (2021)
18. Norkin, A., et al.: HEVC deblocking filter. IEEE Trans. Circuits Syst. Video Technol. **22**(12), 1746–1754 (2012)
19. Pan, Z., Yi, X., Zhang, Y., Jeon, B., Kwong, S.: Efficient in-loop filtering based on enhanced deep convolutional neural networks for HEVC. IEEE Trans. Image Process. **29**, 5352–5366 (2020)
20. Paszke, A., Gross, S., Massa, F., et al.: PyTorch: an imperative style, high-performance deep learning library. In: Proceedings of the 33rd International Conference on Neural Information Processing Systems, pp. 8026–8037 (2019)
21. Ronneberger, O., Fischer, P., Brox, T.: U-net: convolutional networks for biomedical image segmentation. In: Navab, N., Hornegger, J., Wells, W.M., Frangi, A.F. (eds.) Medical Image Computing and Computer-Assisted Intervention (MICCAI 2015), pp. 234–241. Springer, Cham (2015). https://doi.org/10.1007/978-3-319-24574-4_28
22. Sullivan, G.J., Ohm, J.R., Han, W.J., Wiegand, T.: Overview of the High Efficiency Video Coding (HEVC) standard. IEEE Trans. Circuits Syst. Video Technol. **22**(12), 1649–1668 (2012)
23. Zhang, Y., Shen, T., Ji, X., Zhang, Y., Xiong, R., Dai, Q.: Residual highway convolutional neural networks for in-loop filtering in HEVC. IEEE Trans. Image Process. **27**(8), 3827–3841 (2018)

Resolution-Agnostic Neural Compression for High-Fidelity Portrait Video Conferencing via Implicit Radiance Fields

Yifei Li[1], Xiaohong Liu[1(✉)], Yicong Peng[1], Guangtao Zhai[1,2],
and Jun Zhou[1,2(✉)]

[1] Shanghai Jiao Tong University, Shanghai, China
xiaohongliu@sjtu.edu.cn, zhoujun@sjtu.edu.cn
[2] Shanghai Key Laboratory of Digital Media Processing and Transmission, Shanghai,
China

Abstract. Video conferencing has caught much more attention recently.
High fidelity and low bandwidth are two major objectives of video compression for video conferencing applications. Most pioneering methods
rely on classic video compression codec without high-level feature embedding and thus can not reach the extremely low bandwidth. Recent works
instead employ model-based neural compression to acquire ultra-low
bitrates using sparse representations of each frame such as facial land-
mark information, while these approaches can not maintain high fidelity
due to 2D image-based warping. In this paper, we propose a novel low
bandwidth neural compression approach for high-fidelity portrait video
conferencing using implicit radiance fields to achieve both major objectives. We leverage dynamic neural radiance fields to reconstruct high-
fidelity talking head with expression features, which are represented as
frame substitution for transmission. The overall system employs deep
model to encode expression features at the sender and reconstruct portrait at the receiver with volume rendering as decoder for ultra-low bandwidth. In particular, with the characteristic of neural radiance fields
based model, our compression approach is resolution-agnostic, which
means that the low bandwidth achieved by our approach is independent
of video resolution, while maintaining fidelity for higher resolution reconstruction. Experimental results demonstrate that our novel framework
can (1) construct ultra-low bandwidth video conferencing, (2) maintain
high fidelity portrait and (3) have better performance on high-resolution
video compression than previous works.

Keywords: Video conferencing · Neural radiance fields · Neural
compression

1 Introduction

Video conferencing enables individuals or groups to participate in a virtual meeting by using video, which has caught much more attention since the online
lifestyle becomes prevalent. Nowadays, the demand for video conferencing with

G. Zhai et al. (Eds.): IFTC 2023, CCIS 2067, pp. 126–141, 2024.
https://doi.org/10.1007/978-981-97-3626-3_10

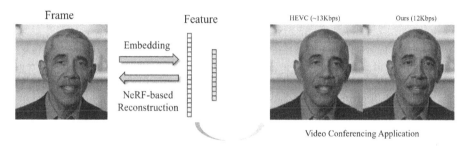

Fig. 1. Illustration of our NeRF-based video compression. The core idea of our framework is frame-feature substitution for extremely low bandwidth. With NeRF-based face reconstruction model ensuring high-fidelity portrait generation, our framework shows significant compression performance for video conferencing application.

the large amount of simultaneous users also determines its extremely low bandwidth limitations in application, which relies more heavily on efficient video compression technologies. Video compression aims to reduce video bandwidth while maintaining high fidelity. Over the past several decades, the dominant video compression methods are based on classic video compression frameworks, such as H.262, AVS [4], H.264, HEVC [2], and VVC [3], which have achieved significant results. However, most classic methods reducing redundancy fully based on images and pixels without high level feature coding, thus can not reach the extremely limited low bandwidth while maintaining acceptable results in present video conferencing scenarios (Fig. 1).

With the development of computer science and deep learning, video, as the main medium for simultaneous auditory and visual outputs, has received extensive attention for its applications and research in related fields [5,15,22,23,40–42,50,57]. At the same time, with the development of computer vision and graphics [13,25,45,52], there are more and more neural network based methods targeting the resolution and quality of videos [6,14,19,30,34,39,49,54–56]. Among them, the field of neural video compression has attracted much attention, where some neural compression methods [7–11] leverage face image generative models to deliver extreme compression by reconstructing video frame from a high-level feature, such as motion keypoints [8,10,12]. Specifically, most previous works use 2D warping based synthesis models to reconstruct portrait images. These warping methods deliver good reconstructions when the difference between the reference and target images is small, but they fail (possibly catastrophically) when there is large head pose movement or occlusion. As a result, lacking of 3D representation, these warping based compression frameworks are not robust in maintaining high fidelity for some cases. Furthermore, most of these generative approaches have restrictions on input resolution (e.g., usually 256×256), which means when it comes to high resolution applications (e.g., typical video conferencing are designed for HD videos), corresponding neural compression will not work. Meanwhile, with the superior capability in multi-view image synthesis of Neural Radiance Fields (NeRF) [16], several feature-conditioned dynamic neural radiance fields [1,17,18,24] have be proposed for talking head and dynamic face reconstruction. Rather than 2D warping, these models propose to use neural radiance fields to reconstruct portrait scene and represent the dynamics (e.g., expressions and head motion) as high-level features. Thanks to implicit 3D representation and volume rendering, these works are capable of producing natural portraits with high fidelity and more specifics (e.g., illumination and reflection) even in large movements. Nevertheless, to the best of our knowledge, the applications of such NeRF-based reconstruction model have not been delivered to neural video compression or video conferencing.

To address the defects of classic video codec and previous neural model-based compression and preserve both high fidelity and ultra-low bandwidth, we propose to leverage Neural Radiance Fields (NeRF) [16] to reconstruct portrait in implicit 3D space for model-based neural compression and video conferencing. Specifically, we propose a novel neural compression framework using implicit neural radiance fields. At the sender, instead of using warping keypoints, we leverage 3D Morphable Face Models (3DMMs) [20] to extract facial expression feature and head pose from portrait frame. Due to its disentanglement of face attributes as a 3D representation, 3DMMs can gain control of face synthesis better. Besides, to obtain higher-level information representation and better compression performance, we propose to employ an attention-based model [21] as encoder for feature embedding, which is called *fine-tuning embedding*. Before the features substituting frames to be transmitted, entropy coding as a lossless coding strategy is employed to compress the features further. Once the features have been received at the receiver, we leverage the feature-conditioned dynamic neural radiance fields to reconstruct the portrait video. It's worth noting that we refer to [1], which has desirable performance in both face and torso rendering, and replace the audio feature with expression feature to build the face reconstruction model employed in our approach. We conduct extensive experiments in both quantitative and qualitative aspects with comparisons to classic video codec and previous model-based video compression. We demonstrate that our approach can reach extremely low bandwidth while maintaining high fidelity for video conferencing application. Furthermore, thanks to the characteristic of NeRF rendering with unlimited resolution [16], our neural compression approach is *resolution-agnostic*.

To summarize, the contributions of our approach are:

- Firstly, we leverage neural radiance fields for extremely low-bandwidth video compression and high-fidelity video conferencing, which is resolution-agnostic. To the best of our knowledge, our approach is the first NeRF-based video compression method.
- Secondly, we holistically construct the framework for NeRF-based video compression and design fine-tuning embedding model to obtain fine-tuned feature as frame substitution to be transmitted for better and adaptive compression performance.
- Lastly, extensive experiments demonstrate that our proposed approach can achieve resolution-agnostic and ultra-low bandwidth with high fidelity pre-

serving for applications in video conferencing, which significantly outperforms classic video codec (HEVC) and previous model-based compression methods.

2   Related Work

Classic Video Codec. Many video applications utilize standard video compression modules, commonly known as codecs, including AVS, H.264/H.265 [2,27], VP8 [26], and AV1 [28]. These codecs employ a technique that divides video frames into key frames (I-frames), capitalizing on spatial redundancies within a frame, and predicted frames (P-/B-frames), leveraging both temporal and spatial redundancies across frames. Over time, these standards have undergone enhancements, incorporating concepts like variable block sizes and low-resolution encoding [28] to optimize performance at lower bitrates.

These codecs demonstrate notable efficiency in their slow modes, if ample time and computational resources to compress videos at high quality are available. Nevertheless, for real-time applications like video conferencing, they still demand a few hundred Kbps, even at moderate resolutions such as 720p. In situations with limited bandwidth, these codecs face challenges and may only transmit at lower quality, experiencing issues like packet loss and frame corruption [29].

Face Animation Synthesis. Historically, face animation synthesis methods can be categorized into warping-based, mesh-based, and NeRF-based approaches. Among these, warping-based methods [9,31–33] are particularly popular within 2D generation techniques. In these methods, source features are warped using estimated motion fields to align the driving pose and expression with the source face. For example, Monkey-Net [35] constructs a 2D motion field from sparse keypoints detected by an unsupervised trained detector. Da-GAN [36] integrates depth estimation to enhance the 2D motion field by supplementing missing 3D geometry information. OSFV [8] attempts to extract 3D appearance features and predict a 3D motion field for free-view synthesis.

Certain traditional approaches [38,43] make use of 3D Morphable Models (3DMM) [20,37], enabling a broad range of animations through disentangled shape, expression, and rigid motions. Models like StyleRig [44] and PIE [46] leverage semantic information in the latent space of StyleGAN [47] to modulate expressions using 3DMM. PIRender [48] employs 3DMM to predict flow and warp the source image.

NeRF [16], a more recent method, represents implicit 3D scenes by rendering static scenes with points along different view directions, which initially gained prominence in audio-driven approaches [1,18,51] due to its compatibility with latent codes learned from audio.

Neural Compression for Video Conferencing. The limitations of classic codecs in achieving extremely low bitrates for high-resolution videos have

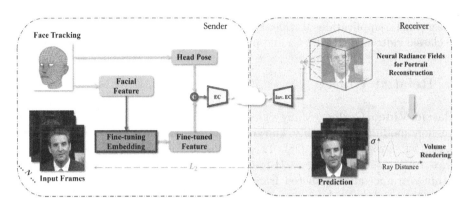

Fig. 2. The overall framework of our proposed method. Face feature is extracted at the sender and substitutes frame to be transmitted with ultra-low bandwidth. At the receiver, NeRF-based model takes the received feature as input to reconstruct portrait frame.

prompted researchers to explore neural approaches for reconstructing videos from highly compact representations. Neural codecs have been specifically tailored for applications such as video streaming, live video, and video conferencing.

However, video conferencing presents distinct challenges compared to other video applications. Firstly, the unavailability of the video ahead of time hinders optimization for the best compression-quality trade-off. Additionally, video conferencing content predominantly consists of facial data, allowing for a more targeted model design for generating facial videos. Several models [7–11] have been proposed over the years, typically utilizing keypoints or facial landmarks as a compact intermediary representation of a specific pose. These representations are then used to compute the movement between two poses before generating the reconstruction. The models may incorporate 3D keypoints [8], off-the-shelf keypoint detectors [9], or a variety of reference frames [11] to enhance prediction.

Neural Radiance Field and Dynamic Rendering. Our approach aligns with recent advancements in neural rendering and novel view synthesis, particularly drawing inspiration from Neural Radiance Fields (NeRF) [16]. NeRF employs a Multi-Layer Perception (MLP), denoted as F, to acquire a volumetric representation of a scene. F, for each 3D point and viewing direction, predicts color and volume density. Through hierarchical volume sampling, F is densely evaluated throughout the scene for a given camera pose, followed by volume rendering to generate the final image. The training process involves minimizing the error between the predicted color and the ground truth value of a pixel.

While NeRF is originally designed for static scenes, several efforts have been made to extend its applicability to dynamic objects or scenes. Some approaches [1,17,18] introduce a time component as input and impose temporal constraints by utilizing scene flow or a canonical frame for talking head and face animation synthesis. For example, AD-NeRF [1] proposes to use an audio feature

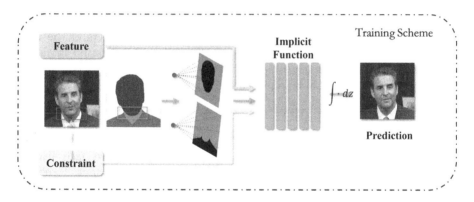

Fig. 3. Training scheme of the NeRF-based reconstruction model. We leverage consistency constraint code to get better generative results.

as additional input with head-torso separate modeling to reconstruct natural and photo-realistic face animation. Nevertheless, NeRF-based face reconstruction model has not been proposed for video compression and video conferencing.

3   Methodology

3.1   NeRF-Based Compression Framework

Our objective is to leverage neural radiance fields to design a video compression framework for extremely low-bandwidth video conferencing with high fidelity. Therefore, the overall framework of our proposed approach can be regarded as a communication system which is composed of the sender, the receiver and transmission. The key insight of the proposed approach is substituting face image with feature which can be represented as low-dimensional vector for transmission. Face tracking model and entropy coding are employed for facial feature extraction and further compression at the sender before transmission. At the receiver, the face animation model based on NeRF is used to reconstruct high-fidelity and photo-realistic portrait frames from the received features. Furthermore, the overall system is end-to-end which is illustrated in Fig. 2.

Face Feature Extraction. To reconstruct high-fidelity portrait frame with low-bandwidth limitation, an appropriate representation of face is essential. Rather than extracting motion keypoints in self-supervised manner described in [7,12], we propose to employ 3DMM [20,37] as face tracking model to extract facial expression feature and head pose for face reconstruction. 3DMMs (3D Morphable Models) utilize a PCA (Principal Component Analysis)-based linear subspace to independently control face shape, facial expressions, and appearance. This approach allows for a disentangled representation of these facial features, enabling more flexible and intuitive manipulation of individual components. This disentanglement is particularly valuable in applications such as face modeling and synthesis, which delivers precise control over specific aspects of the face. Therefore, we employ 3DMM as an intermediate 3D representation model to extract facial expression feature δ and head pose p. Following [37], the primitive facial expression feature can be represented as a 79-dimensional vector. In terms of head pose, a 12-dimensional vector is employed: 9 numbers for the rotation and 3 numbers for the translation.

Fine-Tuning Embedding. However, in fact, the primitive face feature extracted using the pre-trained face tracking model is still redundant. To obtain lower bandwidth transmission and better performance in compression, we leverage an attention-based encoder network [21] to construct a fine-tuning embedding of primitive feature into lower-dimensional and higher-level representation. Specifically, the fine-tuned feature used in our experiment is a 30-dimensional vector.

Further Compression. As for face feature, it's actually represented as vector with floating point values in 16 bits precision, and some classic compression schemes can be employed for further compression. Due to the characteristic of employed reconstruction model, the accuracy of the input features has a significant impact on generative performance. Therefore, the lossless compression scheme is recommended. In our approach, we compress fine-tuned face features further using *Entropy Coding*. Then the coded fine-tuned face feature, together with the coded pose, are transmitted to receiver.

Portrait Frame Reconstruction. At the receiver, portrait frames are reconstructed from received face features using NeRF-based face reconstruction model, which hold the common facial expression and head poses as in *source* input images. Following the recent work of Guo Y *et al.* [1], we employ two individual neural radiance fields to represent head part and torso part separately which demonstrates significant performance in talking-head synthesis. Nevertheless, rather than the audio feature used in [1], we build the reconstruction model with facial expression feature from 3DMM as animation driving in order to maintain consistency in source and reconstructed facial expressions. Furthermore, we propose a learnable constraint to optimize the degree of fit between head and torso for better performance. More details of the reconstruction model are described in Sect. 3.2.

3.2 Neural Radiance Fields for Face Reconstruction

Inspired by audio driven neural radiance fields for talking-head synthesis introduced by Guo Y *et al.* [1], we utilize facial expression feature driven reconstruction model for neural compression. In addition to the view directions (θ, ϕ) and 3D locations (x, y, z), the facial expression feature δ is introduced as an additional input to the neural radiance field which is represented as an implicit function $\mathcal{N}_\Theta$. With the concatenated input vectors $(\delta, \theta, \phi, x, y, z)$, the network estimates color values $\mathbf{c}$ accompanied by volume densities σ along the dispatched rays:

$$\mathcal{N}_\Theta(\delta, \theta, \phi, x, y, z) = (\mathbf{c}, \sigma). \tag{1}$$

Consistency Constraint. In addition, apart from the different selection of driving feature, we observe that there will be a gap between head and torso in reconstruction following the individual optimization strategy introduced in [1], and thus we propose a *learnable constraint code* to improve the consistency between head and torso part, which is substantiated in the ablation study of our experiments. The overall training scheme of the reconstruction model is illustrated in Fig. 3.

Volumetric Rendering of Face Radiance Fields. To generate images from this implicit geometry and appearance representation, we employ volumetric rendering. The process involves casting rays through each individual pixel of a frame, accumulating the sampled density and RGB values along the rays to calculate the final output color. Leveraging head pose tracking with 3DMM, we transform the ray sample points to the canonical space of the head model and then evaluate the dynamic neural radiance field at these locations. It's important to note that the pose P, obtained from head pose tracking, provides us with control over the head pose during test time. This control over head pose allows for dynamic adjustments and customization when rendering the images.

Once the color $\mathbf{c}$ and volume density σ have been predicted by the implicit function $\mathcal{N}_\Theta$, the expected color $\mathcal{C}$ of a camera ray $\mathbf{r}(t) = \mathbf{o} + t\mathbf{d}$ with camera center $\mathbf{o}$ and viewing direction $\mathbf{d} = (\theta, \phi)$ is accumulated as:

$$\mathcal{C}(\mathbf{r}; \Theta, P, \delta) = \int_{b_{near}}^{b_{far}} \sigma_\Theta(\mathbf{r}(t)) \cdot \mathbf{c}_\Theta(\mathbf{r}(t), \mathbf{d}) \cdot T(t) dt, \tag{2}$$

where b_{near} and b_{far} are near bounds and far bounds of sampling along the ray. $T(t)$ is the accumulated transmittance along the ray from b_{near} to t:

$$T(t) = exp(-\int_{b_{near}}^{t} \sigma(\mathbf{r}(x)) dx). \tag{3}$$

Besides, it's worth noting that we use a similar two-stage volumetric integration approach to Mildenhall *et al.* [16].

3.3 Optimization Details

Dataset. We employ HDTF [53] as the main dataset for face animation reconstruction in the applications of video conferencing. We select videos of different identities from HDTF dataset [53]. There are several input resolutions for training: 128×128, 256×256, 512×512 and 1024×1024.

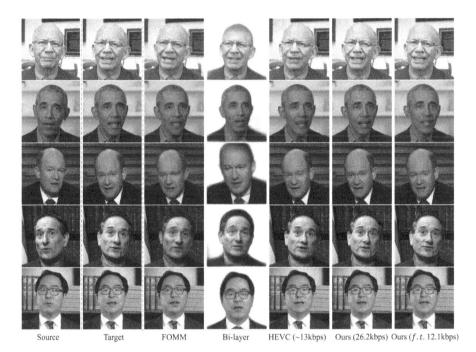

Source   Target   FOMM   Bi-layer   HEVC (~13kbps) Ours (26.2kbps) Ours (f.t. 12.1kbps)

Fig. 4. Qualitative results of the proposed framework compared with previous model-based compression (FOMM [7] and Bi-layer [9]) and classic video codec (HEVC [2]). Our approach, which employs NeRF-based model for high-fidelity reconstruction and feature-frame substitution for ultra-low bandwidth, outperforms other methods in image quality significantly. *f.t.* represents fine-tuning embedding employed in the framework.

Training Loss. As the overall system is end-to-end, we leverage a photo-metric reconstruction error metric over the training images I_i to optimize both the coarse network and fine network:

$$L = \sum_{i=1}^{M} L_i(\Theta_c) + L_i(\Theta_f), \tag{4}$$

where Θ_c and Θ_f are parameters of coarse and fine networks and L_i is:

$$L_i = \sum_{j \in pixels} \|\mathcal{C}(\mathbf{r}_j; \Theta, P_i, \delta_i) - I_i[j]\|^2. \tag{5}$$

4   Experiments

4.1   Overview

The goal of the proposed framework is to construct resolution-agnostic NeRF-based compression for high-fidelity portrait video conferencing with extremely low bandwidth. To demonstrate the significant performance of our approach for applications in video conferencing, we conduct both quantitative and qualitative evaluation compared with state-of-the-art model-based video compression approach and classic video codec and discuss ablation studies of our method.

Metrics and Setting. We measure the performance of reconstruction-based models and classic codec using both quality metrics (**SSIM, PSNR, LPIPS**) and fidelity metrics. Specifically, following [32], we employ **CSIM, AUCON** and **PRMSE** to evaluate the fidelity. Cosine similarity (**CSIM**) is used to evaluate the quality of identity preservation. **PRMSE**, the root mean square error of the head pose angles is leveraged to inspect the capability of the model to properly reenact the pose and the expression of the driver. And **AUCON** represents the ratio of identical facial action unit values between generated images and driving images. As for qualitative evaluation, we design the similar bandwidth of classic codec as other methods and evaluate the quality of images. In terms of quantitative evaluation, we first compare both quality metrics and bitrate-quality trade-off, which is represented as **SSIM/b.r.**, **PSNR/b.r.** and **LPIPS×b.r.**, where **b.r.** represents bitrate. And then we compare the fidelity metrics and bitrate-fidelity trade-off, which is represented as **CSIM/b.r.**, **AUCON/b.r.** and **PRMSE×b.r.**. Furthermore, we also demonstrate the compression performance using rate-distortion curve.

4.2 Qualitative Evaluation

In terms of qualitative evaluation, we compare our method with the SOTA model-based compression Bi-layer [9] and FOMM [7] together with the most available and efficient classic video codec, HEVC. Specifically, we preserve the regular keypoint/landmark settings proposed in Bi-layer and FOMM and employ *Entropy Coding* for further compression as well to make comparisons. For HEVC, we choose the appropriate *Constant Rate Factor* to obtain similar bandwidth as our proposed method and compare the compression performance.

As illustrated in Fig. 4, our method can generate more realistic and high-fidelity results under extremely low bandwidth. Neither Bi-layer nor FOMM can reconstruct high-fidelity portrait due to their 2D warping based method. Classic codec HEVC has little implication on fidelity, while in similar condition (compared to ultra-low bandwidth in our method) there is much distortion that degrades the image quality. Consequently, our proposed framework delivers more appealing results for applications in video conferencing.

4.3 Quantitative Evaluation

With regards to quantitative evaluation, we first compare both the quantitative metrics (quality and fidelity metrics) and trade-off between the bitrate and quality/fidelity represented as **SSIM/b.r.**, **PSNR/b.r.**, **LPIPS×b.r.**, **CSIM/b.r.**, **AUCON/b.r.** and **PRMSE×b.r.**, as shown in Table 1 and

Table 1. Quantitative results over quality metrics and bitrate trade-off.

Methods	Quality				Quality-bitrate Tradeoff		
	L1↓	SSIM↑	PSNR↑	LPIPS↓	SSIM/b.r.↑	PSNR/b.r.↑	LPIPS×b.r.↓
FOMM [7]	0.038	0.77	24.37	0.12	0.04	1.41	2.07
Bi-layer [9]	0.23	0.55	15.88	0.44	0.014	0.41	17.23
HEVC [2]	0.019	0.89	28.83	0.091	<u>0.068</u>	<u>2.22</u>	1.21
Ours	**0.014**	**0.95**	<u>29.97</u>	**0.048**	0.036	1.144	<u>1.19</u>
Ours(*f.t.*)	<u>0.015</u>	<u>0.934</u>	**30.85**	<u>0.05</u>	**0.077**	**2.55**	**0.6**

Table 2. Furthermore, to demonstrate compression performance more clearly, we employ rate-distortion curve analysis in Fig. 5.

Table 2. Quantitative results over fidelity metrics and bitrate trade-off.

Methods	Fidelity			Fidelity-bitrate Tradeoff		
	CSIM↑	AUCON↑	PRMSE↓	CSIM/b.r.↑	AUCON/b.r.↑	PRMSE×b.r.↓
FOMM [7]	0.829	0.856	2.79	0.048	0.0495	48.2
Bi-layer [9]	0.518	0.626	4.86	0.013	0.016	190
Ours	**0.956**	**0.989**	**1.21**	0.036	0.0377	<u>31.7</u>
Ours(*f.t.*)	<u>0.945</u>	<u>0.967</u>	<u>1.29</u>	**0.078**	**0.08**	**15.609**

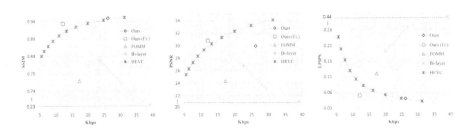

Fig. 5. Rate-distortion curve for our proposed framework compared with existing model-based compression method and classic codec HEVC. The resolution for HEVC codec is 256 × 256.

Resolution-Agnostic Analysis. It's worth noting that besides the significant bitrate-quality trade-off, our NeRF-based compression framework is resolution-agnostic due to the characteristic of neural radiance fields. That is the extremely low bandwidth achieved by our approach is independent of video resolution, while maintaining fidelity for higher resolution reconstruction and compression.

As illustrated in Fig. 6 rate-distortion curve, Bi-layer [9] and FOMM [7] have no support for variation in resolution, while higher resolution has significant affect on performance of HEVC.

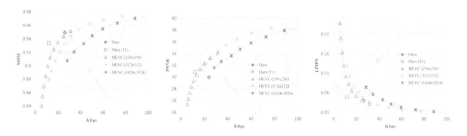

Fig. 6. Rate-distortion curve of resolution-agnostic analysis for our proposed framework compared with classic codec HEVC in several different resolution settings.

Subjective Evaluation. Following [8,12], we conduct subjective evaluation as well. We compress several clips using our framework and HEVC separately and show the compressed clips to users in video conferencing application. With various bitrate settings, we ask the users to choose the preference and compute the percentage as shown in the left side of Fig 7, and to rate the clips by *Mean Opinion Score* (MOS) as shown in the right side of Fig 7. And in extremely low bandwidth setting, our framework shows significant performance compared to HEVC.

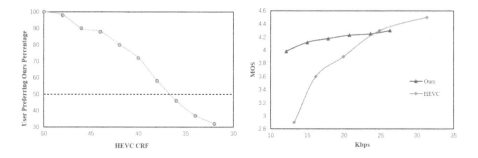

Fig. 7. Subjective evaluation on the proposed framework and HEVC.

4.4   Ablation Study

We also benchmark our performance gain upon our modules. Specifically, we conduct ablations about our proposed *fine-tuning embedding* model and head-torso *consistency constraint* code. As for fine-tuning embedding, we have demonstrated its significant effects on video compression performance from previous experimental results, where fine-tune embedding has little affect on image quality with similar fidelity (PSNR is even higher), and reduces bandwidth significantly. The ablation study of consistency constraint is described in Table 3.

Table 3. Ablation study on head-torso consistency constraint.

Setting	L1	SSIM	PSNR	LPIPS	CSIM	AUCON	PRMSE
w/o. constraint	0.019	0.91	28.68	0.06	0.94	0.958	1.31
w. constraint	**0.015**	**0.934**	**30.85**	**0.05**	**0.945**	**0.967**	**1.29**

5   Conclusion

In this work, we propose to leverage neural radiance fields face reconstruction model for neural video compression. Based on our NeRF-based reconstruction model, we substitute frames with features to be transmitted for video conferencing. With extensive experiments in both qualitative and quantitative aspects, we demonstrate that our novel framework implements resolution-agnostic neural compression with high-fidelity portraits in extremely low bandwidth for video conferencing, which outperforms the existing methods. As for future work, there are more further compression methods for the extracted facial feature besides lossless Entropy Coding, and we plan to leverage deep compression scheme for further feature compression to obtain better performance.

Acknowledgement. This work was supported in part by the Shanghai Pujiang Program under Grant 22PJ1406800.

References

1. Guo, Y., Chen, K., Liang, S., et al.: Ad-nerf: audio driven neural radiance fields for talking head synthesis. In: Proceedings of the IEEE/CVF International Conference on Computer Vision, pp. 5784–5794 (2021)
2. Sullivan, G.J., Ohm, J.R., Han, W.J., et al.: Overview of the high efficiency video coding (HEVC) standard. IEEE Trans. Circuits Syst. Video Technol. **22**(12), 1649–1668 (2012)
3. Bross, B., Chen, J., Liu, S., et al.: Versatile video coding (draft 5). Joint Video Experts Team (JVET) ITU-T Sg **16**, 3–12 (2019)
4. Ma, S., Zhang, L., Wang, S., et al.: Evolution of AVS video coding standards: twenty years of innovation and development. Sci. China Inf. Sci. **65**(9), 192101 (2022)
5. Nie, X., Hu, Y., Shen, X., et al.: Reconstructing and editing fluids using the adaptive multilayer external force guiding model. Sci. China Inf. Sci. **65**(11), 212102 (2022)

6. Shi, Z., Xu, X., Liu, X., et al.: Video frame interpolation transformer. In: Proceedings of the IEEE/CVF Conference on Computer Vision and Pattern Recognition, pp. 17482–17491 (2022)
7. Siarohin, A., Lathuilière, S., Tulyakov, S., et al.: First order motion model for image animation. Adv. Neural Inf. Process. Syst. **32** (2019)
8. Wang, T.C., Mallya, A., Liu, M.Y.: One-shot free-view neural talking-head synthesis for video conferencing. In: Proceedings of the IEEE/CVF Conference on Computer Vision and Pattern Recognition, pp. 10039–10049 (2021)
9. Zakharov, E., Ivakhnenko, A., Shysheya, A.: Fast bi-layer neural synthesis of one-shot realistic head avatars. In: Computer Vision-ECCV, et al.: 16th European Conference, Glasgow, 23–28 August 2020, Proceedings, Part XII, vol. 16, pp. 524–540. Springer (2020)
10. Oquab, M., Stock, P., Haziza, D., et al.: Low bandwidth video-chat compression using deep generative models. In: Proceedings of the IEEE/CVF Conference on Computer Vision and Pattern Recognition, pp. 2388–2397 (2021)
11. Volokitin, A., Brugger, S., Benlalah, A., et al.: Neural face video compression using multiple views. In: Proceedings of the IEEE/CVF Conference on Computer Vision and Pattern Recognition, pp. 1738–1742 (2022)
12. Konuko, G., Valenzise, G., Lathuilière, S.: Ultra-low bitrate video conferencing using deep image animation. In: 2021 IEEE International Conference on Acoustics, Speech and Signal Processing (ICASSP 2021), pp. 4210–4214. IEEE (2021)
13. Liu, M., Wei, Y., Wu, X., et al.: Survey on leveraging pre-trained generative adversarial networks for image editing and restoration. Sci. China Inf. Sci. **66**(5), 1–28 (2023)
14. Shi, Z., Liu, X., Li, C., et al.: Learning for unconstrained space-time video super-resolution. IEEE Trans. Broadcast. **68**(2), 345–358 (2021)
15. Chen, Y., Hao, C., Yang, Z.X., et al.: Fast target-aware learning for few-shot video object segmentation. Sci China Inf. Sci. **65**(8), 182104 (2022)
16. Mildenhall, B., Srinivasan, P.P., Tancik, M., et al.: Nerf: Representing scenes as neural radiance fields for view synthesis. Commun. ACM **65**(1), 99–106 (2021)
17. Gafni, G., Thies, J., Zollhofer, M., et al.: Dynamic neural radiance fields for monocular 4d facial avatar reconstruction. In: Proceedings of the IEEE/CVF Conference on Computer Vision and Pattern Recognition, pp. 8649–8658 (2021)
18. Yao, S., Zhong, R.Z., Yan, Y., et al.: DFA-NeRF: personalized talking head generation via disentangled face attributes neural rendering. arXiv preprint arXiv:2201.00791 (2022)
19. Shi, Z., Liu, X., Shi, K., et al.: Video frame interpolation via generalized deformable convolution. IEEE Trans. Multimedia **24**, 426–439 (2021)
20. Blanz, V., Vetter, T.: A morphable model for the synthesis of 3D faces. In: Seminal Graphics Papers: Pushing the Boundaries, vol. 2, pp. 157–164 (2023)
21. Vaswani, A., Shazeer, N., Parmar, N., et al.: Attention is all you need. Adv. Neural Inf. Process. Syst. **30** (2017)
22. Wang, H., Wu, Y., Li, M., et al.: Survey on rain removal from videos or a single image. Sci. China Inf. Sci. **65**(1), 111101 (2022)
23. Tian, Y., Fu, H., Wang, H., et al.: RGB oralscan video-based orthodontic treatment monitoring. Sci. China Inf. Sci. **67**(1), 112107 (2024)
24. Lombardi, S., Simon, T., Saragih, J., et al.: Neural volumes: learning dynamic renderable volumes from images. arXiv preprint arXiv:1906.07751 (2019)
25. Ma, S., Gao, J., Wang, R., et al.: Overview of intelligent video coding: from model-based to learning-based approaches. Visual Intelligence **1**(1), 15 (2023)

26. Bankoski, J, Wilkins, P., Xu, Y.: Technical overview of VP8, an open source video codec for the web. In: 2011 IEEE International Conference on Multimedia and Expo, pp. 1–6. IEEE (2011)

27. Schwarz, H., Marpe, D., Wiegand, T.: Overview of the scalable video coding extension of the H. 264/AVC standard. IEEE Trans. Circuits Syst. Video Technol. **17**(9), 1103–1120 (2007)

28. Chen, Y., Murherjee, D., Han, J., et al.: An overview of core coding tools in the AV1 video codec. In: 2018 Picture Coding Symposium (PCS), pp. 41–45. IEEE (2018)

29. Fouladi, S., Emmons, J., Orbay, E., et al.: Salsify: low-latency network video through tighter integration between a video codec and a transport protocol. In: 15th USENIX Symposium on Networked Systems Design and Implementation (NSDI 18), pp. 267–282 (2018)

30. Liu, X., Shi, K., Wang, Z., et al.: Exploit camera raw data for video super-resolution via hidden Markov model inference. IEEE Trans. Image Process. **30**, 2127–2140 (2021)

31. Dong, H., Liang, X., Gong, K., et al.: Soft-gated warping-gan for pose-guided person image synthesis. Adv. Neural Inf. Process. Syst. **31** (2018)

32. Ha, S., Kersner, M., Kim, B., et al.: Marionette: few-shot face reenactment preserving identity of unseen targets. Proc. AAAI Conf. Artif. Intell. **34**(07), 10893–10900 (2020)

33. Liu, W., Piao, Z., Min, J., et al.: Liquid warping gan: a unified framework for human motion imitation, appearance transfer and novel view synthesis. In: Proceedings of the IEEE/CVF International Conference on Computer Vision, pp. 5904–5913 (2019)

34. Liu, X., Kong, L., Zhou, Y., et al.: End-to-end trainable video super-resolution based on a new mechanism for implicit motion estimation and compensation. In: Proceedings of the IEEE/CVF Winter Conference on Applications of Computer Vision, pp. 2416–2425 (2020)

35. Siarohin, A., Lathuilière, S., Tulyakov, S., et al.: Animating arbitrary objects via deep motion transfer. In: Proceedings of the IEEE/CVF Conference on Computer Vision and Pattern Recognition, pp. 2377–2386 (2019)

36. Hong, F.T., Zhang, L., Shen, L., et al.: Depth-aware generative adversarial network for talking head video generation. In: Proceedings of the IEEE/CVF Conference on Computer Vision and Pattern Recognition, pp. 3397–3406 (2022)

37. Paysan, P., Knothe, R., Amberg, B., et al.: A 3D face model for pose and illumination invariant face recognition. In: 2009 sixth IEEE International Conference on Advanced Video and Signal Based Surveillance, pp. 296–301. IEEE (2009)

38. Suwajanakorn, S., Seitz, S.M., Kemelmacher-Shlizerman, I.: Synthesizing obama: learning lip sync from audio. ACM Trans. Graph. **36**(4), 1–13 (2017)

39. Liu, X., Chen, L., Wang, W., et al.: Robust multi-frame super-resolution based on spatially weighted half-quadratic estimation and adaptive BTV regularization. IEEE Trans. Image Process. **27**(10), 4971–4986 (2018)

40. Huang, Y., Yang, C., Chen, Z.: 3DPF-FBN: video inpainting by jointly 3D-patch filling and neural network refinement. Sci. China Inf. Sci. **65**(7) (2022)

41. Yi, Z., Song, W., Li, S., et al.: Automatic image matting and fusing for portrait synthesis. Sci. China Inf. Sci. **65**(2), 124101 (2022)

42. Qian, R., Lin, W., See, J., et al.: Controllable augmentations for video representation learning. Visual Intell. **2**(1), 1–15 (2024)

43. Thies, J., Zollhöfer, M., Nießner, M.: Deferred neural rendering: image synthesis using neural textures. ACM Trans. Graph. **38**(4), 1–12 (2019)

44. Tewari, A., Elgharib, M., Bharaj, G., et al.: Stylerig: rigging stylegan for 3d control over portrait images. In: Proceedings of the IEEE/CVF Conference on Computer Vision and Pattern Recognition, pp. 6142–6151 (2020)

45. Fan, D.P., Ji, G.P., Xu, P., et al.: Advances in deep concealed scene understanding. Visual Intell. **1**(1), 16 (2023)

46. Tewari, A., Elgharib, M., Bernard, F., et al.: Pie: portrait image embedding for semantic control. ACM Trans. Graph. **39**(6), 1–14 (2020)

47. Karras, T., Laine, S., Aila, T.: A style-based generator architecture for generative adversarial networks. In: Proceedings of the IEEE/CVF Conference on Computer Vision and Pattern Recognition, pp. 4401–4410 (2019)

48. Ren, Y., Li, G., Chen, Y., et al.: Pirenderer: controllable portrait image generation via semantic neural rendering. In: Proceedings of the IEEE/CVF International Conference on Computer Vision, pp. 13759–13768 (2021)

49. Huang, S., Liu, X., Tan, T., et al.: TransMRSR: transformer-based self-distilled generative prior for brain MRI super-resolution. arXiv preprint arXiv:2306.06669 (2023)

50. Li, K., Guo, D., Wang, M.: ViGT: proposal-free video grounding with a learnable token in the transformer. Sci. China Inf. Sci. **66**(10), 202102 (2023)

51. Shen, S., Li, W., Zhu, Z., et al.: Learning dynamic facial radiance fields for few-shot talking head synthesis. In: European Conference on Computer Vision, pp. 666–682. Springer, Cham (2022)

52. Li, W., Wang, Z., Mai, R., et al.: Modular design automation of the morphologies, controllers, and vision systems for intelligent robots: a survey. Visual Intell. **1**(1), 2 (2023)

53. Zhang, Z., Li, L., Ding, Y., et al.: Flow-guided one-shot talking face generation with a high-resolution audio-visual dataset. In: Proceedings of the IEEE/CVF Conference on Computer Vision and Pattern Recognition, pp. 3661–3670 (2021)

54. Yin, G., Jiang, X., Jiang, S., et al.: Online video streaming super-resolution with adaptive look-up table fusion. arXiv preprint arXiv:2303.00334 (2023)

55. Wu, G., Liu, X., Luo, K., et al.: Accflow: backward accumulation for long-range optical flow. In: Proceedings of the IEEE/CVF International Conference on Computer Vision, pp. 12119–12128 (2023)

56. Wei, B., Wen, Y., Liu, X., et al.: SOFNet: optical-flow based large-scale slice augmentation of brain MRI. Displays **80**, 102536 (2023)

57. Zhou, Z., Meng, M., Zhou, Y., et al.: Model-guided 3D stitching for augmented virtual environment. Sci. China Inf. Sci. **66**(1), 112106 (2023)

Fast QTMT Decision for H.266/VVC via Jointly Leveraging Neural Network and Machine Learning Models

Gongchun Ding⬡, Xiujun Lin⬡, Wenyu Wang⬡, and Dandan Ding$^{(\boxtimes)}$⬡

Hangzhou Normal University, Hangzhou, China
DandanDing@hznu.edu.cn

Abstract. The latest video coding standard H.266/VVC has significantly improved the compression efficiency compared to its predecessor H.265/HEVC. One of the key technologies in H.266/VVC is the QuadTree with nested Multi-type Tree (QTMT), which enhances the coding performance at the cost of increased time complexity. To accelerate the QTMT partitioning process while mitigating performance degradation, this paper models the Coding Unit (CU) partition as a hierarchical decision process and jointly leverages machine learning (ML) and neural network (NN) models for fast CU partition. Specifically, for large-size CUs, we devise an NN model to predict the probability of each candidate partition mode automatically; to further accelerate the above process, we additionally embed an ML algorithm before the NN model, for the fast determination of binary-tree horizontal (BTH) mode, a commonly-used mode in H.266/VVC. On the other hand, for small-size CUs, the neural model is inadequate due to the insufficient pixels for correlation exploration. We thus directly apply the ML model for early terminating the horizontal or vertical partition of each CU. We exemplify the proposed method using typical ML models such as Support Vector Machine (SVM) and Decision Tree (DT) and an NN model of 3.7 MB model size. Experimental results demonstrate that the proposed method achieves 45.04% encoding time reduction over the H.266/VVC reference software VTM-15.0 with only 1.01% BD-BR increase, which remarkably outperforms state-of-the-art works.

Keywords: H.266/VVC · Intra coding · Fast CU partition · Machine learning · Deep learning

1 Introduction

With the prevalence of various video-related applications, such as telemedicine, video conferencing, and short videos, and the increasing demand for higher video resolutions, such as 4K, 8K, and even gigapixel video [1], the video coding community faces substantial challenges to further improve compression efficiency.

Supported by National Natural Science Foundation of China (62171174).

To this end, in July 2020, international standardization committees released the new video compression standard—Versatile Video Coding (H.266/VVC) [2], as a successor of High Efficiency Video Coding (H.265/HEVC) [3].

H.266/VVC offers around 40% BD-BR saving over H.265/HEVC at the expense of a notable increase in computational complexity. Particularly in intra frame coding, H.266/VVC takes 25 times longer than H.265/HEVC [4]. This occurs mainly due to the complex Coding Unit (CU) partition process of H.266/VVC. Specifically, unlike H.265/HEVC which has only quadtree partition, H.266/VVC supports not only quadtree but also horizontal/vertical binary tree and ternary tree partition [5], so-called QuadTree with nested Multi-type Tree (QTMT). This QTMT partition has proven to be one of the most effective tools in H.266/VVC, while its computation complexity is expensive. As shown in Fig. 1, in each layer of the partitioning process, the encoder traverses a maximum of five partitioning modes, including Quad-Tree (QT) splitting, Binary-Tree Vertical (BTV) splitting, Binary-Tree Horizontal (BTH) splitting, Ternary-Tree Vertical (TTV) splitting, and Ternary-Tree Horizontal (TTH) splitting. Previous studies have revealed that disabling binary and ternary tree partitioning can reduce the encoding time by 91.7% under the All Intra configuration of H.266/VVC [6], and testing only one partition at each layer of intra partition process can reduce the encoding time by 97.5% compared to the exhaustive search [7]. As seen, the computational complexity can be significantly reduced by adequately terminating certain partitions. Meanwhile, the coding efficiency is expected to be maintained as much as possible.

A great many works have been devoted to the fast partition problem, using threshold-based algorithm [8–11], Bayesian algorithm [12], machine learning (ML)-based models [13–16], etc. At early times, Tang et al. [8] applied a block-level Canny edge detector to extract edge features and early terminated the partition when the texture within a CU was sufficiently uniform. Liu et al. [17] employed the Scharr edge gradient operator algorithm to describe texture information and set thresholds based on the relationship between texture features and CU partitioning modes. Later, Bayesian classification was introduced, e.g., Zhang et al. [12] utilized the coding information of upper and left CUs as features to calculate the partition probability of current CU. Afterward, ML-based algorithms were widely used with decent performance. Representative algorithms included Chen et al. [18], Yang et al. [14] etc., which treated the recursive CU partition as a hierarchical binary classification problem and used Support Vector Machine (SVM) or Decision Tree (DT) to resolve it.

Recently, Neural Networks (NNs) have also been used to solve the fast CU partition problem and achieved superior performance. For instance, Tissier et al. [19] employed a Convolutional Neural Network (CNN) to predict a set of probability vectors corresponding to the partition probabilities of 4×4 unit boundaries within a 64×64 CU and obtained state-of-the-art performance. Essentially, both ML-based and NN-based models are learning-based methods. ML-based methods, such as SVM and DT, usually model the CU partition as a binary classification problem and utilize manually extracted features for resolution,

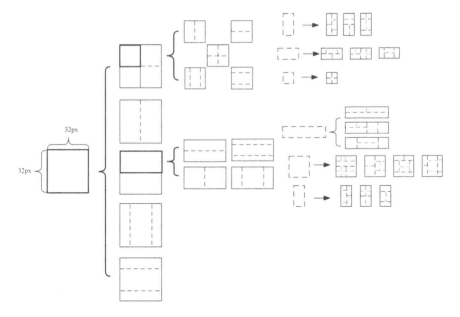

Fig. 1. Recursive Division of 32 × 32 CU. Black, red, and green dotted lines indicate further partition of various CUs. (Color figure online)

which obtain decent performance at low cost. By contrast, NN-based models intelligently extract features from raw pixels, without relying on traditional feature extractors, and usually lead to more precise results. Nevertheless, NN-based models, particularly for large-scale models, require powerful platforms for running, which is unaffordable for practical applications. On the other hand, the effectiveness of NN models is decreased at small-size CUs due to the limited receptive field and insufficient pixels for correlation exploration.

To this end, this paper proposes to take advantage of both ML-based and NN-based models, forming a joint solution to accelerate the CU partition process of H.266/VVC. Specifically, for small-size CUs, we apply an ML model to determine the partition direction of a CU, to skip other candidate partitions; otherwise, we first utilize a lightweight ML model to judge whether the current CU is BTH (often selected in H.266/VVC), and then apply a NN model to predict the probabilities of all candidate modes in a shot. Such a joint utilization of learning-based methods fully exploits the partition characteristics of H.266/VVC and achieves superior performance.

The main contributions of this work are summarized below.

– We propose a learning-based solution that jointly leverages ML and NN models to accelerate the intra QTMT partition of H.266/VVC. Based on the CU size and partition distribution, we model the CU partition process as a hierarchical decision task and develop different models to fasten the decision.

- For large CUs, we first develop an ML model for the early termination of BTH mode due to its high-frequency use in H.266/VVC. Subsequently, a lightweight NN model is devised to predict the probabilities of all candidate modes in a shot. Due to the invalidity of the NN model in small CUs, we specifically apply an ML model to skip horizontal or vertical candidate partitions for small CUs.
- Extensive experimental results confirm the effectiveness of our method. It achieves 45.04% time saving over the reference software of H.266/VVC with only 1.01% BD-BR loss, significantly outperforming state-of-the-art works.

2   Related Works

In the past decades, fast intra CU partition has attracted extensive attention. Associated works can be broadly categorized into three types: statistics-based methods, machine learning-based methods, and deep learning-based methods.

The fundamental idea behind **statistics-based algorithms** [8–10,20,21] is to skip certain partition modes during the encoding process based on a statistical analysis of spatial correlations. These algorithms are computationally lightweight and quite effective in H.265/HEVC which has only quadtree partition, but on the other hand, they heavily rely on prior statistical information. As a result, they are unable to dynamically adjust with video variations and suffer in complex partition scenarios, e.g., in H.266/VVC.

Machine Learning-Based Algorithms [11,13,14,22,23] can make decisions rapidly. Commonly used ML models include SVM, DT, etc. Generally, uniform regions in a frame tend to employ large blocks for encoding, while regions with fine textures tend to use small blocks. Inspired by this point, Liu *et al.* [11] employed SVM to classify CUs into three categories: homogeneous, complex, or uncertain, and different strategies were applied to each category: for homogeneous CUs, the partition process is terminated directly; for complex CUs, it directly moved to the next depth; for uncertain CUs, they were processed with the default encoding process of H.265/HEVC. As for H.266/VVC, Chen *et al.* [13] modeled the CU partition as a binary classification problem and selected three features including entropy, texture contrast, and Haar wavelet to train an SVM model for fast partition. Yang *et al.* [14] categorized the QTMT partition as a hierarchical binary classification problem and used five DT classifiers to make decisions.

Overall, ML-based methods can obtain decent performance with low complexity. However, such performance relies largely on manually selected features. Although using more features may receive better results, the computational complexity is also increased.

Neural Network-Based Algorithms [19,24–28] have been introduced to address CU partition issues of H.266/VVC recent years. On the one hand, NN-based methods can automatically extract features from video frames. On the other hand, NN models can treat the CU partition as a multi-classification problem and predict the probabilities of various partition modes for the current CU in a shot, effectively mitigating the error propagation and accumulation in the decision.

Tissier *et al.* [19] first designed a CNN model to predict the partition information of each 4×4 boundary in a 64×64 CU, and then used this information to train a LightGBM classifier to derive the final partition results. However, this approach requires the information of adjacent reconstructed CUs, hindering parallel implementation in both encoding and decoding. Zhang *et al.* [24] proposed a Global Convolutional Network (GCN) to predict partition probabilities of all candidate modes in a CU. Li *et al.* [25] developed a Multi-Stage Exiting CNN structure (MSE-CNN) and a multi-threshold decision scheme to predict the partition for each 128×128 block. Later, Feng *et al.* [26] represented block partition structures in the form of partition graphs and trained CNN models to predict optimal partition mapping. Instead, Peng *et al.* [27] used partition homogeneity maps to represent the partition structure.

As seen, most previous works apply the NN models to large CUs, such as 64×64 CUs and 128×128 CUs. For small CUs having limited receptive field, NN models are invalid due to the insufficient exploration of pixel correlations.

3   Proposed Method

This section introduces the framework of our proposed method, as illustrated in Fig. 2. The proposed method models the CU partition as a hierarchical decision process and jointly leverages ML and NN models to resolve it. More specifically,

- For high-level CUs, such as large CUs of size 32×32, 32×16, and 16×32, since the BTH mode has a high probability to be selected [22], we first apply an ML model, such as DT, to determine the use of BTH or not. If BTH is selected, the other candidate modes will be all skipped, resulting in significant time savings.
- Otherwise, an NN model is devised to predict the probabilities of all candidate modes of the current CU in a shot, generating a set of probability vectors, corresponding to the six partition modes. Based on predefined thresholds, we select the partition modes with higher probabilities for further processing.
- Instead, for low-level CUs, such as CUs of size 16×8 and 8×16, we directly employ the ML model to skip horizontal or vertical partitions. The NN model is no longer applied because 1) it fails to effectively exploit pixel correlations for probability prediction in these small CUs and 2) it is time-consuming to apply the NN model for small CUs, leading to limited time reduction.

3.1   ML-Based Model

The determination of BTH mode is basically a binary classification problem: BTH partition or non-BTH partition. We train a DT model, which is a tree-structured decision model widely utilized in classification problems, to solve it. Meanwhile, for the determination of the horizontal or vertical direction of small

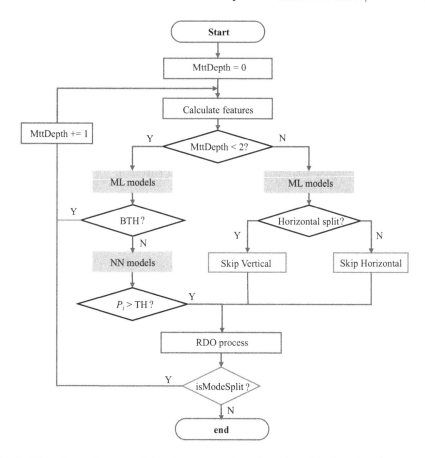

Fig. 2. Flowchart of proposed fast intra partition algorithm. ML-based and NN-based models are jointly utilized to hierarchically early terminate the intra CU partition of H.266/VVC.

CUs, we use SVM instead of DT because the tree structure decision in DT easily leads to error propagation and accumulation, which severely degrades coding performance. Nonetheless, both DT and SVM use the same features, which are detailed below.

Variance. The variance of an image refers to the measure of how much the pixel values in the image deviate from their mean value. It quantifies the spread or dispersion of pixel values in the image. A higher variance indicates that pixel values are far away from the mean. On the other hand, a lower variance implies that pixel values are closer to the mean, indicating a more uniform or less complex image.

$$Var = \frac{1}{H \times W} \sum_{i=0}^{H-1} \sum_{j=0}^{W-1} (x_{ij} - \bar{x})^2, \tag{1}$$

where $\bar{x}$ is the average value of all pixels in a sub-CU. H and W represent the height and width of the sub-CU, respectively. Here, we calculate the variance difference across sub-CUs with horizontal and vertical partitions. We separately compute the eigenvalues of each sub-CU under horizontal and vertical partitions. If a CU is split horizontally, its up and down parts are usually more different than its left and right parts. To this end, we can use the eigenvalues of up and down parts, or left and right parts, to predict whether the two parts have significant differences or not.

Let ΔV_b represent the variance difference of binary splitting and ΔV_t represent that of ternary splitting. They are obtained through:

$$\Delta V_b = \left| V_{bth\_0} - V_{bth\_1} \right| - \left| V_{btv\_0} - V_{btv\_1} \right| \tag{2}$$

and

$$\Delta V_t = \left| V_{tth\_0} - V_{tth\_1} \right| + \left| V_{tth\_1} - V_{tth\_2} \right| \\ - \left| V_{ttv\_0} - V_{ttv\_1} \right| - \left| V_{ttv\_1} - V_{ttv\_2} \right|. \tag{3}$$

Entropy. The entropy of an image represents the amount of information or randomness in the image. It provides insight into the level of complexity or disorder in the image. Higher entropy values indicate that the pixel values are more varied and unpredictable, while lower entropy values suggest that pixel values are more uniform, which is calculated by

$$E_k = -\sum_{i=0}^{255} p(i) \log p(i), \tag{4}$$

where $p(i)$ represents the possibility of ith grayscale. Similarly to ΔV_b and ΔV_t, ΔE_b and ΔE_t are also calculated across sub-CUs.

Contrast. The contrast of an image is a measure of the difference in brightness or color between various parts of the image. Images with higher contrast have more differences in color or brightness between pixels. In this regard, we propose to incorporate the contrast feature as follows:

$$C = \sum_{\delta} \delta(i,j)^2 P_\delta(i,j), \tag{5}$$

where $\delta(i,j) = |i-j|$ represents the degree of difference between adjacent pixels, and $P_\delta(i,j)$ represents the distribution probability of pixels with degree difference δ. Accordingly, ΔC_b and ΔC_t are calculated in a similar way to Eq. (2) and Eq. (3).

Gradient. Gradient is a feature closely related to CU partition, which is widely used in fast encoding algorithms [29]. The Sobel operator is used to calculate the gradient. Corresponding calculation methods of gradients in the vertical direction (G_x) and horizontal direction (G_y) are as follows:

Defining

$$S_x = \begin{bmatrix} -1 & 0 & +1 \\ -2 & 0 & +2 \\ -1 & 0 & +1 \end{bmatrix} \tag{6}$$

and

$$S_y = \begin{bmatrix} +1 & +2 & +1 \\ 0 & 0 & 0 \\ -1 & -2 & -1 \end{bmatrix}, \tag{7}$$

we can compute

$$G_x = \sum_{i=1}^{H} \sum_{j=1}^{W} L \times S_x \tag{8}$$

and

$$G_y = \sum_{i=1}^{H} \sum_{j=1}^{W} L \times S_y, \tag{9}$$

where S_x and S_y represent Sobel operators in the horizontal and vertical directions, respectively. W and H represent the width and height of the current CU, and L denotes the luminance matrix of the current pixel. Finally, gradients (G_x/G_y) and information regarding the CU's dimensions (width and height) are included in the feature set.

3.2   NN-Based Model

The CU partition results are basically affected by a series of factors like Quantization Parameters (QPs), video textures, etc. In contrast to ML models that require explicit features, NN models derive features directly from the input data, based on which probabilities of various candidate modes can be produced. This paper thus devises a lightweight NN model to deal with large CUs.

Model Structure. The structure of our NN model is presented in Fig. 3a. The NN model is built on top of the residual network [30]. It inputs the original CU and outputs a series of probabilities of the candidate partition modes. The main body of this NN model uses three residual blocks for feature extraction and a SENet block [31] for channel correlation exploration. Afterward, the NN model goes through three convolutional layers, a Rectified Linear Unit (ReLU) activation, and a fully connected operation to translate the obtained features into classification results. The Softmax function is employed to convert these results into a probability distribution.

Loss Function. In light of the non-uniform distribution of training samples, where the ternary-tree partition is significantly less than the binary-tree partition, an additional penalty term is introduced into the cross-entropy loss function to improve the model's robustness, which is defined as

$$
L = -\frac{\sum_{n=1}^{N}\left(\frac{1}{p_m}\right)^{x} \cdot \sum_{m\in\mathcal{M}} y_{n,m}\log\left(\hat{y}_{n,m}\right)}{\sum_{n=1}^{N}\left(\frac{1}{p_m}\right)^{x}}, \tag{10}
$$

where $y_{n,m}$ and $\hat{y}_{n,m}$ represent the ground-truth binary label and predicted probability for the nth CU at split mode m. Due to the highly imbalanced proportions for various CU partition modes, for example, the ternary-tree partition is much less than the binary-tree partition, we set a weight p_m on them. x is an adjustable scalar used to determine the importance of penalty weights: the larger the value of x, the larger the penalty. In our experiments, we set $x = 0.3$.

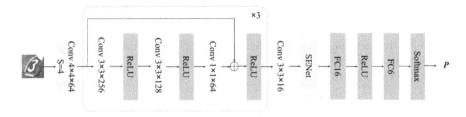

(a) structure of the proposed NN model

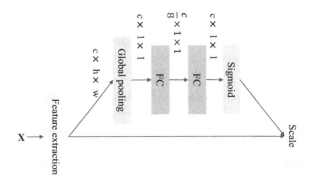

(b) structure of SENet

Fig. 3. Architecture of the proposed NN model. It stacks residual blocks and SENet to extract features from input CUs and generates probabilities of candidate partition modes.

Post-processing. By providing the luminance data of each CU to the proposed NN model, a collection of probability vectors is generated. These vectors correspond to the likelihood of each partitioning mode. Subsequently, a decision is made to retain the modes associated with high probabilities and exclude those with low probabilities. In this way, we effectively reduce the R-D computations. To accommodate various CU levels, distinct thresholds are set as follows:

- The probabilities derived from the NN model are sorted in descending order, with P_k representing the probability of the Kth most probable mode. If $P_1 > \alpha$, the mode with the highest probability is unambiguously selected as the partitioning mode. As illustrated in Fig. 4a, when β is set as 0.15, the results indicate that as α increases, BD-BR loss decreases with time savings, until reaching $\alpha = 0.65$. To this end, α is set as 0.65.
- If $P_1 \leq \alpha$, partition modes with probabilities less than β are omitted, retaining only the top-3 modes. As visualized in Fig. 4b, when α is set as 0.65, enlarging the value of β tends to yield an increase in BD-BR and time savings. In this work, we set $\beta = 0.15$ to maintain our BD-BR performance.

4   Experiments and Results

This section details the experimental settings and compares the results of our proposed method with state-of-the-art works.

Settings . We used the DIV2K dataset [32] which consists of 1000 high-resolution images for training and video sequences officially recommended by the international standardization committee for performance evaluation. These sequences are divided into four categories: Class B (1920×1080), Class C (832×480), Class D (416×240), and Class E (1280×720). Our experiments were performed under the All Intra configuration of the H.266/VVC reference software version 15.0 (VTM-15.0). The hardware platform has an Intel(R) Core(TM) i7-9700K CPU and 2080Ti GPU. Each model was trained for 100k iterations with a batch size of 64, using the Adam optimizer and a learning rate set to 10^{-4}. We use Bjøntegaard Delta Bit Rate (BD-BR) to evaluate the coding performance. Regarding the coding complexity, we define the time reduction (TR) as:

$$TR(\%) = \frac{T_r(i) - T_p(i)}{T_r(i)} \times 100\%, \tag{11}$$

where $T_r(i)$ and $T_p(i)$ represent the total encoding time of the anchor VTM-15.0 encoder and the proposed algorithm, respectively.

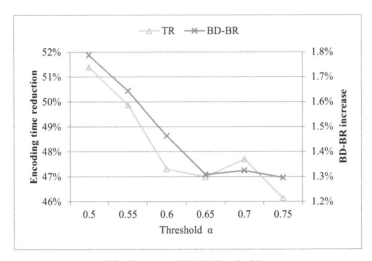

(a) selection of high threshold α

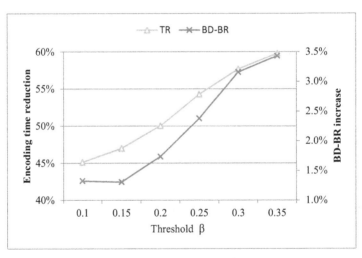

(b) selection of low threshold β

Fig. 4. Coding performance and time saving under different high thresholds α and low thresholds β.

Table 1. Coding performance and run time comparison to state-of-the-art CU partition algorithms over VTM-15.0

Class	He et al. [15]		Chen et al. [13]		Yang et al. [14]		Tissier et al. [7]		Proposed	
	BD-BR	TR	BD-BR	TR	BD-BR	TR	BD-BR	TR	BD-BR	TR
B	0.69%	35.58%	1.52%	55.40%	3.80%	63.43%	1.41%	61.00%	1.00%	50.30%
C	0.91%	23.82%	2.19%	59.00%	2.86%	57.12%	1.20%	37.90%	0.94%	41.10%
D	0.78%	24.13%	1.76%	56.70%	2.15%	54.66%	0.83%	32.50%	0.76%	40.60%
E	1.33%	24.13%	2.47%	56.50%	3.64%	61.86%	2.29%	54.40%	1.46%	47.50%
Average	**0.89%**	**27.59%**	**1.92%**	**56.90%**	**3.12%**	**59.36%**	**1.43%**	**46.5%**	**1.01%**	**45.04%**

Results . Table 1 compares the performance of the proposed approach and state-of-the-art fast CU partition methods [7,13–15]. As shown, the proposed method outperforms most existing works with much less BD-BR increase. For example, in comparison to Tissier *et al.* [7], our method saves almost the same time (45.04% vs. 46.50%) with less BD-BR loss (1.01% vs. 1.43%). Although Yang *et al.* [14] and Chen *et al.* [13] attain much more time saving (56.90% and 59.36%), their BD-BR loss are too large (1.92% and 3.12%), which is unacceptable to many applications. We next give an in-depth analysis of these compared methods.

He *et al.* [15] introduced a classification scheme for fast partition based on the texture complexity of CUs and eventually categorized CUs into three groups: simple, complex, and ambiguous. For the simple and complex CUs, they developed a Random Forest (RF) classifier to directly predict the optimal partitioning mode. In contrast, for ambiguous CUs, another RF classifier was trained to predict whether the partitioning should be prematurely terminated. This strategy led to a reduction of 27.59% in encoding time and a 0.89% increase in BD-BR loss. It is clear that its time saving is very limited. Yang *et al.* [14] analyzed the global information, local information, and context information of CU and trained multiple binary DT models to bypass certain partitions, resulting in a remarkable 59.36% reduction in time complexity. Nevertheless, their performance is largely limited by the handcrafted features, which induced a noticeable performance degradation. Chen *et al.* [13] also employed SVM for CU partitioning, utilizing features such as entropy, contrast, and Haar-like features as inputs to predict the CU partitioning direction. Despite attaining a 56.90% reduction in encoding time, this approach incurred 1.92% BD-BR increase.

Instead of using ML models, Tissier *et al.* [7] designed an NN model to predict CU partition structures. For each 64×64 CU, the NN model generated a probability vector corresponding to the boundaries of each 4×4 unit within the CU. Subsequently, the partitioning mode for each sub-CU was determined using a predefined threshold. Although this approach achieved a time complexity reduction comparable to our method, it was accompanied by another 0.42% increase in BD-BR.

Overall, the proposed method achieves a decent trade-off between encoding time saving and BD-BR loss, which is attractive to practical applications.

5   Conclusion

This paper presents a fast intra partition algorithm that jointly leverages machine-learning models and neural network models. After analyzing the recursive CU partition process in H.266/VVC, we model the partition problem as a hierarchical decision procedure and devise different strategies to tackle it. For small CUs which has a limited number of pixels for local correlation exploration, we directly apply the machine learning model for decision. Otherwise, we apply a neural model to predict the probabilities of all candidate modes of a CU in a shot. Particularly, recognizing that the BTH mode is widely selected in H.266/VVC, we insert another machine learning model to early terminate the BTH mode for efficient processing. Extensive experiments in the sequences defined in MPEG common test condition demonstrate the advancement of the proposed algorithm: it achieves 45% time saving compared with the anchor H.266/VVC with only 1.01% BD-BR loss, which well balances the trade-off between the time reduction and coding performance loss and is attractive to practical applications.

References

1. Brady, D.J., et al.: Multiscale gigapixel photography. Nature **486**(7403), 386–389 (2012)
2. Bross, B., et al.: Overview of the versatile video coding (VVC) standard and its applications. IEEE Trans. Circuits Syst. Video Technol. **31**(10), 3736–3764 (2021)
3. Sullivan, G.J., Ohm, J.-R., Han, W.-J., Wiegand, T.: Overview of the high efficiency video coding (HEVC) standard. IEEE Trans. Circuits Syst. Video Technol. **22**(12), 1649–1668 (2012)
4. François, E., et al.: VVC per-tool performance evaluation compared to HEVC. In: IBC (2020)
5. Huang, Y.-W., et al.: Block partitioning structure in the VVC standard. IEEE Trans. Circuits Syst. Video Technol. **31**(10), 3818–3833 (2021)
6. Saldanha, M., Sanchez, G., Marcon, C., Agostini, L.: Complexity analysis of VVC intra coding. In: 2020 IEEE International Conference on Image Processing (ICIP), pp. 3119–3123. IEEE (2020)
7. Tissier, A., Hamidouche, W., Vanne, J., Galpin, F., Menard, D.: CNN oriented complexity reduction of VVC intra encoder. In: 2020 IEEE International Conference on Image Processing (ICIP), pp. 3139–3143. IEEE (2020)
8. Tang, N., et al.: Fast CTU partition decision algorithm for VVC intra and inter coding. In: 2019 IEEE Asia Pacific Conference on Circuits and Systems (APCCAS), pp. 361–364. IEEE (2019)
9. Song, Y., Zeng, B., Wang, M., Deng, Z.: An efficient low-complexity block partition scheme for VVC intra coding. J. Real-Time Image Process. 1–12 (2022)
10. Fan, Y., Sun, H., Katto, J., Ming, J., et al.: A fast GTMT partition decision strategy for VVC intra prediction. IEEE Access **8**, 107900–107911 (2020)
11. Liu, D., Liu, X., Li, Y.: Fast CU size decisions for HEVC intra frame coding based on support vector machines. In: 2016 IEEE 14th International Conference on Dependable, Autonomic and Secure Computing, 14th International Conference on Pervasive Intelligence and Computing, 2nd International Conference on Big Data Intelligence and Computing and Cyber Science and Technology Congress (DASC/PiCom/DataCom/CyberSciTech), pp. 594–597. IEEE (2016)

12. Zhang, Q., Cui, T., Huang, L., Jiang, B., Zhao, J.: Low-complexity intra coding scheme based on Bayesian and l-BFGS for VVC. Digit. Signal Process. **127**, 103539 (2022)

13. Chen, F., Ren, Y., Peng, Z., Jiang, G., Cui, X.: A fast CU size decision algorithm for VVC intra prediction based on support vector machine. Multim. Tools Appl. **79**, 27923–27939 (2020)

14. Yang, H., Shen, L., Dong, X., Ding, Q., An, P., Jiang, G.: Low-complexity CTU partition structure decision and fast intra mode decision for versatile video coding. IEEE Trans. Circuits Syst. Video Technol. **30**(6), 1668–1682 (2019)

15. He, Q., Wu, W., Luo, L., Zhu, C., Guo, H.: Random forest based fast cu partition for VVC intra coding. In: 2021 IEEE International Symposium on Broadband Multimedia Systems and Broadcasting (BMSB), pp. 1–4. IEEE (2021)

16. Amestoy, T., Mercat, A., Hamidouche, W., Menard, D., Bergeron, C.: Tunable VVC frame partitioning based on lightweight machine learning. IEEE Trans. Image Process. **29**, 1313–1328 (2019)

17. Liu, L., Yang, J.: An adaptive cu split method for VVC intra encoding. Int. J. Inf. Technol. Syst. Approach **16**(2), 1–17 (2022)

18. Zhu, L., Zhang, Y., Pan, Z., Wang, R., Kwong, S., Peng, Z.: Binary and multiclass learning based low complexity optimization for hevc encoding. IEEE Trans. Broadcast. **63**(3), 547–561 (2017)

19. Tissier, A., Hamidouche, W., Mdalsi, S.B.D., Vanne, J., Galpin, F., Menard, D.: Machine learning based efficient GT-MTT partitioning scheme for VVC intra encoders. IEEE Trans. Circuits Syst. Video Technol. (2023)

20. Cui, J., Zhang, T., Gu, C., Zhang, X., Ma, S.: Gradient-based early termination of CU partition in VVC intra coding. In: 2020 Data Compression Conference (DCC), pp. 103–112. IEEE (2020)

21. Wang, Z., Wang, S., Zhang, J., Wang, S., Ma, S.: Probabilistic decision based block partitioning for future video coding. IEEE Trans. Image Process. **27**(3), 1475–1486 (2017)

22. Wu, G., Huang, Y., Zhu, C., Song, L., Zhang, W.: SVM based fast cu partitioning algorithm for VVC intra coding. In: 2021 IEEE International Symposium on Circuits and Systems (ISCAS), pp. 1–5. IEEE (2021)

23. Wang, Z., Wang, S., Zhang, J., Wang, S., Ma, S.: Effective quadtree plus binary tree block partition decision for future video coding. In: 2017 Data Compression Conference (DCC), pp. 23–32. IEEE (2017)

24. Zhang, S., Feng, S., Chen, J., Zhou, C., Yang, F.: A GCN-based fast cu partition method of intra-mode VVC. J. Vis. Commun. Image Represent. **88**, 103621 (2022)

25. Li, T., Xu, M., Tang, R., Chen, Y., Xing, Q.: Deepqtmt: a deep learning approach for fast QTMT-based CU partition of intra-mode VVC. IEEE Trans. Image Process. **30**, 5377–5390 (2021)

26. Feng, A., Liu, K., Liu, D., Li, L., Wu, F.: Partition map prediction for fast block partitioning in VVC intra-frame coding. IEEE Transactions on Image Processing (2023)

27. Peng, Z., Shen, L., Ding, Q., Dong, X., Zheng, L.: Block-dependent partition decision for fast intra coding of VVC. IEEE Trans. Consum. Electron. (2023)

28. Zhao, T., Huang, Y., Feng, W., Xu, Y., Kwong, S.: Efficient VVC intra prediction based on deep feature fusion and probability estimation. IEEE Trans. Multim. (2022)

29. Wen, S., Ding, G., Ding, D.: Paired decision trees for fast intra decision in h. 266/VVC. Displays **80**, 102545 (2023)

30. He, K., Zhang, X., Ren, S., Sun, J.: Deep residual learning for image recognition. In: Proceedings of the IEEE Conference on Computer Vision and Pattern Recognition, pp. 770–778 (2016)

31. Hu, J, Shen, L., Sun, G.: Squeeze-and-excitation networks. In: Proceedings of the IEEE Conference on Computer Vision and Pattern Recognition, pp. 7132–7141 (2018)

32. Agustsson, E., Timofte, R.: Ntire 2017 challenge on single image superresolution: dataset and study. In: Proceedings of the IEEE Conference on Computer Vision and Pattern Recognition Workshops, pp. 126–135 (2017)

End-to-End Image Compression Through Machine Semantics

Jianran Liu[1,2], Chang Zhang[1,2], and Wen Ji[1,3(✉)]

[1] Institute of Computing Technology, Chinese Academy of Sciences, Beijing, China
`jiwen@ict.ac.cn`
[2] University of Chinese Academy of Sciences, Beijing, China
[3] Peng Cheng Laboratory, Shenzhen, China

Abstract. With the increasing demand for AI automated analysis, machine semantics have replaced signals as a new focus in visual information compression. In this paper, we propose a novel end-to-end machine semantic information compression method. To better align machine semantics with tasks, we jointly optimize the entire process of semantic extraction, compression, and inference. Additionally, we introduce a dedicated activation function called StairReLU for machine semantic compression. StairReLU considers the non-linearity in neural networks and quantization in data compression as the same problem, enabling machines to adapt to semantic representations with lower information entropy during the training process. Finally, we conduct end-to-end machine semantic compression experiments on three different datasets. The results demonstrate the superiority of our proposed approach over traditional compression coding methods and incomplete end-to-end compression methods in terms of the trade-off between bit rate and quality.

Keywords: Machine semantics · End-to-end compression · Activation function

1 Introduction

In the era of interconnected big data, a large amount of information is processed by machines. For example, in the context of smart cities [1], extensive surveillance systems continuously collect visual data 24/7, resulting in a massive daily influx of data that needs to be analyzed promptly. In industrial Internet of Things scenarios, to enhance efficiency, ultra-high frame rate capture techniques are employed, capturing billions of frames of information per second [2], which

This work is supported by the National Natural Science Foundation of China (62072440), and the National Key R&D Program of China (2022YFF0902403, 2022YFE0125400, 2023YFB4502805), and the Beijing Natural Science Foundation (L221004).

also generates a significant amount of visual data. These scenarios require low latency and high accuracy, posing challenges for visual data compression and encoding. Traditional hybrid video encoders, developed over several decades, have achieved significant compression of raw visual data, approximately 600 times, while ensuring imperceptible distortion to the human eye, based on the visual signal statistics and the human visual system, with existing standards such as H.266/VVC [3] and AVS3 [4].

However, faced with the rapid growth of visual information and data to be analyzed [5], traditional visual signal compression and encoding methods can no longer meet the demands. Many advancements in visual information compression and encoding systems are based on the classic theories of Claude Shannon in information theory [6], which considers communication systems as transmission pipelines. In these systems, data is collected at the source and then reconstructed at the destination to ensure the most accurate reception of symbols. As we enter the era of "connected intelligence" [7], widely deployed terminal devices generate a large amount of visual data, which is analyzed using AI algorithms for visual task-related analysis. This AI-driven application presents new opportunities for the design of semantic communication systems, leading to a shift from "semantic neutrality" to the need for communication centered around machine semantics [8–10]. Therefore, in specific tasks, extracting machine semantic information from the source and receiving it at the destination for decision-making can significantly improve the efficiency of information transmission.

In this paper, we propose a machine semantic compression method targeting increasingly distributed machine intelligence services and Machine-to-Machine (M2M) application scenarios. Firstly, we introduce an end-to-end machine semantic compression approach. Unlike existing two-stage methods that separate semantic information extraction-compression and machine task inference into two independent stages, our proposed method treats the extraction-compression of semantic information and machine task inference as a complete process and conducts end-to-end training, specifically tailored for visual tasks. Secondly, end-to-end machine semantic compression is often based on a multi-objective joint optimization approach considering rate-task accuracy trade-offs. In the design of the objective function, this paper avoids using abstract trade-off parameters to balance task accuracy losses and rates across different dimensions, enabling more targeted optimization of rate-accuracy distortion in practical network environments. Finally, we propose a coarse-grained activation function called Stair-ReLU that is adapted for the aforementioned end-to-end training process. Stair-ReLU transforms the concept of quantization in traditional image/video compression encoding into an expression of the activation function, allowing for a low-information-entropy data for machine task output. Specifically, the activation function primarily serves as a means to guide machine perception of input data through non-linearization, thereby enhancing the machine's understanding of compacted data.

2   Related Works

2.1   Machine Semantic-Aware Image/Video Compression

This category of methods is typically designed for specific machine vision tasks or a few specific tasks, aiming to highlight machine semantic information in the reconstruction based on pixel-level information. Duan et al. [11] have previously proposed a paradigm of machine semantic compression, which combines distortion of images/videos with multiple task accuracy losses to construct a collaborative optimization objective. Particularly, thanks to the ability of end-to-end deep learning-based encoder-decoders to customize loss/objective functions, task-specific loss functions, and encoding/decoding-related loss functions are weighted and combined to form a hybrid-driven loss [12–14]. During the training process, the upstream encoder-decoder and downstream tasks are jointly trained to achieve a balance between machine vision and human vision. Additionally, in some end-to-end methods, incorporating additional loss terms into the loss function can achieve rate-distortion optimization. For example, [15] introduced a perceptual loss term in the loss function to optimize the latent representation of end-to-end learned image encoding [16] and utilized maximum mean discrepancy (MMD) in the loss term to minimize the difference between feature distributions, thereby ensuring consistency with downstream tasks at the feature level.

Machine semantic-aware image/video compression methods typically exhibit strong specificity and can achieve strong task accuracy performance in specific networks or tasks [17]. In summary, the objectives followed by the aforementioned works can be summarized as:

$$\mathcal{L} = R + \lambda_0 D + \sum_{i=1}^{n} \lambda_i L_i, \tag{1}$$

where R represents the total bitrate of the machine semantic signal, D represents the loss of task accuracy and L represents the reconstruction loss of multiple features, $\lambda_i (i = 0, 1, \cdots, n)$ represents the trade-off parameter, which is used to equalize the importance between the items in the loss term. The choice of λ has a great influence on the final optimization result. For the different dimensions of R, D, and L, the trade-off using λ is a matter of patience.

2.2   Machine Semantic Compression Around Features

Due to differences in understanding features, compression encoding methods in machine compression can be divided into two types:

The first type utilizes extracted features to guide compression encoding by treating features as side information and adjusting the encoder and decoder accordingly. Wang et al. [18] considered the semantic segmentation map of a video as feature-guided video coding using H.265/HEVC [19]. This method preserves the main content of the image at extremely low bitrates. Sun et al. [20] identified objects in the field of view before encoding and encoding them individually, resulting in a structured bitstream. These methods primarily focus on

tasks related to the position of objects in the field of view and effectively eliminate irrelevant redundancy unrelated to video semantics. In [21], a region of
interest (RoI) based method is proposed, which delves into the internal encoding process and reassigns CTUs (Coding Tree Units) based on their importance
to the task. This type of method is driven by the "target" in visual information,
highlighting spatial regions with rich semantic information and carrying machine
vision-related semantic information.

The second type treats features as machine-interpretable semantic information and directly compresses and encodes the extracted features. These methods
generate task-oriented data streams directly based on the statistical properties
of the features. NVIDIA's MAXINE technology [22] selects facial key points
as features for face generation tasks. Facial generation algorithms fit a virtual
dynamic facial image based on key points and facial images, which are then
applied to video calls. Chen et al. [23] attempt to compress the generated feature maps in deep learning computations to improve the generalization of the
encoded features. Yang et al. [24] propose a compact visual representation compression method that designs a codebook before compressing features generated
by neural networks, reducing the dimensionality gap between the generated features and various machine vision features/labels.

As feature-driven methods mainly focus on visual features, the machine
semantics often differ significantly from the original signal-level information.
Therefore, these methods do not pursue the reconstruction of the original data
and achieve significant compression efficiency by removing visual redundancy
almost completely. This paper is inspired by the second approach, which extracts
features from visual signals and guides features to carry machine semantic information while reducing their entropy through end-to-end training, making them
easily compressible and encoded.

3 Approach

3.1 Problem Definition

The purpose of this paper is to generate machine semantics relevant to a specific
machine task and minimize the bitrate of the machine semantics. Firstly, we
define the input digital signal to the system as X and the machine semantic
generation model as $g(\cdot)$. The generated machine semantics F can be represented
as:

$$F = g(X). \tag{2}$$

For machine semantics, different target tasks have different preferences for
semantics. The same machine task can also accept machine semantics at different levels, leading to different methods and complexities for extracting machine
semantics. Here, $g(\cdot)$ represents only the process of generating machine semantics. Therefore, for the entire process of semantic information generation, we
hope to be driven by the quality of a specific task, represented as:

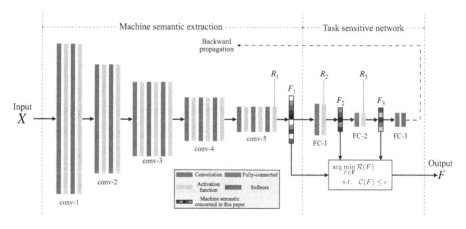

Fig. 1. The proposed method is manifested in the entire end-to-end framework. Here, R_1, R_2, and R_3 represent the activation functions planned to be replaced in this paper, while F_1, F_2 and F_3 represent the machine semantic information that is explored and intended to be outputted.

$$\mathbf{F} = \{F | \forall \mathcal{R}(F) < b : \mathcal{Q} \leq \Phi(F)\}, \tag{3}$$

where $\mathbf{F}$ represents a collection of machine semantic expressions, $\mathcal{R}(\cdot)$ represents the measure of bitrate and $\Phi(F)$ represents the task accuracy achievable by machine semantics F. The Formula 3 implies finding a collection of machine semantics $\mathbf{F}$ with task accuracy greater than $\mathcal{Q}$ among all machine semantics with encoding bitrate less than b and representing this collection as $\mathbf{F}$.

Finally, we aim to find a machine semantic expression in the collection $\mathbf{F}$ that is most suitable for the practical application scenario and has the lowest bitrate:

$$\arg \min_{F \in \mathbf{F}} \mathcal{R}(F)$$
$$s.t. \quad \mathcal{C}(F) \leq c. \tag{4}$$

We consider the extraction and compression of semantic information as a reflection of the computational resources required in practical application scenarios. Here, $\mathcal{C}(F)$ represents the computability or computational resources required to generate machine semantics F and c represents the maximum computational load that can be accommodated in the current application scenario.

The specific methods for addressing the above problem in End-to-End training will be described in the next section.

3.2 End-to-End Training

In this paper, we focus on machine-driven end-to-end machine semantic compression. Therefore, our work is built upon existing end-to-end models. As shown in Fig. 1, we use the VGG-16 [25] model as an example and we highlight the

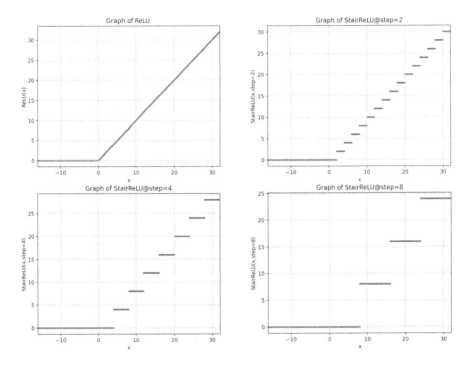

Fig. 2. The proposed StairReLU function, which takes into account both quantization and neuron activation, is compared with the traditional ReLU function in the provided image. We demonstrate three different steps of StairReLU functions, where a larger step indicates a coarser quantization granularity.

important components of the entire network, especially the locations of activation functions. Theoretically, any activation function component can be replaced with our proposed StairReLU. We believe that the activation function in the neural network computation process is functionally similar to the quantization process in signal compression and encoding. Therefore, our goal is to enhance the quantization level of the activation function during the end-to-end training process, resulting in machine semantics outputs with lower information entropy.

Previously, to compress machine semantic information, it needed to be quantized first. Therefore, for the deployment of StairReLU in the neural network, it should be positioned before the machine semantic information is compressed and only deployed at the activation function positions closest to the machine semantics. In this paper, we plan to compress F_1, F_2, and F_3 as shown in Fig. 1. Therefore, the corresponding StairReLU is deployed at the positions of R_1, R_2, and R_3, respectively.

The selection of machine semantic F follows the decision made based on the computational cost of generating that semantic, as described in Eq. 4. Specifically, the computational cost can be measured using the parameter count required to generate the semantic. In the network structure shown in Fig. 1, generating F_1 requires approximately 10% of the total parameter count of the entire network while generating F_2 or F_3 requires over 85% of the total parameter count. However, compared to F_1, F_2 and F_3 have more compact semantic information and lower bitrates.

In summary, the overall approach is still driven by the task objective and the loss function term remains the same as in end-to-end machine task training. The difference lies in the change of activation functions, which leads to the quantization of the machine semantics output during the end-to-end network process. This guides the machine semantics towards sparsity and easier compression.

3.3 StairReLU

In the field of digital signal processing, quantization refers to the process of approximating a large number of possible discrete values with a small number of discrete values to simplify data and achieve compression. In the context of deep learning, the concept of quantization is reflected in the activation functions, aiming to increase the nonlinearity of the neural network model and enable it to learn and perform more complex tasks. Therefore, a reasonable quantization can compress task-related feature vectors while maintaining the accuracy of the machine task.

The commonly used ReLU is a loss function with a relatively large quantization range. It sets all feature elements below 0 to 0, aiming to ensure the dispersion and sparsity of the encoding between neurons. However, for feature elements greater than 0, ReLU keeps their original values unchanged. If entropy coding is applied to these feature elements at this stage, a large number of unquantized feature elements will result in a high bitrate of the encoded data. Therefore, we propose an activation function, StairReLU, which is more inclined towards compression coding for feature data. Similar to ReLU, StairReLU sets negative feature elements with low relevance to the task to 0. For positive feature elements, StairReLU quantizes them according to the step parameter. Figure 2 shows the function graphs of ReLU and StairReLU for $step = 2$, $step = 4$ and $step = 8$.

The expression of StairReLU is defined as:

$$\text{StairReLU}(x, step) = \lceil \frac{x + |x|}{2 \cdot step} \rceil \cdot step, \tag{5}$$

where $x, step \in \mathbb{R}$, $\lceil \cdot \rceil$ represents the ceiling function, which rounds a number up to the nearest integer. The larger the $|step|$, the greater the degree of quantization. Compared to using rate-constrained terms in the loss function or trade-off parameters in end-to-end training, the $step$ provides more intuitive control over the bitrate of machine semantics. In the experimental section, we will further explore and analyze various properties of StairReLU through actual end-to-end training.

4   Experiment

In this section, we provide detailed evidence of the effectiveness of the proposed method from two perspectives: convergence properties and rate-accuracy performance. To this end, we selected three different datasets and three typical neural networks for experimental validation.

4.1   Datasets and Network Architecture

For the datasets, we selected the following three, each belonging to a different category:

Pubfig83+LFW [26]: This dataset is a combination of two face datasets, consisting of a total of 24,618 face images. Among them, 83 individuals are from the PubFig83 dataset, with 2/3 (8,720 faces) used for training and 1/3 (4,282 faces) used for testing. Specifically, 12,066 faces from the LFW dataset are used as distractors to simulate the recognition of non-face subjects within a real-world uncontrolled gallery.

FGVC-Aircraft [27]: This benchmark dataset focuses on the fine-grained visual classification of aircraft. It contains 10,200 aircraft images, with 100 images per each of the 102 aircraft models, most of which are airplanes. Each image is annotated with the corresponding aircraft model label. Among these images, 6,800 are used for training and validation, while the remaining 3,400 images are used for testing.

Caltech101 [28]: The Caltech101 dataset consists of 101 different object categories, with approximately 40–800 images per category. These images are captured by different photographers in various environments, including indoor and outdoor scenes, as well as some computer-generated images. The images have a resolution of 300×200 pixels, and each image is labeled with its corresponding category. For this experiment, we randomly selected 70% of the images for training, while the remaining 30% of the data is used as the test set.

For the selection of neural networks, we chose three typical models: VGG-16 [25], ResNet-34 [29], and Mobilenetv2 [30]. The network architectures, layer configurations, and sizes are set according to the instructions in the original paper. The only modification made is that for different datasets, the dimension of the Softmax layer is set equal to the number of classes in the respective dataset.

4.2   Characteristic of StairReLU

For a newly proposed activation function, one of the most important tasks is to validate its impact on the convergence of the entire task network. We adhere to the cross-entropy loss used in the VGG-16 network:

$$\mathcal{L} = -\frac{1}{N} \sum_{i=1}^{N} \sum_{j=1}^{C} y_{ij} \log(p_{ij}), \tag{6}$$

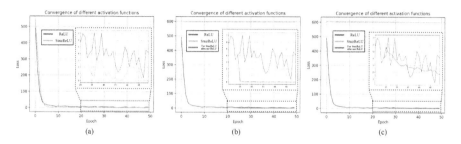

Fig. 3. The impact of StairReLU@step=8 placement on the convergence speed of end-to-end training. Where (a), (b), and (c) represent deploying StairReLU at positions R_1, R_2, and R_3 in Fig. 1, respectively. Specifically, for the cases where StairReLU struggles to converge (b) and (c), we replace the activation function with StairReLU after the 25th epoch.

where N is the number of samples, representing the number of samples in the training set. C is the number of classes, representing the number of categories in the classification task. i represents the index of the sample, ranging from 1 to N. j represents the index of the class, ranging from 1 to C. y_{ij} denotes the value of the true label for sample i on class j. It takes the value 1 if sample i belongs to class j, and 0 otherwise. p_{ij} represents the predicted probability of sample i being classified as class j by the model. It is the output of the model, indicating the estimated probability for sample i belonging to class j. The cross-entropy function guides the network towards more accurate task predictions, while for the compression of machine semantics, we use StairReLU to guide coarse-grained quantization. We replaced R_1, R_2, and R_3 in Fig. 1 with StairReLU@step=8 and recorded the convergence of the loss function during training. Figure 3 shows the gradient descent process when training the Pubfig83 dataset using the VGG-16 network. For R_1, the coarse quantization of StairReLU did not affect the network's convergence. However, for R_2 and R_3, if StairReLU is used for activation at the beginning of training compared to ReLU, it will result in slower convergence speed and extremely challenging gradient descent. Therefore, we propose to train the network with ReLU until a certain point, and then replace ReLU with StairReLU. At this stage, the gradient has already decreased to a lower level, and using StairReLU in this situation can avoid the slow convergence issue in gradient descent.

4.3 Performance of Accuracy and Bitrate

In this subsection, we analyze the performance of the proposed method by combining classification accuracy and the corresponding machine semantics code rate.

First, for StairReLU, we set the step to 2, 4, and 8 to correspond to different levels of quantization. Then, for the dataset and network model mentioned in Sect. 4.1, we conduct separate training, and the results are shown in Table 1. For the rows corresponding to the ReLU function mentioned in Table 1, we train the model for 100 epochs. For the rows corresponding to StairReLU, we first adapt the ReLU for 50 epochs and then continue training with StairReLU for another 50 epochs.

The machine semantics presented in Table 1 are tensors generated after the average pooling layer and the dimensions of machine semantics vary for different networks. Therefore, we describe the coding potential of each machine semantics in an information theory framework by calculating the information entropy of the machine semantics.

The results show that using StairReLU significantly reduces the information entropy of machine semantics while maintaining comparable or even superior task accuracy compared to traditional methods that use ReLU. Occasionally, there may be significant accuracy loss in the model due to the possibility of using a step that is too large for the current model and dataset.

Table 1. Comparison of results between using StairReLU in end-to-end training and using ReLU in end-to-end training. The "Original ReLU" in the table represents the training and inference results obtained without any improvement in quantization.

	Activation function	VGG-16		Resnet-34		Mobilenetv2	
		$H(F)_\downarrow$	Acc.$^\uparrow$	$H(F)_\downarrow$	Acc.$^\uparrow$	$H(F)_\downarrow$	Acc.$^\uparrow$
Pubfig83+LFW	Original ReLU	4.049	0.7505	23.73	0.6683	22.31	0.6136
	StairReLU@*step*=2	1.668	0.7729	1.247	0.6379	0.7483	0.7222
	StairReLU@*step*=4	1.328	0.7698	0.7192	0.6334	0.2301	0.5804
	StairReLU@*step*=8	0.9617	0.7600	0.2431	0.5789	0.0010	0.1164
FGVC-Aircraft	Original ReLU	1.140	0.6472	21.62	0.5055	21.30	0.5028
	StairReLU@*step*=2	0.3960	0.6298	1.177	0.4749	1.266	0.4929
	StairReLU@*step*=4	0.3357	0.6535	0.6620	0.4644	0.7407	0.4260
	StairReLU@*step*=8	0.2657	0.6555	0.1973	0.4005	0.2764	0.0102
Caltech101	Original ReLU	1.564	0.8989	20.85	0.7337	19.85	0.7171
	StairReLU@*step*=2	0.4768	0.8834	0.7340	0.7163	0.7391	0.7020
	StairReLU@*step*=4	0.3871	0.8970	0.1913	0.7121	0.2386	0.5945
	StairReLU@*step*=8	0.2862	0.8992	0.0002	0.6627	0.0039	0.0943

For the accuracy performance in Table 1. In the FGVC-Aircraft and Caltech101 datasets, we use classification accuracy as the measure of task performance. The Pubfig83+LFW dataset involves the presence of confounding data. Therefore, we use precision-recall curves as the evaluation metric and ultimately calculate the average precision (AP) as the evaluation measure. The definitions of precision and recall are as follows:

Precision: The number of correctly identified targets within Pubfig83 divided by the total number of instances classified as Pubfig83.

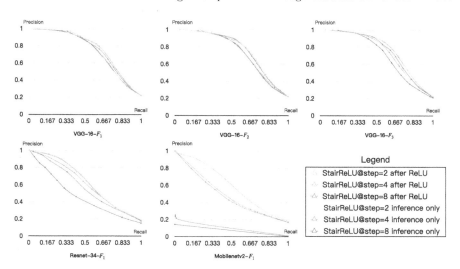

Fig. 4. The AP performance of different neural networks and different levels of machine semantics on the Pubfig83+LFW dataset.

Recall: The number of instances that are targets within Pubfig83 and correctly identified as targets within Pubfig83 divided by the total number of instances in the Pubfig83 dataset.

The AP is obtained by calculating the area under the precision-recall (PR) curve and the formula for calculating AP is

$$\text{AP} = \sum_{i=1}^{n-1} (\text{Rec}_{i+1} - \text{Rec}_i)\text{Pre}_i, \tag{7}$$

where n represents the total number of sampled points in the PR curve and each point on the curve is denoted as $(\text{Rec}_i, \text{Pre}_i)$. Figure 4 showcases the AP performance of different neural networks and different levels of machine semantics on the Pubfig83+LFW dataset. Different from the information presented in Table 1, all the gray curves in Fig. 4 represent the cases where StairReLU was not used in end-to-end training but is employed during inference, serving as a control. The training iterations used in these experiments are consistent with those in Table 1. It is visually evident that employing StairReLU in end-to-end training yields significant advantages.

Finally, we showcase the machine semantics performance across different deep networks, depths, and datasets using R-D curves. The bit rate is obtained by multiplying the dimension of the machine semantics by its information entropy. Figure 5 demonstrates that replacing ReLU with StairReLU during the end-to-end training process significantly enhances the expressive power of machine semantics with low information entropy.

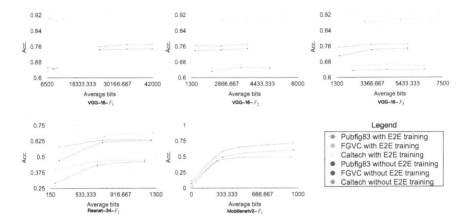

Fig. 5. The R-D curves showcasing the compression performance of machine semantics information across different neural networks. The values representing the bitrate are obtained by calculating the product of the information entropy and the number of machine semantic elements, while the values representing accuracy are based on the evaluation metrics corresponding to the respective datasets.

5   Conclusion

In this paper, we propose the use of StairReLU, a novel activation function, for end-to-end training of neural networks in machine semantics compression. We first present the workflow of end-to-end machine semantics compression and the precise definition of StairReLU. Then, through end-to-end training, we investigate the convergence performance of StairReLU and provide recommendations for its usage. Finally, we demonstrate the effectiveness of the proposed method on three different datasets with five different machine semantics, showing that it significantly reduces the information entropy of machine semantics while maintaining comparable or even superior task accuracy compared to existing methods.

References

1. Ji, W., Xu, J., Qiao, H., Zhou, M., Liang, B.: Visual IoT: enabling internet of things visualization in smart cities. IEEE Netw. **33**(2), 102–110 (2019)
2. Tang, H., et al.: Single-shot compressed optical field topography. Light: Sci. Appl. **11**(1), 244 (2022)
3. Bross, B., et al.: Overview of the versatile video coding (VVC) standard and its applications. IEEE Trans. Circuits Syst. Video Technol. **31**(10), 3736–3764 (2021)
4. Zhang, J., Jia, C., Lei, M., Wang, S., Ma, S., Gao, W.: Recent development of AVS video coding standard: AVS3. In: Proceedings of the Picture Coding Symposium, pp. 1–5. IEEE, Ningbo, China (2019)
5. Simpson, J.: The past, present and future of big data in marketing. Forbes (2020)

6. Shannon, C.E.: A mathematical theory of communication. Bell Syst. Tech. J. **27**(3), 379–423 (1948)
7. Letaief, K.B., Chen, W., Shi, Y., Zhang, J., Zhang, Y.J.A.: The roadmap to 6G: AI empowered wireless networks. IEEE Commun. Mag. **57**(8), 84–90 (2019)
8. Strinati, E.C., Barbarossa, S.: 6G networks: beyond Shannon towards semantic and goal-oriented communications. Comput. Netw. **190**, 107930 (2021)
9. Wang, C.X., Di Renzo, M., Stanczak, S., Wang, S., Larsson, E.G.: Artificial intelligence enabled wireless networking for 5G and beyond: recent advances and future challenges. IEEE Wirel. Commun. **27**(1), 16–23 (2020)
10. Shi, G., Xiao, Y., Li, Y., Xie, X.: From semantic communication to semantic-aware networking: model, architecture and open problems. IEEE Commun. Mag. **59**(8), 44–50 (2021)
11. Duan, L., Liu, J., Yang, W., Huang, T., Gao, W.: Video coding for machines: a paradigm of collaborative compression and intelligent analytics. IEEE Trans. Image Process. **29**, 8680–8695 (2020)
12. Chamain, L.D., Racapé, F., Bégaint, J., Pushparaja, A., Feltman, S.: End-to-end optimized image compression for machines, a study. In: Proceedings of the Data Compression Conference, pp. 163–172. IEEE, Snowbird, United States (2021)
13. Hou, Y., Zheng, L., Gould, S.: Learning to structure an image with few colors. In: Proceedings of the IEEE/CVF Conference on Computer Vision and Pattern Recognition, pp. 10116–10125. IEEE, Virtual (2020)
14. Le, N., Zhang, H., Cricri, F., Ghaznavi-Youvalari, R., Rahtu, E.: Image coding for machines: an end-to-end learned approach. In: Proceedings of the IEEE International Conference on Acoustics, Speech and Signal Processing, pp. 1590–1594. IEEE, Toronto, Canada (2021)
15. Le, N., Zhang, H., Cricri, F., Ghaznavi-Youvalari, R., Tavakoli, H.R., Rahtu, E.: Learned image coding for machines: A content-adaptive approach. In: Proceedings of the IEEE International Conference on Multimedia and Expo, pp. 1–6. IEEE, Montreal, Canada (2021)
16. Yang, Z., et al.: Discernible image compression. In: Proceedings of the 28th ACM International Conference on Multimedia, pp. 1561–1569. ACM, Seattle, United States (2020)
17. Tu, H., Li, L., Zhou, W., Li, H.: Semantic scalable image compression with cross-layer priors. In: Proceedings of the 29th ACM International Conference on Multimedia, pp. 4044–4052. ACM, Chengdu, China (2021)
18. Wang, Y., Xu, J., Ji, W.: A feature-based video transmission framework for visual IoT in fog computing systems. In: Proceedings of the ACM/IEEE Symposium on Architectures for Networking and Communications Systems, pp. 1–8. IEEE, Cambridge, United Kingdom (2019)
19. Sullivan, G.J., Ohm, J.R., Han, W.J., Wiegand, T.: Overview of the high efficiency video coding (HEVC) standard. IEEE Trans. Circuits Syst. Video Technol. **22**(12), 1649–1668 (2012)
20. Sun, S., He, T., Chen, Z.: Semantic structured image coding framework for multiple intelligent applications. IEEE Trans. Circuits Syst. Video Technol. **31**(9), 3631–3642 (2020)
21. Huang, Z., Jia, C., Wang, S., Ma, S.: Visual analysis motivated rate-distortion model for image coding. In: Proceedings of the IEEE International Conference on Multimedia and Expo, pp. 1–6. IEEE, Virtual (2021)
22. NVIDIA Maxine Official Website. https://developer.nvidia.com/maxine

23. Chen, Z., Fan, K., Wang, S., Duan, L., Lin, W., Kot, A.C.: Toward intelligent sensing: intermediate deep feature compression. IEEE Trans. Image Process. **29**, 2230–2243 (2019)

24. Yang, W., Huang, H., Hu, Y., Duan, L. Y., Liu, J.: Video coding for machine: compact visual representation compression for intelligent collaborative analytics. arXiv preprint arXiv:2110.09241 (2021)

25. Simonyan, K., Zisserman, A.: Very deep convolutional networks for large-scale image recognition. arXiv preprint arXiv:1409.1556 (2014)

26. Becker, B., Ortiz, E.: Evaluating open-universe face identification on the web. In: Proceedings of the IEEE Conference on Computer Vision and Pattern Recognition Workshops, pp. 904–911. IEEE, Portland, United States (2013)

27. Maji, S., Rahtu, E., Kannala, J., Blaschko, M., Vedaldi, A.: Fine-grained visual classification of aircraft. arXiv preprint arXiv:1306.5151 (2013)

28. Li, F., Fergus, R., Perona, P.: One-shot learning of object categories. IEEE Trans. Pattern Anal. Mach. Intell. **28**(4), 594–611 (2006)

29. He, K., Zhang, X., Ren, S., Sun, J. Deep residual learning for image recognition. In: Proceedings of the IEEE Conference on Computer Vision and Pattern Recognition, pp. 770–778. IEEE, Las Vegas, United States (2016)

30. Sandler, M., Howard, A., Zhu, M., Zhmoginov, A., Chen, L.C.: Mobilenetv2: inverted residuals and linear bottlenecks. In: Proceedings of the IEEE Conference on Computer Vision and Pattern Recognition, pp. 4510–4520. IEEE, Salt Lake City, United States (2018)

Application of AI

PM$_{2.5}$ Concentration Measurement Based on Natural Scene Statistics and Progressive Learning

Guangcheng Wang[1]($\boxtimes$), Baojin Huang[1], Kezheng Sun[2,3], Lijuan Tang[3], Mengting Wei[4], and Quan Shi[1]

[1] School of Transportation and Civil Engineering, Nantong University, Nantong, China
wangguangcheng0428@163.com
[2] School of Information and Control Engineering, China University of Mining and Technology, Xuzhou, China
[3] School of Electronics and Information, Jiangsu Vocational College of Business, Nantong, China
[4] Institute of Software, Chinese Academy of Sciences, Beijing, China

Abstract. To ensure the well-being of residents and ecological balance, it is essential to conduct continuous and precise PM$_{2.5}$ concentration monitoring. To this end, we have developed a visual-based PM$_{2.5}$ concentration estimation algorithm consisting of two models: a visual feature perception model based on natural scene statistics and a progressive learning-based PM$_{2.5}$ concentration prediction model. The proposed visual feature perception model, drawing from natural scene statistics, pinpoints visual characteristics in the structure and saturation domains, accurately quantifying the loss of color and structural information caused by particulate matter. To build a comprehensive PM$_{2.5}$ concentration prediction model, we integrate multiple sub-PM$_{2.5}$ concentration prediction models using a 'decision-fusion' approach, resulting in our final PM$_{2.5}$ concentration measurement model. Through rigorous testing, we confirm that this method outperforms existing photo-based PM$_{2.5}$ monitoring techniques in terms of both accuracy and efficiency.

Keywords: PM$_{2.5}$ concentration monitoring · Visual perception · Natural scene statistics · Progressive learning

1 Introduction

In the face of rapid urbanization and industrialization, the world is confronted with critical environmental pollution challenges. Air pollution has emerged as a significant factor in influencing both urban sustainability and human well-being. To address these challenges, urgent action is required to mitigate the impact of air pollution and promote

This work was supported in part by the National Science Foundation of China under Grant 62273011 and Grant 62076013; in part by the Beijing Natural Science Foundation under Grant JQ21014; in part by the Nantong Science and Technology Plan Project under JC22022089.

sustainable urban development and enhanced well-being for all [4,8,11,29]. Specifically, fine particulate matter (PM$_{2.5}$), due to its minute size, facilitate residence and dispersion in the atmosphere and are enriched with various harmful substances. Notably, medical research has clearly established that PM$_{2.5}$ near the ground may be inhaled into the human respiratory tract, particularly impacting the human respiratory, cardiovascular, reproductive, and hematological systems, resulting in severe health concerns [3,7,12,26].

PM$_{2.5}$ contains abundant organic compounds, including a variety of polycyclic aromatic hydrocarbons (PAHs) that are highly toxic and have been confirmed as carcinogens, with benzopyrene having the strongest carcinogenic potential [14]. According to the International Agency for Research on Cancer's assessment in October 2013, outdoor air pollution has been listed as one of the human carcinogens [1]. The World Health Organization's Air Quality Guidelines (2005) clearly states that when the annual average concentration of PM$_{2.5}$ reaches 35 μg per cubic meter, the risk of human death is about 15% higher than when the concentration is 10 μg per cubic meter [34]. According to recent studies, in 2019, the novel coronavirus disease (COVID-19) was found to be transmitted through aerosols. Therefore, it is hypothesized that PM$_{2.5}$, being an aerosol itself, could also serve as a carrier for the spread of COVID-19 globally, thus posing a significant threat to human health and safety [6,15,19].

PM$_{2.5}$ pollution poses a serious threat to human health, and also has a significant impact on climate and atmospheric visibility. Aerosol particles have significant uncertainty for global climate change [18]. As PM$_{2.5}$ levels increase in the atmosphere, it can lead to drastic decreases in precipitation in heavily polluted areas, further compounding the negative impact on the environment and human health [32]. Bollasina *et al.*'s groundbreaking research further highlights that the anthropogenic aerosol particle concentration modification plays a pivotal role in the observed decrease in precipitation in South Asia during the mid-20th century, thus highlighting its significant impact on the region's climate and environment [2]. Furthermore, the particulate matter in the atmosphere profoundly weakens the signal intensity of light due to scattering and absorption, thereby significantly reducing the effective range of visibility and impacting visual acuity. Therefore, PM$_{2.5}$ in cities can lead to reduced visibility and the occurrence of "haze" weather and other phenomena. Moreover, Sweerts *et al.* found that the scattering and absorption of solar radiation by aerosols significantly compromises the efficiency of solar photovoltaic power generation in China [23]. This finding underscores the critical need for effective monitoring and regulation of PM$_{2.5}$ concentration to promote human health and enhance the overall atmospheric quality.

To achieve accurate and reliable daily monitoring of PM$_{2.5}$ concentrations, sophisticated electronic instruments have been developed utilizing advanced techniques such as the gravimetric method, β-ray absorption technique, and the tapered element oscillating microbalance approach [5]. Nevertheless, these high-precision electronic instruments possess limitations such as bulky size, high cost, extended sampling period, and the requirement for a stable operating environment, which hinder their widespread implementation for real-time, high-density spatial monitoring of PM$_{2.5}$ [20,24,30]. In view of this, some researchers have successively proposed image-based PM$_{2.5}$ concentration measurement algorithms. This type of algorithm uses image processing technology to extract PM$_{2.5}$ concentration information from images collected by mobile smart devices or surveillance cameras, which has the advantages of fast, convenient and low cost. For instance, Gu *et al.* pioneered a method for determining PM$_{2.5}$ concentration by meticulously analyzing entropy feature disparities between high- and low-concentration PM$_{2.5}$ images across spatial and saturation transformation domains [10]. Wang *et al.* introduced a PM$_{2.5}$ concentration meter that leverages visual saliency technology. This innovative approach calculates the entropy of non-significant regions in the saturation map to estimate PM$_{2.5}$ concentrations [27]. However, it's important to note that the accuracy of this entropy-based monitoring model can be impacted by the diverse range of visual scenarios. In particular, images featuring extensive smooth regions may be incorrectly classified as having a higher PM$_{2.5}$ concentration, potentially leading to inaccuracies in concentration estimation.

To address the challenges of previous methods, Yue *et al.* developed a sophisticated approach for PM$_{2.5}$ concentration estimation [31]. This innovative technique combines structural and color loss estimation to achieve more precise and reliable concentration measurements. By meticulously quantifying structural information loss through precise gradient similarity calculations between image saturation and gray-scale maps, and accurately estimating color information loss by analyzing the intricate Weibull distribution of saturation maps, this method offers unprecedented accuracy and reliability for real-time PM$_{2.5}$ concentration estimation with unparalleled spatial resolution. This groundbreaking technique represents a significant leap forward in the field of PM$_{2.5}$ concentration estimation, setting a new standard for more precise air quality monitoring in the future. Yue *et al.*'s method faces significant challenges in accurately representing image structural loss using gradient similarity between saturation and gray-scale channels of PM$_{2.5}$ images. The absence of gray-scale information in these images greatly limits the method's ability to capture the fine details and nuances of the structure. This limitation can lead to inaccuracies in concentration estimation. Furthermore, Yue *et al.*'s study revealed that the saturation map distribution corresponding to PM$_{2.5}$ images does not follow the Weibull distribution as closely as desired. This observation highlights the need for further research to develop more robust and precise methods for PM$_{2.5}$ concentration estimation. By addressing these limitations, future research can improve the accuracy and reliability of real-time PM$_{2.5}$ concentration estimation with high spatial resolution, ultimately leading to better air quality monitoring and improved public health outcomes. Sun *et al.* [22] and Wang *et al.* [25] introduced the concept of image defogging enhancement for PM$_{2.5}$ concentration estimation, aiming to mitigate the impact of image content diversity on the estimation process. By computing self-similarity based on color, depth, gradient, and entropy in both original and defogged PM$_{2.5}$ images, these methods aim to improve concentration estimation accuracy. However, the current state of defogging algorithm development remains a limiting factor. Improvements in this area are crucial to enhancing the overall estimation accuracy of PM$_{2.5}$ concentrations. Future research should focus on developing more advanced defogging techniques that can effectively remove fog-induced artifacts while preserving important image features for accurate concentration estimation.

To address the limitations of photo-based PM$_{2.5}$ concentration estimation algorithms, we have developed statistical features that aim to mitigate the impact of visual content diversity on the robustness of $PM_{2.5}$ monitoring models. By utilizing a comprehensive statistical analysis, we have created features that can effectively capture the characteristics of $PM_{2.5}$ concentration. Furthermore, we introduce a novel approach called "progressive learning in a 'decision-fusion' manner" to enhance the accuracy of $PM_{2.5}$ concentration estimation. This method leverages sub-prediction models constructed from visual features and progressively integrates them to obtain a more robust and accurate final estimation model. By combining statistical features with the decision-fusion approach, we aim to improve the reliability and accuracy of $PM_{2.5}$ concentration estimation, leading to more effective air quality monitoring and better public health outcomes.

The main contributions of this article are as follows:

1) We propose two novel visual features that leverage natural scene statistics (NSS) in both the saturation and frequency domains to quantitatively assess the color and structural degradation incurred during the imaging process due to $PM_{2.5}$ pollution.
2) We introduce a progressive learning-based $PM_{2.5}$ concentration measurement model, which progressively fuses sub-prediction models generated from our proposed visual features using a "decision-fusion" strategy to produce an accurate $PM_{2.5}$ monitor.
3) The experimental results conducted on a public database demonstrate that the proposed $PM_{2.5}$ concentration measurement algorithm based on NSS and progressive learning outperforms the competing state-of-the-art (SOTA) methods significantly.

2   Proposed Method

As Fig. 1 highlights, the differences between high and low $PM_{2.5}$ concentration images are more pronounced in the saturation and structure domains. To address this, we have devised two distinct types of NSS-based visual features. These features aim to measure the color and structural distortions incurred by particles during the imaging process of $PM_{2.5}$ images. At the same time, we have introduced a $PM_{2.5}$ monitoring device based on progressive learning, which mines sub-prediction models learned from visual features with commonality to build a $PM_{2.5}$ monitoring model. Next, we will introduce the NSS-based visual features and the $PM_{2.5}$ monitoring model based on progressive learning in detail.

2.1   NSS-Based Visual Features in the Saturation Domain

As depicted in Fig. 1, the color and structural degradation of images brought about by particulate matter can be conceptualized as a global degradation. Therefore, we resort to a strategy analogous to that used to assess image quality in the presence of global distortions [13, 16, 17, 35], such as blocking and blur, to extract visual features germane to the concentration of $PM_{2.5}$. To specifically capture saturation information from PM2.5 images, we convert them from the RGB color space to the HSV color space. This conversion process allows us to effectively analyze the color components of the images and

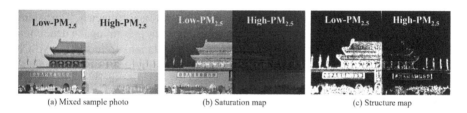

| (a) Mixed sample photo | (b) Saturation map | (c) Structure map |

Fig. 1. Comparisons between pictures captured under high and low PM$_{2.5}$ concentrations. (a) is the mixed sample photo. (b) is the saturation map of (a). (c) is the filtering result of (a) through the Log-Gabor filter.

assess their saturation levels. The RGB to HSV conversion is achieved through a series of mathematical operations:

$$S = \begin{cases} \frac{max(R,G,B)-min(R,G,B)}{max(R,G,B)}, & \text{if } max(R,G,B) \neq 0 \\ 0, & \text{if } max(R,G,B) = 0 \end{cases}, \tag{1}$$

To obtain the saturation map for a given PM$_{2.5}$ image, we first identify the maximum and minimum values of the RGB components. These values are represented by $max(R,G,B)$ and $min(R,G,B)$, respectively. The saturation map S is then computed based on the differences between the maximum and minimum values of the RGB channels. This saturation map provides a measure of color intensity and purity within the image. To enhance the contrast and normalize the saturation map, we subtract the mean and divide by the variance of the pixel values in S. This process results in the mean subtracted contrast normalized (MSCN) coefficient. The MSCN coefficient serves as a visual feature that accounts for the color loss caused by particulate matter. It highlights the variations in saturation levels across the image, providing insights into the spatial distribution and impact of particulate matter on color distortions. By computing the MSCN coefficient, we aim to improve concentration estimation by capturing the salient visual characteristics of PM$_{2.5}$ images. This approach allows us to better analyze and understand the effects of particulate matter on image quality, leading to more accurate concentration estimation. The extraction process for the MSCN coefficient corresponding to the saturation map S is as follows:

$$MSCN_S(x,y) = \frac{S(x,y) - \mu(x,y)}{\sigma(x,y) + C}, \tag{2}$$

$$\mu(x,y) = \sum_{m=-M}^{M} \sum_{n=-N}^{N} \omega_{m,n} S_{m,n}(x,y), \tag{3}$$

$$\sigma(x,y) = \sqrt{\sum_{m=-M}^{M} \sum_{n=-N}^{N} \omega_{m,n} \left(S_{m,n}(x,y) - \mu(x,y)\right)^2}, \tag{4}$$

where the Gaussian weight function $\omega = \{\omega_{m,n} | k = -M, ..., M, n = -N, ..., N\}$ assigns weights to each pixel in the image based on its spatial location. The (x, y) represents the pixel index within the image. Typically, M and N are set to 3, providing a reasonable trade-off between spatial coverage and computational efficiency. The parameter C is a small positive number that serves as a regularizer, preventing the denominator from being zero and introducing stability to the computation. To model the MSCN distribution of $PM_{2.5}$ images in the saturation domain, we utilize the Generalized Gaussian Distribution (GGD) function. The GGD function offers a flexible parametric model that can approximate various types of distributions. It allows us to capture the statistical characteristics of the MSCN values in the saturation domain and build a robust model for concentration estimation. The GGD function is defined as follows:

$$f(x; \alpha, \sigma^2) \quad = \frac{\alpha}{2\beta\Gamma\left(\frac{1}{\alpha}\right)} \exp\left(-\left(\frac{-x}{\beta}\right)^\alpha\right), \tag{5}$$

where $\Gamma(a) = \int_0^\infty t^{(a-1)}e^{-t}dt\,(a > 0)$ is gamma function. $\beta = \sigma\sqrt{\frac{\Gamma\left(\frac{1}{\alpha}\right)}{\Gamma\left(\frac{3}{\alpha}\right)}}$. The parameters α and σ^2 control the shape and variance of the distribution, respectively. The parameters α and σ^2 are employed as the NSS-based visual features to measuring the color loss.

2.2 NSS-Based Visual Features in the Structure Domain

As shown in Fig. 1(c), there are significant differences in the Log-Gabor filter [9] results between low and high concentration $PM_{2.5}$ images. Therefore, we extract distribution parameters as visual features based on NSS by calculating the MSCN coefficient of the $PM_{2.5}$ image to optimize the measurement of image structural loss caused by particulate matter. Specifically, we use the Log-Gabor filter in both horizontal and vertical directions to decompose the $PM_{2.5}$ image and analyze the first layer of the subband image (corresponding to the high spatial frequency). The transformation from the spatial domain to the structural domain of the $PM_{2.5}$ image is as follows:

$$J(i, j) = \ln(|g(i, j)| + K). \tag{6}$$

Among them, $|g(i, j)|$ is the amplitude of the Log-Gabor filter subband coefficient, and $K = 0.1$ is a constant that prevents $g(i, j)$ from being zero. Then, we adopt equations (2)-(5) to extract the statistical parameters (α and σ^2) of the structural domain as NSS-based visual features to measure the structural loss.

2.3 Progressive Learning-Based $PM_{2.5}$ Monitor

The existing feature fusion methods for $PM_{2.5}$ concentration estimation typically involve feeding all types of visual features into a regressor to construct a $PM_{2.5}$ concentration estimation model [22,25,28]. These feature fusion methods assume that visual quality features designed for different types of losses have complementarities, and they ignore differences in the responses of different visual scene contents during the imaging process. To address this challenge, this paper introduces a gradual learning strategy that integrates common visual quality features to establish a robust $PM_{2.5}$ concentration estimation model. The proposed $PM_{2.5}$ concentration estimation model based on gradual learning consists of two primary components: a) A sub-prediction model based on

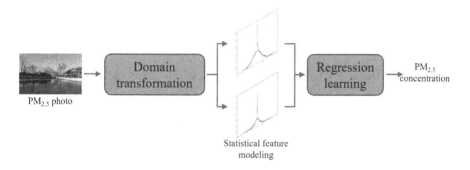

Fig. 2. Framework of the proposed PM$_{2.5}$ concentration estimator.

a single set of visual features; and 2. A "decision-fusion"-based sub-prediction model integration. Specifically, considering that deep forests and deep neural networks have comparable learning capabilities and that deep forests require fewer samples to learn robust models, this work adopts deep forests to learn a mapping from single sets of visual features to PM$_{2.5}$ concentration values to obtain individual prediction models.

$$\hat{Y}_1 = R(X_1), \hat{Y}_2 = R(X_2), \ldots, \hat{Y}_M = R(X_M). \tag{7}$$

Here, $X_1, X_2, \ldots, X_M$ and Y refers to multiple sets of NSS-based visual features and the true PM$_{2.5}$ concentration values mentioned in the previous text. $\hat{Y}_i(i \in 1, 2, \ldots, M)$ represents the predicted PM$_{2.5}$ concentration value corresponding to the i-th type of visual features.

After obtaining the sub-prediction models, they are gradually integrated layer by layer using a "decision-fusion" approach. Specifically, the Euclidean distance between the predicted results of two sub-prediction models is used to measure the complementary characteristics between the two sub-prediction models. When the Euclidean distance between the predicted results of two sub-prediction models is less than the complementary threshold, taking the outputs of the i-th and j-th sub-prediction models, $\hat{Y}_i$ and $\hat{Y}_j$ as an example, $\sqrt{\left(\hat{Y}_i - \hat{Y}_j\right)^2} \leq \Delta$, then the two sub-prediction models are considered complementary and can be used for fusion processing. Here, deep forests are still used to fuse the outputs of the sub-prediction models and perform regression mapping to PM$_{2.5}$ concentration values. Conversely, if the two sub-prediction models are considered mutually exclusive, fusion processing is not considered. By iteratively integrating all sub-prediction models layer by layer using the aforementioned approach, the final PM$_{2.5}$ concentration estimation model is obtained. The entire iterative "decision-fusion" model can be represented as $\min \|\hat{Y} - Y\|^2$, and satisfies $\hat{Y} = R\left(\hat{Y}_{ij}, \hat{Y}_k\right)$, where $i, j, k \in \{1, 2, \ldots, M\}$, $\sqrt{\left(\hat{Y}_i - \hat{Y}_j\right)^2} \leq \Delta$, $\sqrt{\left(\hat{Y}_{ij} - \hat{Y}_k\right)^2} \leq \Delta$. Here, $\|\hat{Y} - Y\|^2$ represents the Euclidean norm of $\hat{Y} - Y$, and $\hat{Y}$ refers to the constructed final PM$_{2.5}$ concentration estimation model. For easier understanding of this work, we draw a flowchart of the proposed PM$_{2.5}$ concentration estimation algorithm, as shown in Fig. 2.

3 Experiments and Discussions

3.1 Experimental Environment

Experimental Data. We conducted an extensive evaluation of our proposed method and compared it to other leading algorithms on the AQID dataset [10]. This benchmark dataset comprises 750 images, spanning a wide range of $PM_{2.5}$ concentrations from 1 to 423 $\mu g/m^3$. To ensure the reliability of the concentration labels, the AQID dataset was carefully curated using a professional instrument, the MetOne BAM-1020. Additionally, all images were captured within one kilometer of the MetOne BAM-1020 device, ensuring accurate representation of the corresponding $PM_{2.5}$ concentrations. The AQID dataset features a diverse range of scenes, including overpasses, squares, roads, parks, lakes, and tall buildings. This diversity ensures that the dataset encompasses a wide range of environmental conditions and scene characteristics. For our evaluation, we allocated 80% of the AQID dataset for training and reserved the remaining 20% for testing, following a standard practice in machine learning.

Evaluation Indicators. In line with previous research [25,31], we employ Pearson's linear correlation coefficient (PLCC), Spearman's rank correlation coefficient (SROCC), and Kendall's rank correlation coefficient (KROCC) to objectively evaluate the accuracy of our $PM_{2.5}$ concentration prediction algorithm. These evaluation metrics are crucial in quantifying the algorithm's ability to predict $PM_{2.5}$ concentrations accurately, as they provide a measure of the correlation between the predicted and actual values. A higher correlation coefficient closer to 1 indicates superior performance, indicating a strong correlation between the predicted and actual values, while a lower coefficient closer to 0 indicates poorer performance. The use of multiple correlation coefficients allows for a comprehensive evaluation, considering both the linear relationship and the rank order between predicted and actual values. This holistic approach ensures a rigorous assessment of the algorithm's predictive capabilities across various environmental conditions and scene configurations.

3.2 Performance Comparison of SOTA Methods

In this study, we set out to validate the accuracy and robustness of our novel $PM_{2.5}$ concentration prediction algorithm, which is based on an innovative combination of natural scene statistics and a progressive learning approach. To establish its superiority, we have chosen five state-of-the-art photo-based $PM_{2.5}$ concentration monitoring methods for comparison. These include the Picture-based Predictor of $PM_{2.5}$ Concentration (PPPC) [10], Yue *et al.*'s method [31], the Image-based $PM_{2.5}$ Predictor with Saliency detection (IPPS) [33], Sun *et al.*'s method [22], and the Multi-modal $PM_{2.5}$ Image Feature Fusion (MIFF) [25]. Each of these algorithms has been briefly described in the introduction of this paper. Our aim is to demonstrate that, through its unique combination of natural scene statistics and progressive learning, our algorithm outperforms these state-of-the-art methods in predicting $PM_{2.5}$ concentrations across diverse environmental conditions and scene configurations.

Table 1. Performance comparison of the proposed method with five SOTA algorithms. The best performance is displayed in bold.

Metrics	PLCC	SROCC	KROCC	Average
PPPC [10]	0.812	0.819	0.608	0.746
Yue [31]	—	0.782*	0.581*	—
IPPS [33]	0.801*	—	0.610*	—
Sun [22]	0.808	0.818	0.612	0.746
MIFF [25]	0.850	0.821	0.620	0.764
Our Method	**0.867**	**0.830**	**0.627**	**0.771**

"*": Experimental results are from the original articles.
"–": Since the original papers' source codes are not open source, these experimental results are not available.

Table 1 presents a comparative analysis of the performance of the proposed PM$_{2.5}$ concentration monitoring method and five state-of-the-art algorithms on the AQID dataset. The results indicate that our proposed algorithm achieved the best performance in terms of PLCC, SROCC, and KROCC, with values of 0.867, 0.830, and 0.617, respectively. Notably, the method proposed by Yue *et al.* focuses primarily on image saturation domain information, neglecting structural domain information. This factor may explain its relatively weaker performance compared to other image-based PM$_{2.5}$ concentration measurement algorithms. Our algorithm's superior performance can be attributed to its unique combination of natural scene statistics and progressive learning, which enables it to effectively capture spatial and temporal variations in PM$_{2.5}$ concentrations. This capability results in more accurate predictions across diverse environmental conditions and scene configurations. PPPC and IPPS measure PM$_{2.5}$ concentration by calculating image saturation and energy entropy in the structure transformation domain, and their performance is also quite similar. The algorithms of PPPC and IPPS, despite their attempts to estimate PM$_{2.5}$ concentrations from multiple domains such as color and structure, fell short in comparison to MIFF and our proposed method, particularly in terms of PLCC performance metrics. The underlying reason for this inferior performance lies in their failure to account for the impact of image content diversity on PM$_{2.5}$ concentration measurement results. MIFF attempted to address this issue by utilizing the defogged image of PM$_{2.5}$ images as reference information in its entropy-based monitoring model. However, even with this addition, MIFF's performance remained wanting compared to our proposed method. Our algorithm outperformed MIFF by 2.00% in PLCC, 1.09% in SROCC, and 1.13% in KROCC, highlighting the superiority of our approach in effectively addressing the challenges posed by image content diversity. The key to our method's superior performance lies in its innovative combination of natural scene statistics and a progressive learning approach. This combination enables the algorithm to effectively capture spatial and temporal variations in PM$_{2.5}$ concentrations, leading to more accurate predictions across diverse environmental conditions and scene configurations. By leveraging natural scene statistics, our method is able to extract meaningful features from images, effectively capturing the complex relationships between $PM_{2.5}$ concentrations and image characteristics. Progressive learning, on the other hand, allows the algorithm to incrementally update its understanding of these relationships, improving its predictive accuracy over time.

Table 2. Performance comparison of the different machine learners-based $PM_{2.5}$ concentration estimators. The best performance is displayed in bold.

Machine Learner	PLCC	SROCC	KROCC	Average
SVR	0.788	0.788	0.562	0.713
RF	0.799	0.786	0.571	0.719
DNN	0.798	0.791	0.577	0.722
Progressive Learning	**0.867**	**0.830**	**0.627**	**0.771**

3.3 Ablation Studies

To comprehensively evaluate the effectiveness of our proposed progressive learning strategy, we conducted a rigorous performance comparison with multiple linear learning algorithms utilized in previous studies [21,22,25,28], including support vector regression (SVR), random forest (RF), and deep neural network (DNN). Table 2 provides a detailed comparison of the PLCC, SROCC, and KROCC values between the estimated $PM_{2.5}$ concentrations obtained from multiple $PM_{2.5}$ concentration monitors based on different learning algorithms and the actual $PM_{2.5}$ concentrations. The SVR- and RF-based models struggled to estimate $PM_{2.5}$ concentrations accurately, highlighting the challenges associated with constructing efficient concentration estimation models using shallow machine learning algorithms. The DNN-based model outperformed its competitors but was still limited by its tendency to converge to local optima when trained with limited data due to weight parameter initialization. In this study, we present a $PM_{2.5}$ monitoring model based on progressive learning, achieving remarkable PLCC, SROCC, and KROCC values of 0.867, 0.830, and 0.627, respectively. When compared to the second-best DNN-based model, our proposed model boosted the PLCC, SROCC, and KROCC values by impressive margins of 8.65%, 4.93%, and 8.67%, respectively. These improvements demonstrate that our $PM_{2.5}$ monitoring model, which is based on progressive learning, effectively mines common visual features to achieve highly accurate $PM_{2.5}$ concentration estimations.

To further validate the effectiveness of our designed NSS-based visual features, we conducted a detailed visualization analysis. Figure 3 presents three RGB images with varying $PM_{2.5}$ concentrations, along with their corresponding saturation and structure maps. The statistical distributions in the saturation and structure transformation domains are also included. The visualizations clearly demonstrate that the NSS-based visual features extracted in the saturation and structure domains effectively capture variations in $PM_{2.5}$ concentration levels. The saturation maps effectively capture changes in

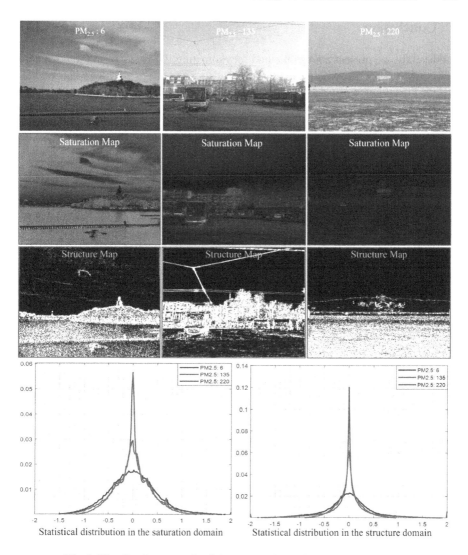

Fig. 3. Visualization example of the proposed NSS-based visual features.

color saturation, while the structure maps highlight variations in image texture and patterns. These visualizations provide valuable insights into the relationship between the NSS-based visual features and PM$_{2.5}$ concentration levels. This analysis further supports the effectiveness of our designed features in capturing important visual patterns associated with PM$_{2.5}$ concentration estimation.

4 Conclusion

In this study, we present a novel method for estimating $PM_{2.5}$ concentration that combines multi-transform domain natural scene statistics and progressive learning. We have designed two unique visual features that are extracted from natural scene statistics and effectively distinguish different levels of $PM_{2.5}$ concentration in the saturation and structural transformation domains. These features offer a more comprehensive understanding of the relationship between visual patterns and $PM_{2.5}$ concentration levels. To further enhance the estimation accuracy, we have developed a progressive learning model that leverages the extracted visual features. This model progressively updates its knowledge based on previous learning experiences, enabling it to refine its estimation as more data becomes available. Experimental results demonstrate that our proposed $PM_{2.5}$ concentration measurement method outperforms existing image-based estimation algorithms. The visual features extracted from natural scene statistics provide valuable insights into the relationship between visual patterns and $PM_{2.5}$ concentration levels.

In the future, we plan to integrate multiple sensor datasets, including infrared and hyper spectral datasets, to enhance the robustness and accuracy of visual-based $PM_{2.5}$ concentration measurement. By leveraging multiple sensor data, we aim to achieve more consistent and reliable $PM_{2.5}$ concentration estimation results that can be used for various applications, such as air quality monitoring and urban planning. Additionally, we will investigate the use of transfer learning techniques to further improve the estimation accuracy. Transfer learning allows us to leverage knowledge gained from previous tasks to improve performance on related tasks, enabling our model to adapt more quickly and effectively to new environments and datasets.

References

1. Aboyans, V., of Death Collaborators, C., et al.: Global, regional, and national age-sex specific all-cause and cause-specific mortality for 240 causes of death, 1990-2013: a systematic analysis for the global burden of disease study 2013. Lancet (British edition) **385**(9963), 117–171 (2015)
2. Bollasina, M.A., Ming, Y., Ramaswamy, V.: Anthropogenic aerosols and the weakening of the South Asian summer monsoon. Science **334**(6055), 502–505 (2011)
3. Particulate matter air pollution and cardiovascular disease: an update to the scientific statement from the American heart association. Circulation **121**(21), 2331–2378 (2010)
4. Chen, Z., Zhang, T., Chen, Z., Xiang, Y., Xuan, Q., Dick, R.P.: Hvaq: a high-resolution vision-based air quality dataset. IEEE Trans. Instrum. Meas. **70**, 1–10 (2021). https://doi.org/10.1109/TIM.2021.3104415
5. Chow, J.: Measurement methods to determine compliance with ambient air-quality standards for suspended particles. J. Air & Waste Mang. Assoc. **45**(5), 320–382 (1995)
6. Daraei, H., Toolabian, K., Kazempour, M., Javanbakht, M.: The role of the environment and its pollution in the prevalence of COVID-19. J. Infect. **81**(2), E168–E169 (2020)
7. Davel, A.P., et al.: Endothelial dysfunction in the pulmonary artery induced by concentrated fine particulate matter exposure is associated with local but not systemic inflammation. Toxicology **295**(1–3), 39–46 (2012)

8. Fekih, M.A., et al.: Participatory air quality and urban heat islands monitoring system. IEEE Trans. Instrum. Meas. **70**, 1–14 (2021). https://doi.org/10.1109/TIM.2020.3034987

9. Fischer, S., Šroubek, F., Perrinet, L., Redondo, R., Cristóbal, G.: Self-invertible 2d log-gabor wavelets. Int. J. Comput. Vis. **75**(2), 231–246 (2007)

10. Gu, K., Qiao, J., Li, X.: Highly efficient picture-based prediction of pm2.5 concentration. IEEE Trans. Indus. Electr.**66**(4), 3176–3184 (2019)

11. Gu, K., Qiao, J., Lin, W.: Recurrent air quality predictor based on meteorology- and pollution-related factors. IEEE Trans. Industr. Inf. **14**(9), 3946–3955 (2018)

12. Guo, Y., Tong, S., Zhang, Y., Barnett, A.G., Jia, Y., Pan, X.: The relationship between particulate air pollution and emergency hospital visits for hypertension in Beijing. China Sci. Total Environ. **408**(20), 4446–4450 (2010)

13. Hu, R., Liu, Y., Gu, K., Min, X., Zhai, G.: Toward a no-reference quality metric for camera-captured images. IEEE Trans. Cybernet. **53**(6), 3651–3664 (2023). https://doi.org/10.1109/TCYB.2021.3128023

14. Kim, K.H., Jahan, S.A., Kabir, E., Brown, R.J.: A review of airborne polycyclic aromatic hydrocarbons (pahs) and their human health effects. Environ. Int. **60**, 71–80 (2013)

15. Liu, Y., et al.: Aerodynamic analysis of SARS-CoV-2 in two Wuhan hospitals. Nature **582**(7813), 557+ (2020)

16. Mittal, A., Moorthy, A.K., Bovik, A.C.: No-reference image quality assessment in the spatial domain. IEEE Trans. Image Process. **21**(12), 4695–4708 (2012)

17. Mittal, A., Soundararajan, R., Bovik, A.C.: Making a "completely blind" image quality analyzer. IEEE Signal Process. Lette. 20(3), 209–212 (2013)

18. Myhre, G., Samset, B.H., Schulz, M., et al.: Radiative forcing of the direct aerosol effect from AeroCom Phase II simulations. Atmos. Chem. Phys. **13**(4), 1853–1877 (2013)

19. Rohrer, M., Flahault, A., Stoffel, M.: Peaks of fine particulate matter may modulate the spreading and virulence of COVID-19. Earth Syst. Environ. **4**(4), 789–796 (2020)

20. Song, S., Li, V.O.K., Lam, J.C.K., Wang, Y.: Personalized ambient pollution estimation based on stationary-camera-taken images under cross-camera information sharing in smart city. IEEE Internet Things J. **10**(17), 15420–15430 (2023). https://doi.org/10.1109/JIOT.2023.3263949

21. Sun, K., Tang, L., Huang, S., Qian, J.: A photo-based quality assessment model for the estimation of pm2.5 concentrations. IET Image Process. **16**(4), 1008–1016 (2022)

22. Sun, K., Tang, L., Qian, J., Wang, G., Lou, C.: A deep learning-based pm2. 5 concentration estimator. Displays **69**, 102072 (2021)

23. Sweerts, B., Pfenninger, S., Yang, S., Folini, D., van der Zwaan, B., Wild, M.: Estimation of losses in solar energy production from air pollution in China since 1960 using surface radiation data. Nat. Energy **4**(8), 657–663 (2019)

24. Wang, G., Shi, Q., Wang, H., Gu, K., Wei, M., Wong, L.K., Wang, M.: Vision-based pm$_{2.5}$ concentration estimation with natural scene statistical analysis. IEEE Trans. Artifi. Intell. 1–11 (2023). https://doi.org/10.1109/TAI.2023.3324892

25. Wang, G., Shi, Q., Wang, H., Sun, K., Lu, Y., Di, K.: Multi-modal image feature fusion-based pm2.5 concentration estimation. Atmospheric Pollut. Res. **13**(3), 101345 (2022)

26. Wang, G., Jiang, R., Zhao, Z., Song, W.: Effects of ozone and fine particulate matter (PM2.5) on rat system inflammation and cardiac function. Toxicology Lett. **217**(1), 23–33 (2013)

27. Wang, X., Wang, M., Liu, X., Zhang, X., Li, R.: A pm2.5 concentration estimation method based on multi-feature combination of image patches. Environ. Res. **211**, 113051 (2022)

28. Xia, Z.: A robust photo-based PM2.5 monitoring method by combining linear and non-linear learning. IET Image Process. (2022)

29. Yang, J., Zeng, Z., Wang, K., Zou, H., Xie, L.: Garbagenet: a unified learning framework for robust garbage classification. IEEE Trans. Artifi. Intell. **2**(4), 372–380 (2021). https://doi.org/10.1109/TAI.2021.3081055

30. Yao, S., Wang, F., Huang, B.: Measuring pm2.5 concentrations from a single smartphone photograph. Remote Sensing **14**(11) (2022). https://doi.org/10.3390/rs14112572, https://www.mdpi.com/2072-4292/14/11/2572

31. Yue, G., Gu, K., Qiao, J.: Effective and efficient photo-based pm2.5 concentration estimation. IEEE Trans. Instrument. Measure. **68**(10), 3962–3971 (2019). https://doi.org/10.1109/TIM.2018.2886091

32. Zhang, H., Zhao, S., Wang, Z., Zhang, X., Song, L.: The updated effective radiative forcing of major anthropogenic aerosols and their effects on global climate at present and in the future. Int. J. Climatol. **36**(12), 4029–4044 (2016)

33. Zhang, H., Peng, D., Chen, W., Xu, X.: Extremely efficient PM2.5 estimator based on analysis of saliency and statistics. Electr. Lett. **55**(1), 30–31 (2019)

34. Zhang, Q., et al.: Effects of meteorology and secondary particle formation on visibility during heavy haze events in Beijing. China Sci. Total Environ. **502**, 578–584 (2015)

35. Zhang, Z., Sun, W., Min, X., Wang, T., Lu, W., Zhai, G.: No-reference quality assessment for 3d colored point cloud and mesh models. IEEE Trans. Circuits Syst. Video Technol. **32**(11), 7618–7631 (2022). https://doi.org/10.1109/TCSVT.2022.3186894

Human-Centered Financial Signal Processing: A Case Study on Stock Chart Analysis

Kaixun Zhang[1], Yuzhen Chen[1], Ji-Feng Luo[1], Menghan Hu[1,2(✉)], Xudong An[3], Guangtao Zhai[2], and Xiao-Ping Zhang[4]

[1] East China Normal University, Shanghai 200241, China
mhhu@ce.ecnu.edu.cn
[2] Shanghai Jiao Tong University, Shanghai 200240, China
[3] Beijing University of Posts and Telecommunications, Beijing 100876, China
[4] Toronto Metropolitan University, Toronto, ON M5B 2K3, Canada

Abstract. In this paper, we explore the "human-centered" financial model. To illustrate this idea, we conducted a case study on the stock chart, referring to stock price chart plus stock volume chart. We first construct the stock chart with professional stock traders' visual attention (SPSTV) dataset, which contains 150 stock charts images associated with eye-movement data from 10 professional stock traders. Based on the SPSTV dataset, the transfer learning and human attention inspired morphological operation are leveraged to develop the stock chart attention model. In validation experiments, compared to other models, SamVgg optimized by transfer learning and human visual attention function performs best with the AUC_Judd, CC, SIM, and NSS of 96.11%, 82.74%, 69.84%, and 2.84, respectively. Through visual comparative analysis, we can find that the visual attention map area after the double optimization strategy is more focused overall and has less excess attention at the edges. This visual optimization will enhance people's observation experience. The proposed model has great potential for two application scenarios: (1) instruct amateur traders how to observe stock charts; and (2) evaluate stock analysis ability of investors. In the future, we will continue to iterate the model and try to apply it in real economic activities to generate benefits.

Keywords: Financial Computer Vision · Financial Signal Processing · Saliency Prediction · Human Attention · Stock Analysis

1 Introduction

Stock market analysis has a strong appeal to investors, financial analysts, researchers, and the general public [21,35]. From the perspective of behavioral economics and socioeconomic theory, stock markets are predictable to a certain extent [6]. Currently, fundamental analysis and technical analysis are the two

G. Zhai et al. (Eds.): IFTC 2023, CCIS 2067, pp. 187–198, 2024.
https://doi.org/10.1007/978-981-97-3626-3_14

main approaches to analyze stock market [1,2,23,26]. For stock market analysis, almost all existing scholars carry out market analysis based on historical data [14]. As illustrations, the mean-variance strategy is utilized for portfolio optimization [21], the Black-Scholes model for predicting market volatility [16], the Ornstein-Ulenbeck process model for statistical arbitrage [3], and Meucci has integrated insights from various models and experts using the entropy pooling approach [19]. Yet, some economists argue that these models' underlying behavioral assumptions, which exclude psychological considerations, might not be precise [29]. Beyond the noted discrepancies between observed human economic actions and established economic models, scholars from the humanities, social sciences, and behavioral sciences decipher and influence the interplay between STEM (science, technology, engineering, and math) and societal institutions, relationships, and values, thereby proactively reducing long-term risks by emphasizing diverse knowledge perspectives and alternative approaches to questions [18]. Moreover, intuitive and non-conscious cognitive processes exert a non-negligible impact on action determination rather than conscious attitudes, motivations and intention [11]. Thus, we believe that the most essential factor that determines the movement of the stock market is human. In other words, the most starting point for the ultimate response of the market is the decision of human. Therefore, if a "human-centered" model can be developed based on the human perspective, we will see the economic markets from a new perspective, which in turn may lead to more accurate and effective analysis of stock market movements under the guidance.

The question now becomes how to build a "human-centered" model. Extant studies suggest that human motion prediction is feasible using deep learning models [10,27], and human-inspired approaches have been applied to many fields, such as robotics [24], image registration [9]. We can consider visual saliency as the temporal accumulation of human visual motion. Hence, to answer this question, we turn our attention to visual saliency prediction models commonly used in computer vision. The aim of visual saliency prediction models is to automatically predict what attracts human attention most in images and videos [8,17,22,31], and these models have been widely used in computer vision tasks such as object detection [25,32,33] and quality assessment [30,34]. In the current work, taking stock chart as an example, we consider that the image elements on the stock chart image may greatly influence the decisions of professional stock traders. Therefore, we try to use visual saliency models to predict where professional stock traders pay attention on stock chart, and the established model can further help other investors especially for the less experienced investors to find the areas which professional stock traders pay the most attention to. By doing so, we can give stock charts the emotions of professional traders, while such a model can establish a resonant relationship between the market and the investors.

To explore the "human-centered" finance model, we created a dataset of stock charts using the Shanghai Composite Index as the data source. A total of 10 professional stock traders were invited to observe the stock charts while performing eye-movement data collection. To capture the eye-movement data from

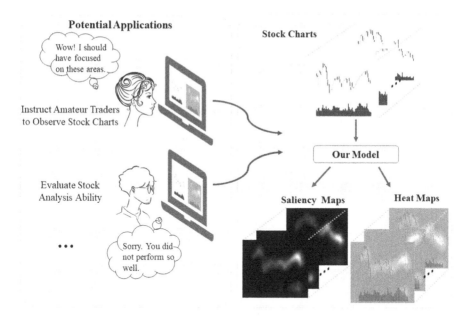

Fig. 1. The right shows usage flow of stock chart attention (SCA) model, where human eye movement is collected using the eye tracking device or mouse, and then analyzed after being converted to saliency maps and heat maps. The left illustrates two potential application scenarios, where the woman is guided to focus on the most interested areas of the professional stock traders, and the actual performance of observing the stock chart is evaluated.

the observations of professional stock traders more accurately, the experimental process is task-oriented: the professional traders need to give their decisions after the observations are finished. Finally, based on the dataset we built, inspired by visual attention models, we construct a model to predict where the professional stock traders view on stock charts. The usage flow and potential application scenarios of the obtained model are shown in Fig. 1. The contributions of this paper are twofold:

1) We construct the stock chart with professional stock traders' visual attention (SPSTV) dataset to assist in developing the "human-centered" stock market analysis model.
2) We develop the stock charts attention (SCA) model by introducing the morphological operation inspired by human attention mechanism to predict where the professional stock traders view on stock charts.

2   Method

Pipeline of the stock charts attention (SCA) model is described in Fig. 3, including the establishment of stock chart with professional stock traders' visual attention (SPSTV) dataset, the development of SCA model and model validation.

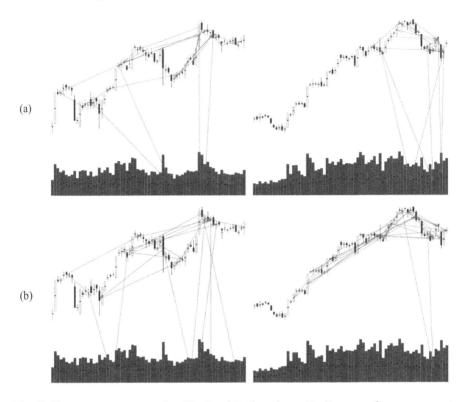

Fig. 2. Eye movement examples. To simplify the schematic diagram of eye movement, the fixations are restricted on the central point of each bar. (a) and (b) are eye movement of two professional stock traders on two exemplified stock charts.

2.1   Stock Chart with Professional Stock Traders' Visual Attention (SPSTV) Dataset

In the current work, we use the Shanghai Composite Index as the data source to construct the SPSTV dataset. The main reason for choosing the Shanghai Composite Index instead of the individual stocks as the data source is that the prices of individual stocks are more susceptible to disruptions from various factors, such as government policies, temporary company decisions and unexpected events. The Shanghai Composite Index can reflect the price movements of all listed stocks on the Shanghai Stock Exchange in a comprehensive manner, with fewer interfering factors. Therefore, this stock index can better demonstrate the advantages of technical analysis, thus making the obtained eye-tracking data more reflective of the high interest areas that the professional stock traders focus on. The historical data of Shanghai Composite Index was downloaded from business.sohu.com, and we selected three relative stable periods, 1997–2005, 2012–2013 and 2015–2017, to create the stock chart. A total of 150 stock chart images were generated by transferring the text data to images via the

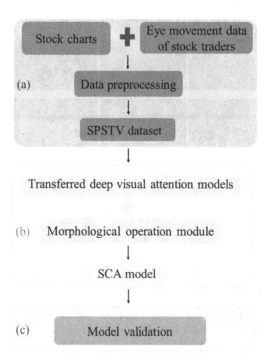

Fig. 3. Pipeline of the stock chart attention (SCA) model (a) Stock chart attention with professional stock traders' visual attention (SPSTV) dataset, where professional stock traders' eye movement data when observing stock charts is collected through an eye tracker, and after preprocessing, it is saved as saliency maps and heat maps. (b) SCA model, where transfer learning in terms of the saliency maps is applied to visual saliency machining learning models and deep learning models, and a morphological operation module imitating human visual characteristics is designed to optimize the models. (c) Model validation, where similarity (SIM), Pearson linear correlation coefficient (CC), area under the curve (AUC), and normalized scanpath saliency (NSS) are used to assess the performance of different models.

MATLAB software, and the resolution of these images was set to 1280×1024 to meet the follow-up eye movement data collection.

Subsequently, 10 professional stock traders were invited to observe the dataset constructed above, and eye-movement data was collected by an eye tracker in parallel. Each subject sat about 65cm away from the eye tracker with 5 screen capture frame-rate. To prevent the effect of fatigue from prolonged observation on the experimental results, we break the experiment process into three segments: after the professional traders observe 50 images, they take a 10-minute break, and then observe the next 50 images. There is one solid gray image between each two images, ensuring that the previous image does not affect the viewing of the latter image. To capture more accurate eye-movement data from the professional traders' observations, our experimental procedure is

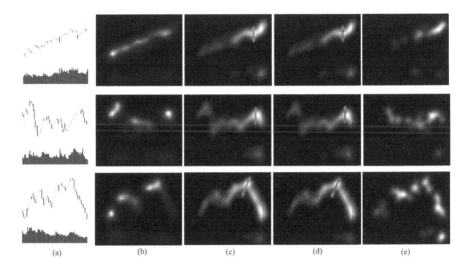

Fig. 4. Visualization of 3 typical predicted results. (a) The test images in SPSTV dataset. (b) Results of original SamVgg model. (c) Results of transferred SamVgg model, where the width of the salient viewing area is measured by the light blue arrow. (d) Results of transferred SamVgg model optimized by the proposed human attention inspired morphological operation, where the width of the salient viewing area is measured by the orange arrow. (e) Groundtruth visual attention map. (Color figure online)

task-oriented, i.e. the professional traders need to give their decisions after the observations. The eye tracker we used is Tobii T120 [12,13,15] with a 19 in. screen whose resolution is 1280×1024. This resolution is consistent with the screen resolution and image resolution.

To generate more representative eye-movement data of professional stock traders, for each image, we map 10 professional stock traders' data together, and then filter the aggregated eye-movement data using a Gaussian filter with 1° of visual angle (36 pixels in this study) to get the final visual attention map of professional stock traders, thus finally getting the SPSTV dataset, which is demonstrated in Fig. 2.

2.2   Stock Chart Attention (SCA) Model

After obtaining SPSTV dataset, the construction of SCA model consists of 2 steps. First, we use the transfer learning method to migrate the pretrained models on natural scene images to SPSTV dataset. Then we propose a morphological operation to further optimize the transferred models considering the characteristics of the stock chart images in SPSTV dataset, and finally obtain the SCA model.

Initial Visual Attention Model: we selected three deep learning attention models namely SamVgg [8], SamResnet [8] and Melnet [7] as the initial models.

These models were pretrained by natural scene images. Since the contents of the images in SPSTV dataset are very different from those of the natural scene images, the above-mentioned pretrained visual attention models are not applicable to SPSTV dataset. This has been verified by our previous experiments (data not shown). Therefore, we randomly divide 60%, 20% and 20% of the SPSTV dataset into training set, validation set and test set, respectively. By means of transfer learning, the initial models will have the ability to predict the behavior of professional stock traders viewing stock charts.

Human Attention Inspired Morphological Operation: The contents of natural scene images are very substantial. By contrast, the image contents in SPSTV dataset are relatively single and do not fill the whole image. This requires us to further adjust the model obtained from the above transfer learning to be more suitable for the economic scene.

Inspired by the fact that the organization of visual space in the lateral geniculate nucleus of brain structure is logarithmic, our visual acuity to the center of visual field is much higher than that to the periphery of visual field [20]. This human vision mechanism is particularly applicable to the images of simple contents, and it will optimize the visual attention map to a greater extent, making it closer to the real situation, and will create a good visual experience. Hence, we design a morphological operation module attached to the end of each model, inspired by this mechanism to make the center field of vision more salient and the boundary more faded.

Specifically, we operate three morphological methods in this module, viz. erosion, opening operation and closing operation. Given a structure element B and a image A, the erosion $(A \ominus B)$ and dilation $(A \oplus B)$ can be expressed as

$$(A \ominus B)_{m,n} = \max_{p,q \in \{1,2,\cdots,b\}} (A_{m+p,n+q} + B_{p,q}), \tag{1}$$

$$(A \oplus B)_{m,n} = \min_{p,q \in \{1,2,\cdots,b\}} (A_{m-p,n-q} - B_{p,q}), \tag{2}$$

where x, y means a pixel in A or B. The opening operation follows the order of first erosion and then dilation while closing operation following first dilation and then erosion.

Suppose the size of B is $b \times b$, and b is a trainable hyper-parameter. Now the target of the module is to find the best morphological method and b.

We adopt "grid search" to find the best pair of morphological method and b, owing to the fact that the number of the parameters to be trained in the morphological operation module is relatively small. Aimed at achieving this goal, we use the Huber Loss, which can accelerate model training and convergence and is more robust for noise. The Huber loss can be explained as

$$Loss_H = \begin{cases} \frac{1}{2}(p - \hat{p})^2 & |p - \hat{p}| \leq a \\ a|p - \hat{p}| - \frac{1}{2}a^2 & \text{otherwise} \end{cases} \tag{3}$$

where p and $\hat{p}$ are the ground truth of pixel value and the predicted pixel value, respectively, and a is an adjustable threshold.

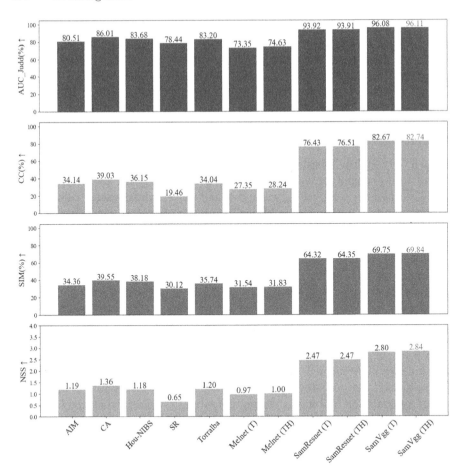

Fig. 5. Model performance comparison. T and TH denotes the models optimized by transfer learning and human attention inspired morphological operation. The best performer is highlighted in red, and no matter which evaluation metric is chosen, SamVgg (TH) performs the best among all models. (Color figure online)

Thus we can obtain more salient center field of vision and more faded boundary in the saliency map.

Stock Chart Attention (SCA) Model: The transferred models were further optimized by the above morphological operation module. All transferred models were implemented in Python using Theano deep learning framework and trained on the SPSTV dataset. The SCA model is used with an initialized learning rate 1×10^{-6}. Considering that the size of the images in SPSTV dataset is 1280×1024, which will cause too large calculation amount, we resized the images to the resolution of 640×512. We set batch size as 1, and the models are trained 9 times.

2.3   Model Validation

We used five widely adopted metrics to evaluate the performance of models: similarity (SIM) [5], Pearson linear correlation coefficient (CC), area under the curve (AUC), normalized scanpath saliency (NSS). AUC is defined as the area under the receiver operating characteristic curve and measures the trade-off between false and true positives at different discrimination thresholds [4]. NSS is a correspondence measure between saliency maps and ground truth, computed by the average normalized saliency at fixated locations [4,28]. SIM measures the intersection between distributions while CC evaluates how dependent or correlated two variables are. In addition, 5 traditional attention models namely AIM, Context-Aware (CA), SR, Hou-NIBS, and Torralba were also selected for model comparison.

3   Experiments and Results

3.1   Results of Test Set and Analysis

From Fig. 5, it can be obviously noticed that compared to the performance of traditional models, deep learning models generally perform much better. This is within expectation, because deep learning is better at learning the characteristics of training sets. Among all traditional and deep learning models, SamVgg (TH) performs best with the AUC_Judd, CC, SIM, and NSS of 96.11%, 82.74%, 69.84%, and 2.84, respectively.

Although the deep visual attention model undergoes transfer learning on SPSTV dataset, it does not consider the features of the images in SPSTV dataset and the gaze characteristics of the professional stock traders. Therefore, the human attention inspired morphological operation was introduced. In Fig. 5, the model improvement is difficult to see from the four metrics. Therefore, Fig. 4 is presented to visually demonstrate the model improvement. As shown in Fig. 4, the attention area was more focused overall after the double optimization, and this effect is marked by the arrows. At the same time, there is less excess attention at the edges of the attention area. This optimization of visual effects can enhance people's observation experience, which in turn is potentially more conducive to future practical applications.

4   Conclusion

In this paper, to build a "human-centered" economic model, we first develop the stock chart database with eye-movement data from professional stock traders, named as stock chart with professional stock traders' visual attention (SPSTV) dataset. Based on SPSTV dataset, we subsequently leverage transfer learning and human attention inspired morphological operation to build the stock chart attention model. Experimental results show that SamVgg (TH) performs best with the AUC_Judd, CC, SIM, and NSS of 96.11%, 82.74%, 69.84%, and 2.84, respectively. Meanwhile, the visual attention map area after the double optimization strategy is more focused overall and has less excess attention at the edge. This visual optimization enhances people's observation experience. In the future, we will continue to refine the dataset to iterate the model, and will try to apply the "human-centered" economic models in real economic activities to generate benefits.

References

1. Anbalagan, T., Maheswari, S.U.: Classification and prediction of stock market index based on fuzzy metagraph. Proc. Comput. Sci. **47**, 214–221 (2015)
2. Ballings, M., Van den Poel, D., Hespeels, N., Gryp, R.: Evaluating multiple classifiers for stock price direction prediction. Expert Syst. Appl. **42**(20), 7046–7056 (2015)
3. Bergault, P., Drissi, F., Guéant, O.: Multi-asset optimal execution and statistical arbitrage strategies under ornstein-uhlenbeck dynamics. SIAM J. Financial Math. **13**(1), 353–390 (2022)
4. Bylinskii, Z., Judd, T., Oliva, A., Torralba, A., Durand, F.: What do different evaluation metrics tell us about saliency models? IEEE Trans. Pattern Anal. Mach. Intell. **41**(3), 740–757 (2018)
5. Chang, Q., Zhu, S.: Human vision attention mechanism-inspired temporal-spatial feature pyramid for video saliency detection. Cognitive Comput, 1–13 (2023)
6. Chen, C., Dongxing, W., Chunyan, H., Xiaojie, Y.: Exploiting social media for stock market prediction with factorization machine. In: 2014 IEEE/WIC/ACM International Joint Conferences on Web Intelligence and Intelligent Agent Technologies, vol. 2, pp. 142–149. IEEE (2014)
7. Cornia, M., Baraldi, L., Serra, G., Cucchiara, R.: A deep multi-level network for saliency prediction. In: 2016 23rd International Conference on Pattern Recognition, pp. 3488–3493. IEEE (2016)
8. Cornia, M., Baraldi, L., Serra, G., Cucchiara, R.: Predicting human eye fixations via an lstm-based saliency attentive model. IEEE Trans. Image Process. **27**(10), 5142–5154 (2018)
9. Feng, J., Ma, L., Bi, F., Zhang, X., Chen, H.: A coarse-to-fine image registration method based on visual attention model. Sci. China Inf. Sci. **57**(12), 1–10 (2014)
10. Gao, H., et al.: Trajectory prediction of cyclist based on dynamic bayesian network and long short-term memory model at unsignalized intersections. Sci. China Inf. Sci. **64**(7), 172207 (2021)
11. Hallsworth, M.: A manifesto for applying behavioural science. Nat. Hum. Behav. **7**(3), 310–322 (2023)
12. Jiang, L., Xu, M., Liu, T., Qiao, M., Wang, Z.: DeepVS: a deep learning based video saliency prediction approach. In: Ferrari, V., Hebert, M., Sminchisescu, C., Weiss, Y. (eds.) Computer Vision – ECCV 2018. LNCS, vol. 11218, pp. 625–642. Springer, Cham (2018). https://doi.org/10.1007/978-3-030-01264-9_37
13. Jiang, M., Huang, S., Duan, J., Zhao, Q.: Salicon: saliency in context. In: Proceedings of the IEEE Conference on Computer Vision and Pattern Recognition, pp. 1072–1080 (2015)

14. Jiang, Z.Q., Xie, W.J., Zhou, W.X., Sornette, D.: Multifractal analysis of financial markets: a review. Rep. Prog. Phys. **82**(12), 125901 (2019)
15. Leifman, G., Rudoy, D., Swedish, T., Bayro-Corrochano, E., Raskar, R.: Learning gaze transitions from depth to improve video saliency estimation. In: Proceedings of the IEEE International Conference on Computer Vision, pp. 1698–1707 (2017)
16. Liang, C., Wei, Y., Zhang, Y.: Is implied volatility more informative for forecasting realized volatility: an international perspective. J. Forecast. **39**(8), 1253–1276 (2020)
17. Lv, Y., Zhou, W.: Hierarchical multimodal adaptive fusion (hmaf) network for prediction of rgb-d saliency. Comput. Intell. Neurosci. **2020** (2020)
18. Marcoci, A., Thresher, A.C., Martens, N.C., Galison, P., Doeleman, S.S., Johnson, M.D.: Big stem collaborations should include humanities and social science. Nat. Hum. Behav., 1–2 (2023)
19. Meucci, A., Nicolosi, M.: Dynamic portfolio management with views at multiple horizons. Appl. Math. Comput. **274**, 495–518 (2016)
20. Niu, Z., Zhong, G., Yu, H.: A review on the attention mechanism of deep learning. Neurocomputing **452**, 48–62 (2021)
21. Nti, I.K., Adekoya, A.F., Weyori, B.A.: A systematic review of fundamental and technical analysis of stock market predictions. Artif. Intell. Rev. **53**(4), 3007–3057 (2020)
22. Pan, J., et al.: Salgan: visual saliency prediction with adversarial networks. In: CVPR Scene Understanding Workshop (2017)
23. Parmar, I., et al.: Stock market prediction using machine learning. In: 2018 First International Conference on Secure Cyber Computing and Communication, pp. 574–576 (2018)
24. Qiao, H., Zhong, S., Chen, Z., Wang, H.: Improving performance of robots using human-inspired approaches: a survey. SCIENCE CHINA Inf. Sci. **65**(12), 221201 (2022)
25. Song, K., Yao, T., Ling, Q., Mei, T.: Boosting image sentiment analysis with visual attention. Neurocomputing **312**, 218–228 (2018)
26. Su, C.H., Cheng, C.H.: A hybrid fuzzy time series model based on anfis and integrated nonlinear feature selection method for forecasting stock. Neurocomputing **205**, 264–273 (2016)
27. Tang, J., Wang, J., Hu, J.F.: Predicting human poses via recurrent attention network. Vis. Intell. **1**(1), 18 (2023)
28. Wang, Y., Bulling, A., et al.: Scanpath prediction on information visualisations. IEEE Trans. Visualiz. Comput. Graph. (2023)
29. Wilkinson, N., Klaes, M.: An introduction to behavioral economics. Bloomsbury Publishing (2017)
30. Wu, J., Zhou, W., Luo, T., Yu, L., Lei, J.: Multiscale multilevel context and multimodal fusion for rgb-d salient object detection. Signal Process. **178**, 107766 (2021)
31. Zhang, Q., Wang, X., Wang, S., Sun, Z., Kwong, S., Jiang, J.: Learning to explore saliency for stereoscopic videos via component-based interaction. IEEE Trans. Image Process. **29**, 5722–5736 (2020)
32. Zhang, X., Jin, T., Zhou, W., Lei, J.: Attention-based contextual interaction asymmetric network for rgb-d saliency prediction. J. Vis. Commun. Image Represent. **74**, 102997 (2021)
33. Zhao, J.X., Liu, J.J., Fan, D.P., Cao, Y., Yang, J., Cheng, M.M.: Egnet: edge guidance network for salient object detection. In: Proceedings of the IEEE/CVF International Conference on Computer Vision, pp. 8779–8788 (2019)

34. Zhou, W., Lei, J., Jiang, Q., Yu, L., Luo, T.: Blind binocular visual quality predictor using deep fusion network. IEEE Trans. Comput. Imaging **6**, 883–893 (2020)
35. Zhou, X., Pan, Z., Hu, G., Tang, S., Zhao, C.: Stock market prediction on high-frequency data using generative adversarial nets. Math. Problems Eng. **2018** (2018)

Unsupervised Event-to-Image Reconstruction Based on Domain Adaptation

Jupo Ma[1,2], Zhenqiang Zhao[1], and Wen Yang[1,2(✉)]

[1] School of Artificial Intelligence, Xidian University, Xi'an, China
{majupo,yangwen}@xidian.edu.cn
[2] Pazhou Lab, Huangpu 510555, China

Abstract. Event camera outputs a stream of asynchronous events, which suffering from a lot of noise, sparse texture, and lacking of static background information. Existing event-to-image reconstruction (E2IR) methods mostly adopt supervised learning approaches. However, it's hard to collect ground-truth images for real events. To tackle this challenge, we present a novel unsupervised E2IR method based on domain adaption (DA) in this paper. First, we design a long-short time event memory integration method to convert the unstructured events into structured tensor. The structured tensor could effectively alleviate the problem of missing background, but is still noisy. The E2IR method requires further learning about how to improve the quality of the structured tensor, similar to what is learned in conventional noisy image enhancement (IE) process. Thus we subsequently propose a novel DA-based strategy by transferring the knowledge from IE to E2IR. To better transfer the knowledge, we additionally design a multi-scale adversarial training method at the image-level features to bridge the domain gap. Experimental results show that the performance of our proposed Multi-scale Domain Adaptation based E2IR (MDAE2I) method is comparable to the state-of-the-art.

Keywords: Event Camera · Event-to-Image Reconstruction · Unsupervised Learning · Domain Adaptation

1 Introduction

Event cameras are novel bio-inspired vision sensors [5]. Each pixel in event camera works independently. When the brightness change reaches a threshold, an event is triggered by the pixel. Compared to conventional frame-based cameras, event cameras have several advantages, such as low latency, high temporal resolution, high dynamic range and so on. However, different from conventional cameras that output intensity-frames at a fixed frame rate by a global shutter,

Supported by the Fundamental Research Funds for the Central Universities.

the output of event camera is a sequence of asynchronous and sparse "events". This form of signal could not offer satisfactory visual experience and hinders the application of exiting frame-based algorithms on event camera. Researchers hope to convert the events into the format of conventional images/videos. As a result, the event-to-image reconstruction (E2IR) task is emerged.

Traditional E2IR methods [1,10,24] mostly approach the reconstruction problem based on handcrafted spatial-temporal features. However, event stream contains a large amount of noise, the quality of reconstructed image may not be satisfactory. Recently, due to development of deep learning, some convolutional neural network (CNN) based E2IR methods [5,23,28] are also proposed. Since it's hard to collect high-quality ground-truth images for event streams, most CNN-based E2IR methods train on the synthetic events [6,18,21,26]. However, due to the complex working mechanisms of event cameras [2,4,7,13,20], the synthetic events might not be realistic, especially in high-speed and high-dynamic-range scenes.

In this paper, we present a novel unsupervised E2IR method based on multi-scale domain adaption (DA) strategy, named as MDAE2I, to reduce the dependency on ground-truth of events. First, we propose a long-short time event memory integration (LSTEMI) method to convert the asynchronous unstructured events into structured tensor. Since event cameras subject to background noise, refractory period, hot pixels and bandwidth limitations, the structured tensor is lack of clear textures. The E2IR method needs to learn about improving the quality and information content of the structured tensor, which is similar to the knowledge learned in noisy image enhancement (IE) [9,11,12,27]. Inspired by that, we next propose to adopt DA-based method to transfer the knowledge from IE (i.e., source domain) to E2IR (i.e., target domain). Specifically, the source domain dataset is defined as noisy images with corresponding pristine images. In order to better bridge the gap between the source domain and target domain, a multi-scale adversarial training strategy at the image-level feature is proposed. Finally, to evaluate the proposed method, a new event dataset is captured with one of the most advanced event cameras – Celex5 [4]. Experimental results verify that our proposed method could effectively perform knowledge transfer from IE to E2IR, thereby realizing high-quality image reconstruction, even without ground-truth for supervision.

The main contribution of this work are summarized as follows:

- A novel unsupervised event-to-image reconstruction method based on the domain adaptation is proposed. Even without ground-truth for supervision, the proposed MDAE2I could reconstruct high-quality images.
- A multi-scale adversarial training strategy at the image-level feature is proposed for domain adaptation. Benefited from the multi-scale DA process, the proposed method could effectively transfer the knowledge from IE to E2IR, so as to achieve high-quality reconstruction on local details (low-level features), regional contours (middle-level features) and global concepts (high-level feature).

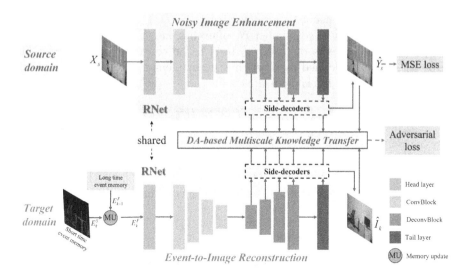

Fig. 1. The whole framework of our proposed method **MDAE2I**.

– A new event dataset captured by Celex5 is established for training and testing. Experimental results show that our proposed method achieves remarkable performance.

2 The Proposed Method

2.1 Formulation of Event-to-Image Reconstruction

The generation process of an event is formulated as

$$\log\left(I\left(x,y,t\right)\right) - \log\left(I\left(x,y,t-\varDelta t\right)\right) \geq \ \text{C} \tag{1}$$

(x,y) represents the spatial location, t represents the timestamp when the event triggered, $t - \varDelta t$ denotes the timestamp of the last triggered event, C is the contrast threshold, $I\left(x,y,t\right)$ denotes the absolute intensity value at time t. Equation 1 represents that a new event at pixel (x,y) will be triggered when the brightness change reaches a threshold. Each event is represented as a tuple

$$e = (x,y,g,t) \tag{2}$$

where g denotes the brightness information about the event, which depends on the event camera type. In general, event signal can be categorized into two types: polarity-event [13] and intensity-event [7]. For polarity-event, $g \in \{-1,+1\}$ represents the direction of brightness change. For intensity-event, $g \in R$ represents the absolute intensity value. In literature, the intensity-event is few studied for E2IR task, although it contains a lot of noise. In this work, we conduct the first attempt to reconstruct images from intensity-events captured by Celex5.

The event stream can be represented as $\varepsilon \doteq \{e_i\}$. We first divide ε into several sub-streams by fixed number N_e of events, i.e., $\varepsilon \doteq \{\varepsilon_k\}$. Next, in order to meet the requirements of CNN, ε_k need to be converted into a image-like tensor E_k^S, which is defined as short-time event memory (STET). By utilizing intensity information, E_k^S is defined as

$$E_k^S(x,y) = \begin{cases} g(x,y,t^*) & if \ event \ triggered \ at \ (x,y) \\ 0 & otherwise \end{cases} \tag{3}$$

t^* is the timestamp of the latest triggered event at location (x,y) in ε_k, $g(x,y,t^*)$ represents the intensity information of the event. Event-to-image reconstruction (E2IR) task aims to convert $\{E_k^S\}$ into a sequence of images $\{\hat{I}_k\}$.

2.2 Reconstruction Method

Overview. As show in Fig. 1, our proposed unsupervised DA-based E2IR method mainly contains two parts: the source domain part for image enhancement (IE) and the target domain part for E2IR. The reconstruction networks in source domain and target domain share the same architecture and weights, so for convenience, the two networks are denoted as the same notation -- $RNet$. In the source domain, $RNet$ directly takes the noisy image X_s as input and outputs the enhanced image $\hat{Y}_s$ with the ground-truth pristine image Y_s is known. In the target domain part, there exists two sub-modules: memory update (MU) module and $RNet$. MU executes the long-short time event memory integration (LSTEMI) process and outputs the structured full-time event memory tensor (FTEM) E_k^F, which is fed into $RNet$ to reconstruct image. Through the multiscale domain adaptation process in $RNet$, the knowledge learned from IE is transferred to E2IR. As a result, $RNet$ could learn how to improve the quality and informative content of the structured tensor E_k^F. Next, We start with introducing the MU module, then goes into the domain adaptation strategy in $RNet$.

Memory Update Module. Event camera responses to dynamic scenes, ignoring the static background. Event stream is sparse and contains a lot of noise. If only the STEM E_k^S is fed into $RNet$, the reconstructed image may contain incomplete background and cluttered texture. Thus, existing E2IR methods [23,25] usually adopt ConvLSTM or ConvGRU to maintain a internal memory state. By taking the internal memory state as an additional input, E2IR methods could reconstruct background effectively.

In our work, by taking the advantage of intensity information captured by Celex5, we design a simple yet effective operation to maintain the event memory. The operation is name as long-short time event memory integration (LSTEMI), which is defined as

$$E_k^F = E_{k-1}^F \odot (1 - \mathbf{M}) + E_k^S \odot \mathbf{M} \tag{4}$$

where E_k^F is defined as the full-time event memory (FTEM) at current step-k, E_{k-1}^F is the previous long-time event memory (LTEM) before current step-k. E_0^F is initialized zeros for all spatial locations. $\odot$ denotes the element-wise product. $\mathbf{M}$ is the mask of locations in E_k^S where the event triggered, i.e., if event is triggered at location (x, y), $\mathbf{M}(x, y) = 1$; otherwise $\mathbf{M}(x, y) = 0$. As a result, in target domain, the E2IR task is formulated as

$$\hat{I}_k = RNet\left(E_k^F\right) \tag{5}$$

Through merging the short and long-time memory, more background information and temporal information could be extracted to reconstruct images. At the same time, taking the FTEM as input of $RNet$ could help to reduce the domain gap between source domain and target domain.

Domain Adaptation Strategy. The main branch of reconstruction network $RNet$ is designed as the encoder-decoder framework as show in Fig. 1. The head layer consists of "Conv + ReLu". ConvBlock is composed of "Conv + Instance Normalization + ReLu" and the stride of convolution is 2 for downsampling. DeconvBlock is set as "Deconv + Instance Normalization + ReLu". DeconvBlock is used for upsampling. In $RNet$, the number of ConvBlock and DeconvBlock is set as $N_L = 4$. The tail layer consists of "Conv + Instance Normalization".

Besides, in order to integrate multi-scale features for reconstruction, side-decoders are added at each level of the DeconvBlocks and the tail layer. Each side-decoder is composed of "Bilinear Upsample + Conv + Tanh". Bilinear Upsample operation upsamples the feature maps from different levels into the same spatial size as the final output image. The output channel of Conv layer in each side-decoder is 1 to predict multi-scale images. The working process of the i-th side-decoders in source domain can be formulated as

$$\hat{Y}_s^i = Dec_{side}^i\left(f^i\right) \tag{6}$$

f^i represents the feature map from the i-th level of the DeconvBlocks and the tail layer, $\hat{Y}_s^i$ represents the multi-scale reconstructed image, and $i = \{1, 2, ..., N_L + 1\}$. By integrating the multi-scale reconstructed images, the final output image is obtained as

$$\hat{Y}_s = \frac{1}{N_L + 1} \sum_{i=1}^{N_L+1} \hat{Y}_s^i \tag{7}$$

In source domain, the supervised loss is adopted for optimization, which is defined as

$$L_{src}^{RNet} = \frac{1}{W \times H}\left(\sum_{i=1}^{N_L+1} \lambda_i \cdot \left\|\hat{Y}_s^i - Y_s\right\|_2^2\right) + \\ \frac{\lambda_{N_L+2}}{W \times H}\left\|\hat{Y}_s - Y_s\right\|_2^2 \tag{8}$$

W, H are the width and height of the reconstructed image, λ_i is the balance weight. In our experiments, $\lambda_1 = \lambda_2 = \cdots = \lambda_{N_L+1} = 0.1$, $\lambda_{N_L+2} = 0.5$.

In the target domain, the structured FTEM tensor E_k^F is set as the input to $RNet$, the working process is formulated as

$$\hat{I}_k = RNet_t\left(E_k^F\right) = \frac{1}{N_L + 1} \sum_{i=1}^{N_L+1} \hat{I}_k^i \tag{9}$$

where,

$$\hat{I}_k^i = Dec_{side}^i\left(f^i\right) \tag{10}$$

$\hat{I}_k^i$ represents the multi-scale reconstructed image from events.

Since it's hard to collect ground-truth for real events, we propose to adopt domain adaptation to transfer knowledge from IE to E2IR, thereby leaning reconstruct high quality images from events. First, a discriminator D inspired by [9] is designed for adversarial learning at the final output image. D takes the final output image $\hat{Y}_s$ or $\hat{I}_k$ as input. At each iteration, the adversarial training has two steps: (1) optimize D with loss L_{adv}^D; (2) optimize $RNet$ with L_{adv}^{RNet}. To stabilize the training process, LSGAN framework is adopted. L_{adv}^D and L_{adv}^{RNet} is defined as

$$L_{adv}^D = E_{\hat{Y}_s}\left\{\left[D\left(\hat{Y}_s\right) - 1\right]^2\right\} + E_{\hat{I}_k}\left\{\left[D\left(\hat{I}_k\right) - 0\right]^2\right\} \tag{11}$$

$$L_{adv}^{RNet} = L_{adv}^{RNet-D} = E_{\hat{I}_k}\left\{\left[D\left(\hat{I}_k\right) - 1\right]^2\right\} \tag{12}$$

The adversarial training at the global image level could align the feature distribution between source domain and target domain. Minimizing L_{adv}^D could optimize D to distinguish $\hat{Y}_s$ from $\hat{I}_k$. Minimizing L_{adv}^{RNet-D} could optimize $RNet$ to reconstruct $\hat{I}_k$ more like $\hat{Y}_s$.

Furthermore, to reconstruct high quality image at all scales, a multi-scale adversarial learning strategy is proposed. We additionally add discriminators D^i for the multi-scale reconstructed images, to reduce the gap between source domain and target domain. The loss function of each D^i is

$$L_{adv}^{D_i} = E_{\hat{Y}_s^i}\left\{\left[D^i\left(\hat{Y}_s^i\right) - 1\right]^2\right\} + E_{\hat{I}_k^i}\left\{\left[D^i\left(\hat{I}_k^i\right) - 0\right]^2\right\} \tag{13}$$

Finally, the loss function of $RNet$ in target domain is

$$L_{adv}^{RNet} = \sum_{i=1}^{N_L+1} \lambda_i \cdot L_{adv}^{RNet-D_i} + \lambda_{N_L+2} \cdot L_{adv}^{RNet-D} \tag{14}$$

where,

$$L_{adv}^{RNet-D_i} = E_{\hat{I}_k^i}\left\{\left[D^i\left(\hat{I}_k^i\right) - 1\right]^2\right\} \tag{15}$$

Through the multi-scale adversarial training at the image-level feature, $RNet$ is optimized to learn transfer multi-scale knowledge from IE task to E2IR task and reduce the domain gap from different scales. As a result, $RNet$ could reconstruct images with better local details (low-level feature), regional contours (middle-level feature) and glob concepts (high-level feature).

3   Experimental Results

3.1   Experiment Setup

Dataset Preparation. In this work, we make the first attempt for the task of unsupervised intensity-event to image reconstruction. While exiting event datasets [21–23] in literature most belong to the polarity-event [2, 13, 16]. Thus, we build a new event dataset by Celex5 as the target dataset. Celex5 is one of the most advanced event cameras, which sensor resolution is up to 800×1280. During data collection, Celex5 is set to operate in "Event Intensity Mode". In this mode, the events captured by Celex5 not only contain polarity information but also intensity information. We collect total 20 event streams in indoor scenes by moving the camera by hand. Each event stream lasts for 15–25 s. We randomly select 16 event streams as training data, and the remaining 4 event streams as testing data.

The source dataset consists of conventional images which can be easily capture by traditional cameras. In our work, we collect 31 pristine videos using a mobile phone, each lasting 11–28 s. The resolution is 720×1280. All the pristine image frames are extracted from these videos to form the source domain dataset. On the other hand, the noisy images is simply obtained by adding synthetic noise to the pristine images. For convenience, two most common noise types, i.e., Gaussian noise and Poisson noise, are adopted in our work. We randomly select 24 videos for training, and the remaining 7 videos for testing.

Besides, by leveraging the videos in source dataset, we additionally build a synthetic event dataset based on the event generative model in V2E [6]. To be consistent with the event format of Celex5, we modify the V2E algorithm to output event with intensity information, i.e., intensity-event. In our experiments, this synthetic dataset is mainly used to retrain other E2IR methods for fairly comparison. Since the ground-truth images are available in the synthetic dataset, we can retrain the selected E2IR methods in supervised learning as in their original papers.

Evaluation Metric. Since there is no ground-truth images for events in our proposed dataset, the widely used metrics PSNR/MSE/SSIM [29]/LPIPS [30] can't be adopted. Considering that E2IR methods aim to reconstruct high-quality images that could offer comfortable visual experience, no-reference image quality assessment (NRIQA) methods are adopted as metrics to measure the performance of different E2IR methods. NRIQA could directly evaluate the perceptual quality of an image without the need for reference image. In our work,

3 NRIQA methods (i.e., NIQE, BIQI and AIGQA) are chosen as the evaluation metrics. NIQE [15] is an "opinion-unaware" and "distortion-unaware" method which is also widely used in conventional image super-resolution task. BIQI [17] is one classical method based on the statistic features. AIGQA [14] is a deep learning based method which mimics the perception mechanism of human brain to measure image quality. The higher the NIQE/BIQI index, the worse the image quality. The higher the AIGQA index, the better the image quality.

Implementation Details. The proposed method is implemented in PyTorch. Adam optimizer with learning rate 10^{-4} is used for optimization. During training, the input tensor is random cropped into 256×256 and the batch size is 8. To stabilize and accelerate the training, adequate number of events are accumulated to ensure that there are triggered events at each location of the full-time event memory tensor E_k^F.

3.2   Quantitative Evaluation

Table 1. Quantitative evaluation of different E2IR methods on the testing set of target dataset. "↑" means higher is better, "↓" means lower is better.

	NIQE(↓)	BIQI (↓)	AIGQA (↑)
E2VID	7.02	39.40	43.74
FireNet	7.12	39.83	42.53
SSLE2I	7.80	46.80	37.73
MDAE2I	**6.62**	**33.07**	**44.79**

Three state-of-the-art CNN-based E2IR methods are adopted for comparison, including E2VID [23], FireNet [25] and SSLE2I [19]. E2VID and FireNet are two supervised methods originally designed for polarity-event to image reconstruction. For a fair comparison, we retrain E2VID and FireNet by intensity-events from the synthetic event dataset. Specifically, STEM is used as the input. SSLE2I is an advanced unsupervised E2IR method by combining the event-based photometric constancy and optical flow estimation. In our experiments, we tried to retrain SSLE2I using intensity-events, but the result is really poor. Thus the polarity information of target dataset is used to retrain SSLE2I.

Table 1 list the mean NIQE index, BIQI index and AIGQA index on the testing event streams of target datasets. Due to the gap between synthetic events and real events, E2VID and FireNet which are trained on synthetic events couldn't generalize to real events well. In addition, events captured by Celex5 suffer from timestamp mismatch problem, which may lead to inaccurate estimation of optical flow in SSLE2I method. Therefore, the performance of SSLE2I is not satisfactory. MDAE2I achieves the best results on all metrics, which shows that our

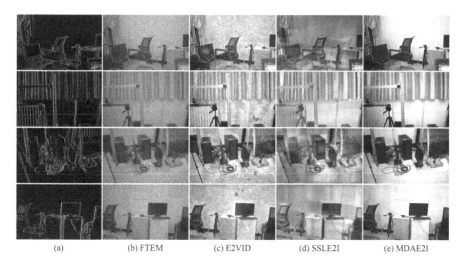

Fig. 2. Reconstructed images from events by different methods. The first column represents the current input tensor (i.e., short-time event memory), the second column is the full-time event memory (FTEM), the third column to the last column are reconstructed images by different E2IR methods.

proposed method is effective to leverage the characters of intensity-events and realize high-quality image reconstruction through knowledge transfer.

3.3   Qualitative Results

In this section, some reconstructed images by different methods are presented, as shown in Fig. 2. To give a more intuitively comparison, the full-time event memory FTEM is also presented in Fig. 2(b). FTEM contains a lot of noise and the visual contrast is poor. Figure 2(c) and Fig. 2(d) show the reconstructed images by E2VID and SSLE2I. The image contrast is improvement to some extent, but new distortion is introduced in the images, such as fake shadows, uneven lighting, etc. In Fig. 2(e), the images reconstructed by MDAE2I achieve the best visual experience: the background is smoother and clearer, the object looks more realistic and the visual contrast is greatly improved. From the above visual comparisons with other E2IR methods, we can conclude that the proposed method achieve remarkable performance. Our method is effective to learn how to reconstruct high-quality images from events by transferring knowledge from conventional image enhancement task. MDAE2I could avoid the degradation of image quality caused by the unrealistic of synthetic events.

Additionally, since the FTEM is similar to conventional noisy image, two popular image denoising methods, i.e., N2N [8] and NAF [3], are also adopted for comparison. N2N is a novel self-supervised image denoising algorithm. NAF is a state-of-the-art supervised image restoration method. Figure 3 presents the denoising results. Due to the complexity and uniqueness of noisy events,

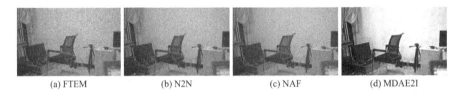

(a) FTEM   (b) N2N   (c) NAF   (d) MDAE2I

Fig. 3. Denoising results of different noisy image enhancement methods on the full-time event memory tensor (FTEM).

conventional image denoising algorithms cannot effectively improve the perceptual quality.

3.4 Ablation Study

Table 2. Results of ablation experiments. "↑" means higher is better.

	AIGQA (↑)
MI2I	42.69
MDAE2I-Enc	43.30
DAE2I	44.12
MDAE2I	44.79

To verify the effectiveness of our proposed techniques, the following ablation experiments are conducted:

1) **MI2I**: This variant model is only trained on the source domain dataset without DA operation.
2) **MDAE2I-Enc**: Instead of doing DA on the image-level, this model adopts DA on the feature-level of encoder layers (i.e., head layer and ConvBlock layers in Fig. 1).
3) **DAE2I**: This variant model does not take the multi-scale adversarial training process, i.e., L_{adv}^{RNet} in Eq. 14 only consists of L_{adv}^{RNet-D}.

Table 2 lists the AIGQA indexes of **MI2I**, **MDAE2I-Enc** and **DAE2I**. There is no DA operation in **MI2I**, the features extracted for reconstruction in the target domain are not aligned with that in the source domain. Therefore, **MI2I** gets the poorest score. Image reconstruction more concerns the image-level features, thus the performance of **MDAE2I-Enc** is inferior than **DAE2I** and **MDAE2I**. Benefiting from the multi-scale domain adaptation strategy, the proposed **MDAE2I** realizes high-quality reconstruction on different scales, include local details (low-level features), regional contours (middle-level features) and global concepts (high-level semantics).

4   Conclusion

In this paper, a novel unsupervised event-to-image reconstruction method based on multi-scale domain adaptation is proposed. By leveraging the characteristics of intensity-event, the long-short time event memory integration could effectively offer background information. A series of ablation studies validate that the proposed image-level multi-scale adversarial leaning strategy can effectively transfer knowledge from image enhancement to E2IR. In conclusion, both quantitative and qualitative experiment results verify that reconstructing high-quality images from events by transferring knowledge from IE is an effective strategy.

References

1. Bardow, P., Davison, A.J., Leutenegger, S.: Simultaneous optical flow and intensity estimation from an event camera. In: 2016 IEEE Conference on Computer Vision and Pattern Recognition (CVPR), pp. 884–892 (2016)
2. Brandli, C., Berner, R., Yang, M., Liu, S.C., Delbruck, T.: A 240×180 130 db 3 μs latency global shutter spatiotemporal vision sensor. IEEE J. Solid-State Circuits **49**(10), 2333–2341 (2014)
3. Chen, L., Chu, X., Zhang, X., Sun, J.: Simple baselines for image restoration. arXiv preprint arXiv:2204.04676 (2022)
4. Chen, S., Guo, M.: Live demonstration: Celex-v: A 1m pixel multi-mode event-based sensor. In: 2019 IEEE/CVF Conference on Computer Vision and Pattern Recognition Workshops (CVPRW), pp. 1682–1683 (2019)
5. Gallego, G., et al.: Event-based vision: a survey. IEEE Trans. Pattern Anal. Mach. Intell. **44**(1), 154–180 (2022)
6. Gehrig, D., Gehrig, M., Hidalgo-Carrió, J., Scaramuzza, D.: Video to events: recycling video datasets for event cameras. In: 2020 IEEE/CVF Conference on Computer Vision and Pattern Recognition (CVPR), pp. 3583–3592 (2020)
7. Guo, M., Ding, R., Chen, S.: Live demonstration: a dynamic vision sensor with direct logarithmic output and full-frame picture-on-demand. In: 2016 IEEE International Symposium on Circuits and Systems (ISCAS), pp. 456–456 (2016)
8. Huang, T., Li, S., Jia, X., Lu, H., Liu, J.: Neighbor2neighbor: self-supervised denoising from single noisy images. In: Proceedings of the IEEE/CVF Conference on Computer Vision and Pattern Recognition (CVPR), pp. 14781–14790, June 2021
9. Isola, P., Zhu, J.Y., Zhou, T., Efros, A.A.: Image-to-image translation with conditional adversarial networks. In: Proceedings of the IEEE Conference on Computer Vision and Pattern Recognition (CVPR), July 2017
10. Kim, H., Handa, A., Benosman, R., Ieng, S.H., Davison, A.: Simultaneous mosaicing and tracking with an event camera. In: Proceedings of the British Machine Vision Conference (2014)
11. Ledig, C., et al.: Photo-realistic single image super-resolution using a generative adversarial network. In: 2017 IEEE Conference on Computer Vision and Pattern Recognition (CVPR), pp. 105–114 (2017)
12. Lee, H.Y., Tseng, H.Y., Huang, J.B., Singh, M., Yang, M.H.: Diverse image-to-image translation via disentangled representations. In: Proceedings of the European Conference on Computer Vision (ECCV), September 2018

13. Lichtsteiner, P., Posch, C., Delbruck, T.: A 128 × 128 120 db 15 μs latency asynchronous temporal contrast vision sensor. IEEE J. Solid-State Circuits **43**(2), 566–576 (2008)
14. Ma, J., et al.: Blind image quality assessment with active inference. IEEE Trans. Image Process. **30**, 3650–3663 (2021). https://doi.org/10.1109/TIP.2021.3064195
15. Mittal, A., Soundararajan, R., Bovik, A.C.: Making a "completely blind" image quality analyzer. IEEE Signal Process. Lett. **20**(3), 209–212 (2013)
16. Moeys, D.P., et al.: A sensitive dynamic and active pixel vision sensor for color or neural imaging applications. IEEE Trans. Biomed. Circuits Syst. **12**(1), 123–136 (2018)
17. Moorthy, A.K., Bovik, A.C.: A two-step framework for constructing blind image quality indices. IEEE Signal Process. Lett. **17**(5), 513–516 (2010)
18. Mueggler, E., Rebecq, H., Gallego, G., Delbruck, T., Scaramuzza, D.: The event-camera dataset and simulator: event-based data for pose estimation, visual odometry, and slam. Int. J. Robot. Res. **36**(2), 142–149 (2017)
19. Paredes-Vallés, F., de Croon, G.C.H.E.: Back to event basics: Self-supervised learning of image reconstruction for event cameras via photometric constancy. In: 2021 IEEE/CVF Conference on Computer Vision and Pattern Recognition (CVPR), pp. 3445–3454 (2021)
20. Posch, C., Matolin, D., Wohlgenannt, R.: A qvga 143 db dynamic range frame-free pwm image sensor with lossless pixel-level video compression and time-domain cds. IEEE J. Solid-State Circuits **46**(1), 259–275 (2011)
21. Rebecq, H., Gehrig, D., Scaramuzza, D.: Esim: an open event camera simulator. In: Proceedings of the 2nd Conference on Robot Learning, vol. 87, pp. 969–982, 29–31 October 2018
22. Rebecq, H., Ranftl, R., Koltun, V., Scaramuzza, D.: Events-to-video: bringing modern computer vision to event cameras. In: 2019 IEEE/CVF Conference on Computer Vision and Pattern Recognition (CVPR), pp. 3852–3861 (2019)
23. Rebecq, H., Ranftl, R., Koltun, V., Scaramuzza, D.: High speed and high dynamic range video with an event camera. IEEE Trans. Pattern Anal. Mach. Intell. **43**(6), 1964–1980 (2021)
24. Reinbacher, C., Graber, G., Pock, T.: Real-time intensity-image reconstruction for event cameras using manifold regularisation. Int. J. Comput. Vis. **126**(12) (2018)
25. Scheerlinck, C., Rebecq, H., Gehrig, D., Barnes, N., Mahony, R.E., Scaramuzza, D.: Fast image reconstruction with an event camera. In: 2020 IEEE Winter Conference on Applications of Computer Vision (WACV), pp. 156–163 (2020)
26. Stoffregen, T., et al.: Reducing the sim-to-real gap for event cameras. In: Vedaldi, A., Bischof, H., Brox, T., Frahm, J.-M. (eds.) ECCV 2020. LNCS, vol. 12372, pp. 534–549. Springer, Cham (2020). https://doi.org/10.1007/978-3-030-58583-9_32
27. Vincent, P., Larochelle, H., Bengio, Y., Manzagol, P.A.: Extracting and composing robust features with denoising autoencoders. In: Proceedings of the 25th International Conference on Machine Learning, pp. 1096–1103 (2008)
28. Wang, L., Kim, T.K., Yoon, K.J.: Eventsr: from asynchronous events to image reconstruction, restoration, and super-resolution via end-to-end adversarial learning. In: 2020 IEEE/CVF Conference on Computer Vision and Pattern Recognition (CVPR), pp. 8312–8322 (2020)

29. Wang, Z., Bovik, A.C., Sheikh, H.R., Simoncelli, E.P.: Image quality assessment: from error visibility to structural similarity. IEEE Trans. Image Process. **13**(4), 600–612 (2004). https://doi.org/10.1109/TIP.2003.819861
30. Zhang, R., Isola, P., Efros, A.A., Shechtman, E., Wang, O.: The unreasonable effectiveness of deep features as a perceptual metric. In: 2018 IEEE/CVF Conference on Computer Vision and Pattern Recognition, pp. 586–595 (2018). https://doi.org/10.1109/CVPR.2018.00068

Adjusting Exploitation and Exploration Rates of Differential Evolution: A Novel Mutation Strategy

Danting Duan[1], Yuhui Zhang[2], Wei Zhong[3(✉)], Long Ye[3], and Qin Zhang[3]

[1] Key Laboratory of Media Audio and Video (Communication University of China), Ministry of Education, Beijing, China
dantingduan@cuc.edu.cn

[2] School of Computer Science and Technology, Dongguan University of Technology, Dongguan, China
yhzhang@dgut.edu.cn

[3] State Key Laboratory of Media Convergence and Communication, Communication University of China, Beijing, China
{wzhong,yelong,zhangqin}@cuc.edu.cn

Abstract. Differential evolution (DE) has attracted significant attention in recent years owing to its high performance in solving continuous problems. Up to now, a large number of variants of DE mutation strategy have been proposed and extensively studied. However, these mutation strategies rarely concentrate on adjusting the exploitation and exploration rates, which can make a great impact on DE's performance. In this paper, a novel mutation strategy capable of visibly adjusting the exploration and exploitation rates is developed for DE algorithms. In the proposed mutation strategy, the difference vector is calculated according to the distance between selected individuals and the gravity center of these individuals. Then, the donor vector is generated by adding this difference vector to the base vector based on an asymmetrical normal distribution that determines the probability of the mutate direction to be inward for exploitation or outward for exploration. Experiments have been carried out on 13 classical benchmark functions and the CEC2013 test suite to study the proposed mutation strategy. The experimental results show that the exploitation and exploration rates have a considerable effect on both the algorithm's convergence rate and the solution accuracy.

Keywords: Differential evolution · Mutation operator · Evolutionary computation

This work was supported by the National Natural Science Foundation of China under Grant Nos. 62271455 and 62106046, the Fundamental Research Funds for the Central Universities under Grant No. CUC18LG024, the Horizontal Research Project under Grant No. HG23004, and the Guangdong Basic and Applied Basic Research Foundation under Grant No. 2019A1515110474.

G. Zhai et al. (Eds.): IFTC 2023, CCIS 2067, pp. 212–226, 2024.
https://doi.org/10.1007/978-981-97-3626-3_16

1   Introduction

Differential Evolution (DE), which first proposed by Storn and Price in 1995 [1–3], is a new form of evolutionary computation (EC). Owing to its high performance in optimizing continuous problems, DE has attracted significant attention. The powerfulness of DE has been demonstrated by its competitive rankings in CEC competitions. After years of development, a large number of DE variants have been proposed [4–7]. Based on this, DE has been applied to solve various real-world problems.

Similar to other EAs, DE is a population-based global optimization algorithm. The algorithm starts by initializing a population of candidate solutions, termed individuals, randomly from the predefined domain. Then the process enters a loop of iteration including three general operators of EA, i.e., mutation, crossover, and selection until the termination criterion is satisfied. In the mutation operator of DE, the difference between two individuals is added to a base individual to generate a donor vector. This difference between individual pair is automatically changed along with the iterations of population, gradually adapt to the natural scaling of a specific problem. In this way, the mutation step length in DE is automatically adjusted during the optimization process. DE's strength owes much to the introduction of the difference vector-based mutation.

Because the mutation operator plays a key role in DE and exhibits a strong influence on its performance, a large amount of research work has been conducted to improve the mutation operator. Some research efforts were devoted to a better tradeoff between convergence speed and robustness [8], whereas some others concentrated on striking a balance between exploitation and exploration capabilities [9,10]. Besides, some mutation strategies were introduced along with adaptive parameter control schemes, such as the DE/current-to-$p$best in [11]. In recent years, alternately using several mutation strategies that are mutually complementary has attracted the attention of some researchers. The work in [12] shows that approaches combining different mutation strategies are very effective. In [13], a self-adaptive variant of DE is proposed, which employs several mutation strategies and adaptively adjusts the using strategy during the search process.

However, to the best of our knowledge, no prior work has focused on adjusting the exploitation and exploration rates of mutation operator by intuitively controlling the mutant direction. As the relative rates of exploitation and exploration are important properties of DE, it provides opportunities to further increase the solution accuracy and convergence speed of the algorithm. In the process of traditional DE mutation operator, after determining the base vector, the step-size and orientation of mutation entirely depend on the difference vector. Although the capability of exploitation and exploration can be tuned by the scale factor F (a low F value gives preference to exploitation whereas a high F value encourages exploration), the mutant direction is out of our control. Figure 1(a) shows the difference vectors formed by all possible pairings of nine individuals. Transporting them to a base vector located at (0, 0) clearly shows their distribution, which is displayed in Fig. 1(b). It can be observed in Fig. 1(b) that each difference vector has a negative counterpart. The probabilities of choosing

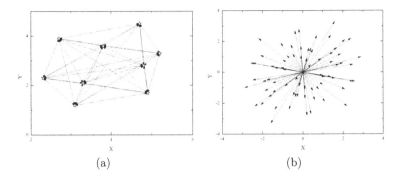

Fig. 1. Distribution of difference vectors.

a difference vector and its negative counterpart are exactly the same. Therefore, if there is a difference vector V drives the base vector toward the inner region of population which facilitates exploitation, there must be another vector V_R (the negative counterpart of V) drives the base vector toward the outer regions and facilitates exploration. In this sense, it is reasonable to consider that the trends of exploitation and exploration in the traditional DE mutation are similar.

In this paper, we introduce a novel mutation strategy that can visibly adjust the exploitation and exploration rates. The model is inspired by the study in [14], where an asymmetrical normal distribution crossover is used to investigate the mean- and parent-centric balance of GA. In the proposed mutation operator, the center of selected individuals is first calculated, then the difference between center and individuals is used to generate donor vector. By introducing the center of selected individuals, we can set our sights on the mutant direction, which is neglected in previous research works. In the mutation, the scale factor is randomly drawn from a novel distribution, called Asymmetric Normal Distribution (AND). The AND contains a control parameter ζ_0 determining the probability of generating a positive number or a negative number. By using the random number generated by AND as scale factor, the probability of driving the base vector toward or outward the center in the mutation can be adjusted. Therefore, instead of using a fixed positive F parameter, ζ_0 in AND is able to tune the probability of exploitation and exploration trends. By controlling the setting of ζ_0, the search behavior of DE can be adjusted. In this paper, we focus on investigating ζ_0 on the performance of DE, which could inspire some interesting future work of DE. Experiments have been carried out on 13 traditional benchmark functions and the CEC2013 test suite with different characteristics. Experimental results indicate that ζ_0 has a considerable effect on controlling the exploitation and exploration of DE, which affects the algorithm's convergence rate and solution accuracy significantly.

The rest of this paper is organized as follows. Section 2 provides an overview of the related work. Section 3 describes the proposed DE framework in detail. In Sect. 4, experiments are carried out on 13 benchmark functions and the CEC2013 test suite for investigation. Finally, concluding remarks are summarized and some pointers to future work are given in Sect. 5.

2   Related Work

Mutation operator is the primary factor that discriminates one DE algorithm from another. The technical name of mutation operator described above is "DE/rand/1", since the base vector is randomly sampled and only one vector difference is added. Besides DE/rand/1, four other mutation strategies that are most frequently used are listed below.

DE/current-to-best/1:

$$V_{i,G} = X_{i,G} + F \cdot (X_{best,G} - X_{i,G}) + F \cdot (X_{r1,G} - X_{r2,G}), \tag{1}$$

DE/best/1:
$$V_{i,G} = X_{best,G} + F \cdot (X_{r1,G} - X_{r2,G}), \tag{2}$$

'

DE/best/2:

$$V_{i,G} = X_{best,G} + F \cdot (X_{r1,G} - X_{r2,G}) + F \cdot (X_{r3,G} - X_{r4,G}), \tag{3}$$

DE/rand/2:

$$V_{i,G} = X_{r1,G} + F \cdot (X_{r2,G} - X_{r3,G}) + F \cdot (X_{r4,G} - X_{r5,G}), \tag{4}$$

where $X_{best,G}$ is the best individual in the current population, indices $r1$, $r2$, $r3$, $r4$ and $r5$ are distinct integers randomly sampled from $[1, NP]$ and all of them are different from index i.

Besides the above strategies, Zhang *et al.* [11] proposed an adaptive differential evolution called JADE along with a new mutation strategy, named DE/current-to-*p*best. DE/current-to-*p*best is an extension of DE/current-to-best. The donor vector is generated in the following manner:

$$V_{i,G} = X_{i,G} + F \cdot (X_{best,G}^p - X_{i,G}) + F \cdot (X_{r1,G} - X_{r2,G}), \tag{5}$$

where $X_{best,G}^p$ is randomly selected from the top $NP \cdot p$ individuals with $p \in (0, 1]$ (individuals are sorted according to their fitness values, the best individual ranks first). Inspired by [11], Segredo *et al.* [10] introduced a similarity-based neighbourhood search method to the exploratory and exploitative variants of JADE, adaptively influencing the choice of neighbours used in the creation of new solutions. Furthermore, Deng *et al.* [8] proposed an improved differential evolution, named NBOLDE, which is based on the neighbourhood variation operator and adversarial learning. In their work, the new evaluation parameters and weighting factors to the neighbourhood model are introduced and a novel neighbourhood strategy is proposed. An experimental comparison of 12 low and high dimensional benchmark functions proves that the NBOLDE algorithm exhibits faster convergence speed, higher convergence accuracy and stronger optimization ability in solving high dimensional complex functions. Later, in order to reduce the burden of selecting suitable mutation strategies and control parameters, Gupta *et al.* [12] proposed an efficient differential evolution framework called EFDE, which employs a novel fitness-based dynamic mutation strategy and control parameters so as to maintain a proper balance between diversity and convergence. Cai *et al.* [9] designed a new search framework for DE that is based on an explicit control strategy to balance the number of explorations and exploits during the search process. Experimental results on benchmark optimisation functions show that the method exhibits excellent performance on complex problems.

3   The Proposed Mutation Strategy Based on AND

In this section, we propose a novel mutation strategy named asymmetric normal distribution mutation (ANDM) with an additional control parameter that can visibly adjust the exploitation and exploration rates. The proposed mutation operator randomly selects θ distinct individuals to generate a donor vector for each target vector. The center of θ individuals is represented by the notation C_θ. The scale factors are randomly drawn from a novel distribution function called asymmetric normal distribution. One of the θ individuals is used as the base vector, and then the scaled difference vectors between other individuals and C_θ are added to the base vector. Thus, a donor vector is built. A more detailed description is given below.

3.1   Implementations

For a target vector $X_{i,G}$, θ distinct individuals are randomly sampled from the population to generate the mutant vector. Assume that the selected individuals are $X_{r1,G}$, $X_{r2,G}$,...,$X_{r\theta,G}$ with $i \neq rj$, $j = 1, 2, ..., \theta$. The mutant vector $V_{i,G}$ is generated as follows:

$$V_{i,G} = X_{r1,G} - \sum_{j=2}^{\theta} (X_{rj,G} - C_\theta) \cdot \omega_j, \tag{6}$$

where C_θ represents the center of θ individuals. To be specific, the center is calculated as:

$$C_\theta = \sum_{j=1}^{\theta} X_{rj,G} \bigg/ \theta. \tag{7}$$

ω_j is a random number drawn from the asymmetrical normal distribution, which is defined as:

$$\omega \sim \begin{cases} 2\zeta_o N(0, \sigma_o^2) & (x \geq 0) \\ 2\zeta_i N(0, \sigma_i^2) & (x < 0) \end{cases}. \tag{8}$$

Here x represents the independent variable in the probability density function, notation $N(0, \sigma^2)$ denotes the normal distribution with mean 0 and standard

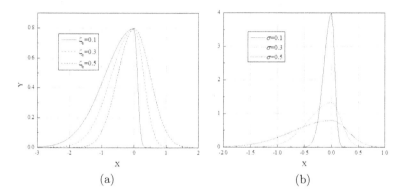

(a)   (b)

Fig. 2. Probability density function of AND. (a) demonstrates the effect of ζ_0 when $\sigma = 0.5$. (b) demonstrates the effect of σ when $\zeta_0 = 0.3$.

deviation σ. ζ_0, σ_0, ζ_i and σ_i are positive real values satisfy the following equations:

$$\zeta_o + \zeta_i = 1, \tag{9}$$

$$\sigma_o = 2\zeta_o\sigma, \tag{10}$$

$$\sigma_i = 2\zeta_i\sigma, \tag{11}$$

where ζ_0 and σ are the introduced parameters of ANDM. ζ_0 is used to determine the area under the probability density function curve when $x > 0$. For example, AND is the same as normal distribution when $\zeta_0 = 0.5$. Meanwhile, σ is used to control the dispersion of the distribution. Graphs of the probability density function with different settings are shown in Fig. 2.

From (6), we can notice that the scale factor F is now replaced by a random number drawn from the novel distribution. The effect of the introduced parameters is displayed in the following part.

3.2   Study of the Search Behavior

We first compare ANDM with DE/rand/1. Figure 3 shows the difference between DE/rand/1 and ANDM while generating a donor vector. DE/rand/1 generates a donor vector by adding the difference between $X_{r2,G}$ and $X_{r3,G}$ to the base vector $X_{r1,G}$, shown in Fig. 3(a). In contrast, the center of $X_{r1,G}$, $X_{r2,G}$, and $X_{r3,G}$ is first calculated in ANDM, as illustrated in Fig. 3(b), where the star denotes the center. Then, the differences between the center and $X_{r2,G}$, $X_{r3,G}$ are added to the base vector $X_{r1,G}$. Actually, there are mainly four situations when generating a trial vector using ANDM. Suppose θ is set to 3, it is easy to expand (6) and we therefore obtain the following equation:

$$V_{i,G} = X_{r1,G} - (X_{r2,G} - C_\theta)\omega_2 - (X_{r3,G} - C_\theta)\omega_3. \tag{12}$$

The four situations are as follows:

1) Both ω_2 and ω_3 are negative.
2) ω_2 is positive and ω_3 is negative.
3) ω_2 is negative and ω_3 is positive.
4) Both ω_2 and ω_3 are positive.

Diagrams of these situations are given in Fig. 3. Figure 3(b), (c) and (d) correspond to situation 1), 3), and 4) respectively. The difference vector generated in situation 2) has just the opposite direction as in situation 3), so it is omitted. If we confine that ω_2 and ω_3 must have the same absolute value, situations 3) is consistent with DE/rand/1 because the first C_θ in (16) is offset by the second C_θ. From Fig. 3, it can be seen that ANDM has more varied forms of generating a donor vector. Therefore, comparing with DE/rand/1, ANDM can increase the population diversity to some extent.

Moreover, the proposed mutation operator has a sense of direction owing to the introduction of the center. After determining the base vector, directions of the difference vectors are then decided by the sign of random numbers drawn from AND. When $\zeta_0 < 0.5$, it is more likely to generate negative numbers, thus the probability of guiding the base vector toward the center of selected individuals is increased. Here, the ratio of the direction being chosen toward the center of individuals is used to represent the exploitation rate. The reasons are

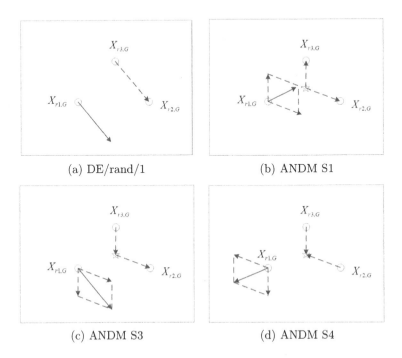

(a) DE/rand/1   (b) ANDM S1

(c) ANDM S3   (d) ANDM S4

Fig. 3. Different ways of generating a donor vector. The stars in (b), (c) and (d) denote the centers of the individuals.

given as follows. The randomly selected individuals constitute a neighborhood of the base vector in the population and the center stands for the neighborhood center. By driving the base vector toward its neighborhood center, the individual can be considered as exploiting its random neighborhood. Especially, with the convergence of the population, the individuals become near, so that the region of the neighborhood shrinks. At this time, the exploitation effect is more significant. In fact, this method is similar to use multi-population technique that the sub-populations are selected at random. In this way, the region of neighborhood is self-adapted during the search process. On the contrary, when $\zeta_0 > 0.5$, the base vector is more likely to drift away from the center. In other words, the base vector tends to escape from its neighborhood and to explore other promising search regions. We define such search behavior as exploitation. Accordingly, when $\zeta_0 = 0.5$, the proposed mutation operator has the same probability of exploitation and exploration.

In Fig. 4, 100 individuals are randomly scattered over $[-10, 10] \times [-10, 10]$, and the base vector is located at $(8, 8)$. Then, we randomly generate 100 difference vectors based on these individuals, and connect them to the base vector. The figure clearly shows the distribution of difference vectors. From Fig. 4, we can notice that ANDM is very similar to DE/rand/1 when $\zeta_0 = 0.5$. In contrast to these, ANDM is more likely to generate donor vectors toward the inner regions when $\zeta_0 = 0.3$.

Besides ζ_0, σ plays an important role in ANDM. The parameter takes the place of scale factor F in DE/rand/1, which is used to control the step-size. From Fig. 2(b), we can learn that a small σ value makes the random number drawn from AND locates around 0, whereas a large σ value increases the probability of generating a large (absolute value) number. That is to say, a small σ value corresponds to small step-size and a large σ value corresponds to large step-size.

4 Numerical Experiments

In this section, DE with the proposed mutation operator is applied to minimize a set of 13 benchmark functions taken from literature [15]. ANDM is compared with DE/rand/1 to show its effectiveness. In addition, experiments on ANDM with different parameter settings are conducted to see the influence of ζ_0 that can adjust the exploitation and exploration rates. Furthermore, to give insights into the performance of ANDM on shifted and rotated functions, CEC2013 benchmarks are adopted.

4.1 Test Functions and Experimental Setup

The selected 13 benchmark functions are listed in Table 1. The characteristics of these functions are briefly discussed as follows. All the benchmarks selected are 30-dimensional real-valued functions. Functions f_1-f_5 are continuous unimodal functions, Function f6 is a discontinuous step function and function f_7 is a unimodal function with noise. Generally, functions f_1-f_7 are used to compare the

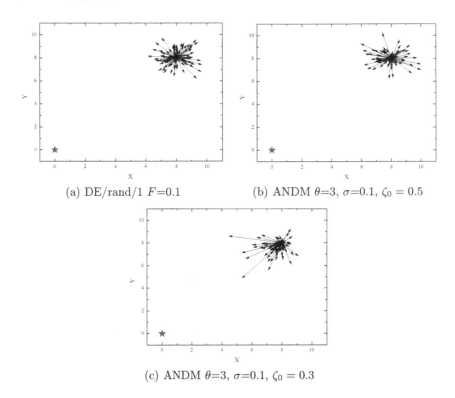

(a) DE/rand/1 F=0.1   (b) ANDM θ=3, σ=0.1, $\zeta_0 = 0.5$

(c) ANDM θ=3, σ=0.1, $\zeta_0 = 0.3$

Fig. 4. Different ways of generating a donor vector. The stars in (b), (c), and (d) denote the centers of the individuals.

convergence rate of different algorithms. Functions f_8-f_{13} are multimodal functions with many local minima, they are used to test the algorithm's ability to escape from local minima and to locate the global optimum, i.e., the ability of global search.

In our experiment, we set the population size NP to 100, and CR is set to 0.1 since it works better than 0.5 and 0.9 on most of the selected benchmark functions. For DE/rand/1, the scale factor F is set to 0.5. θ, σ and ζ_0 are parameters introduced by the proposed mutation operator, for simplicity and comparability(corresponding to the 3 individuals used to generate trial vector in DE/rand/1), θ is set to 3 here. A fixed value 0.5 is assigned to parameter σ corresponding to the fixed setting of F. Finally, ζ_0 is set to 0.8, 0.5, 0.3, and 0.1 respectively to validate the effect which is responsive to the change of probability of exploitation. It can be noticed that a random number drawn from the asymmetrical normal distribution is more like to be in the vicinity of zero, leading to a small scale factor. Therefore, each scaled difference vector is multiplied by a constant c in compensation. So (6) is revised to

$$V_{i,G} = X_{r1,G} - \sum_{j=2}^{\theta} c \cdot (X_{rj,G} - C_\theta) \cdot \omega_j. \tag{13}$$

Table 1. The 13 traditional benchmark functions used in this paper.

Test Function	n	S	f_{min}
$f_1(x) = \sum_{i=1}^{n} x_i^2$	30	$[-100, 100]^D$	0
$f_2(x) = \sum_{i=1}^{n} |x_i| + \prod_{i=1}^{n} |x_i|$	30	$[-10, 10]^D$	0
$f_3(x) = \sum_{i=1}^{n} \left(\sum_{j=1}^{i} x_i \right)^2$	30	$[-100, 100]^D$	0
$f_4(x) = \max_i \{|x_i|, 1 \le i \le n\}$	30	$[-100, 100]^D$	0
$f_5(x) = \sum_{i=1}^{n-1} \left[100(x_{i+1} - x_i^2)^2 + (x_i - 1)^2 \right]$	30	$[-30, 30]^D$	0
$f_6(x) = \sum_{i=1}^{n} (\lfloor x_i + 0.5 \rfloor)^2$	30	$[-1.28, 1.28]^D$	0
$f_7(x) = \sum_{i=1}^{n} i x_i^4 + random[0, 1)$	30	$[-100, 100]^D$	0
$f_8(x) = \sum_{i=1}^{n} -x_i \sin\left(\sqrt{|x_i|}\right)$	30	$[-500, 500]^D$	-12569.5
$f_9(x) = \sum_{i=1}^{n} \left[x_i^2 - 10\cos(2\pi x_i) + 10 \right]$	30	$[-5.12, 5.12]^D$	0
$f_{10}(x) = -20\exp\left(-0.2\sqrt{\frac{1}{n}\sum_{i=1}^{n} x_i^2}\right) - \exp\left(\frac{1}{n}\sum_{i=1}^{n}\cos 2\pi x_i\right) + 20 + e$	30	$[-32, 32]^D$	0
$f_{11}(x) = \frac{1}{4000}\sum_{i=1}^{n} x_i^2 - \prod_{i=1}^{n}\cos\left(\frac{x_i}{\sqrt{i}}\right) + 1$	30	$[-600, 600]^D$	0
$f_{12}(x) = \frac{\pi}{n}\left\{ 10\sin^2(\pi y_i) + \sum_{i=1}^{n-1}(y_i - 1)^2\left[1 + 10\sin^2(\pi y_{i+1})\right] + (y_n - 1)^2 \right\}$ $+ \sum_{i=1}^{n} u(x_i, 10, 100, 4), \quad y_i = 1 + \frac{1}{4}(x_i + 1)$ $u(x_i, a, k, m) = \begin{cases} k(x_i - a)^m, & x_i > a, \\ 0, & -a \le x_i \le a, \\ k(-x_i - a)^m, & x_i < -a \end{cases}$	30	$[-50, 50]^D$	0
$f_{13}(x) = 0.1\{ \sin^2(3\pi x_1) + \sum_{i=1}^{n-1}(x_i - 1)^2\left[1 + \sin^2(3\pi x_{i+1})\right]$ $+ (x_n - 1)\left[1 + \sin^2(2\pi x_n)\right] \} + \sum_{i=1}^{n} u(x_i, 5, 100, 4)$	30	$[-50, 50]^D$	0

In our experiment, c is set to 2.5 empirically. We have tested several c values and we found that $c = 2.5$ is best in line with scale factor $F = 0.5$ in DE/rand/1.

4.2   Results and Discussion

The experimental results of DE/rand/1 and ANDM with settings $\zeta_0 = 0.8$, $\zeta_0 = 0.5$, $\zeta_0 = 0.3$, and $\zeta_0 = 0.1$ are summarized in Table 2. All results are obtained based on 30 independent runs. Wilcoxon rank-sum test is conducted on the experimental results. The best results are marked boldface. It can be seen that the performance of DE/rand/1 and ANDM with $\zeta_0 = 0.5$ are similar. This result is compatible with the analysis that both of them have the same exploitation and exploration rates. Additionally, ANDM with the setting $\zeta_0 = 0.1$ outperforms DE/rand/1 on most of the test function. To give an insight into the algorithms' performance, the convergence graphs of some selected functions are given, shown in Fig. 5. The pairs of lines for DE/rand/1 and ANDM with $\zeta_0 = 0.5$ are almost overlapping. We can learn from the figure that ANDM with setting $\zeta_0 = 0.1$ has a higher convergence rate than DE/rand/1. It is explainable since most of the test functions' global minima are in the center of initialization domain, and ANDM with $\zeta_0 = 0.1$ tends to lead donor vectors toward the center, and thus gives preference to exploitation. Moreover, functions can benefit from the setting $\zeta_0 = 0.1$ even though they are multimodal. This could be explained by two reasons. First, the centers of different neighborhoods may indicate different local

Table 2. Experimental results of DE/rand/1 and ANDM over 30 independent runs on 13 benchmark functions of 30 variables.

FUN	GENS	DE/rand/1 Mean±Std Dev	ANDM $\zeta_0 = 0.8$ MEAN±Std Dev	ANDM $\zeta_0 = 0.5$ Mean±Std Dev	ANDM $\zeta_0 = 0.3$ Mean±Std Dev	ANDM $\zeta_0 = 0.1$ Mean±Std Dev
f_1	1500	3.51E-19±1.07E-19-	6.86E-09±2.04E-09	5.38E-19±1.79E-19	4.55E-28±2.13E-28	**2.52E-37±1.06E-37**
f_2	2000	3.38E-16±7.15E-17-	1.79E-09±3.16E-10	3.99E-16±6.17E-17	1.82E-22±3.88E-23	**5.60E-29±1.65E-29**
f_3	5000	3.00E+03±4.70E+02-	1.18E+04±2.06E+03	2.26E+03±5.25E+02	5.30E+02±1.09E+02	**1.20E+02±3.03E+01**
f_4	5000	2.50E-08±3.50E-09+	6.98E-03±1.16E-03	2.73E-10±6.68E-11	**1.04E-17±3.48E-18**	1.44E+00±9.88E-01
f_5	20000	**2.29E+01±1.60E+00≈**	2.90E+01±1.21E+01	2.77E+01±1.33E+01	2.74E+01±1.51E+01	3.03E+01±2.61E+01
f_6	1500	0.00E+00±0.00E+00≈	0.00E+00±0.00E+00	0.00E+00±0.00E+00	0.00E+00±0.00E+00	0.00E+00±0.00E+00
f_7	3000	8.06E-03±1.24E-03-	1.80E-02±4.03E-03	5.94E-03±1.15E-03	3.64E-03±1.08E-03	**2.52E-03±6.72E-04**
f_8	9000	**−12569.48±1.82E-12≈**	−12565.53±2.13E+01	**−12569.48±1.82E-12**	**−12569.48±1.82E-12**	−12561.59±2.95E+01
f_9	5000	0.00E+00±0.00E+00≈	0.00E+00±0.00E+00	0.00E+00±0.00E+00	0.00E+00±0.00E+00	0.00E+00±0.00E+00
f_{10}	1500	1.74E-10±3.21E-11-	1.19E+00±1.30E+00	2.24E-10±4.59E-11	1.07E-14±2.25E-15	**3.55E-15±0.00E+00**
f_{11}	2000	0.00E+00±0.00E+00≈	3.44E-12±1.70E-12	0.00E+00±0.00E+00	0.00E+00±0.00E+00	0.00E+00±0.00E+00
f_{12}	1500	1.11E-20±4.61E-21-	1.59E-10±5.16E-11	6.13E-21±2.05E-21	3.61E-30±1.82E-30	**1.57E-32±5.47E-48**
f_{13}	1500	6.95E-20±2.18E-20-	1.80E-09±7.68E-10	7.06E-20±3.81E-20	4.41E-29±2.57E-29	**1.35E-32±5.47E-48**

Wilcoxon rank-sum test at a 0.5 significance level is conducted between DE/rand/1 and ANDM $\zeta_0 = 0.1$. "−","+", and "≈" represent that the performance of DE/rand/1 is worse than, better than, and similar to that of ANDM $\zeta_0 = 0.1$, respectively.

optima in the landscape, therefore by using a small ζ_0, the population is able to track the neighborhood centers so as to track the multiple local optima. Second, individuals are very likely to surround the global optimum when the algorithm enters the final phase of the optimization process known as convergence state [16]. Function f_8 is an exception whose global optimum is on the edge of the search domain. Even so, ANDM can find its way out of local minima and stay competitive with DE/rand/1.

4.3   CEC2013 Test Suite Analysis

To have an insight look into the performance of ANDM with $\zeta_0 = 0.1$, experiments on CEC2013 benchmarks f_1-f_{20} are carried out. f_1-f_5 are unimodal functions. f_6-f_{20} are multimodal functions. All functions are shifted and most of them are rotated. More detailed description of the CEC2013 test suite can be found in [17]. The benchmark problems are examined in 30 dimensions and algorithms terminate until they reach the maximum function evaluations, which is set to 300 000. Other settings still follow the previous descriptions. We replicate each run 30 times. The experimental results are reported in Table 3.

Although all CEC2013 benchmark functions are shifted, the performance of ANDM with $\zeta_0 = 0.1$ is promising. From Table 3, it can be observed that ANDM with $\zeta_0 = 0.1$ significantly outperforms DE/rand/1 on 12 out of 20 functions. The following discussion will give a possible reason for these results.

There is a trend that ANDM would gather more offspring (not all) around the center when $\zeta_0 < 0.5$. In another word, it pays more attention on searching some explored regions. However, it should be noticed that this search behavior of ANDM is different from population contraction, and it would not cause the convergence of the population. It is the selection operator that is in charge of the population convergence. Namely, whether the offspring will replace their parents depends on their fitness. Essentially, in an optimization process, there are mainly two cases that should be taken into consideration. The first case

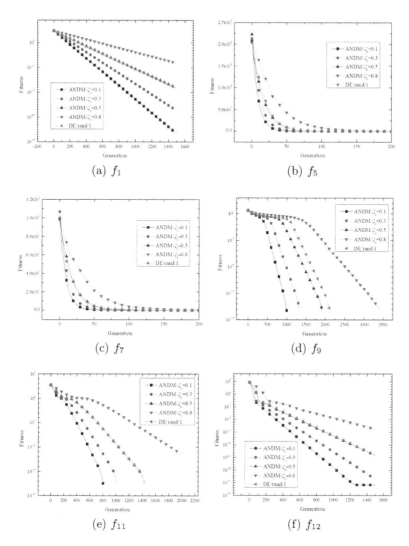

Fig. 5. Evolution of the mean function values derived from DE/rand/1 and ANDM versus the number of generations on some selected functions.

is that the global optimum is close to the neighborhood center. In this case, methods that have a bias toward the center will have greater probabilities to generate high quality offspring. The second case, the global optimum is far away from the neighborhood center. A core method of evolutionary computation which distinguishes it from random search is that it pays more attention on already-found promising regions while still has opportunities to explore the entire search space. In this sense, the proposed method corresponds to the goal. That is to say, when the global optimum lies in an unexplored region, ANDM with $\zeta_0 < 0.5$

Table 3. Experimental results of DE/rand/1 and ANDM over 30 independent runs on CEC2013 benchmark functions.

Function		DE/rand/1 Mean Error±Std Dev	ANDM $\zeta_0 = 0.1$ Mean Error±Std Dev
Unimodal Functions	F_1	0.00E+00±0.00E+0≈	0.00E+00±0.00E+00
	F_2	3.68E+07±6.54E+06-	2.68E+07±6.08E+06
	F_3	1.27E+09±3.86E+08-	7.33E+07±4.88E+07
	F_4	5.91E+04±6.51E+03-	4.14E+04±5.64E+03
	F_5	9.85E-14±3.86E-14-	0.00E+00±0.00E+00
Basic Multimodal Functions	F_6	4.31E+01±2.40E+0≈	4.11E+01±7.39E+00
	F_7	8.84E+01±8.97E+00-	6.59E+01±8.00E+00
	F_8	2.09E+01±5.21E-02≈	2.10E+01±4.74E-02
	F_9	3.12E+01±1.25E+00≈	3.10E+01±1.03E+00
	F_{10}	4.27E+01±1.12E+01-	1.16E+00±5.77E-01
	F_{11}	1.89E-15±1.02E-14≈	6.63E-02±2.48E-01
	F_{12}	1.71E+02±1.30E+01-	1.35E+02±1.14E+01
	F_{13}	1.87E+02±1.47E+01-	1.45E+02±1.33E+01
	F_{14}	4.72E+00±4.24E+00+	1.50E+01±2.28E+01
	F_{15}	6.67E+03±3.30E+02-	6.49E+03±2.50E+02
	F_{16}	2.35E+00±2.98E-01≈	2.31E+00±2.95E-01
	F_{17}	3.04E+01±3.08E-08+	3.06E+01±1.01E-01
	F_{18}	2.22E+02±1.24E+01-	1.90E+02±8.15E+00
	F_{19}	3.88E+00±1.93E-01-	1.94E+00±3.61E-01
	F_{20}	1.27E+01±1.68E-01-	1.21E+01±3.24E-01
−		12	
+		2	
≈		6	

Wilcoxon rank-sum test at a 0.05 significance level are conducted. "−", "+", and "≈" represent that the performance of DE/rand/1 is worse than, better than, and similar to that of ANDM $\zeta_0 = 0.1$, respectively.

still has the ability to locate the global optimum. However, ANDM with $\zeta_0 < 0.5$ might hinder the movement of the individuals, causing a slow convergence rate. Fortunately, this side effect would not last for long. From the results listed in Table III, it can be seen that the benefit of the first case overtakes the drawback on most of the CEC2013 functions.

The results are promising, but it might still be the major concern that too small a ζ_0 value might cause prematurity. As a matter of fact, it does happen (e.g., on F_8 and F_{11}). Although it has been a common view that any constant bias is unacceptable, an adjustable one is probably a good thing. Hence, it would be best to adjust ζ_0 in response to the evolution dynamics, which is an interesting study for future research. Overall, intuitiveness and ease of adjusting the exploitation and exploration rates are the pivotal points of ANDM.

In brief, we can learn from the experimental results that the convergence speed and solution accuracy can be strongly influenced by exploitation and exploration rates. However, as we have mentioned previously, ζ_0 should be adjusted according to the evolution dynamics, therefore the aim of our experiment is not to give a recommend setting that ζ_0 should be somewhat less than 0.5. Instead, it is the great performance gap between parameter setting $\zeta_0 = 0.5$ and $\zeta_0 = 0.1$ that we pay close attention to. The improvement benefits from the change of probability of exploitation and exploration. ANDM can concentrate more efforts on exploiting or on exploring by intuitively tuning the parameter ζ_0. Comparing with DE/rand/1, which makes same efforts to exploit and explore during the whole searching process, it permits more flexibility.

5   Conclusion

In this paper, we propose a novel mutation strategy, which introduces a parameter ζ_0 that can visibly control the exploitation and exploration rates of DE. Experiments have been carried out to investigate the effect of the introduced control parameter. The results show that search behaviors of ANDM agree well with our analysis that a small ζ_0 value less than 0.5 gives preference to exploitation whereas a large ζ_0 value gives preference to the exploration. Another notable outcome is that the exploitation and exploration rates can have a great impact on algorithm's convergence speed and solution accuracy.

Some prospects for the future work are given as follows. Searching for a simpler and more general form of ANDM that can integrate with some state-of-the-art DE variants is worthy of further study. Moreover, since the correlations among performance, θ, and σ are still not clear, understanding it will be beneficial for future research. Last but not the least, as ζ_0 is proved to control the probability of exploitation and exploration of DE, it would be interesting future work to design an adaptive control scheme of ζ_0, to adapt the orientation of mutation to fit the objective function automatically.

References

1. Duan, D., Gong, Y., Huang, T., Zhang, J.: Adaptive clustering-based differential evolution for multimodal optimization. In: 2018 Eighth International Conference on Information Science and Technology (ICIST), pp. 370–376. IEEE (2018)
2. Storn, R., Price, K.: Differential evolution-a simple and efficient heuristic for global optimization over continuous spaces. J. Global Optim. **11**, 341–359 (1997)
3. Huang, T., Duan, D.T., Gong, Y.J., Ye, L., Ng, W.W., Zhang, J.: Concurrent optimization of multiple base learners in neural network ensembles: an adaptive niching differential evolution approach. Neurocomputing **396**, 24–38 (2020)
4. Ahmad, M.F., Isa, N.A.M., Lim, W.H., Ang, K.M.: Differential evolution: a recent review based on state-of-the-art works. Alex. Eng. J. **61**(5), 3831–3872 (2022)
5. Duan, D.T., Mu, N.K., Liao, X.F.: An adaptive differential evolution algorithm based on fuzzy modeling. In: 2018 International Conference on Security, Pattern Analysis, and Cybernetics (SPAC), pp. 290–293. IEEE (2018)
6. Guo, G., Han, L., Wang, L., Zhang, D., Han, J.: Semantic-aware knowledge distillation with parameter-free feature uniformization. Visual Intell. **1**(1), 6 (2023)
7. Li, W., et al.: Modular design automation of the morphologies, controllers, and vision systems for intelligent robots: a survey. Visual Intell. **1**(1), 2 (2023)

8. Deng, W., Shang, S., Cai, X., Zhao, H., Song, Y., Xu, J.: An improved differential evolution algorithm and its application in optimization problem. Soft. Comput. **25**, 5277–5298 (2021)

9. Cai, Z., Yang, X., Zhou, M., Zhan, Z.H., Gao, S.: Toward explicit control between exploration and exploitation in evolutionary algorithms: a case study of differential evolution. Inf. Sci. **649**, 119656 (2023)

10. Segredo, E., Lalla-Ruiz, E., Hart, E., Voß, S.: A similarity-based neighbourhood search for enhancing the balance exploration-exploitation of differential evolution. Comput. Oper. Res. **117**, 104871 (2020)

11. Zhang, J., Sanderson, A.C.: JADE: adaptive differential evolution with optional external archive. IEEE Trans. Evol. Comput. **13**(5), 945–958 (2009)

12. Gupta, S., Su, R.: An efficient differential evolution with fitness-based dynamic mutation strategy and control parameters. Knowl.-Based Syst. **251**, 109280 (2022)

13. Meng, Z., Yang, C.: Two-stage differential evolution with novel parameter control. Inf. Sci. **596**, 321–342 (2022)

14. Someya, H.: Striking a mean-and parent-centric balance in real-valued crossover operators. IEEE Trans. Evol. Comput. **17**(6), 737–754 (2012)

15. Yao, X., Liu, Y., Lin, G.: Evolutionary programming made faster. IEEE Trans. Evol. Comput. **3**(2), 82–102 (1999)

16. Zhan, Z.H., Zhang, J., Li, Y., Chung, H.S.H.: Adaptive particle swarm optimization. IEEE Trans. Syst. Man Cybern. Part B (Cybernetics) **39**(6), 1362–1381 (2009)

17. Liang, J.J., Qu, B., Suganthan, P.N., Hernández-Díaz, A.G.: Problem definitions and evaluation criteria for the cec 2013 special session on real-parameter optimization. Computational Intelligence Laboratory, Zhengzhou University, Zhengzhou, China and Nanyang Technological University, Singapore, Technical Report 201212(34), 281–295 (2013)

Revealing Real Face for Generalized Anti-Spoofing

Weiye Tang[1], Zhiyong Huang[2], and Qiu Shen[1(✉)]

[1] Nanjing University, Nanjing, China
shenqiu@nju.edu.cn
[2] Wuba Intelligent Technology, Hangzhou, China

Abstract. Current researches on Face Anti-Spoofing (FAS) predominantly focus on the detection of spoofing traces in face images. However, these methods may face limitations in generalization since spoofing traces can vary significantly across different domains. Due to poor generalization, which results in overfitting on the training data, cross-domain FAS methods always suffer dramatic degradation. In this paper, our focus is on predicting real faces rather than emphasizing spoofing traces as the primary approach to address the issue. We aim to address the issue of poor generalization by avoiding extracting spoofing traces. Based on this, a generative model named **R**eal **F**ace **G**eneration **N**et (RFGN) is proposed to predicting real faces according to input face images, so that the final decision can be made by simply calculating the distances between original inputs and outputs. The experimental results show that our proposed method can achieve the state-of-the-art (SOTA) performance with a simple structure.

Keywords: Face Anti-spoofing · Face recognition · Generative model

1 Introduction

Face Anti-Spoofing (FAS) has drawn significant attention from both academic and industrial institutions, owing to its critical role in enhancing the security of face recognition systems against various presentation attacks (PAs). These attacks include a range of methods, including print attacks, video-replay attacks, makeup attacks, and 3D mask attacks. FAS has achieved great successes from hand-craft descriptors based methods [15,17,21,25] to deep representation based ones [37,44,56]. Though recent FAS methods perform well on intra-dataset scenarios, they may over-fit on specific domains and attack types, which makes them vulnerable to open-set problems in practice. Accordingly, domain generalization FAS [6,8,19,26,27,29,42,46,49,50,57] that trains models on one or several datasets (source domains) and tests on unseen datasets (target domain) becomes a new hot spot in recent years.

This work was supported in part by the National Natural Science Foundation of China under Grant 62071216, 62231002 and U1936202.

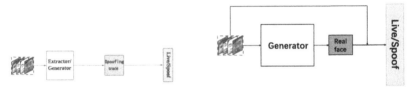

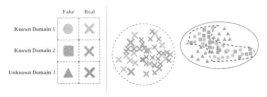

(a) Extracting spoofing trace for FAS. (b) Extracting spoofing trace for FAS.

(c) The distribution of spoofing and real faces.

Fig. 1. Difference between revealing spoofing trace and real face for FAS.

Commonly, FAS methods (no matter hand-craft based or deep learning based methods) are designed to extract the features of spoofing traces to distinguish spoofing faces from real ones [10,20,31,39], as shown in Fig. 1a. This method is effective for intra-dataset FAS because spoofing traces within the same dataset often share common attack types, making it easier to generalize from training to test data. However, the differences in spoofing traces between datasets are more significant due to variations in attack types and materials used. For example, if a model is trained on a dataset without print attack samples, it may not perform well when confronted with print attack scenarios. Similarly, a model trained on a dataset only including paper mask attacks may struggle to perform effectively in silicone mask attacks. Since the training dataset cannot encompass all types of attack methods and materials, methods based on extracting spoofing traces are prone to overfitting. As demonstrated in Fig. 1c, unknown spoofing traces are located out of the designed model over-fitted on known traces, which makes the performance degraded dramatically. To address the limitations of spoof traces, we've chosen not to extract spoofing trace features. Instead, we aim to predict real faces(as shown in Fig. 1b).

In the medical anomaly detection, there are methods based on generative model. Initially, these methods train the Generative Adversarial Net (GAN) using real data to enable the generator to learn the distribution of real data. Subsequently, an encoder is trained to convert images into latent codes that have the ability to produce similar images. Ultimately, regardless of whether the input medical data is normal or abnormal, the model can predict corresponding real images. The classification is determined by the difference between the input and output data, in conjunction with the score computed by the discriminator of GAN.

Inspired by the above method, we propose a generative model called **R**eal **F**ace **G**eneration **N**et (RFGN) which can generate faces without spoofing traces. Generating realistic human faces through GAN is considerably more challenging than generating medical images. It is difficult to train a GAN capable of producing natural-looking faces, as well as an encoder that can map facial features to latent codes. Generative models typically incorporate convolutional layers and upsampling operations to take random noise as input and produce data with the distribution of the training dataset. Given the complexity of generating human faces, it is essential to incorporate additional feature information during the generation process. Therefore, we have chosen for a U-net architecture as the generative network. The encoder within the U-net extracts a hierarchy of features, which are subsequently utilized in the decoder to guide the generation process. To ensure that the generator can accurately predict real faces when processing attack face images, we should provide it with both real and fake data during training. Furthermore, we should incorporate additional supervision when the input consists of attack images.

After training, the Generator is supposed to be able to predict a real face with any input (no matter real or spoofing face). So that, we can make the final decision by easily calculating the difference between input and predicted faces (which may contain spoofing traces and noises) and just comparing to a predefined threshold, without training any classifier. To evaluate the effectiveness of our model, RFGN is tested on different datasets following the cross-domain protocol. The results show that RFGN can easily catch up with state-of-the-art (SOTA) cross-domain FAS methods with more lightweight models (with only 11.4M parameters for training and 9.7M parameters for inference). This is an important evidence that learning a generalized distribution of real face is feasible and effective way to solve the cross-domain FAS problems. Visualization experiments further confirm the findings. We deploy the same framework to predict spoofing traces. The only difference is setting the output of Generator to be spoofing trace, so that the input of Discriminator and distance constraint is calculated by subtracting spoofing trace from input image (which is supposed to be real face). Other modules are kept the same.

The main contributions of this paper are summarized as follows:

- As far as our knowledge extends, our method is the first to utilize a generative approach in cross-domain FAS. Prior approaches had primarily relied on classification methods.
- We explored the difference of revealing real face and spoofing traces in cross-domain FAS with theoretically and experimentally.
- We proposed a generative model with distance constraint and inter-domain constraint to learn a generalized distribution of real faces, which is effective for cross-domain FAS.
- The proposed model can provide a good baseline for cross-domain FAS, as it achieves the SOTA performance with a clear and simple structure.

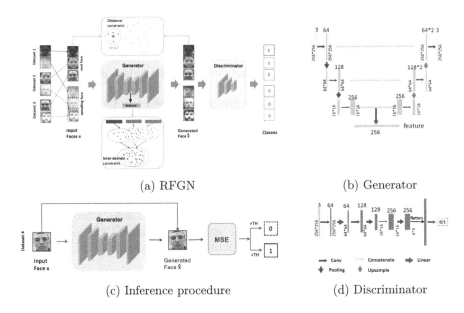

(a) RFGN

(b) Generator

(c) Inference procedure

(d) Discriminator

Fig. 2. The framework of our proposed FAS method. (a) the framework of RFGN, which is used for training; (c) the inference procedure based on the Generator of RFGN; (b) the structure of Generator in RFGN; (d) the structure of Discriminator in RFGN. Real faces are denoted by 1 and solid line box. Spoofing faces are denoted by 0 and dotted box with translucent masks to distinguish from real ones.

2   Related Work

2.1   FAS Methods

At the early stage, hand-crafted features were introduced to implement the FAS tasks, e.g., LBP [2,11,12,36], HOG [24,54], SIFT [41], optical flow motion [5], image quality [14] and rPPG clues [40]. These traditional methods heavily depend on rich task-aware prior knowledge for design, and encountered limited detection accuracy. Benefited from the development of the advanced deep learning architectures and large-scale datasets, deep learning methods becomes the mainstream of FAS. In the early years, FAS is intuitively treated as a binary classification task, which can be directly supervised by binary cross-entropy loss along with some extended losses [7,34,53]. Considering that binary loss may cause unfaithful learning results, pixel-wise auxiliary information (e.g., depth labels [1,30], binary mask label [16,32,48] and reflection maps [22,55]) are introduced to improve the performance. Although the auxiliary task provides fine-grained supervision, it's still challenging to determine if deep black-box models capture intrinsic FAS features. Recently, there's a trend to extract visual spoofing traces by generative model [10,20,31,33,39] and to provide a more intuitive interpretation of the sample's spoofing traces. Overall, existing deep learning methods might easily fall into the local optimum and overfit on the known domains, which encounter great performance degradation in practical applications.

2.2 Cross-Domain FAS Methods

To face the challenges in practical applications with varied conditions (e.g., illumination, facial appearance) and unknown attack types (e.g., masks of new materials), researchers start to pay more attention to cross-domain FAS tasks. Domain adaptation [10,61] is a method that bridges the gap between source and target domains by leveraging knowledge from the target domain. Domain generalization [6,8,19,26,27,29,42,46,49,50,57] trains a model to learn generalized feature representations that can be applied to unseen domains without access to target domain data, making it more practical for real-world deployment. The above methods are all aimed to extract generalized features of spoofing trace by different means. While in this paper, we would like to explore the opposite way, that is predicting real faces from the original ones (no matter they are real or spoofing) to solve the generalization problem of cross-domains FAS.

2.3 Generative Anomaly Detection

In the field of medical anomaly detection, there are already generative methods in use [45]. Typically, they employ Generative Adversarial Networks (GANs) to learn the manifold of normal data. During training, these methods exclusively utilize randomly sampled normal data. Following training, the GAN acquires an understanding of the distribution of normal data and learns how to map medical anatomical images to a latent code. Essentially, this process is the inverse of a GAN, as it aims to determine a latent code, given an image, that can reproduce the same image.

Since the GAN is trained only on normal data, it primarily generates normal data, even when presented with anomaly images. The residual value, which measures the difference between the input and output image, can be leveraged to determine whether an image is normal or abnormal.

3 Proposed Method

In this paper, we do not extract features of spoofing traces but learn the distribution of real faces $\hat{x}$, which is supposed to be more centralized and generalized. Specifically, we propose a generative model named RFGN (shown in Fig. 2a) to realize cross-domain FAS. The Generator is trained to learn the distribution of real faces, so that it can predict a real face with any input (no matter real or spoofing face) to fool the Discriminator. To supervise the training of Generator, we need a discriminator to distinguish real and spoofing faces. Generator and Discriminator are iteratively trained by max-minimizing their adversarial loss functions. After convergence, Generator is assumed to catch the distribution of real face, and Discriminator is capable to distinguish real faces and spoofing faces. Additionally, distance constraint and inter-domain constraint are proposed to improve the generalization ability of Generator for cross domain FAS. Distance constraint is designed to prevent the Generator from working too hard to remove the spoofing trace and harm the quality of original real face. Inter-domain constraint adopt MMD constraint to pull the distribution of data in multiple source domains as close as possible. Based on the above efforts, the inference procedure is quite simple as shown in Fig. 2c.

3.1   The Backbone of RFGN

We use U-Net [38,43], which consists of two parts, i.e., Encoder (**En**) and Decoder (**De**), as our real face prediction network. As shown in Fig. 2b, input image goes through the convolutional layers and pooling layers in the encoder to extract features. And then, the output features are fed to the decoder and go through several convolutional layers and upsampling operations to reconstruct the image. The short-cut structure (denoted by gray arrow) helps aggregate context features and improve the quality of reconstructed images. Due to these advantages, U-Net is able to accomplish the task of revealing real faces according to input face features very well. In order to enable U-Net to learn the manifold of real faces, adversarial learning is necessary. So, we need a Discriminator to supervise the output of Generator. As shown in Fig. 2d, the architecture of Discriminator is composed of several convolutional and pooling layers and one linear layer. It takes a face image as input and outputs feature maps after a series of convolution and pooling operations. Feature maps are flattened as a 1-D feature and go through a linear layer to output a value between 0 and 1.

For the convenience of formula description, we have the following symbol definitions. Suppose there are K (e.g., 3 in Fig. 2a) seen source domains for training. $\mathbf{x}_{l,i} \in R^{N \times N \times 3}$ denotes the i_{th} sample image from the l_{th} domain, where $l \in \{1, \cdots, K\}$ and $N \times N$ denotes the image size. The corresponding label of any input $\mathbf{x}_{l,i}$ (abbreviated as $\mathbf{x}$ for short) is denoted as $y_{l,i}$ (abbreviated as y for short). $y \in \{0, 1\}$ denotes spoofing face and real face respectively. When input a face image $\mathbf{x}$ (no matter real or spoofing) to Generator, the output $\hat{\mathbf{x}}$ is expected to be a real face. The process of generating $\hat{\mathbf{x}}$ is described as Eq. 1.

$$\hat{\mathbf{x}} = \mathbf{G}(\mathbf{x}) = \mathbf{De}(\mathbf{En}(\mathbf{x})) \tag{1}$$

$\hat{\mathbf{x}}$ is then fed into Discriminator which tries to distinguish the real and spoofing face, and outputs a confidence score $\hat{y} \in [0, 1]$, as described in Eq. 2.

$$\hat{y} = \mathbf{D}(\hat{\mathbf{x}}) \tag{2}$$

Accordingly, the network is trained to alternatively minimize the discriminative loss L_D and generative loss L_G.

$$L_D = \mathbb{E}(-log(\mathbf{D}(\mathbf{x}|y=1)) - log(1 - \mathbf{D}(\mathbf{x}|y=0)) \\ - log(1 - \mathbf{D}(\mathbf{G}(\mathbf{x}|y=0)))) \tag{3}$$

L_D consists of three items. The first and second item supervise Discriminator to distinguish whether the input is real or spoofing. The third item enables the Discriminator to distinguish the generated real face from the spoofing input.

$$L_G = \mathbb{E}(-log(\mathbf{D}(\mathbf{G}(\mathbf{x}|y = 1)) - log(\mathbf{D}(\mathbf{G}(\mathbf{x}|y = 0)))) \tag{4}$$

L_G consists of two items. The first item is to ensure that the generated images are still real when the input is real faces. The second item supervises the Generator to generate images which fool the Discriminator even the input images are spoofing.

3.2   Distance Constraints

An important responsibility of RFGN is keeping the real face unchanged while turning the spoofing face to real ones. So, it is beneficial to constrain the quality difference between input and generated faces. L_{DC} is defined to shorten the distance between input and generated faces when input $\mathbf{x}$ is real and enlarge the distance when $\mathbf{x}$ is spoofing, respectively.

$$L_{DC} = \begin{cases} L_{MSE}, y = 1 \\ L_{DIS}, y = 0 \end{cases} \tag{5}$$

Mean Square Error(MSE) loss L_{MSE} is defined to ensure the real faces keep unchanged through the Generator as much as possible.

$$L_{MSE} = \mathbb{E}\,||\mathbf{G}(\mathbf{x}) - \mathbf{x}||_2 \tag{6}$$

Discrepancy loss L_{DIS} is defined to keep a certain difference between spoofing input face and the generated real face.

$$L_{DIS} = \mathbb{E}\left| |\mathbf{G}(\mathbf{x}) - \mathbf{x}| - l_n \right|, y = 0 \tag{7}$$

where l_n is a hyper-parameter, we set it to 0.1 in this paper.

3.3   Inter-domain Constraint

An important advantage of our proposed method is that real faces may have intrinsic consistent features cross different domain, while spoofing traces in different domain may have much difference. Consequently, it is more reasonable to align the distribution of real faces in different domains together. In this paper, an inter-domain loss L_{IC} is proposed to make the distribution of data in multiple source domains as close as possible, to improve the generalization ability of the model.

L_{IC} is calculated by MMD [26] based on the theory that mean estimating expectation is an unbiased estimation. MMD is a function that measures the distance between two sets of data by their features. To obtain input image features, we made modifications to the original version of U–Net by adding a downsample operation after the last output layer of the encoder to get 1-D features as follows.

$$f = \mathbf{P}(\mathbf{En}(\mathbf{x})) \tag{8}$$

where $\mathbf{P}$ is a pooling layer. f is the feature extracted by encoder. As a result, L_{IC} can be calculated as follows.

$$L_{IC} = MMD(f_1, f_2, ...f_l) = \frac{1}{K^2} \sum_{\substack{1 \leq i,j \leq K}}^{i \neq j} \mathrm{MMD}\left(f_i, f_j\right) \tag{9}$$

f_i and f_j represent different features from different source domains.

$$\mathrm{MMD}\left(f_i, f_j\right)^2 = \left\| \frac{1}{n_i} \sum_{m=1}^{n_i} \phi\left(f_{l_j}\right) - \frac{1}{n_j} \sum_{n=1}^{n_j} \phi\left(f_{t_j}\right) \right\|_{\mathcal{H}}^2 \tag{10}$$

where $\phi(\cdot)$ is denoted as a feature map. ϕ maps features to reproducing kernel Hilbert space.

3.4 Overall Loss

To improve the generalization ability of Generator, the Generative loss is extend to L_{GE} as Eq. 11.

$$L_{GE} = L_G + \lambda_1 \cdot L_{DC} + \lambda_2 \cdot L_{IC} \tag{11}$$

where λ_1 and λ_2 are two hyper-parameters. Consequently, the overall loss of RFGN can be described as L_D in Eq. 3 and L_{GE} in Eq. 11, which are used to supervise the optimization of Generator and Discriminator separately.

3.5 Inference Procedure

After finishing the training process, Generator is used for spoofing face detection, as it has a powerful ability of revealing the real face from the input ones. As a result, the inference procedure is very simple as shown in Fig. 2c and Eq. 12. First, feed the image $\mathbf{x}$ into Generator to get a predicted real face image $\hat{\mathbf{x}}$; second, calculate the difference between $\mathbf{x}$ and $\hat{\mathbf{x}}$ (i.e., MSE); Third, make final decision with a given threshold. If the differences are under the threshold, it indicates that input faces are real. On the contrary, if the differences are over the threshold, the input faces are spoofing ones.

$$result = \begin{cases} 1, & MSE(\mathbf{x}, \hat{\mathbf{x}}) \leq \mathbf{T} \\ 0, & MSE(\mathbf{x}, \hat{\mathbf{x}}) > \mathbf{T} \end{cases} \tag{12}$$

where $\mathbf{T}$ is the threshold, which is set equal to l_n (i.e., the hyper-parameter used to determine the distance between the generated face images and the spoofing face images during training).

4 Experiment

To validate whether the proposed framework can learn the generalized features of real faces efficiently, we test the model on multiple challenge datasets following the acknowledged protocols for cross-domain FAS testing in Sect. 4.2. Additionally, visualization experiments are demonstrated in Sect. 4.3 to provide more explicit evidence. Then, comparison experiments with predicting spoofing traces are demonstrated in Sect. 4.4 to answer the question whether revealing real faces is better. Ablation study are executed in Sect. 4.5.

4.1 Experimental Settings

Datasets and Protocols. In this paper, four widely used datasets in cross-domain FAS are used for performance evaluation. They are OULU-NPU [4] (denoted as O), CASIA-FASD [60] (denoted as C), Idiap Replay-Attack [9] (denoted as I), and MSU-MFSD [52](denoted as M). We adopt two protocols in all experiments. In **Protocol 1**, we use four datasets mentioned above. following the prior work, three datasets are used for train and the left one dataset is used for test. In **Protocol 2**, we add a new large Celeba-Spoof [59] as a supplementary dataset for training, referring to the SOTA work with visual transformer (ViT) [18]. Tests on **Proctocol 2** are marked with '†'.

Data Preparation. These datasets are provided in the form of video. So, we take out each frame of the videos, and cut out the face areas by MTCNN [58]. The images are all resized to 256×256.

Implementation Details. Our method is implemented via PyTorch 1.9 on 11G NVIDIA 2080Ti GPUs. The model is trained with Adam optimizer [23]. We only use RGB channels. For training, the hyper-parameters λ_1, λ_2 are both set to 10.

Training Strategy. Inspired by the training strategy of HFN+MP [6], we split the training dataset into two parts for training. In every iteration, one dataset chosen in turn is used for training the Discriminator and the left datasets are used to train the Generator. This strategy can improve the transfer ability of the Generator. Because it can simulate cross-domain tests.

Measurements. We take HTER and Area Under Curve (AUC) to measure the cross-domain performance of FAS. HTER is calculated as illustrated in Eq. 13. AUC means the area under the receiver operating characteristic curve (ROC).

$$HTER = (FAR + FRR)/2.0 \tag{13}$$

where FAR is False Acceptance Rate, FRR is False Reject Rate.

4.2 Performance Evaluation of RFGN

Comprehensive Evaluation on Cross-domain FAS. Cross-dataset test can reveal the generalization ability of FAS method. The better performance (i.e.,

Table 1. Comparison with SOTA cross-domain FAS methods on OULU-NPU, CASIA-MFSD, Replay-Attack, and MSU-MFSD. We mark the top-2 performances in bold.

Method	O&C&M to I		O&C&I to M		O&M&I to C		I&C&M to O		Avg		Param. (M)
	HTER ↓	AUC ↑	HTER ↓	AUC ↑	HTER ↓	AUC ↑	HTER ↓	AUC ↑	HTER ↓	AUC ↑	
Self-DA (2021) [50]	15.60	90.10	15.40	91.80	24.50	84.40	23.10	84.30	19.65	87.65	–
RFM (2020) [47]	17.30	90.48	13.89	93.98	20.27	88.16	16.45	91.16	16.98	90.95	–
D^2AM (2021) [8]	15.43	91.22	12.70	95.66	20.98	85.58	15.27	90.87	16.10	90.83	–
DRDG (2021) [29]	15.56	91.79	12.43	95.81	19.05	88.79	15.63	91.75	15.67	92.04	–
ANRL (2021) [28]	16.03	91.04	10.83	96.75	17.83	89.26	15.67	91.90	15.10	92.24	–
FAS-DR (2021) [42]	11.93	94.95	11.67	93.09	18.44	89.67	16.23	91.18	14.57	92.22	–
NAS-FAS (2020) [57]	11.63	96.98	16.85	90.42	15.21	92.64	13.16	94.18	14.21	93.56	–
FGHV (2022) [27]	16.29	90.11	9.17	96.92	12.47	93.47	13.58	93.55	12.86	93.51	–
PatchNet (2022) [49]	14.6	92.51	7.10	98.46	11.33	94.58	11.82	95.07	11.21	95.15	–
SSDG (2020) [19]	11.71	96.59	7.38	97.17	10.44	95.94	15.61	91.54	11.28	95.31	11.18
HFN+MP (2022) [6]	15.35	90.67	5.24	97.28	9.11	96.09	12.40	94.26	10.53	94.58	45.5
SSAN (2022) [51]	8.88	96.79	6.67	98.75	10.00	96.67	13.72	93.63	9.82	96.46	16.2
SSDG†[19]	7.01	**98.28**	6.58	97.21	12.91	93.92	12.47	94.87	9.72	96.07	11.18
ViT†[18]	9.25	97.15	**1.58**	99.68	5.70	98.91	7.47	**98.42**	6.00	**98.54**	86.39
RFGN	**5.18**	97.31	6.99	96.43	8.93	94.98	9.12	95.22	7.55	95.98	**9.7**
RFGN†	**5.07**	**97.46**	4.86	**99.16**	5.18	**97.31**	7.11	**98.50**	5.55	**98.11**	**9.7**

lower value of HTER or higher value of AUC) reflects the stronger generalization ability. We conduct cross-dataset testing following the LOO strategy: three datasets used for training, and the rest one for testing. The objective performance and computational complexity are compared with latest SOTA methods in Table 1. It is observed that our proposed method RFGN achieves competitive performance, which always takes the top two spots in the performance ranking and takes the first prize in average HTER. It is also interesting that, RFGN has more consistent results on different datasets, while the results of others methods (excluding ViT †) varies significantly. More importantly, RFGN is much smaller than other models in parameters (i.e., 9.7M for inference and 11.4M for training). The other top performance method ViT† has more than 9× parameters. These phenomenons are solid evidence for the hypothesis that learning a generalized distribution of real face for generic FAS is feasible, effective and efficient, and the proposed framework can accomplish this mission perfectly.

Limited Source Domains Test. To evaluate the robustness of our proposed method, we further decrease the number of source datasets from three to two datasets. Obviously, this will increase the difficulty of cross domain testing. We train the models based on MSU-MFSD and Idiap Replay-Attack as source domain datasets, and test it on the left two datasets, OULU-NPU and CASIA-FASD separately. As shown in Table 2, RFGN get the best and more stable performance on both tests. These results are sufficient to prove the superiority of our proposed method.

4.3 Visualization Experiments

Changes When Images Go Through the Generator. We conducted a visualization experiment to verify that the Generator can predict real face no

Table 2. Comparison to face anti-spoofing methods with limited source domains.

Method	M&I to C		M&I to O	
	HTER↓	AUC↑	HTER↓	AUC↑
MS_LBP [36]	51.16	52.09	43.63	58.07
IDA [52]	45.16	58.80	54.52	42.17
ColorTexture [3]	55.17	46.89	53.31	45.16
LBP_TOP [13]	45.27	54.88	47.26	50.21
MADDG [46]	41.02	64.33	39.35	65.10
SSDG [19]	31.89	71.29	36.01	66.88
ANRL [28]	31.06	72.12	30.73	74.10
HFN+MP [6]	30.89	72.48	20.94	86.71
SSAN [51]	30.00	76.20	29.44	76.62
RFGN	**21.22**	**82.14**	**18.18**	**88.36**

Table 3. Performance comparison of predicting real face and predicting spoofing trace for cross-domain FAS.

Method	O&C&M to I		O&C&I to M		O&M&I to C		I&C&M to O	
	HTER↓	AUC↑	HTER↓	AUC↑	HTER↓	AUC↑	HTER↓	AUC↑
RFGN(spoof)†	13.62	88.25	10.29	90.45	14.49	87.37	9.24	93.63
RFGN(real)†	**5.07**	**97.46**	**4.86**	**99.16**	**5.18**	**97.31**	**7.11**	**98.50**

matter the input is real or spoofing. Specifically, t-SNE [35] is used to visualize the features from Discriminator for all samples in the O&C&M training set (including original samples and the corresponding predictions by the Generator). In Fig. 3, we present input images **x** as dots and generated images x̂ as crosses. Cold and warm colors differentiate images with real and spoofing inputs, respectively. The results show that real faces (in blue crosses and green dots) are highly concentrated on the right side. The positions of real faces changes small (even keep unchanged) after going through the Generator. Conversely, the input spoofing faces disperse far away from real ones, and experience significant position changes after going through the Generator. Notably, the generated images of input spoofing faces (in orange dots) move far away from their original images (in red crosses) and towards the area of real images. This visualization experiment confirms that the Generator of RFGN learn the distribution of real faces, which can keep the real faces unchanged and reveal the underlying real face from spoofing ones.

Subjective Illustration. Figure 5 display some examples of input different face images (including real ones and spoofing ones). Images in the first row are input face images **x**. The left four images are real faces and the right four images are spoofing faces. The second row is predicted real images x̂ generated by the

Fig. 3. Visualization of the changes when images go through the Generator.

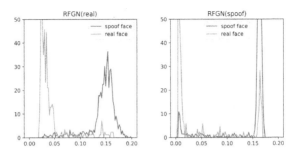

Fig. 4. Histogram of the final values.

Generator of RFGN. The last row is the residual of input faces and predicted faces (i.e., $N(\hat{\mathbf{x}}) = \mathbf{x} - \hat{\mathbf{x}}$). As we expect, when input images are real faces the residual is almost zero, while when input spoofing faces, the residual including spoofing traces are obvious and clearly reflect the attack types. For example, the first spoofing face is replay attack, in which the predicted spoofing trace is obvious as the display has obvious light reflection all over the face. The second and the third are print attack and their predicted spoofing traces mostly around nose and forehead which are non-planar and have much difference when flatten to paper. The last attack is mask attack. The area near eyes in this input image is not blocked by the mask. It can be seen in the spoofing trace image that the eye area is closer to zero than other areas.

4.4   Comparison with Predicting Spoofing Trace

Since RFGN has strong representation ability to reveal the real faces, it is suppose to be able to reveal spoofing traces. Researches maybe suspicious to that predicting spoofing traces can also work well even better. Therefore, comparison experiments based on RFGN are designed to eliminate the suspicion. The main

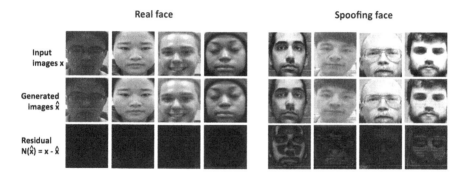

Fig. 5. Subjective visualization of input and output of the Generator in RFGN. Column 1-4 are real faces; Column 5 is replay attack; Column 6 and 7 are print attack; Column 8 is mask attack. $N(\hat{\mathbf{x}})$ is magnified two times for explicit presentation.

structure keep the same with RFGN in Fig. 2a. The only difference is supposing the output of Generator is spoofing faces $N(\hat{\mathbf{x}})$. Accordingly, the input of Discriminator and distance constraint are changed into $x - N(\hat{\mathbf{x}})$. For testing, L2 norm of the predicted spoof traces $N(\hat{\mathbf{x}})$ is calculated and compare with the threshold to make the final decision. The other experimental details remain unchanged. As shown in Table 3, predicting spoof traces (i.e., RFGN(spoof))can work for cross-domain FAS with acceptable performance, which can be ranked in middle position of the list in Table 1. But its performance still fall further behind that of predicting real faces(i.e., RFGN(real)).

To be more intuitive, we compare the histogram of the final values of RFGN(real) (i.e., $MSE(\mathbf{x}, \hat{\mathbf{x}})$) and RFGN(spoof) (i.e., $L2(N(\hat{\mathbf{x}}))$) in Fig. 4. Histograms for real face (orange) and spoofing face (blue) are painted in different colors. It can be observed that, the distribution of real face inputs are around zero, which means the Generator can recognize the real faces and keep them almost unchanged. The distribution of spoofing face inputs are mostly higher than 0.1 (i.e., the threshold used for decision in Sect. 3.5), which means the Generator can pull the spoofing faces far away from its original inputs. It is obvious that, the distribution in RFGN(real) is more separable than that in RFGN(spoof). Specifically, the distribution in RFGN(real) has only one peak for both kinds of inputs respectively, which makes it easy to distinguish the samples with a threshold. while the distribution in RFGN(spoof) has two peak for both kinds of inputs at the same value, which may cause misjudgment. This phenomenon may explain why RFGN(real) is better. Additionally, the distributions in RFGN(real) is wider than that in RFGN(spoof), which may represent better generalization ability.

4.5 Ablation Study

Comparison of Different l_n. Proper value setting of l_n is relatively important to training RFGN. It is used to determine the distance between the generated face images and the spoofing face images. When l_n is too small, the real and spoofing faces become indistinguishable, leading to a decline in performance. Conversely, if l_n is too large, the generated face images may be of poor quality, also resulting a performance drop. As is shown in Table 4, the best performance is achieved when l_n is set to 0.1.

The Effectiveness of Different Constraints. Different losses are reserved during training, in order to observe their effect. This study is test on I&O&C to M task. The experimental results are given in Table 5. L_{MSE} , L_{DIS} and L_{IC} all contribute to performance improvement. L_{MSE} helps improve the quality of generated images and constrain real face input and the output to be consistent. L_{DIS} forces the prediction of spoofing face away from spoofing face distribution and close to real face distribution. L_{IC} can make the features of real faces in multiple domains closer to each other, which is of great help to the generalization ability of the model.

Table 4. Comparison of different l_n on I&O&C to M.

l_n	HTER (%)	AUC (%)
0.08	11.33	92.42
0.1	**6.99**	**96.43**
0.12	9.61	91.91
0.14	11.79	91.63
0.16	15.12	89.16
0.18	16.61	92.72

Table 5. Comparison of different constrains.

L_{MSE}	L_{DIS}	L_{IC}	HTER (%)
			28.7
✓			19.4
✓	✓		15.2
✓		✓	13.8
✓	✓	✓	**6.99**

5   Conclusion

In this paper, we analyzed the limitations of extracting spoofing traces in cross-domain Face Anti-Spoofing (FAS) and propose to revealing real faces alternatively. Comprehensive theoretical analysis and experimental comparison were provided to support the viewpoint that predicting real face is much better in the scenario of cross-domain FAS. Based on such findings, a generative model for cross-domain FAS was proposed by learning a generalized distribution of real faces, which achieved state-of-the-art (SOTA) performance with a clear and simple structure. These results further evaluated the hypothesis and highlighted the potential of revealing real faces in cross-domain FAS. Moreover, the simplicity of the proposed model makes it a good baseline for future researches. There is much potential for improvement and the addition of modules to enhance its generalization ability.

References

1. Atoum, Y., Liu, Y., Jourabloo, A., Liu, X.: Face anti-spoofing using patch and depth-based CNNs. In: 2017 IEEE International Joint Conference on Biometrics (IJCB), pp. 319–328. IEEE (2017)
2. Boulkenafet, Z., Komulainen, J., Hadid, A.: Face anti-spoofing based on color texture analysis. In: 2015 IEEE International Conference on Image Processing (ICIP), pp. 2636–2640. IEEE (2015)
3. Boulkenafet, Z., Komulainen, J., Hadid, A.: Face spoofing detection using colour texture analysis. IEEE Trans. Inf. Forensics Secur. **11**(8), 1818–1830 (2016)
4. Boulkenafet, Z., Komulainen, J., Li, L., Feng, X., Hadid, A.: OULU-NPU: a mobile face presentation attack database with real-world variations. In: 2017 12th IEEE International Conference on Automatic Face and Gesture Recognition (FG 2017), pp. 612–618. IEEE (2017)
5. Brox, T., Malik, J.: Large displacement optical flow: descriptor matching in variational motion estimation. IEEE Trans. Pattern Anal. Mach. Intell. **33**(3), 500–513 (2010)
6. Cai, R., Li, Z., Wan, R., Li, H., Hu, Y., Kot, A.C.: Learning meta pattern for face anti-spoofing. IEEE Trans. Inf. Forensics Secur. **17**, 1201–1213 (2022)
7. Chen, H., Hu, G., Lei, Z., Chen, Y., Robertson, N.M., Li, S.Z.: Attention-based two-stream convolutional networks for face spoofing detection. IEEE Trans. Inf. Forensics Secur. **15**, 578–593 (2019)
8. Chen, Z., et al.: Generalizable representation learning for mixture domain face anti-spoofing. In: Proceedings of the AAAI Conference on Artificial Intelligence, vol. 35, pp. 1132–1139 (2021)
9. Chingovska, I., Anjos, A., Marcel, S.: On the effectiveness of local binary patterns in face anti-spoofing. In: 2012 BIOSIG-Proceedings of the International Conference of Biometrics Special Interest Group (BIOSIG), pp. 1–7. IEEE (2012)
10. Feng, H., et al.: Learning generalized spoof cues for face anti-spoofing. arXiv preprint arXiv:2005.03922 (2020)
11. de Freitas Pereira, T., Anjos, A., De Martino, J.M., Marcel, S.: Can face anti-spoofing countermeasures work in a real world scenario? In: 2013 International Conference on Biometrics (ICB), pp. 1–8. IEEE (2013)
12. de Freitas Pereira, T., Anjos, A., De Martino, J.M., Marcel, S.: *LBP–TOP* based countermeasure against face spoofing attacks. In: Park, J.-I., Kim, J. (eds.) ACCV 2012. LNCS, vol. 7728, pp. 121–132. Springer, Heidelberg (2013). https://doi.org/10.1007/978-3-642-37410-4_11
13. Freitas Pereira, T.d., et al.: Face liveness detection using dynamic texture. EURASIP J. Image Video Process. **2014**(1), 1–15 (2014)

14. Galbally, J., Marcel, S.: Face anti-spoofing based on general image quality assessment. In: 2014 22nd International Conference on Pattern Recognition, pp. 1173–1178. IEEE (2014)

15. Galbally, J., Marcel, S., Fierrez, J.: Biometric antispoofing methods: a survey in face recognition. IEEE Access **2**, 1530–1552 (2014)

16. George, A., Marcel, S.: Deep pixel-wise binary supervision for face presentation attack detection. In: 2019 International Conference on Biometrics (ICB), pp. 1–8. IEEE (2019)

17. Hadid, A.: Face biometrics under spoofing attacks: vulnerabilities, countermeasures, open issues, and research directions. In: Proceedings of the IEEE Conference on Computer Vision and Pattern Recognition Workshops, pp. 113–118 (2014)

18. Huang, H.P., et al.: Adaptive transformers for robust few-shot cross-domain face anti-spoofing. In: Avidan, S., Brostow, G., Cissé, M., Farinella, G.M., Hassner, T. (eds.) ECCV 2022, Part III. LNCS, vol. 13673, pp. 37–54. Springer, Cham (2022). https://doi.org/10.1007/978-3-031-19778-9_3

19. Jia, Y., Zhang, J., Shan, S., Chen, X.: Single-side domain generalization for face anti-spoofing. In: Proceedings of the IEEE/CVF Conference on Computer Vision and Pattern Recognition, pp. 8484–8493 (2020)

20. Jourabloo, A., Liu, Y., Liu, X.: Face de-spoofing: anti-spoofing via noise modeling. In: Proceedings of the European Conference on Computer Vision (ECCV), pp. 290–306 (2018)

21. Kähm, O., Damer, N.: 2D face liveness detection: an overview. In: 2012 BIOSIG-Proceedings of the International Conference of Biometrics Special Interest Group (BIOSIG), pp. 1–12. IEEE (2012)

22. Kim, T., Kim, Y., Kim, I., Kim, D.: BASN: enriching feature representation using bipartite auxiliary supervisions for face anti-spoofing. In: Proceedings of the IEEE/CVF International Conference on Computer Vision Workshops (2019)

23. Kingma, D.P., Ba, J.: Adam: a method for stochastic optimization. arXiv preprint arXiv:1412.6980 (2014)

24. Komulainen, J., Hadid, A., Pietikäinen, M.: Context based face anti-spoofing. In: 2013 IEEE Sixth International Conference on Biometrics: Theory, Applications and Systems (BTAS), pp. 1–8. IEEE (2013)

25. Kumar, S., Singh, S., Kumar, J.: A comparative study on face spoofing attacks. In: 2017 International Conference on Computing, Communication and Automation (ICCCA), pp. 1104–1108. IEEE (2017)

26. Li, H., Pan, S.J., Wang, S., Kot, A.C.: Domain generalization with adversarial feature learning. In: Proceedings of the IEEE Conference on Computer Vision and Pattern Recognition, pp. 5400–5409 (2018)

27. Liu, S., Lu, S., Xu, H., Yang, J., Ding, S., Ma, L.: Feature generation and hypothesis verification for reliable face anti-spoofing. In: Proceedings of the AAAI Conference on Artificial Intelligence, vol. 36, pp. 1782–1791 (2022)

28. Liu, S., et al.: Adaptive normalized representation learning for generalizable face anti-spoofing. In: Proceedings of the 29th ACM International Conference on Multimedia, pp. 1469–1477 (2021)

29. Liu, S., et al.: Dual reweighting domain generalization for face presentation attack detection. arXiv preprint arXiv:2106.16128 (2021)

30. Liu, Y., Jourabloo, A., Liu, X.: Learning deep models for face anti-spoofing: binary or auxiliary supervision. In: Proceedings of the IEEE Conference on Computer Vision and Pattern Recognition, pp. 389–398 (2018)

31. Liu, Y., Liu, X.: Physics-guided spoof trace disentanglement for generic face anti-spoofing. arXiv preprint arXiv:2012.05185 (2020)

32. Liu, Y., Stehouwer, J., Jourabloo, A., Liu, X.: Deep tree learning for zero-shot face anti-spoofing. In: Proceedings of the IEEE/CVF Conference on Computer Vision and Pattern Recognition, pp. 4680–4689 (2019)

33. Liu, Y., Stehouwer, J., Liu, X.: On disentangling spoof trace for generic face anti-spoofing. In: Vedaldi, A., Bischof, H., Brox, T., Frahm, J.-M. (eds.) ECCV 2020. LNCS, vol. 12363, pp. 406–422. Springer, Cham (2020). https://doi.org/10.1007/978-3-030-58523-5_24

34. Lucena, O., Junior, A., Moia, V., Souza, R., Valle, E., Lotufo, R.: Transfer learning using convolutional neural networks for face anti-spoofing. In: Karray, F., Campilho, A., Cheriet, F. (eds.) ICIAR 2017. LNCS, vol. 10317, pp. 27–34. Springer, Cham (2017). https://doi.org/10.1007/978-3-319-59876-5_4

35. Van der Maaten, L., Hinton, G.: Visualizing data using t-SNE. J. Mach. Learn. Res. **9**(11) (2008)

36. Määttä, J., Hadid, A., Pietikäinen, M.: Face spoofing detection from single images using micro-texture analysis. In: 2011 International Joint Conference on Biometrics (IJCB), pp. 1–7. IEEE (2011)

37. Ming, Z., Visani, M., Luqman, M.M., Burie, J.C.: A survey on anti-spoofing methods for facial recognition with RGB cameras of generic consumer devices. J. Imaging **6**(12), 139 (2020)

38. Mirza, M., Osindero, S.: Conditional generative adversarial nets. arXiv preprint arXiv:1411.1784 (2014)

39. Mohammadi, A., Bhattacharjee, S., Marcel, S.: Improving cross-dataset performance of face presentation attack detection systems using face recognition datasets. In: ICASSP 2020-2020 IEEE International Conference on Acoustics, Speech and Signal Processing (ICASSP), pp. 2947–2951. IEEE (2020)

40. Niu, X., Yu, Z., Han, H., Li, X., Shan, S., Zhao, G.: Video-based remote physiological measurement via cross-verified feature disentangling. In: Vedaldi, A., Bischof, H., Brox, T., Frahm, J.-M. (eds.) ECCV 2020, Part II. LNCS, vol. 12347, pp. 295–310. Springer, Cham (2020). https://doi.org/10.1007/978-3-030-58536-5_18

41. Patel, K., Han, H., Jain, A.K.: Secure face unlock: spoof detection on smartphones. IEEE Trans. Inf. Forensics Secur. **11**(10), 2268–2283 (2016)

42. Qin, Y., Yu, Z., Yan, L., Wang, Z., Zhao, C., Lei, Z.: Meta-teacher for face anti-spoofing. IEEE Trans. Pattern Anal. Mach. Intell. (2021)

43. Ronneberger, O., Fischer, P., Brox, T.: U-net: convolutional networks for biomedical image segmentation. In: Navab, N., Hornegger, J., Wells, W.M., Frangi, A.F. (eds.) MICCAI 2015. LNCS, vol. 9351, pp. 234–241. Springer, Cham (2015). https://doi.org/10.1007/978-3-319-24574-4_28

44. Safaa El-Din, Y., Moustafa, M.N., Mahdi, H.: Deep convolutional neural networks for face and iris presentation attack detection: survey and case study. IET Biometrics **9**(5), 179–193 (2020)

45. Schlegl, T., Seeböck, P., Waldstein, S.M., Schmidt-Erfurth, U., Langs, G.: Unsupervised anomaly detection with generative adversarial networks to guide marker discovery. In: Niethammer, M., et al. (eds.) IPMI 2017. LNCS, vol. 10265, pp. 146–157. Springer, Cham (2017). https://doi.org/10.1007/978-3-319-59050-9_12

46. Shao, R., Lan, X., Li, J., Yuen, P.C.: Multi-adversarial discriminative deep domain generalization for face presentation attack detection. In: Proceedings of the IEEE/CVF Conference on Computer Vision and Pattern Recognition, pp. 10023–10031 (2019)

47. Shao, R., Lan, X., Yuen, P.C.: Regularized fine-grained meta face anti-spoofing. In: Proceedings of the AAAI Conference on Artificial Intelligence, vol. 34, pp. 11974–11981 (2020)

48. Sun, W., Song, Y., Chen, C., Huang, J., Kot, A.C.: Face spoofing detection based on local ternary label supervision in fully convolutional networks. IEEE Trans. Inf. Forensics Secur. **15**, 3181–3196 (2020)
49. Wang, C.Y., Lu, Y.D., Yang, S.T., Lai, S.H.: PatchNet: a simple face anti-spoofing framework via fine-grained patch recognition. In: Proceedings of the IEEE/CVF Conference on Computer Vision and Pattern Recognition, pp. 20281–20290 (2022)
50. Wang, J., Zhang, J., Bian, Y., Cai, Y., Wang, C., Pu, S.: Self-domain adaptation for face anti-spoofing. In: Proceedings of the AAAI Conference on Artificial Intelligence, vol. 35, pp. 2746–2754 (2021)
51. Wang, Z., et al.: Domain generalization via shuffled style assembly for face anti-spoofing. In: Proceedings of the IEEE/CVF Conference on Computer Vision and Pattern Recognition, pp. 4123–4133 (2022)
52. Wen, D., Han, H., Jain, A.K.: Face spoof detection with image distortion analysis. IEEE Trans. Inf. Forensics Secur. **10**(4), 746–761 (2015)
53. Xu, Z., Li, S., Deng, W.: Learning temporal features using LSTM-CNN architecture for face anti-spoofing. In: 2015 3rd IAPR Asian Conference on Pattern Recognition (ACPR), pp. 141–145. IEEE (2015)
54. Yang, J., Lei, Z., Liao, S., Li, S.Z.: Face liveness detection with component dependent descriptor. In: 2013 International Conference on Biometrics (ICB), pp. 1–6. IEEE (2013)
55. Yu, Z., Li, X., Niu, X., Shi, J., Zhao, G.: Face anti-spoofing with human material perception. In: Vedaldi, A., Bischof, H., Brox, T., Frahm, J.-M. (eds.) ECCV 2020. LNCS, vol. 12352, pp. 557–575. Springer, Cham (2020). https://doi.org/10.1007/978-3-030-58571-6_33
56. Yu, Z., Qin, Y., Li, X., Zhao, C., Lei, Z., Zhao, G.: Deep learning for face anti-spoofing: a survey. IEEE Trans. Pattern Anal. Mach. Intell. (2022)
57. Yu, Z., Wan, J., Qin, Y., Li, X., Li, S.Z., Zhao, G.: NAS-FAS: static-dynamic central difference network search for face anti-spoofing. IEEE Trans. Pattern Anal. Mach. Intell. **43**(9), 3005–3023 (2020)
58. Zhang, K., Zhang, Z., Li, Z., Qiao, Y.: Joint face detection and alignment using multitask cascaded convolutional networks. IEEE Sig. Process. Lett. **23**(10), 1499–1503 (2016)
59. Zhang, Y., et al.: CelebA-spoof: large-scale face anti-spoofing dataset with rich annotations. In: Vedaldi, A., Bischof, H., Brox, T., Frahm, J.-M. (eds.) ECCV 2020, Part XII. LNCS, vol. 12357, pp. 70–85. Springer, Cham (2020). https://doi.org/10.1007/978-3-030-58610-2_5
60. Zhang, Z., Yan, J., Liu, S., Lei, Z., Yi, D., Li, S.Z.: A face antispoofing database with diverse attacks. In: 2012 5th IAPR International Conference on Biometrics (ICB), pp. 26–31. IEEE (2012)
61. Zhou, F., et al.: Face anti-spoofing based on multi-layer domain adaptation. In: 2019 IEEE International Conference on Multimedia and Expo Workshops (ICMEW), pp. 192–197. IEEE (2019)

Study on Sound Insulation Performance of Membrane-Type Acoustic Metamaterials with Pendulum Arm

Ke Wang[1], Lujin Xiong[1], Shouhao Wu[2($\boxtimes$)], and Jianhua Ji[1]

[1] Shenzhen University, Shenzhen 518060, China
[2] Research Institute of Tsinghua University in Shenzhen, Shenzhen 518071, China
wushouhao@qq.com

Abstract. Membrane-type acoustic metamaterials have attracted attention for their good sound insulation. Inspired by the membrane-type acoustic metamaterial structure of cross pendulum arm three types of pendulum arm structures are proposed in this paper: cross-shaped pendulum arm plus eight-mass block, star-shaped pendulum arm plus four-mass block, and star-shaped pendulum arm plus eight-mass block. In order to compare the sound insulation performance of different structures, the low-frequency sound insulation mechanism of membrane-type acoustic metamaterials is analyzed, and the sound transmission loss of different structures is simulated according to the calculation formula. Through the sound transmission loss curve obtained by the simulation model, it is found that under the condition of the same mass distribution, the star-shaped pendulum arm has better sound insulation performance than the cross-shaped pendulum arm. In the case of the same pendulum arm, the sound insulation performance of the eight-mass evenly distributed block is better than that of the four-mass evenly distributed block. The sound insulation performance of the star-shaped pendulum arm plus the eight-mass block is the best among the three new models. The accuracy of the simulation method is verified by sound insulation experiments.

Keywords: Membrane-Type Acoustic Metamaterials · Pendulum Arm Structures · Sound Transmission Loss · Sound Insulation Performance

1 Introduction

In daily life, noise not only affects people's production and life, but also causes harm to the body; while in the engineering field, noise affects the use of equipment and affects its life, and serious engineering accidents, resulting in property losses, so effective noise reduction is essential. Acoustic metamaterials provide research ideas for noise reduction. Acoustic metamaterials have the characteristics of negative mass density and negative bulk modulus, which enable them to have good low-frequency acoustic performance when the mass is small [1]. Acoustic metamaterials can be categorized into rod-like structures [2], Helmholtz cavity structures [3], plate-type structures [4], Membrane-type acoustic metamaterials [5], and so on, basis on the structure of the constituent units. Among them, membrane-type acoustic metamaterials.

© The Author(s), under exclusive license to Springer Nature Singapore Pte Ltd. 2024
G. Zhai et al. (Eds.): IFTC 2023, CCIS 2067, pp. 245–257, 2024.
https://doi.org/10.1007/978-981-97-3626-3_18

(MAMs) have attracted much attention due to their simple construction, light weight and small footprint.

Yang et al. [6] first proposed MAMs consisting of thin films with additional mass blocks fixed to a frame, which have negative effective kinetic modulus near the resonant frequency and are capable of breaking the acoustic attenuation mass-density law in the range of 100–1000 Hz to achieve low-frequency acoustic isolation at sub-wavelength dimensions. MAMs can be designed to achieve different acoustic effects by designing structures such as thin films, mass blocks and frame rings. Subsequently, a variety of MAMs with different structures have been designed. Naify et al. [7] proposed to change the additional mass blocks of MAMs to coaxial type mass rings, by varying the number of rings, mass distribution, and ring radius size, it was found that these factors affect the peaks, number of isolation peaks, and bandwidths to varying degrees. For the treatment of the rings, double rings and double membranes can be used to form a ring-mode coupled structure [8], or the rings can be split to make the structure with different resonance properties [9]. Zhou et al. [10] proposed a membrane-type acoustic metamaterial structure of the cross pendulum arm with continuous multistate anti-resonant modes in order to solve the problem of discrete anti-resonant modes. It was found that the acoustic isolation obtained from the thin film plus mass block and cross pendulum structure had wider bandwidth and higher acoustic isolation.

Based on the above studies, this paper designs three pendulum arm structures by varying the number of mass blocks and the structure of the pendulum arm to divide the film into several different polymorphic anti-resonance modes. The structures are composed of polyimide films, aluminum pendulum arms, iron mass blocks, and iron frames, which have light and thin application characteristics, and can produce continuous polymorphic anti-resonance modes with good sound insulation performance.

2 Sound Insulation Mechanism of MAMs

MAMs can be treated as a "spring-mass" system during vibration, where the film is the spring and the mass on the film is the mass. When the "spring-mass" system is subjected to external elastic waves, the system will vibrate harmonically under the action of resonance forces. Suppose that in the space Cartesian coordinate system, there is a compact flat film in equilibrium on the plane, and the film is uniformly stretched in all directions. The tensile force on the flat film in unit length is set to N/m. When the membrane is perturbed by an external force in the z-direction, the membrane will deform as a result. If it is perturbed by an external force in the positive z-axis direction, the membrane will bulge, and if it is perturbed by an external force in the negative z-axis direction, then it will concave, and at this point a transverse vibration in the z-axis direction is produced. A small surface element $dxdy$ is taken on the film and when this surface element deforms, its neighboring elements exert a tensile force on the surrounding edges, then the combined force acting on the perpendicular direction on the x and $x + dx$ edges of this surface element is as follows [11]:

$$T \left(\frac{\partial \eta}{\partial x}\right)_{x+dx} \text{错误！未定义书签。} \; dy - T \left(\frac{\partial \eta}{\partial x}\right)_x dy = T \left(\frac{\partial^2 \eta}{\partial x^2}\right) dxdy \tag{1}$$

where η is the displacement in the vertical direction of a point on the film away from the equilibrium position, and similarly the perpendicular combined force acting on the y and y + dy edges of this surface element can be found as follows:

$$T\left(\frac{\partial \eta}{\partial x}\right)_{y+dy} \text{错误! 未定义书签。} dx - T\left(\frac{\partial \eta}{\partial x}\right)_y dx = T\left(\frac{\partial^2 \eta}{\partial y^2}\right)dxdy \qquad (2)$$

Let σ be the surface density, σ dxdy denote the membrane mass per unit area, and t be the time, then the equation of motion of the surface element is shown below:

$$T\left(\frac{\partial^2 \eta}{\partial x^2} + \frac{\partial^2 \eta}{\partial y^2}\right)dxdy = \sigma dxdy\left(\frac{\partial^2 \eta}{\partial t^2}\right) \qquad (3)$$

Organization is available:

$$\nabla^2 \eta = \frac{1}{c^2}\frac{\partial^2 \eta}{\partial t^2} \qquad (4)$$

Equation (4) is the vibration equation of the membrane, where $c = \sqrt{\frac{T}{\sigma}}$, $\nabla^2 = \frac{\partial^2}{\partial x^2} + \frac{\partial^2}{\partial y^2}$ are Laplace operators in two-dimensional rectangular coordinates.

In the "spring-mass" system, the vibration of a circular film belongs to the same distributed parameter system as in the case of other elastomers, i.e., the size of the vibration displacement of a circular film is related to its radial position. The vibration of a circular film can be equated to the vibration of an equivalent mass at the center of the circle under the action of an equivalent spring. The equivalent mass and intrinsic vibration frequency of the circular film can be obtained by analyzing from the energy equivalence point of view and combining with the film vibration equation [12]:

$$M_{en} = mJ_1^2(u_n) \qquad (5)$$

$$f_0 = \frac{1}{2\pi}\sqrt{\frac{K_{en}}{M_{en}}} \qquad (6)$$

where M_{en} denotes the equivalent mass of the film, m is the actual mass of the film, $J_1(u_n)$ is the 1st order column Bessel function, and K_{en} is the equivalent spring constant. When a mass block M is added to the film, the equivalent mass becomes $M + M_{en}$, and the intrinsic frequency of vibration is as follows:

$$f_0 = \frac{1}{2\pi}\sqrt{\frac{K_{en}}{M_{en} + M}} \qquad (7)$$

Equation (7) can be a good explanation for the ability of MAMs to reduce the intrinsic frequency. When the mass of the mass block increases, it is actually the centralized mass that is increasing, which then causes the equivalent total mass to increase, thus decreasing the intrinsic frequency. When the mass of the mass block decreases, it causes the equivalent total mass to decrease, causing the intrinsic frequency to increase. This equation is also an important basis for optimizing membrane-type acoustic metamaterials; when the incident acoustic wave frequency is close to or equal to the intrinsic frequency of the MAMs, the thin film system will undergo the resonance phenomenon. In the resonant state, the sound wave can easily pass through the film, resulting in the acoustic transmission reaching its maximum value, and the acoustic isolation thus becomes the least effective. When the vibrational displacement of the film at the edge of the mass block is opposite to the vibrational displacement at the edge of the entire film structure, the average vibrational displacement of the entire film is almost zero. This anti-phase vibration makes it difficult for sound waves to pass through the film, resulting in optimal sound insulation. The anti-resonance frequency of the MAMs, therefore, is the frequency at which MAMs operate in sound insulation. At this frequency, the transmission of sound waves is extremely low and maximum sound insulation is realized.

3   Low-Frequency Simulation and Analysis of Pendulum-Arm Structures

3.1   Pendulum Arm Design

Figure 1(a) shows cross-shaped pendulum arm MAMs with continuous multi-state anti-resonance modes. Inspired by this, the cross-shaped pendulum arm plus eight-mass block model, the star-shaped pendulum arm plus four-mass block model, and the star-shaped pendulum arm plus eight-mass block model are designed in this paper, as shown in Fig. 1(b), (c), and (d), respectively, and the four structures are named as S_1, S_2, S_3, S_4 in the order of the illustration from left to right.

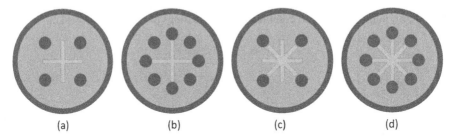

(a)   (b)   (c)   (d)

Fig. 1. (a) cross-shaped pendulum arm plus four-mass block; (b) cross-shaped pendulum arm plus eight-mass block; (c) star-shaped pendulum arm plus four-mass block; (d) star-shaped pendulum arm plus eight-mass block.

All four models consisted of pendulum arm, mass block, frame, and film. The models were circular in shape, with the pendulum arm placed in the center of the film, the mass block placed evenly around the pendulum arm, and the frame, which was a two-ring circle holding the film above and below the film, respectively. The cross pendulum arm consists of two mutually perpendicular pendulum arms, and the star-shaped pendulum arm consists of four pendulum arms, the angle between adjacent pendulum arms is 45°, and the distance from the center of the mass block around the pendulum arm to the center of the film is 20 mm.

The material of the pendulum arm is selected as aluminum, and the length of each pendulum arm is 40 mm, the width of each pendulum arm is 4 mm, and the thickness of each pendulum arm is 2 mm, and the material of the mass block and the frame is made of iron, in which the radius of the mass block is 6 mm, and the thickness of the frame is 2 mm. The outer radius of the frame is 50 mm, the inner radius is 45 mm, and the thickness is 2 mm; the film is made of polyimide with a radius of 50 mm and a thickness of 0.2 mm. The relevant structural and material parameters are shown in Table 1.

Table 1. Thin film structure related parameters

	Length (mm)	Width (mm)	Thickness (mm)	Radius (mm)	Young's modulus (Pa)	Densit (kg/m^3)	Poisson's ratio
Pendulum Arm	40	4	2	/	7.1×10^9	2700	0.32
Mass Block	/	/	2	6	2.0×10^{11}	7800	0.33
Frame	/	/	2	50	2.0×10^{11}	7800	0.33
Film	/	/	0.2	50	1.42×10^9	1420	0.4

The structural morphology of MAMs directly determines their coupled vibration modes, which in turn significantly interfere with the acoustic wave transmission properties [13]. These hybrid anti-resonance modes will put the whole film structure in dynamic equilibrium at certain frequencies, which will effectively improve the sound insulation performance.

3.2 Simulation Modeling of Pendulum-Arm Structures

In this paper, COMSOL Multiphysics software is used to establish a multi-physics field coupling model of MAMs for finite element simulation and analysis of the pendulum-arm structure. The physical field adopts the coupled pressure acoustics and solid mechanics module to model the structure in three dimensions, and the modeling process is as follows: ① Select the physical field computation module as the coupled pressure acoustics and solid mechanics module; ② Establish a circular film and attach a pendulum arm as well as some mass blocks in the center of the film. At the same time, the cylindrical air domain is established so that its cylindrical radius is the same as that of the film, and the symmetry of the air domain is maintained on both sides of the film; ③ Set the film, the pendulum arm, and the mass block as solids, and set the air domain as gases, and assign the corresponding material properties to each part; ④ Set the boundary fixation conditions for the thin-film structure, and determine the size of the film pre-stress.

Taking S as an example, the model is mainly composed of air domain and film structure, as shown in Fig. 2. The cylinder in the figure represents the air domain, and the thin film is in the middle of the air domain, bisecting the air domain. The acoustic wave enters from the inlet of the acoustic wave and passes through the thin film structure and then goes out from the outlet of the acoustic wave.

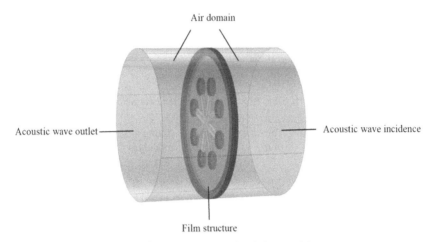

Fig. 2. Film structure simulation model

The model involves the multi-physical field coupling of pressure acoustics and solid mechanics. In the physical field of solid mechanics, the thin film frame and the surrounding area of the film are set as fixed boundaries to limit the radial displacement of the thin film structure; in the physical field of pressure acoustics, the acoustic wave exit is set as a non-reflecting boundary, and the boundaries around the air domain are set as a hard acoustic boundary, and the entire thin film structure is set as an acoustic-structural coupling physical field. The incident wave is radiated by plane wave, the sound pressure of the incident wave is set to 1 Pa, and a perfect matching layer is set at the outlet to absorb the sound wave at the outlet. The relevant parameter settings of the thin-film structure are configured according to Table 1, and then the simulation model is meshed. Due to the small thickness of the film, in order to ensure the accuracy of the calculation, while taking into account the calculation time, the grid division method is chosen to refine the processing, the model grid is divided into 344740 domain cells, 56096 boundary cells and 3108 edge cells, the grid division is shown in Fig. 3.

After meshing, the sound insulation performance needs to be analyzed in the frequency domain, and the frequency range is set to 50–1000 Hz. The sound insulation performance is usually characterized by the sound transmission loss (STL), which refers to the energy lost during the propagation of sound and is expressed in decibels (dB). In the model, the magnitude of the transmission loss is determined by comparing the energy intensity of the sound waves at the incident and exit ports. Integrating the area of the sound pressure of the incident sound wave, the incident sound wave power can be obtained as follows:

$$W_{in} = \int \frac{P_{in}}{2\rho c} dS_{in} \tag{8}$$

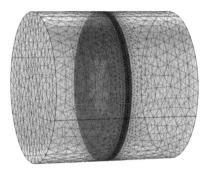

Fig. 3. Model grid segmentation

where P_{in} denotes the incident sound pressure, ρ and c denote the density of air and the speed of sound, respectively, and Sin denotes the area of the incident port. Then the acoustic pressure of the sound wave at the exit port is area-integrated and the power W_{out} is expressed as:

$$W_{out} = \int \frac{P_{out}}{2\rho c} dS_{out} \tag{9}$$

P_{out} denotes the outgoing sound pressure and S_{out} denotes the area of the outgoing port. The equation for STL is shown below [14]:

$$STL = 10lg(\frac{W_{in}}{W_{out}}) \tag{10}$$

3.3 Simulation Analysis of Pendulum-Arm Structures

The simulation frequency range is set to 50–1000 Hz, and the STL curves of each structure can be obtained according to the STL formula as shown in Fig. 4.

In the test range, the bandwidth width of STL above 15 dB is defined as S. The acoustic isolation performance of the four models is compared by comparing the mean, peak and of the STL, and each parameter is shown in Table 2.

From the above, it can be seen that the bandwidth of S_1 is 420 Hz, and the peak sound insulation reaches 61.02 dB, which corresponds to the frequency of 360 Hz. The sound transmission loss curve shows the first sound insulation valley at 90 Hz, and the sound transmission loss is close to zero, and the sound wave continues to propagate forward almost completely through the structure, which is very close to the first-order intrinsic frequency of the structure at this time.

The overall curve trend of the sound insulation curve of S_2 is similar to that of S_1, and the curve shows the first sound insulation valley at the frequency of 90 Hz, and its sound insulation is 0.82 dB. The maximum peak value of the sound insulation is 64.74 dB, which is 3–4 dB larger than that of S_1. In the frequency range of 90–550 Hz, the structure has a slightly poorer performance of the sound insulation compared with that of S_1, but the performance of the sound insulation after 550 Hz is obviously better

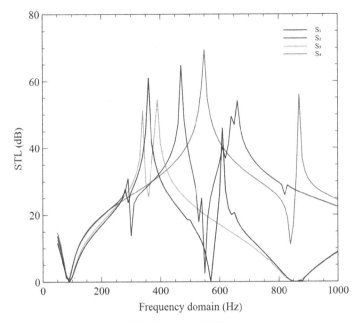

Fig. 4. Simulation model STL curves

Table 2. Simulation model data comparison

Model	Mean(dB)	Peak(dB)	S (Hz)
S_1	15.28	61.02	420
S_2	27.55	64.74	820
S_3	16.01	54.46	450
S_4	28.96	69.43	830

than that of S_1, and the S is 820 Hz. From the perspective of the mean value, the mean value of sound insulation of S_2 is 27.55 dB, and S_1 is 15.28 dB, so S_2 is better in overall sound insulation.

S_3 has a bandwidth of 450 Hz and a mean value of 16.01 dB. Compared to S_1, both S and the mean value have been improved. However, it has a frequency of 340 Hz for the first isolation peak and an isolation of 51.30dB, which reduces the frequency of the first isolation peak compared to S_1, while the isolation has been reduced accordingly.

The STL of S_4 has two valleys and two peaks, the first acoustic peak has a bandwidth of 750 Hz, and the peak acoustic peak has a peak value of 69.43 dB. The first acoustic valley occurs at 90 Hz, and the sound transmission loss is close to zero.The second acoustic valley occurs near 840 Hz, and the sound transmission loss is 11.17 dB. Among the four structures, the mean value, peak value and S bandwidth of S_4 are the largest among the four models, and the separation between the first and second troughs is also farther. Therefore, without considering other special requirements, this model has the best sound insulation performance among the four models in the simulation test.

4   Experimental Validation of Pendulum-Arm Structures

4.1   Experiment and Sample Preparation

The instruments used for the sound insulation test were: AWA8551 impedance tube with a diameter of 100 mm, AWA6223 sound calibrator, AWA6290B signal analyzer, AWA5871 power amplifier and microphone. The experimental samples were made according to the materials and dimensions of the simulated structures. The test samples were fabricated in the following manner: the swing arm, mass block and frame were machined using a milling machine, and the film was cut to a circular film with a diameter of 100 mm. The circular film was fixed to the frame in a wrinkle-free state using 3M spray adhesive, and the mass block and the pendulum arm were glued to the center of the film after the adhesive strength of the 3M spray adhesive had been fully utilized. After fixing, check whether the whole sample will be loosened or not, if it is loosened, it is necessary to carry out the above steps again until the sample is not loosened. The experimental sample is shown in Fig. 5.

Fig. 5. Sample preparation

4.2   Experimental Analysis of Pendulum-Arm Structures

The measurement frequency range of this sound insulation test experiment was 50–1000 Hz. Before the test, a layer of foam was applied around the frame of the specimen and the impedance tube was assembled with petroleum jelly to avoid large sound leakage. The sample was then placed in the impedance tube for testing and the experimental results are shown in Fig. 6.

Similarly in the experimental data also compare the performance of the four structures on the mean, peak and on the STL, the parameters are shown in Table 3.

From the experimental data, it can be seen that the mean value of S_1 is 13.32 dB, the S bandwidth is 387 Hz, the peak value of sound insulation is 27.66 dB, and the frequency corresponding to the peak value of sound insulation is 272.5 Hz. S_2 performs better than S_1 in terms of the mean value, peak value and S value, so the overall acoustic isolation performance of S_2 is better, which is in line with the simulation results. The

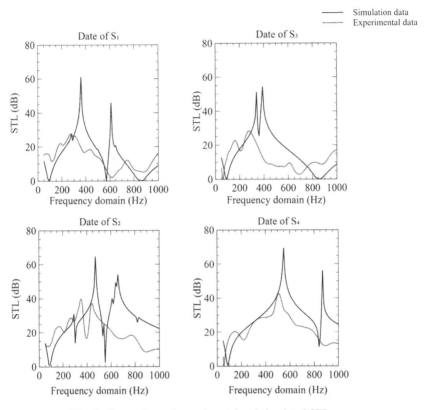

Fig. 6. Comparison of experimental and simulated STL curves

Table 3. Simulation model data comparison

Sample	Mean (dB)	Peak (dB)	S (Hz)
S_1	13.32	27.66	387
S_2	20.41	39.91	709
S_3	13.71	28.36	398
S_4	22.34	42.61	747

S-bandwidth of S_3 is 398 Hz, which is wider than that of S_1 and has the same increase in the mean value, which is similar to the performance of the simulation data. S_4 shows the best level of mean, peak and S value, similar to the simulation, so overall this sample has the best sound insulation performance among the four samples.

Observing Fig. 6, it can be found that the simulation data STL curves and experimental data STL curves of the four structures have roughly the same trend. The simulation results in each model show a smoother performance, and in most cases, the sound insulation at the peak of the sound insulation is higher than the experimental results, and the sound insulation at the valley of the sound insulation is significantly lower than the experimental results. The reason for this is that the clamping of the thin film material is not possible due to the limitations of the glue used to attach the film to the frame, which indirectly affects the effective vibration area of the film, leading to a change in the intrinsic frequency of the structure.

This ultimately led to inconsistencies between the experimentally measured sound transmission loss curves and the frequencies corresponding to the simulation calculations at the peak and trough values of sound insulation. In addition, in the actual testing process, it is difficult to fully satisfy the boundary conditions set in the simulation, and different boundary conditions will have an impact on the sound insulation performance of the structure. Sound leakage also exists during the experimental process, and even if the structure is sealed with petroleum jelly, there is still a possibility of sound wave leakage due to the gap between the frame and the impedance tube. Although there are differences, the STL curves of the two are in good agreement in the trend, proving the correctness of the finite element simulation.

5 Conclusions

In this paper, based on the cross-shaped pendulum arm plus four-mass structure, three different structures of cross-shaped pendulum arm plus eight-mass block, star-shaped pendulum arm plus four-mass block and star-shaped pendulum arm plus eight-mass block are designed by changing the structure of the pendulum arm and the number of mass blocks. This paper analyzes the sound insulation mechanism of MAMs in thin films during vibration, and from the sound insulation mechanism of MAMs, finite element models of the reference structure and the three design structures are established by using COMSOL Multiphysics software, and the STL curves of each model are calculated, and their sound insulation characteristics are compared by comparing the mean, peak, and s-values of the sound insulation quantities.

Under the simulation model, the star-shaped pendulum arm plus four-mass block is compared with the cross-shaped pendulum arm plus four-mass block, the star-shaped pendulum arm has a larger S-band width, a larger mean value, and the second valley of the sound insulation curve is not zero, so on the whole, the acoustic insulation performance of the star-shaped pendulum arm plus four-mass block is better than that of the cross-shaped pendulum arm plus four-mass block. Comparing the cross-shaped pendulum arm plus four-mass block and the cross-shaped pendulum arm plus eight-mass block, it can be seen that the cross-shaped pendulum arm plus four-mass block has the peak frequency of sound isolation relatively backward before 550 Hz, and the bandwidth of this range is close to that of the former. However, after 550 Hz, it has a higher isolation peak and wider bandwidth, while the mean, peak and value perform better than the cross-shaped pendulum arm plus four-mass block.

Among the four models, the star-shaped pendulum arm plus eight-mass block has the largest mean, peak and S values and the best sound insulation. In order to verify the correctness of the simulation, the SLT values of the structure are further analyzed through experiments. The experimental results found that the experimental STL curves are in good agreement with the simulated STL curves in trend, which proves the correctness of the simulation. The model has better sound insulation performance (mean, peak and S) for the star-shaped pendulum arm than the cross-shaped pendulum arm for the same mass block distribution; for the same pendulum arm, the uniform distribution of eight-mass blocks has better sound insulation performance than the uniform distribution of four-mass blocks; meanwhile, the sound insulation performance of the star-shaped pendulum arm plus eight-mass block is the best among the four models. In summary, the three different structures designed enrich the design way between the pendulum arm, mass block and membrane-type acoustic metamaterials to some extent, and provide a new solution idea for the engineering application of low-frequency membrane-type acoustic metamaterials.

Acknowledgments. This study was funded by the Shenzhen Key Technology Research Project (grant number JSGG20200103094001790), the Shenzhen Key Project (grant number KCXFZ20201221173413038), the Basic Research Program (grant number JCYJ20 220809170611004) and Fundamental Research Project of Shenzhen (grant number JCYJ20 200109105216803).

Disclosure of Interests. The authors have no competing interests to declare that are relevant to the content of this article.

References

1. Ding, Y., Liu, Z., Qiu, C., et al.: Metamaterial with simultaneously negative bulk modulus and mass density. Phys. Rev. Lett. **99**(9), 093904 (2007)
2. Zhang, Z., Wang, H., Yang, C., et al.: Vibration energy harvester based on bilateral periodic one-dimensional acoustic black hole. Appl. Sci. **13**(11), 6423 (2023)
3. Nguyen, H., Wu, Q., Xu, X., et al.: Broadband acoustic silencer with ventilation based on slit-type Helmholtz resonators. Appl. Phys. Lett. **117**(13), 134103 (2020)
4. Zhang, Z., Wang, X., Liu, Z.Y., et al.: A study of low frequency sound insulation mechanism of a perforated plate-type acoustic metamaterial. J. Sound Vib. **558**, 117775 (2023)
5. Li, J., Jiang, R., Xu, D., et al.: Study of acoustic transmission losses in particle-reinforced rubber-based membrane-type acoustic metamaterials. Appl. Acoust. **208**, 109379 (2023)
6. Yang, Z., Mei, J., Yang, M., et al.: Membrane-type acoustic metamaterial with negative dynamic mass. Phys. Rev. Lett. **101**(20), 204301 (2008)
7. Naify, C.J., Chang, C.M., McKnight, G., et al.: Transmission loss of membrane-type acoustic metamaterials with coaxial ring masses. J. Appl. Phys. **110**(12), 124903 (2011)
8. Chen, J.S., Chen, Y.B., Chen, H.W., et al.: Bandwidth broadening for transmission loss of acoustic waves using coupled membranering structure. Materials Res. Express **3**(10), 105801 (2016)
9. Lu, Z., Yu, X., Lau, S.K., et al.: Membrane-type acoustic metamaterial with eccentric masses for broadband sound isolation. Appl. Acoust. **157**, 107003 (2020)
10. Zhou, G., Wu, J.H., Lu, K., et al.: Broadband low-frequency membrane-type acoustic metamaterials with multi-state anti-resonances. Appl. Acoust. **159**, 107078 (2020)
11. Ji, Y.L., Li, H.F., Liu, J.B.: Effect of surface tension on acoustic insulation performance of membrane-type acoustic metamaterials. J. Functional Materials **50**(01), 1120–1125 (2019). (in Chinese)

12. Yuan, W., Hu, C.N., Lin, G.C., et al.: Research on low frequency sound insulation of thin film acoustic metamaterials. Machine Design Manufact. Eng. **50**(03), 113–117 (2021). (in Chinese)
13. Ma, F., Huang, M., Wu, J.H.: Acoustic metamaterials with synergetic coupling. J. Appl. Phys. **122**(21) (2017)
14. Thongchom, C., Jearsiripongkul, T., Refahati, N., et al.: Sound transmission loss of a honeycomb sandwich cylindrical shell with functionally graded porous layers. Buildings **12**(2), 151 (2022)

An Anomaly Detection Framework for Propagation Networks Leveraging Deep Learning

Yuewei Wu[1] , Zhenyu Yu[1] , Zhiqiang Zhang[1] , Junyi Chen[1] ,
and Fulian Yin[1,2(✉)]

[1] Communication University of China, Beijing 100024, Chaoyang, China
yinfulian@cuc.edu.cn
[2] State Key Laboratory of Media Convergence and Communication, Beijing 100024, Chaoyang,
China

Abstract. In the Internet era, communication networks are endless, and all kinds of communication anomalies are also dazzling, so it becomes especially important to detect anomalies in social network communication. Graph networks with their excellent ability to capture spatial information have been well applied in the propagation field. In this paper, we develop a graph convolutional deep self-coding framework AD-GCN, which is the first learning algorithm used for anomaly detection in social network propagation. It is based on a deep self-coder, on top of which the popular Graph Convolutional Network (GCN) is introduced to learn the underlying distribution of graph structures and node attributes and to construct the reconstruction error and detect anomalies from both structure and loss perspectives. We have collected a real dataset of hot topics in microblogging and tested accordingly on this dataset to achieve better results.

Keywords: Anomaly detection · Deep self-coder · Graph Convolutional Network

1 Introduction

With the popularization and development of the Internet, the seamless access of various communication devices to the network has made the virtual and real worlds interpenetrate, and human social activities can be recorded, stored and disseminated. The Internet provides a brand-new communication platform for all mankind, and has a profound impact on the life of each of us. At the same time, network technology is also a double-edged sword, its rapid development and wide application, on the one hand, to promote the rapid development of social economy, on the other hand, all kinds of abnormal communication behavior are becoming increasingly rampant, the security of communication has become the basis of national security and social and political stability. Effective measures to identify abnormal communication information will greatly avoid the emergence of network chaos, which is also an important guarantee for the strength of a country.

G. Zhai et al. (Eds.): IFTC 2023, CCIS 2067, pp. 258–268, 2024.
https://doi.org/10.1007/978-981-97-3626-3_19

Regarding anomaly detection, it has been a very important sub-branch of machine learning, and anomaly detection is a very popular research direction in various artificial intelligence fields, such as computer vision, data mining, and NLP, especially in the era of big data, the rate of information dissemination grows by leaps and bounds, and the speed of manual processing of data has been far from catching up with that of the machine, so detecting anomalies in the disseminated data faster and more accurately has become a very important task for us nowadays. How to more accurately capture the differences in structure and attributes between normal and abnormal nodes has always been an extremely important problem in anomaly detection. Samet Akcay et al. (2018) proposed a semi-supervised anomaly detection model, GANomaly, which learns the generation of high-dimensional image space and the inference of the latent space at the same time by introducing a conditional generative adversarial network (GAN) [1]. Ren et al. (2019) proposed a novel algorithm based on spectral residuals (SR) and convolutional neural networks (CNN). The approach is to introduce the SR model from the field of visual saliency detection to time series anomaly detection and innovatively combines SR and CNN to improve the performance of the SR model [2]. Pang et al. (2019) introduced DevNet to the detection of anomalies, which utilizes a small number of labeled anomalies and a priori probabilities to learn anomaly scores directly through the Neural Deviation Network to achieve a more efficient anomaly scoring [3].

Currently, graph neural networks (GNN) are rapidly developing, as graph networks can capture the complex relationships between different nodes in the graph, and also capture the local structure and subgraphs in the graph to deepen the understanding of the graph, and are excellent in dealing with complex relational data [4–6], social networks, molecular structures [7, 8] and so on. Anomaly detection based on graph networks is also receiving much attention, the traditional anomaly detection [9] methods may not be able to capture the nonlinear and irregular relationships between data points well and perform poorly in dealing with real-time data and changing scenarios, while the graph network structure due to its characteristics can well solve the above problems, and the graph network naturally supports semi-supervised learning, which can effectively utilize the unlabeled data and improve the generalization ability of the model, which is useful in anomaly detection.

In this paper, we focus on the application of graph networks (GCN) to social network propagation for anomaly detection [10, 11], and we develop a graph-convolutional deep self-coding framework, AD-GCN, for the first time to use machine learning algorithms for anomaly detection in social network propagation. First, we construct an encoder to set the input of the model as the neighbor matrix and attribute matrix of the nodes in the social network, and learn the embedding of each node using a multilayer graph convolution structure [12–17]. Second, the reconstructors for node structure and node attributes are constructed separately, and the embedding of each node learned by the encoder is used as input to reconstruct the neighbor matrix and attribute matrix of the node [18–20]. Finally, the original matrix and the reconstruction matrix are then used to derive the reconstruction error to identify anomalous nodes in the social network. The main contributions of this paper are as follows:

- We introduce GCN into anomaly detection in social networks and find anomalies from both structural and attribute perspectives of nodes.

- We collect newer real data on microblogging social networks, including but not limited to user relationships. This ensures that our dataset covers a rich set of social network behaviors and relationships and is well suited to test the utility of the model.
- We evaluated our own collected microblogging social network dataset in the AD-GCN model. The model performs well in social network propagation, proving the strength of our dataset.

2 Preliminary

This section gives specific preparations and introduces graph neural networks and deep self-encoders.

2.1 Introduction to Graph Neural Networks

In recent years, graph neural networks have developed rapidly and evolved many variants, and their powerful graph modeling capability gives them a great advantage in processing social network data. In this paper, we use a variant of neural network, GCN, which is based on the adjacency matrix of the graph and the feature matrix of the nodes, and gradually aggregates the neighbor information of the nodes and updates the node representations through multi-layer graph convolution operations. GCN incorporates the Laplace matrix of the graph in its design, which is expressed as in Eq. 1:

$$H^{l+1} = \sigma\left(\tilde{D}^{-\frac{1}{2}}\tilde{A}\tilde{D}^{-\frac{1}{2}}H^l W^l\right) \tag{1}$$

Here H^l is the feature layer of the l-layer in the model, and it is important to note that H^0 is the input to the model here, $H^0 = X$, where X is the attribute matrix of the node at the beginning; $\tilde{A} = A + I_E$, where A is the adjacency matrix and I_E is the unit array; $\tilde{D}$ is the degree matrix of the $\tilde{A}$ matrix, $\tilde{D}_{ii} = \sum_j \tilde{A}_{ij}$; W^l is the learnable weight matrix of the l-layer; σ is the activation function, e.g. $\mathrm{Re}lu(\cdot) = \max(0, \cdot)$, etc. The following is a simple GCN graph network structure, as shown in Fig. 1.

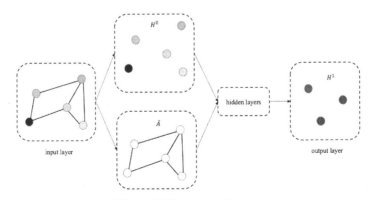

Fig. 1. GCN structure diagram

2.2 Introduction to Deep Self-encoders

Traditional anomaly detection methods are usually based on linear models, and feature extraction of the sample data also generally requires manual extraction, which makes the method potentially less robust in some cases. Deep auto-encoder is a deep neural network that is capable of automatically learning the feature representation of the data end-to-end and has strong nonlinear modeling capabilities for learning the latent representation of the data in an unsupervised manner, which enables it to better adapt to complex data distributions and improve the accuracy of anomaly detection. It learns low-dimensional feature representations of data by stacking multiple encoder and decoder functions, and its simple structure is schematically illustrated in Fig. 2:

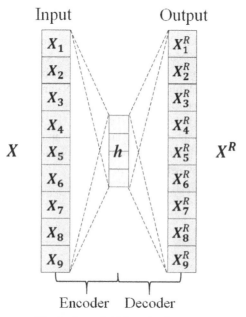

Fig. 2. Deep Self-Encoder Structure

Deep self-encoders are able to extract nonlinear information from high-dimensional data by utilizing multiple linear units and nonlinear activation functions of the encoder and decoder. Its simple workflow can be represented as, given a dataset X, the encoder maps the dataset the dataset to a low-dimensional feature space to obtain a potential low-dimensional feature representation h, which is then fed into the decoder to obtain the recovered data X^R. The learning process can be represented as in Eq. 2:

$$min[dist(X, X^R)] \tag{2}$$

where $dist(\cdot)$ is a measure of distance, and generally we choose the ℓ_2-norm distance to measure the reconstruction error.

3   Proposed Methods

In this section, we present the AD-GCN model, which is based on the deep self-encoder framework and GCN.

3.1   Introduction to the AD-GCN Model

Attribute networks contain not only the structure of the network, but also rich node attributes. The nonlinearity of the data and the interaction of complex modalities lead to how to take an effective approach to capture the latent information of the attribute network becomes a difficult task. GCN is a graph convolution model based on the Laplace spectral transform, which learns new latent representations of hierarchies through the spectral convolution function. GCN can take into account the proximity of the higher-order nodes in learning the embedded representations, which alleviates the sparsity of the network beyond the node linking problem. At the same time, the multilayer nonlinear transformations are utilized to capture the nonlinearity of the data and the complex interaction of the two information modalities in the attribute network. Therefore, we are inspired by Graph Convolutional Networks (GCN) and apply the GCN model to encoding and decoding of deep self-encoders.

We mainly construct the AD-GCN model based on GCN. In this paper, the AD-GCN model mainly consists of a combination of an encoder and two reconfigurators, where the reconfigurators are the node structure reconfigurator and the attribute reconfigurator respectively. Its structure, as shown in Fig. 3:

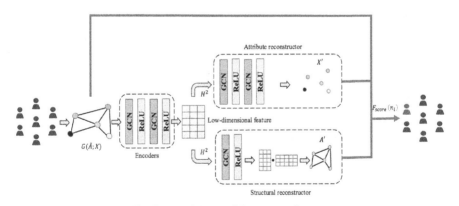

Fig. 3. AD-GCN model structure diagram

First of all, in the encoder part we use a two-layer GCN graph convolutional network structure for dimensionality reduction of the node features, and in the input part of the model we take the attribute matrix of the node as the input of the whole model, and the neighbor matrix of the node is imported into the model as a matrix parameter of the whole model, and the inputs are shown in Eq. 3:

$$input = G\left(\tilde{A}; H^{0}\right) = G(\tilde{A}; X) \tag{3}$$

where H^0 is the input to the first layer of the model; $\tilde{A}$ is the neighbor matrix of the network node after considering itself; X is the attribute matrix of the network node; inside the model we use GCN based graph convolution structure for feature processing, the convolution formula is shown in Eq. 4:

$$H^{l+1} = \sigma\left(\tilde{D}^{-\frac{1}{2}}\tilde{A}\tilde{D}^{-\frac{1}{2}}H^l W^l\right) \qquad (4)$$

where H^{l+1} is the input to the convolutional structure of the l-layer, $\tilde{D}$ is the degree matrix of $\tilde{A}$, $\tilde{D}_{ii} = \sum_j \tilde{A}_{ij}$; W^l is a learnable matrix of the l-layer, and $\sigma(\cdot)$ is a nonlinear activation function. The structure of the encoder model can be expressed as Eqs. 5, 6:

$$H^1 = \sigma\left(\tilde{D}^{-\frac{1}{2}}\tilde{A}\tilde{D}^{-\frac{1}{2}}XW^0\right) \qquad (5)$$

$$H^2 = \sigma\left(\tilde{D}^{-\frac{1}{2}}\tilde{A}\tilde{D}^{-\frac{1}{2}}H^1 W^1\right) \qquad (6)$$

During the model training process, it is necessary to include dropout layers between the layers to prevent overfitting.

Second, the attribute reconstructor also employs a two-layer GCN graph convolution structure to uplift the low-dimensional feature representations of the nodes at the output of the encoder, with the aim of reducing an attribute reconstruction matrix that is as similar as possible to the input attribute matrix of the nodes. The structure of the attribute reconstructor can be expressed as Eqs. 7, 8:

$$H_a^1 = \sigma\left(\tilde{D}^{-\frac{1}{2}}\tilde{A}\tilde{D}^{-\frac{1}{2}}H^2 W_a^0\right) \qquad (7)$$

$$X' = H_a^2 = \sigma\left(\tilde{D}^{-\frac{1}{2}}\tilde{A}\tilde{D}^{-\frac{1}{2}}H_a^1 W_a^1\right) \qquad (8)$$

where X' is the attribute reconstruction matrix. Similarly, dropout layers have to be added between layers during model training to prevent model overfitting.

The structural reconstructor employs a one-layer GCN graph convolution structure and multiplies the convolution output by a matrix transpose, which aims to reduce a structural reconstruction matrix that is as similar as possible to the input node adjacency matrix. The structure of the structural reconstructor can be expressed as Eqs. 9, 10:

$$H_s^1 = \sigma\left(\tilde{D}^{-\frac{1}{2}}\tilde{A}\tilde{D}^{-\frac{1}{2}}H^2 W_s^0\right) \qquad (9)$$

$$A' = H_s^1 H_s^{1T} \qquad (10)$$

where A' is the structural reconstruction matrix. During training, H_s^1 needs to be passed through a dropout layer to prevent model overfitting.

Finally, we come to the construction of the error function, our error function is divided into two main parts: node attribute error and node structure error. The structure error and attribute error represent different aspects of the data. The structure error focuses on the relationships and patterns between data points, while the attribute error focuses on the characteristics of individual data points. The combined use of these two types of errors can provide a more comprehensive anomaly detection performance that covers multiple data dimensions, which can increase the accuracy of anomaly detection and make the system more robust. The node attribute error can be expressed as Eq. 11:

$$L_X = mean\left(\left|X' - X\right|\right) \tag{11}$$

The node structure error can be expressed as Eq. 12:

$$L_A = mean\left(\left|A' - A\right|\right) \tag{12}$$

The error function for the model as a whole can be expressed as Eq. 13:

$$L = \alpha L_X + (1 - \alpha)L_A \tag{13}$$

where α is the loss percentage, which is used to control the proportion of node loss error and structural error in the loss function. Through the above loss function, the AD-GCN model is continuously optimized, with the aim that the encoder can get more accurate low-dimensional features of the nodes, and the reconstructor can restore the original information more completely through that low-dimensional features. After training, when the model converges, we can get the anomaly score of each node, which can be expressed as Eq. 14:

$$F_{score}(n_i) = \alpha\left(x'_i - x_i\right) + (1 - \alpha)\left(a'_i - a_i\right) \tag{14}$$

where, $F_{score}(n_i)$ is the anomaly score of node i, a_i is the original structural characterization of node i, and $a_i{}'$ is the structural reconstruction feature of node i; x_i is the original attribute feature of node i, and $x_i{}'$ is the attribute reconstruction feature of node i. We can set the corresponding discrimination threshold f according to the specific task, together with the anomaly score, to determine whether the node is anomalous or not, which can be expressed as Eq. 15:

$$\begin{cases} F_{score}(n_i) > f & Node\ i\ anomaly \\ F_{score}(n_i) < f & Node\ i\ normal \end{cases} \tag{15}$$

4 Experiment

In this section, we input the real-world collected Sina Weibo social network data into the AD-GCN model to validate the effectiveness of the proposed model.

4.1 Data Description

This paper delves into the poignant case of the microblog hot topic, #Xinzheng No. 3 Middle School teacher's online course death#, serving as a paradigmatic event. The initial catalyst occurred when the deceased's daughter, acting as the primary user, posted a poignant microblog in the early morning of November 2, 2022, exposing the online perpetrator. Our methodology involved designating users who reposted the initial microblog within the first eight hours as seed users. Subsequently, we systematically compiled the attention and fan data of these seed users, progressively extending our data collection to include subsequent users, fan users, and their respective attention and fan data. This step-wise approach was pursued until a dataset of sufficient magnitude was amassed, allowing for the construction of a bona fide microblog network that adheres to the principles of a power-law distribution. The data refinement process commenced with the amalgamation of individual user data files, followed by the identification of cross-correlation relationships among users from the initial dataset of over 10 million entries. Subsequently, redundant cross-correlation relationships were systematically eliminated to enhance data precision. In either case, pairs exhibiting these characteristics were excluded, thus constructing a microblogging network that faithfully reflects real-world dynamics. The culmination of this process yielded a scale-free network structure of interconnected users associated with the studied event. The pertinent parameters characterizing this network are delineated in the subsequent Table 1:

Table 1. The attributes of the graph

Attributes	Nodes	Edges	Average degree	Max. degree	Transitivity
Value	30510	261898	17.168	3636	0.0877

4.2 Data Processing

Since it is usually extremely difficult to obtain anomalous data in real life and our dataset lacks anomalous data, we will artificially add some perturbations in the dataset and construct some anomalous nodes for the purpose of experimentation. This time we plan to construct two types of anomaly nodes: structural anomaly nodes and attribute anomaly nodes. In daily life, some terrorist actions and crowd propagation usually appear in the form of a small group [21], each node in this small group is closely connected with each other, which can be viewed as a line between nodes and nodes in the graph, and we define such a group of nodes as anomalous nodes, firstly, we define the size of the small group as 15, and randomly select 10 such small groups in the dataset. Attribute anomaly, its principle comes from the relationship between node attributes and node structural environment [22], we believe that a certain attribute probability matches a certain structural feature, so we randomly select 150 nodes in the dataset, for each node i, randomly in addition to randomly pick out 50 nodes k, the calculation of node i are respectively different from the attributes of the 50 nodes k, which can be expressed by Eq. 16:

$$Q = |x_i - x_k| \tag{16}$$

where Q denotes the difference between the node attributes and the node attributes, x_i denotes as the attributes of node i and x_k denotes as the attributes of node k. Eventually a node with the largest difference from node i is selected to give its attributes to node i.

In this way we construct node i as an attribute anomaly node, and by repeating this step, 150 attribute anomaly nodes can be constructed, which are also used for the testing of the model.

4.3 Experimental Parameters and Indicators Setting

During our experiments we set the learning rate of the model to 0.005 and the epoch of model training to 20, in addition, for the encoder network we used two graph convolution layers (both 64 neurons), for the node attribute reconstructor we used the symmetric structure of the encoder, and for the node structural reconstructor we used the anomalous graph convolution layer (64 neurons), and in the model we used the Adam [23] algorithm to optimize the loss function.

In the experiments, the ROC-AUC metric was chosen to evaluate the results of the model accordingly:

- **ROC-AUC:** The horizontal coordinate in the ROC plot is the false positive rate (i.e., normal nodes are recognized as abnormal) and the vertical coordinate is the true positive rate (abnormal nodes are recognized as abnormal). The AUC value is obtained by measuring the area under the ROC curve, which takes values ranging from 0 to 1. The larger the AUC, the better the model performance. By looking at the ROC curve and its AUC value, we can evaluate the classification performance of the model under different thresholds, especially when dealing with unbalanced datasets, this metric is often used to evaluate the performance of anomaly detection.

4.4 Experimental Results

In the experiment, because all the data in our scale-free dataset are normal, it is necessary to first pre-process our scale-free dataset with data, add perturbations to construct abnormal nodes in the data to form a new network data, use the processed abnormal network data to test the model, use the method of control variables, set up different loss functions as a percentage of the α, and its observation of the ROC-AUC indexes, and the results of which are shown in Table 2.

From Table 2, we can see that when the α value is extreme, such as only considering the structural error or only considering the attribute error, the AUC index of the model is relatively low and the performance is relatively poor. For our current scale-free network data, the performance of the model reaches better when we take the α value to about 0.4. This reflects that structural anomalies in the scale-free network of this Sina Weibo dataset are more important for the anomaly detection structure of the model.

Table 2. Effect of different α on AUC values

α	0	0.2	0.4	0.6	0.8	1
AUC	0.8913	0.8915	0.8916	0.8914	0.8914	0.8912

5 Conclusion

In this paper, we establish an AD-GCN anomaly detection model and discuss the problem of anomaly detection in social network event propagation. Utilizing the ability of GCN to capture complex features among nodes, combined with a deep autoencoder framework, we embed and reconstruct the nodes learned from GCN into the original attribute network, and then construct the loss function in terms of both attribute anomalies of nodes and structural anomalies of nodes, respectively, and label the anomalous nodes accordingly. The experimental results show that our model performs well in detecting anomalous users in the scale-free network propagation of microblogging trending topics. In future research, we can focus on the adaptability and diversity of the model.

Acknowledgement. This work was supported by the National Natural Science Foundation of China (No. 62372418), The Beijing Natural Science Foundation (No. 4232015), The State Key Laboratory of Media Convergence and Communication, Communication University of China, The Fundamental Research Funds for the Central Universities, The High-quality and Cutting-edge Disciplines Construction Project for Universities in Beijing (Internet Information, Communication University of China).

References

1. Akcay, S., Atapour-Abarghouei, A., Breckon, T.P.: Ganomaly: semi-supervised anomaly detection via adversarial training. In: Jawahar, C.V., Li, H., Mori, G., Schindler, K. (eds.) Computer Vision – ACCV 2018: 14th Asian Conference on Computer Vision, Perth, Australia, December 2–6, 2018, Revised Selected Papers, Part III, pp. 622–637. Springer, Cham (2019). https://doi.org/10.1007/978-3-030-20893-6_39
2. Ren, H., Xu, B., Wang, Y., et al.: Time-series anomaly detection service at Microsoft. In: Proceedings of the 25th ACM SIGKDD International Conference on Knowledge Discovery & Data Mining, pp. 3009–3017 (2019)
3. Pang, G., Shen, C., van den Hengel, A.: Deep Anomaly Detection with Deviation Networks, pp. 353–362 (2019)
4. Akoglu, L., Tong, H., Koutra, D.: Graph based anomaly detection and description: a survey. DMKD **29**(3), 626–688 (2015)
5. Cao, S., Lu, W., Xu, Q.: Deep neural networks for learning graph representations. In: AAAI, pp. 1145–1152 (2016)
6. Hamilton, W., Ying, Z., Leskovec, J.: Inductive representation learning on large graphs. In: NIPS, pp. 1024–1034 (2017)
7. Réau, M., Renaud, N., Xue, L.C., et al.: DeepRank-GNN: a graph neural network framework to learn patterns in protein–protein interfaces. Bioinformatics **39**(1), btac759 (2023)
8. Jha, K., Saha, S., Singh, H.: Prediction of protein–protein interaction using graph neural networks. Sci. Rep. **12**(1), 8360 (2022)
9. Munir, M., Chattha, M.A., Dengel, A., Ahmed, S.: A comparative analysis of traditional and deep learning-based anomaly detection methods for streaming data. In: 2019 18th IEEE International Conference on Machine Learning and Applications (ICMLA), Boca Raton, pp. 561–566 (2019). https://doi.org/10.1109/ICMLA.2019.00105
10. Kaur, R., Singh, S.: A survey of data mining and social network analysis based anomaly detection techniques. Egypt. Inform. J. **17**(2), 199–216 (2016)

11. Rahman, M.S., Halder, S., Uddin, M.A., et al.: An efficient hybrid system for anomaly detection in social networks. Cybersecurity **4**(1), 1–11 (2021)

12. Tan, Q., Liu, N., Hu, X.: Deep representation learning for social network analysis. Front. Big Data **2**, 2 (2019)

13. Alamsyah, A., Rahardjo, B.: Social network analysis taxonomy based on graph representation. arXiv preprint arXiv:2102.08888 (2021)

14. Gidaris, S., Komodakis, N.: Generating classification weights with GNN denoising autoencoders for few-shot learning. In: Proceedings of the IEEE/CVF Conference on Computer Vision and Pattern Recognition, pp. 21–30 (2019)

15. Author, F., Author, S.: Title of a proceedings paper. In: Editor, F., Editor, S. (eds.) Conference 2016, LNCS, vol. 9999, pp. 1–13. Springer, Heidelberg (2016)

16. Ng, I., Zhu, S., Chen, Z., et al.: A graph autoencoder approach to causal structure learning. arXiv preprint arXiv:1911.07420 (2019)

17. Dai, J., Yuan, W., Bao, C., et al.: DAS-GNN: denoising autoencoder integrated with self-supervised learning in graph neural network-based recommendations. Appl. Intell. **53**(14), 17292–17309 (2023)

18. Chow, J.K., Su, Z., Wu, J., et al.: Anomaly detection of defects on concrete structures with the convolutional autoencoder. Adv. Eng. Inform. **45**, 101105 (2020)

19. Cheng, Z., Wang, S., Zhang, P., et al.: Improved autoencoder for unsupervised anomaly detection. Int. J. Intell. Syst. **36**(12), 7103–7125 (2021)

20. Fernandes, G., Rodrigues, J.J.P.C., Carvalho, L.F., et al.: A comprehensive survey on network anomaly detection. Telecommun. Syst. **70**, 447–489 (2019)

21. Skillicorn, D.B.: Detecting anomalies in graphs. In: InISI, pp. 209–216 (2007)

22. Song, X., Mingxi, W., Jermaine, C., Ranka, S.: Conditional anomaly detection. TKDE **19**(5), 631–645 (2007)

23. Kingma, D.P., Ba, J.: Adam: a method for stochastic optimization. arXiv preprint arXiv:1412.6980 (2014)

MABC-Net: Multimodal Mixed Attentional Network with Balanced Class for Temporal Forgery Localization

Haonan Cheng[1], Haixin Yu[2], Li Fang[1], and Long Ye[1,3(✉)]

[1] State Key Laboratory of Media Convergence and Communication, Communication University of China, Beijing, China
{haonancheng,lifang8902,yelong}@cuc.edu.cn
[2] School of Information and Communication Engineering, Communication University of China, Beijing, China
hxyu88@cuc.edu.cn
[3] School of Data Science and Media Intelligence, Communication University of China, Beijing, China

Abstract. As an impactful social task, recognizing and localizing forgery events in videos is getting active attention. Since forgery events occur in both auditory and visual modalities, detailed perception of multimodality is essential for accurate temporal forgery localization (TFL). Currently, most fake videos consist of only a small segment of fake content, which leads to the problem of class imbalance due to large differences in the proportion of fake and real content. Unfortunately, existing methods suffer significantly in performance owing to the fact that they take little account of the problem of class imbalance. To address this issue, we present a multimodal Mixed **A**ttentional network with **B**alanced **C**lass (MABC-Net) for temporal forgery localization. Specifically, we first propose the mixed-attentive feature learning (MAFL) module. This module captures audio-visual temporal features via a mixed learning strategy, which leverages two self-attention blocks and two cross-attention blocks. Moreover, a fusion-balanced localization (FBL) module is designed for alleviating the influence of the class imbalance problem. This benefits from an elegant combination of focal and boundary matching loss functions. Extensive experiments on TFL show that our MABC-Net is superior to the state-of-the-art methods and localizes more precise segment boundaries. Code is available at https://github.com/Tea7374/MABC-Net.

Keywords: temporal forgery localization · multimodal mixed attentional network · class imbalance

1 Introduction

Temporal forgery localization(TFL) is a challenging and important deepfake detection task, which has raised several concerns due to its high societal impact [20,28]. Unlike forgery detection tasks determining the authenticity of the entire

G. Zhai et al. (Eds.): IFTC 2023, CCIS 2067, pp. 269–283, 2024.
https://doi.org/10.1007/978-981-97-3626-3_20

video, the TFL task aims to localize the forgery content, which brings greater challenges for more precise detection (as shown in Fig. 1). This precise task requires not only the exploiting of intra-modal disharmony, but also the characterization of inter-modal cues. Due to the natural correlation between visual and auditory modalities, the audio-visual joint multimodal learning can provide additional information for TFL. In recent years, joint audio-visual deepfake detection works mainly focus on classifying the authenticity of the entire multimedia content based on audio-visual association, such as affective cues [20], phoneme-viseme cues [1], and biometric cues [9]. That is, existing audio-visual deepfake detection models tend to identify the forgery content but cannot localize the forgery content.

However, it is important to locate the timestamps corresponding to the forgery segments. A recent work [4] exploits a boundary aware temporal forgery detection method via a 3DCNN architecture. Since they focus more on the coarse-grained content, detailed information is inclined to be neglected, which makes it difficult to localize short-term forgery segments. Moreover, as suggested in [7], fake content might constitute only small part of a long real video. This may lead to the problem of class imbalance due to large differences in the proportion of fake and real content. Unfortunately, existing methods suffer significantly in performance owing to the fact that they take little account of the problem of class imbalance. Therefore, it is necessity to explore detailed audio-visual joint learning and seek the solution of the imbalance problem.

In this paper, we introduce a novel multimodal **M**ixed **A**ttentional network with **B**alanced **C**lass (MABC-Net) for TFL. To the best of our knowledge, this is the first exploration of the imbalance class problem in the TFL task. To be specific, we first propose a novel mixed-attentive feature learning (MAFL) module composed of mixed attention units to acquire comprehensive and sufficient audio-visual learning. In each mixed attention unit, a self-attention block captures inconsistency features of temporal context within modalities, together with a cross-attention block to obtain the inter-modal correlation features of audio-visual. To alleviate the influence of the class imbalance problem in TFL, we also design a fusion-balanced localization (FBL) module. This module explores to balance the real-fake samples and generate localization proposals with precise temporal boundaries as well as reliable confidence scores simultaneously. By this means, the MABC-Net can obtain detailed audio-visual joint learning and solve the imbalance problem for better TFL performance.

In summary, our main contributions are listed as follows:

- We are the first to discover and address the issue of data imbalance in deepfake localization tasks, which was previously overlooked and seriously affected the precision of TFL.
- We propose a novel approach MABC-Net that combines mixed-attention and focal loss to effectively balance the loss between real and fake segments during model training and improve model localization performance.
- Our proposed approach achieves state-of-art results on the LAV-DF dataset, improving average precision score by up to 10%.

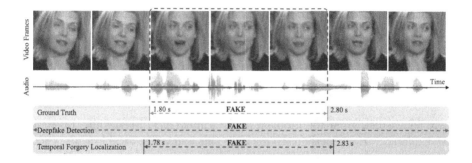

Fig. 1. An illustrative example of the TFL task. TFL aims to temporally localize the fake content in the video, while deepfake detection task aims to classify the authenticity of the entire video.

2   Related Works

2.1   Multimodal Deepfake Video Detection

Multimodal deepfake video detection aims to use visual and auditory cues to determine whether the video is forged. In early detection. [15] explore several feature processing methods with different parameters and different classifiers. [19] incorporate temporal information from audio and video data and create balanced set for training. [14] subsequently focus on different mouth and audio features, using LSTM networks to learn temporal context for video authenticity classification. However, with the development of video generation technology, more and more realistic audiovisual content demands more accurate forgery solutions. In recent years, some methods [7,9] adopt the idea of directly fitting video and audio features using comparative loss, which can preliminarily obtain real and fake video information. [6] start from the perspective of voice face matching, using a universal audio-visual dataset to pre train a voice face matcher, and then fine-tuning it on a deep forgery dataset. [12] use a dense SWIN transformer network to separately determine the authenticity of video and audio features. [25] improve the CBAM [26] model to integrate the features of video and audio streams. [30] utilize attention mechanism to update the features of two modalities and classify the authenticity of videos for both modalities.

Unfortunately, most of the aforementioned methods are ill-suited for the temporal boundary localization of forged video clips. Although [7] demonstrate TFL, the localization performance is not ideal as this method is designed primarily for deepfake detection. [4] propose a baseline model and collect the first and only audio-visual dataset for TFL task. This method maps video and audio features to the same dimension space and uses contrast loss to make the audio and video features of the real video closer in the dimension space, while the forged audio and video features farther away in the dimension space. Then they utilize BMN boundary matching [16] to predict the time boundary of the forged video clip. However, this method obtains insufficient visual and audio correlation information before predicting the temporal boundary, resulting in low localization accuracy. Inspired by the joint learning of audio-visual features in audio-visual analysis tasks [23,29], we introduce attention mechanisms to enhance audio-visual features to address the aforementioned issues.

2.2 Learning Imbalanced Datasets

Many fields suffer from the problem of data imbalance. Meanwhile, researchers have explored various methods to mitigate this issue. The focal loss proposed by [18] has effectively balanced the loss of positive and negative samples by reshaping the standard cross entropy loss. The Balanced Softmax [22] increases the loss weight of tail categories to make the model pay more attention to these tail categories. LDAE [11] is similar to Balanced Softmax and builds upon it by incorporating additional regularization terms. LDAM loss [5] balances stable learning for high-frequency classes and distinction enhancement for low-frequency classes through a distribution-aware margin design. Bal-BCE loss [27] balanced the different classes of loss by adjusting the logit bias. Although the aforementioned losses can address imbalance issues in their filed, our experiments indicate that they are inappropriate for handling the imbalance problem in the TFL task.

3 Method

3.1 Problem Statement

Given a video with T frames as input, we first extract video frames $V = \{v_t\}_{t=1}^T$ and the corresponding audio signals $A = \{a_t\}_{t=1}^T$, where v_t represents the t-th video frame and a_t represents the audio signal corresponding to frame v_t. The task of TFL is to detect the positions of fake video clips or fake audio clips. That is, for a video with M faked clips, our goal is to predict the set of start and end times $\{\hat{t}_{s_i}, \hat{t}_{e_i}\}_{i=1}^M$ of the faked clips to get as close as possible to the real start and end times $\{t_{s_i}, t_{e_i}\}_{i=1}^M$. It can be formulated in the following way:

$$\sum_{i=1}^M \{|t_{s_i} - \hat{t}_{s_i}| + |t_{e_i} - \hat{t}_{e_i}|\} \to 0. \tag{1}$$

However, this task is quite challenging since it is difficult to localize short-term forgery segments in the long real video. Most existing methods for detecting fake videos are unable to locate the temporal boundary of fake video segments or suffer from imbalance problem. Therefore, our final goal is to explore a high accuracy forgery localization method under the unbalanced sample distribution (Fig. 2).

3.2 Mixed-Attentive Feature Learning Module

In faked videos, both visual and audio can be falsified. However, whichever modality is falsified, it can be detected by inconsistencies between visual and

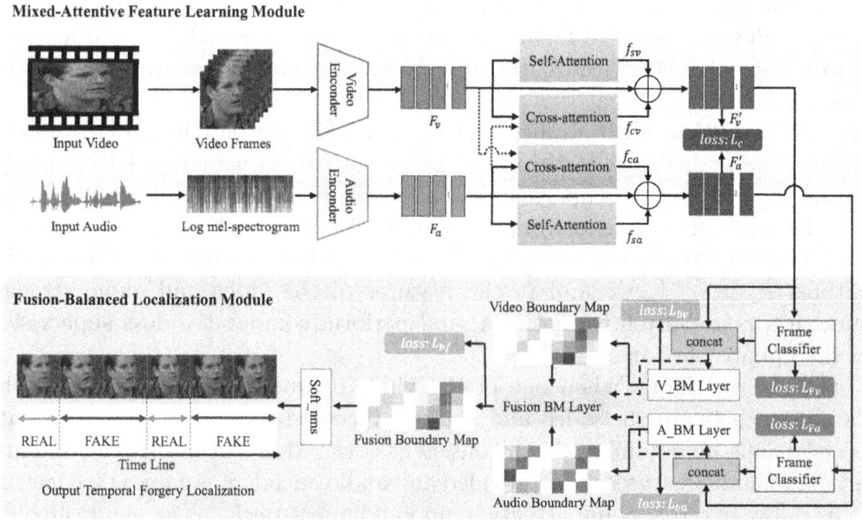

Fig. 2. An overview of our proposed MABC-Net. The proposed framework consists of two parts: the mixed-attentive feature learning module and the fusion-balanced localization module. In the first module, we extract features through video and audio encoders, and then extract deeper correlation features through a mixed-attentive network. In the second module, we locate the temporal boundary of the fake video by classifying multi-modal correlation features based on a sample balancing strategy.

audio. Therefore, we propose Mixed-Attentive Feature Learning (MAFL) for multi-modal learning to extract information from audio-visual inputs.

The MAFL module works in a two-stream manner and consists of two parts: an initial feature extraction unit and a mixed attention unit. The initial feature extraction unit encodes visual and audio separately. Then, the mixed attention unit is adopted to learn further audiovisual relationships which contains a self attention block and a cross attention block. The self attention block is used to capture temporal contextual features within the modality. The cross attention block is introduced to obtain the correlation features between video and audio stream.

Video Encoder. Given a video $V = \{v_t\}_{t=1}^{T}$ with T frames, we first extract its features base on a pre-trained C3D network [24]. The initial video frames are denoted as $V = \{v_t\}_{t=1}^{T} \in \mathbb{R}^{T \times H \times W \times C}$, where C represents the number of color channels, T represents the number of frames, H and W represent the height and width of the video frame. We utilize it as the input to the C3D network to obtain visual feature $F_v \in \mathbb{R}^{C_f \times T}$ through several 3D convolution and pooling operations, where C_f represents the dimension of the feature.

Audio Encoder. Given the input mono audio $A = \{a_t\}_{t=1}^{T} \in \mathbb{R}^{1 \times T}$, we first generate the log-mel spectrum. To be specific, we utilize Fast Fourier Transform (FFT) to extract the mel spectrum of the audio, and take the logarithm to obtain the log-mel spectrum. Then, the generated log-mel spectrum are input to the audio encoder. We finally obtain audio feature $F_a \in \mathbb{R}^{C_f \times T}$ through 2D convolution, where C_f is the feature dimension which is equal to the video feature dimension.

Mixed Attention Unit. Unlike previous work [4] that only learns intra-modal features for audiovisual features, we learn both intra-modal and inter-modal feature relationships. Comparing with previous work, our mixed attention unit provides more fine-grained frame-wise understanding and generates enhanced multi-modal features. After obtaining initial video features $F_v \in \mathbb{R}^{C_f \times T}$ and audio features $F_a \in \mathbb{R}^{C_f \times T}$, we update the features of the video and audio streams through a mixed-attentive network, and perform comparative loss supervision on the updated features.

On the one hand, when one of the video or audio streams is forged, the correlation between the video and audio is inconsistency. Therefore, we locate the fake clips by obtaining this inconsistent correlation feature. After obtaining video and audio features through video and audio encoders, we use video feature F_v as query in cross modal attention, and audio feature F_a as key and value for inter-modality interaction to obtain inconsistent correlation features. The feature calculation formula for cross-modal attention encoding is as follows:

$$f_{cv} = softmax(\frac{F_v F_a^\top}{\sqrt{C_f}})F_a, \tag{2}$$

where C_f is equal to the audio/visual feature dimension and $(\cdot)^\top$ represents the transposition of the matrix.

On the other hand, if both video and audio are forged, we can locate the fake clip by searching for inconsistent features in the temporal context, making the video feature F_v captures its own key information through a self-attention layer. The calculation for self attention encoding is formulated as follows:

$$f_{sv} = softmax(\frac{F_v F_v^\top}{\sqrt{C_f}})F_v, \tag{3}$$

The output generated by the cross-modal attention layer and self-attention layer is fused with the original features after dropout, and new video features are generated after layer normalization. The specific calculation formula is as follows:

$$F_v' = F_v + f_{cv} + f_{sv}, \tag{4}$$

New video features F_v' and the original video feature F_v has the same dimension. The same applies to the update of audio features.

After obtaining the updated feature $F_v' \in \mathbb{R}^{C_f \times T}$ and $F_a' \in \mathbb{R}^{C_f \times T}$, we use contrastive loss [8] to make the difference between real video clips smaller, while the difference between fake video clips becomes larger. The contrastive loss can be computed as follows:

$$L_c = \frac{1}{C_f \times T}[yd^2 + (1 - y)max(margin - d, 0)^2] \tag{5}$$

$$d = \|F_v^{'} - F_a^{'}\|_2 \tag{6}$$

where $y = 0$ indicates that the video clips corresponding to $F_v^{'}$ and $F_a^{'}$ are fake, and $y = 1$ indicates that the video clips corresponding to $F_v^{'}$ and $F_a^{'}$ are real.

3.3 Fusion-Balanced Localization Module

Although previous works explore multi-modal fusion methods initially, they are not applicable to our task. This is due to the fact that in TFL task, the fake clips usually take a very small part of the whole video. Delicate multi-modal fusion methods for imbalance class are still not fully explored. To this end, in this section we first design a fusion strategy to solve the imbalance problem and then generate the final localization result for deepfake detection.

Sample Balanced. Due to the fact that real samples occupy the vast majority of video clips, the loss of real video samples greatly suppresses the loss of fake video samples. To address this problem, we propose a balancing strategy by assigning different weight values to the real and fake samples. Firstly, we need to make preliminary authenticity judgements on the features of video and audio streams to further capture the potential features of fake clip. We use two 1D convolutional classifiers $C_v(\cdot)$ and $C_a(\cdot)$ predicts the authenticity of features $F_{v_i}^{'}$ and $F_{a_i}^{'}$ separately:

$$p^{v_i} = C_v(F_{v_i}^{'}), p^{a_i} = C_a(F_{a_i}^{'}), \tag{7}$$

where $p^{v_i} \in \mathbb{R}^{1 \times T}$ represents the probability of each video frame belongs to the fake class, and $p^{a_i} \in \mathbb{R}^{1 \times T}$ represents the probability of each audio clip belongs to the fake class. To simplify the expression, we use p^{m_i} to denote p^{v_i} and p^{a_i} uniformly, where $m \in \{v, a\}$ represents both visual and audio modalities.

Normally, we usually use the cross entropy loss function to measure the difference between the real sample and the predicted sample when performing classification tasks. However, since our task is to locate the temporal boundary of fake video clip, the fake video clip only occupies a small part of entire video, which causes the imbalance of sample data between the real video and the fake video. Simply using the cross entropy loss function to classify the video or audio of each frame may classify the fake video into the real video, which causes localization errors. Therefore, we introduce the focal loss [18]. Since our sample data has a real video clip label of 0 and a fake video clip label of 1, we find through the results of statistical model localization that when the video is true, the probability p_t given by the model is usually below 0.01. This means that most of the real videos in the sample are simple samples, while the probability distribution of fake video clips is relatively uniform, and there are almost no cases that are very close to 1. Therefore, introducing focal loss is very necessary. Then we finally calculate the classification loss function of each frame as follows:

$$L_{Fm_i}(p_t^{m_i}) = -\alpha_t(1 - p_t^{m_i})^{\gamma} log(p_t^{m_i}), \tag{8}$$

$$p_t^{m_i} = \begin{cases} p^{m_i} & if\, y = 1 \\ 1 - p^{m_i}, & otherwise, \end{cases} \tag{9}$$

where α_t used to adjust the weight of sample categories, γ used to adjust the weights of difficult and easy sample data. p^{m_i} represents the predicted value for each frame of each modality. So the final loss calculation for each modal frame classification is:

$$L_{Fm} = \frac{1}{T} \sum_{i=1}^{T} L_{Fm_i}(p_t^{m_i}). \tag{10}$$

Boundary Prediction. We adopt boundary-matching mechanism for TFL. Specifically, we first splice feature $F_v^{'}$ and $F_a^{'}$ and its corresponding classification output p^{v_i} and p^{a_i} to obtain a boundary matching input with dimension $\mathbb{R}^{(C_f+1) \times T}$. Different from previous boundary sensitive network [17], we adopt Boundary Matching Network (BMN) [16] which has a significant improvement in both generation speed and effectiveness. Firstly, we generate boundary confidence map through a visual boundary matching layer and an audio boundary matching layer. Then, we can obtain the corresponding Video Boundary Map (VBM) and Audio Boundary Map (ABM). Next, VBM and ABM are fused through two weight matrices to obtain the fusion boundary confidence map of the final fused audio and video. The size of all three boundary graphs is $\mathbb{R}^{(D \times T)}$, where D is the proposed maximum duration. Finally, we adopt the soft non maximum suppression proposed in BMN to eliminate duplicates and predict the forged time sets $\{\hat{t}_{s_i}, \hat{t}_{e_i}\}$ of video clips. Here we supervise each boundary matching layer using the simplest mean square error (MSE) loss.

$$L_{bm} = \frac{1}{D \times T} \sum_{i=1}^{D \times T} (\hat{P}^{m_i} - P^{m_i})^2, \tag{11}$$

$$L_{bf} = \frac{1}{D \times T} \sum_{i=1}^{D \times T} (\hat{P}^{f_i} - P^{f_i})^2, \tag{12}$$

where L_{bf} represents the MSE loss for audio-visual dual modality. $\hat{P}^{m_i}$ represents the confidence probability in the boundary graph given by the model. P^{m_i} represents ground truth. So our overall loss function is calculated as:

$$L = \lambda_c L_c + \frac{1}{2} \lambda_{fm} \sum L_{Fm}$$
$$+ \frac{1}{2} \lambda_{bm} \sum L_{bm} + \lambda_{bf} L_{bf}, \tag{13}$$

where $\lambda_c, \lambda_{fm}, \lambda_{bm}, \lambda_{bf}$ are the weights for different losses.

4   Experiments

4.1   Datasets and Evaluation Metrics

Datasets. We evaluate our method on different multi-modal deepfake detection datasets. LAV-DF [4] is a recently proposed dataset explicitly designed for the task of TFL of content driven manipulations. This is the only existing dataset that contains time labels for forged segments. We train and test our model on the LAV-DF dataset. There are a total of 136,304 videos in this dataset, of which 36,431 are real videos. The remaining 99,873 videos contain locally fake clips that are only video forged, only audio forged, and both video and audio forged. Among the fake clips, the longest fake clip time does not exceed 1.6 s, and most of the fake clips are less than 1 s. However, the entire video is usually between 5∼10 s, so the proportion of fake clips is relatively small. We have quantified that the forged segments constitute merely 10% of the entire dataset. We follow the splitting method proposed by [4], i.e., 78,703/31,501/26,100 for training/validation/testing sets, respectively.

We also test the deepfake classification performance of our method on DFDC dataset [10] and FakeAVCeleb dataset [13]. DFDC dataset is a publicly available face swap video dataset, with a total of 128,154 videos sourced from 3,426 actors. We utilize a subset of DFDC with 2,812/394/1,186 for training/validation/testing. FakeAVCeleb dataset contains deepfake visuals and respective synthesized lip-synced fake audios, which uses 490 real videos as a base set and generated 19,500 deepfake videos. We utilize 14,299/1,119/6,126 for training/validation/testing.

Evaluation metrics. We follow the same metrics, namely average precision (AP) and average recall (AR), in this field [4] to evaluate the performance of the localization. We set the Intersection over Union (IoU) thresholds of 0.5, 0.75, and 0.95 for AP. For AR, we set the IoU thresholds to [0.5 : 0.05 : 0.95] and set the number of fake segments to 100, 50, 20, and 10. Our method cannot be directly used for detecting deepfake video classification tasks. So in the classification task, we use the highest confidence score in the predicted segment as the probability of the entire video belongs to a fake video.

Table 1. Performance comparison with the SoTA models on the LAV-DF dataset.

Model	AP@0.5	AP@0.75	AP@0.95	AR@100	AR@50	AR@20	AR@10
MDS [7]	12.78	01.62	00.00	37.88	36.71	34.39	32.15
AGT [21]	17.85	09.42	00.11	43.15	34.23	24.59	16.71
BMN [16]	24.01	07.61	00.07	53.26	41.24	31.60	26.93
AVFusion [2]	65.38	23.89	00.11	62.98	59.26	54.80	52.11
BA-TFD [4]	76.90	38.50	00.25	66.90	64.08	60.77	58.42
Ours (visual-only)	60.62	33.62	0.34	62.93	59.01	52.96	48.40
Ours (audio-only)	59.06	34.52	0.29	62.79	58.58	53.32	49.02
Ours	**83.81**	**48.03**	**00.55**	**69.88**	**67.07**	**64.06**	**62.54**
BA-TFD+ [3]	92.08	75.57	2.04	78,05	76.51	74.36	73.27
BA-TFD+ + ours	**92.31**	**79.08**	**4.58**	**80.14**	**78.69**	**77.27**	**76.20**

4.2   Implementation Details

All experiments are implemented using Pytorch. We train and test our model on four sheets Nvidia RTX 2080Ti. In the comparison experiments with SOTA, we train each model 110 epochs, and in the ablation experiments, we trained each model 80 epochs.

Hyper-parameter Setting. We set the learning rate to $1e^{-5}$ in the experiment. If the loss of the epoch model on the verification set does not decrease every three times, the learning rate will be halved. When the learning rate drops to $1e^{-8}$, the training will stop. The hyper-parameters in loss functions are set to $\lambda_c = 0.1$, $\lambda_{fm} = 2.0$, $\lambda_{bm} = 1.0$, $\lambda_{bf} = 1.0$. For focal loss, we recommend setting $\alpha = 0.5$, $\gamma = 2.0$.

4.3   Comparison with State-of-the-Arts

We compare our MABC-Net with SOTA temporal localization methods on the LAV-DF dataset. As shown in Table 1, compared with the SoTA forgery localization method BA-TFD [4], our results achieve a new SoTA performance in terms of all metrics. The forgery fragment localization results show the most significant improvement at IOU thresholds of 0.5 and 0.75, with an average accuracy improvement of about 7% and 10% respectively. There is also an increase of approximately 3% to 4% in the average recall rate metrics. AGT and BMN are both visual modal localization methods. In addition, we evaluate the positioning results for video output only and audio output only. The results indicate that using only single mode for localization may result in a significant decrease in all metrics. Our results indicate that relying on a single modality alone is insufficient for accurately localizing the temporal boundary of fake video clips. BA-TFD+ [3] adopts a more advanced backbone network, which makes direct comparison unfair. To enable fair comparison, We have retrained the BA-TFD+ model. At the same time, we optimized BA-TFD+ by incorporating our proposed method - mixed-attention combined with focal loss. The optimized BA-TFD+ surpasses the original model on all evaluation metrics.

Table 2. Classification results on DFDC dataset [10] and FakeAVCeleb dataset [13]. The evaluation metric is AUC (%).

Methods	FakeAVCeleb	DFDC
MDS [7]	86.50	91.60
AVFakeNet [12]	83.40	86.20
BA-TFD [4]	84.90	84.60
MABC-Net	**87.04**	**93.94**

We also evaluate the deepfake classification effectiveness of our method by comparing it with previous audio-visual deepfake detection methods on

FakeAVCeleb and a subset of the DFDC dataset. The DFDC has a balanced distribution of real and fake videos, while the FakAVCeleb is highly skewed with many more fake videos than real ones. As shown in Table 2, our method outperforms BA-TFD, which is also a temporal boundary prediction method for fake videos. Our joint audiovisual learning for both intra- and inter-modal can not only achieve more accurate localization, but also improve the performance of fake classification.

4.4 Ablation Study

In this subsection, we discuss the effects of each component in MABC-Net. Experiment results are shown in Table 3.

Mixed-Attentive Module. The mixed attention module is designed to enable the model to find more consistent or inconsistent features between visual and audio modalities, as well as temporal contextual features. To verify its effectiveness, we compare the results of removing the whole mixed attention module (w/o MA), removing the self-attention block (w/o SA) and removing the cross-attention block (w/o CA). As shown in Table 3 (yellow rows), removing mixed attention module may significantly reduce performance on all metrics, especially in AP@0.5 and AP@0.75, which cause over 10% drop in performance. In the experiments of the separately removed modules, the performance of the model with the self-attention block removed is slightly decreased. However, when the cross-attention block is removed, there is a significant decrease in the performance of the model. Therefore, cross-attention plays a significant role in capturing correlation information between video and audio in locating fake video clips temporal boundary.

Table 3. The impact of missing different modules on the MABC Net model.

Model	AP@0.5	AP@0.75	AP@0.95	AR@100	AR@50	AR@20	AR@10
w/o MA	71.04	37.88	00.20	67.22	64.62	61.37	59.23
w/o SA	79.18	43.69	00.52	68.22	65.62	62.69	61.14
w/o CA	76.63	38.79	00.39	67.27	64.12	61.09	59.05
w/o FL	72.22	34.20	00.26	65.98	62.45	58.41	55.94
w/r BCE	77.68	43.03	00.47	68.79	65.80	62.52	60.81
#	81.53	45.22	00.48	69.16	66.06	62.96	61.28
*	53.02	15.72	00.05	57.54	54.68	49.76	44.60
MABC-Net	**83.81**	**48.03**	**00.55**	**69.88**	**67.07**	**64.06**	**62.54**

Focal Loss. We also evaluate the effect of focal loss for the imbalance problem. To verify the necessity of the focal loss, we conducted three experiments: (1) eliminating it, (2) replacing it with cross entropy loss, and (3) replacing it with Bal-BCE Loss. As shown in Table 3 (green rows), after excluding focal loss, After removing the focal loss, the performance of the entire model decreases substantially in all metrics. After replacing focal loss with cross entropy loss, although the performance is improved compared to the upper row, it still drops in all metrics compared to the original model. The "#" represents the model that replaces focal loss with Bal-BCE. While Bal-BCE loss leads to better results than BCE loss, it is still slightly inferior to focal loss. The reason is that Bal-BCE performs well in the long-tail recognition task, but does not focus on hard and easy samples, which is equally important for the model to subsequently perform forgery localization. The "*" represents the model that eliminates mixed attention and replaces focal loss with Bal-BCE. The localization performance of the model has significantly decreased. In summary, after eliminating the mixed attention, neither focal loss nor BalBCE loss can alleviate the impact of data imbalance, no matter which one we adopt. However, when both are incorporated with mixed attention, the model performance sees significant improvement, suggesting that the influence of data imbalance is further eliminated.

4.5 Visualization Results

To qualitatively validate the effectiveness of our MABC-Net, we plot the probability curves of several typical examples as shown in Fig. 3. In each example, the model has a low probability score (close to 0) of being forged in the part far away from the forged fragment. The model usually gives a higher probability score for forged segments and segments closer to forged segments. This probability score is approximately between 0.45 and 0.85. It can be observed from the Fig. 3 that our generated probability curves can effectively locate the forged fragment.

Fig. 3. We visualized the results of four videos on the LAV-DF dataset. The last line of each example represents the score predicted by the model for video forgery.

We further validate the performance of the model by visualizing the distributions of video features. We analyzed 10 videos comprising a total of 2,300 frames. Each data point in the graph represents the features extracted from one frame. As shown in the Fig. 4(a), it can be seen that when there is no mixed attention mechanism, the features of real videos and fake videos are very close in the feature space and most of the features of fake videos are overlapped with the real video features (yellow region in Fig. 4(a)). When we remove the focal loss, it is completely impossible to distinguish between the features of real videos and fake videos in the feature space (shown in Fig. 4(b)). Figure 4(c) shows the feature distribution of the full MABC-Net, it can be observed that features of real videos and fake videos can be well distinguished. It can be noticed that there

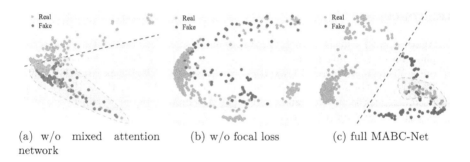

(a) w/o mixed attention network   (b) w/o focal loss   (c) full MABC-Net

Fig. 4. Visualization of the feature distribution in the PCA subspace. Different colors indicate features of different video frames: green → real, gray → fake. (Color figure online)

are some real video features mixed in the fake video features (yellow region in Fig. 4(c)). This is due to that the probability curves do not change abruptly in value between the real and fake segments (as shown in Fig. 3), which may lead to misjudge at the point of the real and fake boundaries. Overall, it can be observed from the feature distribution map that our MABC-Net can effectively distinguish between the features of real and fake video clips.

5 Conclusion

In this paper, we propose MABC-Net, a mixed-attentive temporal localization detection network for the localization of locally fake video. Our MAFL module can obtain consistent, inconsistent, and temporal context features from video and audio streams, making it easier for the model to locate temporal boundary segments of fake video. We further propose a FBL module which balance the real-fake samples and generate localization proposals with precise temporal boundaries. Our approach addresses the problem of sample imbalance that is not sufficiently taken into account by existing forgery localization methods. Furthermore, we demonstrate that simply incorporating a loss function alone does not mitigate the data imbalance issue. In the end, experiments show that our MABC-Net achieves better performance than previous relevant SoTA methods.

Acknowledgement. This work was supported in part by the Natural Science Foundation of China under Grant 62201524, Grant 62271455, and Grant 61971383; and in part by the Fundamental Research Funds for the Central Universities under Grant CUC23GZ016. This work was supported by the Horizontal Research Project under Grant No. HG23002. Supported by Public Computing Cloud, CUC.

References

1. Agarwal, S., Farid, H., Fried, O., Agrawala, M.: Detecting deep-fake videos from phoneme-viseme mismatches. In: Proceedings of the IEEE Conference on Computer Vision and Pattern Recognition Workshops (CVPRW), pp. 2814–2822 (2020)
2. Bagchi, A., Mahmood, J., Fernandes, D., Sarvadevabhatla, R.K.: Hear me out: Fusional approaches for audio augmented temporal action localization. arXiv preprint arXiv:2106.14118 (2021)
3. Cai, Z., Ghosh, S., Gedeon, T., Dhall, A., Stefanov, K., Hayat, M.: "glitch in the matrix!": A large scale benchmark for content driven audio-visual forgery detection and localization. arXiv preprint arXiv:2305.01979 (2023)
4. Cai, Z., Stefanov, K., Dhall, A., Hayat, M.: Do you really mean that? content driven audio-visual deepfake dataset and multimodal method for temporal forgery localization. In: Proceedings of the International Conference on Digital Image Computing: Techniques and Applications (DICTA), pp. 1–10 (2022)
5. Cao, K., Wei, C., Gaidon, A., Arechiga, N., Ma, T.: Learning imbalanced datasets with label-distribution-aware margin loss. Advances in neural information processing systems **32** (2019)
6. Cheng, H., Guo, Y., Wang, T., Li, Q., Ye, T., Nie, L.: Voice-face homogeneity tells deepfake. arXiv preprint arXiv:2203.02195 (2022)
7. Chugh, K., Gupta, P., Dhall, A., Subramanian, R.: Not made for each other- audio-visual dissonance-based deepfake detection and localization. In: Proceedings of the ACM International Conference on Multimedia (ACM MM) (2020)
8. Chung, J.S., Zisserman, A.: Out of time: Automated lip sync in the wild. In: Proceedings of the Asian Conference on Computer Vision Workshops (ACCVW), pp. 251–263 (2017)
9. Cozzolino, D., Nießner, M., Verdoliva, L.: Audio-visual person-of-interest deepfake detection. arXiv preprint arXiv:2204.03083 (2022)
10. Dolhansky, B., Bitton, J., Pflaum, B., Lu, J., Howes, R., Wang, M., Ferrer, C.C.: The deepfake detection challenge (dfdc) dataset. arXiv preprint arXiv:2006.07397 (2020)
11. Hong, Y., Han, S., Choi, K., Seo, S., Kim, B., Chang, B.: Disentangling label distribution for long-tailed visual recognition. In: Proceedings of the IEEE Conference on Computer Vision and Pattern Recognition, pp. 6626–6636 (2021)
12. Ilyas, H., Javed, A., Malik, K.M.: Avfakenet: a unified end-to-end dense swin transformer deep learning model for audio-visual deepfakes detection. Appl. Soft Comput. **136**, 110124 (2023)
13. Khalid, H., Tariq, S., Kim, M., Woo, S.S.: Fakeavceleb: A novel audio-video multimodal deepfake dataset. arXiv preprint arXiv:2108.05080 (2021)
14. Korshunov, P., et al.: Tampered speaker inconsistency detection with phonetically aware audio-visual features. In: Proceedings of the International Conference on Machine Learning (ICML), pp. 1–5 (2019)
15. Korshunov, P., Marcel, S.: Speaker inconsistency detection in tampered video. In: Proceedings of the European Signal Processing Conference (EUSIPCO), pp. 2375–2379 (2018)
16. Lin, T., Liu, X., Li, X., Ding, E., Wen, S.: Bmn: boundary-matching network for temporal action proposal generation. In: Proceedings of the IEEE International Conference on Computer Vision (ICCV), pp. 3889–3898 (2019)
17. Lin, T., Zhao, X., Su, H., Wang, C., Yang, M.: Bsn: boundary sensitive network for temporal action proposal generation. In: Proceedings of the European Conference on Computer Vision (ECCV), pp. 3–19 (2018)

18. Lin, T.Y., Goyal, P., Girshick, R., He, K., Dollár, P.: Focal loss for dense object detection. In: Proceedings of the IEEE International Conference on Computer Vision (ICCV), pp. 2980–2988 (2017)
19. Lomnitz, M., Hampel-Arias, Z., Sandesara, V., Hu, S.: Multimodal approach for deepfake detection. In: Proceedings of the Applied Imagery Pattern Recognition Workshop (AIPRW), pp. 1–9 (2020)
20. Mittal, T., Bhattacharya, U., Chandra, R., Bera, A., Manocha, D.: Emotions don't lie: an audio-visual deepfake detection method using affective cues. In: Proceedings of the ACM International Conference on Multimedia (ACM MM), pp. 2823–2832 (2020)
21. Nawhal, M., Mori, G.: Activity graph transformer for temporal action localization. arXiv preprint arXiv:2101.08540 (2021)
22. Ren, J., Yu, C., Ma, X., Zhao, H., Yi, S., et al.: Balanced meta-softmax for long-tailed visual recognition. Adv. Neural. Inf. Process. Syst. **33**, 4175–4186 (2020)
23. Tian, Y., Li, D., Xu, C.: Unified multisensory perception: weakly-supervised audio-visual video parsing. In: Proceedings of the European Conference on Computer Vision (ECCV), pp. 436–454 (2020)
24. Tran, D., Bourdev, L., Fergus, R., Torresani, L., Paluri, M.: Learning spatiotemporal features with 3d convolutional networks. In: Proceedings of the IEEE International Conference on Computer Vision (ICCV), pp. 4489–4497 (2015)
25. Wang, G., Zhang, P., Xie, L., Huang, W., Zha, Y., Zhang, Y.: An audio-visual attention based multimodal network for fake talking face videos detection. arXiv preprint arXiv:2203.05178 (2022)
26. Woo, S., Park, J., Lee, J.Y., Kweon, I.S.: Cbam: convolutional block attention module. In: Proceedings of the European Conference on Computer Vision (ECCV), pp. 3–19 (2018)
27. Xu, Z., Liu, R., Yang, S., Chai, Z., Yuan, C.: Learning imbalanced data with vision transformers. In: Proceedings of the IEEE Conference on Computer Vision and Pattern Recognition, pp. 15793–15803 (2023)
28. Yang, W., Zhou, X., Chen, Z., Guo, B., Ba, Z., Xia, Z., Cao, X., Ren, K.: Avoid-df: audio-visual joint learning for detecting deepfake. IEEE Trans. Inf. Forensics Secur. **18**, 2015–2029 (2023)
29. Yu, J., Cheng, Y., Zhao, R.W., Feng, R., Zhang, Y.: Mm-pyramid: Multimodal pyramid attentional network for audio-visual event localization and video parsing. In: Proceedings of the ACM International Conference on Multimedia (ACM MM), pp. 6241–6249 (2022)
30. Zhou, Y., Lim, S.N.: Joint audio-visual deepfake detection. In: Proceedings of the IEEE International Conference on Computer Vision (ICCV), pp. 14800–14809 (2021)

Exploiting Diffusion Model as Prompt Generator for Object Localization

Yuqi Jiang[1], Qiankun Liu[1], Yichen Li[1], Hao Jia[2], and Ying Fu[1(✉)]

[1] School of Computer Science and Technology, Beijing Institute of Technology, Beijing, China
{yqjiang,liuqk3,3220231436,fuying}@bit.edu.cn
[2] The 54th Research Institute of China Electronics Technology Group Corporation (CETC54), Shijiazhuang, China

Abstract. Recently, diffusion models have shown unprecedented power in text-to-image generation. The intermediate features in well-trained text-to-image diffusion models have been proven to contain basic semantic and layout information of the synthesized image. Based on such findings, we present a **D**iffusion-model-based **P**rompt generator for **O**bject **L**ocalization, named as **DPOL**. By providing proper text guidance to DPOL, the corresponding object in an image can be localized within two steps: (1) Prompt generation. Conditioned on the text guidance, the image is first inverted into its corresponding latent code and then reconstructed by the diffusion model. The attention maps produced by the diffusion model are used as the location prompt, which contain the coarse position information of the interested objects; (2) Location refinement. The Segment Anything Model (*i.e.*, SAM) is used to get a more accurate position based on the location prompt, which is transformed into the format (in detail, box) that is compatible with SAM. Extensive experiments are conducted to show that our DPOL achieves comparable performance with existing open-vocabulary localization methods, even DPOL requires neither training nor fine-tuning.

Keywords: Diffusion models · Prompt generation · Object localization

1 Introduction

By removing the noise iteratively, Diffusion Model (DMs) [5,10,22,23] can recover useful signals effectively and have been widely used in various tasks, such as natural language processing [8], text-to-image synthesis [16,19,20], object detection [4], object segmentation [2,27], and so on [25,26]. Among these tasks, text-to-image synthesis is the hottest topic, which has achieved great progress with the help of large models and a huge amount of text-image training data [21].

From the perspective of the domain in which DMs work, existing text-to-image DMs can be divided into image-space-based [16,20] and latent-space-based [19] DMs. Just as the name implies, the input and output of image-space-based DMs are both in image-space, and the noises are predicted and removed

G. Zhai et al. (Eds.): IFTC 2023, CCIS 2067, pp. 284–296, 2024.
https://doi.org/10.1007/978-981-97-3626-3_21

directly from images. Though vivid images can be generated, the spatial resolutions of the generated images are limited due to the expensive computational cost. The common practice for image-space-based DMs is to sample images from noises in a smaller resolution and then upsample the synthesized images to a higher resolution with another DM [16,18]. Though the computational burden is reduced, the training and inference cost of multiple DMs are still too expensive to afford. Differently, the input and output of latent-space-based DMs [19] are both latent features, which are of a smaller (*e.g.*, $4\times$) spatial resolution than images. After finishing the sampling of latent features, an auto-encoder is used to construct images from features. Since the auto-encoder is much more lightweight than the DM and constructs the image within one forward, the computational cost is greatly reduced when compared with image-space-based DMs, making the wide utility of DMs (*e.g.*, for image editing and downstream tasks) possible.

Given a text description, the synthesized image is expected to contain the same semantic information as the text. To do this, a text encoder [17] is used to map the provided text description into the text feature, which are further injected into the DM through cross-attention. Specifically, at each stage of the denoising network (usually a U-Net) in the DM, the text feature is mapped to the key and value while the image feature is used as the query. Researchers have found that the image features in well-trained DMs contain basic semantic and layout information. The cross-attention layer produces a higher attention weight for the image features that are well-aligned with text features. In other words, the position of an interested object (indicated by the subject in the text description) can be roughly inferred by the attention map. Based on such findings, lots of works are proposed for image editing [3,9,15]. Attend-and-Excite [3] adjusts the cross-attention values in the DM to strengthen or excite their activations, therefore encouraging the model to generate all the subjects described in the text. Prompt-to-prompt [9] utilizes the cross-attention layer to control the relation between the spatial layout and only substitutes the interested objects while keeping the other parts unchanged. Null-text [15] inverts images into latent codes by optimizing a *null-text* embedding. During the reconstruction stage, the contents of images can be edited with a new text description by changing the attention maps. Apart from these works for image editing, some works [1,29,31] leverage the well-trained text-to-image DMs as representation learners, demonstrating that the learned features in DMs are useful for downstream tasks. For example, RepFusion [29] extracts representations from off-the-shelf DMs and dynamically employs them as supervision for student networks, which shows the superiority of the representations learned by DMs on classification, semantic segmentation, and keypoint detection tasks.

In this paper, we exploit the well-trained text-to-image **D**iffusion model as the **P**rompt generator for **O**bject **L**ocalization, named as **DPOL**. Our goal is to localize the interested objects using text descriptions as guidance without specifically training or fine-tuning the model for the object localization task. Similar to the above-mentioned image editing works, the cross-attention maps in the DM are also leveraged in DPOL. But differently, we use the cross-attention maps to generate the location prompt, rather than to change the content of images. Given a proper text description, the interested objects can be localized within two steps in DPOL: (1) Prompt generation. The input image is first inverted into the latent code using null-text inversion and then reconstructed with the text description as the condition. At each time step in the reconstruction stage, the attention map for the subject in the text description is extracted. All attention maps are averaged to serve as the location prompt, which contains the coarse position information of interested objects. (2) Location refinement. The location prompt is fed into a location refinement model, specifically, the Segment Anything Model (SAM) [12], to get more accurate locations of interested objects. The location prompt from DM is transformed into the formats that are compatible with SAM[1]. The output of SAM can be further used as the location prompt for the next refinement. Experimental results on publicly available dataset show that our DPOL achieves comparable performance with existing open-vocabulary methods, even DPOL requires no training or fine-tuning.

In summary, our contributions are as follows:

- We propose to generate the location prompt of interested objects from the attention maps in diffusion models by using text descriptions as guidance.
- We present a framework, DPOL, for open-vocabulary object localization by marrying the diffusion model with the Segment Anything Model. The proposed DPOL accept flexible text description as the guidance to localize the interested objects.
- Compared with existing open-vocabulary localization models, our DPOL achieves comparable performance without training or fine-tuning.

2   DPOL

The overview of our DPOL is shown in Fig. 1. The whole procedure is divided into two steps: prompt generation and location refinement. The off-the-shelf text-to-image diffusion model (specifically, Stable Diffusion [19]) and Segment Anything Model (*i.e.*, SAM [12]) are the two key components. For better understanding, we first make the preliminaries of Stable Diffusion and SAM, and then explain the prompt generation and location refinement steps in detail.

2.1   Preliminaries

Stable Diffusion aims to map a random noise into an output image with the given text as guidance. To do this, an auto-encoder ϵ_{ae} and a denoising network ϵ_{dn} are exploited. The auto-encoder ϵ_{ae} is trained with a reconstruction task. An image x can be converted into latent space (denoted as z) and then reconstructed back to the image space. Specifically:

$$
\begin{aligned}
z &= \epsilon_{ae}^{e}(x), \\
\hat{x} &= \epsilon_{ae}^{d}(z),
\end{aligned}
\tag{1}
$$

---

[1] The publicly available SAM model only supports boxes and points as prompts.

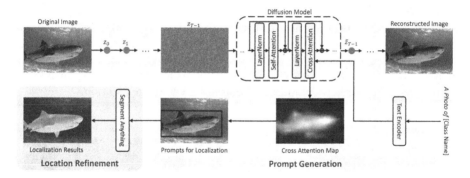

Fig. 1. Pipeline of DPOL. The overall procedure is divided into two steps: prompt generation and location refinement. In the first step, the location prompt is generated based on the attention maps by reverting and reconstructing the input image with a diffusion model conditioned on the provided text description. In the second step, the location prompt serves as the input of the Segment Anything Model. The locations of interested objects are refined iteratively.

where $\hat{x}$ is the reconstructed version of x, ϵ_{ae}^{e} and ϵ_{ae}^{d} are the encoder and decoder of ϵ_{ae}, respectively. Given the well-trained auto-encoder ϵ_{ae} and a text description τ, Stable Diffusion generates images in the latent space. In order to perform sequential denoising, in the training stage, the denoising network ϵ_{dn} is trained to predict artificial noise with the following loss function:

$$\mathcal{L} = \mathbb{E}_{z,\epsilon \sim \mathcal{N}(0,1),c,t}[\|\epsilon - \epsilon_{dn}(z_t, t, c)\|_2^2], \tag{2}$$

where $c = \mathcal{T}(\tau)$ is the text feature obtained by a text encoder $\mathcal{T}$, z_t is the latent code at timestamp t, which is uniformly sampled from $\{0, ..., T-1\}$. In the inference stage, a random noise z_{T-1} is sampled from Gaussian distribution and denoised by the denoising network for T steps to get z_0, which is fed into the decoder ϵ_{ae}^{d} to get the sampled image.

Segment Anything Model comprises three main components: an image encoder, a prompt encoder, and a mask decoder. The image encoder is based on a standard Vision Transformer (ViT) [13] pre-trained by MAE [7]. Following the settings in ViTDet [14], the image features are processed by the transformer blocks with a 14×14 non-overlapped sliding window. Four convolutional layers are equally interleaved within transformer blocks to capture global information between different attention windows. The output of the image encoder is a $16\times$ downsampled embedding of the input image. The prompt encoder is used to map the provided prompts to feature space. According to the types of prompts, different prompt encoders are adopted. The mask decoder is trained to efficiently map the image features, prompt features, and the output token to a mask, which indicates the locations of interested objects. This decoder consists of transformer decoder blocks [24] that are modified to include dynamic mask prediction heads.

The modified transformer decoder block uses cross-attention layers in two directions (prompt-to-image features direction and image-to-prompt features direction) to learn the interaction between the prompt and image features. After running two blocks, the image features are upsampled, and an MLP is used to map the output token to a dynamic linear classifier, which is responsible for computing the mask foreground probability at each image location.

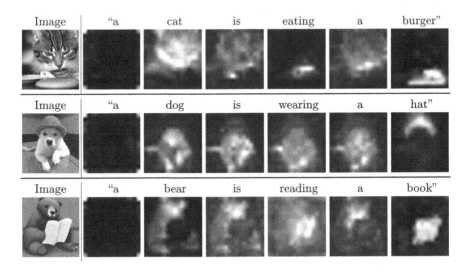

Fig. 2. The cross-attention map of Stable Diffusion [19]. The attention map is extracted from the middle block of the cross-attention layer during the generation of the image.

2.2   Prompt Generation

Given a specific text description, Stable Diffusion [19] demonstrates unprecedented power in generating perfect images. In order to follow the text description, Stable Diffusion utilizes cross-attention layers to relate the image and the text description, and its cross-attention map has been demonstrated that it contains the location information of interested objects (*i.e.*, the subjects in the text description). As demonstrated in Fig. 2, the spatial layout of the image is highly correlated with the cross-attention. Therefore, the location of objects in the synthesized image can be directly acquired by the cross-attention maps, which is the key idea of our DPOL. However, for object localization, such as instance segmentation or detection, only the images are given. We cannot directly obtain the attention map of the cross-attention layer due to the lack of the generation procedure. Therefore, we first invert the given image into its corresponding noisy latent code and then reconstruct the image by the diffusion procedure. At the reconstruction stage, we can acquire the cross-attention maps easily.

Though the image can be inverted by DDIM [5,23], it is mainly designed for the unconditional diffusion model. For Stable Diffusion that applies classifier-free guidance [11], the guidance scale amplifies the error accumulated in the

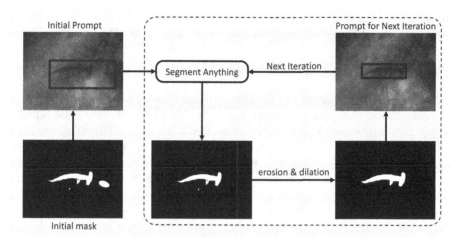

Fig. 3. Pipeline of the location refinement step. The location refinement step is repeated for some iterations to improve the final prediction results.

diffusion process. If directly inverting the clean latent code z_0 into z_{T-1} and diffusing from z_{T-1}, the recovered clean latent code may be far from z_0, resulting in the reconstructed image having obvious differences with the original image. Therefore, we use the power of null-text inversion [15] to invert and reconstruct the image based on Stable Diffusion, which utilizes the diffusion trajectory as the pivot and aims to get the diffusion trajectory of the conditional diffusion model (*i.e.*, Stable Diffusion) close to the DDIM inversion.

To be specific, DDIM inversion produces a diffusion trajectory $z_{T-1}^*, ..., z_0^*$ that contains T steps. Null-text inversion optimizes a null-text embedding ϕ for unconditional sampling in each timestep to enclose the diffusing trajectory with DDIM inversion. The objective function for each timestep t ranging from $T-1, ..., 0$ can be written as

$$\phi_t^* = \arg\min_{\phi_t} \|z_{t-1}^* - \mathrm{DDIM}_{t-1}(\bar{z}_t, \phi_t, c)\|^2, \tag{3}$$

where DDIM_{t-1} represents the DDIM denoising procedure at $t-1$ step, $\bar{z}_t$ is the latent vector of null-text inversion procedure in t step, c is the text embedding for conditional generation, and $\bar{z}_{T-1}$ is initialized using z_{T-1}^*. We finally get the noise vector $\bar{z}_0$ and null-text embedding ϕ.

With null-text inversion, we are able to conduct the diffusion process of a given image, which gives us a chance to extract the cross-attention maps that contain the location information of objects in the given image. In practice, we utilize the cross-attention maps extracted from the middle block of the denoising network. Then, the cross-attention map is resized to the original resolution of the given image. Next, we manually set a threshold to convert the attention map into a binary coarse mask that roughly indicates the location of the interested objects. In order to acquire more accurate locations, we further employ SAM [12] in the location refinement step to refine the mask. To this end, the minimum enclosing bounding box of the coarse mask is used as the prompt for the refinement step.

2.3 Location Refinement

Using the bounding box of the prompt generation step, we are able to conduct a segmentation task using Segment Anything Model (SAM) [12]. The pipeline of location refinement is demonstrated in Fig. 3. Using the bounding box as a prompt, SAM can predict a mask according to the box. However, we observe that the mask predicted by SAM may have many scatter points or may have holes in the mask. Therefore, we further use erosion and dilation as post-processing to refine the mask predicted by SAM. Besides, though the mask can cover most parts of the object right now, we also find that some parts are not contained in the mask. Therefore, we use the predicted mask to form a new bound box as prompt and repeat the above procedure multiple times to improve the quality of the predicted mask.

3   Experiments

In this section, we conduct experiments to prove the effectiveness of our DPOL and perform a thorough analysis. To be specific, we first introduce the implementation details. Then, we compare our DPOL with existing segmentation methods. Next, we discuss the influence of refinement iterations. Finally, we provide the results of simultaneously localizing multiple objects using our DPOL.

3.1   Implementation Details

We conduct all the experiments on the test set of PartImageNet [6] dataset. The provided part masks of an object are merged together to get one mask for the entire object. Considering the time consumption of null-text inversion, we randomly select 300 images to form a new test set including 22 classes. As for our DPOL, the number of iterations in location refinement is set to 20. Each iteration is followed by erosion and dilation for post-processing. Stable Diffusion v1-5 is adopted in DPOL. The Average Precision (AP) of boxes and masks are both provided for evaluation.

3.2   Comparison with Existing Segmentation Methods

To prove the effectiveness of our DPOL, we compare it with two state-of-the-art open-vocabulary instance segmentation methods, *i.e.*, OpenSeeD [30] and MasQCLIP [28]. Both of these two methods require training. In contrast, our DPOL directly utilizes the prior knowledge of Stable Diffusion and SAM, and does not need any additional training or fine-tuning, which avoids the burden on computational resources and time consumption.

Table 1. Box-level localization performance of different methods.

Method	Training-free	AP	AP_{50}	AP_{75}	AP_{Small}	AP_{Medium}	AP_{Large}
OpenSeeD [30]	✘	41.7	47.4	43.6	3.2	36.4	56.1
MasQCLIP [28]	✘	48.7	65.9	49.7	1.0	40.5	62.7
DPOL (Ours)	✔	34.4	50.8	34.2	0.0	27.7	41.5

Table 2. Mask-level localization performance of different methods.

Method	Training-free	AP	AP_{50}	AP_{75}	AP_{Small}	AP_{Medium}	AP_{Large}
OpenSeeD [30]	✘	40.8	49.3	43.9	2.6	34.1	55.2
MasQCLIP [28]	✘	46.1	63.3	48.1	1.1	39.8	59.9
DPOL (Ours)	✔	36.5	53.6	39.0	0.0	26.0	44.8

The qualitative results are provided in Fig. 4. It can be seen that OpenSeeD cannot always identify the objects in the images, *e.g.,* frog, turtle, and crocodile. This reflects the limited ability of OpenSeeD in identifying open-vocabulary objects. As for MasQCLIP, the results show a tendency to predict oversized masks, *e.g.,* shark and snake. Compared with those two methods, our method can accurately segment the required objects in input images, which indirectly reflects the power of the diffusion model as a prompt generator for object localization.

The quantitative results in box-level and mask-level are provided in Table 1 and 2, respectively. Though our DPOL is slightly worse than OpenSeeD and MasQCLIP in AP, considering that our DPOL has not been trained or fine-tuned for the segmentation task and the performance gap is not large, this result is acceptable. Besides, though DPOL is not trained for segmentation or detection, it still outperforms OpenSeeD on AP_{50}. This proves that our DPOL can roughly localize objects in images, but the localization may not be accurate enough, which leads to the lower results of AP_{75}.

3.3 Impact of Refinement Iterations

We also conduct experiments to discover the impact of refinement iterations. We test the results of performing different iterations ranging from 1 to 20. The results are provided in Table 3 and 4, respectively. It can be seen that apparently, more iterations lead to better localization quality in both box-level and mask-level. Especially for the comparison between 1 iteration and 5 iterations, the increase of AP in mask-level can even achieve 4.5%. As the number of iterations increases, the growth trend of AP tends to slow down. Though the results could still be better, considering the computational burden, we choose to use 20 iterations for refinement.

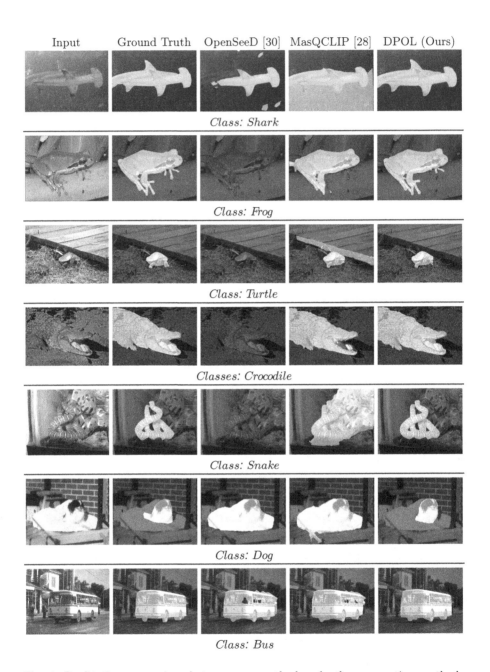

Fig. 4. Qualitative comparison between our method and other competing methods. We average the input image and the segmentation mask for visualization.

Table 3. Mask-level localization performance of DPOL with respect to different refinement iterations. The best results are indicated by **bold**.

Iters	AP	AP_{50}	AP_{75}	AP_{Small}	AP_{Medium}	AP_{Large}
1	30.7	46.1	32.2	**0.6**	**26.3**	30.6
5	35.2	52.3	37.5	0.0	23.5	43.9
10	36.1	53.1	38.6	0.0	25.8	44.2
15	36.2	53.1	38.8	0.0	26.0	44.4
20	**36.5**	**53.6**	**39.0**	0.0	26.0	**44.8**

Table 4. Box-level localization performance of DPOL with respect to different refinement iterations. The best results are indicated by **bold**.

Iters	AP	AP_{50}	AP_{75}	AP_{Small}	AP_{Medium}	AP_{Large}
1	29.0	45.3	28.4	**0.1**	26.3	38.5
5	32.7	48.7	32.5	0.0	24.6	40.1
10	33.7	49.9	33.3	0.0	27.4	40.7
15	33.8	49.8	33.9	0.0	**27.7**	40.6
20	**34.4**	**50.8**	**34.2**	0.0	**27.7**	**41.5**

Input	Results		Input	Results

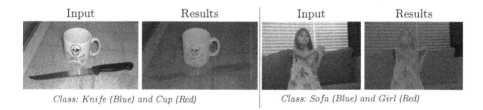

Class: Knife (Blue) and Cup (Red) | *Class: Sofa (Blue) and Girl (Red)*

Fig. 5. Segmentation results of DPOL in handling multiple objects at the same time.

3.4   Results of Localizing Multiple Objects

We also provide the results of localizing multiple objects to prove that DPOL can handle multiple objects at the same time. The results are shown in Fig. 5. It can be seen that our DPOL not only successfully segment multiple objects, but also distinguish their classes, *e.g.,* the knife and cup in the left case, and the girl and the sofa in the right case. This proves the ability of DPOL in localizing multiple objects.

4   Conclusion

In this paper, we leverage the text-to-image diffusion model as a prompt generator for object localization. By marrying the diffusion model (Stable Diffusion) with the Segment Anything Model (SAM), we propose a novel framework,

DPOL, for open-vocabulary object segmentation. Given the text description that contains the interested objects as the subject, we first generate the location prompt based on the attention maps by using Stable Diffusion to invert and reconstruct the input image. The location prompt is transformed into the formats that are compatible with SAM, which produces more accurate locations (*i.e.*, segmentation mask) of the interested objects. The segmentation mask can be further used as the location prompt and fed into SAM for the next iteration of the refinement. Compared with existing open-vocabulary segmentation methods, our DPOL achieves comparable performance even it requires neither training nor fine-tuning. In the future, we will continue to improve the performance of our DPOL for better segmentation results.

References

1. Abstreiter, K., Mittal, S., Bauer, S., Schölkopf, B., Mehrjou, A.: Diffusion-based representation learning. arXiv preprint arXiv:2105.14257 (2021)
2. Amit, T., Shaharbany, T., Nachmani, E., Wolf, L.: Segdiff: image segmentation with diffusion probabilistic models. arXiv preprint arXiv:2112.00390 (2021)
3. Chefer, H., Alaluf, Y., Vinker, Y., Wolf, L., Cohen-Or, D.: Attend-and-excite: attention-based semantic guidance for text-to-image diffusion models. ACM Trans. Graph. **42**(4), 1–10 (2023)
4. Chen, S., Sun, P., Song, Y., Luo, P.: Diffusiondet: diffusion model for object detection. In: Proceedings of the IEEE International Conference on Computer Vision, pp. 19830–19843 (2023)
5. Dhariwal, P., Nichol, A.: Diffusion models beat GANs on image synthesis. In: Proceedings of Advances in Neural Information Processing Systems, vol. 34, pp. 8780–8794 (2021)
6. He, J., et al.: Partimagenet: a large, high-quality dataset of parts. arXiv preprint arXiv:2112.00933 (2021)
7. He, K., Chen, X., Xie, S., Li, Y., Dollár, P., Girshick, R.: Masked autoencoders are scalable vision learners. In: Proceedings of the IEEE Conference on Computer Vision and Pattern Recognition, pp. 16000–16009 (2022)
8. He, Z., Sun, T., Wang, K., Huang, X., Qiu, X.: DiffusionBERT: improving generative masked language models with diffusion models. arXiv preprint arXiv:2211.15029 (2022)
9. Hertz, A., Mokady, R., Tenenbaum, J., Aberman, K., Pritch, Y., Cohen-Or, D.: Prompt-to-prompt image editing with cross attention control. arXiv preprint arXiv:2208.01626 (2022)
10. Ho, J., Jain, A., Abbeel, P.: Denoising diffusion probabilistic models. In: Proceedings of Advances in Neural Information Processing Systems, vol. 33, pp. 6840–6851 (2020)
11. Ho, J., Salimans, T.: Classifier-free diffusion guidance. arXiv preprint arXiv:2207.12598 (2022)
12. Kirillov, A., et al.: Segment anything. arXiv preprint arXiv:2304.02643 (2023)
13. Kolesnikov, A., et al.: An image is worth 16x16 words: transformers for image recognition at scale. In: Proceedings of International Conference on Learning Representations (2020)

14. Li, Y., Mao, H., Girshick, R., He, K.: Exploring plain vision transformer backbones for object detection. In: Avidan, S., Brostow, G., Cissé, M., Farinella, G.M., Hassner, T. (eds.) ECCV 2022. LNCS, vol. 13669, pp. 280–296. Springer, Cham (2022). https://doi.org/10.1007/978-3-031-20077-9_17
15. Mokady, R., Hertz, A., Aberman, K., Pritch, Y., Cohen-Or, D.: Null-text inversion for editing real images using guided diffusion models. In: Proceedings of the IEEE Conference on Computer Vision and Pattern Recognition, pp. 6038–6047 (2023)
16. Nichol, A., Dhariwal, P., Ramesh, A., Shyam, P., Mishkin, P., McGrew, B., Sutskever, I., Chen, M.: Glide: towards photorealistic image generation and editing with text-guided diffusion models. arXiv preprint arXiv:2112.10741 (2021)
17. Radford, A., et al.: Learning transferable visual models from natural language supervision. In: Proceedings of International Conference on Machine Learning, pp. 8748–8763. PMLR (2021)
18. Ramesh, A., Dhariwal, P., Nichol, A., Chu, C., Chen, M.: Hierarchical text-conditional image generation with clip Latents. arXiv preprint arXiv:2204.06125, **1**(2), 3 (2022)
19. Rombach, R., Blattmann, A., Lorenz, D., Esser, P., Ommer, B.: High-resolution image synthesis with latent diffusion models. In: Proceedings of the IEEE Conference on Computer Vision and Pattern Recognition, pp. 10684–10695 (2022)
20. Saharia, C., et al.: Photorealistic text-to-image diffusion models with deep language understanding. In: Proceedings of Advances in Neural Information Processing Systems, vol. 35, pp. 36479–36494 (2022)
21. Schuhmann, C., et al.: Laion-400m: open dataset of clip-filtered 400 million image-text pairs. arXiv preprint arXiv:2111.02114 (2021)
22. Sohl-Dickstein, J., Weiss, E., Maheswaranathan, N., Ganguli, S.: Deep unsupervised learning using nonequilibrium thermodynamics. In: Proceedings of International Conference on Machine Learning, pp. 2256–2265. PMLR (2015)
23. Song, J., Meng, C., Ermon, S.: Denoising diffusion implicit models. arXiv preprint arXiv:2010.02502 (2020)
24. Vaswani, A., et al.: Attention is all you need. In: Proceedings of Advances in Neural Information Processing Systems, vol. 30 (2017)
25. Wolleb, J., Bieder, F., Sandkühler, R., Cattin, P.C.: Diffusion models for medical anomaly detection. In: Wang, L., Dou, Q., Fletcher, P.T., Speidel, S., Li, S. (eds.) MICCAI 2022. LNCS, vol. 13438, pp. 35–45. Springer, Cham (2022). https://doi.org/10.1007/978-3-031-16452-1_4
26. Xia, B., et al.: Diffir: efficient diffusion model for image restoration. arXiv preprint arXiv:2303.09472 (2023)
27. Xu, J., Liu, S., Vahdat, A., Byeon, W., Wang, X., De Mello, S.: Open-vocabulary panoptic segmentation with text-to-image diffusion models. In: Proceedings of the IEEE Conference on Computer Vision and Pattern Recognition, pp. 2955–2966 (2023)
28. Xu, X., Xiong, T., Ding, Z., Tu, Z.: MasQCLIP for open-vocabulary universal image segmentation. In: Proceedings of the IEEE International Conference on Computer Vision, pp. 887–898 (2023)
29. Yang, X., Wang, X.: Diffusion model as representation learner. In: Proceedings of the IEEE International Conference on Computer Vision, pp. 18938–18949 (2023)

30. Zhang, H., et al.: A simple framework for open-vocabulary segmentation and detection. In: Proceedings of the IEEE International Conference on Computer Vision, pp. 1020–1031 (2023)
31. Zhang, Z., Zhao, Z., Lin, Z.: Unsupervised representation learning from pre-trained diffusion probabilistic models. In: Proceedings of Advances in Neural Information Processing Systems, vol. 35, pp. 22117–22130 (2022)

Depression Recognition Based on Pre-trained ResNet-18 Model and Brain Effective Connectivity Network

Xiaoying Zhao, Tingwei Jiang, and Hailing Wang[✉]

Shanghai University of Engineering Science, Shanghai, China
wanghailing@sues.edu.cn

Abstract. Depression has emerged as a primary health burden globally. Therefore, effectively identifying depression has become a significant challenge and obstacle in the field of public health. There are currently numerous issues with using electroencephalography (EEG) signals for depression identification. These issues include neglecting the dynamic characteristics of brain electrical signals, the information transmission relationships among them, and the low recognition accuracy of the features. Regarding the issues mentioned above, this study proposes an effective connectivity method based on transfer entropy to extract brain network features and achieved depression identification using pre-trained models. First, calculate the transfer entropy between all electrodes to obtain the corresponding matrix. Then, convert it into a three-dimensional RGB image, namely a heatmap. The created image is then used as input for pre-trained models, enabling the recognition of depression. In addition, to verify whether high-density EEG signals are beneficial for depression recognition, this study tested the recognition effect using 32-channel and 128-channel respectively. By comparing with other models, it was found that our model achieved the highest accuracy in depression recognition, with the highest accuracy rates achieved on 128 and 32 electrodes being 93.21% and 84.91%, respectively. Furthermore, we observed that the recognition rate of extracted EEG features was improved by 10% points in high-density space compared to low-density space. This indicates that high-density EEG is more effective for depression recognition. Overall, our study presents a novel approach and method for improving the accuracy of depression detection using EEG, which holds significant research implications.

Keywords: Depression · EEG · Effective connectivity · Transfer entropy · ResNet-18

1 Introduction

Major depressive disorder (MDD) is a common mental illness with high prevalence and mortality rates. At present, there are approximately 95 million people with depression in our country, and around 280,000 people commit suicide each year, with 40% of them suffering from depression [23]. Therefore, it is necessary to find simple, objective and accurate methods for detection and assessment, as well as explore biomarkers [13], to address this public health challenge.

Positron Emission Tomography (PET), Functional Magnetic Resonance Imaging (fMRI), and EEG have been widely used in the research of mental diseases. Among them, EEG signals have been extensively applied in depression studies due to their advantages of easy collection, low cost, and high temporal resolution [1, 2, 4, 19, 22].

Traditional methods for feature extraction in depression based on EEG include peak detection, variance analysis, power spectrum estimation, short-time Fourier transform, wavelet transform, etc [12]. In recent years, some researchers have begun to use brain network features for depression identification. Sun et al. [31] employed different coupling methods to construct functional connectivity matrices and binarized the functional networks. Ultimately, they found that the combination of imaginary part of coherence (ICoh) and cluster-span threshold (CST) had the best results. Peng et al. [24] used phase lag index to construct functional connectivity matrices and employed various classifiers for depression detection. They found that the binary linear Support Vector Machine (SVM) classifier had best performance. However, the functional network can only identify connection strength and lack directional information. Considering this limitation, researchers have introduced effective connectivity networks, as it can capture both directional and strength information, to overcome the disadvantages of the functional network. For example, Guirad et al. [10] demonstrated for the first time that the structure of a dynamic connectivity network can perfectly discriminate between a group of people with late-life depression and a group of healthy controls. Saeedi et al. [25] used the brain effective connectivity method to convert 1-D EEG signals into 2-D images. They used a Convolutional Neural Network - Long Short-Term Memory (CNN-LSTM) model for automatic detection of depression and achieved promising recognition outcomes. Khan et al. [18] achieved good accuracy in the classification of MDD and Healthy Controls (HC) subjects of the default mode network regions and three-dimensional (3D) CNN model. Some researchers have also used the effective connectivity of transfer entropy to detect and identify various diseases, achieving promising results.

Indeed, there are several challenges in obtaining clinical EEG data, for example, in most studies there have limited sample sizes. It can be particularly difficult to collect large datasets. However, transfer learning (TL) can significantly reduce the number of parameters and resources required for model development, thereby improving the performance and efficiency of the model. Shahabi et al. [27] a deep TL strategy was proposed based on pre-trained CNNs is developed for classification of Responders and Non-Responders to SSRI antidepressants using EEG data and achieved superior results. Zhang et al. [33] proposed three deep transfer models based on Visual Geometry Group 16 (VGG-16), Visual Geometry Group 19 (VGG-19), and Residual Network 50 (ResNet-50) and the performance of these models in EEG cross-subject seizure detection was evaluated. All of these models achieved high accuracy.

In the study of differentiating MDD and bipolar disorder, Sanchez et al. [26] used Symbolic Transfer Entropy (STE) to extract features from EEG signals. The performance of three widely used classifiers in machine learning was evaluated simultaneously. It was found that the SVM had the best performance. However, in their experiment, the features obtained by using STE for feature extraction were relatively limited and overlooked dynamic features. Additionally, they only extracted features from 42 electrodes, which could result in the loss of some important signal characteristics, resulting in low accuracy in feature recognition. Furthermore, the machine learning also failed to automatically learn higher-level abstract features from raw data, resulting in low performance and generalization ability of the model.

Therefore, in order to further extract the dynamic features and information transmission relationships of the EEG signals, and improve the accuracy of feature recognition, this paper proposes a method based on transfer entropy to extract effective brain network features. Subsequently, depression recognition of EEG signals was implemented by utilizing the pre-trained ResNet-18 model. Furthermore, in order to investigate the potential benefits of high-density EEG signals for depression recognition, this study conducted experiments using both 32-channel and 128-channel setups to evaluate the recognition performance. The specific experimental procedure is as follows. Transfer entropy between each pair of electrodes was calculated first, and then the transfer entropy matrix was converted into a heatmap. Finally, a pre-trained ResNet-18 was used for depression recognition. To better evaluate the performance of the model, we used ten-fold cross-validation and calculated the average accuracy across the ten folds. The experimental results demonstrate that the method of constructing brain networks based on effective connections using transfer entropy can effectively detect depression, with the best performance achieved using 128 electrodes, achieving a recognition accuracy of 93.208%. Therefore, this study provides an effective and reliable objective method for the field of depression detection.

Our contribution is shown as follows:

1. To construct a brain effective connectivity network related to depression and extract dynamic features, we employed a sliding window-based transfer entropy calculation method.
2. We convert the computed TE matrix into a heatmap, which serves as the input for the classification model. Additionally, we propose utilizing the pre-trained deep learning model ResNet-18 for depression recognition.
3. Compared to low-density EEG signals, we found that high-density EEG signals are more advantageous for depression recognition, and they can provide more discriminative information to improve recognition accuracy.

2 Related Work

In recent years, research based on EEG in MDD has been widely developed. For instance, traditional approaches have been employed to extract features from

EEG signals of individuals with depression. Chang et al. [9] employed fast Fourier transform (FFT) to extract spectral data in theta, alpha, and beta frequency bands, aiming to assess the alpha/beta, alpha/theta, and theta/beta ratios can serve as biological markers of depression. In their research on depression recognition based on EEG data, Chang et al. [8] employed the short-time Fourier transform and Hilbert-Huang transform to extract time-frequency features. In addition to employing traditional feature extraction methods, with the advancement of machine learning, some researchers have also used machine learning techniques for feature extraction, recognition and classification of EEG for depression. For instance, the study conducted by Cai et al. [7] compared four classification methods, namely SVM, K-Nearest Neighbors (KNN), Classification Trees, and Artificial Neural Network, to distinguish between individuals with depression and normal controls. The results revealed that KNN achieved the highest accuracy of 79.2%. Jaworska et al. [16] employed various machine learning algorithms, including Random Forest, to individually or collectively analyze three different types of EEG data for predicting antidepressant treatment response. They discovered that when incorporating all features from the three methods together, the classification model achieved an accuracy rate of 88%. Akbari et al. [3] performed analysis and detection of depression EEG signals using SVM and KNN classifiers. Deep learning (DL) is a branch of machine learning. In recent years, there has been a growing utilization of DL methods in the detection of various mental disorders, including the diagnosis of depression. Acharya et al. [1] used a CNN for EEG-based depression screening. It learns automatically and adaptively from input EEG signals to distinguish between EEGs obtained from individuals with depression and those from normal subjects. Additionally, this study revealed that the EEG signals from the right hemisphere of depressed patients were more distinctive than the EEG signals from the left hemisphere. Bagherzadeh et al. [5] conducted a study on the detection of schizophrenia (SZ) from multichannel EEG signals using effective connectivity measure of TE and the hybrid pre-trained CNN-LSTM model. Their findings demonstrated superior performance compared to all recent studies.

An increasing number of studies have demonstrated that depression induces alterations in the topological characteristics of brain networks [17,20]. Zhang et al. [34] conducted an extended investigation into the characteristics of randomized functional brain networks in MDD by analyzing resting-state EEG data. Compared to healthy individuals, patients with MDD exhibited significant randomization of global network metrics. Li et al. [21] studied abnormally increased connectivity of brain functional networks in patients with depression. They found that the brain network of patients with depression appeared randomized and the abnormal network topology of patients with depression was detected in both the prefrontal and occipital regions. Hasanzadeh et al. [14] aimed to validate the topological characteristics of networks in distinguishing between the normal and depressed groups. To achieve this, they utilized three functional connectivity measures, namely correlation, phase lag index (PLI), and imaginary part of coherence (ImC), to construct functional brain networks of two groups. Although the aforementioned studies considered the characteristics of brain functional networks, they overlooked the directionality of connections [31]. In fact, there have been some studies that have applied effective connectivity networks to the investigation of depression. For example, severe depression patients and healthy controls were automatically detected using a method that combines deep learning and effective connectivity. The effective connectivity-based approach was employed to convert one-dimensional EEG signals into two-dimensional images, which were subsequently used as input for the deep learning model. When using features extracted from 19 electrodes for classification, the model achieved an accuracy of 99.245% [25]. The study achieved high recognition rates. But in low-density electrode systems, this led to fewer extracted EEG features. Unable to accurately capture the activity of deep brain structures, which could potentially lead to information loss.

3   Method

3.1   MODMA Dataset

The MODMA dataset [6] is a publicly available multimodal dataset utilized for the analysis of mental disorders. The dataset includes EEG and audio data from clinically depressed patients and matching normal controls (NC). The MODMA dataset consists of three sub-datasets, and the dataset we utilized was collected through traditional means, employing a 128-electrode mounted elastic cap.

This study recruited a total of 24 patients with MDD (11 females and 13 males, age: 30.88 ± 10.37 years), as well as 29 healthy controls (9 females and 20 males, age: 31.45 ± 9.15 years). There were no statistically significant differences between the groups in terms of age and gender. The 24 patients were diagnosed and recommended by proficient psychiatrists from Lanzhou University Second Hospital in Gansu, China, while the 29 healthy control group participants were recruited through poster advertisements. The research process adhered to ethical standards and legal requirements, ensuring that participants voluntarily provided informed consent after a comprehensive understanding of the study's objectives, associated risks, and potential benefits. All MDD patients underwent a structured Mini-International Neuropsychiatric Interview (MINI) that met the diagnostic criteria for major depression based on the Diagnostic and Statistical Manual of Mental Disorders (DSM-IV [11]). The inclusion criteria for all participants were as follows: (1) age between 18 and 55 years old, and (2) primary education level or higher. The exclusion criteria for all participants were as follows: (1) history of alcohol or psychotropic drug abuse or dependence within the past year, and (2) women who were pregnant, lactating, or taking birth control pills. The inclusion criteria for MDD patients were as follows: (1) meeting the diagnostic criteria of MINI [28] for depression and having a Patient Health Questionnaire-9 item (PHQ-9 [29]) score greater than or equal to 5, and (2) no psychotropic drug treatment in the past two weeks. The exclusion criteria for MDD patients were as follows: (1) presence of mental disorders or brain organ damage, (2) presence of a severe physical illness, and (3) presence of severe suicidal tendencies. The exclusion criteria for NC included personal or family history of mental disorders. Before the experiment, self-report measures including the Patient Health Questionnaire-9 (PHQ-9) and the Generalized Anxiety Disorder-7 (GAD-7) [32] were completed by all participants.

3.2 EEG Signal Recording and Preprocessing

During the acquisition of resting-state closed-eye EEG recordings, a HydroCel geodesic sensor net comprising 128 channels and the Net Station data collection software were employed. The recordings had a duration of 5 min, with a sampling frequency of 250 Hz. For accuracy assurance, electrode signals were referenced to Cz, and electrode impedance was kept below 50 kΩ. To mitigate the impact of strong electromagnetic interference, participants underwent data collection individually in a quiet, soundproof room, while the operator monitored their progress from an adjacent room. In the experiment, subjects were required to maintain wakefulness, with any movement of body parts strictly prohibited. The "EEG.data" variable included 129 EEG signals. The specific placement locations are shown in Fig. 1.

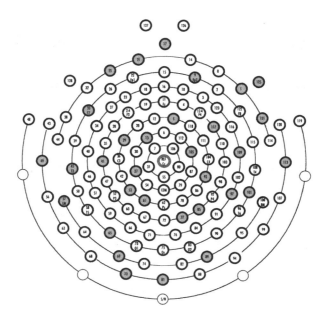

Fig. 1. 128 channel HydroCel Geodesic Sensor Net (HCGSN). The first 128 signals were from the electrode E1 to electrode E128. The last signal from Cz was the reference electrode. The light blue electrodes in the figure are the 32 electrodes selected for the experiment, and the channel selection was performed by selecting every third electrode. (Color figure online)

All the data used in this study were from the publicly available preprocessed dataset MODMA. In order to extract dynamic features related to depression, a non-overlapping sliding window of 1 s was applied to the preprocessed data in this experiment, resulting in several subsequences of length 1 s each. It is important to note that, in order to further investigate the impact of high-density EEG signals on depression identification, we compared the recognition performance between the 128-channel and 32-channel setups. Additionally, these electrodes have been widely used in previous research on depression.

3.3   Transfer Entropy

The depression-related effective brain connectivity network was constructed using the transfer entropy [5] method from each 1-s window of 128 EEG channels and 32 EEG channels. To facilitate the description, we will use 128 EEG channels as an example. This resulted in a 128×128 asymmetric connectivity matrix.

Here is the calculation process of transfer entropy.

Assuming x is independent of y. Equation 1 represents the conditional entropy given the occurrence of x_n and y_n. Here, x_n and y_n represent the EEG signals between different electrodes, ranging from 0 to 127. n represents the time point. p($\cdot$) represents the joint probability distribution.

$$h_1 = - \sum_{x_{n+1}, x_n, y_n} p(x_{n+1}, x_n, y_n) log_2 p(x_{n+1} | x_n, y_n) \tag{1}$$

Equation 2 represents the conditional entropy given the occurrence of x_n alone.

$$h_2 = - \sum_{x_{n+1}, x_n, y_n} p(x_{n+1}, x_n, y_n) log_2 p(x_{n+1} | x_n) \tag{2}$$

Equation 3 represents the transfer entropy of y to x, calculated as the difference between h_1 and h_2.

$$H(Y- > X) = \sum_{x_{n+1}, x_n, y_n} p(x_{n+1}, x_n, y_n) log_2 (\frac{p(x_{n+1} | x_n, y_n)}{p(x_{n+1} x_n)}) \tag{3}$$

By simplifying Eq. 3 using the joint probability distribution, we obtain Eq. 4.

$$H(Y- > X) = \sum_{x_{n+1}, x_n, y_n} p(x_{n+1}, x_n, y_n) log_2 (\frac{p(x_{n+1}, x_n, y_n) p(x_n)}{p(x_{n+1}, x_n) p(x_n, y_n)}) \tag{4}$$

We calculated the TE using Eq. 4 and selected the TE values between the 128 EEG channels to construct a transfer entropy matrix (see Eq. 5) for subsequent analysis. Here, x and y correspond to different EEG signal channels, ranging from 0 to 127. H_{xy} represents the TE value between EEG signal channels x and y. The data dimension of H_{xy} is 128×128.

$$H_{xy} = \begin{bmatrix} H_{00} & H_{01} & \cdots & H_{0n} \\ H_{10} & H_{11} & \cdots & H_{1n} \\ \vdots & \vdots & \ddots & \vdots \\ H_{n0} & H_{n1} & \cdots & H_{nn} \end{bmatrix} \tag{5}$$

3.4   Pre-trained ResNet-18 Model

ResNet-18 [15] is a type of deep convolutional neural network (DCNN) model, and it is one of the smaller models in the ResNet series. Its main characteristics are the use of residual connections and stacked convolutional layers to address the problems of gradient vanishing and insufficient expressive power in deep network training.

The overall structure of ResNet-18 is composed of multiple residual blocks (see Fig. 2). Each residual block consists of two convolutional layers and a skip connection. The skip connection directly passes the input to the output, allowing information to bypass certain convolutional layers through skip connection, thereby alleviating the problem of vanishing gradients. The convolutional layer in each residual block consists of a 3×3 convolutional layer and a 1×1 convolutional layer, which are used to change the number of channels in the feature map. Between each residual block, the size of the feature map is halved and the number of channels is doubled by a convolutional layer with a stride of 2. The last part of the ResNet network model is a global average pooling layer that applies average pooling operation to the output feature map of the last residual block, resulting in a fixed-size feature vector. Then, classification is performed through a fully connected layer, which ultimately outputs the prediction result.

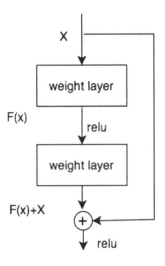

Fig. 2. A residual block.

In the experiment, we convert the transfer entropy matrix constructed from TE values into a three-dimensional RGB image to serve as input for the pre-trained ResNet-18 model. Additionally, adapt the final layer of the model to accommodate a binary classification task specifically focused on depression (see Fig. 3).

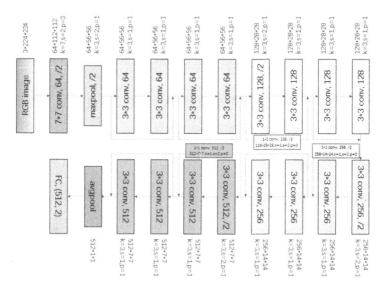

Fig. 3. Structure diagram of the pre-trained ResNet-18 model. (Color figure online)

3.5   Setting of Training Parameters

After data preprocessing and brain network feature extraction, the model data and parameters are initially set for the convenience of subsequent parameter adjustment. The initial parameter details are shown in Table 1. The total amount of data is 530 (53 * 10), and the training set and the test set are divided according

Table 1. Initial model parameter settings.

Parameter	Initial value
Total amount of data	530
Training batch size	8
Validation batch size	8
Number of iterations	15
Learning rate	0.001
Learning rate scheduler	Stochastic Gradient Descent (SGD)
K-fold	10

to 8:2. Ten-fold cross-validation is then performed, and the average accuracy of the ten folds is taken to enhance the generalization ability of the model. To ensure the balance of positive and negative samples across different folds, we employed the Stratified Group K-fold method in Sklearn to partition the dataset. By setting the seed number, the dataset can be partitioned in the same way across different experiments, which achieves the purpose of experiment reproducibility.

In this study, to determine the number of training iterations for each fold experiment, validation was first performed on the pre-trained ResNet-18 network to ascertain the convergence range of iterations (Figs. 4 and 5). It can be observed that the model started to converge approximately around the 15th iteration.

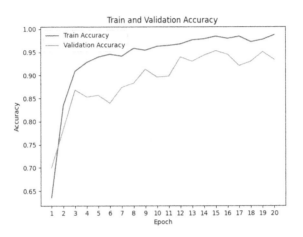

Fig. 4. The accuracy curves of the training and testing sets.

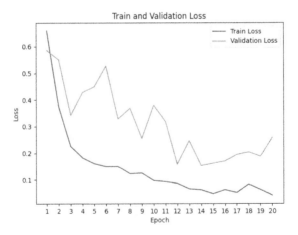

Fig. 5. The loss function curves of the training and testing sets.

4   Result and Discussion

In this section, we will analyze and discuss the final results obtained from the experiment.

The direct application of training deep learning models for the recognition of depression and healthy individuals is challenging to achieve due to the large number of parameters and limited data availability. Based on previous studies, we exclusively manipulated the size of the output layer during pre-trained ResNet-18 model training to achieve discrimination between individuals with depression and those without.

To further demonstrate our model's good classification performance, we compared it with three other pre-trained models and obtained accuracy and standard deviation under different electrode numbers. The comparison results are shown in Table 2 and Table 3. In Table 2, we selected EEG data from 32 electrodes, which is equivalent to feature extraction in low-density spatial locations. Comparing the classification performance of other models, we can see that ResNet-18 achieved the highest accuracy in recognizing depression, demonstrating good recognition performance. To further investigate the potential benefits of high-density EEG signals for depression recognition, we tested the recognition performance using EEG signals from 128 electrodes. In Table 3, it was found that compared to the recognition performance of the 32-electrode setup, the ResNet-18 model achieved a 10% increase in accuracy and a 50% reduction in standard deviation, achieved the highest accuracy of 93.208% among other models. It also demonstrates the stability and superior performance of our model. Furthermore, as the number of electrodes increased, all models showed improved feature recognition accuracy. This indicates that high-density EEG is more effective for recognizing depression and may provide more discriminative information to enhance depression recognition performance.

Table 2. Identification results of 32-channel EEG data.

Model	Accuracy (%)	Standard deviation
VGG-16	61.697	3.685
Efficient Net	63.747	5.119
DenseNet-121	82.077	4.321
ResNet-18	84.907	5.200

In addition, we compared the recognition performance of our model with existing studies. Under the same 128-channel setup, our model achieved the highest accuracy and best performance. This further validates the effectiveness of our model in depression recognition research. The comparison results of each experiment are shown in Table 4.

Based on the transfer entropy calculation function, the transfer entropy matrix is calculated with a window size of 1 s. Then, transform the transfer

Table 3. Identification results of 128-channel EEG data.

Model	Accuracy (%)	Standard deviation
VGG-16	83.775	7.07
Efficient Net	67.358	6.539
DenseNet-121	89.059	4.525
ResNet-18	93.208	2.821

Table 4. Comparison results.

Author	Number of Channels	Classifier	Accuracy (%)
Sun et al. [30]	16	(KNN, NB, DT and LR)	82.31
Khadem et al. [26]	42	(RF, KNN, SVM)	84.90
Sun et al. [31]	128	SVM	87.50
Peng et al. [24]	128	SVM	92.73
Our	32	ResNet-18	84.91
Our	128	ResNet-18	93.21

entropy matrix into a three-dimensional RGB image, namely a heatmap. To avoid the impact of weak color contrast in the heatmap caused by individual extreme values during adaptive heatmap drawing, it is necessary to ensure that the heatmap drawing has a fixed range. Therefore, before drawing the heatmap from the transfer entropy matrix, a 0–1 normalization is necessary to ensure that all transfer entropy matrices are within the same range.

Figure 6 presents the transfer entropy results of a patient with MDD and a healthy individual separately. The red spectrum represents high TE values, while the blue spectrum represents low TE values. The horizontal and vertical axes represent 128 channels, and each element represents the TE value between two channels, with the diagonal element being zero. By comparison, it can be observed that in the prefrontal cortex (PFC) region, the TE values of individual with MDD depicted in Figure (a) are relatively lower than those of the healthy individual depicted in Figure (b). This suggests that the prefrontal cortex function of MDD patients may be affected, which may lead to symptoms such as decreased decision-making ability and difficulty in controlling emotions. We also found that the differences between individual with depression and healthy control mainly reside in the upper portion of the images. As TE values can reflect the direction of information transmission between different brain regions. This suggests that the information transfer between the prefrontal cortex and other brain regions in individuals with depression may be impaired, potentially indicating a reduction in information flow. Therefore, creating three-dimensional RGB images based on effective connections in the brain can better illustrate the differences between the two groups. This further indicates that depressed patients have an abnormal brain network topology.

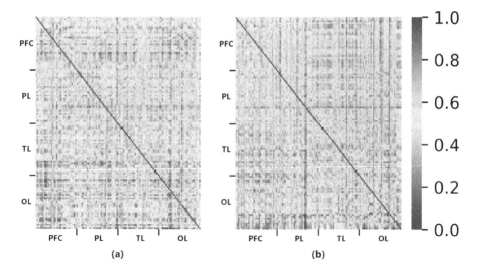

Fig. 6. (a) represents the transfer entropy results for a patient with MDD (ID 02010008). (b) represents the transfer entropy results for a healthy individual (ID 02030004).

5   Conclusion

In order to achieve higher accuracy in identifying healthy subjects and patients with depression, this study utilizes transfer entropy technique for effective connectivity measurement of EEG data. The study also investigates the recognition performance of depression using the pre-trained ResNet-18 model across different electrode configurations. In addition, the study evaluates the performance of the model using 10-fold cross-validation method. We converted the transfer entropy matrix into a heatmap image, which was used as input for the ResNet-18 model to achieve depression identification. Ultimately, we obtained an accuracy of 93.208%. These results demonstrate that the brain network constructed based on transfer entropy can effectively analyze brain function using the ResNet-18 model. Furthermore, compared to all the studies that have detected depression patients from healthy controls in recent years, this study achieved better results. It also demonstrates that high-density EEG is more effective in identifying depression, as it provides more discriminative information and improves the accuracy of recognition.

References

1. Acharya, U.R., Oh, S.L., Hagiwara, Y., Tan, J.H., Adeli, H., Subha, D.P.: Automated EEG-based screening of depression using deep convolutional neural network. Comput. Methods Programs Biomed. **161**, 103–113 (2018)
2. Afshani, F., Shalbaf, A., Shalbaf, R., Sleigh, J.: Frontal-temporal functional connectivity of EEG signal by standardized permutation mutual information during anesthesia. Cogn. Neurodyn. **13**, 531–540 (2019)
3. Akbari, H., et al.: Depression recognition based on the reconstruction of phase space of EEG signals and geometrical features. Appl. Acoust. **179**, 108078 (2021)
4. Ay, B., et al.: Automated depression detection using deep representation and sequence learning with EEG signals. J. Med. Syst. **43**, 1–12 (2019)
5. Bagherzadeh, S., Shahabi, M.S., Shalbaf, A.: Detection of schizophrenia using hybrid of deep learning and brain effective connectivity image from electroencephalogram signal. Comput. Biol. Med. **146**, 105570 (2022)
6. Cai, H., Gao, Y., Sun, S., Li, N., Hu, B.: Modma dataset: a multi-model open dataset for mental- disorder analysis (2020). http://modma.lzu.edu.cn/data/index/
7. Cai, H., et al.: A pervasive approach to EEG-based depression detection. Complexity **2018**, 1–13 (2018)
8. Chang, H., Zong, Y., Zheng, W., Tang, C., Zhu, J., Li, X.: Depression assessment method: an EEG emotion recognition framework based on spatiotemporal neural network. Front. Psych. **12**, 837149 (2022)
9. Chang, J., Choi, Y.: Depression diagnosis based on electroencephalography power ratios. Brain Behav. **13**(8), e3173 (2023)
10. Cosío-Guirado, R., et al.: Diagnosis of late-life depression using structural equation modeling and dynamic effective connectivity during resting fMRI. J. Affect. Disord. **318**, 246–254 (2022)
11. Do, L.: American psychiatric association diagnostic and statistical manual of mental disorders (DSM-IV). In: Encyclopedia of Child Behavior and Development, pp. 84–85 (2011)
12. Greco, C., Matarazzo, O., Cordasco, G., Vinciarelli, A., Callejas, Z., Esposito, A.: Discriminative power of EEG-based biomarkers in major depressive disorder: A systematic review. IEEE Access **9**, 112850–112870 (2021)
13. Group, B.D.W., et al.: Biomarkers and surrogate endpoints: preferred definitions and conceptual framework. Clin. Pharmacol. Therapeut. **69**(3), 89–95 (2001)
14. Hasanzadeh, F., Mohebbi, M., Rostami, R.: Effect of functional connectivity measures on characteristics of EEG based brain networks in MDD patients. In: 6th Basic and Clinical Neuroscience Congress (2017)
15. He, K., Zhang, X., Ren, S., Sun, J.: Deep residual learning for image recognition. In: Proceedings of the IEEE Conference on Computer Vision and Pattern Recognition, pp. 770–778 (2016)
16. Jaworska, N., De la Salle, S., Ibrahim, M.H., Blier, P., Knott, V.: Leveraging machine learning approaches for predicting antidepressant treatment response using electroencephalography (EEG) and clinical data. Front. Psych. **9**, 768 (2019)
17. Kaiser, R.H., Andrews-Hanna, J.R., Wager, T.D., Pizzagalli, D.A.: Large-scale network dysfunction in major depressive disorder: a meta-analysis of resting-state functional connectivity. JAMA Psychiat. **72**(6), 603–611 (2015)
18. Khan, D.M., Yahya, N., Kamel, N., Faye, I.: Automated diagnosis of major depressive disorder using brain effective connectivity and 3d convolutional neural network. IEEE Access **9**, 8835–8846 (2021)

19. Lebiecka, K., Zuchowicz, U., Wozniak-Kwasniewska, A., Szekely, D., Olejarczyk, E., David, O.: Complexity analysis of EEG data in persons with depression subjected to transcranial magnetic stimulation. Front. Physiol. **9**, 1385 (2018)
20. Leistedt, S.J., Linkowski, P.: Brain, networks, depression, and more. Eur. Neuropsychopharmacol. **23**(1), 55–62 (2013)
21. Li, Y., Cao, D., Wei, L., Tang, Y., Wang, J.: Abnormal functional connectivity of EEG gamma band in patients with depression during emotional face processing. Clin. Neurophysiol. **126**(11), 2078–2089 (2015)
22. Liao, S.C., Wu, C.T., Huang, H.C., Cheng, W.T., Liu, Y.H.: Major depression detection from EEG signals using kernel eigen-filter-bank common spatial patterns. Sensors **17**(6), 1385 (2017)
23. Liu, X., Hairston, J., Schrier, M., Fan, J.: Common and distinct networks underlying reward valence and processing stages: a meta-analysis of functional neuroimaging studies. Neurosci. Biobehav. Rev. **35**(5), 1219–1236 (2011)
24. Peng, H., et al.: Multivariate pattern analysis of EEG-based functional connectivity: a study on the identification of depression. IEEE Access **7**, 92630–92641 (2019)
25. Saeedi, A., Saeedi, M., Maghsoudi, A., Shalbaf, A.: Major depressive disorder diagnosis based on effective connectivity in EEG signals: a convolutional neural network and long short-term memory approach. Cogn. Neurodyn. **15**, 239–252 (2021)
26. Sanchez, M.M., et al.: A machine learning algorithm to discriminating between bipolar and major depressive disorders based on resting EEG data. In: 2022 44th Annual International Conference of the IEEE Engineering in Medicine and Biology Society (EMBC), pp. 2635–2638. IEEE (2022)
27. Shahabi, M.S., Shalbaf, A., Maghsoudi, A.: Prediction of drug response in major depressive disorder using ensemble of transfer learning with convolutional neural network based on EEG. Biocybern. Biomed. Eng. **41**(3), 946–959 (2021)
28. Sheehan, D.V., et al.: The mini-international neuropsychiatric interview (MINI): the development and validation of a structured diagnostic psychiatric interview for DSM-IV and ICD-10. J. Clin. Psychiatry **59**(20), 22–33 (1998)
29. Spitzer, R.: Validation and utility of a self-report version of prime-md: the PHQ primary care study. JAMA **282** (1999)
30. Sun, S., Li, J., Chen, H., Gong, T., Li, X., Hu, B.: A study of resting-state EEG biomarkers for depression recognition. arXiv preprint arXiv:2002.11039 (2020)
31. Sun, S., et al.: Graph theory analysis of functional connectivity in major depression disorder with high-density resting state EEG data. IEEE Trans. Neural Syst. Rehabil. Eng. **27**(3), 429–439 (2019)
32. Zeng, H., Yang, C., Dai, G., Qin, F., Zhang, J., Kong, W.: EEG classification of driver mental states by deep learning. Cogn. Neurodyn. **12**, 597–606 (2018)
33. Zhang, B., et al.: Cross-subject seizure detection in EEGs using deep transfer learning. Comput. Math. Methods Med. **2020** (2020)
34. Zhang, M., et al.: Randomized EEG functional brain networks in major depressive disorders with greater resilience and lower rich-club coefficient. Clin. Neurophysiol. **129**(4), 743–758 (2018)

ChatASD: LLM-Based AI Therapist for ASD

Xiaoyu Ren[1], Yuanchen Bai[2], Huiyu Duan[1], Lei Fan[1], Erkang Fei[3], Geer Wu[1], Pradeep Ray[1], Menghan Hu[4], Chenyuan Yan[5], and Guangtao Zhai[1(✉)]

[1] Shanghai Jiao Tong University, Shanghai, China
{windkaiser,huiyuduan,lei.fan,wugeer,pradeep.ray,
zhaiguangtao}@sjtu.edu.cn
[2] Carnegie Mellon University, Pittsburgh, USA
ybai2@andrew.cmu.edu
[3] Shanghai University, Shanghai, China
2741048661@shu.edu.cn
[4] East China Normal University, Shanghai, China
mhhu@ce.ecnu.edu.cn
[5] Shenzhen University Medical School, Shenzhen, China
2022225054@email.szu.edu.cn

Abstract. LLMs have performed significantly in the medical field. While they cover a broad range of topics including internal and surgical diseases, and mental health issues like depression, their depth in specific professional domains, especially Neurodevelopmental Disorders (NDDs) like Autism Spectrum Disorder (ASD), is limited and prone to errors. It is evident that user-friendly, cost-effective, patient, knowledgeable, rational, and interactive LLMs could be an excellent tool, *i.e.*, play a role in autism awareness, diagnosis and treatment. However, the current understanding of autism, the lack of datasets and innovative methods limit this tool's potential. Therefore, in this paper, we conduct the first large-scale study in medical LLMs for autism. The first bilingual autism knowledge dataset with approximately 4500 entries is constructed, including multidimensional information about autism (*e.g.*, education, treatment, inclusivity, *etc.*), real-case diagnostics, and easily confused concepts. Moreover, a LLM for autistic families called ChatASD is introduced, supporting bilingual knowledge dissemination and auxiliary diagnosis. Additionally, a LLM-based diagnostic and treatment pipeline for autistic patients called ChatASD Therapist is proposed, supporting bilingual dialogue and facial video generation. Our dataset and LLM-based tools represent a novel attempt to interact directly with autism patients and their families, providing inspiration for the continued exploration of diagnostic tools for ASD and other NDDs. The constructed database will be available at: https://github.com/DuanHuiyu/ChatASD.

This work was supported by National Key R&D Program of China 2021YFE0206700, NSFC 62225112, 61831015, Shanghai Municipal Science and Technology Major Project 2021SHZDZX0102, STCSM 22DZ2229005, and the Fundamental Research Funds for the Central Universities.
X. Ren, Y. Bai and H. Duan—Equal contribution.

G. Zhai et al. (Eds.): IFTC 2023, CCIS 2067, pp. 312–324, 2024.
https://doi.org/10.1007/978-981-97-3626-3_23

Keywords: Autism Spectrum Disorder (ASD) · Large Language Model (LLM) · Medical Model

1   Introduction

The rise of Large Language Models (LLMs), particularly the popularity of Chat-GPT [1] in 2022, has showcased the extensive knowledge and linguistic interaction capabilities of these massive language models. This includes the non-open source GPT, with its latest version GPT-4 [2] making impressive strides in the multimodal domain, though its implementation details remain undisclosed. Open-source alternatives exist in unimodal domains (*i.e.*, GLM [3,4], LLaMA [5,6], *etc.*), and multimodal domains (*i.e.*, InstructBLIP [7], LLaVA [8,9], *etc.*). Extensive evaluation work has been done on these LLMs, giving us a profound understanding of their abilities and limitations, which lays the groundwork for leveraging them more effectively.

LLMs have also seen numerous explorations in the medical field. However, while they cover a broad range of topics including internal and surgical diseases, and mental health issues like depression, their depth in specific professional domains, especially Neurodevelopmental Disorders (NDDs) like Autism Spectrum Disorder (ASD), is limited and prone to errors.

ASD is a complex neurodevelopmental condition, whose phenotype markers including social communication symptoms, fixated or restricted behaviors or interests [10]. Epidemiologic surveys in recent years have shown that the prevalence of ASD is on the rise globally, with a prevalence of around 1%. ASD treatment requires years of professional therapy, which is time-consuming and economically burdensome. Additionally, children with autism tend to have a poor prognosis and lack the ability to live independently in adulthood, imposing a significant load on families and society. Studies have found that early diagnosis and early intervention can significantly improve core symptoms for individuals with autism [11]. However, there's a disparity in the development across different regions, with a lack of related education and awareness, which means that many families are unaware of ASD-related knowledge, medical interventions, and the urgency and necessity of diagnosis and treatment, leading to missed opportunities for early intervention.

It is evident that user-friendly, cost-effective, patient, knowledgeable, rational, and interactive LLMs could be an excellent tool, *i.e.*, play a role in autism awareness, diagnosis and treatment. However, the current LLM medical methods are often simple fine-tuning, and many are commercial products rather than academic research outputs, lacking rigorous evaluation. Moreover, autism-specific data is even scarcer, and despite the emergence of multimodal datasets, there is still a dearth of large-scale, reliable datasets, particularly in the form of conversational language. In a word, the current understanding of autism, the lack of datasets and innovative methods limit this tool's potential.

In this paper, drawing from medical datasets, professional documents and informative web pages on medical Q&A, using GPT extraction and human evaluation, we have constructed the first bilingual autism knowledge dataset with

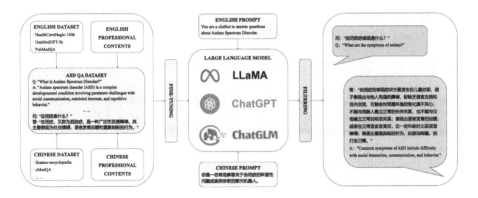

Fig. 1. Overview of ChatASD.

approximately 4500 entries. The data encompass multi-dimensional information about autism (*e.g.*, education, treatment, inclusivity, *etc.*), real-case diagnostics, and easily confused concepts, striving to ensure both breadth and accuracy of knowledge. Furthermore, based on these data, we present the ChatASD model (Fig. 1), a LLM-based tool for autistic families, supporting bilingual knowledge dissemination and auxiliary diagnosis in both Chinese and English. We also propose ChatASD Therapist (Fig. 2), a LLM-based diagnostic and treatment pipeline aimed for autistic individuals, utilizing LLMs with Microsoft Azure's speech recognition api and Sadtalker [12], supporting bilingual dialogue and facial video generation. The contributions of this paper are summarized below:

- We constructed the first bilingual autism knowledge dataset.
- We introduced the ChatASD model, a LLM-based tool for autistic families, supporting bilingual knowledge dissemination and auxiliary diagnosis.
- We proposed the ChatASD Therapist, a LLM-based diagnostic and treatment pipeline aimed for autistic individuals, supporting bilingual dialogue and facial video generation.
- We present the first attempt to interact directly with autistic patients and their families, providing inspiration for the continued exploration of diagnostic tools for ASD and other NDDs.

2   Related Work

2.1   Medical LLM

LLMs have demonstrated powerful contextual memory, long-text coherence, and text generation capabilities, indicating their potential for application in the medical field. There have been numerous trials leveraging LLMs enriched with medical domain knowledge, along with efforts to curate more comprehensive datasets aimed at achieving physician-level performance in question answering. Examples include Med-PaLM-2 [13], IvyGPT [14], *etc.*, which have incorporated fine-tuning and further enhancements through Reinforcement Learning from Human

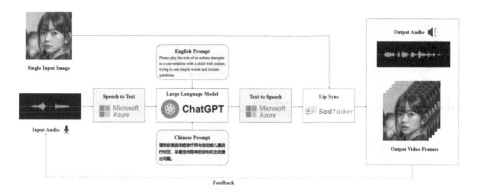

Fig. 2. Overview of ChatASD Therapist.

Feedback (RLHF) in Chinese medical LLMs, such as Zhongjing [15] and BianQue [16]. These also consider the real-world scenario of doctors engaging in multi-turn inquiries based on patients' description and eventually providing consolidated advice, thus mitigating concerns about the sufficiency of user descriptions.

However, these solutions utilize a very limited amount of data on ASD, and most of the data are Artificial Intelligence (AI) - generated without human curation, leading to potential inaccuracies and omissions.

2.2 AI Solutions for Autism

Advancements in AI have significantly contributed to the understanding, diagnosis, and intervention of autism.

AI has aided in understanding and interpreting the challenges and needs associated with ASD in various settings, such as visual attention, which adds to our understanding of ASD. Recent research in the intersection of ASD and AI has achieved remarkable progress in discerning visual attention differences between autistic children and typically developing (TD) controls. This advancement has been propelled by the creation of large-scale eye movement datasets, enabling researchers to refine models to state-of-the-art (SOTA) performance [17–22]. Advanced models [23–26] have been also successful in quantifying atypical visual attention in autistic children across multi-level features, notably highlighting a distinct preference in individuals with autism for low-level features of visual stimuli [27]. Recent studies have expanded this understanding by modeling and analyzing the gaze patterns of children with autism in real-world scenarios. With the rapid development of Virtual Reality (VR) [28–40] and saliency technology [41–45], this has been accomplished through the establishment of datasets using VR, enabling the analysis of omnidirectional visual attention in children, which provides rich information for comprehending their behaviors [46]. In addition to eye movement, it is crucial to study the common characteristics of ASD in more

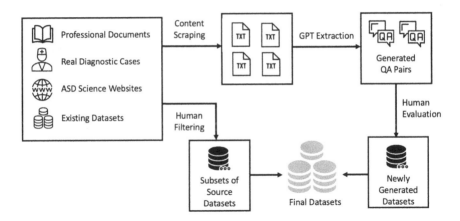

Fig. 3. Dataset Generation Pipeline.

diverse natural settings, including solitary, one-on-one, and group interactions, with the help of both data and the underlying context.

The integration of AI in ASD diagnosis has been long explored and offered insights and methodologies that enhance the diagnostic process. Datasets have been collected, such as a novel crowdsourcing dataset comprising responses to the top 15 questions derived from the Social Responsiveness Scale (SRS) [47], and a dataset based on the Autism Diagnostic Interview-Revised (ADI-R), a widely recognized instrument in the behavioral diagnosis of autism [48]. The application of machine learning techniques in this field has been extensive, aiding in the search for a minimal set of behaviors for autism detection, streamlining the clinical diagnostic process, enabling faster screening, and facilitating earlier treatment [49–51]. However, there are also ongoing discussions regarding diagnostic codes, types of feature selection, evaluation measures, and data class imbalances [52].

AI has not only been instrumental in diagnosis but also in intervention strategies for individuals with ASD. Interactive AI-driven applications, such as VR and AR, have been developed to improve social skills and communication in individuals with ASD [53–57]. Social Robots are also designed to provide a unique and engaging way for children and adults with autism to practice social interactions and communication [58–60].

As an array of unimodal and multimodal Large Language Models emerge as is stated before, they present significant potential in aiding autistic problems, but also require comprehensive evaluation and adaptation prior to actual use.

```
"messages":
[
    {
        "role": "system",
        "content": "'Generate question and answer pairs about Autism Spectrum Disorder
        (ASD) from the provided text. The format should be a list of JSON objects, like
        QAPair: [{"Q": "What is ASD?", "A": "ASD is..."}, ...]. The questions should
        educate the public about ASD. Aim for a diverse set of questions with minimal
        repetition. Additionally, provide a concise key theme for each question in a separate
        list like Themes: ["a", "b", ...]. Formulate the final return as a dictionary with keys
        "QAPair" and "Themes". (Only Json Format as Return).'"
    }
]
```

Fig. 4. Prompt used for Q&A extraction from website and professional document contents.

3   Dataset Generation and Curation

The whole dataset pipeline is shown in Fig. 3. In detail, we began by selecting existing medical datasets and informational contents in both English and Chinese, aiming to encompass a diversity of information on ASD. This includes pathological knowledge, diagnostic and treatment recommendations, social-cultural information, real medical cases, and concepts that are commonly confused. The selection took into account knowledge suitable for public dissemination as well as more specialized content. Utilized datasets include the English datasets: GenMedGPT-5k and HealthcareMagic-100k [61], *etc.*, and the Chinese datasets: Consult [62] and HuaTuo-26M [63], *etc.* Utilized documents include the English source files: Autism Spectrum News[1] and WHO document[2] *etc.*, and the Chinese source files: Alsolife[3] and China Association of Rehabilitation of Disabled persons website[4] *etc.*

Based on the collected contents, we proposed a three-step constructing process: (i) For datasets, we filtered out contents relevant to autism. (ii) For websites and documents, we utilized GPT for extraction. Specifically, to maximize detailed extraction while enhancing content comprehension and minimizing hallucinations, we fed the model in segments of 1000 tokens, preserving the historical information to provide context. We designed a constructing prompt, which is shown in Fig. 4, to consider both accuracy and diversity. (iii) To ensure the high quality of the data, we conducted manual screening, ultimately producing 4506 high-quality Q&A pairs, with 2195 in English and 2311 in Chinese.

---

[1] https://autismspectrumnews.org/.
[2] https://www.who.int/news-room/fact-sheets/detail/autism-spectrum-disorders.
[3] https://www.alsolife.com/.
[4] https://cncard.org.cn/.

Table 1. Finetuning process details of baseline models on the corresponding datasets.

Baseline\Hyper-parameters	Batch_size	Learning_rate	Epochs	Run_time
ChatGLM3-6B (on Chinese dataset)	8	5e−3	10	2 h 12 min
LLaMA-2-7B (on English dataset)	4	1e−4	5	0 h 15 min
gpt-3.5-turbo (on Chinese dataset)	4	1e−5	3	0 h 54 min
gpt-3.5-turbo (on English dataset)	3	1e−5	3	0 h 57 min

4   Experiments

4.1   ChatASD

Baseline Models. We selected ChatGLM3 (ChatGLM3-6B) [3,4] and LLaMA-2 (LLaMA-2-7B) [6] as the baseline models of our ChatASD. And we utilized ChatGPT (gpt-3.5-turbo) [1] for comparison.

For the Chinese encyclopedia, we fine-tuned ChatGLM3 on the Chinese dataset, since it is open source and specifically pretrained on Chinese corpus, demonstrating remarkable Chinese language understanding and generation capabilities. For the English encyclopedia, we finetuned LLaMA-2 on the English dataset, since it is an advanced version of one of the most renowned open-source LLMs, LLaMA [5]. Compared to LLaMA, LLaMA-2 has increased the size of the pretraining corpus by 40% and doubled the context length, demonstrating superior English language understanding and generation abilities. Comparative experiments were conducted with fine-tuned ChatGPT on our constructed dataset, due to its state-of-the-art performance but closed-source nature.

Implementation Details. Following LLaMA-Factory [64], we utilized low-rank adaptation (LoRA) [65] methodology to fine-tune the baseline models on the corresponding constructed datasets. The Chinese dataset was splitted into 2100 training samples and 211 testing samples, and the English dataset was splitted into 2000 training samples and 195 testing samples. Each baseline model was fine-tuned using an NVIDIA GeForce RTX 3090 GPU. The fine-tuning process details are shown in Table 1.

Metrics. We evaluated the models using BLEU-4 (Bilingual Evaluation Understudy) [66] and Rouge-1/2/L (Recall-Oriented Understudy for Gisting Evaluation) [67] metrics, which measure the similarity between the model-generated results and the ground truth in the test set. BLEU-4 calculates the number of 4-gram matches in the model-generated results divided by the total number of 4-grams in the model-generated results, evaluating precision. ROUGE-1/2 calculates the number of 1/2-gram matches in the model-generated results divided by the total number of 1/2-grams in the ground truth, while ROUGE-L calculates the length of the LCSS (Longest Common Subsequence) in the model-generated results divided by the total length of the ground truth, evaluating recall.

Table 2. Quantitative comparison results of different models (ft means the model is fine-tuned on our dataset, the settings of hyper-parameters are shown in Sect. 4.1).

Dataset	Model	BLEU-4	ROUGE-1	ROUGE-2	ROUGE-L
ASD_zh	gpt-3.5-turbo	7.60	26.91	6.36	17.18
	ChatGLM3-6B	6.35	26.19	5.94	16.96
	gpt-3.5-turbo-ft	7.95	26.30	6.98	18.10
	ChatGLM3-6B-ft	**10.06**	**29.33**	**9.15**	**21.12**
ASD_en	gpt-3.5-turbo	7.36	23.44	7.20	13.46
	LLaMA-2-7B	5.67	18.47	5.64	3.91
	gpt-3.5-turbo-ft	12.10	39.74	16.17	30.97
	LLaMA-2-7B-ft	**38.83**	**44.24**	**21.14**	**35.45**

4.2   ChatASD Therapist

The whole pipeline is shown in Fig. 2. Since autistic patients are unable to type, we accessed Microsoft Azure's speech recognition to both sides of LLM, assisting in users with autism to communicate with LLM in person. The audio content of the autistic user is converted into text using Speech-to-Text (STT) from Azure, and then fed into LLM. The response text from LLM is converted into speech using Text-to-Speech (TTS) from Azure, and then fed into SadTalker [12]. After the Lip-sync video is generated, it will replace the therapist in the standby state in the interface. At this time, the user could see the therapist's 3D motion coefficients (*i.e.*, head pose, expression, lip movements, *etc.*) [12], and hear the voice. The above process will loop, supporting a smooth conversation between autistic users and LLM.

Due to the lack of data, we directly inferred GPT-4 [2] as LLM, and the pre-trained model of Sadtalker. Considering the social passivity of autistic users, we designed a prompt to enable LLMs to have the ability to initiate questions (see Fig. 2). All communication between the components in our pipeline is via api.

4.3   Results

As mentioned in Sect. 4.1, we utilized BLEU-4 and Rouge-1/2/L to evaluate the baseline models and fine-tuned models. The quantitative comparison results are shown in Table 2. We can find that on both datasets, the baseline GPT model performs better than the baseline GLM/LLaMA models. However, after fine-tuning with effective hyper-parameters, the GLM/LLaMA fine-tuned models perform better than the GPT fine-tuned model, which demonstrates the benefits of open-source models.

We present two sets of Q&As in Fig. 5, with content about autism knowledge and autism diagnosis. And we compare ChatASD with ChatGPT fine-tuned over our dataset. Note that the conversations listed were originally Chinese conversations, which were then translated into English. We could see that ChatGPT

Fig. 5. Qualitative comparison results of fine-tuned ChatGPT and our ChatASD (The conversation content used in examples are originally Chinese, and are translated to English).

answers in a more general way, while ChatASD answers in a more specific and comprehensive way.

5   Conclusion

In this paper, we present the first bilingual autism knowledge dataset. We introduce the ChatASD model designed for autistic families, supporting bilingual autism knowledge dissemination and auxiliary diagnosis. We also propose the ChatASD Therapist pipeline designed for autistic patients themselves, supporting facial representations and bilingual dialogue between people with autism and LLMs. Our work represents a novel attempt to solve problems in ASD and other

NDDs using LLMs. Hopefully it would provide inspiration for the continued exploration.

There are some shortcomings in our work. Firstly, insufficient data entries related to diagnosis of autism lead to insufficient training of the model's diagnostic capabilities. Additionally, the current dataset consists solely of single-turn Q&A data, which limits the model's understanding of user-provided supplementary information, deviating from real-world medical scenarios. Moreover, the dataset primarily consists of extracted information from authoritative documents, websites, and existing datasets, lacking in up-to-date ASD-related knowledge. In the future, we will address these three issues by enlarging the dataset. And we plan to make it publicly available when it has been reviewed by doctors. Regarding the ChatASD Therapist, the current use of STT and TTS results in the loss of information, *i.e.*intonation, *etc.*. Furthermore, the models used are simply inferred without fine-tuning. In the future, we consider introducing directly the audio modality into the model and constructing a corresponding audio dataset for tuning.

References

1. OpenAI: ChatGPT (2022). https://chat.openai.com/
2. OpenAI: GPT-4 technical report (2023)
3. Zeng, A., et al.: Glm-130b: an open bilingual pre-trained model. arXiv preprint arXiv:2210.02414 (2022)
4. Du, Z., et al.: GLM: general language model pretraining with autoregressive blank infilling. In: Proceedings of the 60th Annual Meeting of the Association for Computational Linguistics (Volume 1: Long Papers), pp. 320–335 (2022)
5. Touvron, H., et al.: LLaMA: open and efficient foundation language models (2023)
6. Touvron, H., Martin, L., Stone, K., et al.: Llama 2: open foundation and fine-tuned chat models (2023)
7. Dai, W., et al.: InstructBLIP: towards general-purpose vision-language models with instruction tuning (2023)
8. Liu, H., Li, C., Li, Y., Lee, Y.J.: Improved baselines with visual instruction tuning (2023)
9. Liu, H., Li, C., Wu, Q., Lee, Y.J.: Visual instruction tuning (2023)
10. Association, A.P., et al.: Diagnostic and statistical manual of mental disorders (DSM-5®). American Psychiatric Pub (2013)
11. Ma, C., Wang, Y.: Research advances on early interventional programs for children with autism spectrum disorders. Chin. J. Child Health Care **28**(1), 57 (2020)
12. Zhang, W., et al.: Sadtalker: learning realistic 3D motion coefficients for stylized audio-driven single image talking face animation. In: 2023 IEEE/CVF Conference on Computer Vision and Pattern Recognition (CVPR), pp. 8652–8661 (2023). https://doi.org/10.1109/CVPR52729.2023.00836
13. Singhal, K., et al.: Towards expert-level medical question answering with large language models, May 2023. https://doi.org/10.48550/arXiv.2305.09617
14. Wang, R., et al.: IvyGPT: interactive Chinese pathway language model in medical domain, July 2023. https://doi.org/10.48550/arXiv.2307.10512
15. Yang, S., et al.: Zhongjing: enhancing the Chinese medical capabilities of large language model through expert feedback and real-world multi-turn dialogue (2023)

16. Chen, Y., et al.: Bianque: balancing the questioning and suggestion ability of health LLMs with multi-turn health conversations polished by chatGPT (2023)
17. Duan, H., et al.: A dataset of eye movements for the children with autism spectrum disorder. In: Proceedings of the ACM Multimedia Systems Conference (ACM MMSys), pp. 255–260 (2019)
18. Duan, H., et al.: Learning to predict where the children with ASD look. In: Proceedings of the IEEE International Conference on Image Processing (ICIP), pp. 704–708 (2018)
19. Duan, H., Min, X., Fang, Y., Fan, L., Yang, X., Zhai, G.: Visual attention analysis and prediction on human faces for children with autism spectrum disorder. ACM Trans. Multimedia Comput. Commun. Appl. (TOMM) **15**(3s), 1–23 (2019)
20. Fang, Y., Duan, H., Shi, F., Min, X., Zhai, G.: Identifying children with autism spectrum disorder based on gaze-following. In: Proceedings of the IEEE International Conference on Image Processing (ICIP), pp. 423–427 (2020)
21. Fan, L., et al.: Screening of autism spectrum disorder using novel biological motion stimuli. In: Zhai, G., Zhou, J., Yang, H., An, P., Yang, X. (eds.) IFTC 2020. CCIS, vol. 1390, pp. 371–384. Springer, Singapore (2021). https://doi.org/10.1007/978-981-16-1194-0_32
22. Shi, F., et al.: Drawing reveals hallmarks of children with autism. Displays **67**, 102000 (2021)
23. Duan, H., Min, X., Shen, W., Zhai, G.: A unified two-stage model for separating superimposed images. In: Proceedings of the IEEE International Conference on Acoustics, Speech and Signal Processing (ICASSP), pp. 2065–2069 (2022)
24. Duan, H., et al.: Develop then rival: a human vision-inspired framework for superimposed image decomposition. IEEE Trans. Multimedia (TMM) (2022)
25. Duan, H., et al.: Masked autoencoders as image processors. arXiv preprint arXiv:2303.17316 (2023)
26. Wang, J., Duan, H., Liu, J., Chen, S., Min, X., Zhai, G.: Aigciqa2023: a large-scale image quality assessment database for AI generated images: from the perspectives of quality, authenticity and correspondence. arXiv preprint arXiv:2307.00211 (2023)
27. Wang, S., Xu, J., Jiang, M., Zhao, Q., Hurlemann, R., Adolphs, R.: Autism spectrum disorder, but not amygdala lesions, impairs social attention in visual search. Neuropsychologia **63**, 259–274 (2014)
28. Duan, H., Shen, W., Min, X., Tu, D., Li, J., Zhai, G.: Saliency in augmented reality. In: Proceedings of the ACM International Conference on Multimedia (ACM MM), pp. 6549–6558 (2022)
29. Wang, Z., et al.: Vision, application scenarios, and key technology trends for 6g mobile communications. Sci. China Inf. Sci. **65**(5), 151301 (2022)
30. Liao, M., Song, B., Long, S., He, M., Yao, C., Bai, X.: SynthText3D: synthesizing scene text images from 3D virtual worlds. Sci. China Inf. Sci. **63**, 1–14 (2020)
31. Duan, H., Min, X., Zhu, Y., Zhai, G., Yang, X., Le Callet, P.: Confusing image quality assessment: toward better augmented reality experience. IEEE Trans. Image Process. (TIP) **31**, 7206–7221 (2022)
32. Duan, H., Guo, L., Sun, W., Min, X., Chen, L., Zhai, G.: Augmented reality image quality assessment based on visual confusion theory. In: Proceedings of the IEEE International Symposium on Broadband Multimedia Systems and Broadcasting (BMSB), pp. 1–6 (2022)
33. Duan, H., Min, X., Sun, W., Zhu, Y., Zhang, X.P., Zhai, G.: Attentive deep image quality assessment for omnidirectional stitching. IEEE J. Sel. Top. Sig. Process. (JSTSP) (2023)

34. Zhu, Y., Zhai, G., Yang, Y., Duan, H., Min, X., Yang, X.: Viewing behavior supported visual saliency predictor for 360 degree videos. IEEE Trans. Circuits Syst. Video Technol. (TCSVT) (2021)

35. Zhou, Z., Meng, M., Zhou, Y., Zhu, Z., You, J.: Model-guided 3D stitching for augmented virtual environment. Sci. China Inf. Sci. **66**(1), 112106 (2023)

36. Zhu, Y., et al.: Audio-visual saliency for omnidirectional videos. In: Lu, H., et al. (eds.) ICIG 2023. LNCS, vol. 14359, pp. 365–378. Springer, Cham (2023). https://doi.org/10.1007/978-3-031-46317-4_29

37. Zhu, X., et al.: Perceptual quality assessment of omnidirectional audio-visual signals. arXiv preprint arXiv:2307.10813 (2023)

38. Cheng, Y., Huang, Z., Quan, S., Cao, X., Zhang, S., Yang, J.: Sampling locally, hypothesis globally: accurate 3D point cloud registration with a RANSAC variant. Vis. Intell. **1**(1), 20 (2023)

39. Cheng, R., Wang, X., Sohel, F., Lei, H.: Topology-aware universal adversarial attack on 3D object tracking. Vis. Intell. **1**(1), 1–12 (2023)

40. Duan, H., Zhu, X., Zhu, Y., Min, X., Zhai, G.: A quick review of human perception in immersive media. IEEE Open J. Immers. Displays (2024)

41. Qiao, H., Zhong, S., Chen, Z., Wang, H.: Improving performance of robots using human-inspired approaches: a survey. Sci. China Inf. Sci. **65**(12), 221201 (2022)

42. Yue, Y., Zou, Q., Yu, H., Wang, Q., Wang, Z., Wang, S.: An end-to-end network for co-saliency detection in one single image. Sci. China Inf. Sci. **66**(11), 1–18 (2023)

43. Tu, D., Min, X., Duan, H., Guo, G., Zhai, G., Shen, W.: End-to-end human-gaze-target detection with transformers. In: Proceedings of the IEEE Conference on Computer Vision and Pattern Recognition (CVPR), pp. 2202–2210 (2022)

44. Sun, Y., Min, X., Duan, H., Zhai, G.: The influence of text-guidance on visual attention. In: Proceedings of the IEEE International Symposium on Circuits and Systems (ISCAS), pp. 1–5 (2023)

45. Tu, D., Min, X., Duan, H., Guo, G., Zhai, G., Shen, W.: IWIN: human-object interaction detection via transformer with irregular windows. In: Avidan, S., Brostow, G., Cissé, M., Farinella, G.M., Hassner, T. (eds.) ECCV 2022. LNCS, vol. 13664, pp. 87–103. Springer, Cham (2022). https://doi.org/10.1007/978-3-031-19772-7_6

46. Ren, X., et al.: Where are the children with autism looking in reality? In: Fang, L., Povey, D., Zhai, G., Mei, T., Wang, R. (eds.) CICAI 2022. LNCS, vol. 13605, pp. 588–600. Springer Nature Switzerland, Cham (2022). https://doi.org/10.1007/978-3-031-20500-2_48

47. Duda, M., Haber, N., Daniels, J., Wall, D.P.: Crowdsourced validation of a machine-learning classification system for autism and ADHD. Transl. Psychiat. **7** (2017). https://api.semanticscholar.org/CorpusID:3911083

48. Wall, D.P., Dally, R.L., Luyster, R.J., Jung, J.Y., DeLuca, T.F.: Use of artificial intelligence to shorten the behavioral diagnosis of autism. PLoS ONE **7** (2012). https://api.semanticscholar.org/CorpusID:1894783

49. Kumar, C.J., Das, P.R.: The diagnosis of ASD using multiple machine learning techniques. Int. J. Dev. Disabil. **68**, 973 – 983 (2021). https://api.semanticscholar.org/CorpusID:236301106

50. Parikh, M.N., Li, H., He, L.: Enhancing diagnosis of autism with optimized machine learning models and personal characteristic data. Front. Comput. Neurosci. **13** (2019). https://api.semanticscholar.org/CorpusID:61485658

51. Shamseddine, H.: Federated machine learning for multi-aspect neurodevelopmental disorders: autism spectrum disorder (ASD) detection. https://api.semanticscholar.org/CorpusID:261730214

52. Thabtah, F.A.: Machine learning in autistic spectrum disorder behavioral research: a review and ways forward. Inform. Health Soc. Care **44**, 278–297 (2019). https://api.semanticscholar.org/CorpusID:46815266

53. Sideraki, A., Drigas, A.: Development of social skills for people with ASD through intervention with digital technologies and virtual reality (VR) tools. Res. Soc. Deve. (2023). https://api.semanticscholar.org/CorpusID:258651607

54. Satu, P., Minna, L., Satu, S.: Immersive VR assessment and intervention research of individuals with neurodevelopmental disorders is dominated by ASD and ADHD: a scoping review. Rev. J. Autism Dev. Disord. 1–19 (2023). https://api.semanticscholar.org/CorpusID:258552129

55. Zhang, Y., Keighrey, C., Murray, N.: A VR intervention based on social story^{TM} to develop social skills in children with ASD. In: Proceedings of the 2023 ACM International Conference on Interactive Media Experiences (2023). https://api.semanticscholar.org/CorpusID:261279463

56. Liu, J., et al.: Designing and deploying a mixed-reality aquarium for cognitive training of young children with autism spectrum disorder. Sci. China Inf. Sci. **64**, 1–3 (2021)

57. Khan, A.T., Li, S., Cao, X.: Human guided cooperative robotic agents in smart home using beetle antennae search. Sci. China Inf. Sci. **65**(2), 122204 (2022)

58. El-Muhammady, M.F., Yusof, H.M., Rashidan, M.A., Sidek, S.N.: Intervention of autism spectrum disorder (ASD) in a new perspective: a review on the deployment of adaptive human-robot interaction (HRI) system in enhancing social skill impairments. 2022 IEEE-EMBS Conference on Biomedical Engineering and Sciences (IECBES), pp. 1–6 (2022). https://api.semanticscholar.org/CorpusID:257859480

59. Simut, R., Verspecht, S., Vanderfaeillie, J.: Can social robots function as models for children with ASD? An intervention study on joint attention skills (2017). https://api.semanticscholar.org/CorpusID:20773757

60. Pérez-Vázquez, E., Lorenzo, G., Lledó, A., Lorenzo-Lledó, A.: Evolution and identification from a bibliometric perspective of the use of robots in the intervention of children with ASD. Technol. Knowl. Learn. **25**, 83–114 (2019). https://api.semanticscholar.org/CorpusID:191674428

61. Li, Y., Li, Z., Zhang, K., Dan, R., Jiang, S., Zhang, Y.: ChatDoctor: a medical chat model fine-tuned on a large language model meta-AI (LLAMA) using medical domain knowledge. Cureus **15**(6) (2023)

62. Zhu, W.: Chatmed-dataset: an GPT generated medical query-response datasets for medcal large language models (2023). https://github.com/michael-wzhu/ChatMed

63. Li, J., et al.: Huatuo-26m, a large-scale Chinese medical QA dataset (2023)

64. hiyouga: LLaMA factory (2023). https://github.com/hiyouga/LLaMA-Factory

65. Hu, E.J., et al.: LoRA: low-rank adaptation of large language models. In: International Conference on Learning Representations (2022). https://openreview.net/forum?id=nZeVKeeFYf9

66. Papineni, K., Roukos, S., Ward, T., Zhu, W.J.: Bleu: a method for automatic evaluation of machine translation. In: Proceedings of the 40th Annual Meeting of the Association for Computational Linguistics, pp. 311–318 (2002)

67. Lin, C.Y.: Rouge: A package for automatic evaluation of summaries. In: Text Summarization Branches Out, pp. 74–81 (2004)

Billiards Hitting Assistance System

Hang Liu, Chaoyi Liu, Jian Zhang$^{(\boxtimes)}$, and Menghan Hu$^{(\boxtimes)}$

Shanghai Key Laboratory of Multidimensional Information Processing, East China Normal University, Shanghai 200241, China
jzhang@ee.ecnu.edu.cn, mhhu@ce.ecnu.edu.cn

Abstract. Performing training sessions to enhance the precision of billiard ball scoring poses inherent challenges. In response, we designed a comprehensive billiard ball hitting assistance system predicated on the utilization of a cellular phone camera. This system leverages the cell phone to capture images, subsequently transmitting them to the server backend for meticulous analysis and processing. The localization module is integrated with the YOLO target detection algorithm, facilitating the precise determination of the billiard ball's spatial coordinates. Simultaneously, the perspective distortion inherent in the billiard table surface is exploited to ascertain the relative positioning of the camera vis-à-vis the billiard table surface, thereby mitigating localization errors attributable to varying shooting perspectives. Furthermore, the shot assistance system undertakes a comprehensive analysis of shot trajectories contingent upon collisions. It furnishes the billiard trainer with a detailed guide on optimal ball striking techniques. Additionally, the system evaluates the likelihood of scoring under diverse positional scenarios by considering the striking angle, and subsequently generates a simulated distribution graph illustrating the probability of scoring. Ultimately, we substantiate the efficacy of this probability distribution algorithm through meticulous simulation-based validation procedures.

Keywords: Billiards · Spatial Localization · Hitting Path · Probability Distribution

1 Introduction

Billiards, as a long-standing sport, has always been loved by many people. In billiards matches, hitting the ball into a hole is one of the key factors to victory, so there are high requirements for the hit rate of billiards. Therefore, how to improve the efficiency of goals is an important link in the process of billiards training. The development of random computer technology has led to the use of machine vision and other methods to monitor billiard tables, which has led to various auxiliary applications [1–7]. For example, robots that can perform sports events [8, 9], automatic scoring systems [10, 11], and existing research on the dynamics of billiards [12, 13]. However, existing research does not analyze the path of hitting the ball and game strategies based on images and videos of billiards matches.

H. Liu and C. Liu—Contributed equally to this work.

G. Zhai et al. (Eds.): IFTC 2023, CCIS 2067, pp. 325–337, 2024.
https://doi.org/10.1007/978-981-97-3626-3_24

The foundation of vision-based billiards hitting assistance system is to locate the position of the billiards ball in the image captured by the camera and predict the hitting path of the billiards ball. In terms of motion trajectory prediction and positioning, Yang et al. proposed a new visual system to measure the trajectory of tennis balls and predict their boundary positions, which can be used for the development of tennis robots [14]. Voeikov et al. proposed a TTNet network to achieve real-time motion detection of table tennis and provide assistance for referee decisions [15]. So, it is of great practical significance to be able to predict and detect trajectories through path prediction algorithms.

The cue ball probability distribution algorithm: The probability distribution model helps users choose reasonable usage intervals by studying probability partitioning, which is very helpful in practical production applications. Niu et al. analyzed the fatigue reliability of full-scale bladed discs under multi-source uncertainty conditions and sensitivity analysis of fatigue design by studying probability distribution [16]. Emanuel estimated the probability of the annual average hurricane rainfall for current and future climates being on the Hurricane Harvey scale by reducing the proportion of large tropical cyclones from three climate analyses and six climate models [17].

This study designs vision-based billiards hitting assistance system, which visually analyzes the actual billiards combat images captured by mobile phones and detects the positions of billiards and ball holes based on object detection. Building upon this foundation, construct a coordinate system derived from the plane of the billiard table, and ascertain the specific coordinates pertaining to each individual billiard ball within this established coordinate framework. Subsequently, leverage this information to devise guidance for achieving optimal ball striking. This initiative aims to provide support for amateur billiards enthusiasts in the training endeavors, while simultaneously offering assistance to competitive athletes during game playback sessions.

The main contributions of the billiards hitting assistance algorithm in this study are as follows:

1. Integration of the YOLO model with the context of billiards was executed to accomplish the task of billiard ball recognition on the billiard table. Subsequently, the error associated with identified billiard balls was mitigated through the application of perspective conversion technology, thereby alleviating lens-related inaccuracies in the camera and enhancing the precision of subsequent predictions.
2. The trajectory prediction algorithm was employed to anticipate the course of the cue ball as it impacts the object ball. This predictive modeling facilitates computer-assisted projection of the impact trajectory, providing users with feedback to enable informed selection of the most optimal striking path and sequence autonomously.
3. The probability distribution of hitting the cue ball at each angle was calculated through geometric mathematics based on the angle between the hole opening and the object ball, helping people choose the most suitable landing position for the cue ball. This can maximize the hitting probability of the player.

2 System Design

2.1 System Design

The system designed in this system realizes the prediction of hitting path and goal probability based on accurate positioning. Users can conduct billiards training on this basis.

Figure 1 shows the overall structure of the billiards hitting assistance system, which consists of a front-end mobile phone and a cloud server. The mobile end interacts with the user as a shooting device to obtain billiards images.

The usage process of the system is as follows: images captured by mobile phones are sent to cloud servers. The cloud server recognizes and analyzes the uploaded images, subsequently providing feedback on the analysis results to the mobile phone. As a human-computer interaction terminal, mobile phones can be used at any time during billiards training. The system backend provides computing services to analyze billiard images uploaded from mobile phones.

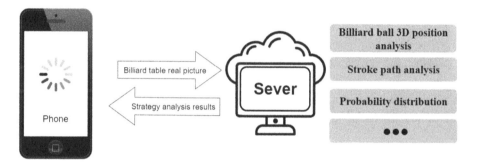

Fig. 1. Billiards hitting assistance system.

2.2 Billiard Localization Algorithm Based on Object Detection

The positioning of the billiard ball in the image is the foundation of the billiard hitting assistance system. This study uses the YOLO model to locate billiards. We obtained 3000 billiards game scene images and annotated them through on-site shooting and capturing relevant game videos. Post-training, the efficiency of recognizing billiards and holes has reached a level of 98%.

Due to perspective distortion, directly captured images cannot be directly used as a basis for determining path planning.

Firstly, in the image captured by the mobile phone, the shape of the billiard table is an irregular quadrilateral. Therefore, perspective conversion is required.

Figure 2 (A) shows a billiard table shot from a side view. Figure 2 (B) shows a billiard table shot from a top-down perspective.

From a top-down perspective, the relative positions of each ball in the image of the billiard table are consistent with the two-dimensional image. However, from a side view perspective, it is difficult to determine the relative position of each billiard ball.

In addition, due to the fact that the center of the billiard ball and the billiard table are not in the same horizontal plane, there is an error between the position of the billiard ball on the billiard table and its actual position in the captured image from a non overhead perspective. This was demonstrated in Fig. 2 (C).

In Fig. 2 (C), the billiard position measurement denotes the positional assessment of the billiard ball, and the billiard position actual is the true position of the billiard ball. The billiard position measurement is determined by the intersection of the extended line connecting the center of the billiard ball from the camera position to the actual position on the billiard table top.

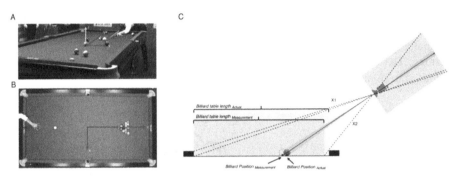

Fig. 2. Perspective distortion and positioning error. (A) A billiard table shot from a side view. (B) A billiard table shot from a top-down perspective. (C) The positioning error was caused by the center of the billiard ball and the tabletop not being in the same horizontal plane.

2.3 Establishment of a Planar Space Coordinate System for Billiards Tables

In Fig. 2 (A), the spatial Cartesian coordinate system of the physical world is established with the center of the billiard table as the origin, the direction of the red arrow being the Y axis, the direction of the blue arrow being the X axis, and the direction of the yellow arrow being the Z axis. In Fig. 2 (B), establish a plane Cartesian coordinate system with the center of the billiard table plane as the origin, the direction of the red arrow as the Y-axis, and the direction of the blue arrow as the X-axis.

In order to reduce the positioning error caused by the center of the billiard ball and the billiard table not being in the same horizontal plane as described in Fig. 2 (C).

The center of the cue ball in the camera is represented by the dotted line observed, but the actual center of the cue ball is the position where the center of the red ball is located. Figure 3 shows the algorithm for calibrating the camera position [18]. Based on the position of the hole in the plane Cartesian coordinate system and the coordinates of the hole in the camera's captured image, the relative position of the camera in the physical world space Cartesian coordinate system can be derived (x_i, y_i, z_i).

Perspective Conversion Algorithm. In order to reduce the impact of perspective distortion, we need to map the coordinates (x, y) of the target billiard ball center in the side

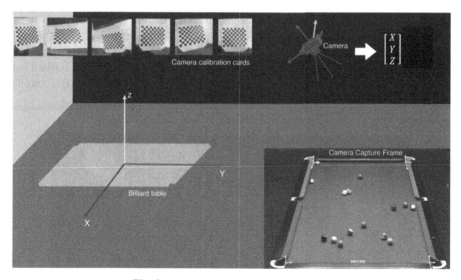

Fig. 3. Determination of camera position.

view captured image to the coordinates (x', y') in the two-dimensional plane of the top view.

The perspective conversion formula is as follows:

$$[x', y', z'] = [x, y, z] * M = [x, y, z] * \begin{bmatrix} a_{11} & a_{12} & a_{13} \\ a_{21} & a_{22} & a_{23} \\ a_{31} & a_{32} & a_{33} \end{bmatrix} \quad (1)$$

where M is the rotation matrix, $(x, y, z = 0)$ is the coordinate of the billiard ball center in the plane Cartesian coordinate system, and $(x', y', z' = 0)$ is the coordinate value of the billiard ball center in the transformed world coordinate system.

In order to calculate the rotation matrix coordinates, we selected the hole openings on the four corners of the billiard table as feature points. Use YOLO to identify the position of the belt opening and determine its coordinates. The second step is to establish a planar Cartesian coordinate system and define the coordinate values of the four feature points in the planar Cartesian coordinate system based on the physical dimensions of the billiard ball; The third step is to input the parameter matrix into the camera, with a matrix format of 3×3; The fourth application requires calling the transformation function in the OPENCV library to solve for the corresponding rotation matrix. After obtaining the rotation matrix, the white sphere coordinates obtained in the plane Cartesian coordinate system can be transformed into the world coordinate system, thus successfully completing the transformation of the white sphere coordinates.

Goal Ball Error Correction. After obtaining the coordinate values of the white ball, the actual position coordinates of the billiard ball can be computed using geometric relationships depicted in the figure (shown in Fig. 4). This calculation relies on the integration of camera coordinates and billiard ball measurement coordinates. In the two-dimensional Cartesian coordinate system, the measurement coordinates of the billiard ball are (x_1, y_1), so the measurement coordinates of the target billiard ball center in the spatial Cartesian coordinate system are (x_1, y_1, r). Assuming the measurement coordinates of the target billiard ball in the two-dimensional Cartesian coordinate system are (x', y'), then the actual coordinates of the tangent point between the target billiard ball and the billiard table in the spatial Cartesian coordinate system are $(x', y', 0)$. From the geometric relationship, it can be seen that:

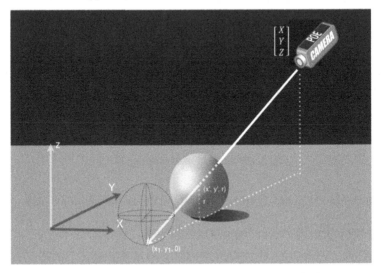

Fig. 4. Relative geometric relationship during position determination process.

$$\frac{x_i - x'}{x' - x_1} = \frac{y_i - y'}{y' - y_1} = \frac{z_i}{r} \tag{2}$$

From this, it can be solved that the actual coordinates of the tangent point between the target billiard ball and the billiard table in the spatial Cartesian coordinate system are $(x', y', 0)$. So, the coordinates of the target ball in the plane Cartesian coordinate system are (x', y').

2.4 Path Prediction Algorithm

To facilitate billiards instructors in coaching the skill of striking billiard balls, we designed a prediction algorithm for the effective goal path of billiards. This path prediction algorithm calculates the final hitting point based on the relative position of the bag mouth, object ball, and cue ball. The line connecting the cue ball and the hitting point is the predicted hitting path.

Mark the position of the center of the object ball as (x_{object}, y_{object}), the coordinates of the upper foot of the bag mouth as (x_{hole1}, y_{hole1}), and the coordinates of the lower

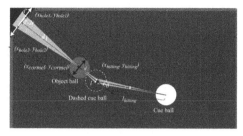 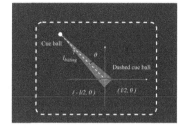

Fig. 5. (A) Analysis of hitting angle. (B) Establish a plane coordinate system with the hitting point as the origin.

foot of the bag mouth as (x_{hole2}, y_{hole2}). Here, first define the distance between the bag mouth as d', the diameter of the table ball as d, and the radius as r. As shown in Fig. 5 (A), the range within which a billiard ball that can accurately enter a hole can move near the hole is $d' - 2r$. The calculation formula for bag opening distance is as follows:

$$d' = \sqrt{(x_{hole1} - x_{hole2})^2 + (y_{hole1} - y_{hole2})^2} \tag{3}$$

From this, we can calculate the movable distance of the cue ball based on the geometric relationship between the two triangles, and assume the distance from the center of the object ball to the bag mouth as d_1. The value of d_1 can be obtained by the following formula:

$$d' = \sqrt{\left(x_{object} - \frac{x_{hole1} + x_{hole2}}{2}\right)^2 + \left(y_{object} - \frac{y_{hole1} + y_{hole2}}{2}\right)^2} \tag{4}$$

The distance that the center of the cue ball can move is assumed to be l, which can be calculated by the following formula.

$$\frac{d_1}{d} = \frac{d' - 2r}{l} \tag{5}$$

This will determine the value of distance l. The next step is to calculate the center coordinates of the hitting point. Assuming that the center coordinates of the hitting point are $(x_{hitting}, y_{hitting})$, and the center coordinates of the bag opening are $\left(\frac{x_{hole1} + x_{hole2}}{2}, \frac{y_{hole1} + y_{hole2}}{2}\right)$, the linear equation between the center coordinates of the ball and the center coordinates of the bag opening can be obtained as follows:

$$y_{hitting} = y_{object} + \frac{(y_{hole1} + y_{hole2})d \times y_{object}}{2d_1} \tag{6}$$

$$x_{hitting} = x_{object} + \frac{(x_{hole1} + x_{hole2})d \times x_{object}}{2d_1} \tag{7}$$

The center coordinates of the cue ball are (x_{cue}, y_{cue}). $l_{hitting}$ is the distance from the cue ball to the scoring point.

$$l_{hitting} = \sqrt{\left(x_{cue} - x_{hitting}\right)^2 + \left(y_{cue} - y_{hitting}\right)^2} \tag{8}$$

Using the hitting point as the origin, the direction from $\left(\frac{x_{hole1}+x_{hole2}}{2}, \frac{y_{hole1}+y_{hole2}}{2}\right)$ to (x_{cue}, y_{cue}) is the y-axis, and the direction perpendicular to the y-axis is the x-axis to establish a planar Cartesian coordinate system as shown in Fig. 5 (B). So in this coordinate system, the coordinates of the hitting point are $(0, 0)$, the two endpoints of the goal point are $\left(-\frac{l_{hitting}}{2}, 0\right)$, $\left(\frac{l_{hitting}}{2}, 0\right)$, and the coordinates of the cue ball is $(l_{hitting} \sin\theta, l_{hitting} \cos\theta)$. Among θ is the angle between the hitting direction of the cut ball and the direction of the line connecting the target ball to the hole; γ is the range of hitting directions in which the cue ball can enter the hole γ, θ it can be calculated using the cosine formula.

2.5 Probability Analysis of Cue Ball Goals

In billiards matches, players frequently find it imperative to position their cue ball strategically for optimal scoring opportunities during gameplay. For a hitting process, the probability of hitting the ball into the hole is not only related to the level of the striking, but also to the placement of the target ball and the cue ball. Therefore, it is meaningful to analyze the probability of hitting a ball into a hole at a specific position between the target ball and the cue ball.

We designed an algorithm to determine the probability of goals based on the different positions of the target ball and the cue ball and calculated the probability distribution of goals relative to the cue ball position.

As shown in Fig. 5 (B), the three parameters θ, γ, and $l_{hitting}$ determine the probability of hitting a hole. The higher the value of θ, the harder it means to hit a thin ball with a large angle, making it difficult for beginners to aim. The higher the value of γ, the higher the fault tolerance of hitting the ball, and it is possible to hit the ball into the hole within a larger range. A high value of $l_{hitting}$ means hitting a long ball.

2.6 Algorithm for Goal Probability Based on Normal Distribution

We used a normal distribution equation to analyze the goal probability of the object ball, and established a normal distribution equation $X \sim N(\mu, \sigma^2)$,

$$f(x) = \frac{1}{\sqrt{2\pi}} e^{-\frac{(x-\mu)^2}{2\sigma^2}} \tag{9}$$

The μ value is defined as 0, while the σ value can be changed independently based on the θ angle calculated earlier and the initial coefficient defined. The initial coefficient is used to describe a player's level. For example, if a player is a master or a novice, the corresponding coefficients are different. The definition of the σ value is as follows:

$$\sigma = a * \theta + b \tag{10}$$

For a master, the success rate of θ goals from different angles are generally relatively high, but for novice billiards players, the success rate is generally higher only when θ is around the $0°$ angle. By adjusting the specific values of a and b, the master and novice can be distinguished. For masters, the a value is generally lower, which can weaken the impact of θ on the master, at the same time, it also indicates that experts have a higher tolerance for tricky angles, while for beginners, the value of a will be higher because beginners have a lower tolerance for θ and are only more likely to score when θ is small. The coefficient b is the remaining influence coefficient, including table quality and club quality, which can be flexibly adjusted. Integrate the above formula to obtain the distribution probability, and the integration formula is as follows:

$$P\left(X \leq \frac{\gamma}{2}\right) = \frac{1}{\sqrt{2\pi}\,\sigma} \int_{-\frac{\gamma}{2}}^{\frac{\gamma}{2}} e^{-\frac{(t-\mu)^2}{2\sigma^2}} dt. \tag{11}$$

Afterwards, based on this integration function, we verified the accuracy of the goal probability. From the perspective of stereotypes, it can be seen that the goal probability distribution analyzed by this algorithm is relatively accurate for balls with different bag openings. The problem of goal probability in different regions is represented by the distribution of three main colors and the gradient of colors. The missing corners in the six images represent the goal strips to be scored. Firstly, after determining the position of the object ball, the probability of it entering each bag opening is calculated separately. The purple area represents that when the cue ball is placed in the purple area without considering special shots such as flipping the bag, the probability of scoring is almost zero. The yellow area represents that when the cue ball is placed in the yellow area, the probability of the cue ball scoring is the highest. The blue area represents the probability of scoring when the cue ball is placed in this area, but it is not as easy to score as the yellow area but easier to score than the purple area (Fig. 6).

Fig. 6. Goal hit rates for different holes.

3 Simulation

This section constitutes a simulation of auxiliary design for billiards striking, encompassing an analysis of the probability of achieving goals in billiards through simulation. Subsequently, constructive feedback is provided to the player with the aim of enhancing their actual goal attainment rate. The simulation was mainly divided into three major groups, which simulated the three major groups of average player hit rate, expert hit rate, and novice hit rate, and analyzed the results (Fig. 7).

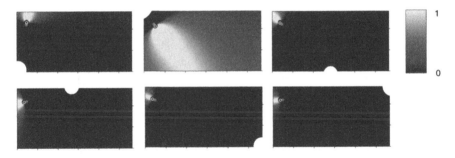

Fig. 7. Average player hit rate.

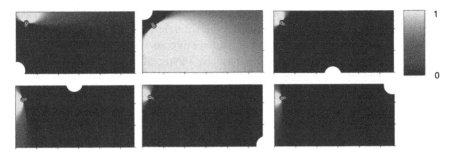

Fig. 8. Hit percentage of advanced players.

Fig. 9. Hitting percentage of junior players.

Through the above figure, it is easy to compare the difference in hit rates among three different levels of players. For experts, the angle of scoring is wide and the success rate of scoring is high; Moderate players take the second place, and for beginners, the comparison is more obvious. The angle of goal scoring is significantly reduced compared to experts. Through the comparison between Fig. 8 and Fig. 9, it can be seen that there is a significant difference. The purple area in the figure above is more difficult for players of different levels to score goals, but the purple and blue areas of beginners are significantly larger than those of advanced players. Generally, it is only easier for beginners to score goals when the hitting angle is relatively small (Fig. 10).

Fig. 10. Comparison of hit rates among players of different levels at the same entrance: leftmost junior player, middle player, right senior player.

The above figure further illustrates that for players of different levels with the same hole opening, their goal hit rates are ranked from left to right, followed by beginners, intermediate players, and senior players. The comparison is still very clear for players of different levels. The hitting area of senior players is significantly higher than that of junior selectors, and intermediate players are slightly inferior to senior players. For beginners, only when the cue ball and object ball are in a straight line, the probability of hitting is relatively high in the yellow area.

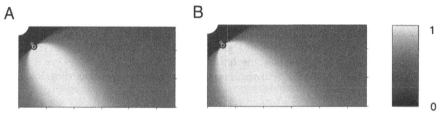

Fig. 11. (A) The algorithm of goal probability distribution calculates the results. (B) Simulation results of goal probability distribution.

In order to verify the effectiveness of algorithm for goal probability, we design a simulation experiment to compare with the calculation results of algorithm for goal probability. The experimental results are shown in Fig. 11. In the simulation experiment, we select 40,000 cue ball positions and simulate 1000 hits at each position. The direction of each impact corresponds to the targeted aiming direction at the point of impact. The hitting direction is sampled according to the normal distribution. Figure 11 (A) shows the result of algorithm for goal probability, and Fig. 11 (B) shows the result of simulation. The experimental results show that the results of the algorithm for goal probability are consistent with the simulation results. This proves that our algorithm for goal probability has some credibility.

4 Conclusion

This study designs relevant hitting assistance algorithms for the sport of billiards. Our algorithm can achieve the following main functions. Firstly, the billiard ball is positioned using the YOLO model to find the billiard ball on the table, which lays the foundation for the subsequent implementation of the algorithm. Secondly, error elimination is achieved. We use perspective conversion technology to find the correct billiard ball position during the observation of billiards in the camera. The third point is the fitting of billiards goal path, which involves fitting the path of the object ball entering the bag. The fourth point is the analysis of billiards goal probability. Through this algorithm, we have achieved feedback to billiards players of different levels when fitting the goal rate contract, helping them analyze more reasonable hitting positions. The next step is to further implement this algorithm and attempt to apply it in practical applications, rather than just staying at the simulation level.

References

1. Zhang, Z., Zhang, W., Chen, W.: Design of intelligent assistant system for billiards hit training. IOP Conf. Ser.: Earth Environ. Sci. **3**, 2021 (1802)
2. Gao, J.Y., He, Q.Y., Zhan, Z.X.: Design of neural network controller for a billiard robot. J. Beijing Univ. Aeronaut. Astronsut. **43**(3), 533–543 (2017)
3. Buric, M., Pobar, M., Ivasic-Kos, M.: Ball detection using yolo and mask R-CNN. In: 2018 International Conference on Computational Science and Computational Intelligence (CSCI), Las Vegas, pp. 319–323 (2018)
4. Zhang, S., Xu, R., Quan, Y.: Large graph layout optimization based on vision and computational efficiency: a survey. Vis. Intell. **1**, 14 (2023)
5. Fan, D.P., Ji, G.P., Xu, P., et al.: Advances in deep concealed scene understanding. Vis. Intell. **1**, 16 (2023)
6. Zhang, B., Zhu, J., Su, H.: Toward the third generation artificial intelligence. Sci. China Inf. Sci. **66**(2), 121101 (2023)
7. Liang, D.K., Chen, X.W., Xu, W., et al.: Special focus on deep learning for computer vision. Sci. China Inf. Sci. **65**(6), 160104 (2022)
8. Jin, L., Zhang, G., Wang, Y., Li, S.: RNN-based quadratic programming scheme for tennis-training robots with flexible capabilities. IEEE Trans. Syst. Man Cybernet.: Syst. **53**(2), 838–847 (2023)
9. Maiorino, A., Muscolo, G.G.: Biped robots with compliant joints for walking and running performance growing. Front. Mech. Eng. (2020)
10. Chin, Y.C., Lai, Y.H., Wang, J.W., Lin, D.C., Wei, M.C., Shih, M.Y.: Automatic score device of table tennis. In: 2015 IEEE/SICE International Symposium on System Integration (SII), Nagoya, pp. 859–864 (2015)
11. Zhang, B.H., Chen, C.Y., Chan, L.C., Fok, W.: Intelligent sports performance scoring and analysis system based on deep learning network. In: 2020 3rd International Conference on Artificial Intelligence and Big Data (ICAIBD), Chengdu, pp. 17–21 (2020)
12. Haar, S., van Assel, C.M., Faisal, A.A.: Motor Learning in Real-World Pool Billiards (2019)
13. Caramiaux, B., Françoise, J., Liu, W., et al.: Machine learning approaches for motor learning: a short review. le centre pour la communication scientifique directe - HAL - Inria, Le Centre pour la Communication Scientifique Directe – HAL, Inria (2020)

14. Yang, Y., Kim, D., Choi, D.: Ball tracking and trajectory prediction system for tennis robots. J. Comput. Design Eng. 1176–1184 (2023)
15. Voeikov, R., Falaleev, N., Baikulov, R.: TTNet: real-time temporal and spatial video analysis of table tennis. Comput. Vision Pattern Recogn. 3857–3865 (2020)
16. Niu, X.P., Wang, R.Z., Liao, D., et al.: Probabilistic modeling of uncertainties in fatigue reliability analysis of turbine bladed disks. Int. J. Fatigue (2021)
17. Emanuel, K.: Assessing the present and future probability of Hurricane Harvey's rainfall. In: Proceedings of the National Academy of Sciences of the United States of America, **114**(48), 12681–12684 (2017)
18. Liu, H., et al.: Angel's girl for blind painters: an efficient painting navigation system validated by multimodal evaluation approach. IEEE Trans. Multim. **25**, 2415–2429 (2023)

Visual Detection System for Industrial Defects

Lei Wang[1], Aiming Xu[1], Zhiyong Huang[2], and Qiu Shen[1(✉)]

[1] Nanjing University, Nanjing, China
shenqiu@nju.edu.cn
[2] Wuba Intelligent Technology, Hangzhou, China

Abstract. An effective industrial inspection system enhances production efficiency, ensures product quality, reduces costs and boosts the factory's core competitiveness throughout the entire production process. Ceramic tiles, widely utilized in building decoration, hold a significant market share. Product quality is essential not just for aesthetic appeal but also for building safety. Detecting surface defects in ceramic tiles poses formidable challenges, including complex background textures, low defect saliency and significant variations in defect scales. This presents important research opportunities in the field of computer vision. This article takes this type of difficult product as an example and starts with the ceramic tile dataset to design a template based industrial defect detection algorithm, including an image acquisition module, a template matching module and a defect detection module. A LoFTR-based template matching algorithm is proposed in this paper for the template matching module to accurately collect and match template images. Use the template images and perspective transformations to eliminate interference from background patterns after acquiring image pairs. At the same time, the system's hardware selection scheme is established, and the YOLOv5 detection network is selected as the baseline model for the performance optimization study.

Keywords: Defect detection · Perspective transformation · Template matching

1 Introduction

The automation of industrial detection not only enhances production efficiency and cuts labor costs but also facilitates early detection and correction of defects, thereby lowering scrap rates and overall production costs. Accurate identification and recording of product defects ensure compliance with quality standards, leading to improved overall product quality. In challenging environments, automated detection systems minimize manual intervention, mitigating accident risks and

This work was supported in part by the National Natural Science Foundation of China under Grant 62071216, 62231002 and U1936202.

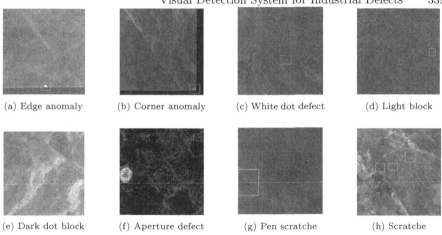

(a) Edge anomaly   (b) Corner anomaly   (c) White dot defect   (d) Light block

(e) Dark dot block   (f) Aperture defect   (g) Pen scratche   (h) Scratche

Fig. 1. Images of ceramic tile defects in various categories

enhancing workplace safety. Moreover, automated detection systems offer flexibility for adjustment to varying product specifications and production requirements, contributing to increased diversity in the production line [12,22,27,29]. However, due to the wide variety of defects, complex texture patterns and surface, defect detection of ceramic tiles remains a major technical challenge that is hindering the development of the ceramic tile industry.

The present industrial defect detection algorithms can be classified into two groups, namely traditional industrial defect detection algorithms and deep learning based industrial defect detection algorithms. Traditional industrial defect detection algorithms mainly rely on image processing, combined with traditional machine learning methods to detect the color, shape and other features of defects. The location where defects appear often exhibits sharp changes in pixel values with obvious mutation characteristics. Therefore, edge detection operators such as Sobel [23], Prewitt [35] and Canny [10] can be utilized to accurately locate the defect areas of industrial products with relatively simple background textures. These edge detection operators mentioned earlier are usually not suitable for defects with complex background textures. In terms of frequency domain characteristics, defects with sudden changes tend to have high-frequency characteristics. Therefore, Wavelet transform, Gabor transform, Fourier transform and other methods can be utilized to convert industrial products with periodic characteristics in the background to the frequency domain to facilitate the detection like Chetverikov et al. [8] and Hou et al. [18].

The field of industrial detection has seen a gradual rise in the use of deep learning algorithms due to their good generalization and robustness in recent years. These algorithms can be divided into two categories based on their characteristics: single-stage detection algorithms and two-stage detection algorithms. Common single stage detection algorithms include SSD [25] and YOLO series algorithms [30–32]. RCNN [15], Fast-RCNN [14] and Faster-RCNN [33] are two-stage detection algorithms that are commonly used. In general, the detection accuracy of a single stage detection algorithm may be slightly lower than that of a two-stage detection algorithm, but it has a detection speed far exceeding that of a two-stage detection algorithm, which is more in line with the real-time requirements of industrial defect detection. The excellent detection performance of YOLO series models has led many researchers to apply them to various industrial defect detection tasks. For example, Zhang et al. [38] applied YOLOv3 to the surface of concrete bridges; Chen et al. [6] modified the YOLOv3 architecture to better adapt to the defects of light-emitting diodes. The high accuracy of two-stage algorithm has also led some scholars to modify the RCNN family of networks, such as Hu et al. [19] who introduced the Faster R-CNN network in the PCB detection task. But invariably these industrial products have two characteristics: simple defects and large differences from the background.

To address defects in industrial products amid complex backgrounds, this article establishes a visual inspection system specifically designed for industrial defect detection. The ceramic tile detection task is intricate and specific, characterized by a multitude of defect types and significant defect size variations. Notably, the challenges include the similarity between defects and the background, as depicted in Fig. 1. Hence, we introduce a template-based algorithm. The system comprises four modules: an image acquisition module, a matching module, an alignment module, and a detection module.

When a detected image enters the system, the algorithm identifies its corresponding template from the template library. This paper presents a template matching algorithm utilizing the LoFTR [36] model to derive feature point matching results for image pairs, enabling the measurement of image similarity. Experimental results demonstrate the effective matching of corresponding templates. Then, upon acquiring the corresponding template, this article employs a perspective transformation method to align and subtract the template image from the target image. This process yields a single-channel residual image, effectively eliminating background interference. Additionally, we address the challenge of homography estimation through a deep learning framework. Finally, the residual channel is concatenated with the original RGB image to create a 4-channel image, which is then sent to the detector. Leveraging YOLOv5, enhancements have been implemented to tackle the intricacies and specificities of ceramic tile tasks, resulting in a significant improvement in accuracy. Specific details can be seen in Fig. 2. However, given the unique nature of ceramic tile inspection tasks and the limited availability of public datasets, we've installed on-site hardware to capture the necessary datasets.

To summarize, our main contributions are:

– We develop a comprehensive system encompassing both hardware and software, addressing the entire process from image acquisition and template matching to detection.
– We capture a dataset of ceramic tiles with the aim of contributing to the ceramic tile testing industry.

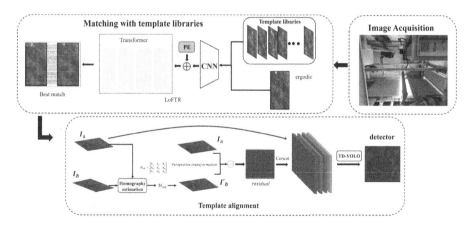

Fig. 2. System work flow. This system consists of four modules: an image acquisition module, a template matching module, a template registration module and a detector.

2   Related Works

Homography Matrix: In the alignment module of this paper, two images are aligned using homography. A homography is a 3×3 matrix which compensates plane motions between two images. It consists of 8°C of freedom (DOF), with each 2 for scale, translation, rotation and perspective respectively. To solve a homography, traditional approaches often detect and match image features, such as SIFT [26], SURF [4], ORB [34], LPM [28] and GMS [5]. Two sets of correspondences were established between two images, following which robust estimation is adopted, such as the classic RANSAC [13], IRLS [16] and MAGSAC [3], for the outlier rejection during the model estimation. A deep homography solution was first proposed by [11] in 2016. The network takes source and target images as input and produces 4 corner displacement vectors of source image, so as to yield the homography. We chose this model [40] as the core of our algorithm for the following reasons: the unsupervised algorithm is more in line with real-world scenarios, and the estimation of the mask allows the model to pay more attention to backgrounds that are similar in the two images.

YOLO: The 8th version of the YOLO series has been updated. For readers who are familiar with YOLO, the overall architecture of YOLO has been established as a backbone+neck architecture since 3th version. Subsequently, FPN and PAN structures have been introduced in the neck section of 5th version. The FPN layer can transmit features containing semantic information from top to bottom, while PAN feature pyramid can transmit features containing spatial position information from bottom to top. The features extracted from different depths of the backbone network are aggregated together to fuse the spatial position information from shallow features into deep features. For industrial defect detection, YOLO series algorithms combine accuracy and speed, and is also rel-

Table 1. EV71YC4MCP1605-BA0 Linear Array CMOS Industrial Camera

Model	EV71YC4MCP1605-BA0
Brand	Teledyne e2 v
Resolution	16384×4
Khz	100
Sensor type	CMOS
Number of lines	4
Picture element	$5\,\mu m$
Spectrum	black and white
Weight	700 g

atively easy to obtain dataset annotation. Therefore, this article selects YOLO as the baseline model to optimize.

3 Structure

3.1 Image Acquisition

Industrial cameras have two imaging modes: line-array imaging and area-array imaging, and the appropriate imaging mode is usually selected according to the shape and movement of the image acquisition object. Area-array cameras are more stable in that they capture all of the image in the lens each time they shoot. Line-array cameras can only capture one row of images at a time, so they must scan each tile individually to generate a complete tile image. There are very small defects on the surface of the tiles, such as white dots, light blocks and dark dot blocks, so the system needs to acquire high-resolution images of the tiles, otherwise it will be difficult for the subsequent defect detection module to detect these small defects. However, due to the technical limitations of image sensors and other aspects, the price of high-resolution area array cameras is very expensive, much higher than that of line array cameras. Therefore, the system in this paper chooses to use a line array camera. This camera offers a resolution of 16384×4 and a line frequency of up to 100 kHz, ensuring an ultra-high signal-to-noise ratio even in low-light conditions. The parameters for camera selection are shown in the Table 1.

3.2 Template Matching

To compute the homography matrix for aligning two images, it is crucial to find the corresponding template in the extensive library and match it with the image to be tested. Consequently, this paper proposes a method for calculating image similarity based on LoFTR [36]. The LoFTR [36] model is utilized to determine the number of matching feature points between images, serving as a measure of similarity between the two images.

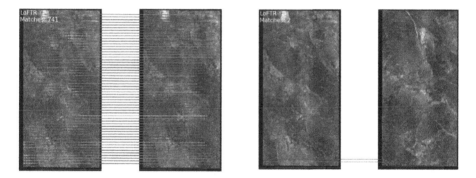

Fig. 3. Comparison of image pairs of tiles with the same background pattern and image pairs of tiles with different background patterns under LoFTR model

As shown in the Fig. 2, the transformer module consists of multiple alternating self-attention and cross-attention layers, with the self-attention layer making each region to focus on the associations of all the regions around it, and the cross-attention layer making the region to focus on the associations with all the regions in the other picture. In this paper, by using adaptive thresholds, the similarity threshold corresponding to the tile image to be detected is obtained; Then, calculate the similarity score between the tile image to be detected and the image in the template library in sequence. If there is a template image that exceed the threshold, it will be directly output as the matching result; Finally, if there are no template images in the template library that exceed the threshold, the template image with the highest similarity score is selected as the matching result output (Fig. 3).

3.3 Template Alignment

After obtaining the corresponding image pairs, the most direct method is to use the template and image for perspective transformation and subtraction to obtain a relatively clean image without background pattern interference. Therefore, the perspective matrix needs to be calculated. Traditional methods use SURF [4] + RANSAC [13] to calculate, which is very easy to fail in the case of repeated textures such as tiles. Therefore, a deep learning method [40] is adopted and the specific idea is as follows: CNN can replace SURF to extract feature points, but it also requires a RANSAC to exclude outliers. Therefore, we add an additional mask to extract the feature map and multiply it with the feature map obtained from the convolutional layer below. This allows the network to pay more attention to the similarities between the two images excluding areas that do not contribute significantly to the results.

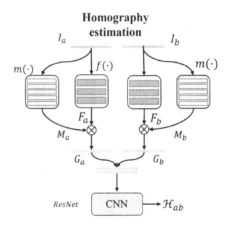

Fig. 4. The specific structure of homography estimation in the template alignment module

In Fig. 4, two input patches, I_a and I_b, undergo processing in two branches. Each branch comprises a feature extractor, denoted as $f(\cdot)$ and a mask predictor, denoted as $m(\cdot)$. This process yields features F_a, F_b and masks M_a, M_b. Subsequently, the obtained features and masks are input into a homography estimator based on ResNet, generating the 8 values of the homography matrix H_{ab}. We adopt an unsupervised approach for training, which is more in line with practical application scenarios. Here, in (1), M_b' is the warped version of M_b, where $F_b' = f(I_b')$ and $I_b' = Warp(I_b, H_{ab})$.

$$L(I_a, I_b') = \frac{\sum_i M_a M_b' \cdot \max(\|F_a - F_b'\|_1 - \|F_a - F_b\|_1 + \text{margin}, 0)}{\sum_i M_a M_b'} \quad (1)$$

3.4   Detector

In the related work section, we provided a concise overview of the YOLOv5 structure. In this context, we have made specific enhancements to the network architecture, tailoring it to the unique demands of ceramic tile tasks. We have named this network TD-YOLOv5.

Firstly, significant variations in both size and aspect ratio characterize defects on the surface of ceramic tiles. For instance, scratches and pen marks typically manifest as slender, large shapes, while white dot defects usually present themselves as dots with edge lengths spanning several pixels. The size discrepancy among these defects can range from tens to hundreds of times and different-scale defects may emerge in distinct regions of the image. Standard convolutional approaches sometimes struggle to effectively adapt to these diverse defect shapes. Addressing this challenge, this article proposes the integration of deformable convolution [9] into the YOLOv5 network. This modification aims to enhance the network's ability to handle the varied shapes encountered in ceramic tile surface

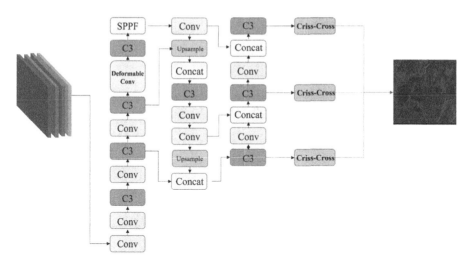

Fig. 5. TD-YOLOv5 network architecture

defect detection tasks. Then, for the intricate task of detecting surface defects on ceramic tiles, the simplicity of the YOLOv5 detection module becomes apparent. To augment the module's capacity to leverage feature information effectively, this article introduces the Criss-Cross attention mechanism [20] grounded in contextual information. This enhancement enables the model to more effectively correlate global contextual features with local features, thereby focusing greater attention on the defect area within the ceramic tile image. As shown in Fig. 5, this article deploys attention modules on all three detection branches. In addition to the aforementioned modifications, to tackle sample inequality, this article also replaces the loss function with Focal Loss [24].

4   Experiment

4.1   Dataset

Utilizing Structure 3.1 for hardware collection, a total of 362 sets of data were captured with a resolution of 8192 × 15840. These datasets underwent meticulous annotation, encompassing both category and location information. The annotation encompasses details for eight distinct categories: Edge anomaly, Corner anomaly, White dot defect, Light block, Dark dot block, Aperture defect, Pen scratch and Scratch, which can be referred to in Fig. 1.

To ensure the experiment closely mirrors real-world production scenarios and to validate the reliability of our proposed method, two distinct datasets were chosen. The first dataset was sourced from the 2021 Guangdong Industrial Intelligent Manufacturing Innovation Competition, while the second dataset was captured and preprocessed in-house. For training purposes, this article employs

	tile 1-1	tile 1-2	tile 1-3	tile 2-1	tile 2-2	tile 2-3	tile 3-1	tile 3-2	tile 3-3	tile 4-1	tile 4-2	tile 4-3	tile 5-1	tile 5-2	tile 5-3
tile 1-1	1276	670	200	4	3	7	5	1	2	1	4	5	1	2	3
tile 1-2	501	1254	276	10	6	9	6	7	8	2	3	2	7	0	2
tile 1-3	190	330	690	3	1	8	4	8	1	6	7	3	1	3	1
tile 2-1	1	3	4	1798	978	809	7	1	3	6	3	1	2	3	3
tile 2-2	8	1	3	1066	1678	1209	3	2	1	3	6	8	3	1	10
tile 2-3	5	8	5	783	872	1502	5	2	5	9	0	2	3	8	0
tile 3-1	1	4	5	8	1	3	978	520	79	2	1	2	5	9	0
tile 3-2	3	3	7	0	7	8	70	987	43	6	4	7	0	3	9
tile 3-3	1	2	5	8	5	0	102	67	140	1	9	0	5	4	3
tile 4-1	4	6	1	9	0	3	7	0	0	1323	899	107	0	1	6
tile 4-2	4	8	9	0	1	3	2	2	1	989	2001	601	2	3	2
tile 4-3	1	2	3	2	2	3	2	8	9	109	738	2098	0	8	1
tile 5-1	3	4	0	2	6	0	0	0	1	5	7	1	908	562	303
tile 5-2	1	8	0	8	6	8	4	7	2	1	1	0	700	829	1392
tile 5-3	4	6	8	5	0	3	7	2	7	1	8	3	460	1290	1683

Fig. 6. Similarity matrix.

the first dataset, while the second, consisting of actual captured data, is reserved for testing. The overall training set comprises 5,676 sets of ceramic tile images, and the test set encompasses 630 sets.

4.2   Experimental Results of Template Matching Algorithm

This article conducted tests on the proposed template matching algorithm based on LoFTR [36] using a real captured tile dataset. To assess the reliability of the image similarity calculation method presented in this study, experiments were conducted on ultra-complex pattern types. Specifically, five ceramic tile images with distinct background patterns were selected, with each pattern featuring three images. For clarity, this article adopts the tile $i - j$ format to name the j-th ceramic tile image with the i-th background pattern. As observed in the Fig. 6, there is a notable difference in the matched scores among different backgrounds.

The running speed of image similarity calculation methods under various downsampling rates was tested in the experimental environment of this article. For the input image with a resolution of 8192 × 15840, the required time is 0.15 s when downsampling 16 times and 0.05 s when downsampling 32 times. The experiments indicate that a significant level of accuracy can still be maintained even after downsampling.

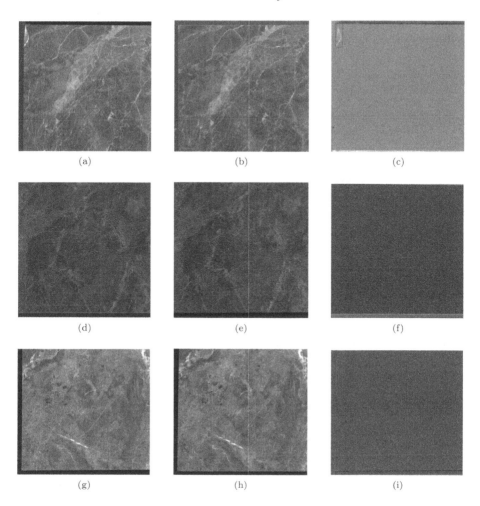

(a)   (b)   (c)

(d)   (e)   (f)

(g)   (h)   (i)

Fig. 7. Residual feature visualization results

4.3 Experimental Results of Template Residual

In Fig. 7, the first column represents tiles with defects. Through alignment with the template tile, residual feature maps are extracted. The green box area in the figure highlights the tile defect region. Based on the visualization results, it is evident that a majority of ceramic tile defects are concealed beneath the intricate background texture of the tile surface, rendering them inconspicuous. The residual features extracted by this method effectively eliminate most background patterns, presenting ceramic tile defects distinctly and clearly.

Table 2. Comparison of experimental results with traditional methods. The bold part indicates that the input is a single channel residual image.

	AC	AC	FT	FT	HC	HC	BMS	BMS	LC	LC	ITTI	ITTI	TD-YOLOv5n	TD-YOLOv5s	TD-YOLOv5m
$\mathfrak{AUC}$ ↑	0.566	0.634	0.542	0.620	0.567	0.637	0.532	0.587	0.542	0.630	0.597	0.748	0.957	0.968	0.970
$\mathfrak{MAE}$ ↓	0.070	0.058	0.082	0.045	0.104	0.040	0.056	0.043	0.081	0.042	0.140	0.076	0.030	0.028	0.020
$\mathfrak{Fscore}$ ↑	0.015	0.035	0.024	0.031	0.028	0.030	0.032	0.038	0.024	0.031	0.030	0.041	0.378	0.401	0.440

Table 3. Comparative experimental results of deep learning methods

method	mAP@0.1	mAP@0.1:0.5	Acc	Rec
YOLOv5n(RGB)	0.406	0.319	0.754	0.581
YOLOv5n(residual)	0.466	0.378	0.773	0.531
RC-YOLOv5n [17]	0.476	0.377	0.784	0.756
Our YOLOv5n	**0.645**	**0.527**	**0.834**	**0.901**
YOLOv5s(RGB)	0.523	0.435	0.803	0.721
YOLOv5s(residual)	0.564	0.458	0.831	0.714
RC-YOLOv5s [17]	0.557	0.461	0.806	0.760
Our YOLOv5s	**0.701**	**0.574**	**0.847**	**0.917**
YOLOv5m(RGB)	0.581	0.481	0.811	0.674
YOLOv5m(residual)	0.635	0.539	0.835	0.751
RC-YOLOv5m [17]	0.636	0.544	0.811	0.876
Our YOLOv5m	**0.724**	**0.625**	**0.853**	**0.934**

4.4   Experimental Results of Detector

This article selects six classic machine learning algorithms, namely AC [1], FT(Frequency-tuned) [2], HC(Histogram-based Contrast) [7], BMS(Boolean Map based Saliency Detection) [39], LC [37] and ITTI [21] as comparative methods. AC relies on local color sparsity, while FT, HC and LC are based on global color sparsity. BMS and ITTI utilize visual attention mechanisms. In addition to RGB images of ceramic tiles, this article explores the use of residual feature maps directly from ceramic tile images. The experimental results in Table 2 reveal that our method outperforms classical machine learning algorithms like ITTI across the three evaluation indicators of $\mathfrak{AUC}$, $\mathfrak{MAE}$ and $\mathfrak{Fscore}$. Notably, ITTI and similar classical machine learning algorithms are widely employed in industrial production for defect detection. These findings indicate that the proposed method exhibits superior detection performance compared to most industrial defect detection algorithms in practical applications, underscoring its high application value and practical significance.

This article chooses YOLOv5 as the baseline model and enhances the input image, which includes modifications to both the backbone and neck components. To our best knowledge, the RC-YOLOv5 [17] model has also been specifically optimized for the detection of ceramic tiles. RC-YOLOv5 incorporates a novel residual structure to bolster feature fusion and information exchange across dif-

Table 4. Ablation studies

	No module	+Homo	+Homo/DC	+Homo/Attention	+Homo/Focalloss	Our
mAP@0.1	0.523	0.620	0.654	0.685	0.654	0.701
mAP@0.1:0.5	0.435	0.520	0.544	0.568	0.548	0.574

ferent layer structures. Additionally, it introduces a Drop-CA mechanism to minimize missed detections. These enhancements make RC-YOLOv5 a suitable choice as our comparative model. Across three different model sizes, the performance of the proposed method in this article notably surpasses that of other comparative methods, as evidenced by superior results in mAP@0.1, mAP@0.1:0.5, Acc and Rec. From Table 3, it's evident that the RC-YOLO model exhibits substantial performance improvements over the original YOLOv5 baseline. However, despite these improvements, its detection performance still lags behind the method proposed in this paper. This observation suggests that the enhancement measures employed in this article are, to some extent, superior to most existing deep learning methods for ceramic tile surface and defect detection, showcasing high application value. The mAP of the improved YOLOv5n, YOLOv5s, and YOLOv5m models in this study is 64.5%, 70.1%, and 72.4%, respectively. These figures represent increases of 23.9%, 17.8%, and 14.3% compared to the original model.

To validate proposed improvements, ablation experiments on the tile defect detection dataset were conducted. The YOLOv5s baseline model served as the baseline, with all experiment models trained on the same dataset and under identical conditions. The results in Table 4 show that optimizing the input image boosts both mAP indicators by almost 0.1. This substantial improvement provides strong evidence for the effectiveness of the proposed improvement measures, centered around the template algorithm. The deep learning-based residual feature extraction method proves to be the most impactful enhancement. Ablation experiments, extending from the foundational optimization of the input module, were performed to scrutinize other enhancement strategies. As shown in Table 4, optimizing the backbone network improves mAP@0.1 by 3.4% and mAP@0.1:0.5 by 2.4%, adjusting the receptive field and scale for better adaptation to varying ceramic tile defects. The detection module optimization results in a substantial 6.5% improvement in mAP@0.1 and a 4.8% enhancement in mAP@0.1:0.5, emphasizing its role in incorporating global contextual features with local ones. Additionally, optimizing the loss function yields a 3.4% improvement in mAP@0.1 and a 2.8% advancement in mAP@0.1:0.5, demonstrating its effectiveness in focusing on indistinguishable samples over easily distinguishable ones.

5   Conclusions

We introduce a comprehensive ceramic tile detection system, encompassing modules for collection, matching, and detection. Additionally, we have implemented improvements to the ceramic tile detector, successfully resolving issues associated with direct failures. These enhancements have proven effective in experiments, surpassing other models that have undergone similar improvements for ceramic tiles.

References

1. Achanta, R., Estrada, F., Wils, P., Süsstrunk, S.: Salient region detection and segmentation. In: Gasteratos, A., Vincze, M., Tsotsos, J.K. (eds.) ICVS 2008. LNCS, vol. 5008, pp. 66–75. Springer, Heidelberg (2008). https://doi.org/10.1007/978-3-540-79547-6_7
2. Achanta, R., Hemami, S., Estrada, F., Susstrunk, S.: Frequency-tuned salient region detection. In: 2009 IEEE Conference on Computer Vision and Pattern Recognition, pp. 1597–1604. IEEE (2009)
3. Barath, D., Matas, J., Noskova, J.: MAGSAC: marginalizing sample consensus. In: Proceedings of the IEEE/CVF Conference on Computer Vision and Pattern Recognition, pp. 10197–10205 (2019)
4. Bay, H., Tuytelaars, T., Van Gool, L.: SURF: speeded up robust features. In: Leonardis, A., Bischof, H., Pinz, A. (eds.) ECCV 2006. LNCS, vol. 3951, pp. 404–417. Springer, Heidelberg (2006). https://doi.org/10.1007/11744023_32
5. Bian, J., Lin, W.Y., Matsushita, Y., Yeung, S.K., Nguyen, T.D., Cheng, M.M.: Gms: grid-based motion statistics for fast, ultra-robust feature correspondence. In: Proceedings of the IEEE Conference on Computer Vision and Pattern Recognition, pp. 4181–4190 (2017)
6. Chen, S.H., Tsai, C.C.: SMD LED chips defect detection using a yolov3-dense model. Adv. Eng. Inform. **47**, 101255 (2021)
7. Cheng, M.M., Mitra, N.J., Huang, X., Torr, P.H., Hu, S.M.: Global contrast based salient region detection. IEEE Trans. Pattern Anal. Mach. Intell. **37**(3), 569–582 (2014)
8. Chetverikov, D., Hanbury, A.: Finding defects in texture using regularity and local orientation. Pattern Recogn. **35**(10), 2165–2180 (2002)
9. Dai, J., Qi, H., Xiong, Y., Li, Y., Zhang, G., Hu, H., Wei, Y.: Deformable convolutional networks. In: Proceedings of the IEEE International Conference on Computer Vision (ICCV) (Oct 2017)
10. Deng, C.X., Wang, G.B., Yang, X.R.: Image edge detection algorithm based on improved canny operator. In: 2013 International Conference on Wavelet Analysis and Pattern Recognition, pp. 168–172. IEEE (2013)
11. DeTone, D., Malisiewicz, T., Rabinovich, A.: Deep image homography estimation. arXiv preprint arXiv:1606.03798 (2016)
12. Du, W., Shen, H., Fu, J., Zhang, G., He, Q.: Approaches for improvement of the X-ray image defect detection of automobile casting aluminum parts based on deep learning. NDT & E Inter. **107**, 102144 (2019)
13. Fischler, M.A., Bolles, R.C.: Random sample consensus: a paradigm for model fitting with applications to image analysis and automated cartography. Commun. ACM **24**(6), 381–395 (1981)
14. Girshick, R.: Fast R-CNN. In: Proceedings of the IEEE International Conference on Computer Vision, pp. 1440–1448 (2015)
15. Girshick, R., Donahue, J., Darrell, T., Malik, J.: Rich feature hierarchies for accurate object detection and semantic segmentation. In: Proceedings of the IEEE Conference on Computer Vision and Pattern Recognition, pp. 580–587 (2014)

16. Holland, P.W., Welsch, R.E.: Robust regression using iteratively reweighted least-squares. Commun. Stat.-Theory Methods **6**(9), 813–827 (1977)
17. Hou, W., Jing, H.: Rc-yolov5s: for tile surface defect detection. The Visual Computer, pp. 1–12 (2023)
18. Hou, Z., Parker, J.M.: Texture defect detection using support vector machines with adaptive gabor wavelet features. In: 2005 Seventh IEEE Workshops on Applications of Computer Vision (WACV/MOTION 2005), vol. 1, pp. 275–280. IEEE (2005)
19. Hu, B., Wang, J.: Detection of PCB surface defects with improved faster-RCNN and feature pyramid network. IEEE Access **8**, 108335–108345 (2020)
20. Huang, Z., Wang, X., Huang, L., Huang, C., Wei, Y., Liu, W.: Ccnet: Criss-cross attention for semantic segmentation. In: Proceedings of the IEEE/CVF International Conference on Computer Vision, pp. 603–612 (2019)
21. Itti, L., Koch, C., Niebur, E.: A model of saliency-based visual attention for rapid scene analysis. IEEE Trans. Pattern Anal. Mach. Intell. **20**(11), 1254–1259 (1998)
22. Jing, J., Zhuo, D., Zhang, H., Liang, Y., Zheng, M.: Fabric defect detection using the improved yolov3 model. J. Eng. Fibers Fabr. **15**, 1558925020908268 (2020)
23. Kanopoulos, N., Vasanthavada, N., Baker, R.L.: Design of an image edge detection filter using the Sobel operator. IEEE J. Solid-State Circ. **23**(2), 358–367 (1988)
24. Lin, T.Y., Goyal, P., Girshick, R., He, K., Dollár, P.: Focal loss for dense object detection. In: Proceedings of the IEEE International Conference on Computer Vision, pp. 2980–2988 (2017)
25. Liu, W., et al.: SSD: single shot multibox detector. In: Leibe, B., Matas, J., Sebe, N., Welling, M. (eds.) ECCV 2016. LNCS, vol. 9905, pp. 21–37. Springer, Cham (2016). https://doi.org/10.1007/978-3-319-46448-0_2
26. Lowe, D.G.: Distinctive image features from scale-invariant keypoints. Int. J. Comput. Vis. **60**, 91–110 (2004)
27. Luo, Q., Fang, X., Liu, L., Yang, C., Sun, Y.: Automated visual defect detection for flat steel surface: a survey. IEEE Trans. Instrum. Meas. **69**(3), 626–644 (2020)
28. Ma, J., Zhao, J., Jiang, J., Zhou, H., Guo, X.: Locality preserving matching. Int. J. Comput. Vis. **127**, 512–531 (2019)
29. Malge, P., Nadaf, R.: Pcb defect detection, classification and localization using mathematical morphology and image processing tools. Intern. J. Comput. Appli. **87**(9) (2014)
30. Redmon, J., Divvala, S., Girshick, R., Farhadi, A.: You only look once: unified, real-time object detection. In: Proceedings of the IEEE Conference on Computer Vision and Pattern Recognition, pp. 779–788 (2016)
31. Redmon, J., Farhadi, A.: YOLO9000: better, faster, stronger. In: Proceedings of the IEEE Conference on Computer Vision and Pattern Recognition, pp. 7263–7271 (2017)
32. Redmon, J., Farhadi, A.: Yolov3: An incremental improvement. arXiv preprint arXiv:1804.02767 (2018)
33. Ren, S., He, K., Girshick, R., Sun, J.: Faster R-CNN: towards real-time object detection with region proposal networks. Adv. Neural Inform. Process. Syst. **28** (2015)
34. Rublee, E., Rabaud, V., Konolige, K., Bradski, G.: ORB: an efficient alternative to SIFT or SURF. In: 2011 International Conference on Computer Vision, pp. 2564–2571. IEEE (2011)
35. Song, Y., Ma, B., Gao, W., Fan, S.: Medical image edge detection based on improved differential evolution algorithm and Prewitt operator. Acta Microscopica **28**(1) (2019)

36. Sun, J., Shen, Z., Wang, Y., Bao, H., Zhou, X.: Loftr: detector-free local feature matching with transformers. In: Proceedings of the IEEE/CVF Conference on Computer Vision and Pattern Recognition, pp. 8922–8931 (2021)
37. Zhai, Y., Shah, M.: Visual attention detection in video sequences using spatiotemporal cues. In: Proceedings of the 14th ACM International Conference on Multimedia, pp. 815–824 (2006)
38. Zhang, C., Chang, C.c., Jamshidi, M.: Concrete bridge surface damage detection using a single-stage detector. Comput.-Aided Civil Infrastructure Eng. **35**(4), 389–409 (2020)
39. Zhang, J., Sclaroff, S.: Saliency detection: a boolean map approach. In: Proceedings of the IEEE International Conference on Computer Vision, pp. 153–160 (2013)
40. Zhang, J., et al.: Content-aware unsupervised deep homography estimation. In: Vedaldi, A., Bischof, H., Brox, T., Frahm, J.-M. (eds.) ECCV 2020. LNCS, vol. 12346, pp. 653–669. Springer, Cham (2020). https://doi.org/10.1007/978-3-030-58452-8_38

A Multimodal Registration and Fusion Diagnostic System Based on Multi-scale Feature

Hongyi Jing[1], Jiannan Liu[2,3(✉)], Jing Han[2,3], and Guangtao Zhai[1]

[1] Institute of Image Communication and Network Engineering, Shanghai Jiao Tong University, Shanghai, China
[2] Department of Oral and Maxillofacial Head and Neck Oncology, Shanghai Ninth People's Hospital, Shanghai Jiao Tong University School of Medicine, Shanghai, China
laurence_ljn@163.com
[3] National Center for Stomatology, National Clinical Research Center for Oral Diseases, Shanghai Key Laboratory of Stomatology, College of Stomatology, Shanghai Jiao Tong University, Shanghai, China

Abstract. The rapid growth in manufacturing and multimodal medical imaging industries, driven by evolving user needs, has led to an increasing demand for advanced digital medical imaging technology and corresponding diagnostic analysis systems. Designing human-centered algorithm systems, including digital consultation, intelligent medical care, and medical imaging for disease diagnosis and treatment tracking, becomes imperative. Given the variations in acquisition equipment and imaging technologies across different modal medical images, disparities in initial pose and spatial characteristics arise. To address this, a multimodal medical image registration algorithm is employed to harmonize data coordinates into a unified spatial coordinate system. This paper proposes a feature analysis and key point extraction network based on deep learning. Methods such as matrix decomposition and unsupervised iterative registration are utilized to achieve precise multimodal medical image registration. Leveraging this registration framework, the study focuses on analyzing latent mandibular deviation as a target disease. Features from diverse modal medical images are extracted and fused through a multi-level feature structure network, facilitating disease classification diagnosis and subsequent parameter analysis.

Keywords: Medical Imaging · Multimodal Registration · Fusion Diagnosis

1 Introduction

In clinical diagnosis, certain diseases cannot be efficiently and accurately diagnosed using single-modality medical imaging data. Additionally, the repetitive examination of medical images across different modalities by doctors may reduce diagnostic and doctor-patient communication efficiency. Multimodal medical images are acquired using diverse equipment and imaging methods, leading to significant variations in spatial coordinate systems and scales due to differing subject postures and states during collection.

© The Author(s), under exclusive license to Springer Nature Singapore Pte Ltd. 2024
G. Zhai et al. (Eds.): IFTC 2023, CCIS 2067, pp. 353–368, 2024.
https://doi.org/10.1007/978-981-97-3626-3_26

Utilizing efficient and accurate automated point cloud registration algorithms becomes essential to align medical digital human data from various modalities into a common reference system. In addressing the three-dimensional medical digital human point cloud registration problem, our focus lies on non-rigid body motion registration [1], defined as follows: Given two-point clouds, the objective of point cloud registration is to determine a non-rigid body motion transformation relationship encompassing scale, rotation, and translation transformations.

After accomplishing multimodal medical image registration and point cloud feature extraction, the deep learning multimodal medical image diagnosis system requires the fusion of features derived from diverse medical image modalities. The creation of an intelligent three-dimensional multimodal medical digital human system facilitates efficient and convenient patient data collection, streamlining processes. Within this system, an integrated background deep learning network and model registration algorithm enable the presentation of diagnostic and treatment analysis through mobile applications, aiding both doctors and patients. Notably, the system boasts high compatibility and portability, allowing seamless integration with existing databases and various access points. This feature enables doctors and patients to access retrospective disease analyses and dynamic disease tracking. Given the disordered nature of point clouds, relative coordinates and offset attention mechanisms are incorporated in the point cloud input embedding stage to better capture local and global features [2]. To optimize the self-attention mechanism for handling large-scale point cloud data, adjacent point sets and sliding window operations are utilized to improve calculation efficiency. Building upon the multimodal medical image registration, the extracted features from the feature extraction network are fused, incorporating a cross-attention mechanism. Subsequently, the network addresses classification problems and conducts parameter analysis for disease diagnosis.

In this paper, we proposed a three-dimensional multimodal medical image registration and fusion diagnosis algorithm. The algorithm begins with embedding the initial point cloud data, followed by employing downsampling and a multi-scale feature extraction network to identify manually labeled key feature points with anatomical significance. The rigid transformation matrix in the coarse registration stage is then calculated using the learned key feature points and matrix decomposition method. To prioritize the facial area in the registration process, facial segmentation is conducted through point cloud segmentation [38]. An unsupervised iterative nearest point algorithm is applied to the facial area, with the addition of a threshold limit in the iterative process to prevent the iterative closest point algorithm from converging to a local optimal solution.

In general, we propose a novel three-dimensional multimodal medical image registration algorithm that can extract facial key points while achieving automated and precise registration, and on this basis, achieving multimodal fusion to complete disease diagnostic classification and disease parameter analysis in clinical practice.

2 Related Work

2.1 Multimodal Registration and Fusion

In the realm of three-dimensional medical imaging data, this paper focuses on using features such as coordinates and normal vectors of point clouds for characterization, excluding features like connecting edges and surfaces. This selective approach enhances algorithm efficiency and reduces the computational cost associated with maintaining edges and surfaces during the downsampling process [3, 4, 37]. The primary objective of three-dimensional point cloud registration is to determine a rigid transformation involving spatial position rotation and translation without altering the inherent shape of the point cloud. Currently, three-dimensional registration between target and source point clouds is a crucial aspect of computer science. The iterative calculation process for three-dimensional point cloud registration typically progresses from coarse to fine [5]. Previous research categorized three-dimensional point cloud registration methods into traditional geometry-based approaches, including the Fast Global Registration (FGR) [6] and Iterative Closest Point (ICP) [7] algorithms, and deep learning-based methods, such as the Deep Closest Point (DCP) [8] algorithm. Traditional geometric methods often rely on the initial pose and shape similarity of point clouds for registration, potentially converging to local optimal values. Multimodal medical image fusion technology involves spatial, informational, and semantic fusion of diverse three-dimensional medical imaging data [29], including computed tomography (CT), magnetic resonance imaging (MRI), and facial scans (FS). These emerging technologies contribute to enhancing the clinical usability and adaptability of medical imaging.

2.2 Medical Imaging Diagnostic Analysis

Leveraging computers for disease diagnosis and predictive analysis has emerged as a prominent trend in recent years within the medical domain. The original dataset contains crucial attributes and characteristics that can be automatically captured by computers. Through this process, the system learns implicit rules and high-order semantic information, facilitating the classification, symptom identification, and prediction of diseases [9, 10]. Artificial intelligence employs various techniques to process input data, including extracting common features and personalized differences from extensive datasets. Additionally, it filters significant features and excludes unimportant ones, considering that redundant or irrelevant characteristics may adversely affect the results. The essence of artificial intelligence lies in selecting the most valuable feature combinations from a plethora of features, eliminating redundant information, and thereby reducing feature dimensionality. This approach accelerates model fitting and enhances the model's generalization ability. When employing artificial intelligence for analysis, it is essential to consider medical images of different modalities. Subsequently, these images are processed based on their specific characteristics to extract both basic and high-order features.

2.3   Optimized Attention Mechanism

The self-attention mechanism [11] is a method of adaptive selection and combination of features, which is implemented through three different matrices: query matrix, key matrix, and value matrix. Since the computational time complexity of the self-attention mechanism is $O(N^2)$, where N is the sequence length, it is a huge overhead for large-scale point cloud data. In this regard, we propose an attention mechanism based on neighboring point sets and sliding windows, which limits feature interaction within the sliding window and reduces the time complexity to O(NM), where M is the length of the sliding window [12, 13]. At the same time, to improve performance, the idea of Laplace transform is used to implement the offset attention mechanism [14], that is, after subtracting the attention feature from the input feature, it undergoes a convolution operation and is added to the input feature.

3   Proposed Method

In the feature analysis and key point extraction network, three-dimensional multimodal medical imaging data undergoes a stepwise downsampling and feature aggregation process to extract local and global features. During the input embedding stage, data encoding occurs through the calculation of adjacent point sets and relative position coordinates [15], addressing the disorder issue inherent in point clouds. Subsequently, a self-attention mechanism based on sliding windows is applied, where the attention matrix is computed solely for each center point and its corresponding neighboring point set. This approach reduces computational complexity, making it adaptable to larger point cloud datasets. Following the features extracted by the sliding window self-attention mechanism, the offset attention mechanism based on Laplace transform is employed for multi-layer processing, ultimately outputting the final extracted features at this scale. The same processing method is applied for feature extraction in the downsampled multi-scale data. The resulting multi-scale features are concatenated, enabling the implementation of various tasks subsequently.

3.1   Input Embedding Module

The embedding module for 3D point cloud data undertakes the processing and transformation of input features to encode information into a high-dimensional feature space. This high-dimensional space is characterized by rich high-order semantics, serving as the foundation for subsequent feature extraction. The initial point cloud input features encompass coordinate information and normal vectors. The point cloud undergoes processing in the embedding module, commencing with a convolutional layer that maintains the size of the feature map, thereby obtaining high-order semantic features. For each center point in the resulting high-order semantic features, M neighboring points are calculated through either nearest point sampling or random sampling [16, 17]. This involves subtracting the central point feature from all neighboring point features to derive relative feature information. Ultimately, the original high-order semantic features and the relative feature information are concatenated, and self-attention mechanism features based on sliding windows are computed to form the final input embedding feature (Fig. 1).

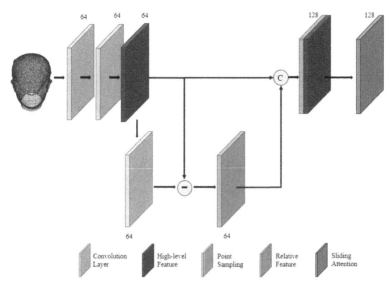

Fig. 1. The computing structure and process of the point cloud input embedding module, which realizes the encoding of point cloud information from original coordinates and normal vectors to high-dimensional feature space.

3.2 Attention Mechanism Based on Sliding Window

In the self-attention mechanism module, the primary factor influencing computational efficiency is the interaction between the characteristics of each point and those of all other points within the point cloud. Points in point cloud data exhibit significant spatial relationships with nearby points, while their correlation with distant points is minimal [18]. The optimization goal is to minimize the necessity for each point to interact with all points in the same point cloud, emphasizing interaction with nearby points that share more spatial relationships. Given the disordered nature of point cloud data, direct utilization of block matrices to simulate the feature interaction of neighboring points is unfeasible. Instead, the process involves identifying the neighboring point set for each point and subsequently calculating the self-attention mechanism. The generation of the neighboring point set can be achieved through fixed sphere radius sampling, where a sphere radius distance r is set, and all points within this space serve as candidate neighboring point sets. To control computational complexity, screening is applied to points within the radius of the sphere, limiting the final size of the neighboring point set. When the number of final neighboring point set points is M, the time complexity of the self-attention mechanism can be compressed to $O(NM)$, which has a linearly increasing relationship with the number of points, greatly optimizing the calculation efficiency, and for each point in the point cloud, it is processed in the form of a sliding window. When interacting with features from a neighboring point set, you can select the closest M points by default, or you can randomly sample M points from the neighboring point set for calculation. After the self-attention mechanism based on the sliding window is multiplied by the query matrix Q and the key matrix K, the feature interaction graph is no longer the original full N*N special graph, but an interactive feature graph with only neighboring points (Fig. 2).

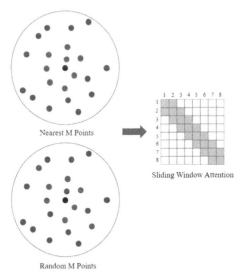

Nearest M Points

Sliding Window Attention

Random M Points

Fig. 2. Schematic diagram of self-attention mechanism sampling and feature map based on sliding window and neighboring point set. This method can reduce the computational complexity of the network and adapt to the disorder problem of point clouds.

3.3 Offset Attention Mechanism

In the graph convolutional neural network, researchers use the Laplacian matrix to process the network. The main form is $L = D-E$, using D-E to replace the adjacency matrix E [19, 31, 32]. You can learn from this idea and apply it to the Transformer network. By subtracting the original input feature matrix from the feature matrix output by the self-attention mechanism, you can learn the different information implicit in it. Then the difference between the two is convolved, and the residual is processed similarly. The features after the convolution are added to the original input features to obtain the final output features, thus enhancing the attention mechanism. Richer semantic information can be learned. The offset attention mechanism refers to the output of the original input feature minus the self-attention mechanism, and this difference information is used for convolution processing. The calculation formula of the offset attention mechanism is as follows:

$$F_{out} = Conv(F_{in} - F_{sa}) + F_{in} \tag{1}$$

Among them, F_{in} is the input feature, F_{sa} is the output feature of the self-attention mechanism, $Conv$ refers to the convolution operation (including pooling and activation function), and $F_{in} - F_{sa}$ is similar to the Laplacian matrix. Replacing the original self-attention mechanism with the offset attention mechanism in the point cloud quality evaluation network will also improve the performance of the network to a certain extent.

$$
\begin{aligned}
\boldsymbol{F}_{in} - \boldsymbol{F}_{sa} &= \boldsymbol{F}_{in} - \boldsymbol{A}\boldsymbol{V} \\
&= \boldsymbol{F}_{in} - \boldsymbol{A}\boldsymbol{F}_{in}\boldsymbol{W}_{V} \\
&= \boldsymbol{F}_{in} - \boldsymbol{A}\boldsymbol{W}_{v}\boldsymbol{F}_{in} \\
&= (\boldsymbol{I} - \boldsymbol{A}\boldsymbol{W}_{v})\boldsymbol{F}_{in}
\end{aligned}
\tag{2}
$$

Among them, $\boldsymbol{A}$ is the Attention matrix, $\boldsymbol{W}_{V}$ is the linear transformation matrix of the input feature, and $\boldsymbol{V}$ is the value matrix in the self-attention mechanism. Because $\boldsymbol{W}_{V}$ is a linear transformation of the input feature, it can be ignored and the previous $\boldsymbol{A}$ matrix can be multiplied by an equivalent transformation matrix $\boldsymbol{W}_{v}$. Finally, after simplification, it can be seen that the offset attention mechanism operates similarly to the Laplace transform on the input features, which can extract richer information.

3.4 Multi-scale Feature Extraction Network

This paper focuses on seven manually marked key feature points: the left and right corners of the eyes, the center of the eyebrows, the base of the columella, the chin, and the left and right ear tragus. The objective is for the network, utilizing multi-scale features, to learn the corresponding coordinates of these key points for a given input point cloud sample. The optimization is guided by the following loss function:

$$
loss = \sum_{i=1}^{K} \sum_{j=1}^{D} (y_{i,j} - \hat{y}_{i,j})^2
\tag{3}
$$

where K is the number of key feature points (here is 7); D is the dimension of key point coordinates (here is 3); $\hat{y}_{i,j}$ is the coordinate of the actual label; $y_{i,j}$ is the coordinate of the predicted point cloud.

The structure of the key feature point learning network is shown in Fig. 3. The leftmost side illustrates the progressive downsampling of the original point cloud using a dynamic method, where the retained center point undergoes recalculations at each step. Subsequently, the encoded features are fed into a multi-layer stacked offset attention layer for further feature extraction. The multi-layer stacked offset attention layer, with its larger receptive field, alleviates concerns about solely considering local neighboring points during attention calculation with sliding windows. Consequently, this facilitates the extraction of local features across a spectrum from a small to a larger range of global features [33, 34]. Following the pooling process, the extracted multi-scale features are concatenated. The linear mapping layer then maps these multi-scale features to the coordinate dimensions of key feature points, specifically the number of key points multiplied by the coordinate dimension of a single key point (7 * 3).

3.5 Multimodal Registration and Fusion

Coarse Registration. After utilizing the 3D point cloud key feature point extraction network to learn and extract key points from both 3D CT data and 3D facial scan data, a preliminary coarse registration rigid transformation matrix (encompassing only

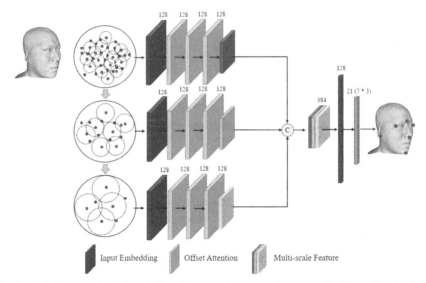

Fig. 3. Architecture of multi-scale key feature points extraction network. The point cloud data of different scales are concatenated with features obtained through input embedding, multi-layer offset attention, and pooling operation, and mapped into coordinates through fully connected layers.

rotation and translation, with no alteration to shape) can be computed using two sets of key feature points. The preliminary rigid transformation matrix is obtained through Singular Value Decomposition (SVD) in matrix decomposition [20]. The formula for rigid transformation is as follows:

$$(\boldsymbol{R}, \boldsymbol{t}) = \begin{matrix} argmin \\ \boldsymbol{R}, \boldsymbol{t} \end{matrix} \sum_{i=1}^{n} w_i ||(\boldsymbol{R}p_i + \boldsymbol{t} + \boldsymbol{N_i}) - q_i||^2 \tag{4}$$

The rotation matrix in the rigid transformation is $\boldsymbol{R}$, and the translation matrix is $\boldsymbol{t}$, and the above formula is optimized using the least squares method. Among them, w_i ($w_i > 0$) is the weight parameter for each point pair, $\boldsymbol{N_i}$ is the noise parameter. After calculating the initial rigid transformation through SVD, the initial pose of the source point cloud can be adjusted appropriately to ensure that the subsequent fine registration algorithm has a good initial state to a certain extent, to prevent the results from entering the local optimal solution too early.

Fine Registration. After the coarse registration stage of point cloud registration, certain discrepancies were identified in the alignment of 3D CT data and 3D facial scan data in the 3D space, particularly in the facial area, where a noticeable deviation was observed. The fine of the registration in the brain part is comparatively high [36]. This discrepancy arises from variations in 3D medical imaging techniques and reconstruction methods across different modalities, resulting in non-identical spatial distributions among different point clouds [21, 22, 35]. 3D facial scan data primarily focuses on surface skin information, whereas CT data includes internal bone tissue information. Consequently, numerous areas in the facial region are absent in the facial scan data but present in 3D CT data. Following the coarse registration stage, it becomes imperative to design a precise registration stage aligned with three-dimensional multimodal medical image data. The fine registration stage in this paper is divided into two main components. The first part involves using point cloud segmentation to filter out crucial areas for registering 3D CT data and 3D facial scan data. Facial region segmentation can be achieved by leveraging previously learned key feature points, directly through the plane formed by the left and right eye corners and chin points. The second part entails applying the unsupervised Iterative Closest Point (ICP) algorithm to these identified areas. This algorithm, a renowned method in the field of 3D point cloud registration, focuses on finding a suitable initial value and approximate transformation matrix between the target point cloud and the source point cloud. The goal is to prevent the registration process from becoming ensnared in local optimal solutions, as follows:

$$E(\boldsymbol{R}, t) = \frac{1}{n} \sum_{i=1}^{n} ||m_i - (\boldsymbol{R}s_i + t)||^2 \tag{5}$$

Among them, $\boldsymbol{R}$ and t are the rotation matrix and translation matrix in the rigid transformation, respectively, and the convergence condition is $||m_i - (\boldsymbol{R}s_i + t)||^2 < \tau$, where τ is the threshold for terminating iterations.

In practical applications, fully circumventing data complexity proves challenging. To address this issue, this paper proposes an ICP algorithm featuring a threshold sphere radius metric. The threshold sphere radius signifies point pairs between the source and target point clouds that need not consider all candidate points throughout the ICP algorithm iteration process. Instead, a sphere radius size is established, and only points within this sphere radius are regarded as candidate points. Initially, in the early stages of iteration, a relatively large threshold sphere radius is set to encourage the algorithm to consider more candidate points, mitigating the risk of entering local optima. In the later stages of iteration, a smaller threshold sphere radius is employed to diminish the impact of noise points on registration results and prevent non-convergence. It mirrors the initial use of a higher learning rate to expedite convergence while minimizing the risk of the model becoming trapped in local optima. Through continual learning, the learning rate decreases, lessening the influence of noise, preventing model oscillations, and facilitating quicker model convergence.

Fusion Diagnosis. In this paper, latent mandibular deviation is the target disease of analysis, chosen due to the inadequacy of diagnosing it solely through facial contour examination. Combining 3D CT and 3D facial scan data is essential to understanding the distribution patterns of key areas. Latent mandibular deviation exhibits a relatively high incidence rate, approximately 35%, in the general population. This condition may lead to condylar absorption in certain cases, resulting in potential mandibular deviation [23]. Due to factors such as gravity and soft tissue compensation, latent mandibular deviation may occur to some extent, making swift analysis and diagnosis challenging based solely on the external contour of the face. This paper focuses on the accurate diagnosis of latent mandibular deviation, employing 3D CT and 3D facial scan data from the same subject. The methodology includes multimodal registration, deep feature information extraction, feature fusion, and the final downstream task output structure. Utilizing a multi-scale feature extraction network for each modality of medical images, the output features undergo cross-attention mechanism application for feature fusion [30]. These cross features are further processed through a fully connected layer, yielding the final classification result for disease diagnosis (Fig. 4).

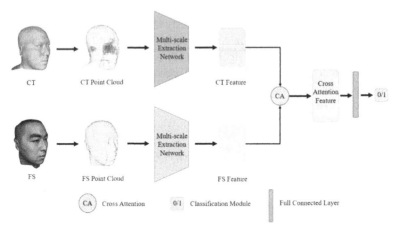

Fig. 4. The process of multimodal medical image fusion diagnosis algorithm, taking latent mandibular deviation as an example. Among them, the cross-attention mechanism is used to interact features of different modalities, and ultimately output the classification results of diseases through the fully connected layer.

4 Experiments

4.1 Datasets Description

This paper used 3D CT and facial scan data from 116 subjects during the multimodal medical image registration stage and manually marked 7 key facial feature points. Meanwhile, because deep learning methods rely on sufficient data, we perform data augmentation operation on the original dataset, randomly rotating each data sample in three-dimensional space (ensuring that each rotation dimension does not exceed 10°), which can also simulate slight perturbations during data collection to some extent. In the subsequent multimodal fusion diagnosis stage of latent mandibular deviation, this paper used 3D CT and facial scan from a population of 120 patients diagnosed with latent mandibular deviation through MRI+X-ray measurement (including 20 males and 100 females) and 95 normal individuals (including 17 males and 78 females).

4.2 Experiment Details

In the stage of completing coarse registration, an important prerequisite is the learning accuracy and error of key feature points in the deep feature network, which will have a significant impact on the final registration result [24]. Therefore, accuracy and error analysis are essential when predicting key feature points. In this paper, the multimodal medical image dataset contains annotations of actual key feature points. In the evaluation set, corresponding indicators will be used to evaluate the accuracy of the key feature points extracted by the deep feature network. When training the key feature point extraction network, two different mean square loss functions with different physical meanings were used for optimization [25]. Assuming that the target point cloud data for training is $\{p_i\}$ and the actual label is $\{p_i^g\}$, define the error E_c based on coordinate fitting separately (Eq. 6) and error E_v based on vector distance (Eq. 7).

$$E_c = \frac{1}{3n} \sum_{i=1}^{n} [\left(p_{i,x} - p_{i,x}^g\right)^2 + \left(p_{i,y} - p_{i,y}^g\right)^2 + (p_{i,z} - p_{i,z}^g)^2] \tag{6}$$

where n is the number of key feature points and the error E_c based on coordinate fitting aims to ensure that the coordinate difference of each point is as small as possible during the actual training process of the network.

$$E_v = \frac{1}{n} \sum_{i=1}^{n} ||p_i - p_i^g||^2 \tag{7}$$

where n is the number of key feature points and the error E_v based on vector distance enables the network to optimize the norm error of vector distance between corresponding feature points during actual training, which has strong practical physical significance (corresponding to the actual distance between points in three-dimensional space).

4.3 Error Analysis of Key Feature Points

After network optimization, we evaluated the coordinate error during the evaluation of the dataset and calculated the error E_c and E_v using mean square error (MSE), root mean square error (RMSE), and mean absolute error (MAE). Simultaneously we calculated the distance metric absolute distance error (ADE) for conversion into actual physical space. The performance of different key point extraction networks on this task is shown in Table 1, which shows that the fitting between the key feature points extracted by the deep key feature point learning network and the actual marked points has achieved good results in our work, and the final actual physical distance error is about 1mm, laying a good foundation for coarse registration and subsequent fine registration stage.

4.4 Multimodal Registration Results

After coarse registration is achieved through two sets of key points in different modalities, the iterative closest point algorithm with threshold constraints is used to achieve the fine registration stage. The comparison results between our method and other multimodal point cloud registration algorithms are shown in Table 2, indicating that our registration method achieves the most accurate registration. In this paper, the experiment on ball radius threshold will simulate a two-stage threshold optimization task. In the first stage, a larger threshold will be used, and in the second stage, a smaller threshold will be used. Different threshold combinations also have different effects on the fine registration results. The specific combinations and registration results are shown in Table 3.

Table 1. Evaluation error results of key feature points extraction.

Net	Data	MSE (E_v)	RMSE (E_v)	MAE (E_v)	ADE (mm)
PointNet++ [26]	FS	5.88330	2.42555	2.37782	1.43654
	CT	7.27898	2.69796	3.46187	2.06065
DGCNN [27]	FS	4.37856	2.09250	2.21485	1.23548
	CT	6.46982	2.54358	2.59841	1.78196
Ours	FS	1.4558	1.2065	1.6075	0.95003
	CT	1.9504	1.3966	1.8286	1.07202

Table 2. Comparison results of different multimodal registration algorithms.

Algorithm	MSE (E_v)	RMSE (E_v)	MAE (E_v)	ADE (mm)
ICP [7]	789.1690	28.0921	33.6459	22.0074
FGR [6]	41.9700	6.4784	9.1486	5.5486
GO-ICP [28]	66.9152	8.1802	9.9890	6.3821
DCP [8]	707.4873	26.5986	32.9791	22.9257
Ours	3.7317	1.9318	2.6644	1.7435

Table 3. Analysis results of threshold in fine registration (ADE, mm).

T1	T2				
	3	4	5	6	7
6	1.92051	1.95841	1.85847	7.95906	1.98415
8	1.82242	1.80464	1.87868	1.86414	1.81797
10	1.81534	1.84143	1.74350	1.88924	1.86530
12	1.88938	1.89107	1.85951	1.86659	1.87584
14	1.93638	1.96127	1.81008	1.95906	2.28741

4.5 Multimodal Fusion Diagnostic Results

For latent mandibular deviation studied in this paper, classification tests were conducted on the dataset using features fused from multimodal medical images, optimized through fully connected layers and binary cross entropy loss functions. The accuracy and AUC index were calculated separately, and the results are shown in Fig. 5. In the process of deep learning iteration, the accuracy rate of 93.6% and the AUC index of 0.974 were finally achieved.

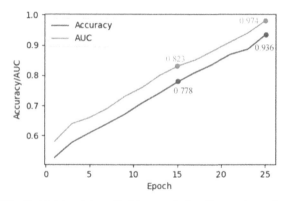

Fig. 5. Multimodal medical images fusion diagnostic results.

4.6 Ablation Study

In the entire registration process, from extracting key point features to coarse registration based on SVD, from facial region segmentation to ICP algorithm based on sphere radius threshold, to verify the optimization effect of each module on the registration of final 3D CT data and 3D facial scan data, ablation experiments were also conducted in the experiment. The results of ablation study are shown in Table 4. It can be seen that coarse registration plays a significant role in adjusting the initial pose, while fine registration of each module also improves the accuracy of the fitting to a certain extent.

Table 4. Results of ablation study on different modules during registration stage.

Strategy	MSE (E_v)	RMSE (E_v)	MAE (E_v)	ADE (mm)
All Modules	3.73169	1.93176	2.66435	1.74350
No SVD	9322.24501	96.55177	97.81120	73.21440
No Segmentation	122.29602	11.05875	13.93787	9.82270
No Threshold	797.78485	28.24509	34.29595	22.17590
No Threshold T1	4.13754	2.03409	2.74864	1.81500
No Threshold T2	9.28368	3.04671	4.32248	2.72348

Another aspect of the ablation study is to analyze the key feature points on the face and to analyze the final registration effect by randomly removing one point from the set of key points. The results are shown in Table 5, which proves that the corresponding full process coarse registration and fine registration algorithms in this paper have high robustness and can adapt to the noise or even loss of certain feature points, as well as the accuracy degradation caused by deep key feature point extraction.

Table 5. Analysis results of key feature point reduction ablation study.

Used Points	MSE(E_v)	RMSE(E_v)	MAE(E_v)	ADE(mm)
All points	3.73169	1.93176	2.66435	1.74350
No right lateral canthus	3.92550	1.98129	2.69748	1.77870
No left lateral canthus	3.76744	1.94099	2.72674	1.74605
No eyebrow center	3.68451	1.91951	2.64563	1.72700
No nasal columella base	3.89423	1.97338	2.77873	1.76168
No mention	4.21674	2.05347	2.81592	1.81840
No right tragus	3.93975	1.98488	2.79246	1.79996
No left tragus	4.33495	2.08205	2.88627	1.87024

5　Conclusion

This paper proposes a 3D point cloud key point extraction network, incorporating multi-scale features and optimizing the self-attention mechanism to accommodate large-scale point cloud data, ultimately achieving precise key point extraction. Building upon this foundation, the paper attains accurate registration of three-dimensional multimodal medical images using coarse and fine registration methods. The fused features from different modalities contribute to clinical disease diagnosis and analysis.

References

1. Chui, H., Rangarajan, A.: A new point matching algorithm for non-rigid registration. Comput. Vis. Image Underst. **89**(2–3), 114–141 (2003)
2. Guo, M.H., Cai, J.X., Liu, Z.N., et al.: PCT: point cloud transformer. Comp. Visual Media **7**, 187–199 (2021). https://doi.org/10.1007/s41095-021-0229-5
3. Zhao, H., Jiang, L., Fu, C.-W., Jia, J.: Proceedings of the IEEE/CVF Conference on Computer Vision and Pattern Recognition (CVPR), pp. 5565–5573 (2019)
4. Liu, Y., Fan, B., Meng, G., Lu, J., Xiang, S., Pan, C.: Proceedings of the IEEE/CVF International Conference on Computer Vision (ICCV), pp. 5239–5248 (2019)
5. Huang, X., Mei, G., Zhang, J., et al.: A comprehensive survey on point cloud registration. arXiv preprint arXiv:2103.02690 (2021)
6. Zhou, Q.-Y., Park, J., Koltun, V.: Fast global registration. In: Leibe, B., Matas, J., Sebe, N., Welling, M. (eds.) ECCV 2016, Part II. LNCS, vol. 9906, pp. 766–782. Springer, Cham (2016). https://doi.org/10.1007/978-3-319-46475-6_47
7. Chetverikov, D., et al.: The trimmed iterative closest point algorithm. In: 2002 International Conference on Pattern Recognition, vol. 3. IEEE (2002)
8. Wang, Y., Solomon, J.M.: Deep closest point: learning representations for point cloud registration. In: Proceedings of the IEEE/CVF International Conference on Computer Vision (2019)
9. Rana, M., Bhushan, M.: Machine learning and deep learning approach for medical image analysis: diagnosis to detection. Multimedia Tools Appl. **82**(17), 26731–26769 (2023)
10. Anwar, S.M., et al.: Medical image analysis using convolutional neural networks: a review. J. Med. Syst. **42**, 1–13 (2018)

11. Vaswani, A., et al.: Attention is all you need. Adv. Neural Inf. Process. Syst. **30** (2017)
12. Beltagy, I., Peters, M.E., Cohan, A.: Longformer: the long-document transformer. arXiv preprint arXiv:2004.05150 (2020)
13. Zhang, P., et al.: Multi-scale vision longformer: a new vision transformer for high-resolution image encoding. In: Proceedings of the IEEE/CVF International Conference on Computer Vision (2021)
14. Bruna, J., Zaremba, W., Szlam, A., LeCun, Y.: Spectral networks and locally connected networks on graphs. In: Proceedings of the International Conference on Learning Representations (2014)
15. Su, J., et al.: Roformer: enhanced transformer with rotary position embedding. arXiv preprint arXiv:2104.09864 (2021)
16. Bhatia, N.: Survey of nearest neighbor techniques. arXiv:1007.0085 (2010)
17. Jones, P.W., Osipov, A., Rokhlin, V.: Randomized approximate nearest neighbors algorithm. Proc. Natl. Acad. Sci. **108**(38), 15679–15686 (2011)
18. Zhang, R., et al.: Nearest neighbors meet deep neural networks for point cloud analysis. In: Proceedings of the IEEE/CVF Winter Conference on Applications of Computer Vision
19. Weideman, J.A.C., Fornberg, B.: Fully numerical Laplace transform methods. Numer. Algorithms **92**(1), 985–1006 (2023)
20. Wu, J.: Rigid 3-D registration: a simple method free of SVD and eigendecomposition. IEEE Trans. Instrum. Meas. **69**(10), 8288–8303 (2020)
21. Wang, J., et al.: A review of deep learning on medical image analysis. Mobile Netw. Appl. **26**, 351–380 (2021)
22. Li, Y., et al.: Medical image fusion method by deep learning. Int. J. Cognit. Comput. Eng. **2**, 21–29 (2021)
23. Evangelista, K., et al.: Prevalence of mandibular asymmetry in different skeletal sagittal patterns: a systematic review. Angle Orthod. **92**(1), 118–126 (2022)
24. Huang, Z., et al.: PF-Net: point fractal network for 3d point cloud completion. In: Proceedings of the IEEE/CVF Conference on Computer Vision and Pattern Recognition (2020)
25. Shi, X., et al.: Geometry-based distance decomposition for monocular 3d object detection. In: Proceedings of the IEEE/CVF International Conference on Computer Vision (2021)
26. Qi, C.R., et al.: PointNet++: deep hierarchical feature learning on point sets in a metric space. Adv. Neural Inf. Process. Syst. **30** (2017)
27. Phan, A.V., et al.: DGCNN: a convolutional neural network over large-scale labeled graphs. Neural Netw. **108**, 533–543 (2018)
28. Yang, J., et al.: Go-ICP: a globally optimal solution to 3D ICP point-set registration. IEEE Trans. Pattern Anal. Mach. Intell. **38**(11), 2241–2254 (2015)
29. Tang, C., Zheng, X., Zhang, W., et al.: Unsupervised feature selection via multiple graph fusion and feature weight learning. Sci. China Inf. Sci. **66**(5), 1–17 (2023)
30. Cheng, G., Lai, P., Gao, D., et al.: Class attention network for image recognition. Sci. China Inf. Sci. **66**(3), 132105 (2023)
31. Ma, X., Li, Z., Song, G., et al.: Learning discrete adaptive receptive fields for graph convolutional networks. Sci. China Inf. Sci. **66**(12), 222101 (2023)
32. Yang, Z., Liang, N., Li, Z., et al.: A convergence algorithm for graph co-regularized transfer learning. Sci. China Inf. Sci. **66**(3), 132104 (2023)
33. Chen, J., Chen, Y., Li, W., et al.: Image co-segmentation based on pyramid features cross-correlation network. Sci. China Inf. Sci. **66**(1), 119101 (2023)
34. Yan, P., Tan, Y., Tai, Y.: Repeatable adaptive keypoint detection via self-supervised learning. Sci. China Inf. Sci. **65**(11), 212103 (2022)
35. Yang, B., Huang, Z., Li, Y., et al.: Hybrid3D: learning 3D hybrid features with point clouds and multi-view images for point cloud registration. Sci. China Inf. Sci. **66**(7), 172101 (2023)

36. Du, L., Wang, H., Zhang, J., et al.: Adaptive structured sparse multiview canonical correlation analysis for multimodal brain imaging association identification. Sci. China Inf. Sci. **66**(4), 142106 (2023)
37. Cheng, Y., Huang, Z., Quan, S., et al.: Sampling locally, hypothesis globally: accurate 3D point cloud registration with a RANSAC variant. Vis. Intell. **1**(1), 20 (2023)
38. Yuan, L., Liu, X., Yu, J., et al.: A full-set tooth segmentation model based on improved PointNet++. Vis. Intell. **1**(1), 21 (2023)

CCDaS: A Benchmark Dataset for Cartoon Character Detection in Application Scenarios

Zelu Qi, Da Pan, Tianyi Niu, Zefeng Ying, and Ping Shi[✉]

School of Information and Communication Engineering, Communication University of China, Beijing, China
{theonqi2001,shiping}@cuc.edu.cn

Abstract. Deep learning's achievements in computer vision have poised cartoon character detection (CCD) as a promising tool for intellectual property protection. However, due to the lack of suitable cartoon character datasets, CCD is still a less explored field and there are many issues need to be addressed to meet the demands of practical applications such as merchandise, advertising, and patent examination. In this paper, we introduce CCDaS, a comprehensive benchmark dataset comprising 55,608 images of 524 renowned cartoon characters from 227 works, including cartoons, games, and merchandise. To our knowledge, CCDaS is the most extensive CCD dataset tailored for real-world applications. Alongside, we also provide a CCD algorithm that can achieve accurate detection of animated images in complex practical application scenarios, called multi-path YOLO (MP-YOLO). Experimental results show that our MP-YOLO achieves better detection results on the CCDaS dataset. Comparative and ablation studies further validate the effectiveness of our CCD dataset and algorithm.

Keywords: Cartoon Character Detection · Image Annotation · Data Augmentation · Convolutional Neural Network · Vision Transformer

1 Introduction

Cartoon character detection is pivotal in the animation industry, which is frequently targeted by copyright infringement. Unauthorized use of cartoon characters on products enables illegal merchants to reap significant profits, egregiously violating copyright laws. Prioritizing intellectual property protection, deploying cartoon character detection algorithms is essential for mitigating infringements and bolstering digital era protections.

Recent studies in cartoon character detection leveraging deep learning have shown significant promise, aided by extensive datasets like Fahad18 [1], ToonNet [2], Manga109 [3] and iCartoonFace [4]. However, challenges persist due to simplistic character styles and limited types of annotations. Specifically, the iCartoonFace dataset, the largest for cartoon face recognition, focuses primarily

G. Zhai et al. (Eds.): IFTC 2023, CCIS 2067, pp. 369–381, 2024.
https://doi.org/10.1007/978-981-97-3626-3_27

on facial features through manual annotations, often overlooking critical aspects such as full-body characteristics. This limitation is evident when distinguishing characters with similar faces but different other features, like Son Goku and Son Gohan we show in Fig. 1. Additionally, real-world applications pose numerous difficulties, such as discolored and distorted cartoon characters. Creating a large-scale, well-annotated cartoon character dataset with diverse sample types is essential.

Another key point in cartoon character detection is to design a method that can effectively solve the complex challenges in real-life scenarios. Challenges include distinguishing between multiple characters with similar faces or dealing with characters of various scales in a single image, where reliance on local features may lead to incorrect or missed detection. Traditional models like Faster R-CNN [5] and YOLO [6] struggle with multi-scale and global feature extraction due to limited receptive fields. To overcome these limitations, we introduce an enhanced, precise approach: Multi-Path-YOLO (MP-YOLO). This method incorporates a multi-path structure into the standard YOLO framework to capture broader semantic information. Additionally, we propose a combined detection mechanism that merges face and body detection modules, enabling the integration of facial and bodily features for comprehensive detection in animated images.

To summarize, our main contributions are as follows:

- We independently collected and built our cartoon character dataset CCDaS for CCD in application scenarios. This dataset contains 524 categories of well-known cartoon characters with 55608 images in total.
- To bridge the style gap between our dataset and real-world commodity images, we enhanced our dataset using Unsupervised Data Augmentation techniques, specifically Style-Augmentation [7] and Cycle-GAN [8].
- We proposed a joint annotating solution by manually annotating both the faces and the whole-bodies of the cartoon characters to avoid confusion in detecting cartoon characters with similar facial features.
- We designed our MP-YOLO algorithm and Cooperate-Detection(Co-Detection) algorithm. Experiments on our CCDaS dataset indicate the effectiveness of our detection model. Moreover, we conduct comparisons with other state-of-the-art object detection algorithms like YOLOv6 [9] and YOLOv7 [10], etc.

The remainder of this article is organized as follows. Section 2 discusses related work. The design of our CCD dataset and our MP-YOLO algorithm is described in Sect. 3. Section 4 provides and discusses the results of our experiments. Section 5 presents the conclusions.

2   Related Work

2.1   Object Detection

Object detection, as the most challenging and fundamental research in computer vision, has been widely used in traffic monitoring, image retrieval, human-computer interaction, and automatic driving. Current CNN-based object detection algorithms can be divided into two main categories: CNN-based two-stage algorithms with higher detection accuracy represented by Faster R-CNN [5], Mask R-CNN [11], D2Det [12], and Sparse R-CNN [13]; CNN-based one-stage algorithms with faster running speed represented by YOLO [6], SSD [14], Mobiledets [15], and Tood [16].

For the past few years, Transformer [17] has been widely used as a structure to obtain global semantic information quickly and efficiently in the field of Natural Language Processing(NLP). In recent research, Vision Transformer has been gradually applied to the field of computer vision. ViT [18] first proposed the use of Transformer Encoders to obtain more global semantic information during the feature extraction process. Afterwards, image recognition models like Mobile-ViT [19], MPViT, Conformer [20] effectively combined CNN and Transformer to acquire better performance on extracting both local and global features. Similarly for object detection, Transformer-based models like DETR [21], MViT [22], DESTR [23], CurveFormer [24] also achieved impressive performance on the benchmark datasets.

2.2   Cartoon Character Detection

The performance of the object detection algorithm hinges on the dataset's quality. For Cartoon Character Detection (CCD), creating a comprehensive and accurately annotated dataset is crucial. Pioneering work by [25] introduced IIIT-CFW, the first large-scale cartoon character dataset containing 8928 annotated images of cartoon faces of 100 public figures to conduct their research about cartoon understanding. [26] developed Sequencity612, featuring 612 comic frames from the Sequencity library. [27] applied DNNs for manga face detection on Manga109, while [2] released ToonNet with 4000 images of 12 characters. [28] utilized IIIT-CFW to refine MTCNN for cartoon face recognition. The iCartoonFace dataset by [4], with 389678 images from 1302 works, emerged as the largest and most comprehensive cartoon dataset. Following this, studies using iCartoonFace [29–31] further advanced CCD. Most recently, [32] developed a fast detection CCD algorithm for 15 cartoon characters, leveraging clustering and cascaded SSD.

In conclusion, the development of computer vision and deep learning has significantly aided CCD. Yet, the application of CCD is complicated by the existence of multi-scale cartoon characters and the high facial resemblance among cartoon characters. This complexity is compounded by the fact that most existing studies concentrate solely on facial aspects, neglecting the crucial whole-body details vital for CCD. Table 1 reports the detailed statistics of the existing CCD datasets, the prevalent large-scale CCD datasets tend to feature images with a singular annotated object, indicating a gap in the richness of data sources. Hence, it's critical to develop a CCD dataset that not only focuses on the distinct features of cartoon characters but also incorporates both facial and whole-body information through a well-annotated, comprehensive dataset.

Table 1. Summary of some existing datasets related to cartoon character recognition and detection.

Dataset	Type	Images	Categories	Annotating Strategy	Objects	Source
Fahad18	Detection	586	18	Face only	Multiple	Screenshots
Sequencity612	Detection	612	--	--	Single	Caricature
Manga109	Detection	21142	--	Face only	Multiple	Caricature
ToonNet	Recognition	4000	12	--	Single	Search Engine(SE)
IIIT-CFW	Detection	8928	100	Face only	Single	SE
iCartoonFace	Detection	389678	5013	Face only	Single	SE & Screenshots
CCDaS	**Detection**	**55608**	**524**	**Face & Whole-body**	**Multiple**	**Multiple Sources**

3   Methodology

In this section, we first present our CCD dataset CCDaS, a large-scale and joint-annotated CCD dataset tailored for application scenarios. Based on CCDaS, we present MP-YOLO, which is designed to handle similar facial features and multi-scale animated images in application scenarios. Our detection model is trained via a collaborative detection approach using joint annotations from CCDaS. The details of our proposed method are discussed in the next section.

3.1   CCDaS: Benchmark CCD Dataset for Application Scenario

Collection of the Cartoon Character Samples. Table 1 reveals that many researchers built cartoon character datasets by extracting images from animations, comics, and artworks, leading to overly simplistic datasets. However, the diverse origins of images significantly complicate the creation of a CCD dataset tailored to application scenarios. To eliminate these biases, we gather images from a broad array of sources and platforms such as search engines (Google, Baidu), online shopping websites (Taobao, JD), and screenshots from animations, comics, and games. We compiled a list of 524 commonly recognized cartoon characters in practical applications and collected approximately 400 images for each character.

The initial samples of our dataset were crude and contained significant noise, leading to a substantial amount of irrelevant or duplicate data among the downloaded images. To this regard, we processed the initial data by manually filtering the useless samples. Meanwhile, we also retained sufficient images from commodities, posters, advertisements, etc., making our dataset more suitable for CCD tasks in application scenarios. To this end, CCDaS contains 55608 images, detailed statistics and distributions of our dataset are reported in Fig. 3.

Annotation of the Cartoon Character Dataset. Current cartoon character datasets mainly annotate facial features, limiting CCD to face recognition and struggling to distinguish characters with similar faces, such as George and Peggy from Peppa Pig and Sun Goku and Sun Gohan from Dragon Ball, share facial similarities but differ significantly in body features, such as costumes and

Fig. 1. Comparisons for different cartoon characters with similar faces. Compared by the faces and whole-bodies of these cartoon characters, we illustrate the necessity of our joint annotation scheme.

hairstyles. This issue is compounded when characters from different series by the same author share identical faces, making accurate character identification based on faces alone problematic in practical applications, as depicted in Fig. 1.

To address these problems, we introduce a joint annotation approach to tackle these issues, separately marking faces with red boxes and whole bodies with green boxes, as illustrated in Fig. 2. This method allows us to train two distinct CCD models using face and body annotations. Based on our joint annotating approach, the total number of annotations of our dataset exceeded 320,000, making it reliable for our training process.

Fig. 2. Illustration for the joint annotating strategy we designed for our CCD dataset CCDaS.

Augmentation of the Cartoon Character Dataset. In application scenarios, cartoon characters face appearance changes, necessitating a CCD dataset with varied character styles. Despite incorporating diverse images, challenges like deformation and discoloration, alongside the legal constraints on using black-and-white design drawings due to intellectual property rights, amplify CCD's complexity and demand for dataset quality.

To address these challenges, we employ Data Augmentation techniques beyond traditional methods like Mixup and Cutout, which only offer limited enhancements. Specifically, we integrate Style-Augmentation and Cycle-GAN to more accurately reflect the various appearances of cartoon characters in application scenarios, enriching the diversity of our dataset, as shown in Fig. 3.

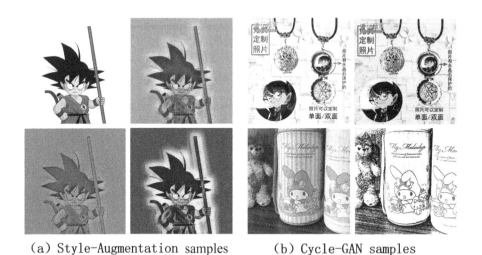

(a) Style-Augmentation samples   (b) Cycle-GAN samples

Fig. 3. Comparisons of the pictures before and after Using Style-Augmentation and Cycle-GAN.

Summary. Leveraging the methodology we proposed, we developed the CCDaS dataset, it contains 524 cartoon characters from 227 cartoon works, game works and product innovations from 13 different countries since 1895, with a total of 55,608 original images and 84,731 enhanced images. Unlike most cartoon character datasets that only collect cartoon characters from cartoons, our dataset also contains cartoon characters from other domains such as merchandise and games. Furthermore, CCDaS distinguishes itself by providing detailed annotations for both the heads and whole bodies of characters, ensuring exceptional annotation accuracy. This comprehensive approach not only broadens the dataset's utility but also enhances its applicability in diverse cartoon character detection scenarios.

3.2   Multi-Path-YOLO

Model Architecture. As we discussed in Sect. 2, CNN-based methods excel in local information extraction but often overlook global and multi-scale details. This leads to frequent false positives and missed detections, thereby reducing accuracy in cartoon character detection in practical applications.

To counter this, we developed MP-YOLO, which combines YOLO's detection capabilities with Vision Transformer, as shown in Fig. 4. MP-YOLO introduces a multi-scale structure and a Transformer encoder for enhanced global feature extraction. It leverages YOLOv5's Focus Layer for downsampling, integrating Transformer-Conv and YOLO Conv blocks for comprehensive feature extraction. We also introduce a novel collaborative detection strategy, fusing facial and body models with a confidence mechanism, notably boosts identification precision for characters with similar features.

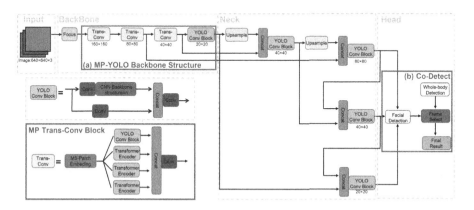

Fig. 4. Overview of our MP-YOLO algorithm: (a)The MP-YOLO backbone structure to improve our model's capability of detecting small-scale and dense cartoon character in application scenarios. (b)The Co-Detection structure to fuse both facial detection model and whole-body detection model for a better performance.

Transformer-Conv Block. Vision Transformers are known for their proficiency in global feature and long-range dependency capture, whereas CNNs, like YOLO, excel in local feature extraction but fall short on global scope due to limited receptive fields. To boost YOLO's global feature extraction capabilities, we merged Transformer Encoders with its CNN structure through a multi-path approach, as shown in Fig. 4(a). This method employs a multi-scale patch embedding(MS-PatchEmbeding) layer from MPViT, producing visual tokens in 3×3, 9×9, and 15×15 sizes for a 640×640 input. These tokens are then processed by respective Transformer Encoders, allowing for precise local feature extraction through the 3×3 patches and effective global feature handling and long-range dependencies capturing with 9×9 and 15×15 patches. Then, we concatenate the features of CNNs and Transformers so that we can obtain rich representations of global features and local features.

Cooperate-Detection. As shown in Fig. 1, cartoon characters with similar faces can be difficult to distinguish by facial features. We propose a solution

Algorithm 1. Co-Detection Algorithm.

Input: Test-set picture P_{in}, cartoon character facial-detecting model M_f, cartoon character whole-body-detecting model M_w.

Output: detected picture with detection frame P_{out}.

1:

2: **Initialize:** set the detection threshold as th, use the FD model M_f and the WD model M_w to detect the cartoon characters in P_{in}, the result of detection frames, categories and confidence is recorded as:

3:

4: $R_f = \{D_f, Cat_f, Conf_f\} = \{(d_{f1}, cat_{f1}, conf_{f1}), \cdots, (d_{fN_1}, cat_{fN_1}, conf_{fN_1})\}$

5:

6: $R_w = \{D_w, Cat_w, Conf_w\} = \{(d_{w1}, cat_{w1}, conf_{w1}), \cdots, (d_{wN_2}, cat_{wN_2}, conf_{wN_2})\}$

7:

8: Combining the result of the FD model and the WD model, the final detection result of detection frames, categories and confidence is renamed as:

9:

10: $R_o = \{D_o, Cat_o, Conf_o\} = \{(d_{o1}, cat_{o1}, conf_{o1}), \cdots, (d_{oN_3}, cat_{oN_3}, conf_{oN_3})\}$

11: **while** $i \in 1, 2, \cdots, N$ and $j \in 1, 2, \cdots, M$ **do**

12:    **if** $\frac{d_{fi} \cap d_{wj}}{d_{fi}} > th$ **then** $R_o = \begin{cases} (d_{fi}, cat_{fi}, conf_{fi}) conf_{fi} > conf_{wj} \\ (d_{wi}, cat_{wi}, conf_{fwi}) conf_{fi} < conf_w \end{cases}$

13:    **else** $R_o = (d_{fi}, cat_{fi}, conf fi)$

14:    **end if**

15: **end while**

16: **return** $P_{out} = P_{in} + R_o$

through a joint annotation approach and a Co-Detection strategy. As depicted in Fig. 2, we annotate both the faces and whole bodies of characters within our dataset. Consequently, we utilize these annotations to separately train a face detection model(FD-Model) and a whole-body detection model(WD-Model). As we show in Fig. 4(b), our Co-Detection structure fuses the detection results of the FD-Model and the WD-Model.

For each input image P_{in}, the FD-Model and WD-Model independently identify the faces and whole bodies of cartoon characters. The detection result of the FD-Model and the WD-Model is recorded as R_f and R_w. Subsequently, a Frame Select Module filters these results to retain only those with the highest confidence levels. Detailed process of our Co-Detection algorithm is illustrated in Algorithm 1.

4 Experiments

4.1 Experimental Setup

During our experiments, we divided CCDaS into three parts: 70% (38,925 original and 84,731 augmented images) for training, 20% (11,122 original images) for validation, and 10% (5,561 original images) for testing. We then created two specialized datasets, CCDaS-face and CCDaS-whole-body, based on our joint annotation process to train the FD-model and WD-model separately. For training, images were resized to 640×640, with a batch size of 32, 300 training iterations, a confidence threshold of 0.6, an initial learning rate of 0.01, and a momentum of 0.937. We employed YOLO's data augmentation techniques, including image translation, flipping, and mosaic, to enrich our training data. Experiments were performed on a system equipped with an Intel Xeon Silver 4114 CPU @ 2.2 GHz, 128G RAM, and an Nvidia Tesla V100-PCIE GPU with 32G video memory, under Ubuntu 18.04 OS.

4.2   Evaluation Metrics

Similarly to other researches about object detection, we characterized the performance of CCD algorithms using the commonly used metrics. Among these metrics, Frames Per Second(FPS) indicates the maximum number of images can be detected per second, for which a higher FPS represents a faster detection speed of the model. Average Precision(AP) is calculated under different Intersections over Union(IoU) ratios and predefined ground truth matching criteria to evaluate the precision rate of detecting small objects or large objects. While Average Recall(AR) is calculated under a maximum number of objects per frame and across scales. Specifically, the AP and AR metrics used in our experiments are described in the following:

- AP: Average Precision with IoUs from 0.50 to 0.95 with a step of 0.05
- AP_{50}: Average Precision with IoU at 0.50(loose metric)
- AP_{75}: Average Precision with IoU at 0.75(strict metric)
- AP_S: Average Precision for objects smaller than 32×32 pixels
- AP_M: Average Precision for objects between 32×32 pixels and 96×96 pixels
- AP_L: Average Precision for objects larger than 96×96 pixels
- AR_{100}: Average Recall for 100 detection results per image
- AR_S: Average Recall for objects smaller than 32×32 pixels
- AR_M: Average Recall for objects between 32×32 pixels and 96×96 pixels
- AR_L: Average Recall for objects larger than 96×96 pixels

4.3   Comparisons with State-of-the-Arts

We compared MP-YOLO against top YOLO variants like YOLOv5-S, YOLOX-S [33], YOLOv6-S, and YOLOv7-S, using our enhanced CCDaS dataset and Co-Detection approach, as shown in Table 2. Results indicate MP-YOLO outperforms YOLOv5-S and YOLOX-S in AP by 3.9%/3.1% and AP S by 1.7%/2.7%, respectively, with similar size and speed. Compared to YOLOv6-S/YOLOv7-S, MP-YOLO reduces parameters by over 107.1%/119.6% while improving AP by 1.1%. In general, we achieved a better CCD result on our CCDaS dataset with a smaller model scale using our proposed method.

Table 2. The comparison between our proposed method and the state-of-the-art real-time, lightweight object detectors.

Model	Params	FPS	AP	AP_{50}	AP_{75}	AP_S	AP_M	AP_L
YOLOv5-S	17.0M	55	63.4%	88.0%	74.0%	43.2%	61.2%	66.3%
YOLOX-S	18.4M	47	64.2%	89.7%	74.6%	42.2%	60.3%	67.4%
YOLOv6-S	34.8M	82	66.2%	90.4%	76.8%	44.6%	62.4%	69.5%
YOLOv7-S	36.9M	78	66.2%	89.8%	78.2%	44.2%	62.3%	70.6%
MP-YOLO	**16.8M**	**54**	**67.3%**	**90.6%**	**77.5%**	**44.9%**	**62.7%**	**70.9%**

4.4 Ablation Studies

Proposed Transformer-Conv Block. To assess our Transformer-Conv Block's impact, we compared MP-YOLO, enhanced with this block, against baseline models. Incorporating three parallel Transformer Encoders along-side the original CSP Block [34], our design aims to better capture long-range dependencies, enhancing accuracy and minimizing background errors. As Table 3 details, the Transformer-Conv Block notably boosts $AP_S/AP_M/AP_L$ by 1.7%/1.5%/4.6% respectively, outperforming the baseline. Additionally, with AR_S at 48.4% and AR_{100} at 72.3%, indicating that our proposed method performed well on detecting small-scale objects and dense objects. The data in Table 3 conclusively show that substituting the traditional CNN backbone with our Transformer-Conv Block enhances performance for CCD tasks.

Table 3. Ablation study on Transformer-Conv Block.

Model	AP_S	AP_M	AP_L	AR_S	AR_{100}
Base(CSP)	43.2%	61.2%	66.3%	46.6%	69.0%
Transformer-Conv	**44.9%**	**62.7%**	**70.9%**	**48.4%**	**72.3%**
Improvement					

Proposed Co-detection Algorithm. To address the challenge of distinguishing cartoon characters with similar faces but different body features, we annotated both aspects and developed separate FD and WD models, later fusing their results using Algorithm 1. To evaluate our Co-Detection Algorithm's efficacy, we conducted tests on both models individually. From the results shown in Table 4, we see that all higher AP values are present on our proposed Co-Detection Algorithm regardless of the baseline YOLOv5-S model or our MP-YOLO model. Specifically, our Co-Detection method enhances AP values by 3.5%, AP_{50} by 2.7%, and AP_{75} by 3.7% with the MP-YOLO model.

Table 4. Ablation study on the Co-Detection Algorithm.

Model	Detect Strategy	AP	AP_{50}	AP_{75}
YOLOv5-S	FD only	60.4%	84.9%	69.7%
	WD only	58.9%	83.1%	68.1%
	Co-Detect	**63.4%**	**88.0%**	**74.0%**
MP-YOLO	FD only	63.8%	87.9%	73.8%
	WD only	62.8%	87.1%	72.9%
	Co-Detect	**67.3%**	**90.6%**	**77.5%**

5   Conclusion

Suffering from the infringement of the patent right of cartoon characters, we aim to propose an effective scheme to reduce the illegal use of cartoon characters. Considering the demands in patent examination and other application scenarios, we built our cartoon character dataset CCDaS with sufficient annotations, which both annotated the face and the whole-body of the cartoon characters. As for our proposed CCD algorithm MP-YOLO, we not only maintained the real-time detection speed and small parameter size of YOLO, but achieved a high detection result for our CCD task. As a result, our approach is competitive with the state-of-the-art and can be effectively used in the patent examination process or other application scenarios. In the future, we would like to explore other CCD methods and continuously improve the accuracy of CCD.

References

1. Khan, F.S., Anwer, R.M., Weijer, J.V.D., Bagdanov, A.D., Lopez, A.M.: Color attributes for object detection. In: Proceedings /CVPR, IEEE Computer Society Conference on Computer Vision and Pattern Recognition (2012)
2. Zhou, Y., Jin, Y., Luo, A., Chan, S., Xiao, X., Yang, X.: Toonnet: a cartoon image dataset and a DNN-based semantic classification system. In: Proceedings of the 16th ACM SIGGRAPH International Conference on Virtual-Reality Continuum and its Applications in Industry, pp. 1–8 (2018)
3. Matsui, Y., et al.: Sketch-based manga retrieval using manga109 dataset. Multimedia Tools Appli. **76**(20), 21811–21838 (2017)
4. Zheng, Y., et al.: Cartoon face recognition: a benchmark dataset. In: Proceedings of the 28th ACM International Conference on Multimedia, pp. 2264–2272 (2020)
5. Ren, S., He, K., Girshick, R., Sun, J.: Faster R-CNN: towards real-time object detection with region proposal networks. Adv. Neural Inform. Process. Syst. **28** (2015)
6. Redmon, J., Divvala, S., Girshick, R., Farhadi, A.: You only look once: unified, real-time object detection. In: Proceedings of the IEEE Conference on Computer Vision and Pattern Recognition, pp. 779–788 (2016)
7. Jackson, P.T., Abarghouei, A.A., Bonner, S., Breckon, T.P., Obara, B.: Style augmentation: data augmentation via style randomization. In: CVPR Workshops, vol. 6, pp. 10–11 (2019)

8. Zhu, J.Y., Park, T., Isola, P., Efros, A.A.: Unpaired image-to-image translation using cycle-consistent adversarial networks. In: Proceedings of the IEEE International Conference on Computer Vision, pp. 2223–2232 (2017)

9. Li, C., et al.: YOLOv6: a single-stage object detection framework for industrial applications. arXiv preprint arXiv:2209.02976 (2022)

10. Wang, C.Y., Bochkovskiy, A., Liao, H.: YOLOv7: Trainable bag-of-freebies sets new state-of-the-art for real-time object detectors. arXiv e-prints (2022)

11. He, K., Gkioxari, G., Dollár, P., Girshick, R.: Mask R-CNN. In: Proceedings of the IEEE International Conference on Computer Vision, pp. 2961–2969 (2017)

12. Cao, J., Cholakkal, H., Anwer, R.M., Khan, F.S., Pang, Y., Shao, L.: D2det: towards high quality object detection and instance segmentation. In: Proceedings of the IEEE/CVF Conference on Computer Vision and Pattern Recognition, pp. 11485–11494 (2020)

13. Sun, P., et al.: Sparse R-CNN: End-to-end object detection with learnable proposals. In: Proceedings of the IEEE/CVF Conference on Computer Vision and Pattern Recognition, pp. 14454–14463 (2021)

14. Liu, W., et al.: SSD: single shot multibox detector. In: Leibe, B., Matas, J., Sebe, N., Welling, M. (eds.) ECCV 2016. LNCS, vol. 9905, pp. 21–37. Springer, Cham (2016). https://doi.org/10.1007/978-3-319-46448-0_2

15. Xiong, Y., et al.: Mobiledets: searching for object detection architectures for mobile accelerators. In: Proceedings of the IEEE/CVF Conference on Computer Vision and Pattern Recognition, pp. 3825–3834 (2021)

16. Feng, C., Zhong, Y., Gao, Y., Scott, M.R., Huang, W.: Tood: task-aligned one-stage object detection. In: 2021 IEEE/CVF International Conference on Computer Vision (ICCV), pp. 3490–3499. IEEE Computer Society (2021)

17. Vaswani, A., et al.: Attention is all you need. Adv. Neural Inform. Process. Syst. **30** (2017)

18. Dosovitskiy, A., et al.: An image is worth 16x16 words: transformers for image recognition at scale. arXiv preprint arXiv:2010.11929 (2020)

19. Mehta, S., Rastegari, M.: Mobilevit: light-weight, general-purpose, and mobile-friendly vision transformer. arXiv preprint arXiv:2110.02178 (2021)

20. Peng, Z., Huang, W., Gu, S., Xie, L., Wang, Y., Jiao, J., Ye, Q.: Conformer: Local features coupling global representations for visual recognition (2021)

21. Carion, N., et al.: End-to-end object detection with transformers. In: Vedaldi, A., Bischof, H., Brox, T., Frahm, J.-M. (eds.) ECCV 2020. LNCS, vol. 12346, pp. 213–229. Springer, Cham (2020). https://doi.org/10.1007/978-3-030-58452-8_13

22. Li, Y., Wu, C.Y., Fan, H., Mangalam, K., Xiong, B., Malik, J., Feichtenhofer, C.: Improved multiscale vision transformers for classification and detection. arXiv preprint arXiv:2112.01526 (2021)

23. He, L., Todorovic, S.: DESTR: object detection with split transformer. In: Proceedings of the IEEE/CVF Conference on Computer Vision and Pattern Recognition, pp. 9377–9386 (2022)

24. Bai, Y., Chen, Z., Fu, Z., Peng, L., Liang, P., Cheng, E.: Curveformer: 3d lane detection by curve propagation with curve queries and attention. arXiv preprint arXiv:2209.07989 (2022)

25. Mishra, A., Rai, S.N., Mishra, A., Jawahar, C.V.: IIIT-CFW: a benchmark database of cartoon faces in the wild. In: Hua, G., Jégou, H. (eds.) ECCV 2016. LNCS, vol. 9913, pp. 35–47. Springer, Cham (2016). https://doi.org/10.1007/978-3-319-46604-0_3

26. Nguyen, N.V., Rigaud, C., Burie, J.C.: Comic characters detection using deep learning. In: 2017 14th IAPR International Conference on Document Analysis and Recognition (ICDAR), vol. 3, pp. 41–46. IEEE (2017)

27. Chu, W.T., Li, W.W.: Manga facenet: face detection in manga based on deep neural network. In: Proceedings of the 2017 ACM on International Conference on Multimedia Retrieval, pp. 412–415 (2017)

28. Jha, S., Agarwal, N., Agarwal, S.: Bringing cartoons to life: Towards improved cartoon face detection and recognition systems. arXiv preprint arXiv:1804.01753 (2018)

29. Zhang, B., Li, J., Wang, Y., Cui, Z., Xia, Y., Wang, C., Li, J., Huang, F.: Acfd: asymmetric cartoon face detector. arXiv preprint arXiv:2007.00899 (2020)

30. Li, Z.: Comparison and analysis of two cartoon face recognition. In: 2021 2nd International Conference on Big Data & Artificial Intelligence & Software Engineering (ICBASE), pp. 478–482. IEEE (2021)

31. Li, Y., Lao, L., Cui, Z., Shan, S., Yang, J.: Graph jigsaw learning for cartoon face recognition. IEEE Trans. Image Process. **31**, 3961–3972 (2022)

32. Wang, Y.: Animation character detection algorithm based on clustering and cascaded SSD. Sci. Program. **2022** (2022)

33. Ge, Z., Liu, S., Wang, F., Li, Z., Sun, J.: Yolox: Exceeding yolo series in 2021. arXiv preprint arXiv:2107.08430 (2021)

34. Glenn., J.: YOLOv5 release v6.1. (2022). https://github.com/ultralytics/yolov5/releases/tag/v6

Driving Dynamics: An In-depth Analysis of Attention Allocation Between Driver and Co-driver in a Simulated Environment

Xinbin Chen[1,3], Di Zhang[1,3], Kai Wang[1,3], Chudan Zhou[1,3], Wenshan Shi[1,3], Zexing Wang[2,3], and Kaijiao Zhang[2,3(✉)]

[1] Communication University of China, Beijing, China
[2] National New Energy Vehicle Technology Innovation Center, Beijing, China
spark_33@163.com
[3] Macau University of Science and Technology, Cotai, China

Abstract. To further improve the visual attention mechanism, this study explores the impact of roles and task assignments on individual attention by analyzing differences in attention allocation between drivers and co-drivers during the driving process. In this experiment, participants were subjected to a road simulation driving test, and eye-tracking technology was employed to analyze the fixation and saccadic behaviors of drivers and co-drivers. This study mainly consists of two parts: First, using indicators such as the percentage of fixation points, total duration of fixations, average duration of fixations, percentage of saccadic counts, and average duration of saccades, we analyze the differences in the fixation behaviors of the driver and the co-driver towards different areas. Secondly, by studying participants' attention levels towards different information, we analyze the disparities in the attention of the driver and the co-driver on different road areas and various traffic information. The study indicates significant differences in attention allocation between drivers and co-drivers due to varying task assignments and distinct responsibilities and expectations for the two roles in the driving task. The research findings have important implications for the improvement of visual attention mechanisms and also provide valuable insights for enhancing vehicle design, increasing driving safety, and developing effective driving training strategies.

Keywords: Simulation driving · dual perspective of driver and co-driver · visual attention allocation · eye-tracking

1 Introduction

1.1 Background

Visual attention mechanism is an important information-processing mechanism in the human visual system. It allows us to focus our attention on the target of interest in complex visual environments, analyze that area in detail, reduce or eliminate interference from other areas, and thereby enhance our perception and cognitive abilities toward the target [1]. Research has shown that human attention biases are closely related to task demands,

G. Zhai et al. (Eds.): IFTC 2023, CCIS 2067, pp. 382–396, 2024.
https://doi.org/10.1007/978-981-97-3626-3_28

and different task types of tasks trigger different visual features [2]. There have been many achievements in the area of research. For example, Borj et al. proposed a unified Bayesian approach to model task-driven visual attention, which can accurately predict human attention and gaze behavior [3]. However, most of these studies focus on specific fixed tasks and overlook the variability and complexity of real-world environments, limiting our understanding of task-driven visual attention in realistic settings.

Research on the attention mechanism of the human visual system has yielded many findings. Firstly, based on theories and hypotheses in cognitive neuroscience, some influential ones include the feature integration theory proposed by Treisman et al., which divides the processing of visual information into an early feature registration stage and a later feature integration stage. This theory is significant for understanding the fundamental principles of attention mechanism, perception, and cognition [4]. Wolfe et al. put forward the guided search theory, which suggests that individuals purposefully acquire information based on their preferences, compare and process it, and finally make decisions. This theory emphasizes the goal-directed nature of individuals and the dynamic adjustment of information processing [5]. Duncan et al. proposed the theory of competitive integration, which suggests that when humans are faced with multiple visual stimuli, these stimuli compete for the limited attention resources of humans. Only the information that wins the competition will be processed and remembered by humans. This theory highlights that attention is allocated to the most salient and essential features [6]. Secondly, visual attention mechanisms can be classified differently based on different criteria. The virtual attention mechanism can be divided into exogenous virtual attention and endogenous visual attention according to whether the eyeball fixation point is consistent with the visual attention focus when the human observes the scene [7]. The former refers to when the eye gaze point and the focus of visual attention are consistent on the same object, while the latter refers to when the eye gaze point and focus are not on the same object.

Visual attention mechanism can be divided into bottom-up visual attention and top-down visual attention according to whether visual attention is directed by knowledge of the brain layer [8]. The former is a data-driven visual processing process, which means that humans will consciously pay attention to the significant areas in the field of vision, while the latter is a task-knowledge-driven visual processing process, which means that humans tend to pay attention to the goals related to cognitive factors such as personal hobbies and knowledge level. Muresan proposed an adaptive traffic signal control method based on deep reinforcement learning. They used a deep Q-network (DQN) as the algorithm for reinforcement learning. They utilized top-down attention mechanisms to select the most relevant information, thereby optimizing the control strategy for traffic signals [9]. Kobylinski et al. proposed a metric called the Visual Attention Convergence Index (VACI) to evaluate the degree of convergence of visual attention in virtual reality experiences. They collected eye-tracking data from participants in virtual reality to understand their attention allocation in different scenes and whether their attention tended to converge on common focal points [10]. In conclusion, it is evident that task-driven research on visual attention occupies a small proportion of all studies on visual attention. However, task-driven approaches can make visual attention mechanisms more applicable to real-world needs. By focusing attention on regions relevant to task objectives, computational efficiency can be improved, and resource allocation can be optimized. Task-driven simulations of real-world scenarios are of utmost importance. Currently, an increasing number of studies are utilizing eye-tracking technology to analyze the visual attention mechanisms of drivers during the driving process [11–14]. However, there is very limited research on how different roles influence visual attention in the same scenario.

This experiment will start from the perspective of simulated driving to study the allocation of attention between the driver and the co-driver during the driving process. We will use the eye tracker to collect real-time visual features of both individuals. On this basis, we will explore the differences in attention behavior between the main driver and the co-driver: including attention to different areas and attention to different traffic conditions. And with this, we will investigate the impact of different roles on this kind of attention behavior.

2 Method

2.1 Research Objective

This experiment will use the Unity simulation platform to construct driving scenarios. The experiment will involve manipulating the traffic conditions that participants encounter. Eye-tracking technology will be used to record the eye movement features of two types of drivers in real time during the experiment. Additionally, a questionnaire will be administered to gather further data. The attention allocation of the two types of drivers will be analyzed through a comprehensive analysis. The following is an introduction to the experimental design.

Experimental Participant. A total of 42 non-professional drivers were recruited to participate in the experiment. The age range of the participants was between 18 and 35 years old. All participants were aware of the experimental procedures and research objectives. Before the experiment, it was ensured that all participants were physically and mentally healthy, emotionally stable, had normal or corrected vision, and had not consumed alcohol or taken medication and that irrelevant variables that could affect the experimental results were excluded.

Experimental Scenarios. In this experiment, we aim to replicate the actual driving conditions for the drivers as closely as possible and have a comprehensive understanding of the overall traffic conditions encountered by the drivers, thus eliminating the individuality and randomness of the experimental results. We used the Unity simulation platform to construct the scenarios to meet these conditions. In the double-lane four-lane urban expressway scenario set up for the experiment, the following potential traffic conditions were implemented:

- Vehicles swiftly passing on the right side of the road.
- Vehicles swiftly passing through a crossroads ahead.
- Pedestrians crossing slowly at a crossroads ahead.
- Landmarks buildings on both sides of the street.

- Road signage guiding the lanes on both sides of the road.

Experimental Procedure. This experiment aims to study the distribution of visual attention between the driver and the co-driver. The experiment is conducted in the experimental scenarios built on the Unity simulation platform with the help of the Logitech G29 Steering Wheel, and the Tobii eye-tracker records the eye movement characteristics of the participants. The following is the complete process for the subjects:

- The subjects sit quietly for ten minutes to calm themselves.
- The subjects are paired, with one person acting as the driver and the other as the co-driver. With the assistance of the staff, they wear and calibrate the eye tracker.
- A five-minute adaptive training session is conducted to familiarize the participants with the operation. This process will not disclose any road information.
- The formal experiment begins, with the driver driving the vehicle from the starting point, following the lane guidance signs, while the co-driver freely observes the road conditions until the vehicle reaches the endpoint and stops.
- And the participants fill out a survey.

3   Analysis of Eye Movement Characteristics

3.1   Delineation of the Driver's Gaze Area

Method of Dividing the Gaze Area. Considering that different areas within the driving field of view contain different road information, delineating the gaze area is crucial because it reflects the driver's focal point when acquiring road and traffic information. Understanding the delineation of the gaze area is critical to comprehend the driver's focus and attention allocation during driving.

This study uses the K-means clustering method to cluster the driver's fixation point coordinates and divides the gaze area based on the clustering results. This method of dividing the gaze area can help understand the underlying patterns within the fixation point coordinate data, making the division more detailed and accurate.

Results of the Division of the Gaze Area. To ensure the representative and validity of the clustering results, five participants with significant differences in personality and driving age were selected from each of the 21 drivers and 21 co-drivers for the fixation point clustering analysis in this study. By constantly adjusting the number of categories, it was finally concluded that the clustering effect of dividing the gaze area into 7 categories was relatively close to the actual situation. Figure 1 shows the clustering result of the gaze point location of one of the participants.

The results of the fixation point clustering were matched with the experimental scenarios. The correspondence between the determined clustering results and the gaze areas is shown in Table 1, and the results of the driver's gaze area division are shown in Fig. 2.

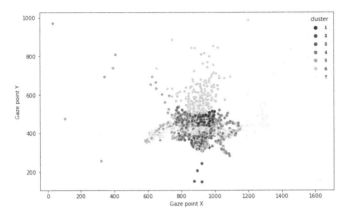

Fig. 1. Clustering results of fixation points

Table 1. Clustering results corresponding to the gaze area

Cluster	Area Name	Contents	AOI
1	Near-Front Area	The area near the front of the current lane, including vehicles	AOI1
2	Instrument panel area	The area where the dashboard is located	AOI2
3	Left Opposing Lane area	The left lane of the current lane, including oncoming vehicles	AOI3
4	Right Same-Direction Lane area	The right lane of the current lane includes vehicles driving in the same direction, vehicles parked on the street, etc.	AOI4
5	Left Street Area	Street view on the left side of the road, including buildings structures	AOI5
6	Far-Front Area	Area in the distant front of the current lane, including traffic lights, vehicles, etc.	AOI6
7	Right Street Area	Street view on the right side of the road, including buildings structures	AOI7

3.2 Analysis of Eye Movement Data

As fixation and saccade are the most closely related and essential indicators of visual characteristics for drivers, they can be used to measure drivers' behavior and attention level to road information during driving, and these two behaviors will be used to analyze the subjects in this study [15].

Analysis of Fixation Behavior. Fixation behavior analysis is a method to study a driver's focus of attention, which can be used to study the difficulty of target object

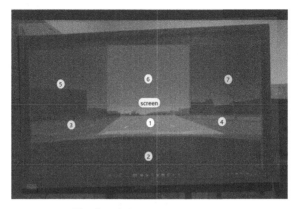

Fig. 2. Division of the gaze area

recognition and the degree of sustained attention of drivers to road information. The percentage of fixation points represents the percentage of all fixation points within an area of interest out of the total fixation points, which can be used to illustrate the distribution of fixations by the participants. The total duration of fixations is the sum of all fixation times in an area of interest, which reflects the subjects' continuous attention to the area of interest and the time consumed in processing the stimulus information [16]. The average duration of fixations is the time spent at each fixation point in an area of interest. The longer the average duration of fixations in a region, and a longer average fixation duration within a specific area indicates more incredible difficulty in acquiring and processing target information [17]. To compare the differences in fixation behavior between primary and secondary drivers in different regions, this paper employs these three metrics for fixation behavior analysis of the two types of drivers.

Percentage of Fixation Points. In this study, we analyzed the gaze area distribution of the driver and the co-driver by using the percentage of fixation points. It records the number of fixation points in each area of interest of the experimental scene and the total number of fixation points within the entire visual range for all participants. The average percentage of gaze points in different areas for both the driver and co-driver is then calculated, resulting in a bar chart as shown in Fig. 3.

From Fig. 3, it is evident that for both the driver and the co-driver, the fixation points are mainly distributed in AOI1 and AOI6, corresponding to the near-front and far-front regions. The percentage of fixation points in the near-front area is as high as 52% and 42% for the drivers and co-drivers, respectively, while the percentages for the far-front area are 35% and 31%, respectively. Meanwhile, it can be seen that the sum of the number of the remaining five regions of the driver and co-driver occupies about 20% of their total fixation points. This indicates that the focus of both the drivers and co-drivers is predominantly on the road ahead, with the driver showing a higher degree of attention. The highest level of attention is paid to the near-front area, which shows that these two types of people need to continuously obtain information about the near-front road condition to judge the feasible driving range and decide the driving direction. Additionally, the co-driver has a higher frequency of fixation points in AOI3, AOI4,

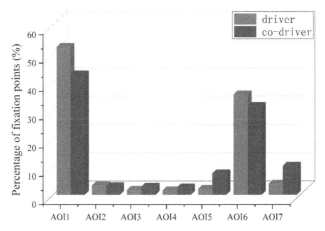

Fig. 3. Percentage of fixation points in different AOI regions of the driver and co-driver

AOI5, and AOI7, suggesting that they pay more attention to the conditions on both sides of the road and the areas on both sides of the street ahead compared to the driver.

Total Duration of Fixations and Average Duration of Fixations. To investigate the differences between the fixation behavior of the driver and the co-driver during driving, this paper presents bar charts and line graphs (see Fig. 4) depicting the total duration of fixation and average duration of fixation time for different gaze areas.

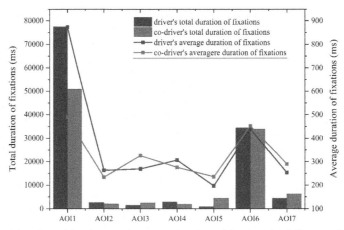

Fig. 4. Total duration of fixations and average duration of fixations in different AOI regions of the driver and co-driver

As shown in Fig. 4, the driver's total duration of fixations in the AOI1 region is significantly higher than the other gaze areas, exceeding that of the co-driver by more than 50%. In addition, the driver's total fixation time is also slightly higher than the co-drivers in AOI2, AOI4, and AOI6 regions. This indicates that during the driving process, the driver spent the majority of his attention time focused on the near-front area of the road and spent more time than the co-driver on the dashboard area, the right-hand lane area, and the far front area. In contrast, the co-driver spent almost five times as much time focusing on the AOI5 region as the driver, and in the AOI7 area, it is 40% higher. This suggests that the co-driver devotes significantly more attention to areas on both sides of the road.

By observing the average duration of fixations for each fixation point in different gaze areas in the figure, it is evident that, for each fixation point in the regions other than the AOI1 and AOI6 regions, both the driver and the co-driver generally maintain an average fixation time of approximately 0.2 to 0.4 s. In particular, the driver usually stayed longer at the fixation point in the right same-direction lane area. In addition, the average fixation duration of the driver in the AOI1 region was approximately twice as long as that of the co-driver.

Analyzing the differences in fixation characteristics between the driver and the co-driver in Fig. 4, the reasons are as follows: drivers need to pay close attention to the information about the road conditions in front of the vehicle and the right-side same-direction lane. This information is essential for accurately judging the traffic environment but is often difficult to obtain and requires constant attention. Furthermore, the driver also pays frequent attention to the dashboard area due to the need to constantly monitor speed and driving conditions. On the other hand, the co-driver is relatively more relaxed during driving and does not need to maintain a high concentration level on road conditions. Conversely, they allocate more time monitoring information on both sides of the road.

Analysis of Saccadic Behavior. Saccadic Behavior Analysis is a study of drivers' saccadic patterns and is primarily used to examine how drivers process and search for information. The percentage of saccade counts is the percentage of all saccade counts within an area of interest relative to the total number of saccades. It can be used to represent how subjects allocate their visual attention. The average duration of saccades is the average time of a saccadic behavior in an area of interest, indicating the time used to search for a target in a region, and can reflect the information-gathering behavior of drivers in that region. In order to compare the differences between the driver and co-driver's saccadic behavior in different areas, this paper analyses the saccadic behavior of the driver and co-driver using the percentage of saccade counts and average saccade duration.

Percentage of Saccade Counts. In this study, we analyzed the distribution of the driver and co-driver's saccadic behavior by the percentage of saccade counts. It depicts the ratio of the number of saccades within various areas of interest for all experimental participants to the total number of saccadic points in a box plot, as shown in Fig. 5.

As can be seen from Fig. 5, the driver and co-driver's saccadic behavior are still mainly concentrated in AOI1 and AOI6, of which 30%–50% of the saccade counts are located in AOI1, and 25%–45% are located in AOI6. This indicates that during the driving process, both two types of people pay special attention to changes in front road conditions and observe them in great detail, necessitating continuous scanning to process changing information and acquire new gaze points. It is worth noting that the driver's percentage of saccade counts in these two regions was about 10% higher than that of the co-driver. This suggests drivers maintain a more vigilant state for front road conditions and increase their saccadic behavior to gather more information.

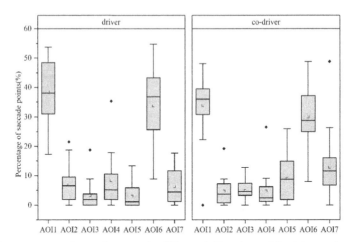

Fig. 5. Percentage of saccade counts in different AOI regions of the driver and co-driver

Further analysis reveals that both drivers and co-drivers have a higher saccade count percentage in other AOI areas compared to the percentage of fixation points in those areas. This suggests that in addition to front road conditions, obtaining information from other areas as assistance during driving is also crucial, and is more often achieved by saccadic behaviors. It can be seen that the percentage of saccade counts in AOI2 and AOI4 was overall significantly higher for the driver than for the co-driver, suggesting that the driver needs to increase the saccadic behavior of the auxiliary area to ensure timely access to traffic information. In contrast, the co-driver's percentage of saccade counts in AOI3, AOI5, and AOI7 was higher overall, suggesting that the co-driver has more interest in conducting more frequent saccades to both sides of the street and the left side of the road for the left-side oncoming lane.

Average Duration of Saccades. When analyzing the saccadic behavior of the experimental participants, in addition to considering the distribution of the saccade counts, this paper also analyses the average saccade duration in different regions by recording the Average duration of saccades of the driver and the co-driver at each saccadic behavior in different gaze areas and calculates their averages, as shown in Fig. 6.

Figure 6 reveals that the drivers and co-drivers have relatively longer average saccade duration in AOI1, AOI4, and AOI6, which is due to the fact that most of the information in front road conditions and the right-side same-direction lane area is dynamic and complex, usually with a long time period, and includes traffic light changes, the movement of the same-direction vehicles, and pedestrian behavior. The acquisition and processing of such information requires more time, thus increasing the average saccade duration. Especially for the driver, the acquisition of such information through saccade requires observing the complete cycle of information changes.

For the other four areas, the average duration of saccades for both the driver and the co-driver is relatively short and almost the same, within 0.5 s overall, because this kind of information is primarily static scenes, which are relatively simple and direct. Both driver and co-driver only need a short scanning time to acquire such information, and there is no significant difference between them.

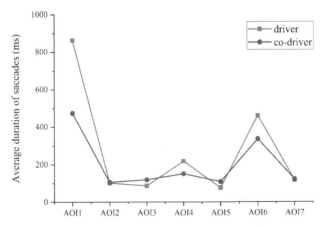

Fig. 6. Average duration of saccades in different AOI regions of the driver and co-driver

4   Analysis of Questionnaire Data

4.1   Data Processing and Research Methods

Data Processing. In this study, we conducted a questionnaire survey on the attention of drivers. We matched the questionnaire items with the gaze areas in the experimental scenarios, which were ultimately categorized into the forward road conditions, roadside conditions on both sides and the road landscape. In addition, in order to explore the differences between drivers and co-drivers' attention to different types of traffic information during driving, we classified the traffic information in the experimental scenarios into static traffic information and dynamic traffic information. Based on the participants' responses to the questionnaire items, we categorized them into different attention levels, including low attention, medium attention, and high attention.

Research Methodology. This study will use non-parametric tests to verify the difference in the distribution of the drivers' and co-drivers' attention in different regions. Since the questionnaire data are ordered as categorical and do not obey normal distribution, many traditional parametric tests such as t-tests and ANOVA are unsuitable. Therefore, non-parametric tests are more appropriate for our analysis.

4.2   Data Analysis

In order to investigate the differences in attention between drivers and co-drivers to different types of information during driving, we analyzed the questionnaire data in terms of differences in attention levels in different areas and differences in attention levels to different types of traffic road conditions.

Differences in Attention Levels in Different Regions. This paper uses non-parametric tests to analyze the differences in the attention levels of the driver and co-driver to the forward road conditions, roadside conditions on both sides and the road landscape, as shown in Table 2 and Fig. 7.

Table 2. Driver and co-driver's attention level for different regions

Region	Role	Low	Medium	High	Z	p
road landscape	driver	14(66.7%)	5(23.8%)	2(9.5%)	−3.213	0.001
	co-driver	3(14.3%)	12(57.1%)	6(28.6%)		
Roadside Conditions on Both Sides	driver	4(19.0%)	13(61.9%)	4(19.0%)	−2.074	0.038
	co-driver	13(61.9%)	4(19.0%)	4(19.0%)		
Forward Road Conditions	driver	0(0.0%)	12(57.1%)	9(42.9%)	2.780	0.005
	co-driver	3(14.3%)	16(76.2%)	2(9.5%)		

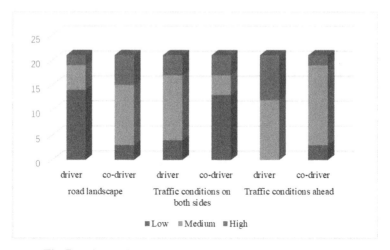

Fig. 7. Driver and co-driver's attention level for different regions

By analyzing the data in Table 2, it can be seen that the p-values for all three regions are less than 0.05, indicating that there is a significant difference between the attention of the driver and the co-driver to all three areas. Upon closer examination of the data, it can be seen that 66.7% of the drivers' attention to the road landscape belongs to a low level, more than 80% of the drivers' attention to the roadside conditions on both sides belongs to a medium-high level, and all of the drivers maintain a medium-high level of attention to the forward road conditions. On the other hand, when observing the attention levels of co-drivers, it is found that only 14.3% of co-drivers have a low level of attention to the road landscape. However, 61.9% of co-drivers have a low level of attention to road conditions on both sides and the majority of co-drivers have a medium level of attention to forward road conditions.

Based on these findings, it can be concluded that the driver pays less attention to the view on both sides of the road relative to the co-driver, but pays significantly more attention to the roadside conditions and the forward road conditions.

Differences in Attention to Different Types of Traffic Information. Similarly, non-parametric tests were used to analyze the differences in attention levels between drivers and co-drivers regarding static and dynamic traffic information as shown in Table 3, and bar charts were created as shown in Fig. 8.

Table 3. Driver and co-driver's attention level for different types of traffic

Traffic	Role	Low	Medium	High	Z	p
static traffic	driver	9(42.9%)	10(47.6%)	2(9.5%)	−2.241	0.025
	co-driver	3(14.3%)	12(57.1%)	6(28.6%)		
dynamic traffic	driver	0(0.0%)	7(33.3%)	14(66.7%)	−3.462	0.001
	co-driver	1(2.4%	17(81.0%)	3(14.3%)		

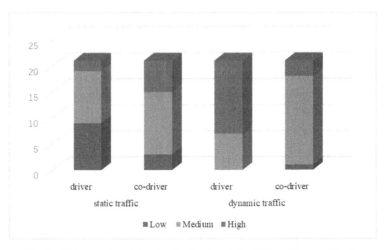

Fig. 8. Driver and co-driver's attention level for different types of traffic

By analyzing the data in Table 3, it can be seen that the p-values for both static and dynamic traffic information are less than 0.05, indicating that there are significant differences in the attention levels of drivers and co-drivers towards these two categories of traffic information. Observation of the data reveals that 42.9% of the drivers pay less attention to static traffic information while driving, whereas only 14.3% of the co-drivers pay less attention to such road conditions. In contrast, concerning the attention levels towards dynamic traffic information, 33.3% of drivers fall into the medium level, while the remaining 66.7% fall into the high level. However, the majority of co-drivers maintain a medium level of attention.

It can be concluded that both types of people are more inclined to pay attention to dynamic traffic information, and the drivers show a higher level of attention to dynamic traffic information and a relatively lower level of attention to static traffic information.

5 Discussion

The results of the experiment show that there is a significant difference in attention allocation between the driver and co-driver while driving. Specifically, the drivers will pay more attention to the areas directly in front of the vehicle, while the co-drivers will pay more attention to the road landscapes or other non-critical areas. The result proves that participants tend to allocate more attention resources to the central areas under high cognitive load [18]. Besides, drivers focus more on dynamic road information while co-drivers focus on static road information more.

These differences in attention allocation may be attributed to the distinct roles carried by the two individuals: the drivers are responsible for direct vehicle control and need to concentrate attention on areas and road information that are most likely to have an impact on the current driving situation, which plays an important role in enhancing road safety. For the co-drivers, they do not have the responsibility of operating the vehicle, and they often serve as companions and navigators, thus assisting the vehicle's operation. This aligns with research by Forlizzi [19], Neider [20], and others, which has confirmed the influence of passengers and co-drivers on the driver.

Incorporating the differences in attention allocation between the driver and co-driver into the design of new driving systems can create a safer driving experience. As Bernhard Maurer [21] has proposed, a shared gaze method can help drivers better obtain road information and complete driving tasks.

6 Conclusion

This study analyzed experiments based on simulated driving using eye-tracking technology, demonstrating the differences in attention allocation between drivers and co-drivers during the driving process. Our results indicate that variations in roles and tasks carried out will affect individuals' attention mechanisms. Throughout the driving process, differences will exist in people's focus range and the degree of attention paid to different road information. The results of this study not only emphasize the complementary roles of the drivers and co-drivers in driving safety but also provide valuable insights for future driving training and car design.

However, this study has certain limitations. Firstly, the relatively small sample size may introduce individual differences that could impact the experimental results, limiting the generalizability of the findings. Secondly, the simulated driving experiment environment cannot fully replicate the complex scenarios under real road conditions, which may cause psychological differences among participants.

Future research should expand the sample size and reduce the impact of the experimental environment. Additionally, researchers could consider incorporating other physiological data and exploring the impact of sensory information beyond vision, such as auditory cues, on attention allocation. This would further advance our understanding of drivers' attention mechanisms. In addition, attention allocation differences should be applied to the construction of more comprehensive attention mechanisms, providing scientific evidence for a safer driving environment and training programs.

References

1. Peters, R., Iyer, A., Koch, C., et al.: Components of bottom-up gaze allocation in natural scenes. J. Vis. **5**(8), 692 (2005)
2. Keller, M., Taube, W., Lauber, B.: Task-dependent activation of distinct fast and slow(er) motor pathways during motor imagery. Brain Stimul. **11**(4), 782–788 (2018)
3. Borji, A., Sihite, D.N., Itti, L.: Probabilistic learning of task-specific visual attention. In: 2012 IEEE Conference on Computer Vision and Pattern Recognition, pp. 470–477. IEEE (2012)
4. Treisman, A.M., Gelade, G.: A feature-integration theory of attention. Cogn. Psychol. **12**(1), 97–136 (1980)
5. Wolfe, J.M., Cave, K.R., Franzel, S.L.: Guided search: an alternative to the feature integration model for visual search. J. Exp. Psychol. Hum. Percept. Perform. **15**(3), 419 (1989)
6. Duncan, J.: Selective attention and the organization of visual information. J. Exp. Psychol. Gen. **113**(4), 501 (1984)
7. Borji, D.S., Itti, L.: Quantitative analysis of human-model agreement in visual saliency modeling: a comparative study. IEEE Trans. Image Process. **22**(1), 55–69 (2013)
8. Treisman, A.: Features and objects: the fourteenth Bartlett memorial lecture. Q. J. Exp. Psychol. **40A**, 201–237 (1988)
9. Muresan, M., Fu, L., Pan, G.: Adaptive traffic signal control with deep reinforcement learning an exploratory investigation. arXiv preprint arXiv:1901.00960 (2019)
10. Kobylinski, P., Pochwatko, G.: Visual Attention Convergence Index for virtual reality experiences. In: Ahram, T., Taiar, R., Colson, S., Choplin, A. (eds.) IHIET 2019. AISC, vol. 1018, pp. 310–316. Springer, Cham (2020). https://doi.org/10.1007/978-3-030-25629-6_48
11. Robbins, C., Chapman, P.: How does drivers' visual search change as a function of experience? A systematic review and meta-analysis. Accid. Anal. Prev. **132**, 105266 (2019)
12. Xia, Y., Zhang, D., Kim, J., Nakayama, K., Zipser, K., Whitney, D.: Predicting driver attention in critical situations. In: Jawahar, C.V., Li, H., Mori, G., Schindler, K. (eds.) ACCV 2018, Part V. LNCS, vol. 11365, pp. 658–674. Springer, Cham (2019). https://doi.org/10.1007/978-3-030-20873-8_42
13. Deng, T., Yan, H., Qin, L., et al.: How do drivers allocate their potential attention? Driving fixation prediction via convolutional neural networks. IEEE Trans. Intell. Transp. Syst. **21**(5), 2146–2154 (2019)
14. Hu, Z., Lv, C., Hang, P., et al.: Data-driven estimation of driver attention using calibration-free eye gaze and scene features. IEEE Trans. Industr. Electron. **69**(2), 1800–1808 (2021)
15. Zhang, C.: Research on driving safety evaluation of icy and snowy roads based on drivers' visual characteristics. Jilin University, Changchun (2017)
16. Li, X.: Research on the influence of typical unfavourable factors on driving behavior performance based on driving simulation experiment. Beijing Jiaotong University, Beijing (2016)
17. Lv, Z., Qi, C., Zhu, S.: Dynamic visual characteristics and loads of drivers under overtaking conditions on grassland highways. Chinese J. Saf. Sci. **32**(04), 15–22 (2022)

18. Engström, J., Johansson, E., Östlund, J.: Effects of visual and cognitive load in real and simulated motorway driving. Transp. Res. F **8**, 97–120 (2005)
19. Forlizzi, J., Barley, W.C., Seder, T.: Where should i turn: moving from individual to collaborative navigation strategies to inform the interaction design of future navigation systems. In: Proceedings of the SIGCHI Conference on Human Factors in Computing Systems, pp. 1261–1270. ACM (2010)
20. Neider, M.B., Chen, X., Dickinson, C.A., Brennan, S.E., Zelinsky, G.J.: Coordinating spatial referencing using shared gaze. Psychon. Bull. Rev. **17**(5), 718–724 (2010)
21. Maurer, B., Trösterer, S., Gärtner, M., et al.: Shared gaze in the car: towards a better driver-passenger collaboration. In: Adjunct proceedings of the 6th International Conference on Automotive User Interfaces and Interactive Vehicular Applications, pp. 1–6 (2014)

Author Index

Printed in the United States
by Baker & Taylor Publisher Services